The Mutual Fund Business

The Mutual Fund Business

Robert C. Pozen
editorial assistance by Sandra D. Crane

The MIT Press
Cambridge, Massachusetts
London, England

This book was set in Times New Roman on the Monotype "Prism Plus" PostScript Imagesetter by Asco Trade Typesetting Ltd., Hong Kong.

Printed and bound in the United States of America.

Library of Congress Cataloging-in-Publication Data

Pozen, Robert C.
  The mutual fund business / Robert C. Pozen.
    p.   cm.
  Includes bibliographical references and index.
  ISBN 0-262-16177-x (alk. paper). — ISBN 0-262-66141-1
  (pbk. : alk. paper)
  1. Mutual funds—United States—Case studies. I. Title.
  HG4930.P63   1998
  332.63′27—dc21   98-4894
                                                        CIP

Contents

Preface

Mutual funds have been one of the fastest growing institutions in the United States. Fund assets have soared from less than $150 billion in 1980 to over $4 trillion by the end of 1997. Since 1996, mutual fund assets have exceeded bank deposits.

Why should you be interested in mutual funds? Mutual funds have the potential to influence several aspects of your life. If you are interested in the stock or bond markets, you are likely to consider investing through mutual funds. When you get a job, you will find that most companies offer a retirement plan for their employees, and many of these plans offer mutual funds as an investment alternative. Some of you may even take a job in the mutual fund industry, which employs more than half a million people and is expanding rapidly.

As the subject of a course, the mutual fund industry brings together a variety of business issues. A study of mutual funds involves an understanding not only of the investment process but also of many other aspects of business. The mutual fund industry has developed innovative marketing and pricing strategies. It has been a leader in applying technology to transaction processing and customer service. It has also expanded globally on both the investment and sales sides.

What is a mutual fund? It is a type of financial intermediary: a corporation or trust through which savers pool their assets for collective investment. In practical terms, savers buy shares of a mutual fund, which in turn invests in various types of securities. Almost every mutual fund is part of a fund complex, a group of funds connected to the same investment adviser.

A mutual fund hires an investment adviser to manage the investments of the fund, and pays an advisory fee to that investment adviser under a management contract approved by the fund's independent directors. A fund is usually categorized into one of three types, according to its principal investments: stock funds, bond funds, and money market funds. Within each category are many subcategories—for example, growth stock, growth and income, and international stock funds.

Investment advisers usually have a trading desk to implement portfolio decisions —to place fund orders to buy or sell shares with securities brokers in various markets. Funds also have custodians, usually banks, to hold portfolio securities (in a segregated account). As substantial owners of stock, mutual funds can have a significant impact on the trading markets, and constitute a potential influence in the corporate governance process.

Every mutual fund has a principal underwriter, typically affiliated with its investment adviser, which organizes the sale of fund shares. Traditionally, the principal underwriter sold fund shares through a broker-dealer network to investors. Since the 1970s, more fund underwriters have sold shares directly (through advertisements or mail) to investors. Since the 1980s, many corporate retirement plans have offered an array of mutual funds to plan participants. During the 1990s, financial planners and fund marketplaces (offering products from many different complexes) have become substantial forces in fund sales.

Over the years, mutual funds have developed a variety of pricing structures. Traditionally, funds charged a front-end sales load of $8\frac{1}{2}\%$, but the front-end load has now dropped to 4% to 5% on average. Alternatively, some funds charge a back-end load when the shareholder leaves the funds. In addition to, or in lieu of, a front-end or back-end sales load, other funds charge an annual distribution fee (called a 12b-1 fee), usually ranging from 0.25% (25 basis points) to 0.75% (75 basis points). Most direct marketed funds are sold without loads or 12b-1 fees, though several do charge a low 12b-1 fee.

Once investors become fund shareholders, they are provided with a broad array of services—for example, automated transactions through phones and checkwriting on money market funds. These services are delivered by the fund's transfer agent, which may be affiliated with its investment adviser or owned by an unrelated third party. The mutual fund industry has been a leader in using technology to process trades and service customers. In particular, the mutual fund industry has attracted retirement assets by delivering recordkeeping, telephonic, and other services through sophisticated computer systems.

All of these areas—fund investments, trading, sales, and servicing—are highly regulated by the Securities and Exchange Commission (SEC) under the Investment Company Act of 1940 (1940 Act). Like other securities laws, the 1940 Act requires mutual funds to make full disclosure to investors through a prospectus. Further, the 1940 Act imposes substantive restrictions on the investments and operations of mutual funds. It also mandates the election of independent directors as the general watchdogs for fund shareholders.

This strict regulation of mutual funds in each country has created substantial barriers to entry to true cross-border sales of mutual funds. Instead, fund sponsors must generally sell clone funds formed specially to meet the legal, accounting, and tax rules of each country. On the other hand, the international investments of U.S. mutual funds have increased dramatically over the last decade. Now there are global, regional, and foreign country funds.

How is this book designed to help students achieve a good understanding of the mutual fund industry? This is a course book with selected readings and case studies designed to stimulate discussion and debate on key issues in the mutual fund industry. It is not a textbook attempting to summarize all relevant facts and present definitive conclusions on every aspect of the industry. The course book is divided into 13 chapters, each of which addresses a separate subject. While most students will (we hope) read all 13 chapters, some will focus on a subset of chapters or even one chapter. For this reason, each chapter is designed to stand alone (with cross references to more detailed treatment in other chapters). While some students may have little background on mutual funds, others may be searching for an intensive look at a particular facet of the fund industry. Hence each chapter starts with an elementary explanation of the subject, and proceeds to a more sophisticated analysis through a case study.

Each chapter is organized in a similar manner. Each begins with an introduction to the subject, followed by several readings from academic and journalistic sources. Then each chapter contains a case study or class exercise that explores in-depth an important facet of the subject, together with a list of specific questions on the case study. The answers to the questions are intended to be discussed in small groups or as a whole class.

The chapters are organized into four main groups. Part I is designed to provide an overview of the mutual fund industry. Chapter 1 explains why investors use financial intermediaries, how a mutual fund operates, and why a mutual fund differs from a bank. Chapter 2 discusses the historical evolution of the mutual fund industry, especially its recent growth spurt, and the role of asset allocation in light of the increasing demand for investment guidance. Chapter 3 completes the overview by outlining the strict regulatory regime under which mutual funds operate, with emphasis on the disclosure documents disseminated to investors.

Part II looks more in detail at portfolio management and equity trading. Chapter 4 reviews the main features of bonds and the U.S. bond market, and then details the functions of portfolio managers for bond funds. Similarly, chapter 5 reviews the key characteristics of U.S. stocks and stock indices, and then focuses on the investment process for portfolio managers of stock funds. Chapter 6 summarizes the operations of the major markets for trading U.S. equities, and then analyzes the role of the fund trading desk in implementing portfolio management decisions.

Part III addresses the marketing and servicing of fund shareholders. Chapter 7 gives an overview of mutual fund marketing, with a focus on the development of new products, pricing structures, and distribution channels. Chapter 8 covers the marketing and servicing of fund shareholders in defined contribution plans including the design of fund arrays, the education of plan participants, and the special responsibilities of plan fiduciaries. Chapter 9 concentrates on the servicing of fund shareholders outside the retirement channel, such as the processing of shareholder transactions, the handling of phone volumes, and the constraining of "hot" money.

Part IV deals in depth with a number of important topics for the mutual fund industry. Chapter 10 analyzes in detail the revenues and expenses of mutual funds and their sponsors, with a case study on a merger of funds. Chapter 11 explores the role of mutual funds as substantial shareholders of publicly traded companies, with a case study on a complicated proxy fight. Chapter 12 explains the significance of technology in the growth of the mutual fund industry, with class exercises involving fund information on the Internet. Chapter 13 reviews the international investments of U.S. mutual funds and the sale of mutual funds to foreign investors, with a case study on exporting a U.S. retirement fund business to Canada.

The materials contained in this course book reflect industry practices and regulations in place, and data available, as of the press date—November 15, 1997. The opinions expressed are those of the author and are not necessarily the opinions of Fidelity Investments.

Acknowledgments

Many people have contributed to the development of the course book and teacher's manual. First, my special thanks to Sandra Crane, for her enthusiastic assistance in compiling materials, developing case studies, and editing the book.

Second, my thanks to many dedicated Fidelity colleagues, who each helped to develop a university session or class exercise covering one of the topics in the book. The following individuals donated their time to developing and class-testing the material: Al Aiello, Steve Akin, Irwin Barnes, George Fischer, Stuart Fross, Bart Grenier, Mike Hudnall, Steve Jonas, Debbie Malins, Kathleen Miskiewicz, Jacques Perold, Anne Punzak, and Roger Servison.

I'd particularly like to thank Jennifer K. Brown, whose coordinating efforts made it possible to teach a full-semester course on mutual funds in the spring of 1997. I also want to thank Dean Eric Hayden, University of Massachusetts, who championed the introduction of the course into the business school's curriculum.

Third, my thanks to numerous colleagues and friends who reviewed significant portions of the material and provided useful suggestions. The key people were: Michael Lipper, Arthur Loring, David Jones, Karen Hammond, and Charlie Brenner. Also thanks to Dan Beckman, Bill Eigen, Drew Elder, Michelle Grenier, Pat Hillman, Judy Hogan, and David Pearlman.

Fourth, my thanks to Chris Regan, Mike Ricciardelli, and Zick Rubin, who helped select a publisher and obtain permissions for pre-publication packets, and Alan Leifer who helped market the book. The staff at the MIT Press was also great to work with.

Fifth, my thanks to the many people who helped to obtain materials and bring the manuscript to a form that could be submitted to the publisher, particularly Bob Difede, Jennifer Traer, Mary Anne Moore, and Lisa Roche.

Finally, my thanks and appreciation to my wife and children, who as usual gave me love and support throughout the whole process of developing the course book.

I   *Overview*

1 Indirect Investing: Mutual Funds versus Commercial Banks

Introduction

This is the first of three general chapters to introduce you to the mutual fund industry. In this chapter, we will look at why investors put their money in mutual funds as opposed to buying individual securities, and then outline the basic operation of a mutual fund as well as a fund complex. We will end with a case study that compares a money market fund account to a bank deposit. In chapter 2, we will review the history of the fund industry and the factors behind its explosive growth. In chapter 3, we will lay out the regulatory framework for mutual funds and their disclosure documents.

Investors have a basic choice: They can invest directly in individual securities, or they can invest indirectly through a financial intermediary. A financial intermediary gathers savings from consumers and invests these monies in a portfolio of financial assets. A mutual fund is a type of financial intermediary—a corporation or trust—through which savers pool their monies for collective investment primarily in publicly traded securities. Other types of financial intermediaries include commercial banks, insurance companies, and pension plans.

A fund is "mutual" in the sense that all of its returns, minus its expenses, are shared by the fund's shareholders. The fund's returns consist of interest and dividends received from the fund's investments, as well as its realized and unrealized gains or losses. The fund's shared expenses consist primarily of an advisory fee for managing the fund's investments and a transfer agency fee for servicing the fund's shareholders, as well as sometimes a 12b-1 fee for distributing the fund's shares.

Most investors are seeking to maximize their returns and minimize their risk, but this combination is not easy to achieve. In general, there is a strong positive relationship between risk and return: In order to achieve higher returns, an investor generally needs to take higher risks (no free lunches!). Although there are many different types of risks associated with securities investing, analysts typically think of securities as having two main types of risk: risk that stems from the market in general, and risk that is specific to the individual company. The latter risk, known as company-specific risk, can be substantially reduced through diversification—a benefit of mutual fund investing. Reading 1.1 in this chapter outlines a framework for risk/return analysis and summarizes some of the relevant work on the subject.

The dominant trend in the United States is toward investing through intermediaries as opposed to investing directly in individual securities. Investors have gravitated toward financial intermediaries because they offer an attractive relationship between risk and return;

they also have advantages over direct investing in terms of securities expertise, administrative costs, and convenience. On the other hand, investing through intermediaries has some inherent disadvantages such as the payment of advisory fees, the possibility of poor performance, and the potential conflicts of interests involved in any fiduciary relationship.

As shown by table 1.0.1, mutual funds have gained assets at a more rapid pace than banks, insurance companies, and other financial intermediaries. (Please note that, although the table shows commercial banks with assets of $4.7 trillion at the end of 1996, their deposits were only $2.8 trillion; the difference is attributable to assets of bank holding companies and nondeposit borrowings of banks.) At the end of 1997, the assets of mutual funds exceeded $4 trillion.

Looking at mutual funds as financial intermediaries, what exactly is the relationship between their investors, the fund, the management company, and other service providers? To answer this question, it is helpful to consider the diagram in figure 1.0.1 as well as readings 1.2 and 1.3 from the *Mutual Fund Fact Book*.

Many people do not realize that a mutual fund is a separate entity—a trust or corporation—with its own board of directors, usually consisting of a majority of independent directors. On the basis of disclosure documents, shareholders-savers provide their money to the fund, and every few years they elect the independent directors of the fund. Each year the independent directors approve an advisory contract with a management company, which invests fund assets in stocks and/or bonds according to the objectives specified in the fund's disclosure documents.

Service providers to a mutual fund may be categorized by their relationship to shareholders, the mutual fund itself, or securities held by the fund. First, as mentioned above, is the *management company* (sometimes called the *investment adviser* or *investment manager*), which contracts with the mutual fund to invest its assets in securities. The management company is also usually the sponsor/creator of the fund. A second category of service providers acts as links between shareholders and the mutual fund; these include the *underwriter* (or *distributor*), which sells fund shares to investors, and the *transfer agent*, which services existing fund shareholders. The underwriter is usually an affiliate of the management company, while the transfer agent may be an affiliate of the management company or an unaffiliated service provider. Still other service providers act as links between the mutual fund and the securities it holds. This third category includes the custodian that holds the assets of the fund in a segregated account, and the brokers that effect securities trades on behalf of the fund. Fund custodians are usually banks, while fund brokers may be independent firms or a combination of independents and affiliates of the fund management company.

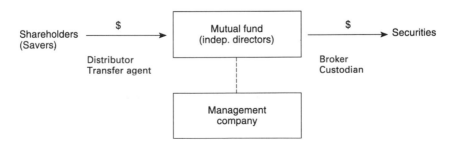

Figure 1.0.1

Table 1.0.1
Assets of major institutions and financial intermediaries (millions of dollars)

	1989R	1990R	1991R	1992R	1993R	1994R	1995R	1996
Depository institutions								
Commercial banks[a]	$3,231,350	$3,337,480	$3,442,190	$3,654,930	$3,891,810	$4,159,760	$4,493,680	$4,710,020
Credit unions[b]	201,920	217,240	239,970	264,700	281,710	293,600	310,660	327,310
Savings institutions[c]	1,512,600	1,357,650	1,171,980	1,078,830	1,029,460	1,013,480	1,016,200	1,034,890
Life insurance	**$1,260,250**	**$1,367,370**	**$1,505,280**	**$1,614,340**	**$1,784,880**	**$1,888,540**	**$2,091,110**	**$2,239,350**
Investment institutions								
Bank-administered trusts[d]	$1,328,481	$1,368,666	$1,585,406	$1,791,526	$2,050,122	$2,043,197	$2,444,823	N/A
Closed-end investment companies	53,626	52,554	72,716	93,467	109,352	103,596	126,094	128,500[e]
Mutual funds[f]	981,955	1,066,892	1,395,498	1,646,259	2,075,366	2,161,495	2,820,355	3,539,205

a. Includes U.S.-chartered commercial banks, foreign banking offices in the U.S., bank holding companies, and banks in affiliated areas.
b. Includes only federal or federally insured state credit unions serving natural persons.
c. Includes mutual savings banks, federal savings banks, and savings & loan associations.
d. Reflects only discretionary trusts and agencies.
e. Preliminary number.
f. Includes short-term funds.
N/A = Not available
R = Revised
Source: Federal Reserve Board, Federal Financial Institutions Examination Council, Investment Company Institute (ICI)

There are many different types of mutual funds (which are explained in detail in chapter 2). But the three main categories are based on the asset class of fund investments: stock funds, bond funds, and money market funds. Most management companies have an array of mutual funds including all three of the main categories. Such an array of mutual funds, all advised by the same management company, is called a *fund complex*. Exhibit 4 of the case study for this chapter lists the array of mutual funds in the T. Rowe Price fund complex. Shareholders are usually allowed to exchange freely among funds in the same complex. In addition, the funds in a complex typically have the same principal underwriter and transfer agent. For this reason, shareholders can make one phone call to purchase or sell several funds in the same complex. Similarly, shareholders periodically receive a consolidated statement containing information on all their fund holdings within the complex.

As mentioned previously, a mutual fund is only one type of financial intermediary. It is a relatively pure form of financial intermediary because there is an almost perfect pass through of money between fund accounts of shareholders-savers and the securities in which the fund invests. Shareholders are told in what types of securities their funds will be invested, and changes in the value of the securities held in the fund portfolio are translated on a daily basis directly to the value of the fund shares held by the shareholders-savers. The management company receives only a fee based on the size of the fund (e.g., 0.6% of fund assets—60 basis points, abbreviated 60 bp) for investing fund assets on behalf of fund shareholders. The management company does not have a participation in either the profits or losses of fund investments (except to the extent that an increase or decrease in the fund's assets affects the amount of the management fee).

By contrast, a commercial bank is not a pure pass-through type of financial intermediary. Through branches and other marketing efforts the bank gathers deposits from savers, although they have no specific knowledge of how their deposits will be used. Bank officers invest the monies of savers in loans or securities the bank deems appropriate at the time. In return for use of their monies, bank depositors usually receive a specified rate of interest that is not directly linked to the performance of the bank's investments in loans or securities. In any event, bank depositors are insured up to $100,000 per separate account by the Federal Deposit Insurance Corporation (FDIC). But, unlike mutual fund investors who are also fund shareholders, bank depositors do not have a role in choosing the directors of a bank, who are elected by its shareholders.

In addition, many banks have trust departments that manage investments for trust, agency, pension, and other fiduciary accounts. To facilitate investments by these fiduciary accounts, some banks have established common and/or collective trust funds that operate to some degree like private mutual funds, though subject to different regulatory and tax regimes. An analysis of bank common and/or collective trust funds is beyond the scope of this book.

After completing reading 1.4 on banking, compare the diagram in figure 1.0.2 of a commercial bank (without a trust department) to the earlier diagram of a mutual fund in figure 1.0.1. Please note that the shareholders of the bank are different from its depositors (savers). Please also note that the bank's managers are officers of the bank itself, in contrast to the fund's managers, who are in a separate entity that has a contract with the fund.

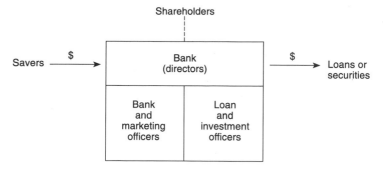

Figure 1.0.2

Questions

In reviewing the material in this chapter, please keep in mind the following questions:

1. What are all the pros and cons of investing directly in individual stocks or bonds, versus investing indirectly through mutual funds?
2. Would your answer to the first question be different for an actively managed versus a passively managed fund? Note: An actively managed fund attempts to outperform a specific benchmark or peer group through superior security selection; a passively managed fund attempts to mimic the returns of an index by investing in a representative sample of the securities composing the index, such as the Standard & Poor's 500.
3. Are mutual fund shareholders, like bank depositors, insured by the FDIC or any other government agency? Does the SEC guarantee that money market funds will always be worth $1 per share?
4. If a money market fund's investments yield interest of 6% per year, what will happen to the return on the fund's shares and to the advisory fee of the fund's manager? If a bank's investments yield interest of 6% per year, what will happen to the return on the bank's deposits and to the profits of the bank?
5. What is the difference between a shareholder of a fund and a shareholder of a bank? Who is an "investor" in the bank? Who do the directors of a fund represent, as opposed to the directors of a bank?

1.1   Money Managers and Securities Research*
R. Pozen

A   The Basic Framework of Portfolio Theory

Economists have developed an extensive body of portfolio theory[1] and empirical evidence on the stock markets. According to portfolio theory, it is a reasonable approximation to characterize every investment by two measures—expected return and risk.[2] Expected return is usually defined as the weighted average of all possible returns[3] from an investment.[4] Risk is usually defined as the average amount of variation among all the possible returns from an investment.[5] As a general rule, risk and return are positively correlated.[6] An investment with a low risk, like a U.S. savings bond, usually has a low return. An investment with a high risk, like a speculative stock, usually has potential for a high return.

Portfolio theory generally assumes that investors are "risk averse": they will avoid investments with increased risks unless compensated by appropriate increases in expected returns.[7] This assumption of risk aversion is probably realistic for most investors,[8] especially for the clients of institutional investors. Although a few gamblers might prefer risky investments solely because of their riskiness, they can better express this preference for risks by trading directly in stock options than by depositing their savings in a financial intermediary with a relatively stable portfolio.[9]

Given the dual characteristics of investment opportunities and the normal preferences of their clients, money managers should try to construct portfolios with the highest return for any given risk level or, in other words, the lowest risk for any given return.[10] In theory, money managers might achieve this objective by either of two approaches—by finding "undervalued" stocks with higher returns than stocks of the same risk category, or by decreasing the aggregate risks of their portfolios without lowering the average returns. . . .

B   The Search for Higher Returns

Most of the securities research purchased by money managers is aimed at discovering undervalued stocks with higher returns than stocks in the same risk category.[11] From a group of 50 very stable stocks, for example, a money manager might try to select the 10 stocks which will show the largest gains during the next year. Researchers (often called analysts) try to discover such undervalued stocks by technical or fundamental analysis. In technical analysis, the researcher examines historical data on prices and volume of stock trading in an attempt to find recurring patterns for individual securities or for the stock market as a whole.[12] For instance, a technical analyst might attempt to predict stock prices on the basis of the volume of short-selling[13] in a particular stock. In fundamental analysis,

---

* Robert C. Pozen, *Money Managers and Securities Research*, 51 N.Y.U.L. Rev. 923 (1976), pp. 923–948.

the researcher examines historical data on corporate earnings and management in an attempt to predict future flows of corporate income for particular companies, industries, or corporations generally. For example, a fundamental analyst might try to predict stock prices in airline companies by projecting the supply and demand for airline services.[14]

1 Technical Analysis

In an extensive set of empirical studies, economists have demonstrated that future changes in stock prices are randomly related to current stock prices.[15] These studies have failed to find any predictable connection of significant magnitude between future changes in stock prices and past data on stock prices, trading volume, and the main chart patterns used by technical analysts.[16] Although these studies have found some statistical dependencies for stock prices within very short and very long time periods, the extra returns from trading strategies based on these dependencies are often offset by the transaction costs of such strategies.[17]

Moreover, technical analysis offers no economic theory of causation between past and future movements of stock prices.[18] It is based on the notion that "largely because of investor psychology, buying and selling patterns recur."[19] Technical analysis focuses exclusively on the internal dynamics of the stock markets; it ignores entirely the earnings of the corporations, which are the ultimate sources of value for the shares traded on the stock markets. . . .

2 Fundamental Analysis

As technical analysts focus on the trading patterns of stocks, so fundamental analysts focus on the earnings of corporations. Since future changes in stock prices are significantly correlated with future changes in corporate earnings,[20] any fundamental analyst who could predict future changes in corporate earnings could thereby predict future changes in stock prices to a substantial degree. The main problem is that future changes in corporate earnings are themselves randomly related to past records of corporate earnings.[21] In other words, a corporation with earnings of $1 million in 1976 is as likely to have earnings of $0.8 million as it is to have earnings of $1.2 million in 1977. For this reason, fundamental analysis will be of economic value only if the analyst uncovers new information about a company's earning potential[22] or makes a new interpretation of existing data about that company. . . .

3 The Social Benefits of Securities Research

[Adherents to the Efficient Market Hypothesis (EMH) do not claim that security analysis is a worthless pursuit. On the contrary, they hold that the workings of efficient markets are vitally dependent on the labors of thousands of analysts and investors; it is just that these poor fellows do not realize, or refuse to believe, that their efforts will not be rewarded. Moreover, we are also told that all those astute financial institutions are paying millions of dollars for research that will not benefit them but will rather fulfill the broader social purpose of keeping our security markets efficient. Adherents to EMH want us to believe this and more. Thus we are to believe that investors and analysts are only selectively rational, that is, they are rational in making the investment decisions which are necessary to keep our securities markets efficient but they are irrational in disbelieving the EMH, which disbelief is essential to the continued efficiency of our security markets. Why, we must ask, should we believe that such an inconsistency in rational behavior on the part of investors and security analysts actually exists? What would happen to the markets' efficiency if investors and analysts refused to expend any longer efforts which cannot benefit them personally? Can true believers in EMH continue to reap the benefits which the work of the disbelievers bestows on them? Can they buy and sell securities with the same degree of confidence as is possessed by those who expend efforts at research?—from Bernstein, 1975][23]

C Lower Risks Through Diversification

While money managers cannot easily find stocks with higher returns in the same risk category, through diversification they can generally decrease the aggregate risk of their investments without decreasing aggregate returns. The basic principle of diversification is that the overall construction of the portfolio, rather than the selection of individual securities, should be the focus of investment decisions.[24] To the extent that the individual securities in the portfolio react differently to the same future events, the aggregate risks of a portfolio of securities is lower than the average of the risks of the individual securities.[25] To take a simplified example, suppose a portfolio consists of two shares of stock—one from Company A that manufactures oil heaters, the other from Company B that manufactures gas heaters. If only oil prices increase, the stock of Company A will decline but the stock of Company B will rise. Conversely, if only gas prices increase, the stock of Company A will rise but the stock of Company B will decline. Since the price movement of each share of stock is offset by the price movement of the other share of stock, the aggregate risk of this portfolio will be lower than the average of the risks of both shares. To decrease the aggregate risk of a portfolio, economists have suggested several types of diversification strategies. . . .

Building on Markowitz's work, William Sharpe proposed a simplified model for ascertaining the efficient frontier of portfolios.[26] Sharpe divided all the risks of a security into two components—alpha and beta coefficients. *Alpha risk* refers to that portion of the price variation of a security attributable to the unique characteristics of the issuer. Since alpha risk by definition is not correlated to the price movements of other securities, it can be eliminated through perfect diversification of a securities portfolio without reducing returns.[27] *Beta risk* refers to that portion of the price variation of a security attributable to the price movements of the stock market as a whole.[28] For example, a stock with a beta of 1.0 will tend to rise and fall with the stock market averages. A stock with a beta of 1.5 will tend to rise 50% more than the stock market when it is rising and to decline 50% more than the stock market when it is declining. Conversely, a stock with a beta of 0.5 will tend to rise 50% less than the stock market when it is rising and to decline 50% less than the stock market when it is declining. Since beta risk by definition represents the degree to which each security reacts in the same way as all other securities, it is impossible to reduce beta risk through diversification without reducing the returns of the portfolio.[29] Thus, given the difficulty of finding undervalued stocks with higher returns than other stocks in the same risk category, Sharpe's efficient frontier is theoretically defined as the securities portfolio at each level of beta risk that has eliminated all alpha risk through perfect diversification. . . .

According to the separation theorem proposed by Sharpe,[30] money managers can attain any beta level selected as an overall investment objective by combining the best portfolio of risky assets (the best risky portfolio) with risk-free assets or borrowed funds. A risky asset (such as a common stock) has a number of possible outcomes so its return may vary; a risk-free asset (such as a United States savings bond) has only one outcome so its return is certain.[31] Under Sharpe's assumptions, the best risky portfolio for all investors is the "market portfolio."[32] While the market portfolio theoretically includes all stocks, the 500 stocks in the Standard & Poor's index are typically used as a proxy for the whole stock market. By definition, a market portfolio contains no alpha risk and has a beta of 1.0; it will move precisely in step with the stock market as a whole. If money managers want an overall beta below 1.0, they should place some of their funds in the market portfolio and some of their funds in a risk-free asset. If money managers want an overall beta above 1.0, they should place all of their funds in the market portfolio and then leverage their investment by borrowing more money to place in the market portfolio. By using the market portfolio in conjunction with risk-free assets or borrowed funds, money managers can theoretically extend the boundaries of the efficient frontier of securities portfolios.[33]

If Sharpe's separation theorem were valid in practice, money managers would have no legitimate reason for purchasing securities research after the selection of an overall investment objective. To attain the maximum return at the selected beta level, money managers would simply employ the market portfolio in conjunction with the correct percentage of risk-free assets or borrowed funds. Sharpe's model for portfolio selection, however, has not been fully supported by empirical studies.[34] These studies suggest that the assumptions behind Sharpe's separation theorem are somewhat unrealistic.[35]

First, Sharpe's market portfolio is the best risky portfolio for all investors only if they have identical expectations, time horizons, and tax rates with respect to each financial asset.[36] If any of these assumptions is not met, then the best risky portfolio will depend on the specific circumstances of each investor. The validity of these assumptions has been questioned for investors generally;[37] the assumptions seem particularly inappropriate for money managers in financial institutions. The time horizon of each money manager is heavily influenced by the liquidity of the outstanding claims by savers against the financial institution. The investment advisers to mutual funds must invest in relatively liquid assets like NYSE-listed stocks since the shares of mutual funds are continuously redeemable. By contrast, the money managers of life insurance companies can invest in relatively illiquid assets like real estate because the payout schedule of their companies is fairly predictable. The tax constraints on investments by money managers are also different for each type of financial institution. For instance, the stock dividends earned by most pension funds are tax-exempt, while the stock dividends earned by most trust accounts are taxable to the trust or the beneficiaries.

Second, Sharpe's separation theorem for attaining beta levels below 1.0 assumes that risk-free assets exist. Although debt securities issued or guaranteed by the United States are typically used as risk-free assets, they are not truly risk-free. There is the extreme possibility that the government of the United States might default on its debts. Apart from that remote possibility, the debt securities of the United States entail the significant risk of less purchasing power through domestic inflation[38] and perhaps through adverse changes in international exchange rates. If money managers conclude that risk-free assets do not exist, then they should not attempt to reach beta levels below 1.0 by allocating funds between the market portfolio and risk-free assets. Instead these money managers should choose the best risky portfolio on the efficient frontier for beta levels below 1.0.[39] A more realistic approach is to recognize several types of assets that are almost risk-free but with different interest rates, tax features, and time dimensions. Money managers choose among these risk-free assets on the basis of their liquidity demands, tax status, and other factors. As a result, each money manager may face different risk-free rates. For example, the risk-free rate may be the interest rate on a three-month Treasury bill for a mutual fund and the interest rate on a six-year insured savings account for a pension fund. Thus, money managers should first find their best risky portfolio on the efficient frontier in light of their actual risk-free rate; if the beta of this best risky portfolio is not as low as their overall investment objective, then they should allocate funds between this best risky portfolio and the appropriate risk-free asset.[40]

Third, Sharpe's separation theorem for attaining beta levels above 1.0 assumes that money managers can borrow large sums of money at the risk-free rate.[41] In practice, the borrowing rates for almost all money managers are substantially above the interest rates on insured savings accounts and United States Treasury bills, typically used as risk-free assets. As money managers try to borrow larger and larger sums, banks will probably increase the interest rate or simply refuse to lend more funds. In addition, under current laws most money managers cannot freely borrow for the purpose of leveraging a market portfolio. The Securities Exchange Act of 1934 and the Investment Company Act of 1940, for instance, severely restrict borrowing by mutual funds. The Tax Reform Act of 1969 imposes a tax on pension funds that borrow directly to purchase securities. State statutes require life insurance companies to maintain substantial reserves and invest certain sums in government securities. Thus, if money managers cannot borrow for practical or legal reasons, they should choose the best risky portfolio on the efficient frontier for beta levels above 1.0.[42] If money managers can borrow sufficient funds but at higher interest rates than their risk-free rate, they should first find their best risky portfolio on the efficient frontier in light of their actual borrowing rate; if the beta of this best risky portfolio is not as high as their overall investment objective, then they should leverage this risky portfolio to the appropriate degree.[43]

Notes

1. For a general introduction to the economic literature, see R. Brealey, *An Introduction to Risk and Return from Common Stocks* (1969). To be precise, the term "portfolio theory" refers to the abstract model on risk and return developed by Professor Harry Markowitz; the term "capital asset pricing theory" refers to the workable model for evaluation of portfolios developed by Professor William Sharpe. But this Article will use portfolio theory to include the contributions of both Professors Markowitz and Sharpe.
2. For a discussion of the reasonableness of this approximation, see Cohen, "The Suitability Rule and Economic Theory," 80 *Yale L.J.* 1604, 1618–19 (1971).
3. Returns include both price increases or decreases, and dividends (if any).
4. For example, suppose stock X had a .35 probability of a 9% return, a .40 probability of an 8% return, a .15 probability of a 7% return and a .10 probability of a 6% return. The expected return of stock X is the weighted average of all these possible returns according to their probability of occurrence, which in this example would be 8%, calculated as follows: $(.35)(9\%) + (.40)(8\%) + (.15)(7\%) + (.10)(6\%) = 8\%$. This example is adapted from Bines, "Modern Portfolio Theory and Investment Management Law: Refinement of Legal Doctrine," 76 *Colum. L. Rev.* 721, 738 (1976).
5. Using the same figures for stock X provided in note 4 supra, the variance of the returns of stock X can be calculated by (1) squaring the difference between each possible return and the expected return;

(2) weighting the squares from step (1) according to their probability of occurrence; and (3) adding together all the weighted squares from step (2).

In the case of stock X, for example, the first step is to calculate the difference between each possible return and the expected return, and then to square the difference. The results are:

$9\% - 8\% = 1\% \times 1 = 1\%$

$8\% - 8\% = 0\% \times 0 = 0\%$

$8\% - 7\% = 1\% \times 1 = 1\%$

$8\% - 6\% = 2\% \times 2 = 4\%$

The second step is to weight the squares from step (1) according to their relative probability of occurrence. The results are:

$1\% \times .35 = .35\%$

$0\% \times .40 = 0\%$

$1\% \times .15 = .15\%$

$4\% \times .10 = .40\%$

The third step is to add together the weighted squares from the second step, which yields a variance of .9% for stock X.

6. J. Lorie & M. Hamilton, The Stock Market: Theories and Evidence 211–27 (1973). But see Modigliani & Pogue, "An Introduction to Risk and Return," *Financial Analysts J.*, May–June 1974, at 69, 77–82, 84–85.

7. J. Cohen, E. Zinbarg & A. Zeikel, *Investment Analysis and Portfolio Management* 739 (1973).

8. Langbein & Posner, "Market Funds and Trust-Investment Law," 1976 *Am. B. Foundation Research J.* 7–8; cf. Friedman & Savage, "The Utility Analysts of Choices Involving Risk," 56 *J. Pol. Econ.* 279, 284, 300–01 (1948).

9. As Bines states: "Plainly, if pure chance is to be an element of a person's investment policy, he requires no professional help to roll the dice." Bines, *supra* note 4, at 759.

10. Money managers cannot simply choose stocks with higher returns at the same risk level because higher returns are generally associated with higher risk stocks. Nor can money managers simply increase returns by choosing high risk stocks, because investors are generally risk averse. Thus, money managers should invest for the highest returns at the particular level of risk selected. Cohen, Zinbarg & Zeikel, *supra* note 7, at 742.

11. See R. Hagin & C. Mader, *The New Science of Investing* 97–106 (1973).

12. Cohen, Zinbarg & Zeikel, *supra* note 7, at 514.

13. A short sale is the sale of a security at time 1 by a seller who does not own the security at time 1, but who effectively promises to deliver by buying the security at time 2. Short sellers hope that the stock price will decline so that the price received for the sale at time 1 will be higher than the price required to buy the stock at time 2.

14. Fundamental and technical analysis can, of course, be used together; they are not mutually exclusive.

15. For a general review of these economic studies, see Fama, "Efficient Capital Markets: A Review of Theory and Empirical Work," 25 *J. Finance* 383 (1970) [hereinafter Fama, "Efficient Capital Markets"]. The randomness is between past data and the *direction* as well as the *amount* of future changes in stock prices. These are, of course, the two critical variables in making investment choices. A money manager who buys a stock at 200, for instance, wants to know whether it will go up to 220 or down to 180.

16. Hagin & Mader, *supra* note 11, at 61–83.

17. *Id.* At 68–69. *See also* Fama & Blume, "Filter Rules and Stock Trading," 39 *J. Bus.* 226–41 (1966).

18. McQuown, "Technical and Fundamental Analysis and Capital Market Theory," *J. Bank Research*, Spring 1973, at 10–11.

19. Bines, *supra* note 4, at 789–90 (footnote omitted).

20. Brealey, *supra* note 1 at 77–81.

21. *Id.* At 88–103; Lorie & Hamilton, *supra* note 6, at 158–63.

22. Cohen, Zinbarg & Zeikel, *supra* note 7, at 753.

23. Bernstein, "In Defense of Fundamental Analysis," *Financial Analysts J.*, Jan.–Feb. 1975, at 4–5.

24. Note, "Fiduciary Standards and the Prudent Man Rule Under the Employment Retirement Income Security Act of 1974," 88 *Harv. L. Rev.* 960, 970–71 (1975) [hereinafter Note, *Fiduciary Standards*].

25. Cohen, *supra* note 2, at 1611–12 & n.39.

26. Sharpe, "A Simplified Model for Portfolio Analysis," 9 *Management Sci.* 277 (1963). The simplified model is often referred to as the Sharpe-Lintner-Mossin model since Lintner and Mossin arrived at models similar to Sharpe's through different methodologies. See Lintner, "Valuation of Risk Assets and the Selection of Risky Investments in Stock Portfolios and Capital Budgets," 47 *Rev. Econ. & Statistics* 13 (1965); Mossin, "Equilibrium in a Capital Asset Market," 34 *Econometrica* 768 (1966).

27. Bines, *supra* note 4, at 752–53; *see* Langbein & Posner, *supra* note 8, at 9–10.

28. Studies indicate that beta accounts for 30–50% of the price movements of listed stocks; the remainder is accounted for by alpha. Cohen, Zinbarg & Zeikel, *supra* note 7, at 769–70 & n.41.

29. See Bines, *supra* note 4, at 753; Langbein & Posner, *supra* note 8, at 9–10. The beta of a portfolio as a whole is defined as the weighted average of the beta of each security in the portfolio. Cohen, Zinbarg & Zeikel, *supra* note 7, at 771.

30. W. Sharpe, *Portfolio Theory and Capital Markets* 69–70 (1970). See also Brealey, *supra* note 1, at 115–22.

31. See Cohen, *supra* note 2, at 1607.

32. See Lorie & Hamilton, *supra* note 6, at 189.

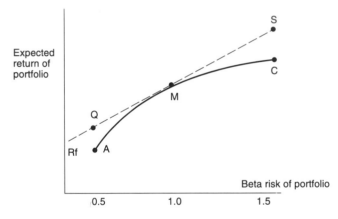

Figure 1.1.1

33. In the above graph, figure 1.1.1, M represents the market portfolio; the curve AMC represents the efficient frontier as defined by Markowitz. The line QMS is called the capital market line. It is derived by drawing a ray from the level of return for risk-free assets (Rf) through the point of tangency with the efficient frontier. This point of tangency will be the market portfolio (M) as long as a number of assumptions are met. See Lorie & Hamilton, *supra* note 6, at 188–89.

Suppose money managers wanted to attain an overall investment objective of 0.5. If they simply constructed a securities portfolio with a beta of 0.5 and with as little alpha as possible through diversification, they would be at point A. If they put half of their funds in the market portfolio (M) and half in risk-free assets, they would be at point Q, clearly superior to point A.

Suppose money managers wanted to attain an overall investment objective of 1.5. If they simply constructed a securities portfolio with a beta of 1.5 and with as little alpha as possible through diversification, they would be at point C. If they invested all their funds plus the same amount of borrowed funds in the market portfolio, they would be at point S, clearly superior to point C.

34. Black, Jensen & Scholes, "The Capital Asset Pricing Model: Some Empirical Tests," in *Studies in the Theory of Capital Markets* 79–82, 113–115 (M. Jensen ed. 1972) [hereinafter *Studies*]; Miller Scholes, "Rates of Returns in Relations to Risk: A Re-examination of Some Recent Findings," in *Studies, supra* at 47, 48–52, 71–72. *See also* Lorie & Hamilton, *supra* note 6, at 210; Modigliani & Pogue, *supra* note 6, at 78–82.

35. See *Editor's Comment:* "Why the Beta Models Broke Down," *Financial Analysts J.*, July–Aug. 1975, at 9 [hereinafter *Editor's Comment*].

36. See Lorie & Hamilton, *supra* note 6, at 200; Sharpe, "Capital Asset Prices: A Theory of Market Equilibrium Under Conditions of Risk," 19 *J. Finance* 425, 433–34 (1964).

37. See Lorie & Hamilton, *supra* note 6, at 205–07.

38. See Cohen, *supra* note 2, at 1619–20 & n.60; Note, "The Regulation of Risky Investments," 83 *Harv. L. Rev.* 622–24 (1970). Money managers can try to minimize the risk of inflation by purchasing three-month Treasury bills instead of long-term government securities. But then money managers pay a premium (in the form of lower interest) for the extremely high liquidity of such Treasury bills, which is not necessary for most money managers. See *Editor's Comment, supra* note 35, at 9.

    The effect of inflation not only creates difficulties for the separation theorem as applied to beta levels below 1.0, but also poses unresolved problems for measuring return and risk that underlie all of portfolio theory. See Biger, "The Assessment of Inflation and Portfolio Selection," 30 *J. Finance* 451 (1975).

39. In the graph in note 40 *infra*, money managers would seek portfolios on the curve AWM for beta levels below 1.0. See J. Francis & S. Archer, *Portfolio Analysis* 130–31 (1971).

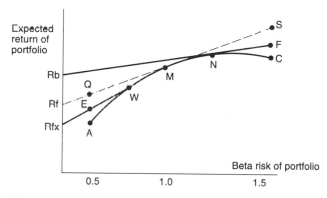

Figure 1.1.2

40. The graph above, figure 1.1.2, is a variation on the graph in note 33 *supra*. The two different risk-free rates on the Y-axis are represented by Rf and Rfx. If Rfx were the risk-free rate for some types of money managers, they would find the best risky portfolio by drawing a line from Rfx to the tangent point on curve AMC, point W in this diagram. To attain an overall beta of 0.5, such money managers would place some funds in portfolio W and some funds in risk-free assets at the Rfx rate. The result would be to attain a beta level of 0.5 at point E. While E is superior to point A on the efficient frontier, it is inferior to point Q on the capital market line.

41. See Lorie & Hamilton, *supra* note 6, at 205–06.

42. In the graph in note 40 *supra*, money managers would seek risky portfolios on the curve MNC.

43. In the graph in note 40 *supra*, Rb represents the actual interest rate for borrowing above the risk-free rate Rf. To find the best risky portfolio, money managers would draw a ray from Rb to its tangent point on AMC, point N. To attain an overall beta of 1.5, such money managers would leverage portfolio N with borrowed funds to attain point F, superior to point C on the efficient frontier, but inferior to point S on the capital market line.

1.2   What Is a Mutual Fund?*

A mutual fund is an investment company that pools money from shareholders and invests in a diversified portfolio of securities. An estimated 63 million individual Americans in 37 million U.S. households own mutual fund shares.

Three Basic Types of Mutual Funds

There are three basic types of mutual funds: stock (also called equity); bond and income; and money market. Money market funds are referred to as short-term funds because they invest in securities that generally mature in about one year or less, whereas stock and bond and income funds are known as long-term funds. Of the total $3.539 trillion invested in mutual funds at the end of 1996, $1.751 trillion was invested in stock funds, $886.5 billion in bond and income funds, and $901.9 billion in money market funds (figures 1.2.1 and 1.2.2).

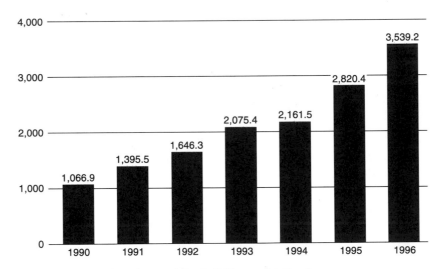

Figure 1.2.1   Assets of mutual funds (billions of dollars)

---

*From Investment Company Institute, *1997 Mutual Fund Fact Book*, 37th edition. Reprinted with permission.

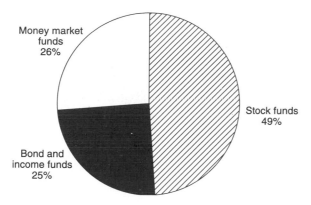

Figure 1.2.2 How mutual funds are invested (year-end 1996)

An investor in a mutual fund is a shareholder who buys shares of the fund. Each share represents a proportionate ownership in all the fund's underlying securities. The securities are selected by a professional investment adviser to meet a specified financial goal, such as growth or income.

It is important to remember that you can lose money in a mutual fund. Because funds invest in securities that rise and fall in value, an investor assumes investment risk, including the possible loss of principal. Unlike bank deposits, mutual funds are not insured or guaranteed by the Federal Deposit Insurance Corporation or any other government agency, nor are they guaranteed by any bank or other financial institution—no matter how or where their shares are sold. Of course, there is also an upside to investment risk. Generally speaking, the greater the investment risk, the greater the potential reward.

Professional Management

The money accumulated in a mutual fund is managed by professionals who decide investment strategy on behalf of shareholders. These professionals choose investments that best match the fund's objectives as described in the prospectus. Their investment decisions are based on extensive knowledge and research of market conditions and the financial performance of individual companies and specific securities. As economic conditions change, the fund may adjust the mix of its investments to adopt a more aggressive or a more defensive posture to meet its investment objective.

Diversification

Fund managers typically invest in a variety of securities, seeking portfolio diversification. A diversified portfolio helps reduce risk by off-setting losses from some securities with gains in others. The average investor would find it expensive and difficult to construct a portfolio as diversified as that of a mutual fund. Mutual funds provide an economical way for average investors to obtain the same kind of professional money management and diversification of investments that are available to large institutions and wealthy investors.

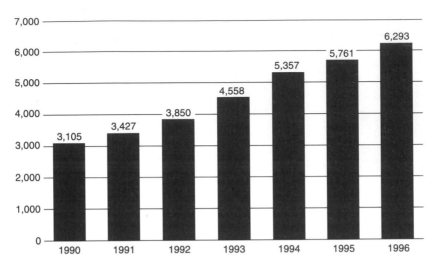

Figure 1.2.3   Number of mutual funds

A Variety of Fund Investments

There are more than 6,200 mutual funds representing a wide variety of investment objectives, from conservative to aggressive, and investing in a wide range of securities (figure 1.2.3). The Investment Company Institute classifies mutual funds into 21 broad categories according to their basic investment objective. There are also specialty or sector funds that invest primarily in a specialized segment of the securities markets. Specialty funds include biotechnology funds, small-company growth funds, index funds, funds that invest in other mutual funds, and social criteria funds. The broad selection of funds arose over the years to meet consumer demand for fund products that help meet a variety of financial objectives.

Daily Pricing

Mutual funds must calculate the price of their shares every business day. Investors can sell (redeem) some or all of their shares anytime and receive the current share price, which may be more or less than the price originally paid. The share price, called net asset value or NAV, is the market value of all the fund's securities, minus expenses, divided by the total number of shares outstanding. The NAV changes as the values of the underlying securities rise or fall, and as the fund changes its portfolio by buying new securities or selling existing ones. Daily NAVs appear in the financial pages of most major newspapers (figure 1.2.4).

When a fund earns money on its portfolio securities, it distributes the earnings to shareholders as dividends or, if the securities are sold for a profit, as capital gains. Shareholders also may elect to reinvest their dividends and capital gains in the purchase of additional fund shares. If the overall value of the securities held by a fund increases, the value of the fund's portfolio increases as well. Dividends and capital gains are paid out to the fund's shareholders in proportion to the number of shares owned. Thus, investors who put $1,000 in the fund get the same investment return per dollar as those who invest $100,000.

How to Read Newspaper Fund Quotes

The following is an example of how mutual fund tables appear in many newspapers. Several funds listed under a single heading indicate a family of funds.

▲ The first column is the abbreviated fund's name. Several funds listed under a single heading indicate a family of funds.

▲ The second column is the Net Asset Value (NAV) per share as of the close of the preceding business day. In some newspapers, the NAV is identified as the sell or the bid price—the amount per share you would receive if you sold your shares (less the deferred sales charge, if any). Each mutual fund determines its net asset value every business day by dividing the market value of its total net assets, less liabilities, by the number of shares outstanding. On any given day, you can determine the value of your holdings by multiplying the NAV by the number of shares you own.

▲ The third column is the offering price or, in some papers, the buy price or the asked price—the price you would pay if you purchased shares. The buy price is the NAV plus any sales charges. If there are no initial sales charges, an NL for no-load appears in this column, and the buy price is the same as the NAV. To figure the sales charge percentage, divide the difference between the NAV and the offering price by the offering price. Here, for instance, the sales charge is 5 percent ($14.18 - $13.47 = $0.71 ÷ $14.18 = 0.050).

▲ The fourth column shows the change, if any, in net asset value from the preceding day's quotation—in other words, the change over the most recent one-day trading period. This fund, for example, gained six cents per share.

▲ A "p" following the abbreviated name of the fund denotes a fund that charges an annual fee from assets for marketing and distribution costs, also known as a 12b-1 plan (named after the 1980 Securities and Exchange Commission rule that permits them).

▲ If the fund name is followed by an "r," the fund has either a contingent deferred sales charge (CDSC) or a redemption fee. A CDSC is a charge if shares are sold within a certain period; a redemption charge is a fee applied whenever shares are sold.

▲ A "t" designates a fund that has both a CDSC or a redemption fee and a 12b-1 fee.

▲ An "f" indicates a fund that habitually enters the previous day's prices, instead of the current day's.

Other footnotes may also apply to a fund listing. Please see the explanatory notes that accompany mutual fund tables in your newspaper.

Fund	NAV	Offer	Chg
Apzbc:			
Axyte	9.95	10.73	...
Bxy Xer	10.37	11.33	-.01
Dar Rppe	7.38	8.07	+.09
Income	3.16	3.45	+.01
Tbqr Ratl	9.97	10.47	+.01
Tbqr Dt	10.19	10.70	-.02
Xypr Apr r	10.05	10.98	-.01
Brlkd:			
Blgr Dfr	15.64	16.46	-.03
Bmo Pnc	8.54	N.L.	-.06
Bto Bmd	7.27	7.65	...
Cmyog:			
MIA p	11.86	12.79	+.01
MIX	11.44	12.33	+.03
MIY P	9.70	10.46	-.01
MBF	11.58	12.49	+.04
MBI	14.18	15.92	+.20
MBR	11.99	12.93	+.03
MRI	13.47	14.18	-.04
MII	7.66	8.25	+.02
MDX	10.00	10.50	...
DMX r	9.74	10.23	...
GYI	6.93	7.47	-.03
JAM	10.01	10.79	-.02
JEL	10.09	10.59	-.06
MTNC	10.25	10.76	-.02
MPRS r	10.12	10.62	+.02
Jellies	20.33	N.L.	+.01
Suiter	23.81	N.L.	+.13
Drxpg:			
Bakc Jau	15.45	16.52	+.06
Cryl Ba	20.68	22.12	+.05
Gryd 3	12.10	12.60	-.04
Frp Dup	9.80	10.45	-.11
Fye Pm	12.61	N.L.	...
Hy Finc	8.19	8.53	-.01
Hx Papie	10.96	11.42	-.06
Lerl Eiy t	10.02	10.95	+.02
Jxt RP	10.90	11.12	-.04
Lante	12.01	13.14	-.02
Mina Si	7.36	7.67	-.01
MsalT t	9.56	9.96	+.01
Nuz Bai	9.85	9.95	...
Oceana	16.49	17.64	+.12
Grxya	15.30	N.L.	+.04
Gsrxab r	12.96	N.L.	-.04
Hilt ltd	10.54	N.L.	-.02
Holpre r	8.40	N.L.	-.02
Hprl Rd	13.58	N.L.	+.07
Nev Sra	16.65	N.L.	-.01
Ow Nort	13.53	N.L.	+.17
Sys Run	5.08	N.L.	-.01
Tqr Hyd	8.73	N.L.	-.02
Tuir IS	10.26	N.L.	-.03
T'rsa Ei	5.11	N.L.	-.01
Veersl Yr	9.49	9.87	+.07
Fdrlk:			
U'nd Eec p	10.18	N.L.	+.03
R'no Ond r	10.77	N.L.	+.02
Itra Nico p	8.54	N.L.	-.06
Gpprl:			
Aiist B	24.00	N.L.	+.01
Cuy Nini	10.76	N.L.	-.03
Eqryti	15.87	16.71	+.02
Ginta Ir	12.00	N.L.	+.01
Gyvt Lis	10.18	N.L.	+.03
Hear /ec	10.40	10.51	-.02
Jbd Hld	10.23	10.77	-.04
JlY sun	14.78	15.40	+.03
Mtri JN	10.93	N.L.	-.01
Op Sec	12.97	13.65	...
Prtn Ta	16.40	17.25	+.03
Rsil Nc	15.33	16.14	-.06
Esrrch R t	9.24	N.L.	-.04
Xiil Ndix	12.13	12.77	+.22
Htoje:			
ACT trp t	47.99	49.22	+.06
ACT asp r	48.89	50.14	+.11
Aal AxC	14.15	14.86	-.03
Batt Pd	10.18	N.L.	+.03
Chrg tt	14.28	15.61	-.01
Dmty E f	11.04	12.07	+.03
Grante	12.02	13.14	-.02
Hdro le	11.53	12.60	-.01
Ilen He	18.82	20.57	+.12
Jl Ncom	11.97	12.84	-.06
Kgn Pod p	15.46	16.58	-.01
Tbq Rati	17.07	18.60	+.08
Tbqr Dt	10.72	11.72	+.01

Figure 1.2.4 [How to read newspaper fund quotes]

Regulation

All U.S. funds are subject to strict regulation and oversight by the Securities and Exchange Commission (SEC). As part of this regulation, all funds must provide investors with full and complete disclosure about the fund in a written prospectus. This document describes, among other things, the fund's investment objective, its investment methods, information about how to purchase and redeem shares, information about the investment adviser, and the level of risk the fund is willing to assume in pursuit of its objective. The SEC requires the placement of a fee table at the front of every prospectus. The descriptions in box 1.2.1 outline all fund fees and expenses and can be used to compare the costs of different funds.

All funds are required to provide their shareholders with annual and semiannual reports that contain recent information on the fund's portfolio, performance, and investment goals and policies. In addition, the investor receives a yearly statement detailing the federal tax status of his or her earnings from the fund. Mutual fund shareholders are taxed on the fund's income directly, as if they held the underlying securities themselves.

Box 1.2.1 Mutual fund fees and expenses

Shareholder Transaction Expenses are fees charged directly to the investor's account for a specific transaction, such as a purchase, redemption, or exchange.

- A *front-end sales charge or "load"* may be attached to the initial purchase of mutual fund shares. This fee is to compensate a financial professional for his or her services. By law, this charge may not exceed 8.5 percent of the initial investment, although most fund families charge less than the maximum.
- A *contingent deferred sales charge*, imposed at the time of redemption, is an alternative way to compensate financial professionals for their services. This fee typically applies for the first few years of ownership and then disappears.
- A *redemption fee* is another type of back-end charge for redeeming shares. It is expressed as a dollar amount or as a percentage of the redemption price.
- An *exchange fee* is the fee, if any, charged when transferring money from one fund to another within the same fund family.

Annual Operating Expenses reflect the normal costs of operating the fund (e.g., maintaining offices, staff, and equipment). Unlike transaction fees, these expenses are not charged directly to an investor's account, but are deducted from fund assets before earnings are distributed to shareholders.

- *Management fees* are ongoing fees charged by the fund's investment adviser for managing the fund and selecting its portfolio of securities. These fees generally average between 0.5 percent and 1 percent of the fund's assets annually.

12b-1 fees, charged by some funds, are deducted from fund assets to pay marketing and advertising expenses or, more commonly, to compensate sales professionals. By law, 12b-1 fees cannot exceed 0.75 percent of the fund's average net assets per year. The fund may also charge a service fee of up to 0.25 percent of average net assets per year to compensate sales professionals.

Similarly, any tax-exempt income received by a fund is generally passed on to the shareholders as tax-exempt.

Mutual funds are regulated under four federal laws designed to protect investors. The Investment Company Act of 1940 requires all funds to register with the SEC and to meet certain operating standards; the Securities Act of 1933 mandates specific disclosures; the Securities Exchange Act of 1934 sets out antifraud rules covering the purchase and sale of fund shares; and the Investment Advisers Act of 1940 regulates fund advisers.

Accessibility

Mutual fund shares are easy to buy. Investors (outside retirement plans) may purchase fund shares either with the help of an investment professional (e.g., a broker, financial planner, bank representative, or insurance agent) or directly, based on the investor's own research and knowledge. Investment professionals provide services to investors—analyzing the client's financial needs and objectives and recommending appropriate funds. They are compensated for those services, generally through a fee for service, a sales commission, or through 12b-1 fees deducted from the fund's assets.

Direct-marketed funds are sold through the mail, by telephone, or at office locations. They typically offer fund shares to the public with a low sales charge or none at all. Funds that do not charge a sales commission are known as "no-loads." Because direct-marketed funds do not usually offer specific investment advice, investors are required to do their own research and determine which funds meet their needs.

Mutual funds may also be offered as investment selections in 401(k) plans and other employee benefit plans.

Shareholder Services

Mutual funds offer a wide variety of services to meet shareholders' needs. These services include toll-free (800) telephone numbers, 24-hour telephone access, touch-tone telephone access to account information and transactions, consolidated account statements, shareholder cost basis (tax) information, exchanges between funds, automatic investments, checkwriting privileges on many money market and some bond funds, automatic reinvestment of fund dividends, and automatic withdrawals. Mutual funds also provide extensive investor education and shareholder communications, including newsletters, brochures, retirement and other planning guides, and websites.

1.3   The Organization and Operation of a Mutual Fund*

Mutual funds are highly regulated financial entities that must comply with a large number of federal laws and regulations. In particular, the Securities and Exchange Commission (SEC) regulates mutual funds under the Investment Company Act of 1940. The 1940 Act imposes restrictions not only on mutual funds but also on their investment advisers, principal underwriters, directors, officers, and employees.

Virtually all mutual funds are externally managed. They do not have employees of their own. Instead, their operations are conducted by affiliated organizations and independent contractors.

Directors

A mutual fund is governed by a board of directors. The directors of a mutual fund have oversight responsibility for the management of the fund's business affairs. They must exercise the care that a reasonably prudent person would take with his or her own business. They are expected to exercise sound business judgment, establish procedures, and undertake oversight and review of the performance of the investment adviser, principal underwriter, and others that perform services for the fund.

A provision of the 1940 Act states that at least 40 percent of a fund's board of directors must be independent of the fund's investment adviser or principal underwriter. Independent fund directors serve as watchdogs for shareholder interests and oversee a fund's investment adviser and others closely affiliated with the fund.

Shareholders

Like shareholders of other companies, mutual fund shareholders have specific rights. These include, with limited exceptions, the 1940 Act requirement that directors be elected by shareholders at a meeting called for that purpose. Material changes in the terms of a fund's investment advisory contract must be approved by a shareholder vote, and funds seeking to change investment objectives or policies deemed fundamental must also seek shareholder approval.

Investment Adviser

An investment adviser is responsible for selecting portfolio investments consistent with objectives and policies stated in the mutual fund's prospectus. The investment adviser

---

*From Investment Company Institute, *1997 Mutual Fund Fact Book*, 37th edition. Reprinted with permission.

places portfolio orders with broker-dealers and is responsible for obtaining the best overall execution of portfolio orders.

A written contract between a mutual fund and its investment adviser specifies the services the adviser performs. Most advisory contracts provide for the adviser to receive an annual fee based on a percentage of the fund's average net assets.

The adviser is subject to numerous legal restrictions, especially regarding transactions between itself and the fund it advises.

Administrator

Administrative services may be provided to a fund by an affiliate of the fund, such as the investment adviser, or by an unaffiliated third party. Administrative services include overseeing the performance of other companies that provide services to the fund and ensuring that the fund's operations comply with federal requirements. Typically, a fund administrator pays for office costs and personnel, provides general accounting services, and may also prepare and file SEC, tax, shareholder, and other reports.

Principal Underwriter

Most mutual funds continuously offer new shares to the public at a price based on the current value of fund assets minus any sales charges. Mutual funds usually distribute their shares through separate organizations designated as principal underwriters. Principal underwriters are regulated as broker-dealers and are subject to National Association of Securities Dealers, Inc. (NASD) rules governing mutual fund sales practices.

Custodian

Mutual funds are required by law to protect their portfolio securities by placing them with a custodian. Nearly all mutual funds use qualified bank custodians. The SEC requires mutual fund custodians to segregate mutual fund portfolio securities from other bank assets.

Transfer Agent

A transfer agent is employed by a mutual fund to conduct recordkeeping and related functions. Transfer agents maintain records of shareholder accounts, calculate and disburse dividends, and prepare and mail shareholder account statements, federal income tax information, and other shareholder notices. Some transfer agents prepare and mail statements confirming shareholder transactions and account balances, and maintain customer service departments to respond to shareholder inquiries.

1.4   How the Banking Industry Operates*

Commercial banks serve as intermediaries between customers who save and customers who borrow. Their principal activities, which we've outlined here, are to collect deposits and disburse loans. However, there's a wide divergence between individual commercial banks in terms of the markets they serve and their sources of earnings.

Other industry concerns that we'll consider are: costs related to obtaining and maintaining adequate funding sources; how to minimize the inherent risks in financing at a given interest rate; Federal Reserve policies and their effect on interest rates; and competitive influences on the retail and commercial strategies of regional and money center banks.

Bank Assets

A commercial bank's earnings are derived from a variety of sources. These "earning assets" include loans (commercial, consumer, and real estate) and securities (investment and trading account).

Loans

Commercial and industrial (C&I) loans can be made on a short-term, medium-term, or long-term basis and may be either secured or unsecured. Often the lowest-yielding of a bank's loans, C&I loans usually include compensating balance requirements, commitment fees, or both, although these requirements are becoming less common in today's intensely competitive environment. Processing costs are relatively low for C&I loans, and pricing (*i.e.*, interest rates and fees) is flexible.

Consumer loans, comprising installment and credit card lending, are usually medium-term in maturity, with predictable principal and interest payments. Credit risk and processing costs are generally higher than for business loans, and yields are subject to usury ceilings in some states.

Secured by a customer's property, commercial and residential real estate loans are generally long-term installment mortgages. Residential mortgages are usually the least risky and, like consumer loans, generate a predictable cash flow. Banks also make commercial real estate loans and or interim construction loans; these medium-term loans generate high yields and high risks.

According to Federal Deposit Insurance Corporation (FDIC) statistics, aggregate loans outstanding were valued at $2.8 trillion on December 31, 1996. Loans secured by real estate accounted for 41% of that sum, while C&I loans totaled 25%, loans to individuals totaled 20%, and other loans totaled 14%.

---

*From Standard & Poor's "Banking" Industry Survey, May 22, 1997, pp. 14–17.

Securities

Investment securities may be taxable (as are U.S. government bonds and other securities) or tax-exempt (such as state and local government securities). The maturities of these financial instruments vary widely. Individuals and institutions such as banks purchase securities as investments. A security's value is typically based on the interest rate it receives, and it will fluctuate with the market level of interest rates.

Banks purchase securities as a means of earning interest on assets while providing the liquidity that banks need to meet deposit withdrawals or to satisfy a sudden increase in loan demand. In addition, securities diversify a bank's risk, improve the overall quality of its earning assets portfolio, and help manage interest rate risk.

Investment securities are also an important source of a bank's earnings, particularly when lending is weak but funds for investing are plentiful. U.S. banks are major participants in the bond market. Municipals are generally longer term and less liquid than U.S. government and Treasury bonds, but their tax-exempt feature is attractive in reducing taxable income.

Trading account securities are interest-bearing securities primarily held for realizing capital gains. Because their trading performance is strongly affected by interest rate trends, they carry a high risk. For that reason, banks have historically held them in small allotments.

Liabilities

A bank's principal liabilities are consumer demand and time deposits; corporate demand and time deposits; foreign deposits and borrowings; negotiable certificates of deposit (jumbo CDs, usually sold in denominations of $100,000 or more); federal funds; other short-term borrowings (such as commercial paper); long-term debt; and shareholder's equity.

Deposits

Consumer savings plans with commercial banks consist of demand deposits, such as checking accounts, and time deposits, which include regular savings, money market, and negotiable order of withdrawal (NOW) accounts as well as six-month money market certificates. These sources of funds have historically proven to be stable and important for banks. The interest rates that they command vary along with overall money market interest rates, and they must be competitive in order to attract and keep depositors.

With deposit interest rates in the range of 3% to 4% over the past few years, deposit growth has been sluggish as consumers seek out higher-yielding alternatives such as mutual funds.

Minimizing Interest Rate Risks

Assets and liabilities can mature or be repriced in periods ranging from overnight to 30 years. Most, however, mature in less than one year, and few extend beyond five years. Interest rate risk occurs when a liability matures or is repriced out of sync with the asset that it's funding.

As a rule, banks don't match assets and liabilities on a one-to-one basis. Instead, assets and liabilities are grouped together into specific time frames, such as overnight, 30 days, 90 days, one year, and the like. Thus, within a given period, banks can determine their interest rate sensitivity.

If more of a bank's liabilities mature or are repriced before assets, the bank is said to be "liability-sensitive" or to have a negative gap. If more assets mature than liabilities, the bank is "asset-sensitive" or has a positive gap. If a bank's assets and liabilities are evenly matched, it's said to be balanced. In a period of falling interest rates, a bank with a negative gap will see net interest margins widen. Conversely, a bank with a positive gap will benefit during a period of rising rates.

The banking industry has become increasingly concerned with limiting its interest rate risk since 1979, when changes in the Federal Reserve's bank policies resulted in high and extremely volatile interest rates. Techniques for managing assets and liabilities have become more sophisticated. For example, interest rate hedging with futures and options and the use of "Macaulay duration" matching, which basically involves balancing liabilities and assets, have become more widespread. Most bank loans now come with variable rates. On the funding side, much of the debt, deposits, and preferred stock dividends also carry variable rates. As a result, much of the interest rate risk has been shifted from the lender to the borrower.

The Fed's Significant Influence

While the capital market deals in long-term investments, the money market is the arena in which banks, corporations, and U.S. government securities dealers can lend or borrow funds for one day to one year. As a major player in this arena, the Federal Reserve has a great deal of influence over the amount of funds available in the banking system on a day-to-day basis.

The Fed has three ways of adjusting the money supply. One is by conducting open-market operations, such as buying and selling Treasury bills. This method has a direct impact on the rate charged for federal funds (reserves loaned by one bank to another, typically overnight, to cover a shortfall in reserve requirements or to profit from excess reserves). Indirectly, it influences the interest rate structure of the economy as a whole.

Rising interest rates curtail demand for borrowing by increasing the cost of funds. This means of restricting money-supply growth also makes banks rely on a greater percentage of more expensive purchased funds. Banks must then become more selective in their lending and perhaps even raise their prime rate, which is the interest rate on loans to large creditworthy corporations.

Second, the Fed can control the money supply and interest rates by raising or lowering banks' reserve requirements on deposits. This is a far more powerful tool than open-market operations and thus is rarely used. Raising reserve requirements reduces banks' abilities to extend loans.

The Fed's most recent change in reserve requirements happened in February 1992, when the Fed tried to stimulate bank lending by lowering the reserve requirement on checking, NOW, and other transaction accounts to 10% from 12%. The Fed's action marked the first change in reserve requirements on these kinds of accounts since 1980. It released about $8 billion in reserves, which then became available for lending.

Finally, the Fed can control the money supply by raising or lowering the discount rate—the interest rate it charges member banks for loans that use government securities as collateral. Small changes in the discount rate can send signals to the bond markets regarding Federal Reserve monetary policy, thus influencing interest rates.

Over the past decade, the Fed has been lauded for reducing price inflation through its effective control of the money supply. It's important to note, however, that the Fed's control over the market isn't absolute, and that monetary policy doesn't always achieve the desired effect.

For example, a tightening in monetary policy is generally intended to reduce demand for bank credit. But initially, it can increase demand for two reasons. Many creditworthy customers substitute short-term borrowings for long-term debt in the hope of obtaining better terms on permanent financing at a later date. And customers tend to borrow in advance of actual needs to ensure that adequate funds are at their disposal.

Interest Rates Impact Bank Profits

The outlook for interest rates has important implications for banks' profits. Because the bulk of bank profits are derived from net interest income (the interest income received on loans minus the interest expense paid for borrowed funds), interest rates determine to a large extent how profitable a bank can be.

Net interest margins (a bank's net interest income divided by its average earning assets) are a common measure of a bank's ability to squeeze profits from its loans. Net interest margins widen or narrow depending on the direction of interest rates, the mix of funding sources underlying loans, and the time period until expiration (or duration) of the investment portfolio.

Falling interest rates have a positive effect on banks for several reasons. One is that net interest margins can expand, at least in the short term. This is because banks are still earning a higher-than-market yield on loans to customers, while the cost of funds goes down more quickly in response to the new, lower rates.

An interest rate decline also enhances the value of a bank's fixed-rate investment portfolio. In addition, it often stimulates loan demand and reduces delinquency rates, because the cost of credit declines. Of course, not all banks are affected equally by rate decreases. Banks that rely more heavily on borrowed funds than on customer deposits to fund loan growth typically reap greater benefits.

In the broadest sense, banks are inherently asset-sensitive because they derive a significant portion of their funding from essentially free sources, such as equity issues or demand deposits. This is especially true of the smaller regional banks that focus on garnering retail (consumer) deposits and have limited access to the purchased money markets. Unless they work to reduce that asset sensitivity, they tend to do better in periods of high interest rates. Money center banks, however, which rely heavily on borrowed funds and have a small retail deposit base relative to their asset size, tend to be liability-sensitive. Thus, they benefit most during periods of falling rates.

Fluctuations in interest rates, while important, don't have an absolute influence over the net interest margins of commercial banks, primarily because of banks' ability to adjust to such fluctuations. In theory, banks can match the maturities of their assets (loans and investments) and liabilities (deposits and borrowings) so that rates earned and rates paid move more or less in tandem and net interest margins remain relatively stable. In practice, however, banks can—and do—deviate from a perfectly balanced position.

Competitive Strategies: Retail and Commercial

Most banks in the United States are small, competing in limited markets for local business. Often these banks have to compete for retail business against money center banks and large regional banks operating in their territories.

Retail banking remains a service-oriented business, and today's banks are increasingly investing in new technology to make banking more pleasant and convenient for customers. Automatic teller machines (ATMs) are widespread. Many bank branches operate drive-through windows, and home banking services are being heavily marketed.

Competition has heated up in the retail market as some banks have expanded and achieved economies of scale through acquisitions. Interstate banks have the servicing advantages of larger ATM networks and more product offerings, such as mutual funds, insurance, and a broader variety of loan products.

The large money center banks compete for large corporate business in the national market. They strive to obtain wholesale business in the international markets, although Citicorp is the only U.S. money center that's truly global in its operating scope. Bankers Trust and J. P. Morgan don't have any consumer operations, and there isn't much overlap in the geographic territories of the other three money-center banks (Bank America, Chase Manhattan, and First Chicago). Money centers do compete against each other in certain categories, however, such as the so-called middle market that encompasses corporations with revenues of $100 million to $500 million.

Industry competition was heightened by the April 1996 merger of Chemical Bank and Chase Manhattan into a single bank known as Chase Manhattan. The new entity, now the largest U.S. bank, has set lofty performance goals for itself, including double-digit earnings growth, a return on equity (ROE) of 18% or better, and an efficiency ratio in the low 50s. (An efficiency ratio measures operating expenses to net revenues.) Other money centers will need to focus on more profitable products and improve efficiency to retain their business positions.

Increasingly, commercial banks must also compete with other types of financial institutions, such as credit card companies and other specialized consumer lending organizations. Meanwhile, the move toward revising or repealing the Glass-Steagall Act, which limits banks' investment underwriting powers, would mean further deregulation of financial markets. For example, commercial banks could make significant inroads into insurance and investment banking markets, where they're now pushing up against the limits of regulation. NationsBank and First Union, in particular, are two commercial banks that are trying to rapidly grow their capital management businesses.

Case Study: **Analyzing Credit Issues in a Money Market Fund**

Money market funds (MM Funds) are the type of mutual fund that is most similar to bank deposits. Both pay income, both do not fluctuate in value, and both are relatively safe. But there are crucial differences between a MM Fund and a bank deposit. The most important difference is that a bank deposit is insured by the Federal Deposit Insurance Corporation (FDIC)—a federally chartered corporation that insures deposits held by commercial banks and thrift institutions—up to $100,000, while MM Funds are not insured by any government agency.

Instead of being insured by the FDIC, MM Funds are subject to strict regulation by the Securities and Exchange Commission (SEC). With regard to taxable money market funds, the type involved in this case study, the SEC imposes three key regulatory restrictions. First, at least 95% of the MM Fund's assets must be invested in the highest quality money market instruments (rated A-1, P-1 or equivalent). Second, the MM Fund may not invest more than 5% of its assets in any single top-rated issuer (other than the federal government), and no more than 1% of its assets in any second-rated issuer. Third, the average maturity of the MM Fund's assets may not exceed 90 days.

MM Funds must determine on a daily basis their net asset value or "NAV" (the current value of the fund's portfolio divided by the number of shares of the fund outstanding). MM Funds generally distribute all net income of the fund as it is earned and use an accounting technique to maintain a constant dollar value for each share, rather than a fluctuating value as do the shares of stock and bond funds. By using amortized cost accounting, distributing all income as received, and rounding NAV to the nearest penny, a MM Fund will usually be able to maintain a NAV of $1 per share. If a MM Fund were to incur losses of $\frac{1}{2}$ of 1% or more on its portfolio, however, its NAV would drop below $1—called "breaking the buck." Such losses would occur mainly in the event of a credit default on a substantial position in one issuer held by a MM Fund, but could also occur in the event of a very severe movement in interest rates for a MM Fund with a relatively long maturity.

Despite these regulatory restrictions, one MM Fund has actually broken the buck and several have come close. In these situations, the investment manager of a MM Fund faces an unattractive set of alternatives, including letting the MM Fund break the buck, or buying the defaulted paper at its face value from the MM Fund and absorbing the loss itself. This is precisely the situation faced by T. Rowe Price in the case study for this chapter.

In-Class Team Discussion

After group discussion, each team should be prepared to answer the following questions:

1. How and why do banks and mutual funds differ from the viewpoint of the sponsoring financial services company?

2. What are the major differences between a bank account and a money market fund from a customer's viewpoint?

3. From the consumer's viewpoint, why would you choose a bank account over a money market fund, or vice versa?

4. Why would T. Rowe Price be so concerned about recognizing a loss in Prime Reserves? Please quantify the accounting issue. What would be the impact of a loss in Prime Reserves on money market funds of other fund sponsors?

5. What alternative courses of action were open to T. Rowe Price in relation to Prime Reserves' holding of MRT paper? What was the best alternative, and why? What was your evaluation of other alternatives?

6. Would T. Rowe Price's stock and bond mutual funds face the same challenge confronting the manager of the Prime Reserve Fund?

7. Would bank management ever face the situation confronting the manager of the Prime Reserve Fund?

8. What does it mean when a bank becomes insolvent? In that event, what happens to the bank depositor?

9. Can a money market fund become insolvent in the same sense as a bank? Can there be a run on a money market fund?

1.5   Threatening to Break a Buck*

On March 12, 1990, Standard & Poor's downgraded the commercial paper of Mortgage & Realty Trust Co. ("MRT") from A-2 to A-3. MRT's access to the commercial paper market was shut off overnight, and previously committed bank credit lines were withdrawn. On March 13, MRT missed a $13 million payment due on maturing medium term notes. A further $97 million of the trust's commercial paper and other indebtedness would be maturing by month's end, as would an additional $200 million within the year. MRT began negotiations with banks and other lenders to try to secure a line of credit sufficient to cover its near-term cash needs.

T. Rowe Price Associates, Inc. ("TRPA") was the single largest holder of MRT paper: $65 million face value of which $42 million was in its Prime Reserve money market fund, and $23 million in various investment advisory accounts. TRPA had to decide whether to intervene and preserve Prime Reserve's unblemished record. Among various alternatives, TRPA could participate in the financing MRT was seeking, and/or it could purchase the MRT paper from the fund and other affected accounts.

Background on T. Rowe Price Associates, Inc.

T. Rowe Price was one of the largest money management organizations in the U.S. At the end of 1989, the firm had $28 billion in assets, of which $17 billion was in mutual funds, and $11 billion in separate accounts (mostly pension funds and endowments). TRPA was one of the few publicly traded independent money management firms. It went public in 1986 at $12 per share, and in March 1990, was trading at around $30. Company insiders owned 23% of the 14.4 million shares outstanding. Exhibits 1–3 contain summary financials; exhibit 4 gives a breakdown of the firm's mutual fund products. The following is an excerpt from the February 1990 Prime Reserves annual report:

The 1980s were ... kind to T. Rowe Price, and we begin the new decade as one of the largest independent investment management firms in the country. During the '80s, our staff tripled in size to over 1,000, the mutual fund assets we manage grew from about $5 billion to $17 billion, and the total number of shareholder accounts expanded from 350,000 to over 1.5 million.

Nonetheless, these years of rapid growth have not changed our dedication to serving individual and institutional investors. We have had no other business since our founding in 1937.

Our strategy, which we believe has served you and us well in good and bad times, rests on several long-held principles:

• Integrity must prevail in every aspect of our business.

- Our time and energy must be devoted to the investment management business, which we know well, and not to unrelated activities which could detract from our primary focus.
- Our shareholders' and other clients' interests come first; if your interests are served, ours will be also over time.
- The money you entrust to us is treated with the same respect and attention we accord our own.
- We strive at all time to deliver the highest quality investment products and services at the lowest reasonable costs.
- We try to talk frankly and openly with you about all aspects of your investments with T. Rowe Price.

Recognizing there is no single or correct way to make money in the financial markets, we have responded to our shareholders' diverse needs by providing a wide range of investments, services, and timely information. In choosing what to offer, however, we try always to make sure we are adding real value and not latching onto short-term trends or fads.

The Prime Reserve Fund

The Prime Reserve Fund dated back to 1976. With assets of $4.8 billion in February 1990, it was by far T. Rowe Price's largest mutual fund. The fund's prospectus described the primary investment objective as:

Preservation of capital, liquidity, and, consistent with these objectives, the highest possible current income by investing in a diversified portfolio of prime domestic and foreign U.S. dollar-denominated money market securities.

The fund's investment restrictions required it to hold at least 65% of total assets in prime money market instruments, i.e., instruments in the highest rating category of a major rating agency: A-1 (Standard & Poor's Corp.), or P-1 (Moody's Investors Service), or F-1 (Fitch Investors Service), or equivalent. Securities could not be purchased if rated less than A-2 or P-2 or F-2 or the equivalent as judged by the fund's board of directors.

Investments could be made in certificates of deposit, bankers' acceptances, and other obligations of banks and savings and loan associations only if they had assets of at least $1 billion. In the case of smaller institutions, investments were limited to the federally insured $100,000 maximum.

Consistent with SEC restrictions, the fund could not purchase an instrument with a maturity greater than one year, and had to maintain an average portfolio maturity of 90 days or less. In addition, at most 5% of the portfolio could be invested (at the time of purchase) in the securities of any one issuer, and at most 25% in any one industry. The SEC restrictions did not apply to securities issued by the U.S. Government and its agencies, or certificates of deposit and bankers' acceptances, although Prime Reserves did limit investments in any one bank or Savings and Loan (S&L) to 5%.

As shown in exhibit 5, the fund's twenty largest holdings accounted for 51.6% of the portfolio and were primarily Euro commercial paper or CDs. The issuers were all financial institutions and nearly all foreign. Exhibit 6 gives the largest holdings of other selected large money market funds including Merrill Lynch's CMA fund which, at $30 billion, was more than twice the size of the next largest fund. Like some of the funds in exhibit 6, Prime Reserve held no U.S. Treasury securities, even though Treasurys made up 26% of total money market fund assets (exhibit 7).

As part of its investment strategy, TRPA tended to position the Prime Reserve portfolio at the most attractive part of the yield curve, viewed in terms of the firm's assessment of the interest rate environment. In March 1990, the portfolio had an average maturity of 38 days. During the prior twelve months, the average maturity had varied between 22 and 53 days, at times deviating from the industry average by as many as 18 days.

Prime Reserve paid T. Rowe Price an annual management fee of 0.44% of assets (exhibit 3). With other costs of 0.31%, its recent twelve-month expense ratio was 0.75%, in line with the current industry average, estimated at 0.73%.

Mortgage & Realty Trust Co.

Mortgage & Realty Trust Co. was a 20-year-old, publicly traded real estate investment trust. It invested primarily in loans secured by commercial real estate, including one- to two-year construction loans, intermediate-term loans used to acquire existing property for physical or economic rehabilitation, and participating loans which provided for sharing in revenues and capital appreciation, with terms of up to 15 years. The Trust also made direct purchases of real estate.

Exhibit 8 contains the Trust's unaudited March 1990 balance sheet. It had $594 million of assets, $405 million of liabilities, and $189 million of net worth. MRT's management argued the Trust was far from insolvent, and that it was merely experiencing a temporary liquidity crisis which asset sales soon would alleviate.

Other Mutual Fund Holders of MRT Paper

Reportedly, there were altogether 10 money market fund holders of MRT paper. Other than the Prime Reserve Fund, only two funds were publicly identified. Alliance Capital's Money Reserves fund held $8.7 million of the paper, and Raymond James Financial's Heritage Cash Trust fund held $12 million. Alliance Capital had $45 billion of assets under management, of which $1 billion was in Money Reserves. Raymond James, whose primary business was brokerage and underwriting, managed some $17 billion through various asset management subsidiaries. Its Heritage Cash Trust fund had $660 million in assets in March 1990.

Previous Cases of Investment Losses in Money Market Funds

The Mortgage & Realty situation was not without precedent. In June 1989, Integrated Resources, a real estate, insurance, and financial services concern, defaulted on some $1 billion of short-term debt. Most of this was in the form of commercial paper issued to fund front-end sales commissions.

The Value Line Cash Fund held $22.6 million (3.2% of its portfolio) of Integrated's paper; Unified Management Corp.'s Liquid Green money market fund held $9 million. Both Value Line and Unified Management chose to "bail out" their fund shareholders by buying the paper for their own accounts at full value. In 1989, Value Line took a $7.5 million after-tax charge to earnings on its holding of Integrated paper.

The Integrated Resources situation represented the first reported instance of default of an instrument purchased by a money market fund. However, it was not the first time money market funds had experienced investment losses. In 1980, anticipating a decline in interest rates, the Institutional Liquid Assets fund lengthened the maturity of its $1.4 billion portfolio of government securities to over 70 days.[1] Instead of falling, rates rose, hurting the fund's performance, and triggering more than $400 million in redemptions in just three days. $2 million of portfolio losses were incurred in selling securities to meet redemptions, an amount for which the fund was reimbursed by Salomon Brothers, the fund's distributor, and the First National Bank of Chicago, the fund's adviser. First National subsequently lost the advisory contract, which was awarded to Goldman Sachs & Co.

The Money Market Fund Industry

Money market mutual funds first appeared in 1974. Like other mutual funds, they were designed to offer small investors the benefits of economies of scale, including particularly diversification, professional management, and investments in odd amounts. In addition, investors usually could receive free checkwriting and wire-transfer privileges (for amounts over some minimum), avoid the early withdrawal penalties of fixed maturity CDs, and receive automatic redemption and next day settlement. Many of the above benefits also were attractive to corporations and other institutions running small short-term portfolios.

Money market funds grew phenomenally between 1978 and 1982 when interest rates surged and Regulation Q limited the rates banks and S&Ls could pay on savings and time deposits. By 1989, there were over 450 money market funds with assets exceeding $350 billion (exhibit 7) and an estimated 20 million accounts. Investment advisory fees on these funds totalled $1.5 billion.

The commercial paper market burgeoned in parallel with money market funds. Corporations increasingly bypassed banks, raising short-term funds directly in the public markets. By the late 1980s, commercial paper issuance exceeded all bank commercial and industrial loans. Money market funds were large buyers, owning about 30% of the $653 billion of commercial paper outstanding in June 1990. In terms of Moody's credit ratings, this total was broken down as follows:

P-1	$462 billion
P-2	79
P-3	9
Non-Prime	6
Not rated	97
Total	$653

Foreign issuers accounted for an increasingly large share of top-rated commercial paper and CDs as the credit quality of U.S. financial institutions and corporations deteriorated.

Calculation of Net Asset Value

Most money market funds, including Prime Reserve Fund, priced their portfolios daily or even more frequently. Securities with maturities longer than 60 days were valued at market. Securities with maturities shorter than 60 days were valued at amortized cost unless this was deemed not to reflect fair value, in which case an alternative "good faith" determination of fair value had to be made.

It was also standard practice for money market funds to maintain a net asset value (NAV) of $1.00 per share. This was accomplished by distributing the net income of the fund as it was earned, and by rounding the NAV to the nearest penny. In addition, money market funds would keep to relatively short maturities, and try to "minimize" credit risk and other exposures. However, as Prime Reserve Fund's prospectus cautioned:

Although [the] Fund believes that it will be able to maintain its net asset value at $1.00 per share under most conditions, there can be no absolute assurance that it will be able to do so on a continuous basis. If the Fund's net asset value per share declined, or was expected to decline, below $1.00 (rounded to the nearest one cent), the Board of Directors of the Fund might temporarily reduce or suspend dividend payments in an effort to maintain the net asset value at $1.00 per share. As a result of such reduction or suspension of dividends, an investor would receive less income during a given period than if such a reduction or suspension had not taken place. Such action could result in an investor receiving no dividend for the period during which he holds his shares and in his receiving, upon redemption, a price per share lower than that which he paid.

Recent Price Competition in Money Market Fund Industry

Historically, yield was an important determinant of the flow of assets between money market funds and alternative savings vehicles like certificates of deposit. Yield was also an important dimension of competition within the mutual fund industry. With the industry expense ratio at 0.73%, low-cost producers like Vanguard—whose money market fund expense ratio was only 0.30%—had an enormous advantage.

In early 1989, in perhaps the most aggressive campaigns in industry history, Fidelity and Dreyfus began marketing their Spartan and Worldwide Dollar funds respectively. The expense ratios of these funds were completely absorbed by the sponsoring companies, giving considerable boost to their yields. When short-term rates were hovering at about 10%, Spartan and Worldwide Dollar were among the few funds able to advertise eye-catching double-digit yields (exhibit 13). Both funds attracted billions of dollars in very short order. On April 30, 1990, Spartan had $8.3 billion in assets, while Worldwide Dollar had $7.1 billion (exhibit 6).

Fidelity guaranteed to keep Spartan's expense ratio beneath 0.45% until 1992. In late 1989, the firm increased the fund's expense ratio to 0.10% (from zero). Dreyfus was less specific about its commitment to maintain a low expense ratio. As of July 1990, Worldwide Dollar's expense ratio was still at zero.

In addition to subsidizing Worldwide Dollar's expense ratio, Dreyfus invested the fund more aggressively than most in higher-yielding Eurodollar securities. Worldwide Dollar also operated under more liberal investment restrictions. For example, the fund could invest up to 15% of its assets in the securities of any one bank, a limitation that moreover applied to only 75% of fund assets. In the fund's prospectus, Dreyfus notes that SEC staff had expressed concern as to whether certain bank obligations should be subject to the statutory 5% limitation governing most mutual fund investments. As shown in exhibit 6, Worldwide Dollar's largest holding on April 30 was a 9% investment in Chrysler Financial. This paper was then rated A-2/P-2 but downgraded to A-3/P-3 in June 1990.

Note

1. *Barron's*, March 26, 1990.

Exhibit 1

T. Rowe Price income statement, December 31, 1989 (dollars in millions)

Management fees:	
Mutual funds	$ 80.9
Private accounts and other	38.0
Administrative fees	32.2
Investment income	5.6
Other revenues	2.8
Total revenues	$159.5
Advertising and promotion expense	11.8
Compensation, administrative, & general	98.7
Total expenses	$110.5
Income before taxes & minority interests	49.0
Income taxes	17.6
Minority interests in consolidates subsidiaries	1.6
Net income	$ 29.7
Earnings per share	$2.00

Exhibit 2

T. Rowe Price balance sheet, December 31, 1989 (dollars in millions)

Assets	
Cash and cash equivalents	$ 40.0
Accounts receivable	24.4
Investments in mutual funds	16.4
Marketable debt securities	19.7
Limited partnership interests	10.5
Property and equipment	10.7
Other assets	5.9
	$127.6
Liabilities and stockholders' equity	
Liabilities:	
Accounts payable and accrued expenses	$ 11.0
Accrued compensation and related costs	5.6
Income taxes payable	2.0
Dividends payable	2.2
Deferred revenues	1.1
Long-term debt	2.6
Minority interests in consolidated subs	1.7
Total liabilities	$ 26.2
Stockholders' equity	101.4
	$127.6

Exhibit 3

Composition of T. Rowe Price management fee revenues, December 31, 1989 (dollars in millions)

	Assets managed	Management fee rate	Revenue running rate
Money market and short-term bond funds	$ 6,200	0.44%	$ 27.3
Equity funds	6,300	0.57	35.9
Fixed-income funds	2,800	0.57	16.0
Municipal bond funds	2,000	0.57	11.4
Total mutual funds	$17,300	0.52%	$ 90.6
Private accounts:			
Equity	$ 5,500	0.42%	$ 23.1
Fixed income	5,400	0.20	10.8
Total private accounts	$10,900	0.30%	$ 33.9
Total	$28,200	0.44%	$124.5

Source: Sanford C. Bernstein & Co., Inc., January 1990.

Exhibit 4

T. Rowe Price mutual funds

Fund (year commenced)	Primary investment objective
Money market:	
Prime Reserve (1976)	Preservation of capital, liquidity and, consistent with these objectives, the highest possible current income by investing in a diversified portfolio of prime domestic and foreign US dollar-denominated money market securities.
Tax-Exempt Money (1981)	Preservation of capital, liquidity, and consistent with these objectives, the highest possible current income exempt from federal income tax by investing in high quality municipal securities which mature in one year or less.
US Treasury Money (1982)	Maximum safety of capital, liquidity and, consistent with these objectives, the highest available current income by investing primarily in short-term US Treasury securities and repurchase agreements on such securities.
California Tax-Free Money (1986)	Highest possible current income exempt from federal and California state income taxes consistent with preservation of principal and liquidity by investing in high quality municipal securities which mature in one year or less.
New York Tax-Free (1986)	Highest possible current income exempt from federal, New York State and New York City Money income taxes consistent with preservation of principal and liquidity by investing in high quality municipal securities which mature in one year or less.

Exhibit 4 (continued)

Fund (year commenced)	Primary investment objective
Stock:	
Growth Stock (1958)	Long-term growth of capital and increasing dividend income through investment primarily in common stocks of well-established growth companies.
New Horizons (1960)	Long-term growth of capital through investment primarily in common stocks of small, rapidly growing companies.
New Era (1969)	Long-term growth of capital through investment primarily in common stocks of companies which own or develop natural resources and other basic commodities, and other selected, non-resource growth companies.
International Stock (1980)	Total return from long-term growth of capital and income principally through investments in marketable securities of established, non-United States issuers.
Growth & Income (1982)	Long-term growth of capital, a reasonable level of current income and an increase in future income through investment primarily in income-producing equity securities which have the prospects for growth of capital and increasing dividends.
New American Growth (1985)	Long-term growth of capital through investment primarily in the common stocks of U.S. companies which operate in the service sector of the economy.
Equity Income (1985)	High current income by investing primarily in dividend-paying common stocks of established companies with favorable prospects for increasing dividend income and, secondarily, capital appreciation.
Capital Appreciation (1986)	Maximum capital appreciation through investment primarily in common stocks.
Science & Technology (1987)	Long-term growth of capital through investment primarily in the common stocks of companies which are expected to benefit from the development, advancement and use of science and technology.
Small-Cap Value (1988)	Long-term capital growth through investment primarily in the common stocks of companies with relatively small market capitalizations which are believed to be undervalued and have good prospects for capital appreciation.
International Discovery (1988)	Long-term growth of capital through investment primarily in the common stocks of rapidly growing, small and medium sized companies based outside the United States.
European Stock (1990)	Long-term capital appreciation by investment primarily in a diversified portfolio of equity securities issued by companies domiciled in Europe.
Taxable bond:	
New Income (1973)	Highest level of income over time consistent with the preservation of capital through investment primarily in marketable debt securities.

Exhibit 4 (continued)

Fund (year commenced)	Primary investment objective
High Yield (1984)	High level of income and, secondarily, capital appreciation through investment primarily in high-yielding, lower-medium and low quality, income-producing debt securities and preferred stocks (including convertible securities).
Short-Term Bond (1984)	Highest level of income consistent with minimum fluctuation in principal value and liquidity through investment primarily in short- and intermediate-form debt securities.
GNMA (1985)	Highest level of current income, consistent with preservation of principal and maximum credit protection by investment exclusively in securities backed by the full faith and credit of the U.S. government, primarily Government National Mortgage Association (GNMA) mortgage-backed securities, and other instruments involving these securities.
International Bond (1986)	High level of current income by investing in an international portfolio of high-quality, nondollar-denominated fixed income securities.
U.S. Treasury Intermediate (1989)	High level of current income consistent with maximum credit protection and an average portfolio maturity of three to seven years by investing primarily in U.S. Treasury securities and repurchase agreements involving such securities.
U.S. Treasury Long-Term (1989)	High level of current income consistent with maximum credit protection and an average portfolio maturity of fifteen to twenty years by investing primarily in U.S. Treasury securities and repurchase agreements involving such securities.
Tax-Free bond:	
Tax-Free Income (1976)	High level of income exempt from federal income tax by investing primarily in longer-term investment-grade municipal securities.
Tax-Free Short-Intermediate (1983)	Higher than money market yields by investing primarily in short- and intermediate-term, high and upper-medium quality municipal securities which make interest payments exempt from federal income tax.
Tax-Free High Yield (1985)	High level of income exempt from federal income tax by investing primarily in long-term medium-to-low quality municipal securities.
New York Tax-Free Bond (1986)	Highest level of income exempt from federal, New York State and New York City income taxes by investing primarily in long-term investment-grade municipal securities.
California Tax-Free Bond (1986)	Highest level of income exempt from federal and California state income taxes by investing primarily in long term, investment-grade municipal securities.
Maryland Tax-Free Bond (1987)	Highest level of income exempt from federal and Maryland state and local income taxes by investing primarily in long-term, investment-grade municipal securities.

Sources: Form 10K for year ended December 31, 1989 and Barron's.

Exhibit 5

Largest holdings of the T. Rowe Price Prime Reserve Fund (2/28/90) (dollars in millions)

Issuer	Value	% Total	Moody's	S&P
Mitsubishi Bank, Ltd. (London)	$ 231	4.8%	P-1	A-1+
Sanwa Bank, Ltd. (London)	230	4.8	P-1	*A-1+
Tokai Bank, Ltd. (London)	168	3.5	P-1	*A-1+
Sumitomo Bank, Limited (London)	150	3.1	P-1	*A-1+
Bank of New York (London)	150	3.1	P-1	A-1
Long Term Credit Bank of Japan (London)	136	2.8	P-1	A-1+
Dai-Ichi Kangyo Bank, Ltd. (London)	133	2.7	P-1	*A-1+
Sumitomo Trust & Banking Co. (London)	130	2.7	P-1	*A-1+
Dresdner Bank AG (London)	130	2.7	P-1	A-1+
Fuji Bank, Ltd. (London)	115	2.4	P-1	*A-1+
Svenska Handelsbanken (London)	113	2.3	P-1	A-1+
Chrysler Financial Corporation[1]	109	2.2	P-2	A-2
Societe Generale (London)	100	2.1	P-1	NR
First Bank System, Inc.	99	2.0	P-2	A-2
Den Danske Bank A/S (London)	98	2.0	P-1	A-1
Citizens Fidelity Bank & Trust Company	95	2.0	P-1	A-1+
Royal Bank of Canada	81	1.7	P-1	A-1+
NCNB National Bank of North Carolina	78	1.6	P-1	A-1
Puget Sound Bancorp	77	1.6	NR	A-2
National City Bank	75	1.5	P-1	A-1
Subtotal	$2,497	51.6%		
U.S. Government & Federal Agencies	0	0.0		
Total fund value	$4,842	100.0%		

Note: Ratings are as of March 1990.
1. Chrysler Financial Corporation downgraded to "A-3" on 6/14/90 and "P-3" on 6/29/90.
*Rating of the parent company.

Exhibit 6

Largest holdings of selected money market funds (dollars in millions)

Fidelity: Spartan (4/30/90)	Value	% Total	Moody's	S&P
Philip Morris Companies, Inc.	$ 330	4.0%	P-2	A-1
General Motors Acceptance Corp.	317	3.8	P-1	A-1+
General Electric Capital Corp.	298	3.6	P-1	A-1+
Citicorp[1]	285	3.4	P-1	A-1+
Sears Roebuck Acceptance Corp.	249	3.0	P-1	A-1
Svenska Handelsbanken, Inc.	234	2.8	P-1	A-1+
Goldman, Sachs & Co.	222	2.7	P-1	A-1+
Barclays Bank PLC	219	2.6	P-1	A-1+
Preferred Receivables Funding Corp.	206	2.5	P-1	A-1
Kansallis North America, Inc.	184	2.2	P-1	A-1+
Bayerische Landesbank GZ	179	2.2	P-1	A-1+
Ford Motor Credit Company	149	1.8	P-1	A-1+
Subtotal	$ 2,873	34.6%		
U.S. Government & Federal Agencies	1,490	17.9		
Total fund value	$ 8,311	100.0%		

Fidelity: Cash Reserves (11/30/89)	Value	% Total	Moody's	S&P
Sanwa Bank, Ltd.	$ 550	5.1%	P-1	A-1+
Salomon, Inc.	492	4.5	P-1	A-1
Chrysler Financial Corporation[2]	456	4.2	P-2	A-2
Eastman Kodak	359	3.3	P-1	A-2
Tokai Bank, Ltd.	356	3.3	P-1	*A-1+
Fuji Bank, Ltd. (Grand Cayman)	350	3.2	P-1	*A-1+
Philip Morris Companies, Inc.	295	2.7	P-2	A-1
Mitsubishi Bank, Ltd. (Grand Cayman)	285	2.6	P-1	A-1+
Grand Metropolitan PLC	281	2.6	P-2	A-1
Sumitomo Bank, Ltd.	260	2.4	P-1	A-1+
General Electric Capital Corporation	248	2.3	P-1	A-1+
Shearson Lehman Hutton Holdings, Inc.	203	1.9	P-1	A-1
Merrill Lynch & Co., Inc.	198	1.8	P-1	A-1
Subtotal	$ 4,334	39.9%		
U.S. Government & Federal Agencies	175	1.6		
Total fund value	$10,860	100.0%		

Exhibit 6 (continued)

Dreyfus: Worldwide Dollar (4/30/90)	Value	% Total	Moody's	S&P
Chrysler Financial Corp.	$ 636	8.9%	P-2	A-2
Mitsubishi Bank, Ltd. (Grand Cayman)	509	7.1	P-1	A-1+
Fuji Bank, Ltd. (Grand Cayman)	426	6.0	*P-1	*A-1+
Chemical Bank (London)	376	5.3	*P-2	*A-2
Goldman, Sachs & Co.	340	4.8	P-1	A-1+
Commercial Credit Co.	288	4.0	P-2	A-2
Oryx Energy Co.	264	3.7	P-2	A-2
Sears Savings Bank	210	2.9	NR	A-2
Columbia Savings—Denver[4]	194	2.7	NR	WR
Philip Morris Companies, Inc.	183	2.6	P-2	A-1
Saitama Bank, Ltd. (London)	171	2.4	P-1	NR
Sumitomo Bank, Ltd. (London)	150	2.1	P-1	*A-1+
Yasuda Trust & Banking Co., Ltd.	135	1.9	P-1	A-1+
Chase Manhattan Corp.	130	1.8	P-2	A-2
Amerco	125	1.8	NR	A-2
Subtotal	$ 4,137	58.1%		
U.S. Government & Federal Agencies	0	0.0		
Total fund value	$ 7,127	100.0%		

Dreyfus: Liquid Assets (12/31/89)	Value	% Total	Moody's	S&P
First National Bank of Chicago	$ 655	8.4%	P-1	A-1
Greenwood Trust Co.	585	7.5	NR	NR
Goldman, Sachs & Co.	394	5.0	P-1	A-1+
Shearson Lehman Hutton Holdings, Inc.	379	4.8	P-1	A-1+
PKBanken North America, Inc.	325	4.1	P-1	A-1+
Morgan Stanley Group, Inc.	309	3.9	P-1	A-1+
Salomon, Inc.	300	3.8	P-1	A-1
Chase Manhattan Corp.	294	3.8	P-2	A-2
Continental Illinois National Bank	290	3.7	P-2	A-2
Chase Manhattan Bank, N.A.[3]	280	3.6	P-1	A-1
Tokai Credit Corp.	275	3.5	P-1	A-1+
State Bank of India Finance Inc.	209	2.7	P-1	A-2
Security Pacific Corp.	209	2.7	P-1	A-1+
Philip Morris Companies, Inc.	199	2.5	P-2	A-1
Citicorp[1]	155	2.0	P-1	A-1+
Subtotal	$ 4,856	62.0%		
U.S. Government & Federal Agencies	0	0.0		
Total fund value	$ 7,836	100.0%		

Exhibit 6 (continued)

Merrill Lynch: CMA (3/31/90)	Value	% Total	Moody's	S&P
General Motors Acceptance Corp.	$ 1,091	3.7%	P-1	A-1+
General Electric Capital Corp.	891	3.0	P-1	A-1+
Ford Motor Credit Company	826	2.8	P-1	A-1+
Citibank, N.A.	805	2.7	P-1	A-1+
Sears Roebuck Acceptance Corp.	796	2.7	P-1	A-1
Dai-Ichi Kangyo Bank, Ltd. (New York)	750	2.5	P-1	A-1+
Fuji Bank, Ltd. (New York)	590	2.0	P-1	*A-1+
American Express Credit Corp.	521	1.8	P-1	A-1+
Associates Corp. of North America	448	1.5	P-1	A-1+
Mitsubishi Bank, Ltd. (New York)	443	1.5	P-1	A-1+
PepsiCo, Inc.	383	1.3	P-1	A-1
ITT Financial Corp.	348	1.2	P-1	A-1
E.I. duPont de Nemours & Co.	348	1.2	P-1	A-1+
Security Pacific National Bank	347	1.2	P-1	A-1+
Mitsui Bank, Ltd. (New York)	330	1.1	P-1	A-1+
Morgan Guaranty Trust Company (London)	313	1.1	P-1	A-1+
Shell Oil Co.	298	1.0	P-1	A-1+
CIT Group Holdings, Inc.	298	1.0	P-1	A-1
Subtotal	$ 9,828	33.0%		
U.S. Government & Federal Agencies	6,463	21.7		
Total fund value	$29,768	100.0%		

Exhibit 6 (continued)

Merrill Lynch: Ready Assets (12/31/89)	Value	% Total	Moody's	S&P
Dai-Ichi Kangyo Bank, Ltd.	$ 617	5.8%	P-1	A-1+
General Electric Capital Corp.	487	4.6	P-1	A-1+
General Motors Acceptance Corp.	440	4.1	P-1	A-1+
Citibank, N.A.	435	4.1	P-1	A-1+
Fuji Bank, Ltd. (New York)	340	3.2	P-1	A-1+
Goldman, Sachs & Co.	308	2.9	P-1	A-1+
Security Pacific National Bank	283	2.7	P-1	A-1+
Ford Motor Credit Co.	269	2.5	P-1	A-1+
Sony Capital Corp.	257	2.4	P-1	A-1
Bankers Trust Company (London)	245	2.3	P-1	*A-1+
Chrysler Financial Corp.[2]	224	2.1	P-2	A-2
Sears Roebuck Acceptance Corp.	211	2.0	P-1	A-1
Long-Term Credit Bank, Japan (New York)	205	1.9	P-1	A-1+
J.P. Morgan & Co., Inc.	200	1.9	P-1	A-1+
Subtotal	$ 4,521	42.5%		
U.S. Government & Federal Agencies	573	5.4		
Total fund value	$10,650	100.0%		

Note: Ratings are as of March 1990.
1. Citicorp downgraded to "P-2" on 5/22/90.
2. Chrysler Financial Corp. downgraded to "A-3" on 6/14/90 and "P-3" on 6/29/90.
3. Chase Manhattan Bank, N.A. downgraded to "P-2" on 6/11/90.
4. Columbia Savings' short-term debt rating of "A-1" withdrawn on 2/15/89; company's subordinated debt downgraded to "D" on 1/6/89.
* Rating of the parent company.

Exhibit 7

Mix of industry money market fund assets (dollars in billions)

	1983	1984	1985	1986	1987	1988	Oct. 1989
Assets	$162	$210	$208	$228	$255	$272	$357
U.S. Treasurys	30%	31%	33%	33%	32%	26%	26%
Certificates of deposit	28	21	17	18	22	23	20
Bankers acceptances	12	9	6	5	4	4	2
Commercial paper	29	37	42	42	39	43	47
All other	1	1	2	3	3	3	4
Total	100%	100%	100%	100%	100%	100%	100%
Average maturity (days)	37	43	37	40	31	28	33
Number of funds	307	329	348	360	389	432	454

Exhibit 8

Balance sheet of Mortgage & Realty Trust, March 1990, unaudited (dollars in millions)

Assets

Mortgage loans and investments:

Construction loans	$ 91	
Standing loans	316	
Long-term amortizing loans	13	
Participating loans and investments	68	
Non-earning mortgage loans	14	
Total mortgage		$502

Real estate:

Investments in real estate equities	51	
Properties acquired through foreclosure and held for sale:		
Earning	7	
Non-earning	20	
Less allowance for losses	(3)	
Total real estate		75
Cash		1
Short-term investments		2
Interest receivable and other assets		14
		$594

Liabilities and stockholders' equity

Liabilities:

Notes payable:

Commercial paper	$167	
Medium-term notes	35	
Bank bid facility	50	
Total public debt	252	
Senior notes	123	
Revolving credit	20	
Total senior debt	395	
Convertible subordinated debentures	1	
Total debt		$396
Accounts payable and accrued expenses		9
Total liabilities		$405
Shareholders' equity		189
		$594

Exhibit 9

The U.S. household balance sheet, December 31, 1979 and 1989 (dollars in billions)

	1979	1989
Financial intermediaries:		
Checkable deposits and currency	$ 256	$ 490
Savings deposits	425	590
MMDAs	0	490
Small CDs	633	1,200
Large CDs	73	45
Total financial intermediaries	$1,387	$ 2,915
Open-market securities:		
Savings bonds	$ 80	$ 120
Treasury and agency debt	154	865
Municipal debt	77	295
Corporate and foreign debt	72	160
Open-market paper	38	140
Subtotal: debt securities	$ 420	$ 1,580
Equities	812	2,100
Total open-market securities	$1,232	$ 3,680
Packaged products:		
Money market & short-term bond funds	$ 40	$ 375
Long-term fixed-income funds	14	295
Equity mutual funds	30	200
Subtotal: mutual funds	$ 84	$ 870
Other packaged products	24	140
Credit balances at brokers	10	45
Total packaged products	$ 118	$ 1,055
Discretionary financial assets	$2,737	$ 7,650
Owner-financed mortgage	89	130
Life insurance reserves	207	325
Pension fund assets	767	2,900
Equity in non-corporate business	1,179	2,430
Total financial assets	$5,580	$13,435
Owner-occupied real estate and land	2,324	4,650
Consumer durables (autos, appliances)	925	1,910
Total assets	$8,829	$19,995

Exhibit 10

Relationship of fixed-income mutual fund inflows to S&L consumer deposit flows

| | New Inflows | | | S&L consumer deposits |
	Money market & short-term bonds	Long-term bonds	Total	
1982	$ 30.4	$ 4.7	$ 35.1	$(14.7)
1983	(43.7)	10.4	(33.3)	41.8
1984	48.8	15.3	64.1	22.5
1985	(5.4)	63.8	58.4	5.4
1986	34.0	99.3	133.3	(11.5)
1987	10.2	6.8	17.0	(9.9)
1988	0.1	(4.5)	(4.4)	(14.0)
1989	81.0	1.0	82.0	(70.0)

Source: Sanford C. Bernstein & Co., Inc., January 1990

Exhibit 11

Comparison of short-term consumer interest rates

		Money market funds	Money market deposit accounts	Thrift 6-month CDs	6-month Treasury bills	A-1/P-1 CP
1984		9.90%	9.19%	10.35%	9.77%	10.12%
1985		7.70	7.51	7.97	7.65	7.95
1986	Q1	7.34%	6.88%	7.74%	6.96%	6.93%
	Q2	6.57	6.48	7.19	6.18	6.45
	Q3	5.88	6.00	6.60	5.60	5.73
	Q4	5.41	5.68	6.17	5.40	6.01
1987	Q1	5.56%	5.62%	6.16%	5.14%	6.23%
	Q2	5.90	5.72	6.59	5.98	6.94
	Q3	6.25	5.85	7.01	6.14	7.90
	Q4	6.73	6.05	7.43	6.46	7.01
1988	Q1	6.48%	6.00%	7.33%	6.04%	6.71%
	Q2	6.46	5.90	7.16	6.46	7.11
	Q3	7.34	6.04	7.60	7.25	8.02
	Q4	8.00	6.22	8.11	7.86	8.65
1989	Q1	8.91%	6.46%	8.72%	8.59%	9.53%
	Q2	9.50	6.61	9.50	8.33	9.70
	Q3	8.68	6.46	8.64	8.00	8.97
	Q4	8.44	6.40	8.34	7.91	8.62

Exhibit 12

The Dreyfus Corporation income statement, 1989 and summary balance sheet, year-end 1989 (dollars in millions)

Income statement:	
Management fees	$186.5
Dreyfus consumer bank	10.2
Other revenues	6.2
Investment income	73.3
Total revenues	$276.2
Advertising & other selling expenses	40.0
Sales, general & administrative	107.4
Interest expense	8.2
Total expenses	$155.6
Income before taxes	120.6
Taxes	35.0
Ordinary income	$85.6
Gain on sale of credit card business	43.2
Net income	$128.8
Earnings per share	$ 3.16
Shares outstanding (millions)	41
Stock price per share (March 1990)	$ 36
Summary balance sheet:	
Assets	
Cash assets	$146
Receivables	59
Investments	677
Fixed and other assets	44
	$926
Liabilities and stockholders' equity	
Accounts payable	$ 34
Other liabilities	175
Stockholders' equity	717
	$926

Exhibit 13

2   Evolution of Funds and Investors

Introduction

This is the second in the trilogy of introductory chapters on mutual funds. The first chapter focused on the functions of financial intermediaries and compared mutual funds to commercial banks. The next chapter will review the regulatory framework for mutual funds with emphasis on disclosure documents for fund investors. This chapter will provide factual background about the evolution of the fund industry, together with ruminations about the industry's future.

Although historians may differ on the exact genesis of modern funds, the origins of the U.S. mutual fund industry can be traced back to Boston. At the beginning of the twentieth century, Boston law firms formed trust divisions to manage the assets of wealthy Boston families. As these families grew and the wealth was dispersed, the mutual fund came into existence as a way to provide commingled management of multiple family accounts. The first U.S. mutual fund (an "open-end" fund, which stands ready to issue and redeem shares to investors) offered to the public was introduced in Boston in 1924. But the growth of the mutual fund industry was soon stymied by the stock crash of 1929 and the Depression of the 1930s. Determined to protect investors better, Congress passed legislation regulating investments and securities markets, including the Securities Act of 1933 that requires full disclosure in all public securities offerings.

In 1935, the Securities and Exchange Commission (SEC) undertook a special study that led to the passage of the Investment Company Act of 1940 (1940 Act). The 1940 Act established the standards by which mutual funds and other types of investment companies must operate, including requirements (detailed in chapter 3) for fund promoting, reporting, product pricing, and portfolio investing. Although the 1940 Act offered better protection to investors, the mutual fund industry grew very slowly during the 1940s and early 1950s.

The industry experienced a small growth spurt during the late 1950s and 1960s, when the economy was strong and the stock market was rising. At that time, most mutual funds invested in stocks and were sold with front-end sales charges or "loads" of $8\frac{1}{2}\%$ of an investor's initial investment in a fund. But this growth spurt gave way to doldrums during the early 1970s: As the stock market declined steadily, it became very difficult to sell stock mutual funds. Instead, investors were mainly interested in short-term or income-oriented investments.

During the 1970s, the industry created money market funds, many of which were sold through direct advertising without the traditional sales load. Money market funds became the savior of the industry during the late 1970s and early 1980s as interest rates, and therefore money fund returns, climbed to double digits while banks were legally prevented from paying more than a specified rate (e.g., 4% or 5%) on most small deposits. By the early 1980s, money market funds accounted for a larger percentage of industry assets than either stock or bond funds. Money market funds allowed fund companies to gather assets from individual investors, who could then exchange easily into stock funds as the stock market took off during the 1980s. At the same time, money market funds became an attractive cash management vehicle for corporations, trust departments, and other institutional investors.

In the late 1970s, the mutual fund industry also introduced tax-exempt funds based on legislation allowing them to pass through to their shareholders tax-exempt interest from municipal debt. These tax-exempt bond and money market funds became increasingly popular after 1986 when Congress eliminated or restricted many other tax-advantaged investment opportunities. Such tax-exempt funds remain one of the core vehicles to attract high net worth investors.

Over the last decade, mutual funds have grown at a fantastic pace. For example, the total assets of mutual funds were less than $800 billion in 1987 and climbed to over $4 trillion in 1997. During the same decade, the assets of commercial banks and insurance companies grew much more slowly. The readings in this chapter delineate a number of factors behind the rapid growth rate of mutual funds during the late 1980s and 1990s. These factors include: a bull market in U.S. stocks, the expansion of tax-advantaged retirement vehicles, the creation of attractive mutual fund products, and the introduction of enhanced services to fund shareholders.

At the same time, mutual fund complexes have developed a broad variety of distribution channels and pricing structures. While later chapters explore these developments in detail, it is useful to summarize the key distribution channels at this point.

The traditional distribution channel was broker-dealers, which sold mutual funds for a front-end sales load charged to the investor at the time of purchase. These sales loads have gradually declined from $8\frac{1}{2}$% in the 1960s to an average of 4% to 5% currently. Alternatively, mutual funds now sold by broker-dealers may offer a back-end load charged to individual shareholders at the time of redemption. The back-end load usually declines the longer a shareholder holds the fund shares—for example, 5% after one year, 4% after two years, etc. In addition to (or in lieu of) loads, brokers now typically receive annual distribution fees, called 12b-1 fees (named after the applicable SEC rule). These 12b-1 fees, which usually range from 25 bp to 75 bp per year of assets under management, are paid by the fund (rather than the individual shareholder) to the distributor.

The advent of money market funds during the 1970s spurred the spread of direct marketed funds. In the direct distribution channel, mutual fund distributors use print ads and mailers to solicit sales from relatively sophisticated investors who are comfortable making their own investment decisions. These investors respond by mail and, more frequently, by calling an 800 number at the fund complex. Most of these direct marketed funds do not charge a sales commission at the front- or back-end; thus, they are called *no-load funds*. Some direct marketed funds, however, do charge low loads (e.g., 2% to 3%) and/or modest 12b-1 fees (e.g., less than 25 bp per year).

Retirement plans represent a third distribution channel, partly institutional and partly retail. Mutual fund complexes are attractive service providers to plan sponsors of 401(k) and other defined contribution plans because they offer a broad array of investment alternatives, refined recordkeeping, and servicing features. After a mutual fund company is chosen by the plan sponsor, it must provide disclosure documents and educational materials to plan participants so they may individually choose to have their play contributions invested in specific funds. In most cases, any sales loads are waived for mutual funds offered to pension plans. Recordkeeping and other service fees (in addition to standard fund expenses) may be negotiated between the mutual fund company and the employer or plan sponsor.

Over the last decade, banks have begun to play a significant role in fund distribution and management, initially in money market and bond funds and spreading to equity funds. Despite various legal restrictions associated with the Glass-Steagall Act (such as commercial banks being prohibited from underwriting public offerings of corporate securities), banks have found ways to offer their own and others' mutual funds to their bank customers in bank offices. Most bank-sponsored funds are sold with loads or 12b-1 fees, although some are sold no-load or with loads waived for fiduciary accounts.

Similarly, insurance companies and financial planners have come to be significant players in certain aspects of the mutual fund industry. Insurance companies have joint ventured with fund sponsors to sell variable annuities—annuity contracts wrapped around a set of mutual funds. These are contracts issued by insurance companies that allow investors to accumulate assets on a tax-deferred basis for retirement or other long-term goals. The return is variable because it depends on the performance of the mutual funds chosen by the investor to fund the annuity contracts. (See chapter 7 for more detail.)

More broadly, financial planners have become major sources of investment advice to mutual fund customers faced with an overwhelming array of choices. Financial planners help fund customers sort out their financial goals, design a general strategy, and select specific funds to implement that strategy. In selecting mutual funds from several fund families, financial planners have been an important user of the mutual fund marketplaces.

Mutual fund marketplaces now allow investors to purchase a broad variety of funds offered by over one hundred fund sponsors, typically through a single brokerage account. This option, initially developed by Charles Schwab & Co. and often called the fourth distribution channel, is now offered by a number of companies including Fidelity Investments and Jack White & Co. In return for a "place" to market its funds, the fund sponsor usually pays an annual fee of 25 bp to 35 bp to the company that runs the marketplace and services the customer accounts. Although the operator of the fund marketplace controls the customer, this mechanism does provide a relatively inexpensive method of distribution for small fund managers.

At the same time, the mutual fund industry has been experiencing a wave of consolidation. In 1994–1997, there were well over 200 announced acquisitions of U.S. investment management companies. For example, Invesco has acquired AIM, while Zurich Insurance has acquired Kemper and Scudder. These acquisitions have occurred because of the increasing need for large expenditures on technology and a broad array of products/services to stay competitive. (See merger case study in chapter 10.) The largest 15 fund sponsors (on a consolidated basis) now control over half of the fund industry's assets, and that proportion is likely to rise over the next decade.

The Internet will be one of the keys to the evolving structure of the mutual fund industry in the twenty-first century. Almost every major fund complex already has a Web site with extensive information on its funds, and the percentage of fund shareholders using the Internet is rising rapidly. Although security concerns have impeded the flow of fund purchases and sales on the Internet, these concerns are in the process of being addressed. (For more information on mutual funds and the Internet, see chapter 12, especially the class exercises.)

What does the future hold in store for the mutual fund industry? The readings will provide some projections of growth and touch on a few of the questions that industry leaders are currently addressing.

Questions

In reviewing the materials in this chapter, please keep in mind the following questions:

1. Over the last fifteen years, the U.S. stock market has risen at an astonishing rate—the Dow Jones Industrial Average has increased ten times from 800 in 1982 to almost 8,000 in 1997. This rise has obviously helped to attract assets to equity mutual funds. Over the next fifteen years, from 1998 to 2012, do you expect the Dow Jones Industrial Average to rise another ten times to 80,000? If not, what does that imply for the growth rate and composition of the mutual fund industry?

2. The demographics in the United States have been favorable to the mutual fund industry. As the Baby Boomers have matured, they have become more oriented toward savings and more disposed toward mutual funds. However, the first wave of the Baby Boomers—born between 1946 and 1950—reaches normal retirement age between 2010 and 2015. What does the retirement of the Baby Boomers imply for mutual funds, directly in terms of savings patterns and indirectly in terms of the stock market?

3. The mutual fund industry has been very creative in developing new products and pricing structures. However, there are now over 6,000 mutual funds, including multiple classes with different pricing arrangements. How will investors respond to this proliferation of products and pricing, and what will this imply for the distribution of mutual funds?

4. The mutual fund industry has led the way in customer service through the use of technology. Now the industry is beginning to use the Internet to disseminate fund information and effect fund transactions. The Internet makes it much easier for savers to obtain information about individual securities and much cheaper to trade these securities. As the Internet develops, will savers make their investment directly, rather than through, financial intermediaries such as mutual funds?

5. The mutual fund industry has recently experienced a wave of mergers and acquisitions. Morgan Stanley has acquired Dean Witter in order to obtain retail distribution, and Franklin has acquired Templeton in order to offer a full product line of funds. Will this trend toward consolidation accelerate or decelerate, and why? Will there be a role for the small fund sponsor in the 21st century?

6. Some banks (e.g., J.P. Morgan and Bankers Trust) have acquired all or part of securities firms, including their asset management divisions. Other banks (e.g., Chase and Citibank) have aggressively built mutual funds into their distribution networks. As the legal barriers between the banking and securities business erode further, will mutual funds become just another banking product? What will happen to the independent mutual fund sponsors like Fidelity and Vanguard?

2.1   History of Mutual Funds*

Mutual funds have been on the financial landscape for longer than most investors realize. In fact, the industry traces its roots back to 19th century Europe, in particular, Great Britain. The Foreign and Colonial Government Trust, formed in London in 1868, resembled a mutual fund. It promised the "investor of modest means the same advantages as the large capitalist ... by spreading the investment over a number of different stocks."

Most of these early British investment companies and their American counterparts resembled today's closed-end funds. They sold a fixed number of shares whose price was determined by supply and demand.

Until the 1920s, however, most middle-income Americans put their money in banks or bought individual shares of stock in a specific company. Investing in capital markets was still largely limited to the wealthiest investors.

A Revolution in Investing

The 75th anniversary of the first modern mutual fund is rapidly approaching. The Massachusetts Investors Trust was introduced in March 1924 and began with a modest portfolio of 45 stocks and $50,000 in assets.

This was the first so-called open-end mutual fund. It introduced concepts that would revolutionize investment companies and investing: a continuous offering of new shares and redeemable shares that could be sold anytime based on the current value of the fund's assets.

The Industry Regulates

The early mutual fund industry was, however, overtaken by events. The 1929 stock market crash and the Great Depression that followed prompted Congress to enact sweeping laws to protect investors and to regulate the securities and financial markets, including the mutual fund industry.

First was the Securities Act of 1933. It required for the first time something easily recognized by today's investor: a prospectus describing the fund. The Securities Exchange Act of 1934 made mutual fund distributors subject to SEC regulations and placed them under the jurisdiction of the National Association of Securities Dealers, Inc., which established advertising and distribution rules.

The most important laws relating to mutual funds and investor protection were adopted in 1940: the Investment Company Act and the Investment Advisers Act. The

---

*From Investment Company Institute, *1997 Mutual Fund Fact Book*, 37th edition.

Investment Company Act of 1940, enacted with strong industry support, has been re-markable in its effectiveness. The Act's core provisions—the requirement that every fund price its assets based on market value every day; prohibitions on transactions between a fund and its manager; leverage limits; and a statutory system of independent directors—are unique to the mutual fund industry.

The 1940 Act imposes regulations not only on mutual funds themselves, but also on their investment advisers, principal underwriters, directors, officers and employees. It mandates that mutual funds redeem their shares anytime upon shareholder request and requires them to pay redeeming shareholders a price based on the next calculated net asset value of the fund's investment portfolio within seven days of receiving a request for redemption.

The Advisers Act requires the registration of all investment advisers to mutual funds with the exception of banks. It also imposes a general fiduciary duty on investment advisers and contains several broad antifraud provisions. It further requires advisers to meet recordkeeping, reporting, disclosure, and other requirements.

It is no wonder that a former SEC Chairman once observed, "No issuer of securities is subject to more detailed regulation than mutual funds."

Mutual Funds Take Root and Grow

Mutual funds began to grow in popularity in the 1940s and 1950s. In 1940, there were fewer than 80 funds with total assets of $500 million. Twenty years later, there were 160 funds and $17 billion in assets. The first international stock mutual fund was introduced in 1940; today there are scores of international and global stock and bond funds.

The complexion and size of the mutual fund industry dramatically changed as new products and services were added. For example, before the 1970s, most mutual funds were stock funds, with a few balanced funds that included bonds in their portfolios. In 1972, there were 46 bond and income funds; 20 years later, there were 1,629.

Innovations in investment and retirement vehicles also swept the industry. In 1971, the first money market mutual funds were established. They offered checkwriting and higher interest rates than bank savings accounts. In 1974, the Employee Retirement Income Security Act (ERISA) was enacted and IRAs were created.

In 1976, the first tax-exempt municipal bond funds were offered, and three years later, the tax-free money market fund was created. It combined the convenience of money market funds and the tax advantages of municipal bond funds. In 1978, the now ubiquitous 401(k) retirement plan was created, as well as the individual retirement plan for the self-employed (or SEP-IRA).

The mutual fund industry also began to introduce even more diverse stock, bond, and money market funds. Today's mutual funds run the gamut from aggressive growth funds to global bond funds to single state tax-exempt money market funds to "niche" funds that may specialize in one segment of the securities market.

Services Mature Too

Over the past 50 years, mutual fund investors have come to receive an unparalleled array and level of services. These include professional management in global securities markets, portfolio diversification, trading and execution services, periodic account statements, tax information, daily liquidity and pricing of portfolios, access to fund personnel, and custody of fund portfolio assets.

Mutual funds are also constantly developing and offering new products, services, and distribution channels to meet consumer demands. Much of what we take for granted today —toll-free 24-hour telephone access, computerized account information, and shareholder newsletters—was unknown or in its infancy 20 years ago.

The Industry Today

The mutual fund industry has enjoyed substantial growth (see figures 2.1.1 and 2.1.2) by avoiding the bumps in the road that have occurred in other financial services sectors. The principles that exemplify the industry's long-standing commitment to shareholders— ensuring strong regulation, educating investors, and promoting opportunities for long-term investing—have guided the industry for the past 50 years, and will continue to do so in the future.

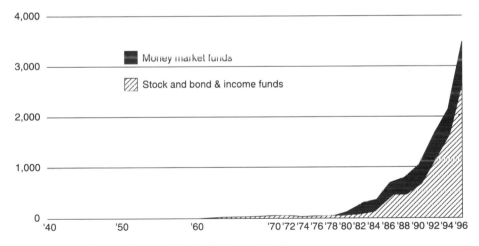

Figure 2.1.1   Assets of mutual funds (billions of dollars)

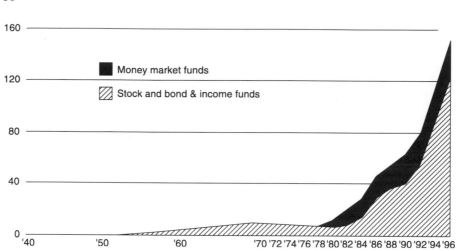

Figure 2.1.2   Mutual fund shareholder accounts (millions)

2.2   Types of Mutual Funds*

Stock Funds

Aggressive Growth Funds seek maximum capital growth; current income is not a significant factor. These funds invest in stocks out of the mainstream, such as new companies, companies fallen on hard times, or industries temporarily out of favor. They may use investment techniques involving greater than average risk.

Growth Funds seek capital growth; dividend income is not a significant factor. They invest in the common stock of well-established companies.

Growth and Income Funds seek to combine long-term capital growth and current income. These funds invest in the common stock of companies whose share value has increased and that have displayed a solid record of paying dividends.

Precious Metals/Gold Funds seek capital growth. Their portfolios are invested primarily in securities associated with gold and other precious metals.

International Funds seek growth in the value of their investments. Their portfolios are invested primarily in stocks of companies located outside the U.S.

Global Equity Funds seek growth in the value of their investments. They invest in stocks traded worldwide, including those in the U.S.

Income-Equity Funds seek a high level of income by investing primarily in stocks of companies with good dividend-paying records.

Bond and Income Funds

Flexible Portfolio Funds allow their money managers to anticipate or respond to changing market conditions by investing in stocks *or* bonds *or* money market instruments, depending on economic changes.

Balanced Funds generally seek to conserve investors' principal, pay current income, and achieve long-term growth of principal and income. Their portfolios are a mix of bonds, preferred stocks, and common stocks.

Income-Mixed Funds seek a high level of income. These funds invest in income-producing securities, including stocks and bonds.

---

*From Investment Company Institute, *1997 Mutual Fund Fact Book*, 37th edition.

Income-Bond Funds seek a high level of current income. These funds invest in a mix of corporate and government bonds.

U.S. Government Income Funds seek current income. They invest in a variety of government securities, including U.S. Treasury bonds, federally guaranteed mortgage-backed securities, and other government notes.

GNMA (Ginnie Mae) Funds seek a high level of income. The majority of their portfolios is invested in mortgage securities backed by the Government National Mortgage Association (GNMA).

Global Bond Funds seek a high level of income. These funds invest in debt securities of companies and countries worldwide, including those in the U.S.

Corporate Bond Funds seek a high level of income. The majority of their portfolios is invested in corporate bonds, with the balance in U.S. Treasury bonds or bonds issued by a federal agency.

High-yield Bond Funds seek a very high yield, but carry a greater degree of risk than corporate bond funds. The majority of their portfolios is invested in lower-rated corporate bonds.

National Municipal Bond Funds—Long-term seek income that is not taxed by the federal government. They invest in bonds issued by states and municipalities to finance schools, highways, hospitals, bridges, and other municipal works.

State Municipal Bond Funds—Long-term seek income that is exempt from both federal tax and state tax for residents of that state. They invest in bonds issued by a single state.

Money Market Funds

Taxable Money Market Funds seek to maintain a stable net asset value. These funds invest in the short-term, high-grade securities sold in the money market, such as U.S. Treasury bills, certificates of deposit of large banks, and commercial paper. The average maturity of their portfolios is limited to 90 days or less.

Tax-exempt Money Market Funds—National seek income that is not taxed by the federal government with minimum risk. They invest in municipal securities with relatively short maturities.

Tax-exempt Money Market Funds—State seek income that is exempt from federal tax and state tax for resident of that state. They invest in municipal securities with relatively short maturities issued by a single state.

2.3   Mutual Fund Ownership and Shareholder Behavior*

U.S. households own the majority of the mutual fund industry's $3.539 trillion in assets. As of year-end 1996, they held $2.626 trillion, or 74.2 percent, of mutual fund assets, while fiduciaries—banks and individuals serving as trustees, guardians, or administrators—and other institutional investors held the remaining $913 billion, or 25.8 percent (see figure 2.3.1).

U.S. Household Financial Assets

In 1996, U.S. households, on net, purchased $543 billion of financial assets, including mutual funds, up 8.7 percent from $499.6 billion in 1995. The increase in net purchases of financial assets was partly financed through higher household saving, which rose 8.3 percent to $274.0 billion. In addition, a pickup in household borrowing in 1996 indirectly helped finance the increase in household purchases of financial assets.

Households directed a significantly higher proportion of their purchases of financial assets to long-term mutual funds in 1996. Stock and bond and income funds garnered a 53.2 percent share of household net acquisitions of financial assets, up from 35.2 percent in 1995.

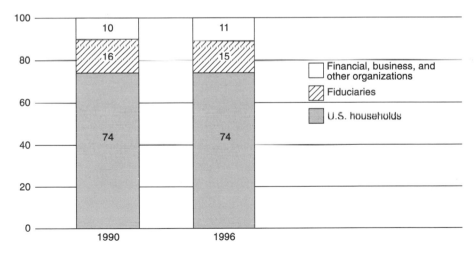

Figure 2.3.1 Composition of mutual fund ownership (percent of total mutual fund assets). Note: Total assets of mutual funds were $1.067 trillion at year-end 1990 and $3.539 trillion at year-end 1996.

---

*From Investment Company Institute, *1997 Mutual Fund Fact Book*, 37th edition. Reprinted with permission.

The increased purchases of long-term fund shares, most of which were equity funds, likely reflected the strong showing of the U.S. stock market, and may have reflected heightened concern about investing for retirement, as the media and financial advisers stressed retirement savings issues and holding stocks for such long-term objectives. Indeed, inflows to long-term funds from private pension plans—largely defined-contribution plans—doubled last year.

Since the late 1980s, mutual funds have captured an increasing share of the growing 401(k) market, which at the end of 1995 amounted to an estimated 38.7 percent of the $675 billion of outstanding plan assets, and industry reports suggest that the share likely increased in 1996.

U.S. Household Net Purchases of Equities

Households were net sellers of corporate stocks in 1996 despite increased investments in equity mutual funds (figure 2.3.2). Through equity funds, households made an estimated $214 billion of net purchases of corporate equities. At the same time, they liquidated $281 billion in direct holdings. These sales primarily were the product of share retirements associated with corporate repurchase programs and with corporate acquisitions and mergers.

Last year's net redemptions of corporate stock marked the third straight year in which households liquidated stock holdings. Indeed, over this period, net sales of equity by households amounted to $207 billion. The magnitude of this liquidation points up the importance of considering the entire scope of household investment activity, not just that involving mutual funds, in considering the flow of cash into the stock market.

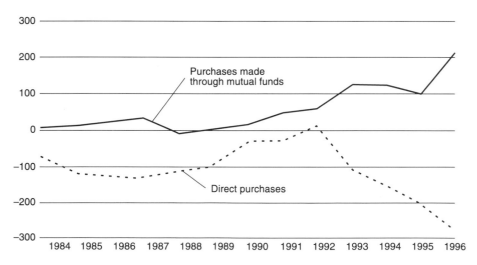

Figure 2.3.2 Purchases of equities by households (billions of dollars). Note: Direct purchases of equities include purchases through closed-end funds, personal trusts, and private defined-contribution plans. Source: Federal Reserve Board, Employee Benefit Research Institute, and Investment Company Institute.

Equity Share of Household Assets

Even though households have been net sellers of corporate equities during the past three years, the share of household financial assets held as equities has increased as a result of rising stock prices. At year-end 1996, the value of household equity holdings, held directly or indirectly, was an estimated $7.3 trillion and amounted to 31.1 percent of household financial assets. Nevertheless, the share of household assets held as corporate equities is below the peak of 33.9 percent reached in 1968 following the run-up in the stock market during the 1960s.

Other Household Balance Sheet Developments

Net purchases of liquid assets—deposits and money market funds—were essentially unchanged, and households also directly bought $11.8 billion in debt securities in 1996. Within the latter class of assets, households continued to liquidate direct holdings of municipal bonds, as they did with indirect holdings through municipal bond funds. This may have reflected concern during the year with the "flat-tax" proposal that many viewed as adversely affecting the tax status of municipal bonds. There also has been a sizable reduction in outstanding tax-exempt bonds over the past three years that perforce has resulted in liquidations by the largest holder of such securities, the household sector. Households were net buyers of government-related securities in 1996, in contrast to outflows from U.S. Government and Ginnie Mae funds.

U.S. Shareholder Characteristics

Investment Company Institute research conducted in 1995 found that the average mutual fund investor is middle class, 44 years old, has financial assets of $50,000, and is likely to be married and employed. The investment decisionmaker in a fund-owning household is most often solely a man (47 percent compared with 32 percent women). Men and women share decisionmaking in 21 percent of households. Shareholders are fairly evenly distributed among age groups, and only 18 percent of sharcholders are retired.

The typical mutual fund investor purchased his or her first fund shares in 1990 or earlier (68 percent). Among these seasoned fund investors, 57 percent also own individual stocks, and 75 percent have Individual Retirement Accounts (see table 2.3.1). Roughly half of seasoned fund investors added money to an existing account in the year preceding the July 1995 survey.

Fund investors have long-term goals. Eighty-four percent cite retirement as one of their investment goals, and 26 percent list saving for their children's or grandchildren's college education.

The typical mutual fund investor owns more than one kind of fund. For instance, investors in equity mutual funds typically hold three different funds, and more than half of them also hold bond and income funds. About 70 percent of equity fund investors bought their first fund shares in 1990 or earlier; half added money to an existing account in the

Table 2.3.1

Household owners of mutual funds demographic and financial characteristics, 1995[1]

	First purchase in 1990 or earlier	First purchase in 1991 or later
Demographic characteristics		
Median age	46	37
Percent of households		
Married	73	63
Employed, full or part-time	79	88
Minor children[2]	41	48
Four year college degree or more	60	55
Financial characteristics		
Median household income	$60,000	$50.000
Median household financial assets[3]	$70,000	$25,000
Percent of households owning:[4]		
Individual stocks	57	48
Individual bonds	27	19
Annuities	29	18
IRA	75	60
401(k)	51	50

1. Characteristics of primary financial decisionmaker in the household.
2. Percent of married households.
3. Excludes assets in employer-sponsored retirement plans.
4. Multiple responses included.

previous year. In addition, 61 percent of all equity fund shareholders and 59 percent of all bond and income fund shareholders own individual stocks. The types of funds owned tend not to differ according to age or financial assets of shareholder, or sex of investment decisionmaker.

Women Investors

Thirty-two percent of fund-owning household investment decisionmakers are solely women. As a group, they are very similar to male household investment decisionmakers except that they tend to be slightly older, are less likely to be married (although half of them are married), and are more likely to be widowed. They are also more cautious investors, tolerating a lower level of risk than the average male decisionmaker, and are slightly more likely to use a financial adviser.

Generational Differences

Generation X (ages 18 to 30 as of 1995) respondents are very interested in mutual fund investing. This group of shareholders has the lowest level of household assets, yet has the second highest portion of its financial assets in mutual funds (38 percent), after those ages 50 to 70. Not surprisingly, Generation X fund owners also have the highest tolerance for investment risk.

Baby Boomer shareholders (ages 31 to 49 as of 1995) have twice as many financial assets in mutual funds as Generation X fund investors, yet a smaller percentage of their assets is invested in funds. Baby Boom fund owners also tend to own more types of funds than Generation X fund owners, who typically have more assets in equity funds. Retirement as a goal for fund investment was high for shareholders of all generations, ranging from 72 percent to 89 percent.

2.4   The Mutual Fund Market: Are Mutual Funds a Product, a Service, or Both?*

Evolving Objective

The objective of the mutual fund industry has changed over the decades. For many years, funds were more of a service than a product, with the service being professional money management. The average investor had relatively few service providers, and each fund had a broad investment objective.

In the last 15 years, mutual funds have evolved to be a product. The average household owns four funds out of a product array numbering 6,000 (see table 2.4.1). The average fund does not have even a five-year track record, and most performance-oriented funds are purchased based on third-party endorsements.

While there is some slight evidence to the contrary, it is not clear that picking mutual funds using any system is much easier than picking stocks. Despite enjoying exceptional returns in recent years, households are confused by the range of choices and the volume of media reporting and recommendations. Such confusion has led managements in the industry to begin to rethink the definition of the business to include more *advice*. This line of thinking has raised more questions than it answers: What is advice? Who should give advice: money managers, discount brokers, retail brokers, or financial planners? Will consumers pay for it, or will it quickly become a free good, bundled with money management? Can retail brokers be transformed from their historical transaction orientation toward a long-term perspective? We try to answer these questions in the Feature (reading 2.6).

It seems to us that the issue of combining service and product will be an important one in the next 5–10 years. The industry's product orientation was very successful in fostering action: Some investors in the large U.S. markets are almost always doing well and excitement can always be created. Good service is often about inaction and directing focus to the long-term and away from the short-term. Whether a happy medium can be found is not yet clear. What is clear is that the serious attempts to meld service and product are about to begin.

In this section of the report we will first discuss household risk-taking from a behavioral finance perspective, and then review the growth outlook for the entire industry. The chapter ends with an assessment of future intra-industry competition.

Risk-Taking from a Behavioral Finance Perspective

Household Risk-Taking: A Determinant of Mutual Fund Growth

The outlook for the retail money management business largely depends on wealthy households' attitude toward risk. After all, what money managers primarily sell is exposure to risky financial assets with a professional management overlay.

---

* From Bernstein Research, "The Future of Money Management in America," 1997 edition, pp. 53–81. Reprinted with permission.

Table 2.4.1

Overview of the mutual fund industry (1983–95)

| | Assets ($ billion) | | | | Share of household discretionary financial assets | No. of open-end funds | Households owning mutual funds (million) | Shareholder accounts (million) | Assets/ account | Accounts/ household |
| | | Institutional | | | | | | | | |
	Retail	Pension assets	Other funds[1]	Total						
1983	$192	$12	$87	$291	6.7%	1,026	9.8	24.6	$11,833	2.5
1987	513	40	217	770	11.5	2,217	22.5	54.5	14,128	2.4
1991	885	86	376	1,347	13.8	3,427	25.4	68.5	19,653	2.7
1995	1,597	338	884	2,820	21.0	5,761	31.5E	131.8	21,405	4.2
Annual growth rate										
1983–87	28%	35%	26%	28%		23%	23%	22%		
1987–91	15	21	15	15		10	3	6		
1991–95	16	41	24	20		14	6	18		

1. Corporate, insurance, and other institutions.

Source: Investment Company Institute, Federal Reserve Board and Bernstein estimates

Relative returns are usually a small portion of total returns. In the last dozen years, the share of financial assets that are under the direct control of households has increased from less than 40% of the total to nearly two-thirds. Some of this change occurred because of the appreciation in initial stock and bond holdings, but a large part came from the investment of marginal savings dollars into riskier assets in packaged form.

In the last five years, about 60% of all cash flows (including reinvested returns) into discretionary financial assets went into mutual funds and unit investment trusts. Why households took this course of action is easy to understand: Short-term rates were falling or low during most of this period, and returns to long-term financial assets were well above previous norms. Treasury-bill yields below 6% typically prompt risk-taking by households, and the experience of the last few years conforms to this pattern.

Another way to judge the behavior of households is to put it in the context of the most fundamental indicator of corporate performance: real profit growth. When Corporate America does well, households want to participate in the prosperity. Since 1950, the profits of publicly held companies have increased at a pace nearly 3% above the rate of inflation. That premium expanded to nearly 7% in the last ten years, and to 13% in the last five years.

Therefore, any assessment of household behavior ultimately reduces to a judgment about the trajectory of real earnings growth. We doubt the sustainability of the recent prosperity, so we are concerned about the risky stance of the household balance sheet.

Historically, the aggregate balance sheet has not been very useful in forecasting behavior because it combined too many very different wealth cohorts. The very wealthy owned the vast majority of risky assets. Most households were outside the purview of the financial markets because of their participation in defined-benefit pension plans, which provided a guaranteed retirement.

In the last decade, however, the number of households with at least some direct exposure to the financial markets has exploded as 401(k)-type plans, IRA rollovers, variable annuities and retail mutual funds enjoyed widespread popularity. The share of equities held individually, in personal trusts and in professionally managed separate accounts, all of which are categories dominated by the wealthy, has declined from around 90% in the 1960s and 1970s to about 70% today. Conversely, the share in self-directed retirement vehicles is now 22% compared to almost nothing 20 years ago. Risk-taking has been democratized.

Technology and Myopic Loss Aversion
Since many more households than in the past are now exposed to the financial markets, we thought it would be interesting to see what the literature on behavioral finance would say about likely future actions. After all, in the 401(k) market in particular, large sums of money are being invested, training individuals to take risk and adopt a long-term horizon. Studies of the psychology of decision-making observe a couple of basic characteristics in behavior.

1. Individuals are usually risk-averse, and evaluate investment outcomes relative to current wealth. Experiments and studies of capital market risk premia[1] show that the slope of the loss function is much steeper than the gain function.
2. Individuals are more willing to take risk if they evaluate their investment portfolios infrequently. The effective holding period is not, for example, just their time to retire-

ment, but is influenced by the periodicity of review. Therefore, if the average 401(k) participants have 25 years to retirement but review their holdings daily they will, over time, think more like a trader.

The combination of natural risk-aversion plus frequent review would appear to lead to myopic loss aversion.

It seems to us that the tenets of behavioral finance will be put to a test ahead. The building blocks of myopic loss aversion are in place: A high share of assets are at risk and portfolios are being reviewed frequently.

Almost without exception, the rhetoric surrounding household behavior is concerned with the long term: goals, financial planning, the dominance of equity returns over long holding periods. Concurrently, the volume of information being provided to individual investors has exploded, and its useful life has grown ever shorter. The business press has expanded symbiotically with the fund industry, with quarterly performance review issues becoming best sellers. Many shareholders read about returns daily. Dedicated cable television networks report every price change, rumor, and earnings announcement—and for the technologically advanced, the same information is available via the Internet. Relatively soon, 401(k) participants will have on-line access to their accounts for both informational purposes and to make asset allocation changes.

In the last five years, the news-hungry households have been reading almost only upbeat stories. Technology has trumpeted the positive trends, and almost everyone experienced (most viscerally only) a record period of real corporate earnings growth. Our best guess is that sometime in the foreseeable future, households will revert to their risk-averse nature. The same sources that transmitted the good news will describe reasons to be fearful. What will be different from past downturns will be both the frequency of information on both fundamentals and asset prices.

Outlook for Growth and Competition

Sources of Mutual Fund Growth

Assets of the U.S. mutual fund industry have expanded at a 23% annual rate over the past 20 years, a 16% rate in the last 10 years, and at a 19% rate since 1991 (see table 2.4.2). During all of those periods, growth from new cash flows excluding reinvested dividends accounted for one-half of the growth rate. We believe that new cash flows and reinvested dividends are loosely correlated, with strong capital gains leading to stronger new flows. Conversely, shrinking assets would be caused by a combination of negative total returns and a cessation of new inflows, especially considering that the underlying redemption rate in the important equity category has averaged 14%–23% of assets in the last decade.

During the 1990s, the rise of 401(k) and other defined-contribution plans and continued rollover activity has accounted for a large share of industry cash flows. Looking out through year-end 1996, new cash flows into the industry during the last five years will total an estimated $925–$950 billion, of which $125 billion probably went into institutional money market funds, $60 billion into other pension accounts (which are often existing relationships converted into pooled form), about $180 billion into 401(k) accounts, and more than $200 billion into IRA/Keogh accounts (mostly the result of rollover activity). This

Table 2.4.2
Mutual fund industry assets under management ($ billion)

	Money market & short-term municipal bonds	Equities	Taxable fixed-income	Municipal bonds	Total funds
1976	$3.7	$42.5	$3.3	$0.5	$50.0
1977	3.9	37.6	4.0	2.3	47.8
1978	10.9	36.8	4.7	2.6	55.0
1979	45.6	39.6	5.1	3.0	93.3
1980	76.4	48.2	5.7	2.9	133.2
1981	186.2	44.8	5.9	3.1	240.0
1982	219.8	58.9	9.1	7.5	295.3
1983	179.4	85.8	11.3	14.6	291.1
1984	233.6	87.0	24.4	20.8	365.8
1985	243.8	124.1	80.4	39.4	487.7
1986	292.1	185.4	163.1	75.6	716.2
1987	316.1	205.4	171.5	77.0	770.0
1988	338.0	216.6	169.0	86.7	810.2
1989	428.1	281.9	166.3	105.7	982.0
1990	498.4	284.2	164.0	120.2	1,066.8
1991	539.6	423.5	230.9	154.2	1,348.2
1992	543.6	556.8	298.8	196.3	1,595.4
1993	565.3	895.9	359.6	254.6	2,075.4
1994	611.4	1,027.9	295.4	227.2	2,161.9
1995	753.0	1,481.2	334.2	253.0	2,821.4
1996E	850.0	1,780.0	375.0	260.0	3,265.0
2001E	$1,250.0	$3,280.0	$580.0	$410.0	$5,520.0
Average annual growth rate					
1976–1996E	31.2%	20.5%	26.7%	36.7%	23.2%
1986–1996E	11.3	25.4	8.7	13.1	16.4
1991–1996E	9.5	33.3	10.2	11.0	19.4
1996E–2001E	8.0	13.0	9.1	9.5	11.1

Source: Investment Company Institute and Bernstein estimates

Table 2.4.3
Mutual fund industry assets under management ($ billion)

	Source of growth		
	Yr/yr asset growth	Net new cash flow	Reinvested return on assets
1976	—	—	—
1977	(4.4)%	0.8%	(5.2)%
1978	15.1	11.9	3.2
1979	69.6	59.8	9.8
1980	42.8	33.7	9.1
1981	80.2	82.4	(2.2)
1982	23.0	15.1	8.0
1983	(1.4)	(7.5)	6.1
1984	25.7	23.4	2.3
1985	33.3	18.7	14.7
1986	46.9	33.7	13.2
1987	7.5	5.6	1.9
1988	5.2	(3.0)	8.2
1989	21.2	9.1	12.0
1990	8.6	4.7	4.0
1991	26.4	17.3	9.1
1992	18.3	11.4	7.0
1993	30.1	14.4	15.7
1994	4.2	4.2	0.0
1995	30.5	8.7	21.8
1996E	15.7	10.0	5.7
2001E	11.1%	5.6%	5.5%

Source: Investment Company Institute and Bernstein estimates

reformation of the retirement system to a defined-contribution model represents the fourth major leg of industry growth since the late-1970s (preceded by money market funds, bond funds, and lately equity funds). The mutual fund industry, with the strongest retail investment franchise, has been the major beneficiary of this fundamental change.

Going forward, we forecast 11% average annual growth for total industry assets (see table 2.4.3). Assuming a 65% dividend reinvestment rate (in recent years this rate has averaged 67%), the internal growth rate of the industry before inflows and redemptions should be about 5%, in contrast to the 7% pace set in the last 20 years. Growth from new cash flow should average 5%–6% a year, which implies that about 60% of household savings cash flows will be captured by the fund industry. The industry's real growth rate has run at 18% a year in the last 20 years and 10% in the last five years. Of course, the base from which growth is being forecast is now almost four times the average asset level of the previous two decades.

This forecast should be viewed in the context of a current expected return of 7.5%–8% for underlying assets. Thus, our outlook could prove to be too pessimistic or wildly optimistic depending on the capital markets' environment. The scenario that would lead to much higher growth would be one of permanently low short-term interest rates in the context of moderate economic growth, prompting a further decline in the equity risk premium. In this setting, individuals will further boost the risk profile of their financial asset holdings. If this extrapolation of the past five years proves correct, industry annual asset growth could be in the 15%–18% range.

There are a number of scenarios under which our baseline forecast could be overly optimistic. If the Federal Reserve Board is forced to raise short-term rates substantially (200 basis points or more), industry net cash flows may fall by 75% from recent levels. It is also possible that some sort of shock will cause investors to reassess the sustainability of corporate profitability and the size of the equity risk premium. Such a shock could be a further precipitous decline in business capital spending, a rising U.S. dollar, or a disruption in oil supplies.

Market Share Trends
Many trends in the mutual fund industry have caused an increase in the concentration of market shares. Inflows into 401(k) plans, which have sourced nearly 20% of total flows, have disproportionately benefited Fidelity and Vanguard, which control more than half of the mutual fund segment of that market. What's more, brokerage firms and banks have effectively narrowed the list of funds actively sold, either formally or informally. A number of large independent fund families have experienced little or no asset growth in the last few years.

There are forces working in the opposite direction. Large proprietary fund complexes have continuously lost market share in the 1990s, thereby reducing concentration (see table 2.4.4). The success of Charles Schwab's Mutual Fund Marketplace has had the same effect on shares by providing a pathway to growth for many small fund groups.

Using numerous yardsticks, our analysis reveals that the net result of these trends has been only a small increase of the concentration of the mutual fund industry in the 1990s. By assets, the largest five fund groups have accounted for approximately one-third of the industry's total (compared to 36% in 1985), and the largest 5% of complexes sourced about two-thirds. It should be noted, though, that the number of industry participants has expanded over time and, with it, the number of firms in the top 5%. Similarly, despite the powerful rise in asset prices, fund complexes with $5 billion or less have consistently included 80%–90% of all sponsors but only a small share of assets. When measured on a net cash flow basis, large firms have gained share in the last few years, primarily due to the success of Fidelity, Vanguard, Putnam, and the American Funds in the retirement business. Among independent load funds, the largest 6–7 sellers (Putnam, American Funds, AIM, Fidelity Advisor, Franklin/Templeton, OppenheimerFunds, and Mass Financial) account for virtually all net sales since 1994.

What is noteworthy is that while aggregate concentration has been fairly stable for decades, the identity of the firms at the top has changed over time. Only two of the largest five firms in 1985 retained that status a decade later.

Table 2.4.4
Market share of assets by type of fund complex

	1985	1986	1987	1988	1989	1990	1991	1992	1993	1994	1995	June 1996	Change 1991– 1996
Direct-marketed funds	24%	24%	25%	26%	28%	29%	31%	32%	33%	34%	35%	36%	4%
Broker-dealer sponsored funds	28	27	26	25	25	24	21	19	18	17	16	15	(5)
Independent load funds	31	33	34	35	34	32	33	33	33	33	33	33	1
Financial planner funds	4	3	3	3	3	4	3	3	4	4	4	4	1
Bank proprietary funds	3	3	3	4	4	5	5	6	6	6	6	6	1
Institutional funds	10	9	9	8	7	7	7	6	6	5	5	5	(2)
Total firms with over $10 bil. in assets	100%	100%	100%	100%	100%	100%	100%	100%	100%	100%	100%	100%	

Source: Investment Company Institute, *Strategic Insight* and Bernstein analysis

The fact that aggregate statistics have been stable in a bull market for equities, despite the weight of evidence that would appear to support a gradual increase in concentration, means that the largest firms held their own in a setting in which they would be otherwise expected to lose share. Sales data also generally reinforces the presumption. It would be an error, though, to put too much emphasis on the role of scale in this industry. Ultimately, investment performance will be a determinant of success, and very large size is its nemesis. Surveys consistently show that the most frequent rationale for account closings is dissatisfaction with investment performance.

What Is the Minimum Scale for a Mutual Fund Complex?

In the last several years, there has much discussion about what is the minimum size for a viable mutual fund complex, with $10 billion an often-cited threshold. We believe there is no single minimum size requirement that can be applied across the industry because distribution and product strategies are so diverse. A small, performance-oriented equity fund family can be enormously successful through broker-dealers, financial planners, or Charles Schwab—if the results are good. On the other hand, a $15 billion load fund group that has produced large capital losses in bond funds would not be helped by a merger with a firm in similar straits.

It is clear that the success of Schwab's Mutual Fund Marketplace product and financial advisor programs has reduced the minimum scale required for growth in the no-load fund arena. Schwab sources the customers and provides the scale. However, the commoditization of fixed-income products combined with the growing demands of the national wirehouses, has raised the scale required for impact in that channel.

Scale is only one dimension to competition in the mutual fund industry. And it will be a long time until it is the only dimension.

Do Brands Count More, or Less?

Business logic tells us that brand power should be of growing importance in the mutual fund industry. After all, it is an industry with 500+ vendors, 6,000+ products, and a customer base that has expanded so quickly as to virtually guarantee declining average sophistication. In the 1990s alone, the number of equity mutual fund shareholder accounts has quadrupled, but the average account size has advanced at only one-third the rate of market returns. Almost inevitably, success has brought with it a customer base with lesser financial resources. The growth of the 401(k) market has caused this shift, with an average participant's age about ten years younger than the rest of the industry and financial resources only half as great.

The customer base is also less sophisticated when it comes to financial knowledge. The Vanguard Group and *Money Magazine* developed a mutual fund investing IQ test, comprised of 20 questions. For example, the first question was:

A mutual fund's performance is best measured by:

a) Yield
b) Income return
c) Total return
d) Capital gains distribution

The right answer is total return (c), with 47% of respondents answering correctly. The average score among the 1,476 people who took the quiz was 49 out of a possible 100, and only 16% received a passing score of 70 or better. Results of the self-selected group who took the quiz via the Internet were somewhat better, with an average score of 71.

Thus, preconditions for brand importance seem to be fully in place. But the stability of brand identities in the money management business may be less than in other industries because relatively short-term performance influences perception and cash flow. While it is possible that brand identities could be rooted in fundamentally different investment philosophies that would be evaluated over decades, that is not how the system has worked. Rather, the brand that has emerged as dominant in the 1990s is not Fidelity, Putnam, or even Merrill Lynch—but instead is Morningstar. Equity funds rated with four or five stars by Morningstar have received 80%–100%+ of all net inflows, depending on the computation method employed. Looked at another way, most of the largest and most successful fund organizations of the 1990s have long had an equity orientation. In an era like the current one, where equities have been prized, they had product lines that were well positioned to benefit from both underlying demand and the move toward ratings. The market share winners of the 1990s tend to have a high proportion of highly ranked funds. Nonetheless, industry advertising expenditures have increased at about the same rate as sales in the last few years.

Going forward, brands will generally count more for three reasons. One is that the investing backdrop is likely to be more difficult than in the recent past. The cardinal rule in predicting household behavior is that individuals are risk-averse and don't like losses. At some point many individuals will absorb losses, and the companies whose funds suffer particularly large declines in value will see their brand franchises harmed, perhaps permanently. The second reason is that the industry will give more advice in some form, which will raise the profile of the organization over that of the product. Third, the average customer is not sophisticated and name awareness will count.

While brand image, on average, should rise in importance, in certain segments it will count less. In the 401(k) segment, for example, brand names are now dominant but will lose some sway ahead. Consultants are beginning to find a role here, and they will hasten the movement toward more open-architecture product configurations and rigorous, comparable performance evaluation tools.

Another area where brands will count less is in the high-end financial planner market. Because a part of the value-added of this channel is to pick and tailor portfolios of funds to the financial goals of moderately high-net-worth individuals, fund obscurity is a virtue.

Price Competition in the Mutual Fund Industry

Pricing in the mutual fund industry has been surprisingly stable in the last decade, with only aggregate loads registering a significant real decline. Equity expense ratios have risen while fixed-income costs have fallen marginally. In fact, equity expense ratios have been rising for several decades, increasing by 30–40 basis points from their levels of the mid-1950s, no doubt because of a major decline in the real average account size and an expansion of what constitutes service.

Fee waiving has the effect of reducing the average fee, but its impact has only been meaningful in the money market fund arena, where *Strategic Insight* estimates about a 20%

net reduction in gross fees. The impact has been half as large in bond products and inconsequential in the equity domain.

In many regards, pricing trends in the mutual fund business defy common sense. The industry is fragmented and the customer is ultimately yield/return sensitive. But only 19% of investors surveyed by the SEC could give an estimate of expenses for their largest mutual funds. Nominal yields have fallen, raising the importance and visibility of costs. Vanguard, a mutual company operating at no profit, has championed and proved the importance of expenses, particularly in fixed-income. With the exception of Vanguard and, possibly, the American Funds, significant differences in pricing have had little impact on market shares. Loads, though, have fallen over time. The vast majority of net inflows into highly rated funds went into no- or deferred-load products.

We think the reason that expense ratios have remained essentially stable is that trailing total returns are still robust. In fact, in the context of ten-year trailing returns, expense ratios are low, not high. In the last ten years, mutual fund expense ratios have equated to 8%–9% of stock and bond total returns. Compared to five decades of returns, the share rises to 11%–18% and equals 14%–15% of current expected returns.

Strong past returns, combined with the fact that at least one product category has been in demand throughout the last 15 years, explain most of industry pricing behavior. When these conditions are not in place, aggregate pricing will begin to trend downward. Relationship pricing tied to advice could be a vehicle through which effective prices will decline.

The move toward wrap-fee-type schemes will accelerate this trend among traditional distributors. The evolution toward ongoing rather than one-time charges raises comparability and visibility. It is easy to envision a setting where incentives will be offered to shareholders to switch balances in fixed-income products. Frequent flyer miles are beginning to appear in the industry, and much more is possible. Aggregate equity expense ratios will erode because indexing will secularly gain share. These changes will most likely occur only gradually. . . .

Intra-Industry Competition

Mutual Fund Distribution: The Battle of the Business Models

As the mutual fund industry has matured, both the number of distribution channels and their rivalry has mushroomed. Each channel has co-opted some of the traditional attributes of competitors, while offering a different value proposition. We anticipate that the historical distinctions among channels will blur further in the years ahead. The reason is the average customer has multiple distributor and product relationships. On the margin, all the channels are vying for the same individual: a fairly high-net-worth business executive or entrepreneur, age 40–64. This customer is the engine of profit growth for distributors. The battle for market share among channels will be fought based on advice/value-added, customer reporting, technology, and price.

While the retail financial services strongly follows the 80:20 rule in that the largest 20% of customers source the vast majority of profitability, the customer bases of the major channels have different characteristics. As shown in table 2.4.5, direct marketers tend to have a considerably younger customer base than do retail brokerage firms. The average retail (non-retirement) customer of the major direct marketers and Charles Schwab is age

Table 2.4.5
Mutual fund customer age mix by distribution channel

	Traditional retail			Insurance company	Defined-contribution pension plan	Total
	Direct	Brokerage firm	Bank			
18–34	22.0%	15.9%	21.8%	19.2%	28.5%	24.0%
35–44	29.9	28.1	28.2	34.9	38.1	32.7
Subtotal	51.9%	44.0%	50.0%	54.1%	66.6%	56.7%
45–64	38.2%	41.7%	34.0%	36.5%	31.9%	34.0%
65+	9.9	14.3	16.0	9.4	1.5	9.3
Total	100.0%	100.0%	100.0%	100.0%	100.0%	100.0%
Memo: Estimated age of core customer base	Upper 40s	58–65	Mid.-50s, but a lot 65+	50s	36–42	

Source: Office of the Comptroller of the Currency, Securities and Exchange Commission and Bernstein estimates

45–50, while the brokerage firm average is in the upper 50s to mid-60s. The bank customer base is, on average, somewhat younger than that of the brokerage firms, but includes a large group at age 65 and over. The average 401(k) plan participant is below 40 years old.

Direct marketers and Charles Schwab are seeking to both grow their customer bases and protect them by broadening product offerings and providing more guidance. Integrated statements, financial planning software, and Internet-based tools are some of the techniques being used in this channel. Brokerage firms are seeking to expand beyond their traditional clientele by moving toward open-architecture schemes, emphasizing goals-based planning and performance evaluation and (ultimately) using lower, relationship pricing. All competitors are vying for the retirement market, in part because of its young demographics.

Interchannel Competition: Market Share Evidence
Measuring the market share performance of the major distribution channels has become virtually impossible due to the proliferation of alternatives. The 401(k) inflows, which are not readily classifiable into any traditional category, are now nearly one-quarter of total inflows. In addition, the funds of direct marketers are available through brokerage firms, banks, insurance companies, variable annuities, and fund marketplaces on both a retail and intermediated basis. Nonproprietary load funds are also used in retirement plans, variable annuities, and wrap-type programs.

In the 1990s, traditional securities firms have lost share to direct marketers and financial planners. As we will discuss ahead, these trends are likely to continue as the brokerage business consolidates and technology enables other distribution approaches. The number of retail brokers has grown at a 4% rate since 1980 and a 2% rate since the 1987 peak. Regional brokerage firms such as Edward D. Jones have been instrumental to industry growth. Average production per broker and their associated earnings have advanced at a 5%–6% annual rate. Overall, retail brokerage systemwide production has grown at an 11% rate since 1980 and 7% since 1987, moderately below the growth rate of the underlying universe of household financial assets. Even in a bull market, the brokerage industry has lost some share to other distribution channels.

Financial Planners Gain Share
Financial planners can take many forms. Traditionally, they were employed by large independent organizations that operated in a manner similar to retail brokerage firms, but offered much higher payouts to their representatives and less support. Typically, production per representative was about 25% that of national brokerage firms at twice the payout. In the 1980s, these firms were large sellers of limited partnerships, but today mutual funds are their largest product category at about one-third of revenues. The registered representatives of the 10 largest firms now total 19,000, up from 12,000 three years ago. Over time, the support provided to reps at these firms has evolved to be closer to that available at national brokerage firms. These commissioned financial planners now account for 7%–8% of mutual fund sales. We suspect that as in the past, the fate of these highly operationally leveraged entities will be tied to the performance of capital markets.

Some commissioned financial planners also provide services on a fee-for-service basis, along with another group which only charges in that manner. This group has increased in size in recent years, to 12,000–15,000. They use service agents such as Charles Schwab, Jack White, and Fidelity for support, and typically charge 1% for service. Their average customer account is about $100,000, or equal in size to the average mutual fund wrap account. Fee-only and fee-based financial planners benefited from the proliferation of mutual funds and have positioned themselves as managers of managers. As such, the planners at the large-end of the market value exclusivity in fund offerings. For them, finding the "undiscovered" fund is some of the value-added of their service; they are gatekeepers. The universal availability of technology and low/no-cost support has enabled the independent financial planner market to grow and to pose a threat (albeit, so far of small proportion) to traditional brokerage firms.

Mutual Fund Marketplaces, Wrap-Fee and Asset Allocation Products
Charles Schwab's Mutual Fund Marketplace and One Source Funds together have emerged as an extraordinarily successful distribution method as assets have grown four-fold since year-end 1992. Assets are equally split between those sourced directly by retail customers and through financial planners. But the average account size of financial advisors is much larger than that of the retail base. Last year, Schwab accounted for about 14%–20% of net inflows into no-load products, and for some fund groups, they accounted for the majority of net sales.

Together, the three major marketplaces—Schwab, Fidelity, and Jack White—have long-term mutual fund assets of about $150 billion. The success of mutual fund marketplaces is attributable to their convenience, low-cost image, and (probably most important) their account statement. To a large extent, they provide much of the integration of information typically offered by retail brokerage firms but without advice and at much lower cost.

In recent years, various forms of mutual fund wrap-fee programs and asset allocation products have enjoyed commercial success. These programs are similar to service offerings of financial advisors using marketplace utilities, as they combine choice and proactive advice. In general, they have at their core the presumption that the advisor can select funds at least well enough to overcome the cost of advice at 100–150 basis points. While all advisor-sold products have this presumption, these offerings make the cost more visible.

Banks as Mutual Fund Distributors

Banks have had some success as distributors of mutual funds, but mostly to the benefit of the leading load fund groups. Approximately one-third of gross sales from 1992–95 went to Putnam, Franklin/Templeton, Fidelity, AIM, and MFS. While commercial banks managed $390 billion of mutual funds at year-end 1995, about $120 billion of the total was gained through acquisition and another $130–$150 billion was converted from other forms of accounts. To build proprietary fund families, banks have aggressively waived fees on proprietary products.

While fee banks have had some success as mutual fund distributors and managers, the list is a short one. What most banks have found is that they do not have an aggressive enough sales culture, nor do they have true access to the portion of their customer bases with appropriate financial resources. We expect banks to continue to make a concerted effort to capture a share of the money management market. A foothold in this market is needed to defend parts of their retail lending business and as service to small businesses.

Mutual Funds and the Internet

The Internet will, over time, accelerate the behavioral and competitive trends that have already emerged in the mutual fund industry. Individuals will receive more information faster than in the past. The greater the velocity of information, the greater the impulse to act upon it. The interactive character of the Internet will lead to more sophisticated performance-evaluation systems, probably including some form of optimization.

If used properly, direct marketers and, possibly, brokerage firms can use on-line access to sophisticated planning and evaluation tools to expand their scope of services and defend existing customer relationships. Another major benefit of the Internet will be customer order entry, which should have a much lower marginal cost than existing methods.

The demographics of the mutual fund industry are well aligned with those of personal computer and Internet users. The Investment Company Institute found in a 1995 survey that more than one-half of fund shareholders have a personal computer and one-sixth are subscribers to on-line services. These shareholders are younger, better educated, and wealthier than average (see table 2.4.6). Another survey revealed about 70% of high-net-worth investors own a personal computer. They are also more likely to be customers of direct marketers. A survey of 1,200 on-line investors found that their preferred fund companies were Fidelity, Vanguard, Twentieth Century, and T. Rowe Price. The rise of on-line technology will further raise the visibility of media information and third-party ratings in the segment of shareholders where they are already important.

Distribution: When Channels Collide

Two conflicting ideas are at the heart of the debate about the distribution of mutual funds. First, control of the customer is thought to be of rising importance. There are a limited

Table 2.4.6
Demographics of mutual fund owners with personal computers

	PC owners	Internet users	All others
Median financial assets	$50,000	$50,000	$40,000
Median age	41	41	44
Share completing graduate school	24%	32%	13%
Share owning mutual funds bought direct	39%	48%	32%

Source: 1995 survey by the Investment Company Institute

number of truly profitable customer relationships and the goal is to capture and retain as many as possible. Selling another product or service to an existing customer typically has a cost of less than one-quarter that of initiating a new relationship. While affluent households have relationships with multiple companies, gaining share of their balance sheet is a key strategic goal. Many strategies are now being employed to build and retain customer relationships, including brokerage firms and intermediaries holding accounts in street names, brokerage firm wrap-fee accounts (which include no-load funds and are intended to increase assets in custody), and the aggressive development of retirement businesses. In the future, relationship pricing—including various bundled services, upfront incentives to transfer assets, and sophisticated portfolio analyses—will be weapons in the battle for key customers. Many of the existing fees, such as those on wrap-fee accounts, will decline ahead.

The second idea about distribution is that each channel has a somewhat different client base, and a key goal is to be represented in all of them. Fidelity, for example, is the largest directly sold mutual fund group, the largest company in the retirement market, among the ten largest fund families by assets through intermediaries and a sales leader in the 1990s, the largest manager of variable annuities, a major factor in the mutual fund marketplaces, and a large manager of defined-benefit pension plan assets. The powerful movement toward open-architecture approaches in the 1990s has to a significant degree commoditized the role of a money manager, who has become a choice on someone else's menu, with a distinct brand identity and track record. Customer control is weak, but the cost of account acquisition, at least so far, is relatively low. Under this approach, scale, breadth, and infrastructure matter less than under a system aimed at customer control.

It seems to us that the movement toward open-architecture is irreversible and that money manager brands will cross channels. While brand awareness will be critical because most customers are unsophisticated, at the margin the mutual fund industry will evolve closer to the model of the defined-benefit pension market. While at first glance it seems inevitable that those organizations with the ultimate customer relationship will be the financial winners, history does not in any way support this presumption. Intermediaries have never been ably to truly price service—and given the rise of technology and alternative distribution approaches, the problem is more likely to get worse. In the end, the largest money managers have had brands which in economic terms were more powerful than those of intermediaries. The rising portability of funds is evidence of this. As distribution approaches proliferate and collide, offering brand name products through many channels will be a viable strategy. Only a few very large managers with proprietary distribution will have true control over customers. . . .

The Mutual Fund Market: Conclusions

Competitive pressures in the mutual fund industry will rise over time. The business still has well above-average growth prospects through cross-selling to existing customers and the retirement market. Yet, funds' penetration of the potentially profitable universe of customers is now virtually complete, awareness of expenses and sales charges is rising, and there are more limited prospects for major innovation. Managements in the industry have enjoyed two decades of near-continuous growth and can be expected to think in expansionary terms.

We expect that, over time, the already-high penetration of the industry will combine with a less favorable cyclical backdrop to cause intermediaries and large managers to adopt an end-game strategy. In this strategy, it pays to expend more to capture the marginal account because there are only a finite number of relationships available. Incentives will be provided to customers to establish relationships. We expect that sales charges will diminish further, fund subsidization will rise, and incentives to concentrate ownership in a given family of funds will rise. We also foresee greater segmentation of the client base, with pricing and service levels differing based upon account or relationship size.

The incredible product proliferation that has characterized the industry for the last decade presents an opportunity for services that organize financial assets and evaluate aggregate risk exposure. This service will take many forms. Direct marketers may offer more-customized asset allocation to important customers, while balanced funds may return to favor and meet the needs of the many investors of relatively modest means who have come to the industry in the 1990s. The catalyst for such an evolution would be poor performance in existing products.

Consolidation will continue in response to the rising cost of brokerage firm distribution, the inadequate scale of many fund groups, and the need to better-utilize fixed overhead bases. More-aggressive price competition will hasten this trend.

Note

1. Benartzi, Shlomo and Thaler, Richard H., "Myopic Loss Aversion and the Equity Premium Puzzle," *Quarterly Journal of Economics*, Vol. CX, Issue 1, February 1995.

Class Exercise: **Allocating Assets Among Funds**

As you are now aware, there are more mutual funds (over 6,000) than stocks listed on the New York Stock Exchange. And there are many different types of funds—not only stock, bond, and money market funds, but also many subcategories of fund objectives (e.g., growth and income funds, international funds, and tax-exempt funds). Thus, it is not surprising that many investors are confused and are looking for advice on which mutual funds to choose. Reading 2.5 (table 2.5.1) summarizes the characteristics of mutual fund shareholders, and reading 2.6 discusses the types of advice investors are currently seeking.

Some investors go to their brokers for advice on mutual funds. These brokers may provide such advice in exchange for sales loads (averaging 4% or 5%), annual distribution charges (12b-1 fees), or both. Alternatively, these brokers may offer so-called wrap programs, in which investors pay an annual fee based on the percentage of their assets in the program. Other investors seek investment advice from financial planners. Pure financial planners are compensated for such advice only by an explicit fee paid by the customer, but many financial planners also receive compensation, directly or indirectly, from the company sponsoring the product sold to the customer or from the customer through sales loads or 12b-1 fees.

Other investors do not choose to pay for advice and buy directly from mutual funds and their underwriters (the direct-marketed funds). These investors believe they can fend for themselves if given appropriate information about particular funds. They may review prospectuses, reports, and other educational information distributed by fund sponsors, as well as articles and analyses published in the press about mutual funds. The direct marketers solicit fund sales from such investors through advertisements in newspapers, magazines, and radio or television, as well as through mailings to potential customers. Most of the direct-marketed funds do not charge any sales loads ("no-load funds"), though some no-load funds have begun to charge annual distribution fees (12b-1 fees). To qualify as a no-load fund, the annual distribution fee must be less than $\frac{1}{4}$ of 1% (25 basis points).

Still other investors are relative newcomers to mutual funds, including new participants in 401(k) plans, who are seeking more basic guidance on how to structure a portfolio of funds that will meet their needs. It is this last category of investors to whom publications such as FundMatch are addressed. The FundMatch is designed to explain to potential customers a few fundamental principles of investing. It also describes in relatively summary terms the main investment alternatives open to these customers. The worksheet in FundMatch is designed as a self-assessment tool for these customers. It requires them to answer questions about their investment objectives as well as constraints, and then through self-scoring to focus on an appropriate mix of mutual funds.

In-Class Team Discussion Outline

First, each student should complete the Fidelity FundMatch worksheet, using his or her personal experience and financial data or creating a fictitious investor. Then after group discussion, each team should be prepared to answer the following questions:

1. What is the objective of diversifying your portfolio? What are the benefits, if any? What are the drawbacks, if any?
2. If an investor's portfolio consisted only of an S&P 500 index fund, would he or she be adequately diversified? Would such a portfolio be inconsistent with other legitimate investor objectives?
3. What is the function of each of the three asset categories mentioned in FundMatch? What other categories, if any, would you add?
4. What are the relative merits of a portfolio of mutual funds versus a portfolio of individual securities?
5. What are the major non-tax factors an investor should consider when building a suitable portfolio? What happens to the relative importance of these factors over time?
6. What consideration should be given to taxes in constructing a portfolio? What happens if one asset does much better than all other assets over time?
7. Does this worksheet provide sufficient guidance to investors seeking to build a suitable portfolio?
8. What are the advantages and disadvantages of using a worksheet versus receiving investment advice from a broker or financial planner?

2.5   Ownership Characteristics of Mutual Fund Households

Table 2.5.1
Ownership characteristics of mutual fund households[1]

	First purchase in 1990 or earlier	First purchase in 1991 or later
Median mutual fund assets	$25,000	$7,000
Median number of funds owned	3	2
Percent		
Household assets in mutual funds[2]	36	28
Fund types owned[3]		
Equity	75	71
Bond and income	50	38
Money market	54	45
Households using purchase channels		
Sales force	65	60
Direct market	33	29
Investment goal[3]		
Retirement	81	77
Children's education	24	27
Risk tolerance profile		
Willing to take:		
Substantial risk with expectation of substantial gain	8	10
Above-average risk with expectation of above-average gain	36	38
Average risk with expectation of average gain	41	36
Below-average risk with expectation of below-average gain	10	13
No risk	6	3
Awareness: Agreed that investing in stock and bond funds involves risk	96	100
Evaluations: Assessed risk of most recent stock or bond fund purchase	67	71
Horizon: Assess mutual fund risk in time frame exceeding five years	65	62

1. Excludes mutual funds in employer-sponsored retirement plans.
2. Excludes any mutual fund assets held in employer-sponsored retirement plans.
3. Multiple responses included.
Source: Investment Company Institute *Mutual Fund Fact Book*, 37th edition (1997)

2.6   Research Feature: On Advice*

How Much Is Enough?

Having delved into the major trends affecting the money management business itself—shifts in growth, competition, pricing, distribution channels, etc.—we should discuss changes occurring in a service that may be playing a more critical role—advice.

Currently, the most widely held view is that individuals need and desire more advice to make investment decisions. The logic behind this view is as follows.

1. The proliferation of investment products, particularly mutual funds, has confused the consumer. There are more than 6,000 open- and closed-end fund offerings, and the average consumer has 4–5 accounts at 2–3 different companies. While most shareholders had investment experience before the 1990s, the average account is less than five years old.

2. The advice channels—brokerage firms, banks, and financial planners—have at least maintained, and possibly gained share of the retail market in recent years. Direct marketers have captured about half of all industry net cash flow, but a smaller share of retail (non-retirement) net flows. Included in the direct marketers' share are financial planners who levy a fee for advice. We believe that these data indicate individuals' interest in buying from intermediaries that provide the needed advice.

3. Select Baby Boomers are thought to have accumulated substantial financial assets through stock options, IPOs and defined-contribution retirement plans. Without adequate expertise or time, they are seeking guidance.

4. Many younger, less sophisticated households are getting exposed to investing for the first time through 401(k) and other defined-contribution retirement approaches. They need more assistance than that traditionally provided by the plans' support materials.

While the overall thrust of the consensus appears at least partially valid, the evidence backing the view is not totally compelling. If there was a ground swell in demand from Baby Boomers for personal advice, we would expect to see an influx of new, younger customers into brokerage firms and other intermediaries. To the contrary, according to industry sources, the average age of the clientele in the advice channels has changed very little in the last few years, and remains about 15 years older than that of direct marketers. Brokers are doing more business with their wealthy, older clientele who have benefited mightily from the performance of the financial markets. While this has propelled their business, this has not translated into share gains. Directly sold products have benefitted at the same time due to the appeal of low-cost service and manageable minimum account sizes.

---

*From "The Future of Money Management in America," 1997 edition, pp. 23–27, Bernstein Research.

Unresolved Issues

That said, we have long thought that the incredible array of product offerings had to create demand for financial planning. Most accounts are new, and it is inconceivable that average retail investors have penetrating insights into the characteristics of their holdings. Investor confusion is building in what has been a very benign environment. Many younger investors are relying on the media for decisionmaking input, which could be dangerous given the media's orientation toward reporting rather than predicting.

Therefore, while there is probably demand for advice, there are still unresolved issues:

- What is advice?
- Who will provide it?
- How much will investors pay for it?

What Is Advice?

The definition of advice is unclear. When individuals talk about "advice," they seem to mean direct guidance on what to do. The guidance can be abstract or administered in a framework and evaluated against predetermined objectives. It frequently encompasses tax considerations and estate planning. Advice often utilizes third-party ratings, such as those provided by Morningstar, Inc. Products such as wrap-fee services and asset allocation funds implicitly are giving advice.

In the hierarchy of needs, after advice comes "assistance," which helps investors narrow choices but with less specificity. Assistance is now provided by almost all fund vendors. Investors also often require "information," which has been made widely available in the media.

In the current discussion, therefore, advice seems to be direct guidance on fund selection, asset allocation and risk-taking. The market at which it is aimed is younger and far less wealthy individuals than the traditional customer base. Typically, about 40% of all customers seek direct advice, 20% need information only, and the remainder are somewhere in between. Different channels are trying to fulfill this demand by altering their traditional approaches to service and price.

Who Will Provide Advice? And at What Price?

Retail brokerage firms with more than 100,000 salespeople are the major providers of investment advice in the U.S. By comparison, there are about 27,000 commission-based financial planners and about another 12,000 operating primarily on a fee basis.

Brokerage firms are trying to move downmarket to serve the needs of a younger, less affluent customer base. They are reorienting their sales forces toward financial planning as the centerpiece of the customer relationship and toward relationship-based and asset-based pricing. This reorientation will be much more easily accomplished with the less experienced representatives that have smaller revenue bases. It will be very difficult to fundamentally alter the behavior of the most established, biggest-producing reps because their existing transaction-based revenue streams are so large. Last year, retail revenues sourced by equities transactions were twice those produced by mutual fund sales. Ultimately, the idea behind financial planning is that both the cost of advice (through asset-based fees) and the performance of the advice given will be visible and easily assessed.

At the other end of the spectrum, discount brokers and direct marketers are beginning to offer portfolio evaluation services and are providing trust services. They are not establishing large sales organizations, but rather are relying on technology as the basis of the service.

Another uncertainty is the amount most new investors will be willing to pay for advice. Historically, the major profit source for advice providers has been high-net-worth households who were price insensitive.

Advice does not come cheap. As a rule of thumb, it costs about 100 basis points of assets. The effective all-in cost of load funds is about 1% above that of no-load funds. Financial planners typically charge a comparable amount, and the effective revenue yield of brokerage firm assets in custody is similar. Broker-sold mutual fund wrap programs add 100–150 basis points on top of existing fund expenses. Programs recently launched by Charles Schwab and Vanguard charge about 50 basis points for financial planning and evaluation services.

Likely Evolutionary Path

To date, advice has been a hard concept to nail down. It is partly a quantitative exercise: portfolio rebalancing, asset class analysis, and risk analysis. However, advice also has a psychological element: convincing individuals that they are doing the right thing, particularly when returns are poor and stress is at its highest.

The psychological aspect of advice is unlikely to be altered, and will depend on personal contact. However, the quantitative aspect of advice-giving probably will undergo great change ahead. It will be more widely available, risk measurement techniques will improve, and funds will be evaluated in a portfolio context rather than singularly. Ultimately, third parties will rate the effectiveness of the quantitative tools, just as they now rate funds. It is easy to foresee a setting where quantitative evaluations are offered as an adjunct to money management services at little or no cost. They will be viewed as a means to unite the customer to the firm.

The movement toward financial planning and asset-based pricing in the brokerage industry will ultimately lead to either lower revenue yields overall or a multi-tiered compensation system, where brokers who perform different functions are paid differently. The true value-added by fund-picking is probably well below 1%–1.5%. Some of the traditional information functions performed by brokers will be facilitated through technology.

Being the arbiter of performance will be critical to the process of advice-giving. We expect some major firms to build or acquire entities that evaluate money manager performance.

2.7

INVESTMENT PLANNING SERIES

Fidelity FundMatch℠

A guide to helping you build a diversified investment portfolio.

How do you choose an asset allocation strategy?
What level of risk are you comfortable with?
Which mutual funds make the most sense for you?

Welcome To Fidelity FundMatch

Your money is just too important to invest without a plan. That's why it's crucial to assess your current situation and analyze your goals before you make key investment decisions or adjust your current portfolio mix.

Using a thoughtful, step-by-step process, the FundMatch method helps you examine your needs and determine the mix of investments that is most appropriate for you. It can also help you diversify your investments in a strategic way across asset classes to maximize return – a process known as asset allocation.

To make it easier for you to use FundMatch, we've organized this guide into three sections.

Laying the Groundwork

This section reviews the factors that influence your investing strategy and explores and defines the principles of:
- diversification
- asset allocation
- risk and return

The FundMatch Worksheet

Based on your individual situation and how you score on the questions, the FundMatch Worksheet will help you determine the mix of investments that might be right for you. Twelve multiple choice questions focus on the key factors that influence your investment decisions, including:
- your time horizon
- your risk tolerance
- the role of an investment in your total portfolio

Your Plan of Action

Here's where you can put the FundMatch method into action. The *Investment Check-Up* chart gives you a way to compare your current investments with the suggested mix from your FundMatch score – and then decide on your next steps. You'll find an array of Fidelity mutual funds to choose from as you implement (or adjust) your investment plan, plus helpful information on other products and services available from Fidelity.

Reviewing Your Plan Periodically

It's important that you take the time to review your plan at least annually to make sure it still meets your needs. As your financial objectives change, you should review your investment strategy to be sure you are comfortable with your investments and that they still fit your goals.

If you have questions about FundMatch, or need additional information about Fidelity products or services, our representatives will be happy to assist you. Just call toll-free anytime, 1-800-544-8888. Or visit your local Fidelity Investor Center to speak with a Fidelity representative in person.

The Importance Of Diversification

Diversification is a time-tested strategy that can help you reduce risk by spreading your money among many different kinds of investments. It works because no two investments typically perform the same way at the same time. Having a diversified portfolio can let you focus on building for the long term instead of trying to time the market.

Spreading your investment over different asset classes can help you meet your investment goals.

Diversification over different asset classes (stocks, bonds, and short-term investments), or asset allocation, is important because not all investments perform the same way at the same time. The more diversified a portfolio – meaning the greater variety of investments – the less likely it is that you will be hurt by the poor performance of a single investment.

Diversified portfolios also tend to provide less volatile returns over the long term. The chart below compares the performance of a diversified portfolio – 40% common stocks (as measured by the S&P 500®), 40% long-term government bonds (as measured by 30-year Treasury bonds), and 20% cash equivalents (short-term instruments) – with a nondiversified portfolio composed entirely of common stocks. The chart also shows how diversification can help stabilize a portfolio.

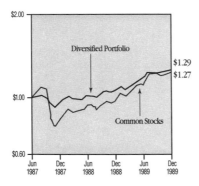

As you can see, the period of comparison includes a major market decline. While both the diversified and nondiversified portfolios ended at approximately the same value during the periods studied, the nondiversified portfolios had more dramatic price swings. Of course, past performance is no guarantee of future results.

Investing over time is a simple strategy that works.

At Fidelity, we believe that a regular investment plan over time is one of the most effective ways to accumulate savings. Investing over time is important because the value of any investment will fluctuate. When you diversify over time, also known as dollar-cost averaging, you buy at many different prices instead of trying to time the market. Even Wall Street experts can't always buy at the lowest price and sell at the highest. Investing regularly over time is an effective way to build savings and meet your investment goals. Although this strategy does not protect you from a loss in a declining market or assure you a profit, over time it should help lower the average cost of your purchase.

Make diversification easy with mutual funds.

Mutual fund investing is one simple way to get a diversified investment. Mutual funds by definition are diversified, because they invest your money in a "basket" of securities, rather than in a single stock or bond. For example, a stock mutual fund would hold a wide range of different stocks at any one time. A bond fund would hold a variety of fixed-income securities. Or you can choose a fund like Fidelity Asset Manager® that holds a number of stocks, bonds, and short-term instruments. With a mutual fund you also get the expertise of a professional money manager, who will watch over the markets and your investment and make decisions about selecting individual securities for the fund.

The chart does not represent the long-term performance potential for common stocks or a diversified portfolio. Source: © *Stocks, Bonds, Bills and Inflation 1996 Yearbook*™, Ibbotson Associates, Chicago (annually updates work by Roger Ibbotson and Rex A. Sinquefield). Used with permission. All rights reserved.

Balancing Risk And Return

Before you determine what investment mix is best for you, it's important to take a closer look at risk and understand how selecting different types of investments can help you manage it. Each of the three types of investments, or "asset classes," has its own associated risks. And with investments, more risk usually means more potential return.

The Relationship Between Risk and Return

Type of Asset Class	Price Fluctuation	Potential for Current Income	Potential for Growth
Stocks	Moderate to high	Low	Moderate to high
Bonds	Low to moderate	High	Low
Short-Term Instruments	Very low	Moderate	Very low

Based on historical performance, as shown on the chart on p.3, an investment in stocks has been more likely to result in a higher return over the long term compared to other asset classes. But investors who need the money on short notice take the risk of having to sell during a market downturn unless they are also invested in some shorter-term instruments.

Stock market investing.

While the stock market as a whole has historically provided superior returns over the long term compared to bonds and short-term instruments, it is important to consider market risk when investing in stocks. Market risk is the risk that your investment will fluctuate in value along with other securities in the market, and your shares may be worth less when you sell them.

Because the share price of a stock can fall as dramatically as it can rise, stock market investing is most appropriate if you are investing for longer-term goals and have the time to wait out any short-term fluctuations in the market.

Investing in bonds.

Bonds historically have been less volatile than stocks. Most pay interest and may be appropriate for investors who want regular income from their investments. Bonds are subject to credit risk, which is the risk of the issuer's defaulting on payment as well as the risk of a decline in the bonds' value when their credit standing deteriorates. Also, bonds do not provide the same opportunity for growth that stocks do.

Bond investors also need to understand interest-rate risk. That's the risk that interest rates will change and therefore affect the price of the bond investment you may be holding. For example, if you hold a bond paying 6% and interest rates rise to 10%, the market value of your bond will decline because current bonds are paying the higher interest rate. This can also work in reverse to produce a gain in your bond price if interest rates were to drop.

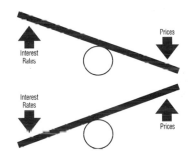

Bond Funds and Interest Rates

When interest rates move up and down, the share price of a bond usually moves in the opposite direction. Bond funds that hold short-term bonds (bonds that are close to maturity) are usually less affected by changes in interest rates than long-term bond funds.

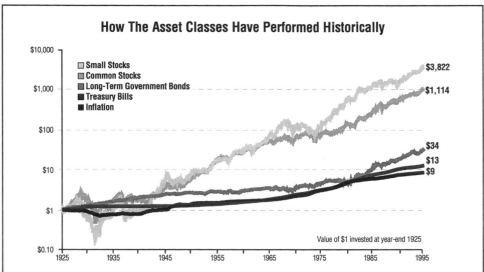

How The Asset Classes Have Performed Historically

Small Stocks
Common Stocks
Long-Term Government Bonds
Treasury Bills
Inflation

$3,822
$1,114
$34
$13
$9

Value of $1 invested at year-end 1925

1925   1935   1945   1955   1965   1975   1985   1995

The total-return data for the above indices include reinvestment of dividends and capital gains. The chart above shows the growth of a one-dollar invest-ment in four types of assets and of inflation since December 31, 1925. While past performance is no guarantee of future results, it will help you see how various investments have fared over the long term. The chart illustrates the principle that different assets can be expected to perform differently over time. Source: © *Stocks, Bonds, Bills, and Inflation 1996 Yearbook*,™ Ibbotson Associates, Chicago (annually updates work by Roger G. Ibbotson and Rex A. Sinquefield). Used with permission. All rights reserved.

Short-term instruments.

Short-term instruments – securities with maturities of one year or less – are the least volatile of the asset classes. Short-term instruments can help you meet short-term investment goals. They also can add some liquidity or stability to a portfolio. Short-term instruments tend to pay lower rates than longer-term bonds, and you should keep in mind that not all short-term instruments are backed by government guarantees or insurance.

Investing in short-term instruments exposes you to the risk that you may lose ground to inflation. This inflation risk is the risk that the returns on your investment may not keep up with inflation. Inflation can eat away at your return, sometimes eroding it entire-ly. For example, during 1996 Treasury bills returned 5.30 percent on average. The same year, the Consumer Price Index, a measure of inflation, rose 3.30 percent. That means that the real gain from money market funds was just 2.00 percent.

Setting up your plan.

The FundMatch Worksheet that begins on the following page can help you develop an asset allocation strategy for a specific invest-ment goal. If you have more than one goal – saving for a down payment and a college education, for instance – you'll want to create a separate plan for each.

The FundMatch Worksheet

Based on common investment principles, the FundMatch Worksheet uses a point system to help you find an asset allocation strategy that matches your investment needs.

To complete the Worksheet, select your best answer for each question and enter the corresponding point value in the space to the right. The point values will vary by question, according to how each factor may influence an investment decision.

Once you've finished, add up the points from questions 1 and 2, then add up the points on questions 3-12. Subtract the sum of 3-12 from the sum of 1 and 2. Compare your total score to the model portfolios you'll find on page 8 to find which one may be most suited to your current needs.

Naturally, the asset allocation that's indicated by your score is just a guide. The decision to invest more conservatively or aggressively than your model suggests is always yours to make. To help you with that decision, the following questionnaire takes into consideration your time horizon, current financial situation, and risk tolerance.

Regardless of your point score, if you're investing for fewer than two years, you may want to consider the Short-Term Portfolio.

Please keep in mind that Fidelity FundMatch is designed to help you plan for a specific investment goal. Should you have multiple investment goals – for short-term and long-term savings, for instance – consider completing a FundMatch Worksheet for each one.

Don't forget, too, that your Worksheet score is based on your *current* assessment of a number of factors. If your personal situation – or market conditions – change, it makes sense to review your investment strategy. At a minimum, you should review your asset allocation on an annual basis.

Your Investment Time Frame

Determining the time frame for your investment is critical to making an investment decision: the longer your investment horizon, the more aggressive you may want to be.

1. In approximately how many years do you expect to need to spend the money you're investing?

2 to 3 years	20
4 to 6 years	38
7 to 10 years	50
More than 10 years	69

2. Do you expect to withdraw more than one-third of the money in this account within seven years (for a home purchase, college tuition, or other major need)?

No	20

If yes, when do you expect to withdraw from the account?

Within 3 years	0
Within 4 to 7 years	12

Subtotal for
Questions 1 and 2

How does this investment fit into your total financial picture?

3. Approximately what portion of your total "investable assets" – the dollar amount of the investments you currently have – will this investment represent?

NOTE: Use the formula below to quickly calculate your investable assets. Do not include your principal residence or vacation home when figuring this total.

It is important to consider this investment in relationship to your total portfolio. The percentage of your portfolio that this investment represents will influence how conservative or aggressive you may want to be.

Less than 25% 0

25% to 50% 1

51% to 75% 2

More than 75% 4

 Points

Amount You Intend To Invest		Total Investable Assets				% Of Assets
$	÷	$	=		× 100 =	%

4. Which ONE of the following describes your expected future earnings over the next five years? (Assume that inflation will average 4%.)

Your expectation for future earnings will help determine how your assets should be allocated. If you're expecting significant earnings increases, it may be appropriate to be somewhat more aggressive.

I expect my earnings increases will far outpace inflation (due to promotions, new job, etc.) 0

I expect my earnings increases to stay somewhat ahead of inflation 1

I expect my earnings to keep pace with inflation. 2

I expect my earnings to decrease (retirement, part-time work, economically depressed industry, etc.) 4

Points

5. Approximately what portion of your monthly take-home income goes toward paying off installment debt (auto loans, credit cards, etc.) other than a home mortgage?

NOTE: Use the formula below to calculate what portion of your income goes toward paying debt.

If a large portion of your income goes toward paying debt, you may need to have cash available for unforeseen circumstances. Or, you may have responsibility for ongoing family obligations. Either can dictate a more conservative approach.

Less than 10% 0

10% to 25% 1

26% to 50% 2

More than 50% 6

Points

Monthly Debt		Monthly Take-Home Income				% Of Income
$	÷	$	=		× 100 =	%

6. How many dependents do you have? (Include children you continue to support, spouse, elderly parents, etc.)

None 0

One 1

2 to 3 2

More than 3 4

 Points

5

7. Do you have an emergency fund? (savings of three to six months' after-tax income)

An emergency fund can provide a cushion against unexpected expenses, so you avoid having to draw on long-term investments to meet immediate needs.

No. 8

Yes, but less than six months after-tax income. 3

Yes, I have adequate emergency funds. 0

8. If you expect to have other major expenses (such as college tuition, home down payment, home repairs, etc.), do you have a separate savings plan for these expenses?

Yes, I have a separate savings plan for these expenses. 0

I do not expect to have any such expenses. 1

I intend to withdraw a portion of this money for these expenses. 3
(**Note**: please answer question 2 accordingly)

I have no separate savings plans for these items at this time. 4

Your Personal Risk Tolerance

9. Have you ever invested in individual bonds or bond mutual funds?
(Aside from U.S. savings bonds.)

Your prior investment experience can help determine your attitude toward investment risk.

No, and I would be uncomfortable with the risk if I did 10

No, but I would be comfortable with the risk if I did 4

Yes, but I was uncomfortable with the risk. 6

Yes, and I felt comfortable with the risk 0

10. Have you ever invested in individual stocks or stock mutual funds?

No, and I would be uncomfortable with the risk if I did 8

No, but I would be comfortable with the risk if I did 3

Yes, but I was uncomfortable with the risk. 5

Yes, and I felt comfortable with the risk 0

11. Which ONE of the following statements best describes your feelings about investment risk?

Your comfort level with investment risk influences how aggressively or conservatively you choose to invest. It should be balanced with your desire to achieve your investment goals.

I would only select investments that have a low degree of risk associated with them (i.e., it is unlikely I will lose my original investment) 12

I prefer to select a mix of investments with emphasis on those with a low degree of risk and a small portion in others that have a higher degree of risk that may yield greater returns. 9

I prefer to select a balanced mix of investments – some that have a low degree of risk, others that have a higher degree of risk that may yield greater returns 5

I prefer to select an aggressive mix of investments – some that have a low degree of risk, but with emphasis on others that have a higher degree of risk that may yield greater returns. 1

I would select an investment that has only a higher degree of risk and a greater potential for higher returns 0

12. If you could increase your chances of improving your returns by taking more risk, would you:

Be willing to take *a lot* more risk with *all* your money?. 0

Be willing to take *a lot* more risk with *some* of your money?. 2

Be willing to take *a little* more risk with *all* of your money? 6

Be willing to take *a little* more risk with *some* of your money? 9

Be unlikely to take much more risk?. 12

Points

Scoring Directions:

A) Write your point score for Questions 1 and 2

B) Add your points from Questions 3 through 12

C) Subtract "B" from "A"

Total Points

See next page for suggested model portfolios.

Should your short-term and bond investments be taxable or tax-free?

It all depends on your tax bracket. If you're in one of the highest federal tax brackets, then you may actually keep more income with tax-free investments than you would with comparable taxable investments. Check the table below, and if you fall into one of those brackets, you may want to consider tax-free money market funds and tax-free bond funds when building your diversified portfolio. (However, if you're investing in an IRA or other tax-deferred retirement account, remember that your money already grows free of taxes.)

1997 Federal Tax Brackets

If you file this type of tax return:	And your taxable income is...	Then your federal tax bracket is...
Single Return	$24,651 – $59,750	28%
	$59,751 – $124,650	31%
	$124,651 – $271,050	36%
	$271,051 and above	39.6%
Joint Return	$41,201 – $99,600	28%
	$99,601 – $151,750	31%
	$151,751 – $271,050	36%
	$271,051 and above	39.6%

What Does Your Score Mean?

Your FundMatch score provides an indication of an asset allocation strategy that may be right for you. Each of the four portfolios below has a different mix of investments, so each one will strike a different balance between risk and return. If you need your money in two years or less, a portfolio made up of short-term/money market instruments can provide you with current income, liquidity, and an element of stability.

If you're investing for less than two years	100% — **Short-Term Portfolio** 100% short-term instruments	Consider a portfolio with 100% short-term instruments regardless of your point score. If you're investing for less than 2 years, short-term investments such as money market funds can provide a stable share price.*
<20 points	50% / 20% / 30% — **Capital Preservation Portfolio** 30% short-term instruments, 50% bonds, 20% stocks	Capital preservation may be more important than long-term growth, so consider a conservative mixture of investments more heavily weighted toward bonds and short-term instruments for your portfolio.
20 – 49 points	40% / 50% / 10% — **Balanced Portfolio** 10% short-term instruments, 40% bonds, 50% stocks	A combination of income and capital growth is indicated. Consider spreading your investments to seek growth combined with less risk over the long term.
50 – 69 points	25% / 70% / 5% — **Growth Portfolio** 5% short-term instruments, 25% bonds, 70% stocks	It suggests that you're willing to take on more risk in an attempt to outperform conservative investments over the long term. Consider emphasizing growth as you choose your investments.
70+ points	15% / 85% — **Aggressive Growth Portfolio** 85% stocks, 15% bonds	Longer-range goals are indicated, and you may want to consider a more aggressive portfolio of 85% stock and 15% bond investments if you can tolerate short-term price swings. If you have other investments that reduce your overall risk, you may wish to consider a 100% stock portfolio.

* Money market mutual funds are not issued or guaranteed by the U.S. government, and there is no assurance that a stable $1 share price will be maintained.

Your Plan Of Action

With your model portfolio as your reference point, developing a plan to achieve the right investment mix requires only a few short steps.

Compare your current mix to the model and decide what changes are necessary.

Use the chart below to compare the asset allocation model indicated by your Worksheet score to your current portfolio. The chart can help you determine the adjustments you may need to make in your investment strategy as you pursue your goals.

Pursue your investment strategy.

Once you determine the kinds of changes you need to make to your investment mix to more closely match your goals, time frame, and risk profile, your next step is to identify the most appropriate investments to fulfill your asset allocation plan.

Investment Check–Up*

	Current Investments		Model Portfolio	Change Suggested
	Market Value	% of Total	% of Total	(+) or (−)
Short-Term Investments				
CDs and other bank deposits	_____			
Money market funds	_____			
Other	_____			
TOTAL SHORT-TERM INVESTMENTS	$_____	_____%	_____%	_____%
Bonds				
Individual bonds	_____			
Bond mutual funds	_____			
Other	_____			
TOTAL BONDS	$_____	_____%	_____%	_____%
Stocks				
Individual stocks	_____			
Stock mutual funds	_____			
Other	_____			
TOTAL STOCKS	$_____	_____%	_____%	_____%
TOTAL FOR 3 ASSET CLASSES	$_____	100%	100%	_____%

*Include bank accounts and CDs, investments at other firms and, if you're saving for retirement, Qualified Plan money you have in 401(k)s. Do not include investments such as real estate, precious metals, and limited partnerships.

Fidelity Makes It Easy To Diversify Your Investments

Whether you plan to invest in mutual funds, individual securities, or both, to create a more diversified portfolio, Fidelity makes it easy to get started.

Invest with a Mutual Fund Leader.

Fidelity Investments has become synonymous with mutual funds because of the simple, but powerful, philosophy we follow – to manage your investments, stock by stock, country by country, trade by trade, year by year – all with the goal of delivering consistent long-term performance for our investors. With over $438 billion in assets under management, Fidelity is America's leading mutual fund company. No other company can match the resources we dedicate to investment research. We've built the mutual fund industry's deepest and broadest research capabilities. Our research professionals follow virtually all the world's markets and over 6,000 companies every year. With Fidelity's range of professionally managed mutual funds, you can tailor your portfolio precisely to your needs – from equity funds to international funds, from fixed income funds to money market funds.[1]

The lists of Fidelity mutual funds on pages 11–12 provide an overview of the kinds of Fidelity money market, bond, and stock mutual funds you may want to consider as you implement your asset allocation plan. Or consider one of our Asset Manager funds below. Naturally, you'll need a prospectus for any fund you're considering. Please read it carefully before you invest.

Get access to a wide range of mutual funds and individual securities.

A Fidelity brokerage account gives you a full range of investment choices as you adjust your portfolio to match your model mix. With a brokerage account you can invest in Fidelity funds plus:

- select from over 3,000 more funds from other investment companies through Fidelity's FundsNetwork®[2] – including 600 funds without paying a transaction fee to Fidelity.[3]
- trade stocks and options at substantial savings compared with full cost firms.
- purchase a variety of individual bond and money market investments, plus UITs, CDs, U.S. Treasuries, Ginnie Maes, and more.

With all this available, it's easy to diversify and manage your investment in one comprehensive account. A single, consolidated brokerage account statement will show all your activity and all your holdings, with up-to-date valuations of every security.

Fidelity Asset Manager Funds – a one-step approach to diversification

Fidelity offers a convenient way to put the FundMatch ideas to work with the Fidelity Asset Manager funds. With a single investment, these funds let you diversify your investment across a carefully allocated mix of short-term vehicles, bonds, and stocks.

Each of the funds has a benchmark percentage allocation called the "neutral mix," which represents the way the fund's investments will be allocated over the long term.

The Asset Manager funds take advantage of a team approach to investing. Once the fund's manager determines the overall allocation of assets among stocks, bonds, and short-term/money market instruments, a team of managers who specialize in each asset class employs Fidelity's vast resources to seek out the best investment opportunities.

● Stocks ● Bonds ● Short-term instruments

Fidelity Asset Manager: Income℠

For investors scoring up to 20 points on the Worksheet. Its goal is a high level of income, and capital appreciation where appropriate. The fund's neutral mix is 20% stocks, 50% bonds, and 30% short term/money market instruments.

Fidelity Asset Manager®

For investors scoring between 20 and 49 points on the Worksheet. Its goal is high total return with reduced risk over the long term. The neutral mix is 50% stocks, 40% bonds, and 10% short-term/money market instruments.

Fidelity Asset Manager: Growth℠

For investors scoring between 50 and 69 on the Worksheet. Its goal is to maximize total return over the long term. The neutral mix is 70% stocks, 25% bonds, and 5% short-term/money market instruments.

[1] A portion of income from these funds may be subject to state taxes and the federal alternative minimum tax. An investment in a money market fund is neither insured nor guaranteed by the U.S. government and there is no assurance that the fund will maintain a stable $1 share price. [2] For more information on the FundsNetwork® program, call for a *FundsNetwork® Performance Directory*. Fidelity Brokerage Services, Inc., or its brokerage affiliate may receive remuneration for providing certain recordkeeping and shareholder services to the fund families. [3] All fees described in the fund's prospectus still apply.

Choose From A Wide
Array Of Fidelity Mutual Funds

In addition to the Asset Manager funds described on the previous page, we've included a further selection of Fidelity funds you may wish to consider as you make your investment decisions.

Money Market funds

Money Market funds offer a place where your short-term investments can earn high current yields while remaining more stable and accessible than longer-term investments. They also provide an interim investment while you are searching for the right growth or income opportunity. All Fidelity money market funds offer checkwriting, so they are among the most liquid investments available. In addition, all of Fidelity's money market funds are offered without a sales charge. All funds seek to maintain a $1 share price.

Fund Name	Investment Objective
Fidelity Cash Reserves	Seeks income while maintaining a stable $1.00 share price. Invests in high-quality U.S. dollar-denominated short-term money market securities.
Fidelity Municipal Money Market Fund	Seeks income free from federal income tax while maintaining a stable $1.00 share price. Invests in high-quality, short-term municipal money market securities of all types.

Bond funds

Bond funds can play an important role in your portfolio by adding stability, balance and growth. They also may help you achieve a variety of investment objectives, including portfolio diversification, current income, protection of principal, and tax reduction. The chart below highlights just a few of Fidelity's bond funds. All are available without a sales charge.

Fund Name	Investment Objective
Taxable	
Fidelity Capital & Income Fund	Seeks income and capital growth. Invests mainly in lower-quality debt securities and common and preferred stocks.
Fidelity Ginnie Mae Fund	Seeks high current income. Invests in mortgage securities issued by the Government National Mortgage Association.
Fidelity Investment Grade Bond Fund	Seeks high current income by investing normally in investment-grade debt securities. Managed to react to interest rate changes similarly to bonds with maturities between 4 and 10 years.
Fidelity Short-Intermediate Government Fund	Seeks as high a level of current income as is consistent with preservation of capital. Invests in government securities and instruments related to U.S. Government securities, while normally maintaining an average maturity of 2–5 years.
Fidelity Short-Term Bond Fund	Seeks high current income with preservation of capital. Invests primarily in investment-grade securities. Average maturity will be 3 years or less.
Municipal	
Fidelity Limited Term Municipal Income Fund	Seeks high current income free from federal income tax with preservation of capital by investing in investment-grade municipal securities with an average maturity of 12 years or less.
Fidelity Municipal Income Fund	Seeks high current income free from federal taxes by investing normally in investment-grade municipal securities. Managed to react to interest rate changes similarly to municipal bonds with maturities between 8 and 18 years.

Stock funds

Stock funds can play an important role in your portfolio, particularly if your goal is long-term growth, because over time stocks historically have outperformed other types of investments. Their potential for growth means stock funds can also serve as a hedge against inflation, helping to prevent erosion of an investment's value.

Some stock funds also pursue current income in combination with growth. The dividends offered in growth and income stock funds may help to cushion your portfolio against the volatility typical of more aggressive stock funds that focus primarily on capital appreciation and growth.

Fund Name	Investment Objective
Fidelity Contrafund	Seeks capital appreciation. Invests mainly in the equity securities of companies that are undervalued or out of favor.
Fidelity Disciplined Equity Fund	Seeks long-term growth by investing mainly in a broadly diversified portfolio of common stocks that are determined through both technical and fundamental analysis to be undervalued. The fund seeks to maintain industry diversification similar to that of the Standard & Poor's 500 Index®.
Fidelity Equity-Income II Fund	Seeks reasonable income and also considers the potential for growth by investing mainly in income-producing equity securities.
Fidelity Growth & Income Portfolio	Seeks high total return through a combination of income and growth by investing mainly in equity securities of companies that pay current dividends and offer potential growth of earnings.
Fidelity Growth Company Fund	Seeks capital appreciation by investing mainly in equity securities of those companies believed to have above-average growth.
Fidelity Magellan® Fund	Seeks capital appreciation by investing mainly in a broad mix of stocks: large and small, at home and abroad. America's largest stock fund.
Fidelity Overseas Fund*	Seeks long-term growth of capital by investing mainly in equity securities outside the U.S.
Fidelity Puritan® Fund	Seeks high income and preservation of capital, and considers the potential for long-term growth, through a broadly diversified portfolio of stocks and bonds. Its income-oriented strategy has produced regular quarterly dividends since 1947.

*Foreign investments involve risks that are in addition to those of U.S. investments, including political and economic risks as well as the risk of currency fluctuations. These risks may be magnified in emerging markets.

Fidelity Makes It Easy
To Put Your Plan Into Action

At Fidelity, we believe that, given the right tools and information, you're the one who's best qualified to make your own financial decisions. So we make it easy to access a wealth of information and assistance – over the phone, via the computer, and in person.

By phone

- You can discuss your investments with a Fidelity representative anytime – 24 hours a day, 7 days a week – by calling us at the toll-free number below.

- As a Fidelity investor, you can use our automated TouchTone Xpress℠ service to get account updates, obtain mutual fund and stock quotes, and exchange or trade securities around the clock.

By computer

- At our Web site, you'll find investment news, performance data, and fund details for every Fidelity fund, plus News InSite for international and U.S. market news.

- With a Fidelity brokerage account, you can actively manage your investments from your desktop with Fidelity On-Line Xpress+® software that combines powerful portfolio management and research tools with direct access to your Fidelity account.

In person

If you prefer to meet in person with a Fidelity representative, visit one of our 82 Fidelity Investor Centers nationwide. Call our toll-free number for an appointment at the Investor Center nearest you.

Questions?
Call toll-free 1-800-544-8888
24 hours a day

. . .

TDD Service for the hearing impaired:
1-800-544-0118 (9 a.m. to 9 p.m. ET)

. . .

http://www.fidelity.com

An annual mutual fund maintenance fee will be deducted from accounts with balances of less than $2,500 as of the valuation date (assessed annually). This fee does not apply to accounts using regular investing programs. For customers with $30,000 or more in assets with Fidelity, mutual fund maintenance fees will be waived. The $30,000 waiver will be determined by aggregating, on the valuation date, all assets maintained by Fidelity Service Company, Inc., or Fidelity Brokerage Services, Inc. (excluding assets maintained through Fidelity Institutional Retirement Services Company or Fidelity Investments Tax-Exempt Services Company, such as 401(k) or 403(b) plan assets) which are registered under the same Social Security number or which list the same Social Security number for the custodian of a Uniform Gifts/Transfers to Minors Act account.

For more complete information on any fund offered through Fidelity, including charges and expenses, please call for a free prospectus.
Read it carefully before you invest or send money.

3   Regulation of Mutual Funds and Required Disclosure

Introduction

This is the third and last introductory chapter on mutual funds. We have already covered the basic concept of financial intermediation and the operation of the mutual fund, as well as the historical evolution and growth spurt of the fund industry. In this chapter, we will look at the regulation of mutual funds, with emphasis on the disclosure documents provided to fund investors.

We focus early on regulation of mutual funds because they are so strictly regulated. It is almost impossible to think about launching a new fund product without consulting a lawyer on how to make sure that a product complies with the Investment Company Act of 1940 (1940 Act). This act spells out numerous restrictions and requirements designed to protect investors in entities that primarily invest in securities. It is based on the premise that such entities should be more closely regulated than industrial or operating companies, which are not covered by the Act. It also does not cover other entities that primarily hold liquid assets, such as insurance companies or pension funds, since they are subject to separate regulatory schemes.

To begin with, it is useful to understand the legal composition of a mutual fund, and specifically to dispel the myth that a mutual fund is a mere product. A mutual fund is a legal entity, a trust, or corporation organized under the laws of a state, distinct from the fund's investment manager. For this reason, fund trustees or directors are subject to fiduciary duties under state law. In addition, all mutual funds are subject to an elaborate layer of federal regulation. Mutual funds are classified as "open-end, management investment companies" under the 1940 Act, and must meet certain diversification requirements as well as certain income distribution requirements of the Internal Revenue Code.

Mutual funds have a dynamic portfolio of securities, which may vary in composition as the portfolio manager buys and sells specific securities based on specific investment objectives. In contrast, passive investment companies like unit investment trusts (UITs) offer interests in a fixed portfolio of securities; there is no significant change in the portfolio of securities held by the unit investment trust after it is initially assembled (unit trusts in the U.K. are a different matter).

Within the class of management companies, there are open-end and closed-end funds. An open-end fund continuously sells shares to the public and stands ready to redeem shares every day at its net asset value, or NAV (the value of a single share, computed by adding up the fund's assets, subtracting its liabilities, and then dividing the result by the number of shares outstanding). By contrast, a closed-end fund offers new shares episodically (if at all) and does not provide a redemption privilege. Once issued, shares of a closed-end fund are traded on an exchange similar to shares of industrial companies, and may trade at above or below NAV. In most cases, closed-end funds trade at a price below their NAV (the discount).

Management companies are broken down further into diversified and nondiversified funds. Most mutual funds meet the 1940 Act's definition of diversification: As to 75% of the assets of the fund, the fund may not acquire more than 10% of the voting securities of any one issuer *and* may not invest more than 5% of total fund assets in any one issuer. Thus, in theory, a diversified mutual fund could invest 25% of its assets in one issuer and 75% of its assets in 15 issuers (i.e., 5% in each issuer). In practice, most diversified mutual funds hold more than 50 positions and rarely invest more than 10% of their assets in any one issuer. By contrast, nondiversified mutual funds often concentrate their investments in a smaller number of companies.

Whether or not they meet the 1940 Act's tests for diversification, all mutual funds must meet the diversification and income distribution requirements of the Internal Revenue Code (the Code) in order to qualify for tax pass-through treatment. A tax pass-through means that the mutual fund (which, you may recall, is a corporation or trust) pays no corporate tax; instead, the dividends, interest, and capital gains on its investments are distributed to fund shareholders, according to their proportionate ownership of the fund, who are then taxed on the distributions. In practice, most fund shareholders choose to have their fund distributions automatically reinvested in additional fund shares.

While the Code's diversification requirements are less stringent than those in the 1940 Act, the Code's income distribution requirements force every mutual fund to pay out to their shareholders each year almost all dividends and interest payments received as well as the net capital gains realized by the funds. Realized capital losses may be used to offset realized capital gains before fund distributions, but realized capital losses in excess of realized capital gains are not distributed and instead are carried forward to the next tax year. While the tax pass-through is a big advantage for mutual funds, the annual distribution of all realized gains needed to qualify for pass-through reinforces a significant disadvantage to holders of mutual fund shares as compared to holders of individual securities: Holders of mutual fund shares have no control over the timing of realized gains. For example, a fund shareholder cannot choose to delay the realization of a capital gain in appreciated shares sold by the fund, even if he or she would have preferred to wait until the next tax year.

The 1940 Act was passed a few years after Congress enacted the core disclosure statute for securities offerings—the Securities Act of 1933 (1933 Act). The 1933 Act requires all public issuers of securities to disseminate a prospectus disclosing all material facts to potential investors. The 1933 Act, together with other general antifraud provisions in the securities laws, also generally prohibits material misrepresentations and omissions in connection with the purchase or sale of securities. The 1933 Act, however, does not prohibit or prescribe conduct by issuers. As long as these issuers are prepared to tell the world what they are doing, they have broad freedom to conduct their business as they please.

By contrast, the 1940 Act prohibits a broad range of conduct and mandates various types of fund behavior. For example, the 1940 Act requires mutual funds (technically open-end investment companies that redeem shares daily) to concentrate on relatively liquid securities that can be converted fairly quickly to cash and to value these securities each day. The 1940 Act establishes severe restrictions on the ability of mutual funds to issue debt or effect short sales—selling a security one does not own, in the hopes of buying it back later at a lower price. Most important, the 1940 Act contains extensive prohibitions on transactions between mutual funds and their affiliates, broadly defined to include anyone holding more than 5% of the voting stock of a fund or its manager and any entity if more than 5% of its voting stock is held by the fund or its manager. As an illustration, someone who owns 6% of a fund's investment adviser would be prohibited from buying portfolio securities from that fund. This extensive range of prohibitions may be waived only in special circumstances as determined by the Securities and Exchange Commission (SEC) through a rule or exemptive order.

The 1940 Act also gives special powers to "disinterested" directors or trustees of a mutual fund, often called the independent directors of a fund. Under the 1940 Act, an independent director may not be affiliated with the fund's investment adviser and must meet other tests of independence. Independent directors must constitute at least 40% of all mutual fund boards, and a majority of the board if the fund's principal underwriter is affiliated with the fund's adviser. In most funds, the independent directors act as a nominating committee for new directors; this procedure is required if the fund has adopted a 12b-1 plan.

The key function of the independent directors is periodically to approve the management contract between the fund and its investment adviser. Although independent directors rarely fire a fund's adviser, they do negotiate for better fees and services from the adviser. In addition, the independent directors negotiate and approve the contracts between the fund and other service providers (e.g., transfer agents and custodial banks). Under many SEC rules and exemptions, independent directors must approve in advance, or review periodically, specific actions by the fund's investment adviser. More generally, independent directors are supposed to serve as "watchdogs" on behalf of fund shareholders—as their elected representatives, monitoring the activities of the fund adviser and other service providers.

Even in the disclosure area, mutual funds are subject to relatively strict rules because mutual funds are continuously offering their shares to investors. As a result, mutual funds become subject to many of the same rules that apply to initial public offerings (IPOs) of industrial companies. Most important, the SEC severely restricts public advertisements at the time of a securities offering and requires the delivery of a lengthy prospectus in connection with the public sale of a security. As explained in the readings and class exercise, the SEC is in the process of rethinking its prospectus requirements for mutual funds and soon will permit the use of a short-form prospectus in question-and-answer format. The current SEC rules rigidly restrict fund advertisements containing fund performance numbers to information whose "substance" already appears in the fund's prospectus. Again, the SEC will soon replace this restriction with a more flexible standard focused more on preventing material omissions and misrepresentations.

A mutual fund must clear its prospectus through the SEC, which sets and interprets the rules for prospectus disclosure. While the SEC never actually "approves" the issuance of any prospectus, it does have a right to stop a prospectus from being distributed. To avoid such a confrontation, mutual fund sponsors go through a lengthy comment and negotiation process with the SEC staff. The SEC also sets the legal framework for fund advertising, which is interpreted and administered by the National Association of Securities Dealers (NASD). The NASD is a self-regulatory organization for securities brokers and dealers, which has the power to discipline member firms for violating its rules. All sales and advertising material (other than prospectuses) must be submitted for review to the NASD. In addition, mutual funds must still pay state registration fees for sales to investors in that state, although states no longer review fund prospectuses. Instead, the states focus on monitoring the activities of small investment advisers and policing the sales practices of local broker-dealers.

All the rules and regulations for mutual funds are vigorously enforced by public and private parties. The SEC may bring various types of enforcement actions against funds, their advisers, and their directors for material violations of the federal securities laws. Similarly, the NASD may bring disciplinary proceedings against any member firm or employee thereof for material violations of its fund advertising or sales rules. Fund share-holders have an express right of action under section 36(b) of the 1940 Act to challenge fund advisory fees that they believe are excessive, and may sue under applicable provisions of state or federal law for breaches of fiduciary duty by their fund's adviser or directors. Fund shareholders may also bring individual or class actions under the 1933 Act or other federal anti-fraud provisions for material misrepresentations or omissions in their fund's prospectus.

Subject to such a broad range of public and private lawsuits, most fund complexes have retained legal counsel to the funds and their independent directors separate from the legal counsel to the fund adviser. With guidance from separate counsel, the independent directors usually ask the fund adviser for extensive amounts of data in connection with the renewal of the advisory contract. In addition, independent directors in some complexes rely on the external auditor of the fund to monitor compliance with certain regulatory requirements. In litigation, judges have given considerable weight to the business judgment of independent directors who have evaluated relevant information with the assistance of an independent counsel.

The readings for this chapter summarize the key legal provisions regulating mutual funds, especially the rules on advertising and promoting the sale of mutual funds.

Questions

In reviewing the materials in this chapter, please keep in mind the following questions:

1. Should mutual funds be subject to more extensive regulation than industrial companies under the federal securities laws? If so, why?
2. What are the critical differences between mutual funds and closed-end funds? In what types of circumstances would investors be likely to buy closed-end funds?
3. Why do sophisticated investors try not to buy shares of a mutual fund immediately before its annual distribution of realized gains? What happens to its unrealized gains?
4. Does the 1940 Act regulate conflicts of interest too strictly or too leniently? Should the 1940 Act distinguish between actual and potential conflicts?
5. Are independent directors effective "watchdogs" for fund shareholders? What types of evidence would support your conclusions?
6. Are the disclosure rules for initial public offerings appropriate for mutual funds since most are continuously offering shares to the public? Should the SEC limit print advertising to short descriptions of the fund without performance numbers?

3.1   The Work of the SEC*

Introduction

Under the Securities Exchange Act of 1934, Congress created the Securities and Exchange Commission (SEC). The SEC is an independent, nonpartisan, quasi-judicial regulatory agency.

The SEC's mission is to administer federal securities laws and issue rules and regulations to provide protection for investors and to ensure that the securities markets are fair and honest. This is accomplished primarily by promoting adequate and effective disclosure of information to the investing public. The laws administered by the Commission are the:

- Securities Act of 1933;
- Securities Exchange Act of 1934;
- Public Utility Holding Company Act of 1935;
- Trust Indenture Act of 1939;
- Investment Company Act of 1940; and
- Investment Advisers Act of 1940.

The Commission also serves as adviser to federal courts in corporate reorganization proceedings under Chapter 11 of the Bankruptcy Reform Act of 1978. The Commission reports annually to Congress on administration of the securities laws.

The Commission is composed of five members appointed by the President, with the advice and consent of the Senate, for five-year terms. The Chairman is designated by the President. Terms are staggered; one expires on June 5 of every year. Not more than three members may be of the same political party.

Under the direction of the Commission, the staff ensures that publicly held companies, broker-dealers in securities, investment companies and advisers, and other participants in the securities markets comply with federal securities laws. (e.g., Among other things, the staff reviews registration statements and periodic reports, conducts examinations and inspections, makes rules and regulations, conducts investigations, and brings enforcement actions against violators.) The SEC does not guarantee the value or merit of a particular investment. The Commission cannot bar the sale of securities of questionable value. The investor must make the ultimate judgment of the worth of securities offered for sale.

The SEC's staff is composed of lawyers, accountants, financial analysts and examiners, engineers, investigators, economists, and other professionals. The staff is divided into divisions and offices (including 11 regional and district offices), each directed by officials appointed by the Chairman.

---

*Office of Public Affairs, Policy Evaluation and Research, United States Securities and Exchange Commission, June 1997.

Securities Act of 1933

This "truth in securities" law has two basic objectives:

- to require that investors are provided with material information concerning securities offered for public sale; and
- to prevent misrepresentation, deceit, and other fraud in the sale of securities.

A primary means of accomplishing these objectives is disclosure of financial information by registering offers and sales of securities. Most offerings of debt and equity securities issued by corporations, limited partnerships, trusts, and other issuers must be registered. Federal and most other domestic government debt securities are exempt. Certain transactions qualify for exemptions from registration provisions.

Purpose of Registration

Registration is intended to provide adequate and accurate disclosure of material facts concerning the company and the securities it proposes to sell. Thus, investors may make a realistic appraisal of the merits of the securities and then exercise informed judgment in determining whether to purchase them.

Registration requires, but does not guarantee, the accuracy of the facts represented in the registration statement and prospectus. However, the law does prohibit false and misleading statements under penalty of fine, imprisonment, or both. Investors who purchase securities and suffer losses have important recovery rights under the law if they can prove that there was incomplete or inaccurate disclosure of material facts in the registration statement or prospectus. If such misstatements are proven, the following could be liable: the issuing company, its responsible directors and officers, the underwriters, controlling interests, the sellers of the securities, and others. These rights must be asserted in an appropriate federal or state court (not before the Commission, which has no power to award damages).

Registration of securities does not preclude the sale of stock in risky, poorly managed, or unprofitable companies. In fact, it is unlawful to represent that the Commission approves or disapproves of securities on their merits. The only standard which must be met when registering securities is adequate and accurate disclosure of required material facts concerning the company and the securities it proposes to sell. The fairness of the terms, the issuing company's prospects for successful operation, and other factors affecting the merits of investing in the securities (whether price, promoters' or underwriters' profits, or otherwise) have no bearing on the question of whether or not securities may be registered....

Securities Exchange Act of 1934

By this Act, Congress extended the disclosure doctrine of investor protection to securities listed and registered for public trading on our national securities exchanges. Thirty years later, the Securities Act Amendments of 1964 extended disclosure and reporting provisions to equity securities in the over-the-counter market. This included hundreds of companies with assets exceeding $1 million and shareholders numbering 500 or more. Today, securities of thousands of companies are traded over-the-counter. The Act seeks to ensure fair and orderly securities markets by prohibiting certain types of activities and by setting forth rules regarding the operation of the markets and participants. . . .

Investment Company Act of 1940

The Public Utility Holding Company Act of 1935 required Congress to direct the SEC to study the activities of investment companies and investment advisers. The study results were sent to Congress in a series of reports filed in 1938, 1939, and 1940, causing the creation of the Investment Company Act of 1940 and the Investment Advisers Act of 1940. The legislation was supported by both the Commission and the industry.

Activities of companies engaged primarily in investing, reinvesting, and trading in securities, and whose own securities are offered to the investing public, are subject to certain statutory prohibitions and to Commission regulation under this act. Also, public offerings of investment company securities must be registered under the Securities Act of 1933.

Investors must understand, however, that the Commission does not supervise the investment activities of these companies and that regulation by the Commission does not imply safety of investment.

In addition to the registration requirement for such companies, the law requires that they disclose their financial condition and investment policies to provide investors complete information about their activities. This Act also:

- prohibits such companies from substantially changing the nature of their business or investment policies without stockholder approval;
- bars persons guilty of securities fraud from serving as officers and directors;
- prevents underwriters, investment bankers, or brokers from constituting more than a minority of the directors of such companies;
- requires that management contracts and any material changes be submitted to security-holders for their approval;
- prohibits transactions between such companies and their directors, officers, or affiliated companies or persons, except when approved by the SEC;
- forbids such companies to issue senior securities except under specified conditions and upon specified terms; and
- prohibits pyramiding of such companies and cross-ownership of their securities.

Other provisions of this Act involve advisory fees, adviser's fiduciary duties, sales and repurchases of securities issued by investment companies, exchange offers, and other activities of investment companies, including special provisions for periodic payment plans and face-amount certificate companies.

In addition to enforcing the requirements described above, the Commission may institute court action to remove management officials who have engaged in personal misconduct constituting a breach of fiduciary duty.

Investment companies also must file periodic reports and are subject to the Commission's proxy and insider trading rules. . . .

3.2   Securities Regulation in a Nutshell*
David L. Ratner

---

§26.   Coverage of the 1940 Act

The Investment Company Act (ICA) (i) requires every investment company to register with the SEC, (ii) imposes substantive restrictions on the activities of a registered investment company and persons connected with it, and (iii) provides for a variety of SEC and private sanctions.

Under ICA §3(a), an investment company is an entity which (a) "is ... engaged: *primarily* ... in the business of investing, reinvesting, or trading in securities," or (b) is "engaged" in that business and more than 40% of its assets consist of "investment securities" (i.e., all securities other than government securities and securities of majority-owned subsidiaries).

(a)   Types of Investment Companies
Most investment companies are organized as corporations, although they may also be set up in trust, partnership, or other forms. Most of the regulatory provisions use corporate terms such as "directors" and "shareholders," so that appropriate modifications must be made when other forms are used.

The Act divides investment companies into three classes: "face-amount certificate companies," which issue fixed-income debenture-type securities; "unit investment trusts," which offer interests in a fixed portfolio of securities, and the most important class, "management companies," which includes all other types of investment companies. ICA §4.

"Management companies" are further divided into "open-end" and "closed-end" companies, ICA §5(a), and into "diversified" and "non-diversified" companies, ICA §5(b). "Open-end companies," commonly known as "mutual funds," are those which offer redeemable securities. They generally offer shares on a continuous basis, at a price related to current net asset value (i.e., the current market value of the fund's portfolio divided by the number of shares of the fund outstanding), and stand ready to redeem shares at any time at the shareholder's request, also at net asset value or at a price related to it. "Closed-end companies" are more similar to other types of corporations; at any time, they have a fixed number of shares outstanding, which are traded either on an exchange or in the over-the-counter market, at prices which reflect supply and demand and may be substantially above or below the net asset value.

An investment company is "diversified" if, with respect to at least 75% of its portfolio the securities of any single issuer do not account for (a) more than 5% of the investment

---

* From David L. Ratner, *Securities Regulation in a Nutshell*, 4th ed. (St. Paul, Minn.: West Publishing Co., 1992), pp. 215–241. Reprinted with permission of the West Group.

company's assets, or (b) more than 10% of the outstanding voting securities of that issuer. (These diversification requirements are similar to those which permit an investment company to qualify for special tax treatment under §851(b)(4) of the Internal Revenue Code.) Since diversification depends on the amount of investment in a single issuer, an investment company which invests solely in a single industry or geographical area is still considered "diversified." . . .

Specialized Investment Media
The Act excludes from coverage banks, insurance companies, savings and loan associations, finance companies, oil and gas drilling funds, charitable foundations, tax-exempt pension funds, and other special types of institutions. ICA §§ 3(c)(3)–(13). However, insurance companies and banks have been held to be subject to the Act when they publicly offer investment plans or services in which the rate of return varies depending on the performance of a separate fund of securities. . . .

§ 27. Regulation of Fund Activities

Registration and Reporting Requirements
An investment company registers with the SEC by filing a notification of registration setting forth a statement of its investment policy and other specified information, ICA § 10. A registered company must file annual reports with the Commission, ICA § 30, and maintain specified accounts and records, ICA § 31.

Protection of Assets
As a safeguard against looting of investment company assets, all securities must be held in the custody of a bank or stock exchange member, or under strict procedures laid down by the SEC. ICA § 17(f), Rule 17f-2. Larceny or embezzlement from an investment company is a federal crime, ICA § 37, and officers and employees who have access to the company's cash or securities must be bonded. ICA § 17(g), Rule 17g-1.

Capital Structure
An open-end company (mutual fund) may not issue any "senior security" (debt or preferred stock) other than notes to evidence bank borrowings. ICA § 18(f). A closed-end company may issue not more than one class of debt securities and not more than one class of preferred stock, provided that it has an asset coverage of at least 300 percent, in the case of debt, or 200 percent, in the case of preferred stock. ICA §§ 18(a), (c). No registered management company may issue any rights or warrants to purchase any of its securities. ICA § 18(d). An investment company may not make any public offering of its securities until it has a net worth of at least $100,000. ICA § 14(a).

Dividends
No dividends may be paid from any source other than accumulated undistributed net income, or net income for the current or preceding fiscal year, unless accompanied by a written statement disclosing the source of such payment. Under the tax laws, an investment company must pay dividends to its shareholders amounting to at least 98 percent of

its taxable ordinary income each year to avoid double taxation of its income to itself and its shareholders. Internal Revenue Code § 852(a)(1).

Investment Activities

An investment company may not purchase securities on margin, sell short, or participate in joint trading accounts. ICA § 12(a). It may not incur underwriting commitments aggregating more than 25% of the value of its total assets. ICA § 12(c). Unless authorized by the vote of the holders of a majority of its voting securities, it may not borrow money, issue senior securities, underwrite any securities, purchase or sell real estate or commodities, make loans, change its investment policy with respect to concentration or diversification, change its subclassification, or change the nature of its business so as to cease to be an investment company. ICA § 13(a).

Investment companies, unlike trusts, insurance companies, and other types of institutional investors, are not limited to a "legal list" in making investments, nor are they subject to the "prudent Man" rule. The managers, therefore, cannot be held liable for losses resulting from investments which turned out badly or might have been deemed "imprudent" by a conservative investor. The managers are subject to SEC sanctions, however, if they fail to provide the kind of investment management and supervision which they have advertised in their sales literature or statements of policy. Managed Funds, SA Rel. 4122 (1959); Financial Programs, SEA Rel. 11312 (1975); Chase, IAA Rel. 449 (1975). In such situations, the directors of the fund may also be held civilly liable, under state law, for damages caused by the mismanagement. Lutz v. Boas, 39 Del.Ch. 585, 171 A.2d 381 (1961). In Brouk v. Managed Funds, 286 F.2d 901 (8th Cir.1961), the court held that such mismanagement did not give rise to an implied right of action against the directors under the Investment Company Act, but subsequent decisions have recognized such a right of action. See Fogel v. Chestnutt, 668 F.2d 100 (2d Cir.1981).

Fund Investments in Other Funds

As a result of its unpleasant experience in the 1960s with The Fund of Funds, a large European-based mutual fund which invested heavily in the shares of American mutual funds, the SEC urged Congress to prohibit any investment company from acquiring shares of any other investment company. The 1970 amendments, however, did not impose a complete prohibition. Instead, they limited such investment so that no investment company can own more than 3% of the stock of another investment company nor invest more than 5% of its assets in any one investment company or more than 10% of its assets in other investment companies generally. [Further amended in 1996 to permit situations in which the acquired company and the acquiring company are part of the same group of investment companies (commonly referred to as a complex). This amendment allows for "funds-of-funds" within the same complex.—ed. note] ICA § 12(d).

---

§ 28.   Management and Control

(a) Shareholders, Directors, and Officers

All shares of stock issued by an investment company must have equal voting rights, and voting trusts are prohibited, ICA §§ 18(i), 20(b). Solicitations of proxies from investment company shareholders are subject to approximately the same rules that apply under SEA § 14 to solicitations of shareholders of listed companies. ICA § 20(a), Rules 20a–1, 2, 3.

In addition to their voting rights under the laws of an investment company's state of incorporation, shareholders are entitled to vote on: changes in investment policy or status, ICA § 13(a); approval or assignment of investment advisory contracts, ICA § 15(a); filling of more than a specified number of vacancies in the board of directors, ICA § 16(a); sale of stock of a closed-end company below net asset value, ICA § 23(b); and appointment of independent public accountants, ICA § 32(a).

The Act contains a number of provisions designed to insure the integrity of directors and officers and the independence of the board of directors. Under ICA § 9(a), no person who has been convicted within 10 years of a securities-related felony or is enjoined from securities-related activities may serve as a director or officer or in certain other specified capacities. And ICA § 17(b) prohibits any provisions indemnifying directors or officers against liabilities to the company arising out of their willful misfeasance, bad faith, gross negligence of reckless disregard of duty.

To assure the existence of independent voices on the board of directors, ICA § 10(a) provides that no more than 60% of the members of the board may be "interested persons" of the company. (There is an exception for "no-load" funds managed by registered investment advisers, which are required to have only one "non-interested" director. ICA § 10(d).) The term "interested person" was introduced by the 1970 amendments, and represents a significant broadening of the category of "affiliated persons" which was the standard prior to 1970. In addition to "affiliated persons," who are persons in a direct control relationship with the investment company or its adviser, ICA § 2(a)(3), the term "interested person" includes any broker-dealer or affiliate of a broker-dealer, any person who has served as legal counsel to the company within the past two years, any member of the immediate family of an affiliated person, and any other person whom the SEC determines to have had "material business or professional relationship" with the company or its principal executive officer within the past two years. ICA § 2(a)(19).

(b) Management Compensation

In contrast to most business corporations, which are managed by their own officers, acting under the supervision of the board of directors, investment companies, particularly mutual funds, normally contract with a separate entity known as the "investment adviser" to provide all management and advisory services to the investment company for a fee. In fact, the normal procedure is for the investment advisory organization (which may be a partnership or a privately or publicly held corporation) to create one or more mutual funds as "corporate shells" to serve as vehicles for pooling the investments of a large number of small customers.

In an effort to protect the shareholders of an investment company from overreaching by the adviser, ICA § 15(a) provides that an investment adviser must serve under a written contract approved initially by a vote of the shareholders and thereafter approved annually by the board of directors of the investment company. . . .

A new provision was added to ICA § 36, under which an investment adviser is "deemed to have a fiduciary duty with respect to the receipt of compensation for services" from an investment company. This duty is specifically made enforcible in the courts, either by the SEC or in a suit by a fund shareholder, which does not require prior demand on the directors. Daily Income Fund v. Fox, 464 U.S. 523 (1984).

While the Congressional reports on this amendment refer to the developments which led up to the legislation, they do not define the content of the adviser's "fiduciary duty." It has been held, however, to bar an adviser from increasing its fees, even with shareholder approval, where the increase was of no benefit to the investment company. See Galfand v. Chestnutt, 545 F.2d 807 (2d Cir. 1976)...

As an additional measure to assure adequate consideration of advisory fees by an investment company's board of directors, the 1970 amendments also added ICA §15(c), under which any amendment or renewal of the advisory contract must be approved by a majority of the *disinterested* directors, who are under a duty to request "such information as may reasonably be necessary to evaluate the terms of [the] contract."...

§29. Transactions with Affiliates

One obvious possibility for abuse by the persons in control of an investment company is to cause the investment company to buy securities from them, or to sell securities to them, at a price which is more favorable to them than to the investment company. Under ICA §17(a), therefore, it is illegal for any affiliated person, promoter, or principal underwriter of an investment company to sell securities or other property to the company, or buy them from the company, or to borrow from the company, subject to certain limited exceptions. However, under ICA §17(b), the SEC is authorized, upon application, to exempt a proposed transaction from the prohibition of §17(a) if it finds that the transaction (1) is fair and reasonable and does not involve overreaching on the part of any person concerned, (2) is consistent with the policy of the investment company, and (3) is consistent with the general purposes of the Act. Under this standard, the SEC must be satisfied that the transaction is fair, not only to the investment company, but to all other parties to the transaction. E.I. du Pont v. Collins, 432 U.S. 46 (1977)....

§30. Sale of Fund Shares

As noted above, investment companies are divided into "closed-end" and "open-end" companies. Closed-end companies, like other corporations, issue a fixed number of shares to the public in a one-shot underwritten offering. Open-end companies, or "mutual funds," make a continuous offering of shares at a price related to the current "net asset value" (i.e., the current market value of the fund's portfolio, divided by the number of shares outstanding). Mutual funds are in turn divided into "load" and "no-load" funds. Load funds distribute their shares to the public either through securities dealers or (in the case of a few large fund complexes) through their own "captive" sales forces, charging a sales commission, or "load," ranging up to $8\frac{1}{2}\%$ of the public offering price. No-load funds sell shares directly to the public through the mail, charging the current net asset value, with no sales charge added. The principal underwriter of a fund's shares must operate under a written contract renewed at least annually by the shareholders or directors of the fund, ICA §15(b).

(a) Disclosure Requirements

The disclosure requirements of the Securities Act of 1933 (SA) apply to investment companies, but with certain modifications. Under ICA §24(a), an investment company's registration statement, instead of containing the information required by Schedule A to the 1933 Act, may set forth certain of the information contained in the company's reports under ICA §30. And ICA §24(b) requires that any sales literature used by a mutual fund to supplement the information contained in its prospectus must be filed with the SEC. In addition, since mutual funds make continuous offerings of their shares, ICA §24(e)(3) modifies SA §§11 and 13 to provide that the effective date of the most recent amendment to a fund's registration statement is deemed to be the effective date of the registration statement and the date of commencement of the fund's public offering. (In the absence of this provision, people who purchased fund shares several years after the commencement of the fund's public offering would have no right of action under SA §§11 and 12.)

The SEC was strongly criticized for imposing unduly strict limitations on what mutual funds can say in their advertising. Accordingly, in 1979 it took three steps which drastically reduced the restrictions: (a) it adopted a new Rule 482 under the 1933 Act, under which an advertisement in the print or broadcast media which contains only information that could be included in a statutory prospectus (but not necessarily all of such information) satisfies the prospectus delivery requirements of §5 of that Act; (b) it rescinded its detailed "Statement of Policy" governing the contents and method of presentation of investment company sales literature; and (c) it adopted a new Rule 156 under the 1933 Act, specifying the factors which would be taken into account in determining whether investment company sales literature would be considered false or misleading under the general antifraud provisions. See SA Rels. 6034, 6116, 6140 (1979).

To enhance the ability of mutual fund investors to compare the costs of different funds, the SEC in 1988 revised its disclosure forms to require all funds to feature prominently in their prospectuses a standardized fee table showing how large a bite management fees, sales charges, and other expenses will take out of a $1,000 investment over various periods of time.

(b) Controls on Prices

Closed-End Companies

To prevent "dilution" of the interests of existing shareholders, ICA §23(b) prohibits closed-end companies from issuing shares at a price below their current net asset value without the consent of a majority of their shareholders. Since the shares of closed-end companies normally trade in the market at substantial discounts from net asset value, this provision makes it extremely difficult for existing closed-end companies to make additional offerings of their shares.

Open-End Companies

ICA §22 contains a complicated set of provisions governing the prices at which shares of open-end companies, or "mutual funds," can be sold to the public. ICA §22(a) authorizes the NASD to adopt rules prescribing the methods of computing the price at which its members may purchase shares from the fund and resell them to the public, for the purpose of preventing dilution or unfair discrimination between different purchasers or holders of fund shares.

ICA §22(d) provides that no fund shares may be sold to the public "except at a current offering price described in the prospectus." If a particular fund states in its prospectus that its shares are offered at current net asset value plus a sales load of $8\frac{1}{2}$%, no dealer may sell shares of that fund to the public at any other price. The price-fixing provisions of §22(d), like other "retail price maintenance" statutes, have been defended by the industry on the ground that they are essential to the maintenance of an "orderly distribution system." In its 1966 Mutual Fund Report to Congress, the SEC pointed out how the statutory restraint on competition had produced uneconomically high sales charges for mutual fund shares, but stopped short of recommending that §22(d) be repealed. Instead, it persuaded Congress to modify ICA §22(b) (which had previously contained a prohibition against "unconscionable or grossly excessive" sales loads) to give the NASD authority to fix maximum sales loads so that the public offering price "shall not include an excessive sales load but shall allow for reasonable compensation for sales personnel, broker-dealers, and underwriters, and for reasonable sales loads to investors." The NASD, operating under this "reasonable" standard, eventually adopted rules, effective June 1, 1976, under which sales loads may not exceed $8\frac{1}{2}$% (the previously prevailing figure).

Contractual Plans

One special problem of sales loads arises in connection with so-called "contractual plans" sold on a "front-end load" basis. Under these plans, an investor signs up to make monthly investments in a mutual fund over a period of years (although he is not in fact contractually obligated to complete the plan). Under ICA §27, the sales load on the completed plan may not exceed 9% of the total payments; however, up to 50% of each of the first 12 monthly payments can be deducted for sales compensation. Thus, the typical sales load on a 10-year plan will be 50% of each of the first 12 payments and approximately $4\frac{1}{2}$% of each of the remaining 108 payments.

The problem with this system is that, while it provides a strong incentive to sales reps to get investors started on a plan, it imposes a very heavy sales load on the substantial percentage of investors who stop making payments after a year or two. The SEC, in its 1966 Mutual Fund Report, recommended that Congress prohibit the front-end load and require all fund shares to be sold on a level-load basis. Congress, however, adopted an intermediate approach under which funds may continue to sell shares on a front-end load basis, provided that the fund either (a) does not deduct more than 20% of any payment for sales load, or (b) agrees that the investor may redeem her shares at any time during the first 18 months of the plan and receive (1) the current value of her shares, plus (2) the amount by which the total sales load she has paid exceeds 15% of her total payments into the plan. ICA §§27(d), (g). Contractual plans currently account for a very small percentage of mutual fund sales.

Payment of Distribution Costs by Fund

ICA §12(b) prohibits a mutual fund from acting as distributor of its own securities, except in compliance with SEC rules. Prior to 1980, this provision effectively barred the funds themselves from bearing any part of the cost of selling fund shares, meaning that these costs had to be paid out of the sales loads received by the underwriter, or, in the case of funds sold on a "no-load" basis, by the management company. In 1980, the Commission adopted ICA Rule 12b–1, under which a fund can act as distributor of its own shares and bear all or part of the cost of distribution, provided it is pursuant to a plan approved by the directors and shareholders of the fund. Abuses soon developed with respect to these "12b–1 plans." The SEC has brought a number of proceedings against fund managers for using fund assets for expenses unrelated to sales, and the NASD has barred funds which impose 12b–1 charges [higher than 25 bp] from advertising themselves as "no-load" funds.

3.3   Protecting Investors: A Half Century of Investment Company Regulation*,[1]

A   Application of the Securities Act and Rules to Investment Company Advertising

1   General Considerations

When Congress enacted the Investment Company Act of 1940,[2] the Securities Act already regulated the offer and sale of investment company securities. While the Investment Company Act contained provisions that either supplemented the Securities Act or harmonized the scheme of regulation under the two statutes, it did not make any fundamental changes in the way investment companies could distribute their shares to the public. As a result, even though investment companies, particularly mutual funds, almost certainly were not the type of issuer Congress had foremost in mind when drafting the Securities Act, investment companies continued to be subject to its provisions.[3]

The central provision of the Securities Act, section 5,[4] contains prohibitions regarding the use of interstate commerce to offer and sell securities to the public. Absent an exemption, under section 5(c) it is illegal for an issuer or underwriter to offer a security for sale to the public using jurisdictional means until a registration statement is filed with the Commission.

Section 5 also contains prohibitions regarding the dissemination of written selling material to investors during the offering period. Section 5(b)(1) makes it unlawful to use interstate commerce to transmit any prospectus relating to a security with respect to which a registration statement has been filed unless the prospectus meets the requirements of section 10 of the Securities Act.[5] "Prospectus" is broadly defined in section 2(10) to include any advertisement or other communication, "written or by radio or television, which offers any security for sale or confirms the sale of any security."[6] Thus, advertisements are considered prospectuses under the Securities Act if they offer a security for sale. Because the term "offer" is defined and interpreted broadly to encompass any attempt to procure orders for a security,[7] written advertisements relating to a security or aiding in the selling effort with respect to a security generally must be in the form of a section 10 prospectus.

Investment companies primarily use two types of section 10 prospectuses: the statutory prospectus specified in section 10(a); and a prospectus permitted under section 10(b) that "omits in part or summarizes" information in the section 10(a) prospectus.[8] A security cannot actually be sold until the registration statement becomes effective,[9] and the section 10(a) prospectus must be delivered no later than the delivery of the security or the confirmation of the sale, whichever occurs first.[10]

There is a limited exception to the general requirement that written offers after the filing of a registration statement be in the form of a section 10 prospectus. So-called "supplemental sales literature" may be used after the effective date of a registration state-

---

*United States Securities and Exchange Commission, Division of Investment Management, May 1992.

ment if accompanied or preceded by the statutory prospectus.[11] Thus, advertisements not meeting the requirements of section 10 may be used after the effective date if the statutory prospectus is printed in the advertisement (or was sent previously to each person receiving the advertisement). In addition, the use of specific types of advertisements such as "tombstone" advertisements are permitted under very limited circumstances, without prior delivery of the statutory prospectus.

The advertising restrictions and the prospectus delivery requirements are intended to foster an environment for making rational decisions based on the full disclosures contained in the filed registration statement.[12] The requirements also are intended to limit the potential for high pressure salesmanship, undue expectations, and appeals to emotion in the sale of securities.[13] It is possible, however, under the Securities Act to sell a security orally and to send the statutory prospectus later, either with the security or the confirmation of the sale (whichever is earlier), because section 5(b)(1) limits only the use of a prospectus, and "prospectus" is defined to include written—but not oral—communications. Thus, investors do not necessarily receive full, written disclosure before they decide to purchase a security.[14]

As discussed above, many investment companies are continuously subject to the advertising restrictions of the Securities Act. Mutual funds engage in continuous offerings. UITs are continuously subject to the Securities Act because the trusts' sponsors typically operate secondary markets in which sponsors offer to buy back trust units from existing unit holders and sell them to new unit holders. Because the sponsor, as the trust's depositor, is an "issuer" under section 2(4) of the Securities Act,[15] all offers and sales by the sponsor in the secondary market, unless otherwise exempt, are subject to the Securities Act.

The greater impact of the Securities Act on these investment companies compared to other issuers cannot be traced to any particular congressional concern. Instead, it is simply a product of a statute that treats issuers that distribute their shares continuously the same as issuers that distribute their shares periodically. . . .

B The Interplay of Rules 482 and 134

In the fifty-two years since the enactment of the Investment Company Act, Congress and the Commission have attempted to accommodate the unusual requirements of investment companies within the federal securities laws. The result now is a somewhat anomalous situation in which one kind of advertisement, the rule 134 tombstone, may be used to promote investment company shares creatively, perhaps even irresponsibly, subject only to the antifraud provisions and to the prohibition against the inclusion of any performance information. While the rule 482 omitting prospectus advertisement *may* use performance information, the substance of the information also must be in the statutory prospectus, and is subject to the stricter liabilities of section 12(2) of the Securities Act. [In 1996, Congress gave the SEC rulemaking authority to eliminate the "substance of" requirement in rule 482. When the SEC adopts these rules, fund advertisements will be allowed to contain performance numbers as long as the advertisements are not false or misleading, and comply with any other conditions imposed by the SEC.—ed. note]

Moreover, although rule 482 permits mutual funds to advertise performance information, they may do so only because of an attenuated link to the "substance of" requirement.

To make the rule workable, investment companies have not been required to put actual performance figures in the statutory prospectuses, which would have resulted in investment companies constantly having to "sticker" their section 10(a) prospectuses. Rather, advertisements are deemed to meet the "substance of" standard of rule 482 as long as the section 10(a) prospectus describes the methodology used to calculate the performance figures.[16]

The interplay between rule 134 and rule 482 has some ironic and unintended consequences. When reviewing advertisements, employees of the National Association of Securities Dealers, Inc. must try to discern which rule the sponsor is or should be relying upon to publish the advertisement.[17] As a practical matter, the only distinguishing feature is the inclusion or absence of performance information. If an advertisement contains such information, it must conform to rule 482's requirements, including the "substance of" requirement. If an advertisement does not contain performance data, it may be subject only to rule 134.[18]

Notes

1. This is a report of the Division of Investment Management. The Commission has expressed no view regarding the analysis, findings, or conclusions herein.
2. Investment Company Act of 1940, 15 U.S.C. §80a.
3. One possible explanation is that the predominant form of investment company in existence in 1940 was closed-end. See Chapter 11. Unlike open-end companies, closed-end companies usually engage in traditional underwritten offerings of a fixed number of shares, and in most cases do not offer their shares to the public on a continuous basis.
4. 15 U.S.C §77e.
5. Section 10 and Schedule A of the Securities Act set forth specific information required in section 10 prospectuses, as modified by the rules and regulations of the Commission adopted pursuant to its powers under section 10.
6. 15 U.S.C. §77b(10).
7. Section 2(3) defines the term "offer" to include "every attempt or offer to dispose of, or solicitation of an offer to buy, a security or interest in a security, for value." 15 U.S.C. §77b(3). See, also, e.g., In the Matter of Carl M. Loeb, Rhodes & Co., 38 S.E.C. 843, 848 (1950) (holding that the statutory definitions of "offer" and "prospectus" are intentionally broad so as to include any document designed to procure orders for a security).
8. See *infra* note 18 for a discussion of generic advertisements and newsletters.
9. Securities Act §5(a), 15 U.S.C. §77e(a).
10. See Securities Act §§2(10), 5(b)(1)–(2), 15 U.S.C §§77b(10), 77e(b)(1)–(2).
11. Under section 2(10)(a), supplemental sales literature is not considered to be a prospectus, and thus is not subject to section 5(b)(1) of the Securities Act. Many investment companies use supplemental sales literature extensively, often as an insert in the prospectus.
12. See *Federal Supervision of Traffic in Investment Securities in Interstate Commerce, H.R. Rep.* No. 85, 73d Cong., 1st Sess. 8 (1933).
13. See *id.* at 2.
14. The Commission has imposed requirements to encourage the pre-sale distribution of preliminary prospectuses, but the requirements do not affect the vast majority of mutual fund sales.
15. 15 U.S.C. §77b(4).
16. See Dechert Price & Rhoads (pub. avail. Nov. 20, 1979).
17. For the rules governing the filing of advertisements with the NASD, see Securities Act rule 497(i)(17 C.F.R §230.497(i)) and Article III, section 35 of the NASD Rules of Fair Practice, Nat'l Ass'n Sec. Dealers, Sec. Dealers Manual (CCH) q 2195.

18. Two other communication formats utilized by investment companies deserve mention. "Generic" advertisements, which do not name any particular fund, have been permitted since 1972 as a way to promote the investment company industry generally. Sec. Act Rel. 5248 (adopting rule 135a under the Securities Act). 17 C.F.R. §230.135a. In addition, funds distribute newsletters that often combine articles of general interest (non-offering material or "free writing") with separately designated rule 134 and rule 482 material. The Division has issued guidelines for the preparation of newsletters. See Letter from Kathryn B. McGrath, Director, Division of Investment Management, Securities and Exchange Commission, to Matthew P. Fink, Senior Vice President and General Counsel, Investment Company Institute (Jan. 29, 1990).

Class Exercise: **Designing a Profile Prospectus**

Almost everyone agrees that the full prospectus for a mutual fund is too long, too complex, and too boring for most investors. As a result, most investors do not read all of the full prospectus; instead, they read at most a few pages and usually rely on other sources of information, such as press articles, rating services, and friends' suggestions.

To make fund disclosure documents simpler and more readable, the SEC and the fund industry have developed a short-form prospectus called the profile. The profile is designed to provide investors with the key items of information about a fund in an easy to read Q and A format. The SEC requires all funds to answer the same questions in the same sequence in order to facilitate comparisons.

The profile does not do away with the full prospectus, however. The cover of the profile must offer an 800 number for investors to call if they want to be sent the full prospectus before purchasing a fund. In addition, the profile must offer to send investors a copy of the fund's latest annual or semiannual report if they wish to learn more about the fund. After an investor chooses to purchase a fund on the basis of the profile, the investor must receive the full prospectus along with confirmation of his or her purchase.

Thus, the profile is premised on a multitier system of disclosure. Investors may obtain more or less information from fund disclosure documents depending on their needs or desires. The profile is designed to provide the key information necessary for a purchase; an existing shareholder may use a full prospectus to find out more detailed information about taxes or fund wires. But some investors may want the full prospectus and the fund's annual report before purchasing; these documents can be easily obtained for free by calling an 800 number.

Set forth below are a few articles to provide background on the profile for use in completing the class exercise. The exercise asks you to draft your own profile on the basis of the full prospectus for the Fidelity Growth and Income Portfolio included in your course materials.

In-Class Team Discussion Questions

After discussing the information an investor needs to make a decision about a fund, working as a group, each team should outline the contents of a readable short-form prospectus for the Fidelity Growth and Income Portfolio. In drafting the outline, please keep in mind the following questions:

1. What are the key pieces of information an investor needs to decide whether to invest in a fund?
2. How would you report fund performance? Which time periods would you choose, and why? Do you think funds should be required to compare past performance with a benchmark? How do you recommend that performance numbers be updated?

3. How do you recommend that the prospectus disclose the risks associated with investing in the fund, so that prospective investors could compare the relative riskiness of different funds?

4. What fees, specifically, should the fund company be required to disclose? Would you require that all fees that appear in the full prospectus also appear in the short-form prospectus?

5. What information does the investor need to know about the process of purchasing or selling shares of the fund? And what other information does the investor need regarding the logistics of doing business with the fund company?

6. In your opinion, should the short-form prospectus be distributed to prospective investors in lieu of the Section 10(a) prospectus? Or, should the short-form always be accompanied by the more detailed prospectus?

7. Do you think all fund underwriters should be required to distribute prospectuses in the same format (with the same questions)? Or, should there be different rules for different types of funds, for example, money market vs. bond vs. stock funds?

8. Should there be special types of profiles for investors in mutual funds used in 401(k) plans, as compared to retail investors? Should fund profiles be allowed to be displayed on the Internet?

3.4   Taking the Mystery out of the Marketplace: The SEC's Consumer Education Campaign*

Arthur Levitt

I've certainly come to the right place to discuss the English language.

George Orwell blamed the demise of the English language on politics. It's quite possible he never read a prospectus.

You each have before you a paragraph we've selected from a mutual fund prospectus. It was chosen pretty much at random—you can find something written like it in many, if not most, prospectuses, so the actual fund doesn't matter. Now, the national press corps is among the most informed people in our nation. You're also familiar with the arcane language of boardroom and bar—you know that a "frivolous suit," for example, is not something you buy at Brooks Brothers. And you're well-versed in writing and deciphering the English language.

At the risk of C-Span's ratings, and the Press Club's reputation as a lively luncheon spot, I'm going to read the first few lines of that paragraph aloud:

Maturity and duration management decisions are made in the context of an intermediate maturity orientation. The maturity structure of the portfolio is adjusted in anticipation of cyclical interest rate changes. Such adjustments are not made in an effort to capture short-term, day-to-day movements in the market, but instead are implemented in anticipation of longer terms, secular shifts in the levels of interest rates (i.e., shifts transcending and/or not inherent to the business cycle)....

That was only half the paragraph. Is it understandable?

Why should we care about how fund prospectuses are written? Because there's a new economic fact of life in America, one whose significance has not yet sunk in. For the first time in history, investment company assets have surpassed commercial bank deposits. We've gone from a nation of savers to a nation of investors. The latest figures from the Federal Reserve confirm this trend: The number of American families with investments in mutual funds or the stock market has risen from one out of four—already pretty impressive—to one out of three.

This mass movement into our securities markets has provided new opportunities for investors—and new opportunities for America. But it's also increased risk, and it's led to a great deal of confusion. Investors are not as informed as they should be. It's a complex field, inhabited by creatures with names like "collateralized mortgage obligation," "bull-bear butterfly spread," and "inverse floater." And there are misconceptions even about such basic products as mutual funds.

Last November, a Commission survey showed that two-thirds of those who bought mutual funds through banks mistakenly believed that bank-sold money market funds were federally insured. And the problem's not limited to banks—almost 40 percent of those surveyed believed that mutual funds purchased from a stockbroker were federally insured.

---

*From remarks delivered at the National Press Club, Washington, D.C., October 13, 1994.

These people are just plain wrong. No mutual fund is federally insured—even if you bought it at a desk 5 feet away from your bank teller; even if it's named "The Rock Solid Honestly Safe U.S. Government Guaranty Trust Savings Fund." Investor confusion is so widespread that we've begun a series of town hall meetings across the country—to convey some basic facts about investing, and to encourage people to protect themselves by asking tough questions. After 30 years in and around the industry, that's the most important investment lesson I know. Unfortunately, it's a lesson few investors know.

I'm here today as part of a campaign to change that, by educating investors.

I've already met with people in New Jersey and Chicago. Tomorrow I'll speak at the Florida Crime Prevention Association meeting and at the Florida Atlantic University. I'm not just answering questions, however—I'm also asking them. And in my own conversations at these forums so far, I've learned something about the needs and knowledge of individuals looking to the capital markets for financial security and success.

I asked how many people could precisely measure the performance of their portfolios from this year to last—about one-quarter could. I asked how many people trusted their brokers—only a fifth did. Less than a fifth actually read their prospectuses....

Our greatest challenge at the SEC today is how to deal with the confusion and lack of information among investors. We need to do better. We've got to take the mystery out of our marketplace....

Let me now tell you about two more initiatives to reduce confusion in the marketplace, both being announced for the first time today.

If you didn't before, you know now that prospectuses can be tough to read. The prose trips off the tongue like peanut butter. Poetry seems to be reserved for claims about performance.

In fairness, much of the reason for the arcane language has to do with well-founded legal concerns.

I wish I could say that the SEC had nothing to do with the status quo, but I can't. We've contributed to the situation, albeit with the best intentions—and so have our fellow regulators and the courts. We ask funds to simplify and clarify their discussions of derivatives, for example. Within days, battalions of fund managers and lawyers descend on paneled conference rooms, thousands of legal pads slap down on shiny tables, and a new contest begins between the forces of Clarity and the forces of Confusion.

It's no wonder many investors wouldn't know a derivative if they saw one. The law of unintended results has come into play: Our passion for full disclosure has created fact-bloated reports, and prospectuses that are more redundant than revealing.

The answer can't be simply to make a rule requiring fund prospectuses to be clear and concise. We already have a rule that requires fund prospectuses to be clear and concise. The problem is that clarity and conciseness often collide with legal requirements.

We can do better. But it's obvious that rulemaking only goes so far. I've decided to try a different tack. I'm asking funds to compete with one another to make prospectuses more consumer-friendly, in two distinct ways: first, through clear language; and second, through the inclusion of a single page that covers the essentials.

First, clear language: It's my hope to have prospectuses begin to speak a new language —the English. I've recruited someone you all know to help me. Warren Buffett is the Chairman and CEO of Berkshire Hathaway. He's deservedly famous as a successful manager and investor.

But there's one other thing he's famous for, and that is the clarity of his company's annual reports. That's why, when I began to think about ways to make prospectuses clearer, I immediately called him and asked him to translate the first paragraph I read to you today into plain English. Here's the result, which is also on the sheet you have:

We will try to profit by correctly predicting future interest rates. When we have no strong opinion, we will generally hold intermediate-term bonds. But when we expect a major and sustained increase in rates, we will concentrate on short-term issues. And, conversely, if we expect a major shift to lower rates, we will buy long bonds. We will focus on the big picture and won't make moves based on short-term considerations.

That's the whole paragraph, and I think it's a real improvement.

Warren's success with that paragraph in particular, and with clear communication in general, proves it can be done. The ball is now in the industry's court. Mutual funds compete for business all the time. Let's see if they can't also compete for clarity of communication.

For our part, I've asked the staff to re-evaluate the process by which it comments on prospectuses. I've emphasized the need to limit the number and nature of the comments we give. We simply cannot give comments that can be answered only by technical, incomprehensible prose.

I'm announcing today that we've created some incentives for funds to write clearer prospectuses. To recognize those who are trying to do the right thing, we're instituting an expedited review process for funds that come in with a prospectus they want to make more readable. At the same time, I'm putting the industry on notice that, in commenting on fund registration statements sent to us for review, we're going to feel free to talk about the clarity of language used, in addition to legal technicalities. We want a higher standard of clarity.

To me, it makes good business sense to have a readable prospectus—a clear and concise product description is a salesman's best friend. I've asked my staff to do better; now I'm asking the industry to do the same.

Out second goal is to make the information in prospectuses less encyclopedic. As writers, you all know that it's easy to write a long story; what's hard is to get the same story into a few inches of column space, or 60 seconds of TV time. You wrestle with this problem every day.

So does the mutual fund industry—and they do so in good faith. One way to compress information in prospectuses is to provide investors with a one-page stand-alone summary of a fund's main features. There's a pending proposal before the Commission known as the "off-the-page prospectus," which attempts to meet this goal. When I first came to the SEC, I thought this proposal might be a good solution. The SEC has begun using focus groups to learn more from investors themselves about their needs, and in those groups, people have told us that a single page would not provide them with enough information to make an investment decision.

What our focus groups did like, however, was having the traditional prospectus include a single page summary, with standard information in a standard format. We've been tracking this question for more than a year now, and our latest study is being conducted as I speak. But preliminary results seem to confirm that while people want a single-page summary, most of them want it along with the traditional prospectus.

Industry leaders know that investors don't want to work their way through several pounds' worth of dense prose in order to find the nuggets of information they need. They know that a clear prospectus can help sales. So we knew the response would be positive if we asked funds to create a Profile Prospectus—that is, a prospectus with a single-page summary.

Today, I'm pleased to announce that seven major mutual fund groups have already stepped forward to pilot the Profile Prospectus: Capital Group, Fidelity, Vanguard, T. Rowe Price, Scudder, Dreyfus, and IDS. We hope more funds will join them. Because if funds compete for clarity, the winner will not be any single fund—it will be 38 million Americans who invest in mutual funds—that's 38 million and growing every day.

We have within our grasp a chance to help them—a chance to change the way they buy funds—a chance to make it easier to them to make comparisons, and easier to get right to the key issues they need to know before investing. When all is said and done, that's what these initiatives are about—people reaching for a better life—a new home, children through college, or a decent retirement. People looking to our capital markets as never before, for future financial security and success.

We've already become a nation of investors.

It's time we became a nation of educated investors.

3.5   The Profile Prospectus: An Assessment by Mutual Fund Shareholders*

Background

In October 1994, Arthur Levitt, Jr., Chairman of the U.S. Securities and Exchange Commission (SEC), launched an innovative project to improve disclosure about mutual funds. He called upon mutual fund companies to develop a concise or "profile" prospectus that would contain information essential to an investment decision. In response to Chairman Levitt's initiative, the Investment Company Institute[1] and eight mutual fund groups,[2] in consultation with the SEC's Division of Investment Management and with the Investment Companies Committee of the North American Securities Administrators Association (NASAA), developed a prototype of a profile prospectus that established 11 critical areas to be addressed in fund disclosure:

1. the fund's goals or objectives;
2. its investment strategies;
3. its risks;
4. the kind of investors for whom the fund might be an appropriate investment;
5. a table showing fees and expenses of the fund;
6. a graphic depiction of the variability of the fund's performance over time, in the form of a bar chart presenting the fund's total return in each of the last ten years, accompanied by standardized SEC performance data of the fund;
7. the name of the fund's investment adviser;
8. how investors may purchase shares of the fund, including any minimum investments;
9. how investors may redeem their shares;
10. when and how distributions are made by the fund; and
11. other services the fund offers to investors.

In August 1995, the SEC approved use of prototype versions of the profile prospectus for a one-year trial period. Participating fund groups have developed profile prospectuses for 38 equity, bond, and money market funds and provided them to prospective investors. In addition, the Institute and fund groups participating in the project have undertaken research to determine how shareholders assess the profile prospectus. The research methods and results are summarized below. This research represents, to the Institute's knowledge, the most extensive survey ever conducted of U.S. investors regarding the content and format of mutual fund disclosure.

---

*From report to the U.S. Securities and Exchange Commission by the Investment Company Institute, May 1996.

Research Methods

The Institute undertook research to determine whether the profile prospectus provides the information that investors seek before purchasing a mutual fund and whether the profile prospectus enables investors to obtain key investment information more readily than the prospectus currently in use (the Section 10(a) prospectus).

. . .

Research Results

The studies conducted by the Institute and its members provide important information about the needs of fund shareholders and the potential of the profile prospectus to serve as a model for effective disclosure. The research findings are presented in a two-volume report, *The Profile Prospectus: An Assessment by Mutual Fund Shareholders*, submitted to the SEC by the Institute on May 20, 1996.

As SEC Chairman Levitt observed in August 1995, research of this kind should help the Commission determine "what, if any, permanent changes to fund disclosure should be made" and "whether investors should be able to rely on a stand-alone profile . . . in deciding to invest in funds."[3] In light of the research findings summarized below, the Institute has recommended that the SEC propose rulemaking that would authorize the use of the profile prospectus, with enhancements to the prototype, and subject to strict conditions governing future use.[4]

1. The Section 10(a) prospectus is not meeting the needs of many investors for making investment decisions.

*   **Many investors do not use or read the Section 10(a) prospectus.** Half of all recent fund investors surveyed by the Institute did not consult or use the Section 10(a) prospectus for *any* purpose before making their most recent purchases of a mutual fund.[5] Most investors who made no use of the Section 10(a) prospectus expressed a lack of a full understanding of mutual fund investing.

*   **Investors find the Section 10(a) prospectus to be neither easy to use nor easy to understand.** In the Institute's survey, fewer than 36 percent of all respondents reported that it was very easy locating or understanding key investment items in the Section 10(a) prospectus. Investment risk posed the greatest challenge, with little more than one-fifth saying that locating or understanding the risk information was very easy (figure 3.5.1)

2. Mutual fund investors strongly favor the contents, format, and overall utility of the profile prospectus.

*   **Investors believe the profile prospectus contains the right amount of information for making investment decisions.** Seventy percent of the recent fund buyers surveyed by the Institute stated that the profile prospectus provided them with the right amount of information with which to make investment decisions. Moreover, the format of the profile prospectus appealed equally to those investors who had used the Section 10(a) prospectus in their most recent purchases and to those who had not, an indication that the profile prospectus would be used broadly by both groups if it were available.

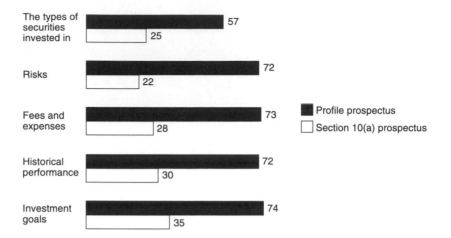

Figure 3.5.1 Ease of locating selected information in the Section 10(a) and Profile prospectuses (percent of buyers indicating very easy to locate). Far more recent buyers found it very easy to locate important information in the profile prospectus. Note: Number of respondents varies. Source: The Profile Prospectus: An Assessment by Mutual Fund Shareholders, Volume 1, Institute Research (Investment Company Institute, May 1996).

Scudder's survey of prospective investors found more than 80 percent saying that the profile prospectus was just the right length and more than 85 percent indicating that each of the 11 items in the profile prospectus was very useful in making an investment decision. Seventy-nine percent of respondents to Vanguard's survey of prospective investors rated the profile prospectus as excellent or good for providing sufficient information for making investment decisions.

- **Investors can readily locate and easily understand information presented in the profile prospectus.** A majority of the recent fund investors surveyed by the Institute said it was very easy to locate key investment items in the profile prospectus, and a majority said it was very easy to understand the discussions of these items. For example, 72 percent of respondents said it was very easy to locate information on fund risks in the profile prospectus, and 56 percent said it was very easy to understand the discussion.

More than 90 percent of fund inquirers responding to Fidelity's survey thought the profile prospectus' discussions of fund performance, goals, and risks were useful. Also in Fidelity's survey, more than three-fifths of the prospective buyers thought the profile prospectus was better than the Section 10(a) prospectus for finding information and for presenting information clearly. In Scudder's survey, more than 80 percent indicated that the profile prospectus was easy to read, was well-organized, and made it simple to focus on key issues about the fund.

- **Investors regard the profile prospectus to be more useful than the Section 10(a) prospectus for making investment decisions.** Nearly 60 percent of recent fund buyers surveyed by the Institute rated the overall usefulness of the profile prospectus higher than that of the Section 10(a) prospectus. Even the majority of those investors who used a Section 10(a) prospectus in their most recent purchases rated the profile prospectus higher. In addition, two thirds of all recent buyers would place the profile prospectus at or near the top of their list of information sources. In contrast, 57 percent put the Section 10(a) prospectus at the middle or bottom of the list.

In Fidelity's survey of prospective investors, more than half rated the profile prospectus as better than the Section 10(a) prospectus for making investment decisions. In Dreyfus' survey of prospective investors, 49 percent said the profile prospectus was extremely useful for making fund investment decisions.

• **Professional financial advisers view the profile prospectus as assisting investors in their investment decisions.** In Capital Research's survey of financial advisers, 87 percent preferred the profile prospectus over the Section 10(a) prospectus for helping investors make an investment decision. In addition, the majority of advisers responding to American Express' survey gave higher marks to the layout, length, and content of the profile prospectus than to the Section 10(a) prospectus. For example, 56 percent of advisers rated the length of the profile prospectus as excellent, while only 10 percent of respondents gave the Section 10(a) prospectus this rating.

3. The majority of investors who do not currently use the Section 10(a) prospectus would use the profile prospectus, if it were available.

• **The Institute survey of recent fund buyers found that 61 percent of those who had not consulted a Section 10(a) prospectus for any purpose stated they would be very likely to use the profile prospectus, if it were available.** Moreover, even among those who do use the Section 10(a) prospectus, 71 percent would be very likely to use the profile prospectus.

Research of the participating mutual fund companies also found that investors would use the profile prospectus. In Scudder's survey of prospective investors, 64 percent found the profile prospectus to be very useful for making investment decisions. In Vanguard's survey, 57 percent of prospective investors preferred the profile prospectus over the Section 10(a) prospectus for evaluating fund investments.

4. Mutual fund shareholders would prefer to be provided with the profile prospectus for investment decisionmaking.

• **A substantial majority of mutual fund investors would like to receive the profile prospectus, provided the Section 10(a) prospectus would be available upon request.** Two thirds of recent fund investors surveyed by the Institute indicated that, in making an investment decision, they would like to receive the profile prospectus by itself or with the option of obtaining a Section 10(a) prospectus from the fund company.

Institute members' research also indicated that mutual fund investors would like the opportunity to use the profile prospectus in this fashion. For example, 62 percent of the shareholders in American Express' survey would prefer to receive the profile prospectus, either alone or with the option of requesting a Section 10(a) prospectus.

Fidelity's survey of fund inquirers found that 61 percent favored receiving the profile prospectus along with an 800 telephone number through which the Section 10(a) prospectus could be requested.

• **Professional financial advisers would use the profile prospectus with current and prospective customers.** In Capital Research's survey of professional financial advisers, 78 percent said they were very likely or extremely likely to use the profile prospectus in face-to-face meetings with investors. In American Express' adviser survey, 75 percent said that they would prefer to send investors the profile prospectus, either alone or with the option to request a Section 10(a) prospectus.

Definitions

Section 10(a) Prospectus   The Section 10(a) prospectus refers to the prospectus that funds currently deliver to shareholders pursuant to Section 10(a) of the Securities Act of 1933.

Profile Prospectus   The "profile prospectus" refers to the prototype prospectus developed at the initiative of the SEC to address investor needs for simple and more understandable disclosure when making investment decisions. It is limited to information on the 11 areas prescribed by the SEC.

Notes

1. The Investment Company Institute is the national association of the U.S. investment company industry. Its membership includes 5.876 open-end investment companies ("mutual funds"), 448 closed-end investment companies, and 10 sponsors of unit investment trusts. Its mutual fund members had assets of $2.994 trillion as of March 31, 1996, accounting for approximately 95 percent of total industry assets, and had over 38 million individual shareholders in mid-1995.
2. The eight fund groups are American Express Financial Corporation; Bank of America N.T. & S.A.; Capital Research and Management Company; The Dreyfus Corporation; FMR Corp. (Fidelity); Scudder, Stevens & Clark, Inc.; T. Rowe Price Associates, Inc.; and The Vanguard Group, Inc.
3. Remarks by Chairman Levitt at a press conference to announce the distribution of the profile prospectus to investors (July 31, 1995).
4. See letter from Paul Schott Stevens, Senior Vice President and General Counsel, Investment Company Institute, to Barry Barbash, Director, Division of Investment Management, Securities and Exchange Commission (May 20, 1996).
5. Previous Institute research found that a far smaller percentage of survey respondents—26 percent—indicated they had used the Section 10(a) prospectus as a source for mutual fund information. Whereas the current Institute research study is limited to recent purchasers, respondents to the earlier Institute study were broadly representative of all mutual fund shareholders. See Piecing Together Shareholder Perceptions of Investment Risk (Investment Company Institute, Spring 1993) at page 26.

3.6 Less Is ... Less*
Pat Regnier

Despite their detractors, prospectuses fill a necessary role. The law requires fund companies to get a prospectus in the hands of any interested investor before selling him or her any shares. This isn't just bureaucratic red tape: For all its flaws, the mutual-fund prospectus is one of the major reasons fund investing is so transparent today. These ponderous documents lay out for shareholders the rules by which the managers of their funds are supposed to play, and are often the only free source of information specifying the special risks a fund might take on. (They are also, incidentally, a primary source for Morningstar and other third-party information providers.)

So the prospectus can't be scrapped, but maybe it can be modified so that it's easier to use. To this end, the Securities and Exchange Commission and a group of large fund companies have an experiment in the works. In August, shareholders of 24 funds—Fidelity, Scudder, and American funds among them—received "fund profiles" in the mail. These short-form versions of the standard prospectus are just three pages long (with lots of white space), are easy to read, and have a clear, standardized format. Every profile addresses the same 11 basic questions, including "What are the significant risks?" and "How has the fund performed?"

These profiles are now only supplemental to conventional prospectuses, but many in the fund industry clearly have bigger plans. In heartily endorsing profile prospectuses in a press release, the Investment Company Institute suggested that they might eventually be suitable as stand-alone documents, with the full prospectuses distributed only on an investor's request. A Fidelity press release echoes this sentiment, citing the positive response from some focus-group participants to argue that "from the investor point of view, less is truly more."

Is it? Are those focus-group participants really getting what they need from a three-page brochure? A closer look at some of these profile prospectuses suggests that they have some pretty serious limitations. They simply can't offer the kind of detailed information about the risks a fund takes that complete prospectuses can. Worse, some of these documents sacrifice clarity for the sake of brevity, and could potentially mislead less-experienced investors.

For example, the profile prospectus of Scudder Emerging Markets Income described the fund's investment objectives and risks in just a few sentences. It explains that the fund buys high-yield emerging-markets debt, and that it courts more risk than funds that invest in developed markets. "Political events, changes in perceived credit-worthiness, fluctuating national interest rates, and movements in foreign currencies will affect the value of the fund's holdings," reads the profile. This is, as far as it goes, accurate and essential information.

---

*From *Morningstar Investor*, November 1995. Reprinted with permission.

Investors will miss a lot, though, if they don't take the time to read through the long-form prospectus. Investors face credit risk, interest-rate risk, and currency risk in any foreign debt market, but emerging-markets debt is perilous beyond conventional expectations. Scudder's statutory prospectus does a good job of laying out the specific potential pitfalls, including hyperinflation, "inexperienced foreign intermediaries" (i.e., possibly incompetent traders), nationalization (seizure) of corporate assets, military coups, radical currency devaluations, and the fact that many of these "markets" aren't actively trading (liquid) markets at all. This information really matters, as any investor who has recently owned an emerging-markets bond fund can attest. Many of these funds scored double-digit losses last year as Mexico's economy, markets, and political structure seemed to fall apart. This fund got away with a comparatively mild 8% hit—still bad enough to merit advance warning.

Scudder's profile comes up short mostly because its corresponding prospectus is so much more effective. Bond Fund of America's profile, meanwhile, is just plain spotty. For one thing, it omits mention of management's freedom to use derivatives. This is an unfortunate oversight: Bond Fund of America's losses last year were exacerbated by a small stake in inverse floaters.

This fund's profile has failings other than that of omission, however. It states that the fund invests at least 60% of its assets in high-quality issues, which means a fair amount of the portfolio resides in junk bonds. The description of risk reads as follows: "Investing in bonds involves risk, including credit risk (the possibility that the bond issuer will default on its obligation) and market risk (when interest rates rise, bond prices fall and vice versa). Lower-rated bonds are subject to greater price fluctuations and risk of loss than higher-rated bonds." This isn't exactly wrong, it's just not the whole picture.

Except for the junkiest of junk, lower-rated issues (which carry higher coupons to compensate for their added credit risk) often hold up better when rates go up than do their lower-coupon, investment-grade peers. The risks of the fund's investment-grade holdings —which include those inverse floaters—should get at least as much attention as the junk bonds.

The point here is really not to chide Scudder, American, or any of the other families participating in the profile experiment. To the contrary, they deserve some credit for confronting a difficult problem. If long-form prospectuses aren't being read, it doesn't matter how good the information is that can be culled from them. The fund profile is the first serious stab at tailoring the presentation of prospectus information for the interest level and time demands of the average individual investor. The problem is that here less is, in fact, too much less. Three lightly inked pages just can't hold enough information, especially if investors are asked to go out of their way to get more.

This experiment isn't a washout, though. Properly beefed up, fund profiles could help investors screen through a number of mutual-fund options, or could be used as guides for longer documents. Furthermore, the question-and-answer format is a real improvement over the scattershot presentation of many standard prospectuses. There's no reason why the profile's elegantly simple approach couldn't be imported to a prospectus with more-complete answers.

Details can be boring, but attention to them is vital to effective investing. The task for the SEC and the industry isn't to eliminate complexity, but to make that complexity manageable.

3.7

Please read this prospectus before investing, and keep it on file for future reference. It contains important information, including how the fund invests and the services available to shareholders.

To learn more about the fund and its investments, you can obtain a copy of the fund's most recent financial report and portfolio listing, or a copy of the Statement of Additional Information (SAI) dated September 25, 1997. The SAI has been filed with the Securities and Exchange Commission (SEC) and is available along with other related materials on the SEC's Internet Web site (http://www.sec.gov). The SAI is incorporated herein by reference (legally forms a part of the prospectus). For a free copy of either document, call Fidelity at 1-800-544-8888.

Mutual fund shares are not deposits or obligations of, or guaranteed by, any depository institution. Shares are not insured by the FDIC, Federal Reserve Board, or any other agency, and are subject to investment risks, including possible loss of principal amount invested.

GAI-pro-0997

Fidelity
Growth & Income
Portfolio
(fund number 027, trading symbol FGRIX)

Growth & Income seeks high total return through a combination of current income and capital appreciation by investing mainly in equity securities.

Prospectus
September 25, 1997

Fidelity Investments®

82 Devonshire Street, Boston, MA 02109

This page
intentionally
left blank

Contents

Key Facts

The Fund at a Glance

Goal: High total return through a combination of current income and capital appreciation. As with any mutual fund, there is no assurance that the fund will achieve its goal.

Strategy: Invests mainly in equity securities of companies that pay current dividends and offer potential growth of earnings.

Management: Fidelity Management & Research Company (FMR) is the management arm of Fidelity Investments, which was established in 1946 and is now America's largest mutual fund manager. Foreign affiliates of FMR may help choose investments for the fund.

Size: As of July 31, 1997 the fund had over $34.2 billion in assets.

Who May Want to Invest

The fund may be appropriate for investors who are willing to ride out stock market fluctuations in pursuit of potentially high long-term returns. The fund is designed for those who seek a combination of growth and income from equity and some bond investments.

The value of the fund's investments and the income they generate will vary from day to day, and generally reflect market conditions, interest rates, and other company, political, or economic news both here and abroad. In the short-term, stock prices can fluctuate dramatically in response to these factors. Over time, however, stocks have shown greater growth potential than other types of securities. The prices of bonds generally move in the opposite direction from interest rates. When you sell your shares, they may be worth more or less than what you paid for them. By itself, the fund does not constitute a balanced investment plan.

 The Spectrum of Fidelity Funds

Broad categories of Fidelity funds are presented here in order of ascending risk. Generally, investors seeking to maximize return must assume greater risk. Growth & Income is in the **Growth and Income** category.

- **Money Market** Seeks income and stability by investing in high-quality, short-term investments.

- **Income** Seeks income by investing in bonds.

➤ **Growth and Income** Seeks long-term growth and income by investing in stocks and bonds.

- **Growth** Seeks long-term growth by investing mainly in stocks.

Expenses

Shareholder transaction expenses

are charges you may pay when you buy or sell shares of a fund. In addition, you may be charged an annual account maintenance fee if your account balance falls below $2,500. See "Transaction Details," page 27, for an explanation of how and when these charges apply.

Maximum sales charge on purchases and reinvested distributions	**None**
Deferred sales charge on redemptions	**None**
Exchange fee	**None**
Annual account maintenance fee (for accounts under $2,500)	**$12.00**

Annual fund operating expenses

are paid out of the fund's assets. The fund pays a management fee to FMR. It also incurs other expenses for services such as maintaining shareholder records and furnishing shareholder statements and financial reports. The fund's expenses are factored into its share price or dividends and are not charged directly to shareholder accounts (see "Breakdown of Expenses" page 16).

The following figures are based on historical expenses of the fund and are calculated as a percentage of average net assets of the fund. A portion of the brokerage commissions that the fund pays is used to reduce the fund's expenses. In addition, the fund has entered into arrangements with its custodian and transfer agent whereby credits realized as a result of uninvested cash balances are used to reduce custodian and transfer agent expenses. Including this reduction, the total fund operating

expenses presented in the table would have been 0.71%.

Management fee	0.50%
12b-1 fee	**None**
Other expenses	0.23%
Total fund operating expenses	**0.73%**

Examples: Let's say, hypothetically, that the fund's annual return is 5% and that its operating expenses are exactly as just described. For every $1,000 you invested, here's how much you would pay in total expenses if you close your account after the number of years indicated:

After 1 year	$ 7
After 3 years	$ 23
After 5 years	$ 41
After 10 years	$ 91

These examples illustrate the effect of expenses, but are not meant to suggest actual or expected costs or returns, all of which may vary.

 Understanding Expenses

Operating a mutual fund involves a variety of expenses for portfolio management, shareholder statements, tax reporting, and other services. These costs are paid from the fund's assets; their effect is already factored into any quoted share price or return.

Key Facts - continued

Financial Highlights

The financial highlights table that follows has been audited by Coopers & Lybrand L.L.P., independent accountants. The fund's financial highlights, financial statements, and report of the auditor are included in the fund's Annual Report, and are incorporated by reference into (are legally a part of) the fund's SAI. Contact Fidelity for a free copy of the Annual Report or the SAI.

Selected Per-Share Data

Years ended July 31	1997	1996	1995	1994[F]	1993	1992	1991	1990	1989	1988
Net asset value, beginning of period	$ 28.20	$ 25.10	$ 22.17	$ 21.90	$ 21.34	$ 19.92	$ 17.10	$ 18.56	$ 14.56	$ 17.44
Income from Investment Operations										
Net investment income	.46[C]	.49	.43	.45	.53	.50	.46	.58	.76[D]	.55
Net realized and unrealized gain (loss)	11.44	3.99	4.14	1.07	3.02	1.94	3.10	(.02)	3.86	(1.58)
Total from investment operations	11.90	4.48	4.57	1.52	3.55	2.44	3.56	.56	4.62	(1.03)
Less Distributions										
From net investment income	(.48)	(.48)	(.40)	(.48)	(.59)	(.38)	(.52)	(.75)	(.62)	(.50)
From net realized gain	(1.12)	(.90)	(1.24)	(.77)	(2.40)	(.64)	(.22)	(1.27)	—	(1.35)
Total distributions	(1.60)	(1.38)	(1.64)	(1.25)	(2.99)	(1.02)	(.74)	(2.02)	(.62)	(1.85)
Net asset value, end of period	$ 38.50	$ 28.20	$ 25.10	$ 22.17	$ 21.90	$ 21.34	$ 19.92	$ 17.10	$ 18.56	$ 14.56
Total return[A,B]	44.16%	18.39%	21.95%	7.08%	19.10%	12.75%	21.89%	3.22%	32.66%	(6.04)%

Ratios and Supplemental Data

	1997	1996	1995	1994	1993	1992	1991	1990	1989	1988
Net assets, end of period (In millions)	$ 34,284	$ 19,206	$ 12,106	$ 8,757	$ 6,646	$ 4,199	$ 2,686	$ 1,910	$ 1,428	$ 1,188
Ratio of expenses to average net assets	.73%	.75%	.78%	.83%	.83%	.86%	.87%	.87%	.89%	1.02%
Ratio of expenses to average net assets after expense reductions	.71%[E]	.74%[E]	.77%[E]	.82%[E]	.83%	.86%	.87%	.87%	.89%	1.02%
Ratio of net investment income to average net assets	1.43%	1.82%	2.21%	2.09%	2.67%	2.49%	2.62%	3.43%	4.76%	3.69%
Portfolio turnover rate	38%	41%	67%	92%	87%	221%	215%	108%	97%	135%
Average commission rate[G]	$ .0433									

[A] Total returns do not include the former one time sales charge.
[B] The total returns would have been lower had certain expenses not been reduced during the periods shown.
[C] Net investment income per share has been calculated based on average shares outstanding during the period.
[D] Net investment income per share contains a special dividend of $.09 per share.
[E] FMR or the fund has entered into varying arrangements with third parties who either paid or reduced a portion of the fund's expenses.
[F] Effective August 1, 1993, the fund adopted Statement of Position 93-2, "Determination, Disclosure, and Financial Statement Presentation of Income, Capital Gain, and Return of Capital Distributions by Investment Companies." As a result, net investment income per share may reflect certain reclassifications related to book to tax differences.
[G] For fiscal years beginning on or after September 1, 1995, a fund is required to disclose its average commission rate per share for security trades on which commissions are charged. This amount may vary from period to period and fund to fund depending on the mix of trades executed in various markets where trading practices and commission rate structures may differ.

Performance

Mutual fund performance is commonly measured as *total return*. The total returns that follow are based on historical fund results and do not reflect the effect of taxes.

The fund's fiscal year runs from August 1 through July 31. The tables below show the fund's performance over past fiscal years compared to different measures, including a comparative index and a competitive funds average. The chart on page 8 presents calendar year performance.

Average Annual Total Returns

Fiscal periods ended July 31, 1997	Past 1 year	Past 5 years	Past 10 years
Growth & Income	44.16%	21.56%	16.72%
S&P 500	52.14%	20.66%	14.96%
Lipper Growth and Income Funds Average	43.83%	18.15%	13.01%

Cumulative Total Returns

Fiscal periods ended July 31, 1997	Past 1 year	Past 5 years	Past 10 years
Growth & Income	44.16%	165.44%	369.31%
S&P 500	52.14%	155.75%	303.48%
Lipper Growth and Income Funds Average	43.83%	131.27%	242.79%

Understanding Performance

Because this fund invests in stocks, its performance is related to that of the overall stock market. Historically, stock market performance has been characterized by volatility in the short run and growth in the long run. You can see these two characteristics reflected in the fund's performance; the year-by-year total returns on page 8 show that short-term returns can vary widely, while the returns in the mountain chart show long-term growth.

Example: Let's say, hypothetically, that you had $10,000 invested in the fund on August 1, 1987. From that date through July 31, 1997, the fund's total return was 369.31%. Your $10,000 would have grown to $46,931 (the initial investment plus 369.31% of $10,000).

$10,000 Over Ten Years

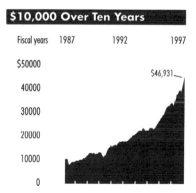

Fiscal years	1987	1992	1997

$46,931

Key Facts - continued

Year-by-Year Total Returns										
Calendar years	1987	1988	1989	1990	1991	1992	1993	1994	1995	1996
Growth & Income	5.77%	22.98%	29.60%	-6.80%	41.84%	11.54%	19.53%	2.27%	35.38%	20.02%
S&P 500	5.10%	16.61%	31.69%	-3.10%	30.47%	7.62%	10.08%	1.32%	37.58%	22.96%
Lipper Growth & Income Funds Average	1.82%	15.99%	23.62%	-4.34%	29.07%	8.93%	11.58%	-0.94%	30.82%	20.78%
Consumer Price Index	4.43%	4.42%	4.65%	6.11%	3.06%	2.90%	2.75%	2.67%	2.54%	3.32%

Percentage (%)
■ Growth & Income

Explanation of Terms

Total return is the change in value of an investment over a given period, assuming reinvestment of any dividends and capital gains. A *cumulative total return* reflects actual performance over a stated period of time. An *average annual total return* is a hypothetical rate of return that, if achieved annually, would have produced the same cumulative total return if performance had been constant over the entire period. Average annual total returns smooth out variations in performance; they are not the same as actual year-by-year results.

Yield refers to the income generated by an investment in the fund over a given period of time, expressed as an annual percentage rate. Yields are calculated according to a standard that is required for all stock and bond funds. Because this differs from other accounting methods, the quoted yield may not equal the income actually paid to shareholders.

Standard & Poor's 500 Index (S&P 500®) is a widely recognized, unmanaged index of common stocks.

Unlike the fund's returns, the total returns of the comparative index do not include the effect of any brokerage commissions, transaction fees, or other costs of investing.

The Consumer Price Index is a widely recognized measure of inflation calculated by the U.S. Government.

The competitive funds average is the the Lipper Growth & Income Funds Average. As of July 31, 1997, the average reflected the performance of 565 mutual funds with similar investment objectives. This average, published by Lipper Analytical Services, Inc., excludes the effect of sales loads.

Other illustrations of fund performance may show moving averages over specified periods.

The fund's recent strategies, performance, and holdings are detailed twice a year in financial reports, which are sent to all shareholders. For current performance or a free annual report, call 1-800-544-8888.

Total returns and yields are based on past results and are not an indication of future performance.

The Fund in Detail

Charter

Growth & Income is a mutual fund: an investment that pools shareholders' money and invests it toward a specified goal. The fund is a diversified fund of Fidelity Securities Fund, an open-end management investment company organized as a Massachusetts business trust on October 2, 1984.

The fund is governed by a Board of Trustees which is responsible for protecting the interests of shareholders. The trustees are experienced executives who meet periodically throughout the year to oversee the fund's activities, review contractual arrangements with companies that provide services to the fund, and review the fund's performance. The trustees serve as trustees for other Fidelity funds. The majority of trustees are not otherwise affiliated with Fidelity.

The fund may hold special shareholder meetings and mail proxy materials. These meetings may be called to elect or remove trustees, change fundamental policies, approve a management contract, or for other purposes. Shareholders not attending these meetings are encouraged to vote by proxy. Fidelity will mail proxy materials in advance, including a voting card and information about the proposals to be voted on. The number of votes you are entitled to is based upon the dollar value of your investment.

FMR and Its Affiliates

The fund is managed by FMR, which chooses the fund's investments and handles its business affairs. Fidelity Management & Research (U.K.) Inc. (FMR U.K.), in London, England, and Fidelity Management & Research (Far East) Inc. (FMR Far East), in Tokyo, Japan, assist FMR with foreign investments.

Steven Kaye is Vice President and manager of Growth & Income, which he has managed since January 1993. Previously, he managed other Fidelity funds. Mr. Kaye was assistant director of equity research from 1989 to 1990. Mr. Kaye joined Fidelity in 1985.

Fidelity investment personnel may invest in securities for their own accounts pursuant to a code of ethics that establishes procedures for personal investing and restricts certain transactions.

Fidelity Distributors Corporation (FDC) distributes and markets Fidelity's funds and services.

Fidelity Service Company, Inc. (FSC) performs transfer agent servicing functions for the fund.

FMR Corp. is the ultimate parent company of FMR, FMR U.K., and FMR Far East. Members of the Edward C. Johnson 3d family are the predominant owners of a class of shares of common stock representing approximately 49% of the voting power of FMR Corp. Under the Investment Company Act of 1940 (the 1940 Act), control of a company is presumed where one individual or group of individuals owns more than 25% of the voting stock of that company; therefore, the Johnson family may be deemed under the 1940 Act to form a controlling group with respect to FMR Corp.

FMR may use its broker-dealer affiliates and other firms that sell fund shares to carry out the fund's transactions, provided that the fund receives brokerage services and commission rates comparable to those of other broker-dealers.

Investment Principles and Risks

Growth & Income seeks high total return through a combination of current income and capital appreciation by investing mainly in equity securities. The fund expects to invest the majority of its assets in domestic and foreign equity securities, with a focus on those that pay current dividends and show potential earnings growth. However, the fund may buy debt securities as well as equity securities that are not currently paying dividends, but offer prospects for capital appreciation or future income.

The value of the fund's domestic and foreign investments varies in response to many factors. Stock values fluctuate in response to the activities of individual companies and general market and economic conditions. Bond values fluctuate based on changes in interest rates and in the credit quality of the issuer. Investments in foreign securities may involve risks in addition to those of U.S. investments, including increased political and economic risk, as well as exposure to currency fluctuations.

FMR may use various investment techniques to hedge a portion of the fund's

risks, but there is no guarantee that these strategies will work as FMR intends. Also, as a mutual fund, the fund seeks to spread investment risk by diversifying its holdings among many companies and industries. Of course, when you sell your shares of the fund, they may be worth more or less than what you paid for them.

FMR normally invests the fund's assets according to its investment strategy. The fund also reserves the right to invest without limitation in preferred stocks and investment-grade debt instruments for temporary, defensive purposes.

Securities and Investment Practices

The following pages contain more detailed information about types of instruments in which the fund may invest, strategies FMR may employ in pursuit of the fund's investment objective, and a summary of related risks. Any restrictions listed supplement those discussed earlier in this section. A complete listing of the fund's limitations and more detailed information about the fund's investments are contained in the fund's SAI. Policies and limitations are considered at the time of purchase, the sale of instruments is not required in the event of a subsequent change in circumstances.

FMR may not buy all of these instruments or use all of these techniques unless it believes that they are consistent with the fund's investment objective and policies and that doing so will help the fund achieve its goal. Fund holdings and recent investment strategies are

The Fund in Detail - continued

detailed in the fund's financial reports, which are sent to shareholders twice a year. For a free SAI or financial report, call 1-800-544-8888.

Equity Securities may include common stocks, preferred stocks, convertible securities, and warrants. Common stocks, the most familiar type, represent an equity (ownership) interest in a corporation. Although equity securities have a history of long-term growth in value, their prices fluctuate based on changes in a company's financial condition and on overall market and economic conditions. Smaller companies are especially sensitive to these factors.

Restrictions: With respect to 75% of total assets, the fund may not purchase more than 10% of the outstanding voting securities of a single issuer.

Debt Securities. Bonds and other debt instruments are used by issuers to borrow money from investors. The issuer generally pays the investor a fixed, variable, or floating rate of interest, and must repay the amount borrowed at maturity. Some debt securities, such as zero coupon bonds, do not pay current interest, but are sold at a discount from their face values.

Debt securities have varying levels of sensitivity to changes in interest rates and varying degrees of credit quality. In general, bond prices rise when interest rates fall, and fall when interest rates rise. Longer-term bonds and zero coupon bonds are generally more sensitive to interest rate changes.

Lower-quality debt securities (sometimes called "junk bonds") are considered to have speculative characteristics, and involve greater risk of default or price changes due to changes in the issuer's creditworthiness, or they may already be in default. The market prices of these securities may fluctuate more than higher-quality securities and may decline significantly in periods of general or regional economic difficulty.

The following table provides a summary of ratings assigned to debt holdings (not including money market instruments) in the fund's portfolio. These figures are dollar-weighted averages of month-end portfolio holdings during the fiscal year ended July 1997, and are presented as a percentage of total security investments. These percentages are historical and do not necessarily indicate the fund's current or future debt holdings.

Restrictions: Purchase of a debt security is consistent with the fund's debt quality policy if it is rated at or above the stated level by Moody's Investors Service (Moody's) or rated in the equivalent categories by Standard & Poor's (S&P), or is unrated but judged to be of equivalent quality by FMR. The fund currently intends to limit its investments in lower than Baa-quality debt securities to less than 35% of its assets.

Exposure to Foreign Markets.

Foreign securities, foreign currencies, and securities issued by U.S. entities with substantial foreign operations may involve additional risks and considerations. These include risks relating to political or economic conditions in foreign countries, fluctuations in foreign currencies, withholding or other taxes, operational risks, increased regulatory burdens, and the potentially less stringent investor protection and disclosure standards of foreign markets. Additionally, governmental issuers of foreign debt securities may be unwilling to pay interest and repay principal when

Fiscal Year Ended July 1997 Debt Holdings, by Rating

	Moody's Investors Service (as a % of investments)		Standard & Poor's (as a % of investments)	
	Rating	Average of total investments	Rating	Average of total investments
Investment Grade				
Highest quality	Aaa	0.6%	AAA	0.6%
High quality	Aa	0.0%	AA	0.0%
Upper-medium grade	A	0.0%	A	0.0%
Medium grade	Baa	0.0%	BBB	0.0%
Lower Quality				
Moderately speculative	Ba	0.4%	BB	0.3%
Speculative	B	0.1%	B	0.2%
Highly speculative	Caa	0.0%	CCC	0.0%
Poor quality	Ca	0.0%	CC	0.0%
Lowest quality, no interest	C		C	
In default, in arrears	—	0.0%	D	0.0%
		1.1%		1.1%

Refer to the fund's SAI for a more complete discussion of these ratings.

The fund does not necessarily rely on the ratings of Moody's or S&P to determine compliance with its debt quality policy. Securities not rated by Moody's or S&P amounted to 0.1% of the fund's investments. This percentage may include securities rated by other nationally recognized statistical rating organizations, as well as unrated securities. Unrated lower-quality securities amounted to 0.1% of the fund's investments.

For foreign government securities not individually rated by a nationally recognized statistical rating organization, FMR assigns the rating of the sovereign credit of the issuing government.

The Fund in Detail - continued

due and may require that the conditions for payment be renegotiated. All of these factors can make foreign investments, especially those in developing countries, more volatile than U.S. investments.

Asset-Backed Securities include interests in pools of debt securities, commercial or consumer loans, or other receivables. The value of these securities depends on many factors, including changes in interest rates, the availability of information concerning the pool and its structure, the credit quality of the underlying assets, the market's perception of the servicer of the pool, and any credit enhancement provided. In addition, these securities may be subject to prepayment risk.

Mortgage Securities include interests in pools of commercial or residential mortgages, and may include complex instruments such as collateralized mortgage obligations and stripped mortgage-backed securities. Mortgage securities may be issued by agencies or instrumentalities of the U.S. Government or by private entities.

The price of a mortgage security may be significantly affected by changes in interest rates. Some mortgage securities may have a structure that makes their reaction to interest rates and other factors difficult to predict, making their price highly volatile. Also, mortgage securities, especially stripped mortgage-backed securities, are subject to prepayment risk. Securities subject to prepayment risk generally offer less potential for gains during a declining interest rate environment, and similar or

greater potential for loss in a rising interest rate environment.

Repurchase Agreements. In a repurchase agreement, the fund buys a security at one price and simultaneously agrees to sell it back at a higher price. Delays or losses could result if the other party to the agreement defaults or becomes insolvent.

Adjusting Investment Exposure. The fund can use various techniques to increase or decrease its exposure to changing security prices, interest rates, currency exchange rates, commodity prices, or other factors that affect security values. These techniques may involve derivative transactions such as buying and selling options and futures contracts, entering into currency exchange contracts or swap agreements, purchasing indexed securities, and selling securities short.

FMR can use these practices to adjust the risk and return characteristics of the fund's portfolio of investments. If FMR judges market conditions incorrectly or employs a strategy that does not correlate well with the fund's investments, these techniques could result in a loss, regardless of whether the intent was to reduce risk or increase return. These techniques may increase the volatility of the fund and may involve a small investment of cash relative to the magnitude of the risk assumed. In addition, these techniques could result in a loss if the counterparty to the transaction does not perform as promised.

Direct Debt. Loans and other direct debt instruments are interests in amounts owed to another party by a company, government, or other borrower. They have additional risks beyond conventional debt securities because they may entail less legal protection for the fund, or there may be a requirement that the fund supply additional cash to a borrower on demand.

Illiquid and Restricted Securities.

Some investments may be determined by FMR, under the supervision of the Board of Trustees, to be illiquid, which means that they may be difficult to sell promptly at an acceptable price. The sale of some illiquid securities, and some other securities, may be subject to legal restrictions. Difficulty in selling securities may result in a loss or may be costly to the fund.

Restrictions: The fund may not purchase a security if, as a result, more than 10% of its assets would be invested in illiquid securities.

Other Instruments may include securities of closed-end investment companies and real estate-related instruments.

Cash Management.

The fund may invest in money market securities, in repurchase agreements, and in a money market fund available only to funds and accounts managed by FMR or its affiliates, whose goal is to seek a high level of current income while maintaining a stable $1.00 share price. A major change in interest rates or a default on the money market fund's investments could cause its share price to change.

Diversification.

Diversifying a fund's investment portfolio can reduce the risks of investing. This may include limiting the amount of money invested in any one issuer or, on a broader scale, in any one industry.

Restrictions: With respect to 75% of its total assets, the fund may not purchase a security if, as a result, more than 5% would be invested in the securities of any issuer. The fund may not invest more than 25% of its total assets in any one industry. These limitations do not apply to U.S. Government securities.

Borrowing.

The fund may borrow from banks or from other funds advised by FMR, or through reverse repurchase agreements. If the fund borrows money, its share price may be subject to greater fluctuation until the borrowing is paid off. If the fund makes additional investments while borrowings are outstanding, this may be considered a form of leverage.

Restrictions: The fund may borrow only for temporary or emergency purposes, but not in an amount exceeding $33\frac{1}{3}\%$ of its total assets.

Lending

securities to broker-dealers and institutions, including Fidelity Brokerage Services, Inc. (FBSI), an affiliate of FMR, is a means of earning income. This practice could result in a loss or a delay in recovering the fund's securities. The fund may also lend money to other funds advised by FMR.

Restrictions: Loans, in the aggregate, may not exceed $33\frac{1}{3}\%$ of the fund's total assets.

The Fund in Detail - continued

Fundamental Investment Policies and Restrictions

Some of the policies and restrictions discussed on the preceding pages are fundamental, that is, subject to change only by shareholder approval. The following paragraphs restate all those that are fundamental. All policies stated throughout this prospectus, other than those identified in the following paragraphs, can be changed without shareholder approval.

The fund seeks high total return through a combination of current income and capital appreciation.

With respect to 75% of its total assets, the fund may not purchase a security if, as a result, more than 5% would be invested in the securities of any one issuer and may not purchase more than 10% of the outstanding voting securities of a single issuer. These limitations do not apply to U.S. Government securities.

The fund may not invest more than 25% of its total assets in any one industry. This limitation does not apply to U.S. Government securities.

The fund may borrow only for temporary or emergency purposes, but not in an amount exceeding $33\frac{1}{3}$% of its total assets.

Loans, in the aggregate, may not exceed $33\frac{1}{3}$% of the fund's total assets.

Breakdown of Expenses

Like all mutual funds, the fund pays fees related to its daily operations. Expenses paid out of the fund's assets are reflected in its share price or dividends; they are neither billed directly to shareholders nor deducted from shareholder accounts.

The fund pays a **management fee** to FMR for managing its investments and business affairs. FMR in turn pays fees to affiliates who provide assistance with these services. The fund also pays **other expenses,** which are explained on page 17.

FMR may, from time to time, agree to reimburse the fund for management fees and other expenses above a specified limit. FMR retains the ability to be repaid by the fund if expenses fall below the specified limit prior to the end of the fiscal year. Reimbursement arrangements, which may be terminated at any time without notice, can decrease the fund's expenses and boost its performance.

Management Fee

The management fee is calculated and paid to FMR every month. The fee is calculated by adding a group fee rate to an individual fund fee rate, and multiplying the result by the fund's average net assets.

The group fee rate is based on the average net assets of all the mutual funds advised by FMR. This rate cannot rise above 0.52%, and it drops as total assets under management increase.

For July 1997, the group fee rate was 0.2964%. The individual fund fee rate is 0.20%.

The total management fee rate for the fiscal year ended July 31, 1997 was 0.50%.

FMR has sub-advisory agreements with FMR U.K. and FMR Far East. These sub-advisers provide FMR with investment research and advice on issuers based outside the United States. Under the sub-advisory agreements, FMR pays FMR U.K. and FMR Far East fees equal to 110% and 105%, respectively, of the costs of providing these services.

The sub-advisers may also provide investment management services. In return, FMR pays FMR U.K. and FMR Far East a fee equal to 50% of its management fee rate with respect to the fund's investments that the sub-adviser manages on a discretionary basis.

Other Expenses

While the management fee is a significant component of the fund's annual operating costs, the fund has other expenses as well.

The fund contracts with FSC to perform transfer agency, dividend disbursing, shareholder servicing, and accounting functions. These services include processing shareholder transactions, valuing the fund's investments, handling securities loans, and calculating the fund's share price and dividends.

For the fiscal year ended July 1997, the fund paid transfer agency and pricing and bookkeeping fees equal to 0.21% of its average net assets. This amount is before expense reductions, if any.

The fund also pays other expenses, such as legal, audit, and custodian fees; in some instances, proxy solicitation costs; and the compensation of trustees who are not affiliated with Fidelity. A broker-dealer may use a portion of the commissions paid by the fund to reduce that fund's custodian or transfer agent fees.

The fund's portfolio turnover rate for the fiscal year ended July 1997 was 38%. This rate varies from year to year.

 Understanding the Management Fee

The management fee FMR receives is designed to be responsive to changes in FMR's total assets under management. Building this variable into the fee calculation assures shareholders that they will pay a lower rate as FMR's assets under management increase.

Your Account

Doing Business with Fidelity

Fidelity Investments was established in 1946 to manage one of America's first mutual funds. Today, Fidelity is the largest mutual fund company in the country, and is known as an innovative provider of high-quality financial services to individuals and institutions.

In addition to its mutual fund business, the company operates one of America's leading discount brokerage firms, FBSI. Fidelity is also a leader in providing tax-sheltered retirement plans for individuals investing on their own or through their employer.

Fidelity is committed to providing investors with practical information to make investment decisions. Based in Boston, Fidelity provides customers with complete service 24 hours a day, 365 days a year, through a network of telephone service centers around the country.

To reach Fidelity for general information, call these numbers:

• For mutual funds, 1-800-544-8888

• For brokerage, 1-800-544-7272

If you would prefer to speak with a representative in person, Fidelity has over 80 walk-in Investor Centers across the country.

Types of Accounts

You may set up an account directly in the fund or, if you own or intend to purchase individual securities as part of your total investment portfolio, you may consider investing in the fund through a brokerage account.

You may purchase or sell shares of the fund through an investment

professional, including a broker, who may charge you a transaction fee for this service. If you invest through FBSI, another financial institution, or an investment professional, read their program materials for any special provisions, additional service features or fees that may apply to your investment in the fund. Certain features of the fund, such as the minimum initial or subsequent investment amounts, may be modified.

The different ways to set up (register) your account with Fidelity are listed in the table that follows.

The account guidelines that follow may not apply to certain retirement accounts. If you are investing through a retirement account or if your employer offers the fund through a retirement program, you may be subject to additional fees. For more information, please refer to your program materials, contact your employer, or call your retirement benefits number or Fidelity directly, as appropriate.

 Fidelity Facts

Fidelity offers the broadest selection of mutual funds in the world.

• Number of Fidelity mutual funds: over 235

• Assets in Fidelity mutual funds: over $470 billion

• Number of shareholder accounts: over 32 million

• Number of investment analysts and portfolio managers: over 273

Ways to Set Up Your Account

Individual or Joint Tenant
For your general investment needs

Individual accounts are owned by one person. Joint accounts can have two or more owners (tenants).

Retirement
To shelter your retirement savings from taxes

Retirement plans allow individuals to shelter investment income and capital gains from current taxes. In addition, contributions to these accounts may be tax deductible. Retirement accounts require special applications and typically have lower minimums.

- **Individual Retirement Accounts (IRAs)** allow anyone of legal age and under $70\frac{1}{2}$ with earned income to invest up to $2,000 per tax year. Individuals can also invest in a spouse's IRA if the spouse has earned income of less than $250.

- **Rollover IRAs** retain special tax advantages for certain distributions from employer-sponsored retirement plans.

- **Keogh or Corporate Profit Sharing and Money Purchase Pension Plans** allow self-employed individuals or small business owners (and their employees) to make tax-deductible contributions for themselves and any eligible employees up to $30,000 per year.

- **Simplified Employee Pension Plans (SEP-IRAs)** provide small business owners or those with self-employed income (and their eligible employees) with many of the same advantages as a Keogh, but with fewer administrative requirements.

- **SIMPLE IRAs** provide small business owners and those with self-employed income (and their eligible employees) with many of the advantages of a 401(k) plan, but with fewer administrative requirements.

- **403(b) Custodial Accounts** are available to employees of most tax-exempt institutions, including schools, hospitals, and other charitable organizations.

- **401(k) Programs** allow employees of corporations of all sizes to contribute a percentage of their wages on a tax-deferred basis. These accounts need to be established by the trustee of the plan.

Gifts or Transfers to a Minor (UGMA, UTMA)
To invest for a child's education or other future needs

These custodial accounts provide a way to give money to a child and obtain tax benefits. An individual can give up to $10,000 a year per child without paying federal gift tax. Depending on state laws, you can set up a custodial account under the Uniform Gifts to Minors Act (UGMA) or the Uniform Transfers to Minors Act (UTMA).

Trust
For money being invested by a trust

The trust must be established before an account can be opened.

Business or Organization
For investment needs of corporations, associations, partnerships, or other groups

Requires a special application.

Your Account - continued

How to Buy Shares

The fund's share price, called net asset value per share (NAV), is calculated every business day. The fund's shares are sold without a sales charge.

Shares are purchased at the next share price calculated after your investment is received and accepted. Share price is normally calculated at 4 p.m. Eastern time.

If you are new to Fidelity, complete and sign an account application and mail it along with your check. You may also open your account in person or by wire as described on page 21. If there is no application accompanying this prospectus, call 1-800-544-8888.

If you already have money invested in a Fidelity fund, you can:

• Mail in an application with a check, or
• Open your account by exchanging from another Fidelity fund.

If you are investing through a tax-sheltered retirement plan, such as an IRA, for the first time, you will need a special application. Retirement investing also involves its own investment procedures. Call 1-800-544-8888 for more information and a retirement application.

If you buy shares by check or Fidelity Money Line®, and then sell those shares by any method other than by exchange to another Fidelity fund, the payment may be delayed for up to seven business days to ensure that your previous investment has cleared.

Minimum Investments	
To Open an Account	**$2,500**
For Fidelity IRA, Rollover IRA, SEP-IRA and Keogh accounts	$500
To Add to an Account	**$250**
For Fidelity IRA, Rollover IRA, SEP-IRA and Keogh accounts	$250
Through regular investment plans*	$100
Minimum Balance	**$2,000**
For Fidelity IRA, Rollover IRA, SEP-IRA and Keogh accounts	$500

*For more information about regular investment plans, please refer to "Investor Services," page 24.

These minimums may vary for investments through Fidelity Portfolio Advisory Services, a Fidelity College Savings Plan account, or a Fidelity Payroll Deduction Program account in the fund. There is no minimum account balance or initial or subsequent investment minimum for certain retirement accounts funded through salary deduction, or accounts opened with the proceeds of distributions from Fidelity retirement accounts. Refer to the appropriate program materials for details.

	To Open an Account	To Add to an Account
Phone **1-800-544-7777**	• Exchange from another Fidelity fund account with the same registration, including name, address, and tax-payer ID number.	• Exchange from another Fidelity fund account with the same registration, including name, address, and tax-payer ID number. • Use Fidelity Money Line to transfer from your bank account. Call before your first use to verify that this service is in place on your account. Maximum Money Line: up to $100,000.
Mail	• Complete and sign the application. Make your check payable to "Fidelity Growth & Income Portfolio." Mail to the address indicated on the application.	• Make your check payable to "Fidelity Growth & Income Portfolio." Indicate your fund account number on your check and mail to the address printed on your account statement. • Exchange by mail: call 1-800-544-6666 for instructions.
In Person	• Bring your application and check to a Fidelity Investor Center. Call 1-800-544-9797 for the center nearest you.	• Bring your check to a Fidelity Investor Center. Call 1-800-544-9797 for the center nearest you.
Wire	• Call 1-800-544-7777 to set up your account and to arrange a wire transaction. Not available for retirement accounts • Wire within 24 hours to: Bankers Trust Company, Bank Routing #021001033, Account #00163053. Specify the complete name of the fund and include your new account number and your name.	• Not available for retirement accounts. • Wire to: Bankers Trust Company, Bank Routing #021001033, Account #00163053. Specify the complete name of the fund and include your account number and your name.
Automatically	• Not available.	• Use Fidelity Automatic Account Builder. Sign up for this service when opening your account, or call 1-800-544-6666 to add it.

TDD — Service for the Deaf and Hearing-Impaired: 1-800-544-0118

21   **Prospectus**

Your Account - continued

How to Sell Shares

You can arrange to take money out of your fund account at any time by selling (redeeming) some or all of your shares. Your shares will be sold at the next share price calculated after your order is received and accepted. Share price is normally calculated at 4 p.m. Eastern time.

To sell shares in a non-retirement account, you may use any of the methods described on these two pages.

To sell shares in a Fidelity retirement account, your request must be made in writing, except for exchanges to other Fidelity funds, which can be requested by phone or in writing. Call 1-800-544-6666 for a retirement distribution form.

If you are selling some but not all of your shares, leave at least $2,000 worth of shares in the account to keep it open ($500 for retirement accounts).

To sell shares by bank wire or Fidelity Money Line, you will need to sign up for these services in advance.

Certain requests must include a signature guarantee. It is designed to protect you and Fidelity from fraud. Your request must be made in writing and include a signature guarantee if any of the following situations apply:

• You wish to redeem more than $100,000 worth of shares,
• Your account registration has changed within the last 30 days,
• The check is being mailed to a different address than the one on your account (record address),
• The check is being made payable to someone other than the account owner, or
• The redemption proceeds are being transferred to a Fidelity account with a different registration.

You should be able to obtain a signature guarantee from a bank, broker (including Fidelity Investor Centers), dealer, credit union (if authorized under state law), securities exchange or association, clearing agency, or savings association. A notary public cannot provide a signature guarantee.

Selling Shares in Writing

Write a "letter of instruction" with:

• Your name,
• The fund's name,
• Your fund account number,
• The dollar amount or number of shares to be redeemed, and
• Any other applicable requirements listed in the table that follows.

Unless otherwise instructed, Fidelity will send a check to the record address. Deliver your letter to a Fidelity Investor Center, or mail it to:

Fidelity Investments
P.O. Box 660602
Dallas, TX 75266-0602

	Account Type	Special Requirements
Phone **1-800-544-7777**	All account types except retirement	• Maximum check request: $100,000. • For Money Line transfers to your bank account; minimum: $10; maximum: up to $100,000.
	All account types	• You may exchange to other Fidelity funds if both accounts are registered with the same name(s), address, and taxpayer ID number.
Mail or in Person	Individual, Joint Tenant, Sole Proprietorship, UGMA, UTMA	• The letter of instruction must be signed by all persons required to sign for transactions, exactly as their names appear on the account.
	Retirement account	• The account owner should complete a retirement distribution form. Call 1-800-544-6666 to request one.
	Trust	• The trustee must sign the letter indicating capacity as trustee. If the trustee's name is not in the account registration, provide a copy of the trust document certified within the last 60 days.
	Business or Organization	• At least one person authorized by corporate resolution to act on the account must sign the letter. • Include a corporate resolution with corporate seal or a signature guarantee.
	Executor, Administrator, Conservator, Guardian	• Call 1-800-544-6666 for instructions.
Wire	All account types except retirement	• You must sign up for the wire feature before using it. To verify that it is in place, call 1-800-544-6666. Minimum wire: $5,000. • Your wire redemption request must be received and accepted by Fidelity before 4 p.m. Eastern time for money to be wired on the next business day.

TDD — Service for the Deaf and Hearing-Impaired: 1-800-544-0118

Your Account - continued

Investor Services

Fidelity provides a variety of services to help you manage your account.

Information Services

Fidelity's telephone representatives are available 24 hours a day, 365 days a year. Whenever you call, you can speak with someone equipped to provide the information or service you need.

Statements and reports that Fidelity sends to you include the following:

• Confirmation statements (after every transaction, except reinvestments, that affects your account balance or your account registration)
• Account statements (quarterly)
• Financial reports (every six months)

To reduce expenses, only one copy of most financial reports and prospectuses will be mailed to your household, even if you have more than one account in the fund. Call 1-800-544-6666 if you need copies of financial reports, prospectuses, or historical account information.

 24-Hour Service

Account Assistance
1-800-544-6666

Account Transactions
1-800-544-7777

Product Information
1-800-544-8888

Retirement Account Assistance
1-800-544-4774

TouchTone Xpress^{SM} ◄☎►
1-800-544-5555

◄☎► *Automated service*

Transaction Services

Exchange privilege. You may sell your fund shares and buy shares of other Fidelity funds by telephone or in writing.

Note that exchanges out of the fund are limited to four per calendar year, and that they may have tax consequences for you. For details on policies and restrictions governing exchanges, including circumstances under which a shareholder's exchange privilege may be suspended or revoked, see page 30.

Systematic withdrawal plans let you set up periodic redemptions from your account.

Fidelity Money Line® enables you to transfer money by phone between your bank account and your fund account. Most transfers are complete within three business days of your call.

Regular Investment Plans

One easy way to pursue your financial goals is to invest money regularly. Fidelity offers convenient services that let you transfer money into your fund account, or between fund accounts, automatically. While regular investment plans do not guarantee a profit and will not protect you against loss in a declining market, they can be an excellent way to invest for retirement, a home, educational expenses, and other long-term financial goals. Certain restrictions apply for retirement accounts. Call 1-800-544-6666 for more information.

Regular Investment Plans

Fidelity Automatic Account Builder[SM]
To move money from your bank account to a Fidelity fund

Minimum	Frequency	Setting up or changing
$100	Monthly or quarterly	• For a new account, complete the appropriate section on the fund application.
		• For existing accounts, call 1-800-544-6666 for an application.
		• To change the amount or frequency of your investment, call 1-800-544-6666 at least three business days prior to your next scheduled investment date.

Direct Deposit
To send all or a portion of your paycheck or government check to a Fidelity fund[A]

Minimum	Frequency	Setting up or changing
$100	Every pay period	• Check the appropriate box on the fund application, or call 1-800-544-6666 for an authorization form.
		• Changes require a new authorization form.

Fidelity Automatic Exchange Service
To move money from a Fidelity money market fund to another Fidelity fund

Minimum	Frequency	Setting up or changing
$100	Monthly, bimonthly, quarterly, or annually	• To establish, call 1-800-544-6666 after both accounts are opened.
		• To change the amount or frequency of your investment, call 1-800-544-6666.

[A] *Because its share price fluctuates, the fund may not be an appropriate choice for direct deposit of your entire check.*

Shareholder and Account Policies

Dividends, Capital Gains, and Taxes

The fund distributes substantially all of its net income and capital gains to shareholders each year. Normally, dividends are distributed in March, June, September, and December. Capital gains are distributed in September and December.

Distribution Options

When you open an account, specify on your application how you want to receive your distributions. If the option you prefer is not listed on the application, call 1-800-544-6666 for instructions. The fund offers four options:

1. Reinvestment Option. Your dividend and capital gain distributions will be automatically reinvested in additional shares of the fund. If you do not indicate a choice on your application, you will be assigned this option.

2. Income-Earned Option. Your capital gain distributions will be automatically reinvested, but you will be sent a check for each dividend distribution.

3. Cash Option. You will be sent a check for your dividend and capital gain distributions.

4. Directed Dividends® Option. Your dividend and capital gain distributions will be automatically invested in another identically registered Fidelity fund.

For retirement accounts, all distributions are automatically reinvested. When you are over $59\frac{1}{2}$ years old, you can receive distributions in cash.

When the fund deducts a distribution from its NAV, the reinvestment price is the fund's NAV at the close of business that day. Cash distribution checks will be mailed within seven days.

Taxes

As with any investment, you should consider how your investment in the fund will be taxed. If your account is not a tax-deferred retirement account, you should be aware of these tax implications.

Taxes on distributions. Distributions are subject to federal income tax, and may also be subject to state or local taxes. If you live outside the United States, your distributions could also be taxed by the country in which you reside. Your distributions are taxable when they are paid, whether you take

---

 Understanding Distributions

As a fund shareholder, you are entitled to your share of the fund's net income and gains on its investments. The fund passes its earnings along to its investors as **distributions.**

The fund earns dividends from stocks and interest from bond, money market, and other investments. These are passed along as **dividend distributions.** The fund realizes capital gains whenever it sells securities for a higher price than it paid for them. These are passed along as **capital gain distributions.**

---

them in cash or reinvest them. However, distributions declared in December and paid in January are taxable as if they were paid on December 31.

For federal tax purposes, the fund's income and short-term capital gain distributions are taxed as dividends; long-term capital gain distributions are taxed as long-term capital gains. Every January, Fidelity will send you and the IRS a statement showing the taxable distributions paid to you in the previous year.

Taxes on transactions. Your redemptions – including exchanges to other Fidelity funds – are subject to capital gains tax. A capital gain or loss is the difference between the cost of your shares and the price you receive when you sell them.

Whenever you sell shares of the fund, Fidelity will send you a confirmation statement showing how many shares you sold and at what price. You will also receive a consolidated transaction statement every January. However, it is up to you or your tax preparer to determine whether this sale resulted in a capital gain and, if so, the amount of tax to be paid. Be sure to keep your regular account statements; the information they contain will be essential in calculating the amount of your capital gains.

"Buying a dividend." If you buy shares when the fund has realized but not yet distributed income or capital gains, you will pay the full price for the shares and then receive a portion of the price back in the form of a taxable distribution.

Effect of foreign taxes. Foreign governments may impose taxes on the fund and its investments and these taxes generally will reduce the fund's distributions. However, an offsetting tax credit or deduction may be available to you. If so, your tax statement will show more taxable income or capital gains than were actually distributed by the fund, but will also show the amount of the available offsetting credit or deduction.

There are tax requirements that all funds must follow in order to avoid federal taxation. In its effort to adhere to these requirements, the fund may have to limit its investment activity in some types of instruments.

Transaction Details

The fund is open for business each day the New York Stock Exchange (NYSE) is open. Fidelity normally calculates the fund's NAV as of the close of business of the NYSE, normally 4:00 p.m. Eastern time.

The fund's NAV is the value of a single share. The NAV is computed by adding the value of the fund's investments, cash, and other assets, subtracting its liabilities, and then dividing the result by the number of shares outstanding.

The fund's assets are valued primarily on the basis of market quotations. Short-term securities with remaining maturities of sixty days or less for which quotations are not readily available are valued on the basis of amortized cost. This method minimizes the effect of changes in a security's market value. Foreign securities are valued on the

Shareholder and Account Policies - continued

basis of quotations from the primary market in which they are traded, and are translated from the local currency into U.S. dollars using current exchange rates. In addition, if quotations are not readily available, or if the values have been materially affected by events occurring after the closing of a foreign market, assets may be valued by another method that the Board of Trustees believes accurately reflects fair value.

The fund's offering price (price to buy one share) is its NAV. The fund's **redemption price** (price to sell one share) is its NAV.

When you sign your account application, you will be asked to certify that your social security or taxpayer identification number is correct and that you are not subject to 31% backup withholding for failing to report income to the IRS. If you violate IRS regulations, the IRS can require the fund to withhold 31% of your taxable distributions and redemptions.

You may initiate many transactions by telephone. Fidelity may only be liable for losses resulting from unauthorized transactions if it does not follow reasonable procedures designed to verify the identity of the caller. Fidelity will request personalized security codes or other information, and may also record calls. You should verify the accuracy of your confirmation statements immediately after you receive them. If you do not want the ability to redeem and exchange by telephone, call Fidelity for instructions.

If you are unable to reach Fidelity by phone (for example, during periods of unusual market activity), consider placing your order by mail or by visiting a Fidelity Investor Center.

The fund reserves the right to suspend the offering of shares for a period of time. The fund also reserves the right to reject any specific purchase order, including certain purchases by exchange. See "Exchange Restrictions" on page 30. Purchase orders may be refused if, in FMR's opinion, they would disrupt management of the fund.

When you place an order to buy shares, your order will be processed at the next offering price calculated after your order is received and accepted. Note the following:

• All of your purchases must be made in U.S. dollars and checks must be drawn on U.S. banks.
• Fidelity does not accept cash.
• When making a purchase with more than one check, each check must have a value of at least $50.
• The fund reserves the right to limit the number of checks processed at one time.
• If your check does not clear, your purchase will be cancelled and you could be liable for any losses or fees the fund or its transfer agent has incurred.

To avoid the collection period associated with check and Money Line purchases, consider buying shares by bank wire, U.S. Postal money order, U.S. Treasury check, Federal Reserve check, or direct deposit instead.

Certain financial institutions that have entered into sales agreements with FDC may enter confirmed purchase orders on behalf of customers by phone, with payment to follow no later than the time when the fund is priced on the following business day. If payment is not received by that time, the financial institution could be held liable for resulting fees or losses.

When you place an order to sell shares, your shares will be sold at the next NAV calculated after your request is received and accepted. Note the following:

• Normally, redemption proceeds will be mailed to you on the next business day, but if making immediate payment could adversely affect the fund, it may take up to seven days to pay you.
• Fidelity Money Line redemptions generally will be credited to your bank account on the second or third business day after your phone call.
• The fund may hold payment on redemptions until it is reasonably satisfied that investments made by check or Fidelity Money Line have been collected, which can take up to seven business days.
• Redemptions may be suspended or payment dates postponed when the NYSE is closed (other than weekends or holidays), when trading on the NYSE is restricted, or as permitted by the SEC.

Fidelity reserves the right to deduct an annual maintenance fee of $12.00 from accounts with a value of less than $2,500, subject to an annual maximum charge of $24.00 per

shareholder. It is expected that accounts will be valued on the second Friday in November of each year. Accounts opened after September 30 will not be subject to the fee for that year. The fee, which is payable to the transfer agent, is designed to offset in part the relatively higher costs of servicing smaller accounts. This fee will not be deducted from Fidelity brokerage accounts, retirement accounts (except non-prototype retirement accounts), accounts using regular investment plans, or if total assets with Fidelity exceed $30,000. Eligibility for the $30,000 waiver is determined by aggregating Fidelity accounts maintained by FSC or FBSI which are registered under the same social security number or which list the same social security number for the custodian of a Uniform Gifts/Transfers to Minors Act account.

If your account balance falls below $2,000, you will be given 30 days' notice to reestablish the minimum balance. If you do not increase your balance, Fidelity reserves the right to close your account and send the proceeds to you. Your shares will be redeemed at the NAV on the day your account is closed.

Fidelity may charge a fee for special services, such as providing historical account documents, that are beyond the normal scope of its services.

FDC may, at its own expense, provide promotional incentives to qualified recipients who support the sale of shares of the fund without reimbursement from the fund. Qualified recipients are securities dealers who have sold fund shares

Shareholder and Account Policies - continued

or others, including banks and other financial institutions, under special arrangements in connection with FDC's sales activities. In some instances, these incentives may be offered only to certain institutions whose representatives provide services in connection with the sale or expected sale of significant amounts of shares.

Exchange Restrictions

As a shareholder, you have the privilege of exchanging shares of the fund for shares of other Fidelity funds. However, you should note the following:

• The fund you are exchanging into must be available for sale in your state.
• You may only exchange between accounts that are registered in the same name, address, and taxpayer identification number.
• Before exchanging into a fund, read its prospectus.
• If you exchange into a fund with a sales charge, you pay the percentage-point difference between that fund's sales charge and any sales charge you have previously paid in connection with the shares you are exchanging. For example, if you had already paid a sales charge of 2% on your shares and you exchange them into a fund with a 3% sales charge, you would pay an additional 1% sales charge.
• Exchanges may have tax consequences for you.
• Because excessive trading can hurt fund performance and shareholders, the fund reserves the right to temporarily or permanently terminate the exchange privilege of any investor who

makes more than four exchanges out of the fund per calendar year. Accounts under common ownership or control, including accounts with the same taxpayer identification number, will be counted together for purposes of the four exchange limit.
• The exchange limit may be modified for accounts in certain institutional retirement plans to conform to plan exchange limits and Department of Labor regulations. See your plan materials for further information.
• The fund reserves the right to refuse exchange purchases by any person or group if, in FMR's judgment, the fund would be unable to invest the money effectively in accordance with its investment objective and policies, or would otherwise potentially be adversely affected.
• Your exchanges may be restricted or refused if the fund receives or anticipates simultaneous orders affecting significant portions of the fund's assets. In particular, a pattern of exchanges that coincides with a "market timing" strategy may be disruptive to the fund.

Although the fund will attempt to give you prior notice whenever it is reasonably able to do so, it may impose these restrictions at any time. The fund reserves the right to terminate or modify the exchange privilege in the future.

Other funds may have different exchange restrictions, and may impose fees of up to 1.00% on purchases, administrative fees of up to $7.50, and redemption fees of up to 1.50% on exchanges. Check each fund's prospectus for details.

II *Portfolio Management and Equity Trading*

4 Portfolio Management of Bonds

Introduction

This is the first of three chapters on portfolio management. This chapter will focus on bonds and bond funds; the next chapter will focus on stocks and stock funds; and the final chapter in the trilogy will discuss brokerage transactions for funds.

Bonds represent borrowings by companies or governmental institutions needing money. These monies can be supplied by banks through loans or by securities underwriters through bonds. A borrower will consider the relative costs, repayment dates, and other factors in deciding whether to take out a loan or issue a bond. In both cases, the monies being provided to the borrower are directly or indirectly being supplied by savers. If a borrower issues bonds, they will be bought by individuals or by financial intermediaries such as mutual funds that have gathered monies from savers. If a borrower takes out a bank loan, the loan will be funded by bank deposits that have been gathered from savers. Savers will consider the relative risks and returns of buying bonds directly, purchasing shares in a bond fund, or making deposits in a bank.

A bond represents a contractual obligation by the issuing company, as opposed to stocks, which represent equity ownership in the company. Interest and principal repayments are specified for each bond at issuance, so that cash flows are relatively certain (unless the issuer declares bankruptcy). In contrast, the periodic cash flow from stocks (i.e., dividends) is subject to a discretionary vote of the company's directors, and the company's obligations to pay its bonds are senior to any claims of its stockholders. For these reasons, bonds are generally considered less risky than stocks.

Bond funds provide investors with a convenient way to buy a diversified pool of bonds with a relatively predictable income stream. Most bond funds concentrate on a particular segment of the bond market (e.g., government or corporate) and a specified average maturity (e.g., short-term or long-term). Municipal bond funds invest in bonds issued by state and local governments, and pay their shareholders income that is exempt from federal tax (and sometimes state taxes as well).

A portfolio manager (PM) selects the specific bonds for each bond fund. A PM's objective may be to replicate the return of an index representing the relevant segment of the bond market—for example, intermediate-term federal government bonds. This approach is called *passive management* or *indexing*. Most PMs are "active" managers in that they attempt to beat the return of the relevant index or competitor bond funds with similar investment objectives. As explained below, active PMs try to outperform by selecting bonds on the basis of credit analysis, interest rate timing, or other strategies.

This chapter will outline the major sectors of the bond market, the basic characteristics of bonds, and the main measures used to analyze bonds. It will then describe the investment objectives and benchmarks of bond funds, three of the key investment strategies employed by bond PMs, and the roles of the various professionals involved in bond fund management. The chapter ends with a case study that puts you in the place of a PM of a bond fund faced with a challenging set of decisions.

Major Sectors of the Bond Market

There are five major sectors of the bond market: governments, mortgage backed securities, corporates, municipals, and foreign governments. Since U.S. mutual fund managers primarily focus on dollar-denominated bonds, we will concentrate here on the size and composition of the U.S. bond market (see table 4.0.1). The largest sector of the bond market consists of bonds issued by the U.S. government, which borrows to finance its ongoing operations. In recent years, large deficits have resulted in Treasury issuance of $150 billion to $300 billion per year. In spite of its huge indebtedness, obligations of the U.S. Treasury are thought to be among the most secure investments in the world. This is because the United States is a large and wealthy country and because U.S. dollars are widely accepted as a base currency around the world. The Treasury issues bonds on a monthly and quarterly basis, and currently has about $2.7 trillion in outstanding debt. (Federal agencies have also issued about $0.9 trillion in outstanding debt.)

Mortgage backed securities (MBS) make up the next largest sector. MBS are packages of home mortgage loans that are combined and structured to suit the needs and preferences

Table 4.0.1
U.S. dollar bonds outstanding at year-end 1996 (Nominal value; U.S. dollars in billions)

U.S. Treasury securities	2,682.3	28%
U.S. agency mortgage pass-throughs[a]	1,711.0	18%
Other U.S. agency securities[a]	923.5	10%
Non-agency mortgage securities[b]	346.9	4%
Municipals	1,049.6	11%
Corporates[c]	1,910.0	20%
Foreign bonds (Yankees)[d]	175.9	2%
Eurodollar bonds[d,e]	784.3	8%
Total publicly issued U.S. bonds	9,583.4	100%

a. Includes budgeted and sponsored Federal agencies
b. Consists of non-Government agency pass-throughs and collateralized mortgage obligations (CMOs); Includes single-family, residential, multi-family and commercial mortgages.
c. Includes straight, convertible and floating-rate debt, tax-exempt corporate bonds, medium-term notes (MTNs), and asset-backed securities.
d. Includes straight, convertible and floating-rate debt.
e. Includes U.S. dollar-denominated bonds issued in Japan.
Source: Salomon Brothers "How Big Is the World Bond Market" 1997 Update

of investors. The most common type of MBS is known as a *pass-through* security, so named because all principal and interest payments from the mortgages of which they are composed "pass through" to bond holders in a prespecified manner. The largest issuers of MBS are U.S. government-sponsored entities commonly known as Fannie Mae (FNMA), Ginnie Mae (GNMA), and Freddie Mac (FHLMC). Because home mortgage loans can be prepaid by homeowners at any time, MBS are also highly susceptible to early prepayment (e.g., the risk of receiving principal payments earlier than expected), thus making it difficult to project exact maturity dates. The size of the MBS market is currently about $2.1 trillion.

Corporate bonds are issued by large corporations. Smaller corporations generally fund their operations with bank loans. Junk bonds are the "high yielding" subset of the corporate market for corporations with poorer credit. The size of the corporate bond market is roughly $1.9 trillion at present.

Municipal bonds are issued by states and local municipalities in the United States. The proceeds of these bonds are generally used to finance the construction of capital projects such as hospitals, highways, and schools. Periodic interest payments and coupon income from municipal bonds are exempt from income taxes. This tax exemption makes municipal bonds attractive to individuals in the highest tax brackets. The size of the municipal market is roughly $1.0 trillion at present.

Foreign government bonds include those issued by large industrialized nations such as Germany and Japan and smaller "emerging markets" such as Argentina and Thailand. Foreign governments currently have about $6.0 trillion in outstanding bonds. Foreign companies currently have about $1.0 trillion in outstanding bonds.[1]

Basic Characteristics of Bonds

Bonds have four key characteristics, set at the time of issuance, which can be ascertained from the face of the bond and/or the underlying bond documents:

Par value (or face value) is the principal amount that investors will be paid when the bond comes due. For instance, if an investor owned $10,000 par value of a bond, that investor would be entitled to receive $10,000 when the bond matured.

Coupon is the rate of interest the bond will pay, expressed as an annual percentage of the par value. The term derives from actual coupons that bond owners would periodically clip from a bond certificate and exchange for payment. For instance, a bond might bear a 6% coupon; if the investor held $10,000 par value, he or she would receive $600 per year in coupon payments.

Maturity is the date the bond comes due; the issuer is required to pay investors their principal on the maturity date. For instance, a bond with ten years to maturity from 1/1/1998 would mature on 1/1/2008. Most bonds mature within 30 years of their issuance date, although bonds have been issued with up to a 100-year maturity (a century bond).

Call provisions written into the bond contract are stipulations that allow the issuer to redeem (or "call") the bond before the final maturity. Issuers often exercise call options in order to refinance their debt at lower interest rates. Treasury bonds are typically issued with no call options; they will stay outstanding until maturity. However, many corporate and municipal bonds, as well as all MBS, have the possibility of early retirement.

Elements of Bond Analysis

In analyzing bonds, investors can use the following six mathematical calculations to compare the return and/or risk characteristics of different bonds over time:

Current yield is found by dividing the annual coupon interest by the current market price. Although current yield is a measure of return, it ignores other sources of return that will affect the total yield of a bond, such as interest earned on interest and the gain or loss experienced over the purchase price of the bond at maturity.

Yield to maturity (YTM) is the annual rate of return an investor would realize if he or she bought a bond at a particular price, received all the coupon payments, reinvested the coupons *at this same YTM rate*, and received the principal at maturity. YTM is also known as the bond's internal rate of return (IRR). The YTM calculation allows investors to compare bonds with different coupons, maturities, and prices. Bonds are typically quoted for trading purposes using this measure.

Price is the amount that an investor pays for a bond, expressed as a percentage of par value. Thus, a price of 97.5 for a $10,000 par value bond means that the investor pays $9,750 (97.5% of $10,000) for the bond. Generally, the YTM of a bond is determined first, and the price of the bond is then calculated to produce that YTM. The formula equating price and yield for a bond paying annual coupons for *n* years is:

$$\text{Price} = \frac{Coupon_1}{(1+\text{YTM})} + \frac{Coupon_2}{(1+\text{YTM})^2} \ldots + \frac{Coupon_n + Principal}{(1+\text{YTM})^n}$$

Note: Since YTM is in the denominator of the fraction, the price and yield of a bond will move in opposite directions—if the yield rises, the price will fall; and if the price rises, the yield will fall. This inverse relationship is important in bond portfolio management. For example, no one will pay full price for a bond with a 5% coupon rate when other similar bonds pay 8%—the 5% bond will sell at a discount from par, or less than 100 cents on the dollar. The exact price would be worked out from the formula above; the bond in the example would sell for a price that produces a YTM of 8%.

The **yield curve** is a graph showing yields for bonds of various maturities, typically using a benchmark group of bonds, such as U.S. Treasuries. In general, longer maturities offer higher yields, so the yield curve is upward sloping. It is upward sloping because longer maturities typically carry more risk of inflation or other adverse developments. A recent example of a yield curve is shown in figure 4.0.1.

A **yield spread** is the yield of a particular bond minus the yield of a benchmark yield curve at the bond's maturity. For instance, a ten-year bond that had a yield of 6.75% on January 6, 1997, corresponds to the ten-year U.S. Treasury yielding 6.51%, and would have a yield spread of 0.24% (check that on the yield curve in figure 4.0.1). In general, a yield spread is compensation for risk—it is a premium the bond pays to induce investors to take risk.

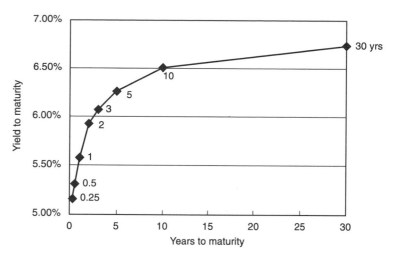

Figure 4.0.1   U.S. Treasury yield curve, 1/6/97

Duration is the percentage a bond's price will change if its yield is changed by 1% (100 basis points or 100 bp). For instance, if a bond has a duration of 7, and its yield rises from 5% to 6%, we would expect the price to drop (remember, price and yield move in opposite directions) by 7% (duration multiplied by change in yield). Duration can be thought of as the average time it takes for an investor to receive principal and interest payments on a bond, weighted by the present value of these payments. The most important factor in determining a bond's duration is its maturity; longer maturities cause longer durations. But a bond's duration will be shorter than its maturity if the investor receives interest payments before the bond matures. In today's Treasury market (as of October 1997), five-year maturities have durations of about 4.2, ten-year maturities have durations of about 7.2, and thirty-year maturities have durations of about 13.1.

Investment Objectives and Benchmarks

In selecting bonds for any bond fund, the PM must follow the fund's investment objective as stated in its prospectus. The Securities and Exchange Commission (SEC) currently requires a fund to invest at least 65% of its assets according to its name, and the SEC will soon increase the 65% to 80%. For example, at least 65% (going to 80%) of the California Municipal Bond Fund must be invested in bonds issued by California municipalities.

The key division for bond funds is between taxable and tax-exempt bond funds. In the taxable area, bond funds may invest primarily in high-grade corporate bonds, junk bonds (below investment grade), asset-backed bonds (e.g., MBS), foreign bonds, or federal government bonds. Interest derived from federal government bonds is generally subject to federal, but not state, income tax. In the tax-exempt area, bond funds are invested in municipal bonds from jurisdictions across the nation or within a specific state. The income derived from national tax-exempt bond funds is not subject to federal income tax, but most of the income is likely to be subject to state income tax. The income derived from state tax-exempt bond funds is "double-tax free"—subject to neither federal nor state income taxes for residents of that state.

Consistent with the bond fund's investment objective, the active PM selects bonds in an effort to beat the return of the market—defined in terms of a market index or a competitive universe. A market index is a hypothetical portfolio of bonds designed to represent a segment of the bond market. The index is created and maintained by an independent provider (two of the largest providers of bond indices are Lehman Brothers and Salomon Smith Barney). The providers price each bond in the market index periodically and calculate many statistics for the index, including its average duration, yield, and total return. A PM can use these indices to understand what constitutes a neutral position in line with the relevant segment of the bond market. Then the PM can choose to buy more or less of a particular bond than it makes up proportionately of the index.

A competitive universe is a set of bond funds with similar investment objectives. For example, all of the short-term U.S. government bond funds would constitute a competitive universe. The competitive universe is created and maintained by an independent measuring firm such as Lipper Analytical Services, Inc. On a monthly, quarterly, and yearly basis, these firms rank all funds in the competitive universe according to their total returns. The first quartile represents the best performing funds of the competitive universe, while the fourth quartile represents the worst performing funds.

Instead of trying to outperform an index or competitive universe, a relatively small number of bond funds aim to equal the return of a particular market segment. To achieve that objective, the PM would buy bonds (or a representative sample of such bonds) in the same proportion as they constitute of the relevant index. These bond funds are known as *index funds* and their management is called *passive*.

Three Types of Investment Strategies

In this chapter we will focus on the active PM for bond funds. The active PM seeks to beat the relevant index or competitive universe by employing one or more strategies including duration management, credit selection, and prepayment prediction.

Duration management is also known as *market timing*. This strategy involves altering the average duration of the bonds in a fund depending on the PM's outlook for interest rates. The general level of interest rates fluctuates over time, depending on such macroeconomic factors as inflation, economic growth, and the Federal Reserve's monetary policy. If a PM is expecting yields to fall, he or she would buy bonds with longer durations and sell bonds with shorter durations. The PM would need to do this until the average duration in the fund was longer than the market's average duration. Then, if yields fell as expected, the portfolio would rise in price more than average—in other words, it would beat the market. Conversely, if the PM expected yields to rise, the PM would shorten up the fund's average duration.

Duration management is a powerful performance tool. If a PM really can predict the course of interest rates, the fund will surely beat the market. Unfortunately, predicting the direction of interest rates is very difficult. Predicting macroeconomic variables amounts to predicting what vast numbers of people, companies, and governments will do—and that is never easy. In addition, the market quickly incorporates into bond yields any new information bearing upon interest rates. This market efficiency makes it hard for any one fund manager to predict interest rates correctly and consistently.

Another important strategy is known as *credit selection*: choosing a bond in anticipation of changes in its credit rating. A credit rating tells investors about an issuer's ability to pay interest and principal (that is, the risk of default). A bond's credit rating is an important factor in determining its yield spread, since the rating measures an important risk associated with holding such a bond. Credit ratings are assigned to bonds by independent agencies such as Moody's Investors Service and Standard & Poor's Corporation. From strongest to weakest, Standard & Poor's ratings run AAA, AA, A, BBB, BB, B, CCC, CC, C, and D. Bonds rated BB or below are not considered investment grade. The U.S. government has a credit rating of AAA, while junk bonds have ratings of BB or lower.

Credit selection involves overweighting the bonds of certain issuers and underweighting the bonds of others. If the PM expects an issuer's credit ratings to be upgraded, he or she is likely to expect that the yield spread of its bonds would also tighten. A tightening yield spread causes a bond's price to rise relative to the market, and hence to provide the bond with a superior return. Conversely, a widening yield spread will cause a bond to lag behind the market. While credit selection is an important performance tool, it is not as powerful as duration management. A fund may own many bonds poised for upgrade, but it would take quite a few to equal the impact of one correct interest rate forecast. On the other hand, a change in credit quality is more amenable to analysis than the course of interest rates, since credit judgments require understanding of only one company at a time.

A third strategy is *prepayment prediction*. As noted above, call provisions in many bonds allow the issuer to repay them before maturity. This is a serious potential problem for holders of bonds, who are likely to have high yielding bonds bought back from them if interest rates drop. Thus, one of the PM's strategies may be to hold callable bonds with low prepayment risk relative to their yield spread. The most important application of this strategy involves MBS.

MBS are highly vulnerable to early retirement through calls because the home mortgages underlying MBS will usually be refinanced when interest rates fall. Bond analysts study the patterns of these prepayments and create models that predict how quickly MBS with different coupons will be retired. By comparing the output of such models with the yield spreads available in the market, the PM tries to forecast which MBS will do well and which will do poorly, and adjust the fund's holdings accordingly. Although forecasting the speed of prepayments for MBS is a less powerful performance tool than duration management, it is more achievable. Prepayment prediction involves analyzing fewer aspects of the behavior of fewer people than predicting interest rates.

All three of these strategies can be used separately to beat the market, or they can be used in combination. There are many other strategies as well. In each case, the PM must not only choose which bonds to acquire, but also how much risk to take. In the case of duration management, that means deciding how much of a difference in duration the portfolio should have relative to the overall market. In the case of credit selection, this means deciding how large a percentage of the portfolio a particular company or municipality should represent. In the case of prepayment forecasting, this means deciding how much exposure to a particular type of call provision a portfolio should have.

Roles of Investment Professionals

There are four main categories of bond fund professionals: portfolio managers, credit analysts, quantitative analysts, and traders.

The **Portfolio Manager** makes buy and sell decisions for one fund or a group of similar funds. As discussed above, the PM must keep the fund invested within its written guidelines. In addition to looking for bonds that will outperform the market, the PM manages the aggregate risk exposure of the fund including the construction of an adequately diversified portfolio. The PM must also invest new cash in times of shareholder purchases and sell bonds to raise cash for shareholder redemptions. Therefore, the PM must monitor the liquidity of the fund's holdings and its cash position.

The **Credit Analyst** evaluates the security of the cash flows that will support the payments of interest and principal of the bond, for the purpose of predicting the credit ratings and default risk of particular issuers. In principle, public credit ratings should incorporate all available information about an issuer. In practice, the rating agencies have so many issuers to follow that they cannot keep up. Thus, the lags between changes in issuers' credit quality and changes in their public credit ratings present opportunities. The questions asked by a credit analyst are detailed in the readings. These questions explore a bond issuer's historic and projected financial performance, the current status of its balance sheet, the competitive and regulatory environment, the potential for event risk, and the quality of management. These questions are approached by studying financial statements, by talking with management, customers, and competitors as well as suppliers, by touring facilities, by reading trade journals, by attending conferences, and by reading Wall Street research. On the basis of information from many sources, a credit analyst looks for bonds whose risk premiums (yield spread) do not reflect his or her view of their true risks. A successful credit analyst is one who can predict changes in credit ratings and yield spreads ahead of the rest of the market.

The **Quantitative Analyst** researches the structural aspects of bonds, such as valuing yield spreads, estimating duration, and modeling the prepayment behavior of MBS. He or she also searches for market inefficiencies and tries to quantify the risks and expected rewards associated with portfolio strategies. Quantitative analysts apply sophisticated mathematical modeling techniques to large sets of historical data. These data include not only bond prices and yields, but also macroeconomic and demographic variables. The quantitative analyst advises the PM about the risks and prospective returns of different types of bonds.

The **Trader** is the primary contact with the Wall Street broker-dealers. The trader executes trades for funds—often specializing in a particular sector of the market. As the execution specialist, the trader makes important decisions about which dealers to trade with, how to obtain the highest prices possible for sales, and how to obtain the lowest possible prices for new purchases. The trader coordinates his or her activities closely with the PMs and contributes important market information to investment discussions. At some mutual fund complexes, the PM doubles as the trader.

The PM, credit analyst, quantitative analyst, and trader work together as a team. Each has specialized skills and access to particular information. They share their perspectives and information and collaborate in the management of the bond funds. Their goal as a team is to deliver the best return possible while keeping the fund's risk within shareholders' expectations.

Questions

In reviewing the materials in this chapter, please keep in mind the following questions:

1. What advantages and disadvantages do bonds offer investors relative to stocks? What type of investors are likely to be interested in bond funds versus stock funds?
2. Why would an investor put money in a bond fund instead of a money market fund or bank deposit?
3. What are the advantages and disadvantages of owning a bond fund vs. individual U.S. Treasury bonds? Is the answer different for individual municipal bonds or high-yield bonds?
4. Why does the yield curve normally slope upward? In what circumstances would the yield curve slope downward?
5. If a bond with a duration of 3.0 experienced a widening of its yield spread from 0.40% to 0.60% (while the benchmark yield remained constant), by how much would its price change?
6. If a company's credit rating is upgraded, what will be the impact on the yield spread and price of the company's bonds? Why?
7. Does a bond with a higher coupon rate have higher risk? Does a bond with a higher yield to maturity (YTM) have higher risk?
8. Why do investment managers of bond funds employ credit analysts when there are public ratings on so many bonds issued by the rating agencies?
9. Why should a portfolio manager monitor the liquidity of a bond fund's holdings? What percentage of a bond fund should be held in cash?
10. Which bond fund has higher risk: a fund with an average maturity of 10 years, or a fund with an average duration of 9 years?

Note

1. All bond market size estimates come from *How Big Is the World Bond Market*, Salomon Brothers, September 1997.

4.1   Introduction to *Bond Markets, Analysis and Strategies**
Frank Fabozzi

Overview of Bond Features

In this section, we provide an overview of some important features of bonds. A more detailed treatment of these features is presented in later chapters. The bond *indenture* is the contract between the issuer and the bondholder, which sets forth all the obligations of the issuer.

Type of Issuer

A key feature of a bond is the nature of the issuer. There are three issuers of bonds: the federal government and its agencies, municipal governments, and corporations (domestic and foreign). Within the municipal and corporate bond markets, there are a wide range of issuers, each with different abilities to satisfy their contractual obligation to lenders.

Term to Maturity

The *term to maturity* of a bond is the number of years over which the issuer has promised to meet the conditions of the obligation. The *maturity* of a bond refers to the date that the debt will cease to exist, at which time the issuer will redeem the bond by paying the principal. The practice in the bond market, however, is to refer to the "term to maturity" of a bond as simply its "maturity" or "term." As we explain below, there may be provisions in the indenture that allow either the issuer or bondholder to alter a bond's term to maturity.

Generally, bonds with a maturity of between 1 to 5 years are considered "short-term." Bonds with a maturity between 5 and 12 years are viewed as "intermediate-term," and "long-term" bonds are those with a maturity of more than 12 years.

There are three reasons why the term to maturity of a bond is important. The most obvious is that it indicates the time period over which the holder of the bond can expect to receive the coupon payments and the number of years before the principal will be paid in full. The second reason that term to maturity is important is that the yield on a bond depends on it. The "shape" of the yield curve determines how term to maturity affects the yield. Finally, the price of a bond will fluctuate over its life as yields in the market change. The volatility of a bond's price is dependent on its maturity. More specifically, with all other factors constant, the longer the maturity of a bond, the greater the price volatility resulting from a change in market yields.

Principal and Coupon Rate

The *principal value* (or simply "principal") of a bond is the amount that the issuer agrees to repay the bondholder at the maturity date. This amount is also referred to as the *redemption value, maturity value, par value,* or *face value.*

---

*From Frank J. Fabozzi, *Bond Markets, Analysis and Strategies*, 2d ed. Prentice-Hall, 1993. Reprinted by permission of Prentice-Hall, Inc., Upper Saddle River, N.J. © 1993.

The *coupon rate*, also called the *nominal rate*, is the interest rate that the issuer agrees to pay each year. The annual amount of the interest payment made to owners during the term of the bond is called the *coupon*. The coupon rate multiplied by the principal of the bond provides the dollar amount of the coupon. For example, a bond with an 8% coupon rate and a principal of $1,000 will pay annual interest of $80. In the United States and Japan, the usual practice is for the issuer to pay the coupon in two semiannual installments. For bonds issued in European bond markets or the Eurobond market, coupon payments are made only once per year.

Note that all bonds make periodic coupon payments, except for one type that makes none. These bonds, called *zero-coupon bonds*, made their debut in the U.S. bond market in the early 1980s. The holder of a zero-coupon bond realizes interest by buying the bond substantially below its principal value. Interest then is paid at the maturity date, with the exact amount being the difference between the principal value and the price paid for the bond.

Floating-rate bonds also exist. For these bonds coupon rates are reset periodically according to some predetermined benchmark. Although the coupon rate on most floating-rate bonds is reset on the basis of some financial index, there are some issues where the benchmark for the coupon rate is a nonfinancial index, such as the price of a commodity. Second, while the coupon on floating-rate bonds benchmarked off an interest rate benchmark typically rises as the benchmark rises, and falls as the benchmark falls, there are issues whose coupon interest rate moves in the opposite direction from the change in interest rates. Such issues are called *inverse floaters*; institutional investors use them as hedging vehicles.

In the 1980s, new structures in the high-yield (junk bond) sector of the corporate bond market have provided variations in the way coupon payments are made. One reason is that a leveraged buyout or a recapitalization financed with high-yield bonds, with consequent heavy interest payment burdens, places severe cash flow constraints on the corporation. To reduce this burden, firms involved in LBOs and recapitalizations have issued *deferred-coupon bonds* that let the issuer avoid using cash to make interest payments for a specified number of years. There are three types of deferred-coupon structures: (1) deferred-interest bonds, (2) step-up bonds, and (3) payment in kind bonds. Another high-yield bond structure requires that the issuer reset the coupon rate so that the bond will trade at a predetermined price.

In addition to indicating the coupon payments that the investor should expect to receive over the term of the bond, the coupon rate also indicates the degree to which the bond's price will be affected by changes in interest rates. All other factors constant, the higher the coupon rate, the less the price will change in response to a change in interest rates. Consequently, the coupon rate and the term to maturity have opposite effects on a bond's price volatility.

Embedded Options

It is common for a bond issue to include a provision in the indenture that gives either the bondholder and/or the issuer an option to take some action against the other party. The most common type of option embedded in a bond is a *call feature*. This provision grants the issuer the right to retire the debt, fully or partially, before the scheduled maturity date.

Inclusion of a call feature benefits bond issuers by allowing them to replace an old bond issue with a lower-interest cost issue if interest rates in the market decline. A call provision effectively allows the issuer to alter the maturity of a bond. For reasons explained in the next section, a call provision is detrimental to the bondholder's interests.

The right to call an obligation is also included in all mortgage loans and therefore in all securities created from these loans. This is because the borrower (i.e., the homeowner) has the right to pay off a mortgage loan at any time, in whole or in part, prior to the stated maturity date of the loan.

An issue may also include a provision that allows the bondholder to change the maturity of a bond. An issue with a *put provision* included in the indenture grants the bondholder the right to sell the issue back to the issuer at par value on designated dates. Here the advantage to the investor is that if interest rates rise after the issue date, thereby reducing a bond's price, the investor can force the issuer to redeem the bond at par value.

A *convertible bond* is an issue giving the bondholder the right to exchange the bond for a specified number of shares of common stock. Such a feature allows the bondholder to take advantage of favorable movements in the price of the issuer's common stock. An *exchangeable bond* allows the bondholder to exchange the issue for a specified number of common stock shares of a corporation different from the issuer of the bond.

Some issues allow either the issuer or the bondholder the right to select the currency in which a cash flow will be paid. This option effectively gives the party with the right to choose the currency the opportunity to benefit from a favorable exchange rate movement.

The presence of embedded options makes the valuation of bonds complex. It requires investors to have an understanding of the basic principles of options. The valuation of bonds with embedded options frequently is complicated further by the presence of several options within a given issue. For example, an issue may include a call provision, a put provision, and a conversion provision, all of which have varying significance in different situations.

Risks Associated with Investing in Bonds

Bonds may expose an investor to one or more of the following risks: (1) interest-rate risk; (2) reinvestment risk; (3) call risk; (4) default risk; (5) inflation risk; (6) exchange-rate risk; (7) liquidity risk; and (8) volatility risk.

Interest-Rate Risk

The price of a typical bond will change in the opposite direction from a change in interest rates: As interest rates rise, the price of a bond will fall. As interest rates fall, the price of a bond will rise. If an investor has to sell a bond prior to the maturity date, an increase in interest rates will mean the realization of a capital loss (i.e., selling the bond below the purchase price). This risk is referred to as *interest-rate risk* or *market risk*. This risk is by far the major risk faced by an investor in the bond market.

As noted earlier, the actual degree of sensitivity of a bond's price to changes in market interest rates depends on various characteristics of the issue, such as coupon and maturity. It will also depend on any options embedded in the issue (e.g., call and put provisions), which are also affected by interest rate movements.

Reinvestment Risk

Calculation of the "yield" of a bond assumes that the cash flows received are reinvested. The additional income from such reinvestment, sometimes called "interest-on-interest," depends upon the prevailing interest rate levels at the time of reinvestment, as well as on the reinvestment strategy. Variability in the reinvestment rate of a given strategy because of changes in market interest rates is called *reinvestment risk*. This risk is that the interest rate at which interim cash flows can be reinvested will fall. Reinvestment risk is greater for longer holding periods, as well as for bonds with large, early, cash flows, such as high-coupon bonds.

It should be noted that interest-rate risk and reinvestment risk have offsetting effects. That is, interest-rate risk is the risk that interest rates will rise, thereby reducing a bond's price. In contrast, reinvestment risk is the risk that interest rates will fall. A strategy based on these offsetting effects is called immunization.

Call Risk

As explained earlier, many bonds include a provision that allows the issuer to retire or "call" all or part of the issue before the maturity date. The issuer usually retains this right in order to have flexibility to refinance the bond in the future if the market interest rate drops below the coupon rate.

From the investor's perspective, there are three disadvantages to call provisions. First, the cash flow pattern of a callable bond is not known with certainty. Second, because the issuer will call the bonds when interest rates have dropped, the investor is exposed to reinvestment risk, i.e., the investor will have to reinvest the proceeds when the bond is called at relatively lower interest rates. Finally, the capital appreciation potential of a bond will be reduced, because the price of a callable bond may not rise much above the price at which the issuer will call the bond.

Even though the investor is usually compensated for taking call risk by means of a lower price or a higher yield, it is not easy to determine if this compensation is sufficient. In any case, the returns from a bond with call risk can be dramatically different from those obtainable from an otherwise comparable noncallable bond. The magnitude of this risk depends upon various parameters of the call provision, as well as on market conditions. Call risk is so pervasive in bond portfolio management that many market participants consider it second only to interest-rate risk in importance.

Default Risk

Default risk, also referred to as *credit risk*, refers to the risk that the issuer of a bond may default, i.e., will be unable to make timely principal and interest payments on the issue. Default risk is gauged by quality ratings assigned by commercial rating agencies such as Moody's Investor Service; Standard & Poor's Corporation; Duff & Phelps; McCarthy, Crisanti & Maffei; and Fitch Investors Service, as well as the credit research staffs of securities firms.

Because of this risk, bonds with default risk trade in the market at a price that is lower than comparable U.S. Treasury securities, which are considered free of default risk. In other words, a non-U.S. Treasury bond will trade in the market at a higher yield than a Treasury bond that is comparable otherwise.

Except in the case of the lowest-rated securities, known as "high-yield" or "junk bonds," the investor is normally more concerned with the changes in the perceived default risk and/or the cost associated with a given level of default risk than with the actual event of default. Even though the actual default of an issuing corporation may be highly unlikely, the impact of a change in perceived default risk, or the spread demanded by the market for any given level of default risk, can have an immediate impact on the value of a bond.

Inflation Risk

Inflation risk or *purchasing-power risk* arises because of the variation in the value of cash flows from a security due to inflation, as measured in terms of purchasing power. For example, if investors purchase a bond on which they can realize a coupon rate of 7%, but the rate of inflation is 8%, the purchasing power of the cash flow actually has declined. For all but floating-rate bonds, an investor is exposed to inflation risk because the interest rate the issuer promises to make is fixed for the life of the issue. To the extent that interest rates reflect the expected inflation rate, floating-rate bonds have a lower level of inflation risk.

Exchange-Rate Risk

A nondollar-denominated bond (i.e., a bond whose payments occur in a foreign currency) has unknown U.S. dollar cash flows. The dollar cash flows are dependent on the exchange rate at the time the payments are received. For example, suppose an investor purchases a bond whose payments are in Japanese yen. If the yen depreciates relative to the U.S. dollar, then fewer dollars will be received. The risk of this occurring is referred to as *exchange-rate* or *currency risk*. Of course, should the yen appreciate relative to the U.S. dollar, the investor will benefit by receiving more dollars.

Liquidity Risk

Liquidity or *marketability* risk depends on the ease with which an issue can be sold at or near its value. The primary measure of liquidity is the size of the spread between the bid price and the ask price quoted by a dealer. The wider the dealer spread, the more the liquidity risk. For an investor who plans to hold the bond until the maturity date, liquidity risk is less important.

Volatility Risk

The price of a bond with certain types of embedded options depends on the level of interest rates and factors that influence the value of the embedded option. One of these factors is the expected volatility of interest rates. Specifically, the value of an option rises when expected interest rate volatility increases. In the case of a bond that is callable, or a mortgage-backed security, where the investor has granted the borrower an option, the price of the security falls, because the investor has given away a more valuable option. The risk that a change in volatility will affect the price of a bond adversely is called *volatility risk*.

Note

1. A majority of the securities backed by a pool of mortgages are guaranteed by a federally sponsored agency of the U.S. government. These securities are classified as part of the mortgage-backed securities market rather than as U.S. government agency securities.

4.2   Credit Analysis for Corporate Bonds*
Jane Tripp Howe

Industry Considerations

The first step in analyzing a bond is to gain some familiarity with the industry. Only within the context of an industry is a company analysis valid. For example, a company growing at 15 percent annually may appear attractive. However, if the industry is growing at 50 percent annually, the company is competitively weak. Industry considerations can be numerous. However, an understanding of the following eight variables should give the general fixed income analyst a sufficient framework to properly interpret a company's prospects.

Several of these variables should be considered in a global context. For example, it is not sufficient to consider the competitive position of the automobile industry without considering its global competitive position. As trade barriers fall, the need to become globally competitive increases.

Economic Cyclicality

The economic cyclicality of an industry is the first variable an analyst should consider in reviewing an industry. Does the industry closely follow GNP growth, as does the retailing industry, or is it recession-resistant but slow growing, like the electric utility industry? The growth in earnings per share (EPS) of a company should be measured against the growth trend of its industry. Major deviations from the industry trend should be the focus of further analysis. . . .

Growth Prospects

A second industry variable related to economic cyclicality is the growth prospects for an industry. Is the growth of the industry projected to increase and be maintained at a high level, such as in the nursing industry, or is growth expected to decline, as in the defense industry? Each growth scenario has implications for a company. In the case of a fast-growth industry, how much capacity is needed to meet demand, and how will this capacity be financed? In the case of slow-growth industries, is there a movement toward diversification and/or a consolidation within the industry, such as in the trucking industry? A company operating within a fast-growing industry often has a better potential for credit improvement than does a company whose industry's growth prospects are below average.

Research and Development Expenses

The broad assessment of growth prospects is tempered by the third variable—the research and development expenditures required to maintain or expand market position. The

*From *The Handbook of Fixed Income Securities*, 4th ed., ed. Frank J. Fabozzi and T. Dessa Fabozzi. Copyright © The McGraw-Hill Companies, Inc., 1995. Reprinted with permission.

technology field is growing at an above-average rate, and the companies in the industry should do correspondingly well. However, products with high-tech components can become dated and obsolete quickly. Therefore, although a company may be well situated in an industry, if it does not have the financial resources to maintain a technological lead or at least expend a sufficient amount of money to keep technologically current, its position is likely to deteriorate in the long run. In the short run, however, a company whose R&D expenditures are consistently below industry averages may produce above-average results because of expanded margins. . . .

Competition

Competition is based on a variety of factors. These factors vary depending on the industry. Most competition is based on quality and price. However, competition is also derived from other sources, such as airlines operating in bankruptcy that are able to lower their costs and thereby gain a cost advantage. . . .

   Competition within an industry directly relates to the market structure of an industry and has implications for pricing flexibility. An unregulated monopoly is in an enviable position in that it can price its goods at a level that will maximize profits. Most industries encounter some free market forces and must price their goods in relation to the supply and demand for their goods as well as the price charged for similar goods. In an oligopoly, a pricing leader is not uncommon. . . .

Sources of Supply

The market structure of an industry and its competitive forces have a direct impact on the fifth industry variable—sources of supply of major production components. A company in the paper industry that has sufficient timber acreage to supply 100 percent of its pulp is preferable to a paper company that must buy all or a large percentage of its pulp. . . .

   A company that is not self-sufficient in its factors of production but is sufficiently powerful in its industry to pass along increased costs is in an enviable position. RJR Nabisco is an example of the latter type of company. Although RJR Nabisco has major exposure to commodity prices for ingredients, its strong market position has enabled it to pass along increased costs of goods sold.

Degree of Regulation

The sixth industry consideration is the degree of regulation. The electric utility industry is the classic example of regulation. Nearly all phases of a utility's operations are regulated. The analyst should not be as concerned with the existence or absence of regulation per se but rather with the direction of regulation and the effect it has on the profitability of the company. . . .

Labor

The labor situation of an industry should also be analyzed. Is the industry heavily unionized? If so, what has been the historical occurrence of strikes? What level of flexibility does management have to reduce the labor force? When do the current contracts expire, and what is the likelihood of timely settlements? The labor situation is also important in non-unionized companies, particularly those whose labor situation is tight. What has been the turnover of professionals and management in the firm? What is the probability of a firm's employees, such as highly skilled engineers, being hired by competing firms? . . .

Accounting

A final industry factor to be considered is accounting. Does the industry have special accounting practices such as those in the insurance industry or the electric utility industry? If so, an analyst should become familiar with industry practices before proceeding with a company analysis. Also important is whether a company is liberal or conservative in applying the generally accepted accounting principles. The norm of an industry should be ascertained, and the analyst should analyze comparable figures....

Financial Analysis

Having achieved an understanding of an industry, the analyst is ready to proceed with a financial analysis. The financial analysis should be conducted in three phases. The first phase consists of traditional ratio analysis for bonds. The second phase, generally associated with common stock research, consists of analyzing the components of a company's return on equity (ROE). The final phase considers such nonfinancial factors as management and foreign exposure, and includes an analysis of the indenture.

Traditional Ratio Analysis

There are numerous ratios that can be calculated in applying traditional ratio analysis to bonds. Of these, eight will be discussed in this section. Those selected are the ratios with the widest degree of applicability. In analyzing a particular industry, however, other ratios assume significance and should be considered. For example, in the electric utility industry, allowance for funds used in construction as a percent of net income is an important ratio that is inapplicable to the analysis of industrial or financial companies.

Pretax Interest Coverage

Generally, the first ratio calculated in credit analysis is pretax interest coverage. This ratio measures the number of times interest charges are covered on a pretax basis. Fixed-charge coverage is calculated by dividing pretax income plus interest charges by total interest charges. The higher the coverage figure, the safer the credit. If interest coverage is less than 1x, the company must borrow or use cash flow or sale of assets to meet its interest payments. Generally, published coverage figures are pretax as opposed to after-tax because interest payments are a pretax expense. Although the pretax interest coverage ratio is useful, its utility is a function of the company's other fixed obligations. For example, if a company has other significant fixed obligations, such as rents or leases, a more appropriate coverage figure would include these other fixed obligations.... The analyst should also be aware of any contingent liabilities such as a company's guaranteeing another company's debt.... Although the company being analyzed may never have to pay interest or principal on the guaranteed debt, the existence of the guarantee diminishes the quality of the pretax coverage. In addition, the quality of the guaranteed debt must be considered.

Once pretax interest coverage and fixed-charge coverage are calculated, it is necessary to analyze the ratios' absolute levels and the numbers relative to those of the industry. For example, pretax interest coverage for an electric utility of 4x is consistent with a AA rating, whereas the same coverage for a drug company would indicate a lower rating.

Leverage

A second important ratio is *leverage*, which can be defined in several ways. The most common definition, however, is long-term debt as a percent of total capitalization. The higher the level of debt, the higher the percentage of operating income that must be used to meet fixed obligations. If a company is highly leveraged, the analyst should also look at its margin of safety. The margin of safety is defined as the percentage by which operating income could decline and still be sufficient to allow the company to meet its fixed obligations.

The most common way to calculate leverage is to use the company's capitalization structure as stated in the most recent balance sheet. In addition to this measure, the analyst should calculate capitalization using a market approximation for the value of the common stock. When a company's common stock is selling significantly below book value, leverage will be understated by the traditional approach....

The degree of leverage and margin of safety varies dramatically among industries. Finance companies have traditionally been among the most highly leveraged companies, with debt to equity ratios of 10:1. Although such leverage is tolerated in the finance industry, an industrial company with similar leverage would have a difficult time issuing debt.

In addition to considering the absolute and relative levels of leverage of a company, the analyst should evaluate the debt itself. How much of the debt has a fixed rate, and how much has a floating rate? A company with a high component of debt tied to the Prime rate may find its margins being squeezed as interest rates rise if there is no compensating increase in the price of the firm's goods. Such a debt structure may be beneficial during certain phases of the interest-rate cycle, but it precludes a precise estimate of what interest charges for the year will be. In general, a company with a small percentage of floating-rate debt is preferable to a similarly leveraged company with a high percentage of floating-rate debt.

The maturity structure of the debt should also be evaluated. What is the percentage of debt that is coming due within the next five years? As this debt is refinanced, how will the company's embedded cost of debt be changed? In this regard, the amount of original-issue discount (OID) debt should also be considered. High-quality OIDs were first issued in sizable amounts in 1981, although lower quality OIDs have been issued for some time. This debt is issued with low or zero coupons and at substantial discounts to par. Each year, the issuing company expenses the interest payment as well as the amortization of the discount. At issuance, only the actual bond proceeds are listed as debt on the balance sheet. However, as this debt payable will increase annually, the analyst should consider the full face amount due at maturity when evaluating the maturity structure and refinancing plans of the company.

The existence of material operating leases can understate the leverage of a firm. Operating leases should be capitalized to give a true measure of leverage. This approach is particularly enlightening in industries such as the airline industry, where leverage for the three major carriers increases from approximately 70 percent to 90 percent when leases are considered.

A company's bank lines often comprise a significant portion of a company's total long-term debt. These lines should be closely analyzed in order to determine the flexibility afforded to the company. The lines should be evaluated in terms of undrawn capacity as well as security interests granted. In addition, the analyst should determine whether the line contains a Material Adverse Change (MAC) clause under which the line could be withdrawn. For example, a company that has drawn down its bank lines completely and is in jeopardy of activating its MAC clause may have trouble refinancing any debt.

Cash Flow

A third important ratio is cash flow as a percent of total debt. Cash flow is often defined as net income from continuing operations plus depreciation, depletion, amortization, and deferred taxes. In calculating cash flow for credit analysis, the analyst should also subtract noncash contributions from subsidiaries. In essence, the analyst should be concerned with cash from operations. Any extraordinary sources or uses of funds should be excluded when determining the overall trend of cash-flow coverage. Cash dividends from subsidiaries should also be questioned in terms of their appropriateness (too high or too low relative to the subsidiary's earnings) and also in terms of the parent's control over the upstreaming of dividends. Is there a legal limit to the upstreamed dividends? If so, how close is the current level of dividends to the limit?

Net Assets

A fourth significant ratio is net assets to total debt. In analyzing this facet of a bond's quality, consideration should be given to the liquidation value of the assets. Liquidation value will often differ dramatically from the value stated on the balance sheet. At one extreme, consider a nuclear generating plant that has had operating problems and has been closed down and whose chance of receiving an operating license is questionable. This asset is probably overstated on the balance sheet, and the bondholder should take little comfort in reported asset protection. At the other extreme is the forest products company whose vast timber acreage is significantly understated on the balance sheet. In addition to the assets' market value, some consideration should also be given to the liquidity of the assets. A company with a high percentage of its assets in cash and marketable securities is in a much stronger asset position than a company whose primary assets are illiquid real estate.

The wave of takeovers, recapitalizations, and other restructurings has increased the importance of asset coverage protection. Unfortunately for some bondholders, mergers or takeovers may decimate their asset coverage by adding layers of debt to the corporate structure that is senior to their holdings. While the analyst may find it difficult to predict takeovers, it is crucial to evaluate the degree of protection from takeovers and other restructurings that the bond indenture offers....

In addition to the major variables discussed above, the analyst should also consider several other financial variables including intangibles, unfunded pension liabilities, the age and condition of the plant, and working capital adequacy.

Intangibles

Intangibles often represent a small portion of the asset side of a balance sheet. Occasionally, particularly with companies that have or have had an active acquisition program, intangibles can represent a significant portion of assets. In this case, the analyst should estimate the actual value of the intangibles and determine whether this value is in concert with the balance sheet valuation. A carrying value significantly higher than market value indicates a potential for a write-down of assets. The actual write-down may not occur until the company actually sells a subsidiary with which the intangibles are identified. However, the analyst should recognize the potential and adjust capitalization ratios accordingly.

Unfunded Pension Liabilities

Unfunded pension liabilities can also affect a credit decision. Although a fully funded pension is not necessary for a high credit assessment, a large unfunded pension liability that is 10 percent or more of net worth can be a negative. Of concern is the company whose unfunded pension liabilities are sufficiently high to interfere with corporate planning. For example, a steel company with high unfunded pension liabilities might delay or decide against closing an unprofitable plant because of the pension costs involved. The analyst should also be aware of a company's assumed rate of return on its pension funds and salary increase assumptions. The higher the assumed rate of return, the lower the contribution a company must make to its pension fund, given a set of actuarial assumptions. Occasionally, a company having difficulty with its earnings will raise its actuarial assumption and thereby lower its pension contribution and increase earnings. The impact on earnings can be dramatic. In other cases, companies have attempted to "raid" the excess funds in an overfunded retirement plan to enhance earnings....

Age and Condition of Plant

The age of a company's plant should also be estimated, if only to the extent that its age differs dramatically from industry standards. A heavy industrial company whose average plant age is well above that of its competitors is probably already paying for its aged plant through operating inefficiencies. In the longer term, however, the age of the plant is an indication of future capital expenditures for a more modern plant. In addition, the under-depreciation of the plant significantly lowers inflation-adjusted earnings....

Working Capital

A final variable in assessing a company's financial strength concerns the strength and liquidity of its working capital. Working capital is defined as current assets less current liabilities. Working capital is considered a primary measure of a company's financial flexibility. Other such measures include the current ratio (current assets divided by current liabilities) and the acid test (cash, marketable securities, and receivables divided by current liabilities). The stronger the company's liquidity measures, the better it can weather a downturn in business and cash flow. In assessing this variable, the analyst should consider the normal working capital requirements of a company and industry. The components of working capital should also be analyzed. Although accounts receivable are considered to be liquid, an increase in the average days a receivable is outstanding may be an indication that a higher level of working capital is needed for the efficient running of the operation.

The state of contraction or expansion should also be considered in evaluating working capital needs. Automobile manufacturers typically need increased working capital in years when automobile sales increase.

Analysis of the Components of Return on Equity

Once the above financial analysis is complete, the bond analyst traditionally examines the earnings progression of the company and its historical return on equity (ROE). This section of analysis often receives less emphasis than the traditional ratio analysis. It is equally important, however, and demands equal emphasis. An analysis of earnings growth and ROE is vital in determining credit quality because it gives the analyst necessary insights into the components of ROE and indications of the sources of future growth. Equity analysts devote a major portion of their time examining the components of ROE, and their work should be recognized as valuable resource material.

A basic approach to the examination of the components of return on equity is presented in a popular investment textbook by Jerome B. Cohen, Edward D. Zinbarg, and Arthur Zeikel.[1] Their basic approach breaks down return on equity into four principal components: pretax margins, asset turnover, leverage, and one minus the tax rate. These four variables multiplied together equal net income/stockholders' equity, or return on equity.

$$\left(\frac{\text{Nonoperating pretax income}}{\text{Sales}} + \frac{\text{Operating pretax income}}{\text{Sales}}\right)$$

$$\times \frac{\text{Sales}}{\text{Assets}} \times \frac{\text{Assets}}{\text{Equity}} \times (1 - \text{Tax rate}) = \frac{\text{Net Income}}{\text{Equity}}$$

In analyzing these four components of ROE, the analyst should examine their progression for a minimum of five years and through at least one business cycle. The progression of each variable should be compared with the progression of the same variables for the industry, and deviations from industry standards should be further analyzed. For example, perhaps two companies have similar ROEs, but one company is employing a higher level of leverage to achieve its results, whereas the other company has a higher asset-turnover rate. As the degree of leverage is largely a management decision, the analyst should focus on asset turnover. Why have sales for the former company turned down? Is this downturn a result of a general slowdown in the industry, or is it that assets have been expanded rapidly and the company is in the process of absorbing these new assets? Conversely, a relatively high rise in asset-turnover rate may indicate a need for more capital. If this is the case, how will the company finance this growth, and what effect will the financing have on the firm's embedded cost of capital?

The analyst should not expect similar components of ROE for all companies in a particular industry. Deviations from industry norms are often indications of management philosophy. For example, one company may emphasize asset turnover, and another company in the same industry may emphasize profit margin. As in any financial analysis, the trend of the components is as important as the absolute levels. . . .

The importance of adjusting financial statements to capture differences among firms was highlighted in November 1993 by S&P's introduction of "adjusted key industrial financial ratios." In calculating its adjusted ratios, S&P eliminates nonrecurring gains and losses. In addition, S&P includes operating leases in all of its calculations. . . .

Nonfinancial Factors

After the traditional bond analysis is completed, the analyst should consider some non-financial factors that might modify the evaluation of the company. Among these factors are the degree of foreign exposure and the quality of management. The amount of foreign exposure should be ascertainable from the annual report. Sometimes, however, specific country exposure is less clear because the annual report often lists foreign exposure by broad geographic divisions. If there is concern that a major portion of revenue and income is derived from potentially unstable areas, the analyst should carefully consider the total revenue and income derived from the area and the assets committed. Further consideration should be given to available corporate alternatives should nationalization of assets occur. Additionally, the degree of currency exposure should be determined. If currency fluctuations are significant, has management hedged its exposure?

The quality and depth of management is more difficult to evaluate. The best way to evaluate management is to spend time with management, if possible. Earnings progress at the firm is a good indication of the quality of management. Negative aspects would include a firm founded and headed by one person who is approaching retirement and has made no plan for succession. Equally negative is the firm that has had numerous changes of management and philosophy. On the other hand, excessive stability is not always desirable. If one family or group of investors owns a controlling interest in a firm, they may be too conservative in reacting to changes in markets. Characteristics of a good management team include depth, a clear line of succession if the chief officers are nearing retirement, and a diversity of age within the management team.

Indenture Provisions

An indenture is a legal document that defines the rights and obligations of the borrower and the lender with respect to a bond issue. An analysis of the indenture should be a part of a credit review in that the indenture provisions establish rules for several important spheres of operation for the borrower. These provisions, which can be viewed as safeguards for the lender, cover such areas as the limitation on the issuance of additional debt, sale and leasebacks, and sinking-fund provisions.

The indentures of bonds of the same industry are often similar in the areas they address. Correlation between the quality rating of the senior debt of a company and the stringency of indenture provisions is not perfect. For example, sometimes the debt test is more severe in A securities than in BBB securities. However, subordinated debt of one company will often have less restrictive provisions than will the senior debt of the same company. In addition, more restrictive provisions are generally found in private placement issues. In analyzing a company's indenture, the analyst should look for the standard industry provisions. Differences in these provisions (either more or less restrictive) should be examined more closely. In this regard, a more restrictive nature is not necessarily preferable if the provisions are so restrictive as to hinder the efficient operation of the company.

Bond indentures should be analyzed in conjunction with the covenants of bank lines. Frequently, bank lines can be more restrictive than bond indentures. The analyst should focus on the most restrictive covenants. . . .

The Rating Agencies and Brokerage Houses

There is no substitute for the fundamental analysis generated by the fixed-income analyst. The analyst has many sources of assistance, however. The major sources of assistance are the public rating agencies and brokerage houses that specialize in fixed-income research.

Rating Agencies

Four rating agencies provide public ratings on debt issues: Standard & Poor's Corporation, Moody's Investors Service, Fitch Investors Service, and Duff & Phelps/MCM Investment Research Co.

Standard & Poor's (S&P) and Moody's are the most widely recognized and used of the services, although Duff & Phelps/MCM and Fitch are frequently cited. Fitch was revitalized in 1989 by a new investor group. S&P and Moody's are approximately the same size, and each rates the debt securities of approximately 2,000 companies. If a company desires a rating on an issue, it must apply to the rating agency. The agency, in turn, charges a one-time fee of generally $5,000 to $20,000. For this fee, the issue is reviewed periodically during the life of the issue, and at least one formal review is made annually.

All of the rating agencies designate debt quality by assigning a letter rating to an issue. Standard & Poor's ratings range from AAA to D, with AAA obligations having the highest quality investment characteristics and D obligations being in default. In a similar fashion, Moody's ratings extend from Aaa to C, and Fitch's from AAA to D. Duff & Phelps, historically, assigned numerical ratings from 1 to 17, with 1 analogous to a AAA.

In June 1989, Duff & Phelps/MCM changed its ratings to match the scales used by Moody's and Standard & Poor's. Duff & Phelps/MCM's ratings currently extend from ΛΛΛ to CCC.

Public ratings are taken seriously by corporate managements because a downgrade or an upgrade by a major agency can cost or save a corporation thousands of dollars in interest payments over the life of an issue. In the event of downgrade below the BBB− or Baa3 level, the corporation may find its bonds ineligible for investment by many institutions and funds, by either legal or policy constraints. Corporations therefore strive to maintain at least an investment-grade rating (Baa3 or higher) and are mindful of the broad financial parameters that the agencies consider in deriving a rating.

Many factors promote the use of agency ratings by investors, bankers, and brokers. Among these strengths are the breadth of companies followed, the easy access to the ratings, and the almost universal acceptance of the ratings. On the other hand, the ratings are criticized for not responding quickly enough to changes in credit conditions and for being too broad in their classifications.

The slow response time of the agencies to changes in credit conditions is certainly a valid criticism. There are few instances in which the lag is significant in terms of a dramatic change, but the market generally anticipates rating changes. The rating agencies have become increasingly sensitive to this criticism and have been quicker to change a rating in light of changing financial parameters. On the other hand, the agencies recognize the financial impact of their ratings and their obligation to rate the long-term (as opposed to the short-term) prospects of companies. They therefore have a three- to five-year perspective and deliberately do not change a rating because of short-term fluctuations.

Standard & Poor's has addressed this criticism directly by creating *Creditwatch*, a weekly publication of companies whose credit ratings are under surveillance for rating changes. These potential rating changes can be either positive or negative. The basis for potential change can emanate from a variety of sources, including company and industry fundamentals, changes in the law, and mergers. Duff & Phelps/MCM also has *Watch List*, [a listing] of companies that are potential upgrades or downgrades. Additionally, subscribers to the agencies' services have access to agency analysts to discuss individual companies or industries.

Investors who are concerned that the ratings are too broad in their classifications have several options among the brokerage-house services that offer more continuous ratings.

Brokerage-House Services

Numerous brokerage houses specialize in fixed-income research. Generally, these services are available only to institutional buyers of bonds. The strength of the research stems from the in-depth coverage provided, the statistical techniques employed, and the fine gradations in rating. On the other hand, the universe of companies that these firms follow is necessarily smaller than that followed by the agencies.

In spite of the numerous services available, the market continues to demand more fixed-income research. To partially satisfy this demand, many independent analysts are evaluating segments of the market previously not covered or inadequately covered.

Conclusion

This chapter has emphasized a basic method for analyzing corporate bonds. A format for analysis is essential. However, analysis of securities cannot be totally quantified, and the experienced analyst will develop a second sense about whether to delve into a particular aspect of a company's financial position or to take the financial statements at face value. All aspects of credit analysis, however, have become increasingly important as rapidly changing economic conditions and increasingly severe business cycles change the credit quality of companies and industries.

Note

1. *Investment Analysis and Portfolio Management* (Homewood, Ill.: Richard D. Irwin, 1977).

4.3 Guidelines in the Credit Analysis of General Obligation and Revenue Municipal Bonds*

Sylvan G. Feldstein

Introduction

Historically, the degree of safety of investing in municipal bonds has been considered second only to that of U.S. Treasury bonds, but beginning in the 1970s, ongoing concerns have developed among many investors and underwriters about the potential default risks of municipal bonds....

In analyzing the creditworthiness of either a general obligation or revenue bond, the investor should cover five categories of inquiry: (1) legal documents and opinions, (2) politics/management, (3) underwriter/financial advisor, (4) general credit indicators and economics, and (5) red flags, or danger signals.

The purpose of this chapter is to set forth the general guidelines that the investor should rely upon in asking questions about specific bonds.

The Legal Opinion

Popular opinion holds that much of the legal work done in a bond issue is boilerplate in nature, but from the bondholder's point of view the legal opinions and document reviews should be the ultimate security provisions because, if all else fails, the bondholder may have to go to court to enforce his or her security rights. Therefore, the integrity and competency of the lawyers who review the documents and write the legal opinions that usually are summarized and stated in the official statements are very important.

The relationship of the legal opinion to the analysis of municipal bonds for both general obligation and revenue bonds is threefold. First, the lawyer should check to determine whether the issuer is indeed legally able to issue the bonds. Second, the lawyer is to see that the issuer has properly prepared for the bond sale by enacting the various required ordinances, resolutions, and trust indentures and without violating any other laws and regulations. This preparation is particularly important in the highly technical areas of determining whether the bond issue is qualified for tax exemption under federal law and whether the issue has been structured in such a way as to violate federal arbitrage regulations. Third, the lawyer is to certify that the security safeguards and remedies provided for the bondholders and pledged by either the bond issuer or third parties (such as banks with letter-of-credit agreements) are actually supported by federal, state, and local government laws and regulations.

General Obligation Bonds

General obligation bonds are debt instruments issued by states, counties, towns, cities, and school districts. They are secured by the issuer's general taxing powers. The investor should review the legal documents and opinion as summarized in the official statement to determine what specific *unlimited* taxing powers, such as those on real estate and personal property, corporate and individual income taxes, and sales taxes, are legally available to the issuer, if necessary, to pay the bondholders. Usually for smaller governmental jurisdictions, such as school districts and towns, the only available unlimited taxing power is on property. If there are statutory or constitutional taxing power limitations, the legal documents and opinion should clearly describe how they affect the security of the bonds.

For larger general obligation bond issuers, such as states and big cities that have diverse revenue and tax sources, the legal opinion should indicate the claim of the general obligation bondholder on the issuer's general fund. Does the bondholder have a legal claim, if necessary, to the first revenues coming into the general fund? This is the case with bondholders of state of New York general obligation bonds. Does the bondholder stand second in line? This is the case with bondholders of state of California general obligation bonds. Or are the laws silent on the question altogether? This is the case for most other state and local governments. . . .

Revenue Bonds

Revenue bonds are issued for project or enterprise financings that are secured by the revenues generated by the completed projects themselves, or for general public-purpose financings in which the issuers pledge to the bondholders tax and revenue resources that were previously part of the general fund. This latter type of revenue bond is usually created to allow issuers to raise debt outside general obligation debt limits and without voter approvals. The trust indenture and legal opinion for both types of revenue bonds should provide the investor with legal comfort in six bond-security areas:

- The limits of the basic security.
- The flow-of-funds structure.
- The rate, or user-charge, covenant.
- The priority of revenue claims.
- The additional-bonds test.
- Other relevant covenants.

Limits of the Basic Security

The trust indenture and legal opinion should explain what the revenues for the bonds are and how they realistically may be limited by federal, state, and local laws and procedures. The importance of this is that although most revenue bonds are structured and appear to be supported by identifiable revenue streams, those revenues sometimes can be negatively affected directly by other levels of government. For example, the Mineral Royalties Revenue Bonds that the state of Wyoming sold in December 1981 had most of the attributes of revenue bonds. The bonds had a first lien on the pledged revenues, and additional bonds could only be issued if a coverage test of 125 percent was met. Yet the basic revenues themselves were monies received by the state from the federal government as royalty payments for mineral production on federal lands. The U.S. Congress was under no legal obligation to continue this aid program. Therefore, the legal opinion as summarized in the official statement must clearly delineate this shortcoming of the bond security.

Flow-of-Funds Structure

The trust indenture and legal opinion should explain what the bond issuer has promised to do concerning the revenues received. What is the order of the revenue flows through the various accounting funds of the issuer to pay for the operating expenses of the facility, payments to the bondholders, maintenance and special capital improvements, and debt-service reserves? Additionally, the trust indenture and legal opinion should indicate what happens to excess revenues if they exceed the various annual fund requirements.

The flow of funds of most revenue bonds is structured as *net revenues* (i.e., debt service is paid to the bondholders immediately after revenues are paid to the basic operating and maintenance funds, but before paying all other expenses). A *gross revenues* flow-of-funds structure is one in which the bondholders are paid even before the operating expenses of the facility are paid. Examples of gross revenue bonds are those issued by the New York Metropolitan Transportation Authority. However, although it is true that these bonds legally have a claim to the fare-box revenues before all other claimants, it is doubtful that the system could function if the operational expenses, such as wages and electricity bills, were not paid first.

Rate or User-Charge Covenants

The trust indenture and legal opinion should indicate what the issuer has legally committed itself to do to safeguard the bondholders. Do the rates charged only have to be sufficient to meet expenses, including debt service, or do they have to be set and maintained at higher levels to provide for reserves? The legal opinion should also indicate whether or not the issuer has the legal power to increase rates or charges of users without having to obtain prior approvals by other governmental units.

Priority of Revenue Claims

The legal opinion as summarized in the official statement should clearly indicate whether or not others can legally tap the revenues of the issuer even before they start passing through the issuer's flow-of-funds structure. An example would be the Highway Revenue Bonds issued by the Puerto Rico Highway Authority. These bonds are secured by the revenues from the Commonwealth of Puerto Rico gasoline tax. However, under the commonwealth's constitution, the revenues are first applied to the commonwealth government's own general obligation bonds if no other funds are available for them.

Additional-Bonds Test

The trust indenture and legal opinion should indicate under what circumstances the issuer can issue additional bonds that share equal claims to the issuer's revenues. Usually, the legal requirement is that the maximum annual debt service on the new bonds as well as on the old bonds be covered by the projected net revenues by a specified minimum amount. This can be as low as one times coverage. Some revenue bonds have stronger additional-bonds tests to protect the bondholders. For example, the state of Florida, Orlando–Orange County Expressway Bonds have an additional-bonds test that is twofold. First, under the Florida constitution the previous year's *pledged historical revenues* must equal at least 1.33

times maximum annual debt service on the outstanding and to-be-issued bonds. Second, under the original trust indenture, *projected revenues* must provide at least 1.50 times the estimated maximum annual debt service on the outstanding and to-be-issued bonds.

Other Relevant Covenants

Lastly, the trust indenture and legal opinion should indicate whether there are other relevant covenants for the bondholder's protection. These usually include pledges by the issuer of the bonds to insure the project (if it is a project-financing revenue bond), to have the accounting records of the issuer annually audited by an outside certified public accountant, to have outside engineers annually review the condition of the capital plant, and to keep the facility operating for the life of the bonds....

The Need to Know Who *Really* Is the Issuer

Still another general question to ask before purchasing a municipal bond is just what kind of people are the issuers? Are they conscientious public servants with clearly defined public goals? Do they have histories of successful management of public institutions? Have they demonstrated commitments to professional and fiscally stringent operations? Additionally, issuers in highly charged and partisan environments in which conflicts chronically occur between political parties or among political factions or personalities are clearly bond issuers to scrutinize closely and possibly to avoid. Such issuers should be scrutinized regardless of the strength of the surrounding economic environment.

For General Obligation Bonds

For general obligation bond issuers, focus on the political relationships that exist among chief executives such as mayors, county executives, and governors, and among their legislative counterparts. Issuers with unstable political elites are of particular concern. Of course, rivalry among politicians is not necessarily bad. What is undesirable is competition so bitter and personal that real cooperation among the warring public officials in addressing future budgetary problems may be precluded. An example of an issuer that was avoided because of such dissension is the city of Cleveland. The political problems of the city in 1978 and the bitter conflicts between Mayor Kucinich and the city council resulted in a general obligation note default in December of that year.

For Revenue Bonds

When investigating revenue bond issuers, it is important to determine not only the degree of political conflict, if any, that exists among the members of the bond-issuing body, but also the relationships and conflicts among those who make the appointments to the body. Additionally, the investor should determine whether the issuer of the revenue bond has to seek prior approval from another governmental jurisdiction before the user-fees or other charges can be levied. If this is the case, then the stability of the political relationships between the two units of government must be determined....

In addition to the above institutional and political concerns, for revenue bond issuers in particular, the technical and managerial abilities of the staff should be assessed. The professional competency of the staff is a more critical factor in revenue bond analysis than it is in the analysis of general obligation bonds. The reason is that, unlike general obligation bonds, which are secured in the final instance by the full faith and credit and unlimited taxing powers of the issuers, many revenue bonds are secured by the ability of the revenue projects to be operational and financially self-supporting. . . .

On the Financial Advisor and Underwriter

Shorthand indications of the quality of the investment are (1) who the issuer selected as its financial advisor, if any, (2) its principal underwriter if the bond sale was negotiated, and (3) its financial advisor if the bond issue came to market competitively. Additionally, since 1975 many prudent underwriters will not bid on competitive bond issues if there are significant credit-quality concerns. Therefore, it is also useful to learn who was the underwriter for the competitive bond sales as well.

Identifying the financial advisors and underwriters is important for two reasons: the need for complete, not just adequate, investment risk disclosures [and] . . . the importance of firm reputation for thoroughness and integrity. . . .

General Credit Indicators and Economic Factors in the Credit Analysis

The last analytical factor is the economic health or viability of the bond issuer or specific project financed by the bond proceeds. The economic factors cover a variety of concerns. When analyzing general obligation bond issuers, one should look at the specific budgetary and debt characteristics of the issuer, as well as the general economic environment. For project-financing, or enterprise, revenue bonds, the economics are primarily limited to the ability of the project to generate sufficient charges from the users to pay the bondholders. These are known as pure revenue bonds.

For revenue bonds that rely not on user charges and fees but instead on general purpose taxes and revenues, the analysis should take basically the same approach as for the general obligation bonds. For these bonds, the taxes and revenues diverted to the bondholders would otherwise go to the state's or city's general fund. . . .

For General Obligation Bonds

For general obligation bonds, the economic concerns include questions in four specific areas: debt burden, budget soundness, tax burden, and the overall economy.

Debt Burden

In relation to the debt burden of the general obligation bond issuer, some of the more important concerns include the determination of the total amount of debt outstanding and to be issued that is supported by the general taxing powers of the issuer as well as by earmarked revenues. . . .

The debt of the general obligation bond issuer includes, in addition to the general obligation bonds outstanding, leases and "moral obligation" commitments. Additionally, the amount of the unfunded pension liabilities should be determined. Key debt ratios that reveal the burden on local taxpayers include determining the per capita amount of general obligation debt as well as the per capita debt of the overlapping or underlying general obligation bond issuers. Other key measures of debt burden include determining the amounts and percentages of the outstanding general obligation bonds as well as the outstanding general obligation bonds of the overlapping or underlying jurisdictions to real estate valuations. These numbers and percentages can be compared with most recent year medians, as well as with the past history of the issuer, to determine whether the debt burden is increasing, declining, or remaining relatively stable.

Budgetary Soundness

Concerning the budgetary operations and budgetary soundness of the general obligation bond issuer, some of the more important questions include how well the issuer over at least the previous five years has been able to maintain balanced budgets and fund reserves. How dependent is the issuer on short-term debt to finance annual budgetary operations? How have increased demands by residents for costly social services been handled? That is, how frugal is the issuer? How well have the public-employee unions been handled? They usually lobby for higher salaries, liberal pensions, and other costly fringe benefits. Clearly, it is undesirable for the pattern of dealing with the constituent demands and public-employee unions to result in raising taxes and drawing down nonrecurring budget reserves. Last, another general concern in the budgetary area is the reliability of the budget and ac-counting records of the issuer. Are interfund borrowings reported? Who audits the books?

Tax Burden

Concerning the tax burden, it is important to learn two things initially. First, what are the primary sources of revenue in the issuer's general fund? Second, how dependent is the issuer on any one revenue source? If the general obligation bond issuer relies increasingly upon a property tax, wage and income taxes, or a sales tax to provide the major share of financing for annually increasing budget appropriations, taxes could quickly become so high as to drive businesses and people away. Many larger northern states and cities with their relatively high income, sales, and property taxes appear to be experiencing this phenomenon. Still another concern is the degree of dependency of the issuer on inter-governmental revenues, such as federal or state revenue sharing and grants-in-aid, to finance its annual budget appropriations. Political coalitions on the state and federal levels that support these financial transfer programs are not permanent and could undergo dra-matic change very quickly. Therefore, a general obligation bond issuer that currently has a relatively low tax burden but receives substantial amounts of intergovernmental monies should be carefully reviewed by the investor. If it should occur that the aid monies are reduced, as has been occurring under many federal legislative programs, certain issuers may primarily increase their taxes, instead of reducing their expenditures to conform to the reduced federal grants-in-aid.

Overall Economy

The fourth and last area of general obligation bond analysis concerns the issuer's overall economy. For local governments, such as counties, cities, towns, and school districts, key items include learning the annual rate of growth of the full value of all taxable real estate for the previous 10 years and identifying the 10 largest taxable properties. What kinds of business or activity occur on the respective properties? What percentage of the total property tax base do the 10 largest properties represent? What has been the building permit trend for at least the previous five years? What percentage of all real estate is tax-exempt, and what is the distribution of the taxable ones by purpose (such as residential, commercial, industrial, railroad, and public utility)? Last, who are the 5 largest employers? Concerning the final item, communities that have one large employer are more susceptible to rapid adverse economic change than communities with more diversified employment and real estate bases. For additional information that reveals economic health or decline, one must determine whether the population of the community over the previous 10 years has been increasing or declining by age, income, and ethnicity and how the monthly and yearly unemployment rates compare with the national averages as well as with the previous history of the community.

For state governments that issue general obligation bonds, the economic analysis should include many of the same questions applied to local governments. In addition, the investor should determine on the state level the annual rates of growth for the previous five years of personal income and retail sales and how much the state has had to borrow from the Federal Unemployment Trust Fund to pay unemployment benefits. This last item is particularly significant for the long-term economic attractiveness of the state because under current federal law, employers in states with large federal loans in arrears are required to pay increased unemployment taxes to the federal government.

For Revenue Bonds

Water and Sewer Revenue Bonds
Water and sewer revenue bonds are issued to provide for a local community's basic needs and as such are not usually subject to general economic changes. Because of the vital utility services performed, their respective financial structures are usually designed to have the lowest possible user changes and still remain financially viable. Generally, rate covenants requiring that user charges cover operations, maintenance, and approximately 1.2 times annual debt-service and reserve requirements are most desirable. On one hand, a lower rate covenant provides a smaller margin for unanticipated slow collections or increased operating and plant maintenance costs caused by inflation. On the other hand, rates that generate revenues more than 1.2 times the annual debt-service and reserve requirements could cause unnecessary financial burdens on the users of the water and sewer systems. A useful indication of the soundness of an issuer's operations is to compare the water or sewer utility's average quarterly customer billings to those of other water or sewer systems. Assuming that good customer service is given, the water or sewer system that has a relatively low customer billing charge generally indicates an efficient operation and therefore strong bond-payment prospects.

Key questions for the investor to ask include the following:

- Has the bond issuer through local ordinances, required mandatory water or sewer connections? Also, local board of health directives against well water contamination and septic tank usage can often accomplish the same objective as the mandatory hookups.
- Does the issuer have to comply with an EPA consent decree and thereby issue significant amounts of bonds?

- What is the physical condition of the facilities in terms of plant, lines, and meters, and what capital improvements are necessary for maintaining the utilities as well as for providing for anticipated community growth?
- For water systems in particular, it is important to determine if the system has water supplies in excess of current peak and projected demands. An operating system at less than full utilization is able to serve future customers and bring in revenues without having to issue additional bonds to enlarge its facilities.
- What is the operating record of the water or sewer utility for the previous five years?
- If the bond issuer does not have its own distribution system but instead charges other participating local governments that do, are the charges or fees based upon the actual water flow drawn (for water revenue bonds) and sewage treated (for sewer revenue bonds) or upon gallonage entitlements?
- For water revenue bonds issued for agricultural regions, what crop is grown? An acre of oranges or cherries in California will provide the grower with more income than will an acre of corn or wheat in Iowa.
- For expanding water and sewer systems, does the issuer have a record over the previous two years of achieving net income equal to or exceeding the rate covenants, and will the facilities to be constructed add to the issuer's net revenues?
- Has the issuer established and funded debt and maintenance reserves to deal with unexpected cash-flow problems or system repairs?
- Does the bond issuer have the power to place tax liens against the real estate of those who have not paid their water or sewer bills? Although the investor would not want to own a bond for which court actions of this nature would be necessary, the legal existence of this power usually provides an economic incentive for water and sewer bills to be paid promptly by the users.

Additional bonds should be issued only if the need, cost, and construction schedule of the facility have been certified by an independent consulting engineer and if the past and projected revenues are sufficient to pay operating expenses and debt service. Of course, for a new system that does not have an operating history, the quality of the consulting engineer's report is of the uppermost importance.

Red Flags for the Investor

In addition to the areas of analysis described above, certain red flags, or negative trends, suggest increased credit risks.

For General Obligation Bonds

For general obligation bonds, the signals that indicate a decline in the ability of a state, county, town, city, or school district to function within fiscally sound parameters include the following:

- Declining property values and increasing delinquent taxpayers.
- An annually increasing tax burden relative to other regions.
- An increasing property tax rate in conjunction with a declining population.
- Declines in the number and value of issued permits for new building construction.

- Actual general fund revenues consistently falling below budgeted amounts.
- Increasing end-of-year general fund deficits.
- Budget expenditures increasing annually in excess of the inflation rate.
- The unfunded pension liabilities are increasing.
- General obligation debt increasing while property values are stagnant.
- Declining economy as measured by increased unemployment and declining personal income.

For Revenue Bonds

For revenue bonds, the general signals that indicate a decline in credit quality include the following:

- Annually decreasing coverage of debt service by net revenues.
- Regular use of debt reserve and other reserves by the issuer.
- Growing financial dependence of the issuer on unpredictable federal and state-aid appropriations for meeting operating budget expenses.
- Chronic lateness in supplying investors with annual audited financials.
- Unanticipated cost overruns and schedule delays on capital construction projects.
- Frequent or significant rate increases.
- Deferring capital plant maintenance and improvements.
- Excessive management turnovers.
- Shrinking customer base.
- New and unanticipated competition.

Case Study: **Choosing Between Bond Fund Investments**

This case is designed to put you in the position of a portfolio manager of a bond fund who is confronted with a challenging set of decisions. She had purchased some bonds issued by Hillsborough Water and Sewer System (Hillsborough W&S), located in southern Florida, with the expectations that the yield on the bond would go down, the bonds would appreciate in value, and the fund would sell them for a significant gain. The opposite has happened, however; the yield on the bond has gone up, the price of the bond has declined, and the fund is now facing a loss.

At the same time, the portfolio manager was being shown by an in-house analyst bonds issued by the state of Massachusetts. This was in 1993, when Massachusetts was just finishing a very difficult time and was starting to show some credit improvement that was starting to be recognized by the rating agencies. Moreover, the in-house analyst believed that these Massachusetts bonds might be upgraded again by the rating agencies.

The portfolio manager has several alternatives. First, she could admit that she had been wrong on Hillsborough W&S, sell the bonds at a loss, and put the money into cash. Second, she could add to her position in Hillsborough W&S at the higher yield, assuming she had sufficient cash flow to support the purchase. Third, she could sell the Hillsborough bonds at a loss and reinvest the proceeds in these Massachusetts GOs (general obligation bonds).

The questions set forth below are intended to make you go through the same steps in the investment process as would the portfolio manager. These include consulting the credit analyst and the trader, evaluating the relative risks of the two bonds, and assessing the implications for her whole portfolio. The final question focuses on the relationship between the case and the general points made in this chapter about managing a bond portfolio.

In-Class Team Discussion

After group discussion of the case, each team should be prepared to answer the following questions:

1. What questions should Anne ask the credit analyst about Massachusetts GOs?
2. What questions should Anne ask the trader about Massachusetts GOs?
3. What questions should Anne ask the credit analyst about Hillsborough W&S?
4. What questions should Anne ask the trader about Hillsborough W&S?
5. What are the relative risks of these two bonds?
6. What questions should Anne ask herself about diversification and liquidity?
7. What bond portfolio management strategies are exemplified by these investment decisions?

4.4 Trustworthy Municipal Bond Fund

The Situation

Trustworthy Investments was a large manager of mutual funds.[1] At Trustworthy, tax-exempt funds were managed by a group consisting of 8 portfolio managers, 15 analysts, and 3 traders (exhibit 6). Anne Preston described the fund management process at Trustworthy: "It is a team effort with the portfolio managers working closely with the bond analysts and traders. I view the portfolio manager as a coordinator of resources, and the decisions he or she makes are based on market information provided by the traders and the credit information provided by analysts."

Since Trustworthy employed its own traders, the portfolio managers were freed from monitoring the execution of the trade and were able to manage more than one fund. Anne Preston managed a number of tax-exempt bond funds including the Trustworthy Municipal Bond Fund.

The Trustworthy Municipal Bond Fund was designed for investors seeking income exempt from federal income taxes (exhibit 8). Municipal Bond Fund investors tended to be extremely tax-conscious and many wanted to avoid as much federal taxation as possible. The fund's prospectus required it to be in bonds rated BBB. In addition, the fund was invested in bonds all along the yield curve, generally maintaining a dollar weighted average duration of 7–8 years.

The portfolio managers gave close consideration to a number of factors when evaluating an investment opportunity. These included attempting to anticipate possible changes in interest rates and positioning the duration of the portfolio at a level consistent with this outlook but also in accordance with fund objectives. In addition, the portfolio managers would pay close attention to their in-house credit analysis rather than be dependent simply on credit ratings. Preston explained: "The credit agencies for the most part lag the market. The market may start to price a particular bond higher if it feels that there is a change in the underlying credit or a change in the environment that will benefit the bond issuers. Rating agencies, however, are slow to revise their ratings owing to the large number of issuers in the market and the difficulties associated with following all of them minutely. Our analysts try to stay ahead of the rating agencies and alert us to the possibility of any such changes so that we may benefit from them."

The portfolio managers also had to make tradeoffs between choosing a bond for its high current income and buying a bond that was selling at a discount for its capital gain opportunity. Internally, Trustworthy evaluated the performance of its portfolio managers on the basis of total return, measured against other funds with similar objectives. (Total return is the sum of coupon income or dividends and any change in principal value, divided by initial value.)

Finally, the portfolio managers had to remain cognizant of the need to be diversified not only to control portfolio risk, but also to preserve liquidity so that the fund could move out of its investments quickly if necessary. Liquidity was especially needed in environments where portfolio managers feared large shareholder redemptions, which, in turn, could force them to sell in a declining market. With higher-rated bonds generally being more liquid than lower-rated bonds, portfolio managers are often faced with the choice between buying more liquid bonds with lower yields versus less liquid bonds with higher yields.

Hillsborough Florida Water and Sewer Bonds

Hillsborough Water and Sewer Utility (HW&S) was a municipality that supplied water and sewer facilities to residents in southern Florida. HW&S derived revenues from two sources: connection fees charged to new subscribers and usage fees charged to all subscribers depending on their monthly water usage.

In 1991, HW&S had proposed a debt offering consisting of a mixture of current income and zero-coupon bonds.[2] In their proposed offering, HW&S had projected an optimistic revenue growth rate of 7%–8% per annum with about 40% of the debt repayment being dependent on connection fees to be collected from new customers. When S&P was approached to rate the new issue, it expressed concerns about the ability of the utility to meet the debt repayment schedule principally because it was so dependent on acquiring new customers. Further, S&P pointed out that because the utility already had the highest water rates in the state—it had recently modernized its equipment—there was little possibility that it could increase its revenues from further rate increases. As a result the new issue was only able to get a rating of BBB+. Prior to the offering, HW&S had been rated A− by S&P and Baa by Moody's. Moody's continued to rate HW&S as Baa.

The lower rating by S&P had a number of unfavorable consequences. Among these consequences was that most retail investors (mostly older wealthy individuals) were reluctant to buy lower rated bonds. Owing to the subsequent lack in demand, the bonds sold at a substantial discount when issued in 1991.

Commonwealth of Massachusetts General Obligation Bonds

As with other general obligation bonds, the Commonwealth of Massachusetts GOs are secured by a pledge of the full faith and credit and taxing power of the state. In the late 1980s and the early 1990s, Massachusetts faced a difficult period financially and economically. Indeed by 1991, the "Massachusetts miracle" touted by Michael Dukakis during the 1988 Presidential campaign had all but disappeared. From 1988 to 1991, the Commonwealth lost more than 10.0% of its employment base and saw its unemployment rate rise to 9.0% compared with 6.8% for the nation as a whole. The state, which had historically operated with modest surplus or balanced operations, faced the emergence of a structural imbalance where its revenues were not sufficient to pay its ongoing operating expenses. As a result, Massachusetts weighed in with poor financial performance punctuated by operating deficits that ballooned to more than $1.2 billion in 1990. The net effect of this trying financial period was the complete drawdown of the Commonwealth's existing budgetary reserves and significant increases in the overall debt burden of the state. In response to the foregoing, Moody's and S&P downgraded the credit ratings of Massachusetts from Aa and AA in 1988 to Baa and BBB in 1990.

In 1991, Dukakis was replaced as governor by the more fiscally conservative William Weld. Weld set about reducing the size of state government, effectuating tax cuts to stimulate the economy, and undertaking deficit financings to resolve the accumulated deficit. Fortunately, from 1991 to 1993, Massachusetts saw its economy stabilize and, following the imposition of fiscal discipline on state finances, a return to balanced operations. Moreover, the Commonwealth continuously added to its Stabilization Fund with the fund balance growing to more than $309 million in 1993 from just $59 million in 1991. To recognize some of this improvement, Massachusetts GOs had been upgraded to A by Moody's Investor Service and A by Standard & Poors in 1992.

What to Do About Hillsborough Water & Sewer

On July 7, 1993, the HW&S bonds were brought to Anne Preston's attention by Bill Roche, a bond trader at Trustworthy. The bonds were trading at a yield of 5.15%. Municipal bonds had lagged behind the tremendous run-up in the stock and taxable bond markets, mainly owing to municipal issuers taking advantage of low interest rates and refinancing their debt, and the uncertainty about President Clinton's plan to raise taxes. Preston was, however, willing to purchase the bonds for their short-term capital gain potential.

Before deciding, Preston had consulted Joe Brown, the Trustworthy credit analyst following Hillsborough Water & Sewer. He described current market opinion as viewing HW&S as a BBB credit with little room for future improvement; however, he felt that the credit had actually improved in light of a number of changes. HW&S no longer had the highest water rates in Florida, as a number of other water and sewer facilities had raised their rates after being forced to update their equipment to ensure compliance with the safe drinking-water act. In addition, HW&S now was able to meet 100% of its debt service requirements through usage fees owing to an impressive growth in its customer base. Preston could hope that the credit improvement would be recognized by the rating agencies. She decided to invest $9.25 million in the coupon-bearing HW&S bonds on July 7 for the account of the Trustworthy Municipal Bond Fund.

It was now August 5 and the bonds had declined in price to yield 5.35%, 90 basis points higher than typical AAA-rated bonds. Preston evaluated her options. She could sell the bonds and cut her losses, or she could hold the bonds and wait for the market to recognize the credit improvement in HW&S. However, if the bill to raise taxes currently before Congress was defeated, municipal bonds could fall further.

A third alternative involved the purchase of the Massachusetts general obligation bonds. Anne Preston knew that Susan DiAngelo, the analyst following the Commonwealth of Massachusetts' credit for Trustworthy, felt that the ongoing improvement in the economic and financial conditions of the state warranted an internal rating of A+. Susan saw additional upside in the bond longer term and anticipated upgrades from both Moody's and S&P over the next six months to A1 and A+, respectively. Because Susan saw this potential upside for the bonds, there was a substantial possibility that yield spreads on these bond relative to a AAA bond would decrease, resulting in positive price movement. Anne Preston knew that she could sell the Hillsboroughs and purchase these bonds. Trader Bill Roche remarked that he expected if the 5.50% Massachusetts GOs were upgraded to A+, the bonds would trade at a price to yield 5.30%

Notes

1. This case is not a depiction of actual events; it was written for discussion purposes only.
2. Zero coupon bonds were typically more expensive to issue in an environment in which the market desired current income. However, HW&S had insufficient revenues to pay interest on current income bonds. The issuer believed that with a rising customer base and rising water rates, it would have little difficulty redeeming the zero coupon bonds at maturity.

Exhibit 1

Current Date	08/05/93			
Issuer	Hillsborough W&S		Massachusetts G.O.	
Coupon	5.25%		5.50%	
Maturity	08/01/2000		08/01/2007	
Rating	BBB+		A	
Modified duration	5.8		9.7	
	YTM	Price	YTM	Price
	4.75%	102.94	5.00%	104.99
	4.85%	102.35	5.10%	103.97
	4.95%	101.75	5.20%	102.96
	5.05%	101.16	5.30%	101.96
	5.15%	100.58	5.40%	100.97
	5.25%	100.00	5.50%	100.00 ⟸ Current
Current ⟹	5.35%	99.42	5.60%	99.04
	5.45%	98.85	5.70%	98.09
	5.55%	98.28	5.80%	97.15
	5.65%	97.72	5.90%	96.23
	5.75%	97.15	6.00%	95.31

Exhibit 2

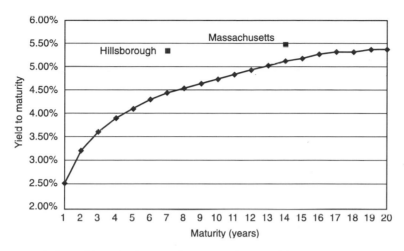

Description of Standard & Poor's Corporation municipal bond ratings

Exhibit 3

Municipal bond defaults*

Year	No. issues	Volume ($ millions)
1983	25	2,300
1984	47	498
1985	56	374
1986	150	1,287
1987	175	1,683
1988	139	899
1989	105	1,091
1990	162	1,964
1991	252	4,919
1992	174	2,081

*"Default" includes bond issues in which technical abrogations of covenants have occurred but principal and interest payments remain on schedule. Some of these defaults need not result in any losses to investors.
Source: Bond Investors Association and Fidelity Investments

Exhibit 4

Municipal ratings changes by Standard & Poor's Corp.

	1990	1991	1992	1993 (through 9/93)
Upgrades	140	145	396	127
Downgrades	465	607	478	157
Upgrades/downgrades	30%	24%	83%	81%

Source: Bond Investors Association and Fidelity Investments

Exhibit 5

AAA   Debt rated AAA has the highest rating assigned by Standard & Poor's to a debt obligation. Capacity to pay interest and repay principal is extremely strong.

AA   Debt rated AA has a very strong capacity to pay interest and repay principal and differs from the highest-rated debt and issues only in small degree.

A   Debt rated A has a strong capacity to pay interest and repay principal. Whereas it normally exhibits adequate protection parameters, adverse economic conditions or changing circumstances are more likely to lead to a weakened capacity to pay interest and repay principal for debt in this category than in higher-rated categories.

BBB   Debt rated BBB is regarded as having an adequate capacity to pay interest and repay principal. Whereas it normally exhibits adequate protection parameters, adverse economic conditions or changing circumstances are more likely to lead to a weakened capacity to pay interest and repay principal for debt in this category than in higher-rated categories.

BB   Debt rated BB has less near-term vulnerability to default than other speculative issues. However, it faces major ongoing uncertainties or exposure to adverse business, financial, or economic conditions which could lead to inadequate capacity to meet timely interest and principal payments.

B   Debt rate B has a greater vulnerability to default but currently has the capacity to meet interest payments and principal repayments. Adverse business, financial, or economic conditions will likely impair capacity or willingness to pay interest and repay principal. The B rating category is also used for debt subordinated to senior debt that is assigned an actual or implied BB or BB– rating.

CCC   Debt rated CCC has a currently identifiable vulnerability to default, and is dependent upon favorable business, financial, and economic conditions to meet timely payment of interest and repayment of principal. In the event of adverse business, financial, or economic conditions, it is not likely to have the capacity to pay interest and repay principal.

CC   Debt rated CC is typically applied to debt subordinated to senior debt which is assigned an actual or implied CCC debt rating.

C   The rating C is typically applied to debt subordinated to senior debt which is assigned an actual or implied CCC debt rating. The C rating may be used to cover a situation where a bankruptcy petition has been filed but debt service payments are continued.

CI   The rating CI is reserved for income bonds on which no interest is being paid.

D   Debt rated D is in payment default. The D rating category is used when interest payments or principal payments are not made on the date due even if the applicable grace period has not expired, unless S&P believes that such payments will be made during such grace period. The D rating will also be used upon the filing of a bankruptcy petition if debt service payments are jeopardized.

The ratings from AA to CCC may be modified by the addition of a plus or minus to show relative standing within the major rating categories.

Source: Standard & Poor's Corp.

Exhibit 6

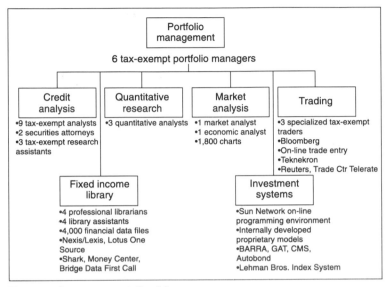

Trustworthy tax-exempt fixed-income resources.

Exhibit 7

Relationship between duration, maturity, coupon, and yield-to-maturity (calculated assuming semi-annual coupon payments)

Yield-to-maturity	Coupon	Duration (years)				
		5-year maturity	10-year maturity	15-year maturity	20-year maturity	30-year maturity
	0%	5.0	10.0	15.0	20.0	30.0
	3%	4.7	8.7	12.2	15.2	20.0
3%	5%	4.5	8.2	11.2	13.8	18.0
	7%	4.4	7.8	10.6	13.0	16.9
	3%	4.7	8.6	11.8	14.3	17.7
5%	5%	4.5	8.0	10.7	12.9	15.8
	7%	4.3	7.6	10.1	12.0	14.9
	3%	4.6	8.4	11.3	13.3	15.4
7%	5%	4.5	7.8	10.2	11.9	13.7
	7%	4.3	7.4	9.5	11.1	12.9

Note: The duration of a bond is the weighted-average time to receipt of its coupons and principal. The duration of fixed-rate debt is also an approximate measure of sensitivity of price to changes in yield-to-maturity. Specifically, the percentage change in price is approximately equal to the negative of the duration of the bond multiplied by the change in yield-to-maturity.

Exhibit 8

Trustworthy Municipal Bond Fund*
Fund Manager: Anne Preston
The Municipal Bond Fund's objective is to obtain a high level of current tax-exempt income consistent with preservation of capital. The Fund generally acquires longer-term (20–40 years) tax-exempt bonds which have credit characteristics consistent with rating agencies' definitions of "A" or better, although it may purchase bonds with BBB credit characteristics.
Portfolio Breakdown   Net assets: $1,005,604,218

Categories	12/31/94	12/31/93
State general obligations	7.1	3.5
Local general obligations	6.1	4.7
Special tax	9.4	6.0
Lease rental	8.3	8.2
Water, sewer, & gas utilities	7.2	10.3
Electric utilities	16.6	21.4
Ind. revenue/pollution control	1.8	3.6
Transportation	10.2	6.0
Health care	14.8	20.5
Universities/student loans	4.1	6.9
Housing	3.2	3.5
Pooled loans/other	1.7	0.2
Escrowed/special oblig./pre-ref.	4.8	3.8
Total municipal bonds	95.3	98.6
Short-term obligations	6.9	2.1
Receivables less liabilities	2.1	(0.8)
	100.0%	99.9%
Net assets ($000)	1,005,604	1,258,068
Net asset value ($)	7.36	8.69
Weighted average years to maturity	17.0	21.4
Duration	8.8	8.6

Exhibit 8 (continued)

Categories		12/31/94	12/31/93
Ratings breakdown (Expressed as a % of total net assets)			
	AAA	40.3	36.7
	AA	23.9	25.0
	A	25.7	27.7
	BBB	12.2	11.4
		102.1%	100.8%
Maturity distribution (Expressed as a % of total net assets)			
	Years		
	0–1	6.9	2.1
	1–5	3.2	2.4
	5–10	6.7	3.1
	10–15	16.3	8.2
	15–20	32.2	22.0
	20+	36.8	63.0
		102.1%	100.8%
Top 5 states by % of net assets			
		CA 12.9	CA 14.1
		NY 11.6	PA 8.6
		MA 8.8	NY 8.5
		TX 8.6	MA 5.9
		IL 5.7	WA 5.6

*Hypothetical: For description purposes only.

5   Portfolio Management of Stocks

Introduction

This is the second chapter on portfolio management. The first chapter reviewed bonds and bond funds; the third chapter discusses brokerage transactions for mutual funds. This chapter will focus on stocks, stock indices, and stock funds.

We will begin with the basics. A share of stock represents ownership of a company and participation in the profits and losses of the company. Shares are initially sold by the company to investors (in a public or private offering), and then may be traded among investors (through an exchange or over-the-counter market). Generally, if a company does well and profits rise, the stock should appreciate in value and the company should have the ability to pay higher dividends. If a company falters, the stock price will probably fall and the company will possibly cut or stop paying dividends.

In other words, the annual return from a traded share of stock is the sum of its annual change in market price (which may be a positive or negative number) and the amount of its annual dividends, divided by the beginning-of-year price. Dividends constitute the portion of a company's profits distributed to shareholders. Dividends may take various forms, mainly in cash and occasionally in more stock. The amount and form of a company's dividend is declared for each dividend period (usually quarterly) at the discretion of its board of directors.

Thus, the level of profits or losses and potential dividends investors receive from a share of stock is uncertain. By contrast, a bond (discussed in chapter 4) represents a fixed obligation of the company, which must pay interest on the bond (if it can) regardless of the company's profits. Although the market value of a bond may fluctuate from time to time, the company must pay the principal (face value) due on the bond at maturity. The primary exception to the company's obligations to pay interest and principal on its bonds is when a company declares bankruptcy, at which time a bankruptcy court will decide what will be received by bondholders (whose claims as creditors are senior to stockholders' claims).

In general, capital stock is divided into two categories: preferred stock and common stock. While the readings summarize the characteristics of preferred stock and other equity instruments, we will focus here on common stock as well as indices of common stock. Indices are groups of stocks that attempt to represent the performance of a whole stock market or market segment—such as technology stocks or small-cap stocks. Common stock indices serve as benchmarks for portfolio managers—the baseline against which their performance is measured. Active portfolio managers try to beat their benchmarks by selecting what they believe are undervalued stocks and/or by overweighting industries they believe will be relative outperformers. Passive managers (of index funds) try to track their indices as closely as possible by selecting securities designed to be representative of all securities in the index.

This chapter will first review the main analytic measures applied to shares of common stock, as well as the use of stock indices and competitive universes. Then it will examine the responsibilities of stock fund managers and the role of security analysts in the investment process. (The role of stock traders is discussed in chapter 6.) The chapter ends with a class exercise on an important ethical issue: personal trading in stocks by employees of a mutual fund complex.

Measures of Stocks

The current value of a company—its market capitalization—is based on the total value of its outstanding stock. Specifically, the market capitalization of a company is determined by multiplying the number of its outstanding shares of common stock by the current market price of each share. For example, a company with 10 million shares of common stock outstanding selling for $21 per share would have a market cap of $210 million. Portfolio managers may use market capitalization as a screen for investments (e.g., a "large-cap" manager may buy only securities with market "caps" above $5 billion or $7 billion). Security analysts may compare the market cap to book value (the company's assets minus its liabilities) for an indication of how investors value a company's future prospects.

The market price of a share of common stock is typically analyzed in terms of various financial measures:

Price/Earnings Ratio (P/E), also known as the **P/E multiple**, is simply the price of a share of stock divided by its earnings per share (sometimes most recent reported, sometimes projected). This ratio gives an indication of how much investors are willing to pay for a company's potential earning power. The higher the multiple, the more investors are willing to pay. Stocks are often classified by their P/E ratio: those with a high P/E (e.g., 40) are typically young or fast-growing companies, while those with a low P/E (e.g., 8) are typically in low-growth or mature industries. Low P/E stocks also may include companies that have underperformed, or companies that are stable but unexciting earners.

Price/Book Ratio (P/B) is computed by dividing the price of a share of stock by its book value (the company's assets minus its liabilities) per share, and is often used as a measure of relative value for stocks. Analysts may compare the stock's P/B ratio to its own over time or to comparable industry ratios. P/B, like P/E, is often used in determining the attractiveness of a security.

Price/Cash Flow Ratio (P/CF) is found by dividing the price of a share of stock by a measure of cash flow per share (often net income plus depreciation). P/CF is often used as a supplement to P/E, since cash flow is less subject to accounting distortions than are net earnings.

Dividend Yield is the rate of return paid on a stock, as measured by dividends. This measure is expressed as a percentage of the current market price of a share of stock. For example, a stock selling for $25 per share that pays an annual dividend of $1 has a dividend yield of 4% ($1/$25). As a general rule, low P/E stocks have higher dividend yields than high P/E stocks, which sometimes pay no dividends at all.

Stocks are also typically placed into one of several categories based on the anticipated movement of company earnings underlying these stocks:

Cyclical Stocks represent ownership interest in companies that tend to experience upward and downward changes in their net earnings that are correlated with the health of the economy in general. Earnings tend to rise quickly when the economy turns up and fall quickly when the economy turns down. Examples of cyclical industries are automobiles and housing.

Growth Stocks represent ownership interests in companies with opportunities for above-normal increases in revenue or earnings. Because of their growth potential, these companies (e.g., Microsoft) often sell at relatively high P/E ratios. Since these companies tend to reinvest earnings back into the business rather than pay dividends, growth stocks tend to have relatively low dividend yields.

Value Stocks represent ownership interests in companies in mature industries with relatively low prospects for earnings and revenue growth, or companies with assets whose value has not yet been recognized by other investors. These stocks (e.g., electric utilities) often sell at low P/E ratios and/or tend to have relatively high dividend yields.

Stock Indices and Competitive Universes

Similar to a bond index, a *stock index* is a hypothetical portfolio of stocks that is maintained by an independent provider (two of the largest stock index providers are Standard & Poor's and Frank Russell Company). The providers price each stock in the market index periodically and calculate the index's price change and total return. Indices were created to provide a gauge of the activity of the general market, by measuring and reporting value changes in a representative sample of securities.

Almost everyone has heard of the Dow Jones Industrial Average index (DJIA), but it is composed of only 30 large, primarily industrial, stocks. Although it is the oldest and most quoted U.S. stock indicator, it represents only a narrow part of the performance of the overall U.S. stock market. A better representative may be the Standard & Poor's 500 index, which is designed to represent the overall market and is composed of stocks of 500 large companies that trade in the United States, or, even better, the Wilshire 5,000 index, which includes all listed stocks of companies headquartered in the United States for which prices are readily available. There are countless other indices composed of U.S. and/or international stocks that are designed to represent a broad market.

Some indices are narrower, and may focus on stocks of a particular industry or market sector, or on stocks with specific financial characteristics. An illustration of the latter is the division of the Russell 1,000 index (largest 1,000 U.S. listed securities) into value and growth indices. The Russell 1,000 Value (R1V) includes the securities in the Russell 1,000 that share certain characteristics, such as a relatively low price/earnings (P/E) ratio, a relatively low price/book ratio, and a relatively high dividend yield. By contrast, the Russell 1,000 Growth (R1G) includes the securities from the Russell 1,000 that share opposite characteristics, such as a relatively high P/E ratio, a relatively high price/book ratio, and a relatively low dividend yield. For small capitalization stocks, a popular index is the Russell

2,000, which comprises the next 2,000 largest U.S. stocks after the large-cap stocks in the Russell 1,000 (i.e., the stocks ranked from 1,001 to 3,000 by market capitalization). There are also indices focused on mid-cap stocks (e.g., S&P Mid-Cap 400), between the large and small capitalization companies.

Mutual fund managers often rely on indices to gauge their performance. While some managers may simply aim for high absolute returns, or returns that beat other managers with similar strategies, mutual funds increasingly use indices to represent "the market" that they try to outperform. For instance, in order to beat the Russell 2,000, a portfolio manager for a small-cap stock fund is likely to concentrate on stocks with market capitalizations below a certain level. An active manager will try to outperform the relevant benchmark by various methods—for example, buying large positions in certain stocks included in the benchmark (stock selection) or overweighting sectors (industries) in the benchmark. A passive manager will follow the applicable index as closely as possible by seeking to minimize tracking error.

Mutual fund managers are also judged by their performance relative to a competitive universe. A competitive universe is a group of competing mutual funds that share the same investment objective. The funds in a competitive universe are ranked by total return and are often divided into four quartiles. The better performers (top 25%) compose the first quartile, while the poorer relative performers (bottom 25%) are in the fourth quartile. Independent measuring firms, such as Lipper Analytical Services, Inc., Standard & Poor's Micropal, and Morningstar, Inc., generate monthly, quarterly, and annual rankings of mutual funds by their total returns relative to their competitive universes.

The key question in these rankings is whether a fund is being considered in the appropriate competitive universe. In stock funds, the competitive universes are grouped around several standard investment objectives—for example, capital appreciation, growth, and equity income. Some competitive universes, however, are very small—only four funds make up the universe of SEC-registered, Canadian stock funds. Moreover, some funds do not neatly fit into one competitive universe because their investment objective is subject to varying interpretation.

By contrast, there is a standard definition of total return for mutual funds. The total return of a fund is calculated by summing dividends received and any change in price (which can be positive or negative), and dividing by the cost of the initial investment. For the purpose of calculating total return, all fund distributions are normally assumed to be reinvested in additional shares of the same fund.

Responsibilities of Equity Portfolio Managers

As mentioned above, there are two main approaches to portfolio management, passive management and active management:

Passive management is an approach where the investment objective is simply to equal the return on a market index. This could be done by purchasing all of the component securities of the index in identical proportions. Since some indices contain very large numbers of stocks, however, passive management can be accomplished by purchasing a statistically representative sample of stocks whose combined total return will closely approximate that of the index.

Active management is an approach where the investment objective is to beat the return of an index, or to achieve a return near the top of a competitive universe. Active management may involve overweighting and underweighting securities and/or sectors of the market relative to the benchmark index, though some managers ignore indices entirely and simply try to pick the best stocks.

We will focus on the active *portfolio manager* (PM). On a day-to-day basis, the active PM makes buy and sell decisions for one fund or a group of similar funds. There are several subcategories of active managers. Fundamental managers examine individual companies and industrial sectors, analyze financial ratios, and talk to management. "Top-down" managers tend to invest their funds first by deciding on broad sector positions based on economic themes—for example, heavily investing in energy stocks in anticipation of oil price changes—and then deciding on individual companies. "Bottom-up" managers tend to pick specific companies, and let sector allocations follow from individual stock-by-stock decisions. Quantitative managers, by contrast, input reams of data into computer models in order to find securities with good prospects. This is often called the "black box" approach. Quantitative managers sometimes use computer screens to identify potentially interesting stocks for further analysis by fundamental managers.

Some actively-oriented fund complexes have a team approach to PM decisions—groups of investment professionals make portfolio decisions for the fund. Other complexes make one individual responsible for choosing securities for the whole fund or a designated portion of the fund. Some complexes promulgate an "approved" list of stocks from which a PM may choose; other complexes allow each PM to select any stock, as long as it is consistent with the fund's name and/or investment universe.

A PM is often obliged to invest a certain percentage of the fund's assets in securities covered by the fund's name. The SEC is increasing the name test (which requires a fund to invest according to its name) from 65% to 80% of a fund's assets, which is measured at the time of security acquisition. The name test must be met by a fund whose name has a common meaning—for example, the Biotechnology or Energy Fund. But the names of many funds are so vague—for example, Putnam Voyager or American Century Ultra—that they are not subject to the SEC's name test. A fund's investment universe may be limited geographically—for example, the Canada or Far East Fund; by the type of security—for example, the OTC or Convertible Bond Fund; or by the market capitalization of a company—for example, the Large Cap or Small Cap Fund.

Less specifically, a fund's investment universe may be defined by its fundamental investment policies. These policies describe the types of securities in which the mutual fund tends to invest. For example, a fund's fundamental policy may be to focus on finding companies that are poised to make a comeback or that are likely to increase their dividends. The fundamental policies of some funds may constrain a PM's investment strategy by setting specific criteria for portfolio characteristics—for example, an equity-income fund, which must hold a portfolio with above average dividend yields. Other funds may be designed to allow the PM more flexibility—a "go-anywhere" fund, which may change strategy according to conditions in the market.

Within these broad investment policies, a PM must decide how to position his or her fund. One important strategic decision is how many stocks a fund will hold. A fund

Table 5.0.1
Portfolio strategy: Sector weighting

Sector	Mutual fund sector weighting 12/31/96	S&P 500 sector weighting 12/31/96	Differential
Finance	23.51%	15.15%	8.36%
Technology	18.57	13.83	4.74
Health	11.00	10.56	0.44
Nondurables	10.85	11.19	−0.34
Industrial machinery	5.97	5.64	0.33
Basic industries	5.05	6.01	−0.96
Retail wholesale	4.86	4.42	0.44
Energy	4.64	8.95	−4.31
Media leisure	4.24	4.14	0.10
Utilities	4.12	9.96	−5.84
Durables	3.63	4.24	−0.61
Aerospace/defense	2.11	2.52	−0.41
Services	0.53	0.69	−0.16
Construction	0.40	0.50	−0.10
Precious metals	0.28	0.58	−0.30
Holding companies	0.24	0.29	−0.05
Transportation	0.00	1.33	−1.33
Total	100.00%	100.00%	0.00%

concentrated in 25 or 30 names is generally considered to be more aggressive than a fund spread across 100 names. A second strategic choice is how to position a fund relative to the market—the fund's beta as explained by reading 1.1 in chapter 1. If a PM anticipates a rising market, the PM will hold a portfolio with a relatively high beta—a portfolio that tends to go up higher than a rising market and tends to go down lower than a falling market. Conversely, if a PM anticipates a declining market, the PM will hold a portfolio with a relatively low beta. A third strategic question is how big a sector bet a PM wants to make. A PM may stay close to the sector weightings in the fund's benchmark and focus on stock picking. Alternatively, a PM may overweight some sectors and underweight others in an effort to beat the fund's benchmark. The latter strategy is illustrated by table 5.0.1. For someone managing against the S&P 500 index, this table shows an overweighting in finance and technology, with an underweighting in energy, utilities, and transportation.

Consistent with a fund's investment universe and strategy, the active PM tries to find a diversified portfolio of stocks that he or she believes will outperform the fund's benchmark. For example, on the basis of securities research (discussed below), a PM may come to believe that a new drug developed by Merck & Co. is likely to be approved for sale earlier than anticipated, resulting in increased market share and higher earnings than expected by most Wall Street analysts. Therefore, this PM would probably decide to purchase Merck & Co. in a higher percentage than its portion of the relevant market index (called *overweighting*). Conversely, a PM might be concerned about the government's antitrust investigation into Microsoft, and underweight that stock relative to the appropriate market

Table 5.0.2
S&P 500: Top 10 securities as of 12/31/96

	Security name	Index end weight
1	General Electric Co.	2.88%
2	Coca-Cola Co.	2.32
3	Exxon Corp.	2.15
4	Intel Corp.	1.90
5	Microsoft Corp.	1.75
6	Merck & Co., Inc.	1.69
7	Philip Morris Co., Inc.	1.62
8	Royal Dutch Petroleum (NY Shs)	1.62
9	International Business Machines Corp.	1.38
10	Proctor & Gamble Co.	1.30
	Top 10 total	18.61%

index. As illustrated by table 5.0.2, the top 10 stocks in the S&P 500 constitute over 18% of the total market capitalization of that index. Thus, suppose a PM is managing a $10 billion equity mutual fund with the S&P 500 as its benchmark. If that fund holds millions of shares of Coca-Cola, the PM may still be betting against that stock unless the fund's holdings of Coca-Cola constitute at least 2.3% of the fund's total assets.

After a PM decides on a stock, he or she gives a purchase or sell order to the trading desk, which is part of the investment adviser's operations. The *trader* implements the investment decisions of the PM by allocating orders to markets and/or broker-dealers. The trader tries to obtain the highest prices possible for sales and the lowest possible prices for new purchases. The trader also provides the portfolio manager with information about how the market and particular stocks are responding to events or news. At some mutual fund complexes the portfolio manager doubles as the trader. (For a more detailed discussion of fund trading, see chapter 6.)

In addition to choosing stocks, portfolio managers need to take into account other factors relating to the management of a mutual fund. These include the cash flows resulting from shareholder purchases and redemptions, as well as the liquidity of individual securities and market sectors. Continuous cash inflows to a fund cause the manager to look for ways to put that cash to work quickly, by buying more of existing securities or by seeking new investments. Heavy redemptions may require the manager to sell some of the fund's holdings in order to handle the cash outflows, even if the timing of the sale is not optimal. Cash flow can be particularly high in sector funds or other funds which concentrate investments in a specific security type. Liquidity of securities (the ability to buy and sell quickly) is especially important in thinly traded markets, such as certain foreign markets and the U.S. markets in small capitalization stocks. (See case study in chapter 9.)

Finally, on a regular basis portfolio managers should carefully analyze the sources of their over- and under-performance relative to their indices and peer groups. Such analysis is called *performance attribution*, which typically includes a list of stocks and sectors that have most contributed to and detracted from the fund's performance.

Types of Securities Research

PMs of actively managed funds rely on *research analysts* to supply investment recommendations concerning which stocks to buy or sell. Most investment advisers have in-house analysts, who produce proprietary research for their own PMs. In addition, most PMs obtain research from outside analysts at Wall Street firms (commonly referred to as Street research). Security analysts, if they do well, can often go on to become PMs.

There are many different research methodologies used by mutual funds. The main types of research are fundamental, technical, and quantitative (which can be either fundamental or technical). The remainder of this introduction describes the main types of analysts and the research methods employed by each. The readings go into more detail on the approaches taken by security analysts.

The *fundamental analyst* rates stocks based on his or her research into the operations and finances of a company with a focus on estimating its future earnings. These analysts tear apart the public disclosures of companies, interview company managements, and make stock recommendations to PMs.

The *technical analyst* looks at data such as past price movements and trading volume to estimate future prices rather than looking at earnings of companies. Observations from the general stock market as well as individual securities can lead to the development of trading techniques, and ultimately, investment recommendations.

The *quantitative analyst*, who may use fundamental or technical data or a combination of both, develops mathematical models to assist in finding stocks that meet certain investment criteria. The quantitative analyst inputs vast amounts of data into a computerized model, which can then act as a screen for desirable stocks, categorized according to previously assigned criteria.

How Companies Are Researched

Fundamental equity research involves evaluating not only a specific company, but also its competitive position within its industry as well as the industry's position in the market. The following are general questions that a fundamental equity analyst may ask:

- **Historical financial performance**   What has the trend been in revenues, costs and profit margins? Are the drivers of that performance still in place, or have things changed significantly?
- **Projected performance**   What is the projected trend in unit growth versus pricing? What is the breakdown of revenues by operating units? What areas will experience growth versus areas that might stagnate?
- **Breakdown of financial performance**   Is demand for the company's products strong? What is the supply relative to demand? Are prices for its raw materials stable, or subject to increases? Does the company have excess cash flow from operations, and what is management's intended use for that cash flow?
- **Current financial position**   What is the current cash position? Are receivables going up or down? How are sales? What is the current inventory level? Any lost contracts?

- **Competitive environment** Who are the important competitors the company faces, how large and strong are those competitors, and what are their announced plans? Is there pricing pressure?
- **Regulatory environment** Do the existing regulations protect the company from competition? Are those regulations likely to change in an adverse way?
- **Event risk** Are there impending regulatory or legislative changes? If the company has foreign operations, could currency fluctuations in a country have an impact on the firm? Is there risk of adverse government actions, such as an oil embargo?
- **Quality of management** Are the senior managers of the company experienced, with strong track records? As unanticipated problems occur, will the managers make good decisions about how to respond?

The analyst typically approaches these questions by studying financial statements, by talking with management, competitors, and suppliers, by touring facilities, by reading trade journals, by attending conferences, and by reading Wall Street research. Much of this boils down to anticipating change ahead of the market. By absorbing information from many sources, analysts try to assemble a complete picture of an industry. They then look for stocks whose current price does not reflect their view of the company's value. If they believe the stock is underpriced, they will recommend buying the stock. If they believe the stock is overpriced, they will recommend selling the stock (or simply not buying it).

Rather than talking to companies and poring over financial statements, technical analysts study price and volume data to try to predict future price moves. The types of data technical analysts use include the following:

- **Aggregate market data** The strength and duration of advances versus declines, as well as new absolute and relative price highs over significant time periods, may warn of improving or weakening trends.
- **Relative strength to the market** Slower price declines at major market lows or initial underperformance at major market highs often telegraph major turns in stocks and groups of stocks.
- **Sentiment** Analysts may assess investor optimism (or pessimism) through short interest, put-call ratios, and investor surveys.
- **Supply/demand relationship** Data such as money flows and volume trends indicate buying and selling patterns of individual and institutional investors.

Quantitative research involves designing and applying computer models to predict stock returns or identify specific stocks that are likely to outperform or underperform over a given investment horizon. While there are many different variables used in quantitative models, most analysts follow a similar path in designing and testing these models, including hypothesis formulation, identification of key characteristics, model design, rigorous testing and validation, and application. In addition, most quantitative analysts carefully monitor the real-time performance of their models to ensure that performance does not degrade over time.

Questions

In reviewing the materials in this chapter, please keep in mind the following questions:

1. What is the difference between the book value and market value of a company? What is the relationship of each of these financial measures to a company's earnings? Which is more useful to the securities analyst?

2. If you are worried about a sharp decline in the stock market, would you generally be better off holding a stock with a high P/E ratio or a stock with a high dividend yield? Why?

3. The S&P 500 outperformed the Russell 2,000 and S&P Mid-Cap 400 in 1995, 1996, and 1997. Would you predict that this pattern will continue in 1998 thru 2000, or that the relationship among these indices will be cyclical?

4. Can a domestic growth fund or international stock fund beat its index, but fall within the third quartile of its competitive universe? Or lose to its index but be in the top quartile of its competitive universe?

5. Suppose a PM who manages against the S&P 500 as the fund's benchmark puts 1% of the fund's assets in the common stock of General Electric. Is the PM betting for or against General Electric and for or against other stocks in the S&P 500?

6. Suppose a PM who is managing against the Russell 1,000 as a benchmark invests the fund so that the percentage of its assets invested in each sector matches each sector's percentage weight in the index. How does that PM expect to add value through active management of the fund?

7. Would the price movement of a stock relative to other stocks in the same industry over the last year be significant to a technical analyst, a fundamental analyst or both? Why?

8. Suppose a PM who has intensely studied a high tech company's financial statements and industry data believes that the company's earnings are likely to be higher than Wall Street's estimates. Before buying the company's stock, should the PM ask a company official to confirm one of the PM's assumptions about the company's research expenditures? Should the PM ask a company official to confirm rumors about a potential merger involving the company?

5.1   The Stock Market: What the Stock Market Has to Offer*
John M. Dalton

"Businesses" usually evolve, over time, from one-man operations (sole proprietorships) to partnerships and ultimately to full-fledged corporations. Corporations traditionally meet their short-term cash requirements, for carrying inventory or for similar reasons, by borrowing from banks. When corporations need long-term financing, they may sell ownership interests in the company (common stocks and preferred stocks) to the public—or borrow from the public by selling bonds.

There are two major subdivisions to the stock market: the primary market and the secondary market. The *primary market* involves only new issues, while the *secondary market* handles "used" items. . . .

In this text we refer to this entire market, both primary and secondary, as the well-functioning "stock market."

Why Stocks Are Offered

Stocks exist to enable companies in need of long-term financing to "sell" pieces of the business—stocks (equity securities)—in exchange for cash. This is the principal method of raising business capital other than by issuing bonds. When the stocks of these corporations, which have been issued and are owned by the public at large—including both individual investors and institutions—they are said to be *publicly held*. These publicly held shares can be easily traded (sold) to other investors in the stock market, and are thus said to be *liquid*, or readily converted to cash.

The primary stock market is for newly issued shares, both common stock and preferred stock, which are sold by the issuer (the corporation in need of capital) to the investing public. Stock brokerage firms usually serve as intermediaries in these transactions, buying the new securities at wholesale prices from the issuer and then reselling them to the investing public at retail prices. This is, effectively, what happens when you buy a new car. General Motors produces the car, a "new issue," and then sells it to you through a dealer. You exchange cash for the car, General Motors gets the bulk of the cash, and the dealer earns a commission for his efforts in arranging the transaction.

The Size of the Stock Market

Approximately 4,000 different stock issues are currently traded on stock exchanges throughout the United States, (so-called *listed* securities) and about 25,000 other issues are

---

traded over the counter. Generally speaking, the older, better established companies opt for listing on one or more exchanges, while the over-the-counter (OTC) market is where newer and smaller companies are traded. There are some notable exceptions to this, and quite a few companies that are able to meet the most exacting exchange listing requirements prefer to stay OTC....

[At the end of 1996, the New York Stock Exchange—the largest U.S. exchange—had 2,907 listed companies with total market capitalization of $7.3 billion and handled an average daily trading volume of 412 million shares. At the end of 1996, Nasdaq—the automated quotation system for the OTC market—had 5,556 listed companies with total market capitalization of $1.5 billion and handled an average daily trading volume of 544 million shares.—ed. note]

Why Individuals and Institutions Buy Stocks

Stocks are purchased as investments, to make additional money on the money invested. There are many other investment vehicles including real estate, precious metals, and rare paintings, but investing in stocks offers a great number of advantages. Among these advantages are the relatively low commission costs, the ease with which purchased securities can be safeguarded (brokerage firms will hold them for clients upon request), the speed at which they can be bought and sold, the ability to determine your investments' exact market value in a matter of minutes, and, most importantly, their "track record." Over the long term, investments in stocks have proven to be an excellent way to more than keep pace with the erosive effects of inflation.

Dividends

Many common stocks and all preferred stocks pay dividends. Most dividend-paying stocks make their distributions on a quarterly basis (four times a year). That schedule is not a legal requirement, but most companies stick to it. The amount and timing of dividend payments are at the discretion of the corporation's board of directors. Most profitable corporations share their profits with their investors by paying them a cash dividend. A very general rule is that one-half the profit gets paid to the shareholders, and the remaining half gets reinvested in the company. Companies in an aggressive growth period might elect to reinvest most, or even all, of their profits to fuel expansion, paying only token cash dividends or even none at all.

There is no law that states that a company *must* pay a dividend on its common shares, even if the company is profitable. The board of directors can raise, reduce, or eliminate a company's dividend rate. Dividends on common stock are flexible, therefore, but companies try to maintain a fairly even flow of dividends, increasing the dividend when the company enjoys a growth in net earnings. A company with an annual dividend rate of $1.20 would most probably be paying out $0.30 per quarter. In this instance the annual rate would be $1.20; the quarterly rate would be $0.30. (Dividends may also be paid in additional shares of stock [*stock dividends*] in lieu of, or in addition to, cash.)

The expected receipt of dividend income is sometimes justification enough for investing in a given stock, particularly if the yield on the investment exceeds the return afforded by savings accounts or CDs. Stocks that pay out a fairly generous dividend are known as *income stocks*. These are generally popular with individuals or institutions that are satisfied with the rate of return in and of itself. Such dependable income producers are usually in stable industries such as utilities and food stocks. While the receipt of income is important to many investors and, as stated previously, sometimes the *only* reason for purchasing a stock, most investors hope to gain an additional return in the form of *capital gains.*

Capital Gains

When a stock is purchased at a given price, then subsequently sold at a higher price, the resultant profit is known as a *capital gain.* Trying for such "buy-low, sell-high" profits over a short time span is a speculative activity known as *short-term trading.* Often the securities are held only for a single day, sometimes for as little as several hours! Most individual and institutional investors, however, have a much longer time horizon and will hold stocks for many years.

Companies that are expected to grow over time are known as *growth stocks.* Investors buy such stocks in anticipation that their per-share value will increase over time as the company prospers, and as its per-share earnings and dividends increase. When stocks that have been held for more than a year are sold at a profit, the profit is *long-term.* Short-term profits are the result of profitable trades on securities that have been held for one year or less. A capital gain will also result from a *short sale* that is subsequently purchased (covered) at a lower price.

Investors sometimes purchase securities only for their capital gains potential. Many growth stocks pay out very little in dividends, sometimes not at all. It is probably fair to say that relatively conservative investors are attracted to income stocks, while those who are more adventurous, and more willing to take risks, gravitate toward growth stocks. While certain stocks are dividend payers with little chance for spectacular growth in price (cash cows), and others offer small dividend potential but a chance for capital gains (*venture capital, special situations*), many stocks—probably *most* stocks—offer possible rewards both through dividends *and* capital gains.

Ultimately, that is why stocks are purchased: for dividends and/or capital gains—for *investment.* Most well-rounded portfolios have a balance between income situations and stocks with capital gains potential. Some investors achieve this aim by buying a package of securities with such a mix, typically exemplified by growth and income mutual funds.

Short Selling

Most of us think of making a "killing" by buying something at a low price and subsequently selling it at a much higher price. With most investment vehicles (undeveloped real estate, rare paintings and coins, art treasures), this is the only way to profit. Such investments rarely produce income while they are held, unlike stocks, and one's only hope for gain is to be astute enough to buy at the right times—at a low price—and to sell later at a higher price. The "buy-low, sell-high" principle is, after all, the essence of making capital gains. The stock market affords another method for striving for capital gains, and that is through the medium of the *short sale*.

Investors (and speculators) who believe a stock is selling at a bargain price will purchase it in anticipation of later selling the security at a higher price. They are *bullish* on the stock and expect it to increase in price. But what about investors who believe a security is *overpriced*? Such situations also offer the opportunity for capital gains through the medium of the short sale. Someone who thinks that a stock is selling at too high a price, and that it will decline, is said to be *bearish* on the stock. As unlikely as it sounds, it is possible (at least in the stock market) to sell this supposedly overpriced item first, and to buy it later! That's right: first sell at the high price and then buy at the low price. The difference between the sale price and the purchase price represents the investor's profit or loss. Naturally she wishes the stock to *decline* in value after she sells it, so that the purchase (the *covering* transaction) will be at a lower price.

Let's look at an example. John Bear believes that XYZ stock is overpriced at $89 per share and that it is due for a fall. He *shorts* (sells short) 100 shares at $89 and then keeps his fingers crossed. XYZ does decline in price, and Mr. Bear covers the short position by buying 100 shares of XYZ at $76 per share. He first *sold* for $8,900 and then *purchased* for $7,600, making a profit of $1,300. Instead of buying at a low price and then selling at a high price, Mr. Bear first sold at a high price and then bought at a low price. It's backwards, but it works!...

Risks and Rewards of Investing

When we buy a lottery ticket, we know that our maximum loss will be the price of the ticket. The same thing is true when we buy a stock; the most we can lose is what we paid for the stock. While the lottery offers a grand prize, there is no definitive "prize" when you purchase a stock for investment. But how high can a stock price go? Some have been going up for years—and are still going up! Stocks therefore (at least in theory) have unlimited profit potential. Investing in the stock market has proven to be extremely rewarding over time. Although stocks go up and down, sometimes rather dramatically, they generally have been in an uptrend for more than 60 [now 70] years. Historically stocks have "returned" (dividends and capital gains) more than 10 percent annually, more than keeping pace with inflation. That's probably their greatest attraction; they are a proven investment medium that outpaces inflation.

There is no magic formula for making money in the stock market, but *patience* probably comes closest. Five years generally "bridges" most market declines, and, for those prepared to wait out a bear market, the market is *comparatively* safe. There have been only six losing five-year periods in the last 60 such periods. Patient investors who hold a well diversified portfolio of stocks have been rewarded handsomely. Most financial advisors consider stocks a *must* investment for virtually all investors.

Brokerage accounts are insured, by SIPC, for $500,000. This is *not* insurance against bad judgment in the selection and/or timing of stock purchases, but purely protection against the failure (bankruptcy) of brokerage firms. It is always a possibility that you will lose everything you have invested in an individual stock. Even if you don't lose everything, substantial losses can—and too often do—occur. The market does *fluctuate*, and that is both the good news and the bad news. One can profit from an upward move (selling long) and from a downward move (selling short). Guess incorrectly and you can certainly lose with either approach.

For investors who own securities, their potential loss is their entire investment, while there is no limit (theoretically) to the amount they can make. Short sellers have very different risks and rewards. Since the short seller makes his maximum profit from a downward movement in a stock's price, he is hoping that the stock falls in price as far as possible. In effect, he is hoping that the stock goes bankrupt so that he can "cover" for zero and thus make a profit equal to the proceeds of the original short sale. That's as far down as a stock can go—to zero—so that's the price at which the short seller maximizes profit potential.

The short seller is a bear who wants the stock's price to decline. What the short seller *doesn't* want is for the stock to go up! Remember, he has sold the stock at what he believes is too high a price and hopes to buy it back more cheaply. He doesn't want to have to buy it back at a higher price since this will result in a loss. There is no limit to the amount the short seller can lose. That's the inherent danger in short selling—the specter of unlimited losses.

While the short seller's profit is limited, the buyer has an unlimited profit potential—but can lose his entire investment. A further consideration for the short seller is that the stock he sold was borrowed from someone else and that it must ultimately be returned. If he shorts a dividend-paying stock, he will not receive the dividends but will have to pay them out! Since he has borrowed the stock, he must make good the dividends to the one he borrowed the stock from. This results in a negative cash flow for the short seller.

In a broad sense, bonds and money market funds are safest, while preferred stocks have slightly more risk and common stocks are the riskiest of all. The offset is that the high-risk situations offer the most potential reward. In general, the higher the potential risk is, the higher the potential reward. While stocks are generally risky, they have outperformed all other financial instruments over the long term. For all but the most ultra-conservative investors, one of the greatest risks might be to *not* invest in stocks!

Common Stocks

All corporations *must* issue common stock. These shares of common stock represent ownership in the corporation. The total number of shares that investors (both individuals and institutions) own at any one time is known as the *outstanding shares*.

An owner of common stock has, in effect, a "piece of the action." Common stocks are a type of *equity* (ownership) security. If a company has 1,000 shares of common stock outstanding, and you own 100 of those shares, then you are a 10 percent *owner* of the corporation (100 ÷ 1000 = 10 percent).

The rights of the common stockholder vary from company to company, but normally they include the following:

1. The right to vote.
2. The right to dividends.
3. Residual rights.

The Right to Vote

Almost all common stocks carry the right to vote. Occasionally a company will issue several different classes of common stock, only some of which may be voting stock. This is comparatively rare. Shareholders vote for, among other things, the selection of directors who are elected to see that the company is operated in accordance with the terms of the corporate charter. The directors appoint a slate of officers who attend to day-to-day operations of the corporation. Shareholders are also asked to vote on extraordinary events such as mergers and acquisitions, changes in the company's capitalization, stock splits, and other unusual actions.

Voting is usually conducted either on a statutory basis or a cumulative basis. Under *statutory voting* (the most common method), if four different directorships are up for election and you own 100 voting common shares, then you can cast up to 100 votes for your favorite for each of the four seats. If you favor Mary, John, Lucy, and Pete, then you may give each of those candidates a maximum of 100 votes. Under this method, holders of more than half the voting shares have absolute control over the directorships since they will always outvote everyone else. Fifty-one-percent ownership thus assures 100 percent control. Under *cumulative voting*, you may "save" your votes and split them up any way you wish. Given the same four directorships, you might opt to vote none of your 100 shares for Mary, John, or Lucy, but instead vote 400 shares for Pete. Cumulative voting thus gives minority shareholders their best chance at gaining representation on the board of directors.

The Right to Receive Dividends

Common stockholders have the right to receive dividends *when, as, and if* declared by the board of directors. The dividend is under their absolute control and is not vested in the corporation's officers. Generally, while bonds pay a fixed amount of interest and preferred stocks pay a fixed amount of dividend, the dividend on common stock varies, usually in direct proportion to the company's earnings. Growth stocks usually exhibit a long-term pattern of increasing dividends through the years.

Residual Rights

When a company is dissolved, either voluntarily or involuntarily, many claims must be satisfied before the common stockholders can claim any "salvage" rights. Even though they are the owners of the company, their claims come dead last. All salaries and taxes must first be satisfied, then general creditors and bondholders are paid, then preferred shareholders. And *then* common shareholders get to share whatever may be left. Usually there is nothing left for the common stockholder since even the bondholders and holders of the preferred issues rarely get paid in full. Some rare exceptions to this occur when a company is overly rich in assets. In such cases the company may be "worth more dead than alive," and the common shareholders benefit when the company is dissolved.

The *par value* of a common stock is *not* an important consideration. Par value bears no direct relationship to a common stock's initial price, its dividend rate, or what it is worth in the current marketplace or in dissolution (book value). A company's par value is of use only to accountants. For most U.S. corporations, a par value of between $0.01 and $1.00 is usually assigned, and sometimes a common stock is listed as having *no* par value!

Preferred Stocks

Many corporations issue preferred stock, although they are under no legal obligation to do so. Preferred shares generally pay a fixed dividend which is announced when the shares are first offered in the marketplace. Most corporations have only one class of common stock outstanding, but, for corporations that do elect to issue preferred stock, they usually issue several different such issues over time. When we say that someone owns "XYZ," it is understood that we are referring to common stock. Just "XYZ" is description enough; we don't have to say "XYZ common stock." When referring to preferred stocks, however, we must add something to the description of the preferred stock to distinguish it from the *other* issues of preferred stock that that same company probably issued. To avoid confusion, companies elect to name their different preferred issues in several ways. (See table 5.1.1.)

Method 1. ABC company preferred issues are distinguished, one from the other, by the dollar amount of the *annual* dividend. . . .

Method 2. The different CYA company preferred issues show a percent (%) rather than a dollar amount. This is the percent of each preferred stock's par value that the company has agreed to pay annually as the dividend on that particular issue. While many preferred stocks have a $100 par value, some do not. . . .

Method 3. RFQ company uses only letters of the alphabet rather than dollar values or percentages. Now there is no way you can figure the amount of the dividend just from the security's name. You will have to look it up in one of the security industry's information service manuals such as Moody's, Value Line, or Standard and Poor's.

The Senior Aspects of Preferred Stock

This type of equity security is called "preferred" for several reasons. For one, a company must pay dividends on all its preferred stock issues, in full, before it can pay anything to the common shareholders. The preferred stockholder also comes before the common stockholder with respect to salvage rights. When the company is dissolved, either voluntarily or involuntarily, the preferred stockholders must receive their issue's par value and accrued cash dividends before anything may be distributed to the common stockholders. Within a given company, its preferred issues are certainly "safer" than the company's common stock, with respect to both dividends and salvage value. In a broad sense, preferred issues are purchased for fairly safe income and not for capital gain possibilities. They are "preferred" by the more conservative investor over common stocks.

Table 5.1.1

Method 1	Method 2	Method 3
ABC $8.00 preferred	CYA 7 percent preferred	RFQ A preferred
ABC $10.00 preferred	CYA 11 percent preferred	RFQ B preferred
ABC $12.60 preferred	CYA 13.2 percent preferred	RFQ C preferred

Types of Preferred Stock

Cumulative Preferred

Virtually all preferred issues are *cumulative*. This means that, if the company skips a quarterly dividend, it is still owed to the preferred shareholder. If the company is struggling through bad times, they will almost certainly reduce or even eliminate the dividend on the common stock. If they get in a real cash bind, they will also skip the preferred stock dividend. While the "skipped" common stock dividend is gone forever, the preferred dividend becomes an arrearage and is still owed to the preferred shareholders. When the company ultimately recovers, all such passed-over preferred dividends must be paid before dividend payments to the common shareholders may resume. This is another example of the preferred stock's relative safety.

Callable Preferred

Some preferred issues are *callable*. This means that the issuing corporation reserves the right to retire the preferred issue by paying the stockholders a certain amount of cash. When a preferred issue is called, the shareholder has no other option than to surrender the stock. The minimum call price is par, which is the amount for which the issue was originally sold to the investing public. Callability is an undesirable trait for a preferred stock, at least insofar as the *shareholder is concerned.*

New preferred stocks are issued at the then-prevailing rates of return. If interest rates are high, then new preferred issues will also have a high return. If, sometime after a callable preferred issue is sold to the public, interest rates fall dramatically, then the company will refinance the existing issue by "calling" it and issuing other securities at a cheaper rate of interest. This saves the company money since they are replacing a high dividend rate with a lower rate, just as a homeowner refinances a mortgage when rates decline below the original mortgage rate. A shareholder who purchased a callable preferred when interest rates were high will have it called away from her just when things are getting good—when her return on the preferred she purchased is higher than newly issued preferreds. Thus, with a callable preferred, an investor cannot "lock up" a high rate of return.

Callable preferreds are usually not callable immediately after issuance. There is traditionally a grace period during which the issue is not callable, the first five years after issuance being fairly standard. When the issue ultimately becomes subject to call, the company usually offers a few "extra" dollars over par as compensation. . . .

Convertible Preferred

Some preferred issues are *convertible. This* option permits the shareholder to exchange preferred shares for other securities, usually common stock of the same corporation. The preferred shareowner has complete control over when, or if, he converts. You cannot convert back into preferred once you have exchanged your shares for common stock. It's a one-time deal.

The number of shares of common stock that you will receive for each exchanged share of preferred is known as the *conversion ratio*. Financial publications usually express the exchange feature as a *conversion price*. A conversion price can be changed to a conversion ratio simply by dividing the issue's par value by the conversion price. Thus a convertible preferred ($50 par) with a conversion price of $25 has a conversion ratio of 2. In other words, each preferred share can be exchanged for two shares of common stock ($50 ÷ $25). Most investors find it easier to work with the conversion ratio....

Stock Rights

Some common stocks have a *preemptive rights* feature. This means that existing shareholders will be given the first opportunity to buy any new common shares that are sold to the public. The general rule is that "old" shareholders are issued one right for each share they own. These rights may be surrendered, with a cash payment known as the *subscription price*, for the new shares. Shareholders not wishing to subscribe for the new shares may sell their rights in the open market. This feature permits shareholders to maintain their same proportion of ownership in the company, should they choose to do so. For example, Ms. Claudette Morgan owns 100 shares of XYZ. Since a total of 10,000 shares of XYZ are outstanding, she owns 1 percent of the company (100 ÷ 10,000). If another 10,000 shares were issued, and Claudette did *not* purchase any of these new shares, her ownership would be reduced to only 0.5 percent (100 ÷ 20,000). If the company had a preemptive rights feature, and Ms. Morgan chose to use her rights and subscribe to 1 percent of the new shares, she would then own 200 shares and would remain a 1 percent owner (200 ÷ 20,000). A rights offering lasts about one month. During this time the rights are traded on the same exchange or marketplace as are the old shares of stock.

Since the subscription price is set somewhat under the current market price for the old shares, the rights have value. After all, using them gives you the ability to buy stock at a discount, and so save some money. It's similar to the value of a discount coupon. When a shareholder receives rights, she must determine whether to subscribe to the new shares. If the rights are *not* used, they should definitely be sold for their intrinsic value. It would be foolish neither to use nor to sell rights.

Stock Warrants

While rights are usually issued on old shares, warrants are normally issued as a feature of new offerings. Warrants are, essentially, long-term rights. Typically, they offer holders the right to purchase common shares at a fixed price (the subscription price) for periods of up to ten years, sometimes even longer. They are often issued as a "sweetener" on a new issue of bonds to make the new offering more attractive to the investing public. While rights are issued with a positive value (they allow the purchase of stock at a price *less* than the stock's current market price), warrants are "out of the money" at the time they are issued. They permit the purchase of the company's stock at a *higher*-than-current price so that, at least at the time of the issuance, they have no value. What's their attraction? Since they have so long to run (up to 10 years or more), investors believe that *sometime* during their long life the underlying common stock's market price might rise to well above the subscription price, and thus the warrants would then have real value. Warrants are generally considered to be speculative. They are very similar to a "deep out-of-the-money call." Warrants do not necessarily trade on the same exchange or marketplace as does their underlying common stock....

5.2   Two Illustrative Approaches to Formula Valuations of Common Stocks*

Benjamin Graham

Of the various approaches to common stock valuation, the most widely accepted is that which estimates the average earnings and dividends for a period of years in the future and capitalizes these elements at an appropriate rate. This statement is reasonably definite in form, but its application permits the widest range of techniques and assumptions, including plain guesswork. The analyst has first a broad choice as to the future period he will consider; then the earnings and dividends for the period must be estimated, and finally a capitalization rate selected in accordance with his judgment or his prejudices. We may observe here that since there is no *a priori* rule governing the number of years to which the valuer should look forward in the future, it is almost inevitable that in bull markets investors and analysts will tend to see far and hopefully ahead, whereas at other times they will not be so disposed to "heed the rumble of a distant drum." Hence arises a high degree of built-in instability in the market valuation of growth stocks, so much so that one might assert with some justice that the more dynamic the company the more inherently speculative and fluctuating may be the market history of its shares.[1]

When it comes to estimating future earnings few analysts are willing to venture forth, Columbus-like, on completely uncharted seas. They prefer to start with known quantities —e.g., current or past earnings—and process these in some fashion to reach an estimate for the future. As a consequence, in security analysis the past is always being thrown out of the window of theory and coming in again through the back door of practice. It would be a sorry joke on our profession if all the elaborate data on past operations, so industriously collected and so minutely analyzed, should prove in the end to be quite unrelated to the real determinants of the value—the earnings and dividends of the future.

Undoubtedly there are situations, not few perhaps, where this proves to be the rueful fact. But in most cases the relationship between past and future proves significant enough to justify the analyst's preoccupation with the statistical record. In fact the daily work of our practitioner consists largely of an effort to construct a plausible picture of a company's future from his study of its past performance, the latter phrase inevitably suggesting similar intensive studies carried on by devotees of a very different discipline. The better the analyst he is, the less he confines himself to the published figures and the more he adds to these from his special study of the company's management, its policies, and its possibilities.

The student of security analysis, in the classroom or at home, tends to have a special preoccupation with the past record as distinct from an independent judgment of the company's future. He can be taught and can learn to analyze the former, but he lacks a suitable equipment to attempt the latter. What he seeks, typically, is some persuasive method by

---

which a company's earnings record—including such aspects as the average, the trend or growth, stability, etc.—plus some examination of the current balance sheet, can be transmuted first into a projection of future earnings and dividends, and secondly into a valuation based on such projection.

A closer look at this desired process will reveal immediately that the future earnings and dividends need not be computed separately to produce the final value. Take the simplest presentation:

(1) Past earnings times X equal future earnings.
(2) Future earnings times Y equal present value.

This operation immediately foreshortens to:

(3) Past earnings times XY equal present value.

It is the XY factor, or multiplier of past earnings, that my students would dearly love to learn about and to calculate. When I tell them that there is no dependable method of finding this multiplier they tend to be incredulous or to ask, "What good is security analysis then?" They feel that if the right weight is given to all the relevant factors in the past record, at least a reasonably good present valuation of a common stock can be produced, one that will take probable future earnings into account and can be used as a guide to determine the attractiveness or the reverse of the issue at its current market price.

In this article I propose to explain two approaches of this kind which have been developed in a seminar on common-stock valuation. I believe the first will illustrate reasonably well how formula operations of this kind may be worked out and applied. Ours is an endeavor to establish a comparative value in 1957 for each of the 30 stocks in the Dow Jones Industrial Average, related to a base valuation of 400 and 500, respectively, for the composite or group. (The 400 figure represented the approximate "Central Value" of the Dow Jones Average, as found separately by a whole series of formula methods derived from historical relationships. The 500 figure represented about the average market level for the preceding twelve months.)

As will be seen, the valuations of each component issue take into account the four "quality elements" of profitability, growth, stability, and dividend pay-out, applying them as multipliers to the average earnings for 1947–56. In addition, and entirely separately, a weight of 20% is given to the net asset value.

The second approach is essentially the reverse of that just described. Whereas the first method attempts to derive an independent value to be compared with the market price, the second starts with the market price and calculates therefrom the rate of future growth expected by the market. From that figure we readily derive the earnings expected for the future period, in our case 1957–66, and hence the multiplier for such future earnings implicit in the current market price.

The place for detailed comment on these calculations is after they have been developed and presented. But it may be well to express the gist of my conclusions at this point, viz.:

(1) Our own "formula valuations" for the individual stocks, and probably any others of the same general type, have little if any utility in themselves. It would be silly to assert that Stock A is "worth" only half its market price, or Stock B twice its market price, because these figures result from our valuation formula.

(2) On the other hand, they may be suggestive and useful as composite reflections of the past record, taken by itself. They may even be said to represent what the value would be, assuming that the future were merely a continuation of past performances.

(3) The analyst is thus presented with a "discrepancy" of definite magnitude, between formula "value" and the price, which it becomes his task to deal with in terms of his superior knowledge and judgment. The actual size of these discrepancies, and the attitude that may possibly be taken respecting them, are discussed below.

Similarly, the approach which starts from the market price, and derives an implied "growth factor" and an implied multiplier therefrom, may have utility in concentrating the analyst's attention on just what the market seems to be expecting from each stock in the future, in comparison or contrast with what it actually accomplished in the past. Here again his knowledge and judgment are called upon either to accept or reject the apparent assumptions of the marketplace.

Method 1: A Formula Valuation Based Solely on Past Performance in Relation to the Dow Jones Industrial Average as a Group

The assumptions underlying this method are the following:

(1) Each component issue of the Dow Jones Industrial Average may be valued in relation to a base value of the average as a whole by a comparison of the statistical records.

(2) The data to be considered are the following:

(a) *Profitability*—as measured by the rate of return on invested capital. (For convenience this was computed only for the year 1956.)

(b) *Growth of per-share earnings*—as shown by two measurements: 1947–56 earnings vs. 1947 earnings, and 1956 earnings vs. 1947–56 earnings. (It would have been more logical to have used the 1954–56 average instead of the single year 1956, but the change would have little effect on the final valuations.)

(c) *Stability*—as measured by the greatest shrinkage of profits in the periods 1937–38 and 1947–56. (The calculation is based on the percentage of earnings retained in the period of maximum shrinkage.)

(d) *Payout*—as measured by the ratio of 1956 dividends to 1956 earnings. In the few cases where the 1956 earnings were below the 1947–56 average we substituted the latter for the former, to get a more realistic figure of current payout.

These criteria demonstrate the quality of the company's earnings (and dividend policy) and thus may control the multiplier to be applied to the èarnings. The figure found under each heading is divided by the corresponding figure for the Dow Jones group as a whole, to give the company's relative performance. The four relatives were then combined on the basis of equal weights to give a final "quality index" of the company as against the overall quality of the group.

The rate of earnings on invested capital is perhaps the most logical measure of the success and quality of an enterprise. It tells how productive are the dollars invested in the business. In studies made in the relatively "normal" market of 1953 I found a surprisingly good correlation between the profitability rate and the price-earnings ratio, after introducing a major adjustment for the dividend payout and a minor (moderating) adjustment for net asset value.

It is not necessary to emphasize the importance of the growth factor to stock-market people. They are likely to ask rather why we have not taken it as the major determinant of quality and multipliers. There is little doubt that the expected future growth is in fact the major influence upon current price-earnings ratios, and this truth is fully recognized in our second approach, which deals with growth expectations as reflected in market prices. But the correlation between market multipliers and past growth is by no means close.

Some interesting figures worked out by Ralph A. Bing show this clearly.[2] Dow Chemical, with per-share earnings growth of 31% (1955 vs. 1948) had in August 1956 a price-earnings ratio of 47.3 times 1955 earnings. Bethlehem Steel, with corresponding growth of 93%, had a multiplier of only 9.1. The spread between the two relationships is thus as wide as fourteen to one. Other ratios in Mr. Bing's table show similar wide disparities between past growth and current multipliers.

It is here that the stability factor asserts its importance. The companies with high multipliers may not have had the best growth in 1948–55, but most of them had greater than average stability of earnings over the past two decades.

These considerations led us to adopt the simple arithmetical course of assigning equal weight to past growth, past stability, and current profitability in working out the quality coefficient for each company. The dividend payout is not strictly a measure of quality of earning power, though in the typical case investors probably regard it in some such fashion. Its importance in most instances is undeniable, and it is both convenient and plausible to give it equal weight and similar treatment with each of the other factors just discussed.

Finally, we depart from the usual Wall Street attitude and assign a weight of 20% in the final valuation to the net assets per share. It is true that in the typical case the asset value has no perceptible influence on current market price. But it may have some long-run effect on future market price, and thus it has a claim to be considered seriously in any independent valuation of a company. As is well known, asset values invariably play some part, sometimes a fairly important one, in the many varieties of legal valuations of common stocks, which grow out of tax cases, merger litigation, and the like. The basic justification for considering asset value in this process, even though it may be ignored in the current market price, lies in the possibility of its showing its weight later, through competitive developments, changes in management or its policies, merger or sale eventuality, etc.

The above discussion will explain, perhaps not very satisfactorily, why the four factors entering into the quality rating and the fifth factor of asset value were finally assigned equal weight of 20% each.

The actual application of our illustrative method can now be explained by working through the figures for the first company in the group, Allied Chemical & Dye. Following are data used in computing the "value" of ACD relative to a 400 and a 500 valuation for the Dow Jones Industrial Average (see table 5.2.1).

In table 5.2.2 we supply the "valuation" reached by this method for each of the 30 stocks in the Dow Jones Industrial Average. Our table includes the various quality factors, the average earnings, and the asset values used to arrive at our final figures.

In about half the cases these "valuations" differ quite widely from the prices ruling on August 5 last, on which date the D. J. Average actually sold at 500. Seven issues were selling at 20% or more above their formula value, and an equal number at 20% or more

Table 5.2.1

	D.J. Ind. Av.	Allied C. & D.	"Quality" factors: Ratio of ACD to D.J.
Earned per share			
1956	$ 36.00	$ 4.74	
1947–1956	27.00	4.50	
1947	21.80	3.73	
1938 (unadjusted)	6.01	5.92	
1937 (unadjusted)	11.49	11.19	
Dividends 1956	23.15	3.00	
Net asset value 1956	275.00	40.00	
Profitability:			
1956 earnings/1956 net assets	13.0%	11.85%	91%
Growth			
A: 1947–56 vs. 1957–59	26%	21%	
B: 1956 vs. 1947–56	30%	5%	
A plus B	56%	26%	46%
Stability:			
1938 earnings/1937 earnings	52.3%	53%	101%
Payout:			
1956 dividend/1956 earnings	64.3%	64%	100%
Average of four quality factors			84%

Formula to produce value of 400 for D.J. Ind. Av.:

"Value" equals 1/5 net assets plus 12.5 × 1947–56 earnings or 55 plus 12.5 × 27.50 or 400.

Corresponding "valuation" of Allied Chem. & Dye, (including Quality Factor of 84%):

Value equals 1/5 × 40 plus 0.84 × 12.5 × 4.50 or 55.

Formula to produce value of 500 for D.J. Ind. Av.:

Value equals 1/5 net assets plus 16.2 × 1947–56 earnings or 500.

Corresponding "valuation" of Allied Chem. & Dye:

Value equals 1/5 × 40 plus 0.84 × 16.2 × 4.50 or 69.

below such value. At the extremes we find Westinghouse selling at a 100% "premium," and United Aircraft at about a 50% "discount." The extent of these disparities naturally suggests that our method is technically a poor one, and that more plausible valuations could be reached—i.e., ones more congruous with market prices—if a better choice were made of the factors and weights entering into the method.

A number of tests were applied to our results to see if they could be "improved" by some plausible changes in the technique. To give these in any detail would prolong this report unnecessarily. Suffice it to say that they were unproductive. If the asset-value factor had been excluded, a very slight change would have resulted in favor of the issues which were selling at the highest premium over their formula value. On the other hand, if major

Table 5.2.2
Formula valuations of Dow Jones Industrial issues

Company	Quality factors				Avg. factor	Earnings 1947–56	Book value	Indicated value basis		Price 8/5/57
	Profit.	Growth	Stability	Payout				D.J. 400	D.J. 500	
Allied Ch.	91	46	94	100	84	4.50	40	55	69	89
Am. Can	81	70	137	107	99	2.61	28	39	48	44
Am. S. & Ref.	101	39	100	81	80	5.43	51	65	85	54
Am. T. & T.	54	40	165	130	97	9.90	150	151	185	173
Am. Tob.	98	27	111	104	85	6.58	59	82	102	72
Beth. St.	95	138	0	97	83	2.88	31	36	45	49
Chrysler	91*	0	38	51	45	8.15	74	66	80	77
Corn. Prod.	100	65	114	98	94	1.96	40	31	37	31
Du Pont	154	198	100	109	140	5.60	41	107	136	199
East. Kod.	136	100	148	85	117	3.49	28	57	63	104
Gen. Elec.	139	129	84	127	120	1.87	14	31	39	68
Gen. Foods	138	99	141	79	114	2.42	20	39	49	49
Gen. Motors	160	119	95	104	120	2.48	20	42	53	45
Goodyear T.	108	207	129	83	132	4.18	43	78	98	76
Int. Harv.	58*	0	91	98	62	3.70	49	39	47	35
Int. Nickel	164	263	119	90	159	3.86	31	83	105	92
Int. Paper	100	46	0	101	62	6.40	55	61	76	101
Johns Man.	93	96	44	100	83	3.07	29	38	47	45
Nat. Dist.	73*	0	62	118	63	2.47	26	25	31	26
Nat. Steel	95	96	101	88	95	5.71	68	79	99	75
Proc. & Gam.	110	46	105	103	91	2.61	21	34	42	49
Sears Roe.	112	56	144	84	99	1.82	15	26	32	28
S. O. Cal.	124	113	134	65	109	3.09	24	47	59	58
S. O. N. J.	130	166	97	80	118	2.85	24	47	59	67
Texas Corp.	126	171	81	66	111	3.48	34	56	70	74
Un. C. & C.	138	92	108	100	110	3.73	27	53	67	117
Un. Aircr.	158	361	181	66	192	3.65	35	96	121	62
U. S. Steel	99	239	0	67	101	3.51	47	54	67	69
Westinghouse	65*	0	0	83	37	3.79	43	27	32	64
Woolworth	69*	0	116	109	74	3.58	40	41	51	42
D.J. Ind. Av.	(13.0)	(56)	(52.3)	(64.3)	100	27.50	275	400	500	500

* Based on 1947–56 Average earnings vs. 1956 book value plus adj.

emphasis had been placed on the factor of past growth, some of our apparently under-valued issues would have been given still larger formula values; for table 5.2.2 shows that more of the spectacular growth percentages occur in this group than in the other—e.g., United Aircraft, International Nickel, and Goodyear.

It is quite evident from table 5.2.2 that the stock market fixes its valuation of a given common stock on the basis not of its past statistical performance but rather of its expected future performance, which may differ significantly from its past behavior. The market is, of course, fully justified in seeking to make this independent appraisal of the future, and for that reason any automatic rejection of the market's verdict because it differs from a formula valuation would be the height of folly. We cannot avoid the observation, however, that the independent appraisals made in the stock market are themselves far from infal-lible, as is shown in part by the rapid changes to which they are subject. It is possible, in fact, that they may be on the whole a no more dependable guide to what the future will produce than the "values" reached by our mechanical processing of past data, with all the latter's obvious shortcomings.

Method 2

Let us turn now to our second mathematical approach, which concerns itself with future growth, or future earnings, as they appear to be predicted by the market price itself. We start with the theory that the market price of a representative stock, such as any one in the Dow Jones group, reflects the earnings to be expected in a future period, times a multiplier which is in turn based on the percentage of future growth. Thus an issue for which more than average growth is expected will have this fact shown to a double degree, or "squared," in its market price—first in the higher figure taken for future earnings, and second in the higher multiplier applied to those higher earnings.

We shall measure growth by comparing the expected 1957–66 earnings with the actual figures for 1947–56. Our basic formula says, somewhat arbitrarily, that where no growth is expected the current price will be 8 times both 1947–56 earnings and the expected 1957–66 earnings. If growth G is expected, expressed as the ratio of 1957–66 to 1947–56 earnings, then the price reflects such next decade earnings multiplied by 8 times G.

From these assumptions we obtain the simple formula:

Price equals $(E \times G) \times (8 \times G)$, or $8G^2 \times E$,
where E is the per-share earnings for 1947–56.

To find G, the expected rate of future growth, we have only to divide the current price by 8 times 1947–56 earnings, and take the square root.

When this is done for the Dow Jones Average as a whole, using its August 5, 1957, price of 500, we get a value of 1.5 for G—indicating an expected growth of 50% for 1957–66 earnings vs. the 1947–56 actuality. This anticipates an average of $41.00 in the next decade, as against $27.50 for the previous ten years and about $36.00 in 1956. This esti-mate appears reasonable to the writer in relation to the 500 level. (In fact he started with this estimate and worked back from it to get the basic multiplier of 8 to be applied to issues with no expected growth.) The price of 500 for the D. J. Average would represent in turn a

Table 5.2.3

Formula calculations of expected growth of earnings of Dow Jones Industrial issues, as indicated by August 5, 1957, price

Company	Price 8/5/57	Average earnings 1947–56	Exp. growth 1957–66 vs. 1947–56	Indicated earnings 1957–66	Indicated multiplier*	Earnings 1956	Exp. incr. 1957–66 vs. 1956	Act. incr. 1956 vs. 1947–56
Allied Ch.	89	$ 4.50	+58%	$ 7.22	12.6	$ 4.74	+52%	+6%
Am. Can	44	2.61	46	3.83	11.6	2.92	33	12
Am. S. & R.	54	5.43	12	6.10	9.0	6.67	(–8)	23
Am. T. & T.**	173	9.90	47	14.70	11.8	10.74	36	14
Am. Tob.	72	6.58	18	7.80	9.4	7.51	4	14
Beth. St.	49	2.88	44	4.15	11.5	3.83	8	33
Chrysler	77	8.95	4	9.28	8.3	2.29	(large)	(–76)
Corn Prod.	31	1.96	41	2.76	11.4	2.36	18	12
Du Pont	199	5.60	112	11.85	17.0	8.20	45	47
East. Kod.	104	3.49	93	6.62	15.4	4.89	36	37
Gen. Elec.	68	1.87	113	4.00	17.0	2.45	62	31
Gen. Foods	49	2.42	59	3.86	12.7	3.56	9	45
Gen. Motors	45	2.48	51	3.74	12.1	3.02	24	22
Goodyear T.	76	4.18	42	5.96	11.4	6.03	(–1)	47
Int. Harv.	35	3.70	8	4.02	8.6	3.14	29	(–15)
Int. Nickel	92	3.86	62	6.30	13.0	6.50	(–3)	68
Int. Paper	101	6.40	40	9.03	11.2	7.05	28	11
Johns Man.	45	3.07	36	4.21	10.9	3.50	20	14
Nat. Dist.	26	2.47	15	2.86	9.2	2.11	36	(–15)
Nat. Steel	75	5.71	28	7.32	10.2	7.09	3	25
Proc. & Gam.	49	2.61	53	3.99	12.2	3.05	30	20
Sears Roebuck	28	1.82	38	2.53	11.0	2.20	16	18
S. O. Cal.	58	3.09	55	4.78	12.4	4.24	12	39
S. O. N. J.	67	2.85	72	4.99	13.8	4.11	21	44
Texas Corp.	74	3.48	62	5.66	13.0	5.51	3	59
Un. C. & C.	117	3.73	99	7.43	15.9	4.86	53	32
Un. Air.	62	3.65	45	5.31	11.6	7.66	(–32)	93
U. S. Steel	69	3.51	57	5.55	12.6	6.01	(–8)	73
Westinghouse	64	3.79	45	5.53	11.6	.10	(large)	(–97)
Woolworth	42	3.58	22	4.39	9.8	3.57	23	0
D. J. Ind. Av.	500	$27.50	50	$41.25	12.0	$35.80	15	30

* Dec. 1956 price ÷ Indicated 1957–66 Earnings.

** The basic formula is less applicable to AT&T than to industrial issues.

multiplier of 8×1.5, or 12, to be applied to the expected future earnings of $41. (Incidentally, on these assumptions the average current formula value of about 400 for the Dow Jones Average would reflect expectations of a decade-to-decade growth of 35%, average earnings of $37.10 for 1957–66, and a current multiplier of 10.8 for such future earnings.)

In table 5.2.3 we set forth the results of applying this second approach to the 30 Dow Jones issues. (The figures for Am. Tel. & Tel. might well be ignored, since utility issues should take a different basic formula.) The main interest in the table lies in the disparities it indicates between the expected future growth, implicit in the market prices, and the actual growth during the past decade. Ten of the companies (plus AT&T) sold at prices anticipating at least twice the Dow Jones Average rate of growth, comparing 1957–66 with 1956. Of these only two, Du Pont and General Electric, had actually shown distinctly better than average growth in the last ten years. Conversely, eight of the companies were indicating less than half the average expected rate of growth, including five for which actual declines from 1956 levels were apparently predicted. Yet of these eight companies, no less than five had actually shown far greater than average growth in the past decade.

This leads us to our final observations, which tie our two tables together. The ten companies previously mentioned, for which unusually rapid growth is anticipated, include seven of those shown in table 5.2.2 as selling significantly above their formula valuation. Again, the eight for which subnormal or no growth is expected include six which were selling substantially below their formula valuations.

We conclude that a large part of the discrepancies between carefully calculated formula values and the market prices can be traced to the growth factor, not because the formulas underplay its importance, but rather because the market often has concepts of future earnings changes which cannot be derived from the companies' past performance. The reasons for the market's breaking with the past are often abundantly clear. Investors do not believe, for example, that United Aircraft will duplicate its brilliant record of 1947–56, because they consider that a company with the United States Department of Defense as its chief customer is inherently vulnerable. They have the opposite view with regard to Westinghouse. They feel its relatively mediocre showing in recent years was the result of temporary factors, and that the electric manufacturing industry is inherently so growth-assured that a major supplier such as Westinghouse is bound to prosper in the future.

These cases are clear cut enough, but other divergencies shown in our table are not so easy to understand or to accept. There is a difference between these two verbs. The market may be right in its general feeling about a company's future, but the price tag it sets on the future may be quite unreasonable in either direction.

It is here that many analysts will find their challenge. They may not be satisfied merely to find out what the market is doing and thinking, and then to explain it to everyone's satisfaction. They may prefer to exercise an independent judgment—one not controlled by the daily verdict of the marketplace, but ready at times to take definite issue with it. For this kind of activity one or more valuation processes, of the general type we have been illustrating, may serve a useful purpose. They give a concrete and elaborated picture of the past record, which the analyst may use as a point of departure for his individual exploration and discoveries in the field of investment values.

Notes

1. On this point the philosophically inclined are referred to the recent article of David Durand, "Growth Stocks and the Petersburg Paradox," *The Journal of Finance* (September 1957): 348–63. His conclusion is that "the growth stock problem offers no great hope of a satisfactory solution."
2. R. A. Bing, "Can We Improve Methods of Appraising Growth Stocks?" *Commercial and Financial Chronicle* (September 13, 1956).

5.3   Portfolio Management: Seven Ways to Improve Performance*,[1]
Richard H. Jenrette

The Portfolio manager today faces increasing pressures to improve investment performance. These pressures come at a time when the task of obtaining what are considered good results is becoming increasingly difficult, reflecting the huge size of assets under institutional management, the growing sophistication of professional managers generally, and hence the competition between managers, and, of course, the challenge of the market itself.

Given the pressures to improve performance, what are some of the ways to improve results? I would like to outline seven steps which we believe are essential to superior investment results.

Step 1.   Set Your Bogey—Define and Analyze What You Are Trying to Beat

The first step toward improving investment results is to gain agreement with the client as to what you are trying to accomplish. This, of course, usually involves agreement at the outset as to what funds, if any, are going to be set aside, more or less permanently, as fixed-income holdings and what percentage of funds are eligible for equity-type investments with a less predictable return.

For the equity portion, we see a growing use of the popular market averages— Standard & Poor's or Dow Jones Industrial—as a benchmark for measuring performance. The objective or account bogey increasingly assigned the portfolio manager is to do better than the market, as represented by one of the averages. The University of Chicago studies, showing a 7%–8% average annual return from common stock over long periods of time suggest that "beating the market" is indeed a worthwhile goal. Particularly for the large institution whose own buying and selling of securities has a sharp market impact, and whose cash flow frequently reaches its peak simultaneously with the market, equalling the market is a very good performance. For the smaller and more flexible fund, a stated return above the market might be appropriate. In any case, for the equity portion of a portfolio, a bogey relative to the market is more realistic, in my judgment, than one put in terms of absolute percentage gains.

If doing better than the "market" is the account objective, and increasingly it seems to be, the logical first step is to examine in detail the thing that you are trying to beat. At DLJ [Donaldson, Lufkin, & Jenrette], we obtain a monthly updated industry diversification for the Standard & Poor's 500 index, which we use as a measure of the market. We prefer the S&P because it offers a finer analytical tool for portfolio composition than averages such as the Dow Jones which uses a far smaller and unweighted number of stocks. With the

---

S&P we have full and accurately-weighted industry representation (except for banks and insurance companies). . . .

The S&P average is nothing more than a starting point—but at least it is that. Common sense suggests that if you are favorably disposed toward a certain industry, and if your objective is to do better than the S&P average, then you should seriously consider giving the particular industry a greater weight in your portfolio than is found in the S&P. For example, about six months ago our firm became quite optimistic over prospects for the oil industry. When we mentioned this fact to many of our institutional clients, they agreed but replied they already had a large position in oils. On examination, we found that this usually meant 8%–10% of the common stock portfolio. Yet at that time, the S&P average actually contained a 16% weight for oils. Holding a lower percentage in oils actually implied a negative judgment of the industry's prospects.

Applying the S&P point of reference generally, you might say that the investor whose objective is to equal the performance of these averages probably should not stray too far from the industry diversification of these averages in constructing his own portfolio. Similarly, if your objective is to do substantially better than the averages, you should see to it that your portfolio does differ—in the right way, of course—from the market averages' weighting.

Many of our clients have questioned the use of the S&P as an account bogey on the very valid grounds that (1) you can't invest in the averages, and (2) this is a "no-decision" bogey, and comparisons should be made with "decision" alternatives such as other mutual funds, common trusts of banks, privately managed pension funds, etc. In general, I am in agreement with this line of reasoning. There is a practical problem, however, in deciding what is a comparable fund for purposes of comparison. Moreover, the nature of the capital one is managing may preclude some of the investment practices of some of the swifter mutual funds.

Nevertheless, the practice of comparing one's performance with decision alternatives (as opposed to the no-decision S&P) does have considerable merit and may gain increasing acceptance. To the extent one does find himself compared to certain mutual funds, one can still follow the approach outlined in analyzing the composition of the S&P. We do this through quarterly breakdowns of institutional portfolios along the lines of the S&P industry diversification. Such an analysis, for example, recently disclosed a below-average market weighting in oils (less than the S&P 16%) for most of the aggressive funds. In view of our favorable view of oil industry prospects, this suggested a substantial accumulation of oil industry shares by the funds potentially was in the offing. These same funds also had 10% plus in airlines, suggesting no room for further accumulation. All this is a part of knowing what your competition is and deciding when and where you are going to differ from the competition, if at all.

Step 2. Know Your Limitations

Knowing your limitations is an important prerequisite to determining how you are going to manage the portfolio. How flexible can you be? Some funds have a portfolio turnover rate which would not be acceptable to many investors or trustees. Do you have discretion over the account, or do you have to go before a committee and then call up or write 500 clients, and then sweat out a painful buying and selling process in the order room? Does the character of the capital you manage prohibit certain types of investments or make them meaningless to overall performance?

Unless you have discretion and the ability to act quickly, you may as well forget about "fashion investing"—buying stocks currently in vogue but which may drop from favor quickly. At the other end of the spectrum, you may also be constrained from such "contrary opinion" approaches as buying depressed stocks or turnarounds—if your limitations prelude flexibility. Turnarounds often backfire and depressed stocks often keep going down for fundamental reasons not at first apparent.

In short, if you lack flexibility perhaps you are limited to fairly orthodox, middle-of-the-road quality companies, with a diversification weighting that resembles the market averages or your leading competitors, such as other funds. Moreover, if you lack flexibility, you had better operate on a considerably longer time span than many institutions currently appear to be.

Step 3.   Have an Investment Philosophy

Most of us have an investment philosophy—usually reflected in the kind of company we are most comfortable buying. Some investors, for example, have an inherent bias toward small growth companies, some are most disposed toward turnarounds, some like to "play" the business cycle, some buy strong fundamentals without regard to price or price/earnings ratio, others avoid all investments that have a trace of cyclicality.

While we believe everyone should have an investment philosophy, we see certain dangers in a rigid approach, such as all the foregoing imply. At DLJ we have evolved a fairly simple investment philosophy which we believe is flexible to meet changing circumstances. It has led us to a variety of investments over the last seven years.

Rule No. 1:   Buy Relative Earnings Growth

By this, I refer to companies whose earnings are growing faster than overall corporate profits—for the time span in which we are making the investment. The concept of investing in relative earnings growth rests simply on the belief that the market will always show greatest interest in those companies showing the largest earnings gains—relative to overall corporate profits. The time span in which you choose to look for relative earnings growth relates back to step 2 above (how flexible can you be) and will vary from one investor to the next. We have usually used a time span of 1–3 years in which we look for relative earnings growth. Some institutions with a high degree of flexibility are operating on a shorter time span. Others, with little flexibility, might be well advised to use longer than a three-year span. It is surprising how short a time span many institutional investors are operating on today, which creates unusual opportunities for the investor willing to look just a little bit into the future. The important point is to concentrate the weight of your portfolio in companies showing much more rapid gains in earnings than the economy as a whole—during the time span in which you can operate.

Rule No. 2:   At a Reasonable Relative Price-earnings Ratio

Here again one must apply the relative test. How does the stock's current multiple look relative to its historical relationship to the market's multiple? Under these guidelines, the ideal investment is a company whose earnings not only have been and are still moving up relative to corporate profits generally, but also with a price/earnings ratio which has been moving down relative to the market—despite the above-average earnings growth. A vulnerable pattern would be declining or level relative earnings and an increasing relative multiple. Stocks demonstrating this pattern usually soon begin to lag the market, assuming, of course, that there is no reason to expect a reversal of the downward relative earnings trend. Stocks like Sears Roebuck and General Foods showed this pattern from early 1963 to early 1966.

As a guide to implementing this philosophy of concentrating the portfolio in companies and industries experiencing relative earnings growth, we use Standard & Poor's computer tapes to compute relative price, earnings, price/earnings and yields for roughly 900 companies and 80 industry groups on a quarterly basis. The charts derived from this data have proved a valuable tool in identifying relative earnings trends which have not been reflected in price/earnings ratios. There is usually a sufficient lag between the emergence of relative earnings growth and price to permit accumulation of a substantial position.

The chief advantage of this rather simple philosophy of investing in relatively growing earnings at a reasonable relative multiple is its adaptability. The search for relative earnings growth might lead one to stress cyclical stocks at a given time (such as was appropriate in the 1962–66 period of rapid industrial expansion) or high growth rate stocks, or in another environment, the moderate but predictable growth industries such as utilities, foods, etc. (suitable in the 1955–60 hiatus in corporate profits growth in the U.S.)

1966 provided a new challenge to investing in relatively increasing earnings. Recognition that bond yields would increase significantly in 1966 might have helped put the expected large corporate earnings increase in 1966 in perspective. As things turned out, the yield available to investors on high grade bonds at their peak had increased by about 25% over year-end 1965. This compares with an earnings increase of 10%–15% for corporate profits. Corporate earnings thus declined relative to the increase in bond yields in 1966. The subsequent result was a considerable reduction in the total market price/earnings ratio.

Step 4.   Develop an Investment Strategy

Having an investment strategy is essential to implementation of the investment philosophy just described. The strategy selected must encompass the time span for which you are investing. It grows out of your assessment of the *character* of the economy over this span. I place particular stress on the word character since we believe directional change and the general economic environment are far more important in developing investment strategy than is a detailed, specific forecast of GNP.

For example, is the economy likely to be characterized by price inflation or are deflationary pressures at work? Are wage increases running ahead of productivity gains as appears to be the case now? What is the net effect on profit margins? What segments of the economy are most vigorous? Capital goods, government, or consumer spending? In effect, you are trying to decide which stream to be fishing in, and the answers to these questions will provide a set of criteria which can be used to test existing or proposed commitments.

Out of your assessment of the character of the economy comes a strategy. Should the portfolio be weighted toward economy-oriented areas such as capital goods and other cyclical industries, or should it be skewed away from business cycle exposure, with heavy weighting in such groups as utilities, insurance, food, or other consumer non-durables? Should one avoid labor-intensive industries, such as the current environment suggests? Should one stick to "quality" companies (such as in the early stages of market recovery) or are some of the "second-line" companies likely to be the main beneficiaries of the environment you foresee? What attitude should be taken toward high multiple growth stocks?

Evolving an appropriate strategy for changing economic and market conditions is admittedly difficult but absolutely essential to superior results.

Step 5.   Concentrate the Portfolio

You may be right in your choice of strategy and have brilliant company selection, but if the portfolio manager lacks courage to implement the program the good effort will be subverted.

Over-diversification is probably the greatest enemy of portfolio performance. Most of the portfolios we look at have too many names. As a result, the impact of a good idea is negligible. Moreover, the greater the number of companies in the portfolio the more difficult it is for the fund manager to stay on top of developments affecting these companies....

The chief roadblock to portfolio concentration in taxable funds is reluctance to take capital gains. While we could discourse at length on this subject, in our judgment the penalties involved in realizing capital gains from time to time are more than offset by the benefits of flexible management, which inherently involves change.

It is surprising that this reluctance to realize capital gains is also quite often found in tax-free funds. In all honesty, many of us as portfolio managers are reluctant to eliminate a holding with a big gain—which stands as a reminder of past wisdom! As focus increasingly shifts to overall investment performance under some of the new measurement systems, I fear we may be far less comfortable holding securities with large unrealized gains if their potential no longer justifies retention.

Step 6.   Flexibility

This brings us to the next key element in superior portfolio management, and this is flexibility. Nothing is more certain than change, and it seems rather obvious that flexibility is needed to meet changing circumstances. Yet most of us yearn for some sort of panacea which will carry us through without having to make change. Some portfolio managers seem to fear that making a change in the portfolio is tantamount to admitting a mistake. This fear is based on the mistaken view that there are "stocks for all seasons." Few companies are appropriate to all environments.

If flexibility is a key element in portfolio performance, it is surprising how few of us have structured our own organizations to respond to change. The rigidities built into most investment organizations are staggering. It is hardly surprising so few changes are made considering the red tape involved in implementing change. Because of this red tape, the relatively few organizations that have organized to act quickly enjoy a significant and growing competitive advantage over their more encumbered competitors.

Chiefly responsible for this inflexibility is our industry's reluctance to accept discretionary power over client funds—or to insist on it. It seems to us that the investment manager is going to be judged on results—regardless of whether the client concurs. We may as well face this responsibility and accept capital only on terms which permit us to do a first-rate management job.

Step 7.   Keep Score

Buttressed by a 30-year bull market, the investment community, at least until recently, has seldom found it necessary to report results to its clients. Elaborate client appraisals give all sorts of information, but we rarely see one that reports the most important single piece of information in which the client should be interested, namely the performance of the fund. Even rarer are references to other published indices such as the market averages, which might be used for comparison purposes. If it is understandable why investment managers have not wished to make their clients more performance-oriented, it is nonetheless surprising how few of us bother to keep score for our own edification as professional investment managers. Interesting possibilities exist to go behind performance measurement figures to analyze why the account did better or worse than its objective.

In closing, I would like to say again that performance measurement is here to stay, whether we welcome it with open arms or not. The result is a much more competitive environment, stressing the need to turn performance measurement into an aid to better performance in line with objectives.

Note

1. Reprinted from the transcript of an address given to the New York Society of Security Analysts, October 19, 1966, with permission of Richard H. Jenrette.

Class Exercise: Drafting a Code of Ethics

Over the last few years, press reports have focused on the issue of personal trading in securities by investment professionals and other employees at mutual fund complexes. As a practical matter, the issue has revolved around personal trading of stocks. This exercise is intended to provide you with background on the issue of personal trading, and an opportunity to come to grips with the practical issues related to personal trading, by drafting a Code of Ethics for a mutual fund complex.

The SEC requires every mutual fund and its investment adviser to adopt a Code of Ethics meeting certain criteria. First, the code must be reasonably designed to prevent fraudulent and manipulative practices. Second, the code must require "access persons"— those with access to information about fund trades—to file reports on their trading at least quarterly with the fund adviser. Third, the code must include reasonable procedures to maintain records of personal trading and to enforce the provisions of the code.

This approach gives mutual fund complexes considerable leeway in fashioning rules on personal trading that are appropriate for the particular fund complex. However, the Investment Company Institute (ICI)—the trade organization for mutual funds—has published detailed guidelines for "best practices" on personal trading, and these guidelines have been accepted by most fund complexes. The SEC reviews both the substance and enforcement of a complex's Code of Ethics through the examination and inspection process. The SEC also has instituted enforcement actions in cases where it finds that fund personnel are violating the code and/or provisions of the federal securities laws.

By contrast, neither federal nor state laws require Codes of Ethics for personal trading by employees of other financial institutions, such as commercial banks, insurance companies, or pension funds. The employees of these financial institutions are subject mainly to general fiduciary restrictions against certain conflicts of interest. Indeed, the SEC does not impose the requirements of a Code of Ethics on investment advisers to entities other than mutual funds; for example, an investment adviser to a hedge fund has no SEC obligation to adopt a Code of Ethics.

Let us begin our discussion of the Code of Ethics by focusing on two polar approaches to regulating personal trading by fund complex employees. On the one hand, Congress could enact legislation that would ban all personal trading by employees of mutual fund advisers and their affiliates. A modified ban would prohibit all personal trading in securities other than mutual funds. What would be the pros and cons of such a ban?

On the other hand, the SEC could simply rely on existing antifraud and antimanipulation rules together with a system for reporting and monitoring trades by fund-related personnel. It is already illegal to front-run a fund—that is, for such personnel to buy or sell a stock for their own account on the basis of advance knowledge of what a fund will be trading. Would it be sufficient to have a compliance officer review all trades by fund-related personnel, reported pursuant to a code requirement, in order to ascertain whether anyone had engaged in fraudulent or manipulative conduct?

Between these poles, of course, lie many intermediate approaches to restricting but not banning personal trading.

In-Class Discussion Questions

After reading the background materials for this exercise, your team should attempt to draft the key provisions of a model Code of Ethics for a medium-size fund complex including various types of stock, bond, and money market funds. In the process, your team should be prepared to answer the following questions:

1. Who precisely will the code be regulating? What are the relevant categories of fund-related personnel and should they be regulated differently in some respect?
2. What types of transactions should be regulated by the code? Should the code treat differently trades in various kinds of securities (stocks, bonds, treasuries, mutual funds, etc.)? Should the code have special provisions for securities transactions other than trades on a U.S. stock exchange (e.g., initial public offerings and private placements)?
3. What will be the code's regulatory strategy (e.g., prohibitions, disclosure, or advance approval) toward various transactions? What transactions by which people should be subjected to the strictest regulatory strategies?
4. How will the code be enforced? How often will reports be submitted and by whom? How will disputes be resolved about possible violations of the code? What types of sanctions should be imposed for code violations?

5.4   Report of the Advisory Group on Personal Investing*

A   Statutory Standards

The federal securities laws prohibit outright certain types of transactions by investment company personnel. Some of these restrictions apply broadly to all participants in the marketplace. For example, Section 10(b) of the Securities Exchange Act and Rule 10b-5 thereunder have been interpreted to proscribe trading on the basis of material, nonpublic information or communicating this information in breach of a fiduciary duty ("insider trading" and "tipping"). The prohibition on insider trading applies to "any person" and not just investment company personnel.

The insider trading prohibition must be distinguished from the focus of recent media discussions and of this report: the latter concerns personal trading activities by investment company personnel that do *not* constitute insider trading but *may* involve fraud or raise other conflict issues. The federal securities laws impose additional layers of protection to address these latter concerns. For example, investment company personnel are prohibited from:

- purchasing or selling securities for a personal account in order to profit from a subsequent purchase or sale by an investment company ("front-running");
- placing the investment company in securities in order to receive personal investment opportunities, bribes, or kickbacks; or
- purchasing or selling securities from the investment company.

B   Rule 17j-1

In addition to these statutory proscriptions, the personal investing activities of investment company personnel are subject to strict regulation by the Commission. Investment Company Act Rule 17j-1, the linchpin of the commission's regulatory authority, was the product of a lengthy gestation period. Over thirty years ago, in its landmark 1963 *Special Study of the Securities Markets*, the Commission noted that personal trades by investment company personnel in securities held by an investment company they advise may raise a conflict of interest. The *Special Study* noted:

broad industry awareness of the problem raised by the conflict of interest which may exist when an individual or entity privy to a mutual fund's investment recommendations and decisions engages in trading for his, her, or its own account in securities purchased or sold by the fund. The almost universal existence of policies aimed at dealing with the problem and the adoption of such a policy in 1962 by the industry's principal trade organization, the Investment Company Institute, are evidence of this awareness.

---

* Investment Company Institute, May 9, 1994, pp. 6–12, 16–17. [Footnotes deleted.] Reprinted with permission.

The issue resurfaced three years later in the Commission's report on the *Public Policy Implications of Investment Company Growth.* In the *Public Policy Implications* report, the Commission requested that Congress give it specific authority to adopt rules for the protection of investors in connection with securities transactions by investment companies and by persons affiliated with investment companies, or their investment advisers or principal underwriters. With the industry's support, Congress added Section 17(j) to the Investment Company Act in 1970. Section 17(j), as enacted, expressly contemplated that investment company personnel would, and could, engage in "the purchase or sale ... of ... securit[ies] held or to be acquired by [a] registered investment company" with which they are employed or affiliated. Consequently, Section 17(j) does not ban personal investing, but rather authorizes the Commission to adopt rules and regulations necessary to prevent any trading practices that might prove "fraudulent, deceptive, or manipulative."

Among other things, Section 17(j) specifically authorizes the Commission, by rule, to require "the adoption of codes of ethics by registered investment companies and investment advisers of, and principal underwriters for, such investment companies...." The Senate Report accompanying the bill enacting Section 17(j) noted that the provision gave the Commission broad authority "to draw flexible guidelines to prohibit [affiliated] persons ... from engaging in securities transactions for their personal accounts when such transactions are likely to conflict with the investment programs of their companies."

The Commission's subsequent rulemaking reflected a delicate balance between the appropriateness of prohibiting conduct that might disadvantage investment company shareholders and the desirability of utilizing individual compliance efforts to take account of the facts and circumstances unique to each investment company. The initial version of the rule, proposed in 1972, contained specific trading prohibitions and would have mandated that codes of ethics violations be reported to the Commission. The proposed rule was withdrawn in 1976 and reproposed two years later, in an effort to provide greater flexibility to investment companies in adapting their codes of ethics to their specific operations. Two years later, after further comments and revisions, Rule 17j-1 was promulgated in its current form.

In brief, the Rule:

- prohibits directors, officers and employees of investment companies (and their investment advisers and principal underwriters) from engaging in fraudulent, manipulative or deceptive conduct in connection with their personal trading of securities held or to be acquired by the investment company;
- requires investment companies (and their investment advisers and principal underwriters) to adopt codes of ethics and procedures reasonably designed to prevent trading prohibited by the rule;
- requires every "access person" to file reports with the firm concerning his or her personal securities transactions, within 10 days of the end of the quarter in which the transaction was effected; and
- requires investment companies (and their investment advisers and principal underwriters) to maintain records related to the implementation of their procedures.

Several features of the rule are worth particular note. First, Rule 17j-1 specifically exempts from any of its terms (and presumably *any* limitations on personal transactions by investment company personnel) transactions in "securities issued by the Government of the United States, bankers' acceptances, bank certificates of deposit, commercial paper, and shares of registered open-end investment companies."

Second, Rule 17j-1 defines the term "access person" quite broadly. With respect to an investment adviser, for example, the term "access person" is defined to include any director, officer, and general partner, as well as any employee "who, in connection with his or her regular functions or duties, makes, participates in, or obtains information, regarding the purchase or sale of a security by a registered investment company, or whose functions relate to the making of any recommendations with respect to such purchases or sales." Moreover, the filing requirement was extended to transactions involving any security in which the access person has "any direct or indirect beneficial ownership," a provision broad enough to encompass accounts held by immediate family members in the same household and certain trust accounts if the access person has influence or control over those accounts. As a result, many investment companies have elected to treat all of their employees *and* their immediate family members as access persons and to require them to file the quarterly reports required under Rule 17j-1.

Finally, these procedures, particularly the reporting requirement, were designed to enable each investment company complex to detect and to prevent potential conflicts of interest, including those that may not be addressed specifically by Commission regulations, in a manner deemed most effective for its particular business structure and operations. As the Commission stated when it adopted Rule 17j-1:

[T]he variety of employment and the institutional arrangements utilized by different investment companies renders impracticable a rule designed to cover all conceivable possibilities. Moreover, as a matter of policy, the Commission believes the introduction and tailoring of ethical restraints on the behavior of persons associated with an investment company can best be left in the first instance to the directors of the investment company.

Thus, the Commission purposely crafted Rule 17j-1 to be broad in its scope and flexible in its application, to permit personal investment activities but to mandate the implementation through codes of ethics of standards and procedures deemed necessary to prevent abusive practices. The Commission expressly stated its expectation "that an effective code of ethics will be designed, in part, to eliminate conflict of interest situations where access persons improperly are able to gain personal benefit through their relationship with the investment company." . . .

C   Comparison with Standards of Other Asset Managers

Today, there are numerous vehicles other than investment companies through which investors obtain professional money management. These include, for example, employee benefit plans, bank common trust funds and collective investment funds, insurance company separate accounts, commodity pools, and hedge funds. *All* of these vehicles present identical opportunities for conflicts of interest and other abuses in connection with personal trading. In considering what additional safeguards might be appropriate for investment companies, the Advisory Group therefore reviewed the approaches taken by other asset management vehicles and those who regulate them.

The Advisory Group finds that the close scrutiny of personal investing in the investment company industry contrasts starkly with the regulatory framework for personal investing in other industries. The personal investing of no other category of investment manager is subject to a regulatory regime as strict, comprehensive, or detailed as that governing investment company personnel. Although each of the other pooled investment vehicles is subject to some form of regulation, there is nothing comparable to the specific mandates in Rule 17j-1 (*i.e.*, those concerning codes of ethics, quarterly reporting by a broad category of employees, and detailed recordkeeping), or the Commission's active inspection and enforcement program in this area.

. . .

5.5   Keeping Both Hands in View*

Ever since the insider-dealing upsets of the 1980s, Wall Street stockbrokers determined to trade securities for themselves as well as their clients have shouldered a heavier regulatory burden in doing so. Now it is the turn of mutual fund managers, whose business the Securities and Exchange Commission (SEC) is beginning to think warrants stricter supervision. Among the firms whose managers the Commission wants to know more about is the biggest mutual fund runner of them all, Boston-based Fidelity Investments.

This is no coincidence. Fidelity has $268 billion in funds under management. It is also known for its competitive and performance-driven culture. A fund manager who does not trade actively on his own account is apt to be viewed as a wimp. It is said within the firm that some money managers have made more in recent years from trading on their own behalf than from salaries and bonuses.

These is nothing necessarily wrong, let alone illegal, about this. Fidelity is not alone in believing that allowing a manager to risk his own money encourages him to get sharp and stay sharp. And it may be expedient to let him do so. If a successful fund manager cannot back his hunches with his own money, he is likely to move to a more accommodating employer or to set up his own, potentially far more lucrative, hedge fund (a largely unregulated investment pool for sophisticated investors).

Yet those who criticise the practice have some reason to do so. A fund manager may easily be distracted from his clients' interests by his own. Worse, the two may conflict. A money manager might well want to buy a share for himself in the knowledge that he would later buy that company's stock in bulk for his fund, so pushing up its price. The conflict can be controlled, and in good firms it is; but it is hard to deny that the potential for abuse exists.

Fidelity reckons its internal rules are among the toughest in the industry, and it has 100 people in its compliance department implementing them. The company allows a manager to trade a share so long as he makes the trade at least five days before or after he has dealt in the stock for his fund, and provided that he clears it in advance with the trading desk and reports each month to the compliance department. (He need not trade through Fidelity's own discount-broking company.) Such rules ought to mean that fund investors are adequately protected against "front-running." Yet things are rarely cut and dried.

Take, for example, a fund manager at any firm who buys a share for his own account six days after he has bought it for his fund. A week later his fund receives an inflow of new money and he buys more of the same stock for his fund. Front-running? Or he might buy a share for his own account on what seems a good tip and then tell his firm's research analysts about it; they do their homework and then recommend the stock to funds within the group. Has the money manager acted unethically?

Whatever conclusions the SEC eventually draws from them, its researches into mutual fund managers seem bound to throw up trading patterns which look odd. The scale of some Fidelity managers' personal-account trading has apparently been enormous, amounting to several hundreds of trades a year. If Fidelity's 5m American investors become aware of this, they are bound to wonder if the fund managers they are paying spend more time worrying about their own portfolios than those of their clients. Suspicion will grow if managers' own investments are shown to have proven extremely profitable. At stake is Fidelity's public image in America's vast retail-investment heartland, an image which has been crucial for a company whose marketing prowess has made it the Procter & Gamble of the mutual fund industry.

Cracking Down

Officially, the SEC neither confirms nor denies that it is investigating Fidelity, which is its standard response to questions about individual cases. Fidelity, for its part, denies press reports that the agency has asked it for managers' personal trading records.

The word from on high within the SEC, however, is that a decision has been taken to direct more vigorous regulatory attention to mutual funds. Americans have now entrusted $2 trillion of their savings to them, and there is no government safety net (such as deposit insurance for bank deposits) slung beneath the funds in case things go wrong. Public confidence is all; and that has been sapped by the sacking this month of John Kaweske, a star money manager at another mutual fund company, Invesco, for allegedly failing to report to his employer certain trades for his personal account.

Fidelity employees have been told not to talk to the press about any SEC investigation. But fund managers were urged at a compliance meeting in November to tone down their personal trading (a Fidelity spokeswoman says simply that "procedures were clarified"). Among those who traded actively for themselves are believed to be three well-known Fidelity fund managers, Lawrence Greenberg, Michael Gordon, and Jeffrey Vinik. Mr. Vinik manages Fidelity's $33 billion flagship Magellan Fund and Mr. Gordon its Blue-Chip Fund. Both funds returned a more-than-respectable 25% or so last year to investors.

Attitudes toward own-account trading vary widely among investment management companies. John Bogle, who is chairman of the $125 billion Vanguard Group and a frequent critic of his industry, says that in his view anyone managing an equity mutual fund should be forbidden to trade on his own account, for the potential conflicts of interest involved are simply too great. If a manager wants to invest, he should do so in his own fund or someone else's. But Vanguard does not enforce this policy, since it farms out active equity-fund management to other companies.

If the SEC pursues the issue and finds abuse, Mr. Bogle's view could one day become the industry's. Meanwhile, front-running and similar sins are not the only mutual fund matters in which the SEC is interested these days. Another is the allocation of hot new issues and other desirable investments among funds within a mutual fund group, especially if in-house funds (partnership accounts, or employee pension funds) are favoured at the expense of ordinary mutual funds. The agency is also looking at soft-dollar commissions (fund managers' practice of routing trades to dealers in exchange for rebates in the form of Reuters screens and the like), with a view to demanding more disclosure. To further this regulatory push, the SEC wants to hire another 150 or more examiners to specialise in mutual funds.

The problem for Fidelity, and for other mutual fund companies with a public reputation to protect, is that greater scrutiny by the Securities and Exchange Commission is almost bound to uncover some misconduct in a business which has grown so fast. The extraordinary success of the mutual fund industry has pushed it from the sidelines of financial services to centre stage. It must now live with the regulatory consequences.

5.6   Managers' Personal Trades: What the SEC Wants You to Know*
Ann Wozencraft

If your mutual fund allowed its manager to trade for himself at the same time that he was trading for you, wouldn't you want to know?

The Securities and Exchange Commission believes that you should be able to know that information, and easily. So it has proposed that fund prospectuses disclose their policies on such personal trading by fund managers and other employees. To further protect investors against abuses, the SEC wants to mandate that fund directors keep a closer eye on personal trading.

The agency's action is the latest to arise from increasing concerns about such trading. The mutual fund industry, which controls $3 trillion in assets, has long been debating the issue, recognizing that potential conflicts of interest may exist when portfolio managers buy or sell the same securities for their personal accounts as they do for their funds.

When Jeffrey N. Vinik, for example, came under scrutiny in several news reports earlier this year for the large number of personal trades he made while managing the Fidelity Magellan fund, some investors wondered why fund managers were allowed to trade for their own accounts at all.

Though Fidelity said an internal review of Mr. Vinik's personal trades showed no conflict with the firm's policies, and the SEC found no cause to investigate, the issue to many was one of perception.

"If I were a director, I would have reservations about portfolio managers trading for their own account," Arthur Levitt Jr., the chairman of the SEC, said at a mutual fund conference in late May. "With millions of investors migrating from insured bank accounts, this industry can hardly afford even the appearance of conflicts."

The debate over personal-trading policies has intensified since 1994, after John J. Kaweske, a fund manager for Invesco, was dismissed that January for not reporting his personal trades.

Now the SEC is in the final stages of finetuning a proposed amendment to the regulation, known as Rule 17j-1, that addresses potential conflicts in personal trading. The proposal to change the rule, which was adopted in 1980 under the Investment Company Act of 1940, is an effort to give investors better access to personal-trading policies.

"Personal trading is an evolving issue that must be continually monitored to make sure proper procedures are in place," said Barry Barbash, head of the SEC's investment management division. In a report two years ago, the SEC found that 1 in 10 mutual fund managers made personal trades more than 41 times a year and that some made them more than twice as often.

While Mr. Barbash said the fund industry had not had any major problems in the personal-investing arena, he added that there would always be the potential for conflicts of

---

*From *The New York Times*, July 21, 1996. Reprinted with permission.

Box 5.6.1 . . . And how rules are enforced

The five largest mutual fund companies follow these compliance procedures governing personal trading as recommended by the Investment Company Institute:

- All trades must be cleared in advance. (At Capital Research, trades over $25,000 must also be cleared by a special committee.)
- Investment activity is monitored after clearance is given.
- Records of personal transactions are automatically supplied to the company's compliance officer by the broker.
- Personal holdings must be disclosed annually.
- Employees must certify that they have complied with the ethics code.

---

interest by fund managers. One type of abuse is known as front-running; it occurs when a fund manager buys or sells stock for his or her own account immediately before buying or selling a large amount of that same stock for the mutual fund, which can influence the stock price in the fund manager's favor.

"You'd like to believe every fund manager is an angel, but, unfortunately, there is always someone who will abuse that trust," Mr. Barbash said.

To try to keep a high level of public trust, the SEC requires that investment firms set ethics policies that establish personal-trading guidelines and that mutual fund employees abide by rules that discourage managers from using their insider positions for selfish gains.

The industry has generally taken a strong stand on personal-investing restrictions. In May 1994, the Investment Company Institute, the national association of investment firms, released a report that found that most firms' ethics codes largely exceeded legal requirements.

Still, the report made a number of recommendations to improve personal-investing activities and compliance. And in a follow-up report released in April 1995, the Institute found that 85 percent of its members, representing 97 percent of fund assets, had adopted the recommendations, with many going beyond them (see box 5.6.1). The report found no reason to recommend banning personal trading, as long as proper restrictions were in place and compliance procedures were followed.

The 10 largest mutual fund companies all have ethics policies, but shareholders of funds and potential investors do not always have access to them. The SEC wants to change that.

"We're not saying whether personal investing by portfolio managers should or should not be allowed," Mr. Barbash said. "We acknowledge it's an ethical issue best left to fund companies. But we are saying that it's of enough interest to many shareholders that mutual fund companies should disclose publicly where they stand on personal trading."

The SEC proposal is intended to update Rule 17j-1, which requires all investment companies to adopt codes of ethics and procedures to detect and prevent improper personal trading; directs all those with access to how a fund invests to file quarterly reports on their personal securities transactions, and requires maintenance of substantial records of these transactions. A vote by the commissioners is expected in the next few months.

The proposed changes include requiring each fund to disclose in its prospectus its policy on personal trading by portfolio managers. Funds would also have to file a copy of their codes with the SEC so investors have better access to the information.

Though funds currently are not required to release their codes of ethics to the public, some funds do make their policies available to shareholders.

Among the five largest fund companies, two, Capital Research and Management and the Franklin Templeton Group, will provide copies of their codes to investors who request them. Anticipating the rule change, Merrill Lynch Asset Management—where the personal trading rules apply to all employees—has said it expects to make its code available, and until then its compliance director, Jerry Weiss, has agreed to discuss the policy with investors who wish to do so.

"Shareholders need to know that looking out for them is our No. 1 goal," Mr. Weiss said. "Our personal interests take a second seat."

Fidelity Investments and Vanguard, the two biggest fund companies, will not release their full codes of ethics to the public, but they will discuss the key provisions of the codes over the telephone with shareholders.

"It's a very long and technical document, so if you had to send it to everyone it would be very costly," said Robert Pozen, general counsel and a managing director of Fidelity. "A summary is a much better communication device that is much more geared to what fund investors are interested in."

As the SEC presses for disclosure of codes, it is also pushing for more involvement by the boards of investment companies and for improved monitoring of the fund managers' reports on personal trading. While each board now determines its own oversight procedures, the SEC wants to set minimum standards, primarily requiring directors to sign off on each fund's annual report covering personal trading by managers and others.

"We want to get the fund companies' codes of ethics in the sunlight," Mr. Barbash said. "Then investors can decide whether they like what they see."

Mutual fund leaders say most investors would already be happy, noting that plenty of reporting and verification procedures are already in place in ethics codes—particularly since the Investment Company Institute panel made its recommendations.

"It's in all of our best interests to have the perception that not only are these fund managers trustworthy people," said Jack Brennan, Vanguard's president and chief executive, "but that we have very tight rules that govern what we do."

Paul Haaga, senior vice president of Capital Research and Management, which oversees the American Funds group, said: "We're fiduciaries entrusted with other people's money. Shareholders come first."

In a letter to the SEC on the personal-trading proposals, the Investment Company Institute said it supported a "brief and clear" disclosure as to whether employees "are permitted to engage in personal securities transactions," and, if so, under what general restrictions and procedures. But it recommended that the SEC eliminate the proposal that investment companies be required to specifically disclose whether staff members may invest in "securities that may be purchased or held by" the company. Such disclosure, the institute argues, "creates a pejorative implication that such investing is inherently suspect."

For that and other reasons, the Securities Industry Association, in a letter to the SEC, opposed the proposed disclosure in prospectuses of information concerning personal investment policies.

Table 5.6.1

Code of ethics: How investments are restricted.... Here are the rules governing personal trading by fund managers and other employees with knowledge of fund trading that are in effect at the five largest mutual fund companies.

Company	Fidelity Investments	Vanguard Group	Capital Research and Management	Merrill Lynch Asset Management	Franklin Templeton Group
Assets under management	$391.9 billion	$208.5 billion	$155.1 billion	$147.0 billion	$106.8 billion
Participation in initial public offering	Prohibited.	Prohibited.	Prohibited.	Prohibited.	Prohibited.
Private placement investments	Restricted.	Restricted.	Restricted.	Restricted.	Restricted.
Holding period (minimum time between purchase and sale of the same security)	60 calendar days.	60 calendar days.	60 calendar days.	60 calendar days.	60 calendar days.
Blackout period (ban on trading in a security before and after the company's funds trade in it)	7 calender days.	7 calendar days. If a Vanguard fund buys the same security within 7 days of an employee's purchase, the employee must hold the security for at least six months.	7 calendar days.	After a Merrill Lynch fund buys a security, employees may not sell it for 30 days or buy it for 15 days. After a Merrill Lynch fund sells a security, employees may not sell it for 7 days of buy it for 30 days.	5 business days.
Short selling	Employees may not sell short any securities in which Fidelity funds hold a long position, but short positions are allowed on securities Fidelity funds do not own, against the S&P 100 and 500 indices, and "against the box."	Prohibited.	Prohibited. Writing options is also prohibited.	Banned from selling a security short if the Merrill Lynch manager's fund or private account holds a long position in the same security.	No special restrictions.

With more than 7,000 mutual funds vying for investor dollars, competition is fierce, and experts say funds without stringent ethics policies on personal investing are hurting themselves in investors' eyes.

Perception is important in the fund industry, said A. Michael Lipper, president of Lipper Analytical Services, because the relationships between investors and fund managers are so distant. Still, an ethics policy is only one of many elements investors must examine in choosing a fund; others are expenses, management fees, and general compliance history, he said.

"It's a plus, but it's a safety factor that only works if there's a problem," Mr. Lipper said. "If I saw a fund that had a loose ethics policy but I liked it for every other aspect, I don't think I'd refuse to put money in. I might just put in less."

Of particular concern lately have been fund companies' policies on short sales, which involve bearish bets in which investors sell borrowed shares, hoping to profit by replacing them later with less expensive shares. The panel did not address the issue specifically, but it recommended more broadly that mutual fund companies ban short-term trading profits reaped within 60 days, a policy that the five biggest mutual fund companies have embraced.

While Fidelity recently barred its investment staff from profiting in personal accounts by betting against stocks in which Fidelity mutual funds held a long position, it gives more freedom to its employees than most other mutual fund companies do. For example, short positions are allowed "against the box," regardless of whether Fidelity has a position in that security. Shorting against the box means selling short the same number of shares of a security that an investor already owns, resulting in favorable tax treatment. Short positions are also allowed on securities that Fidelity funds do not own, and against the Standard & Poor's 500 and the S&P 100 indexes.

"We think it's important to let managers trade for their personal accounts," said Robyn S. Tice, a Fidelity spokeswoman. "As long as personal investing is subject to the appropriate safeguards, we think it benefits our shareholders by improving the skills of our investment professionals. It's an important element of personal freedom."

Vanguard, meanwhile, allows its employees a little less freedom, by prohibiting personal trading in the securities of companies with which Vanguard has a relationship, like publicly traded companies that have Vanguard 401(k) plans.

Both Vanguard and Capital ban short sales. At Merrill Lynch, no decision-making manager can sell a security short if that employee's fund holds a long position in the same security. Both Smith Barney Asset Management and T. Rowe Price ban short-selling, except against the box.

At Franklin Templeton Group, there is no blanket restriction on short sales, but they are subject to the same ethical restrictions as any other transactions.

"We discourage it because if you can't turn a profit within 60 days, you probably don't want to do it," said Deborah Gatzek, Franklin Templeton's general counsel. (See table 5.6.1.)

6 Brokerage Transactions for Mutual Funds

Introduction

This is the last of three chapters on portfolio management. So far we have looked at bond funds and stock funds from the viewpoint of investment selection. In this chapter, we will look at the implementation of investment decisions through the trading desk.

Most investment managers to mutual funds have a relatively small trading organization or division that typically works in concert with the corresponding portfolio management group. The trading function is kept separate from the portfolio management function for several reasons. First, this separation allows the portfolio managers to concentrate on their primary task of selecting stocks and structuring portfolios. Second, the separation allows the fund traders to develop specialized expertise in implementing the investment decisions of portfolio managers. Third, the separation provides an independent check on the relations between portfolio managers and Wall Street firms (or the counter-parties to fund transactions).

This chapter will focus on equity trading, and begins by reviewing in detail the operation of stock exchanges and over-the-counter dealer markets. We then will focus on the role of the fund trader in the investment process and expand on terminology of mutual fund trading. Finally, there will be a case study involving a fund trader attempting to execute large orders for the funds in a mutual fund complex.

U.S. Equity Markets

In the United States, there are two main ways to trade stocks: on exchanges or using the over-the-counter market (OTC). In its most basic form, an exchange is a physical place (the exchange floor) at which a limited number of brokers (member firms) trade a limited number of stocks called *listed securities*. The New York Stock Exchange (NYSE) is the largest stock exchange in the country, and is an order-driven exchange. On such an exchange, one specialist (representing a broker-dealer firm) undertakes the obligation to maintain simultaneous buy and sell quotations for each listed stock in return for exclusive control over the trading of that stock on the exchange floor. When buy (or sell) orders come from member firms (brokers) to the specialist's post, they are matched with other public sell (or buy) orders or with the specialist's inventory. An exception to this process may occur when the order specifies a price that cannot immediately be matched, in which case the order is held in the specialist's book for future matches.

The difference between the buy and sell quotations maintained simultaneously by each specialist is called the *spread*, which represents a key source of profits for the specialist. The specialist runs a continuous auction and is charged with making orderly markets, which includes committing small amounts of the specialist's own capital to facilitate trading, if necessary. After trades are consummated at the specialist's post, they are sent back to member firms, which exchange securities for cash in a centralized clearance and settlement system. The member firms also charge commissions to their customers for acting as their agents in executing trades. Commissions represent charges for the services of the member firm in their brokerage functions and use of the exchange floor.

In contrast, the over-the-counter (OTC) market has no physical trading floor; it is a network of telephone lines and a computerized quotation system through which trades can be made. It is not limited to single specialists with exclusive trading rights, but rather has multiple market makers for each security traded OTC. If firms choose to become market makers in certain stocks, they make bids and offers through a computerized quote system (called NASDAQ—the NASD's Automated Quotation system) or through daily "pink sheets" for smaller stocks. The price and volume of trades are then negotiated verbally by phone or electronically by computer. But no one dealer is required to be a market maker in any OTC stock. As a result, popular and heavily traded stocks attract many market makers, while thinly traded or obscure stocks may have no market maker.

The OTC market operates through brokers and dealers. As brokers, or agents, for their customers, firms try to negotiate trades with the dealer offering the best quotation in the relevant stock, like exchange members who send orders on an agency basis to the specialist. But most mutual funds do not use a broker for OTC trades; instead they go directly to the firms that act as OTC dealers in the relevant stock. As dealers for their own accounts, firms buy or sell shares directly with their customers, like specialists who match public orders with their own inventories. In the OTC market, customers typically pay the dealers a spread between the current buy and sell quotations. Thus, as compared to brokers who earn commissions on exchange trades, OTC dealers make money on the spread between the bid and offered price.

If a stock is listed on the NYSE, a trade in that stock can be executed there by a broker (or on a regional exchange with unlisted trading privileges in that stock). If a stock is traded in the OTC market, a trade in that stock can be negotiated through one of several dealers that make a market in that stock. In addition, there are various electronic markets and matching services that can be used by institutional investors to help execute a trade. These systems, such as Instinet or POSIT, allow the submission of anonymous bids, which become trades if the "other side" (a match) is found in the system.

A fund management company may have an affiliated broker-dealer (e.g., Merrill Lynch or Paine Webber) and may use that broker-dealer to transact on the fund's behalf under certain circumstances. An affiliated dealer is not legally permitted to execute a *principal* trade with a fund (see discussion of affiliated transactions in chapter 2) since such a trade would involve a purchase or sale by the fund of a security owned by an affiliate. Such principal transactions may involve potential conflicts of interest for the affiliated dealer, so they are prohibited (unless special permission is granted by the SEC via an exemption from the relevant rules). For example, a fund advised by Merrill Lynch Asset Management would not be permitted to buy a stock from Merrill Lynch as an OTC dealer in that stock. By contrast, an affiliated broker of a fund adviser may execute exchange trades as *agent* for the fund, subject to the oversight of the independent directors. For example, Merrill Lynch may act as agent in transmitting an order to the NYSE for a fund advised by Merrill Lynch Asset Management. The independent directors generally review the costs and quality of fund trading, with special scrutiny of agency trades executed by affiliated brokers.

Roles and Responsibilities of Mutual Fund Traders

Fund traders allocate fund orders to buy or sell securities to securities dealers or brokers; they do not actually execute the trades themselves. Fund traders are not securities dealers who continuously make markets for securities and trade as principals with mutual funds. Nor do they act as securities brokers, bringing fund trades as agent to the stock exchanges and receiving commissions for their services. In other words, fund traders perform an important role in the investment management process, and are typically compensated through salary plus bonus rather than through a commission or spread.

The objective of a fund trader is to place each fund trade with the securities broker or dealer likely to provide the fund with the best execution. In this regard, a fund trader uses many information sources (typically provided through computer terminals) to assist their decision making process in selecting among trading alternatives. These alternatives, explained in the chapter's readings, include the place to trade (exchange floor, upstairs market, OTC, or crossing networks), the broker to use, and the time over which to execute the trade.

No trader can guarantee best execution of a trade for a fund; this is a goal the trader seeks to achieve. In an exchange transaction, the trader seeks the best total price—the lowest purchase price plus the lowest commission on a buy, and the highest sale price minus the lowest commission on the sale. In an OTC transaction, the trader seeks the best net price, since mutual funds generally effect OTC trades directly with a dealer and pay no commission on such trades. The federal securities laws, however, expressly permit an investment adviser to pay more than the lowest commission available on fund trades if the adviser determines in good faith that the amount of the commission is reasonable in relation to the research and other brokerage services it receives from the broker-dealer, viewed in terms of either the particular transaction or the adviser's overall responsibilities for its managed accounts. For example, a trader for a fund adviser may decide not to send trades to a discount broker with low commissions for execution-only services, and instead to send those trades to a full-service broker that regularly provides useful securities research to the adviser or actively shops for matches on difficult fund trades. The practice of using commissions to pay for research is called *soft dollars*—"soft" because the research is paid for through higher commissions or through directing more business to the broker, rather than by a separate cash remittance.

The large size of some trades for mutual funds can make them difficult to execute through the normal exchange process. First, specialists may not have the capital needed to acquire blocks of 100,000 or more shares, or may not be willing to commit such an amount because of the risks involved. These risks are the second problem: finding buyers or sellers for these large blocks might depress or inflate the market price (and reduce returns) before the trade is completed. Third, NYSE Rule 113 prohibits the exchange specialist from directly contacting institutions to ascertain their interest in buying or selling a large block.

Therefore, rather than trade a large order in bits and pieces on the floor, mutual funds often negotiate a block trade directly with another institution (typically a broker-dealer) in an "upstairs" transaction. Investment banking firms known as block houses (e.g., Goldman Sachs) help to match institutions for large trades, and receive a negotiated commission for their efforts. For example, the investment banking firm (dealer) may buy the stock from the mutual fund and then immediately sell most of the shares to institutions that have committed to different amounts of the block while retaining a small portion of the block for the firm's own account. Block trading, especially the decisions that must be made by a fund trader, is further illustrated in the case study.

In order to reduce transaction costs associated with fund trades, including block trades, the SEC permits two funds in the same complex to "cross" a security without using a broker or dealer. Let's take a simple illustration from a fund complex that gives each portfolio manager full responsibility to select securities—that is, the complex does not have an "approved" list of securities. If the portfolio manager of Fund A sends the trading desk an order to sell 40,000 common shares of General Electric at 90 and soon afterward a different portfolio manager for Fund B in the same complex sends the trading desk an order to buy 40,000 common shares of General Electric at $90\frac{1}{4}$, the trader may "cross" the two orders at the last reported price of an NYSE trade at $90\frac{1}{8}$ so that both funds save $\frac{1}{8}$ per share on the bid-ask spread as well as brokerage commissions. Such interfund trades must be executed in accordance with an SEC rule that imposes pricing, recordkeeping, and other requirements including quarterly review of crossing procedures by the fund's independent directors.

If two or more mutual funds in the same complex want to buy or sell the same stock at the same time, it may not be feasible to fill all the orders promptly at the same price. The best illustration is an initial public offering, where a complex receives an allocation of 100,000 shares as compared to total buy orders for 200,000 shares on the trading desk. In such situations, the desk must follow reasonable allocation procedures—for example, allocating buy orders by relative size of fund, or allocating sell orders by relative amount of fund holdings.

Crosses between funds and allocations among funds are both subject to review by the independent directors of the funds. Under applicable SEC rules and exemptive orders, the independent directors are supposed to make sure that the fund trading desk has adopted reasonable procedures to address the potential conflicts between and among funds in the same complex. As mentioned above, the independent directors also review with special scrutiny agency transactions effected for the fund by a broker affiliated with the fund's manager.

More generally, independent directors review the cost and quality of executions effected for the funds by the trading desk. This review is based on extensive data about which brokers are executing how many trades at what average commission rate. To evaluate these data, the independent directors must be apprised of the particular situation of each broker. For example, which brokers are executing the difficult trades involving a capital commitment, and which brokers supply valuable research and market information as well as execution services?

The operations of the trading desk are also subject to review by the SEC examiners as part of their regular examinations of fund complexes. The SEC examiners look to see if a complex has procedures reasonably designed to obtain the best execution for the funds.

Like the independent directors, the SEC examiners focus on areas of potential conflict among the funds (e.g., crosses and allocations) and between the funds and their adviser.

Questions:

In reviewing the materials in this chapter, please keep in mind the following questions:

1. What is the difference between a primary offering and secondary market for stock? Why does the management of the issuer of stock—the company—care- about the trading price of its stock?
2. What are the functions and limitations of an NYSE specialist in a listed stock? Compare and contrast the NYSE specialist to an OTC market maker in any stock.
3. The bid-ask quotes used to be expressed in intervals of $\frac{1}{8}$, which have recently moved to intervals of $\frac{1}{16}$, which will move to decimal points over the next few years. Will these movements in bid-ask quotes help or hinder mutual funds in executing stock trades?
4. Suppose a fund trader requests a broker affiliated with the fund's adviser to execute an OTC trade as agent for the fund. Does such an execution violate the affiliated person rules of the 1940 Act or present any other conflict of interest?
5. Suppose a fund trader places an order to buy 5,000 shares of an exchange-listed stock with Broker F, which charges a commission of 5 cents per share, although Broker D would charge a commission of 4 cents per share for the same trade. Is such a placement permissible? If so, on what grounds?
6. Suppose a complex has a $1 billion diversified growth fund and a $100 million financial services fund. Both place orders at the same time to buy 100,000 shares of an initial public offering of an insurance company. If the trader received only 150,000 shares of the offering, how should they be allocated between the two funds?
7. Suppose a trader receives a market order to buy 20,000 shares of Ford from Fund B and a limit order to sell 20,000 shares of Ford at $80\frac{1}{4}$ from Fund S in the same complex. If the last reported trade for Ford on the consolidated tape was at $80\frac{1}{8}$, may the trader cross these two trades at $80\frac{1}{4}$ to save transaction costs for both funds?
8. Are there any economies of scale in a trader bunching together orders from five funds in the complex, each to buy 2,000 shares of Intel? Would your answer be the same if each of the five funds wanted to buy 100,000 shares of Intel?

Glossary of Trading Terms

Broker   An individual or firm in the securities business that executes trades as agent for the customer. In contrast to a dealer, a broker does not itself buy securities from a customer or sell its own securities to a customer.

Capital gain or **capital loss**   Profit or loss from the sale of a security. A capital gain, under current Federal income tax laws, may be classified as either short-term (12 months or less) or long-term. Short-term gains are taxed as ordinary income. The maximum long-term capital gains rate is 28% if the security is held 12 months to 18 months, and 20% if the security is held 18 months or more.

Commission   The fee paid to brokers for executing trades on an exchange. These are set through negotiation between broker and customer.

Confirmation   An acknowledgment issued to shareholders after each transaction which occurs in their account, reflecting the price and other details of the transaction.

Dealer   Individual or firm in the securities business acting as principal rather than agent. Typically, a dealer buys for its own account and sells to a customer from its own inventory. The same individual or firm may function, at different times, either as broker or dealer.

Derivative security   A security whose value depends on the value of another underlying security such as a common stock or bond. Options, futures, rights, and warrants are examples of derivative securities.

Floor broker   A member of the exchange who executes orders on the floor of the exchange for a member firm.

Last sale price   The last reported price (on the tickertape for stocks) at which a trade in a security was executed. Last sale price is often different from the quotation, which represents the current offer and bid prices.

Limit order   An order that is to be executed only at a specific price or better.

Long   Signifies ownership of securities: "I am long 100 Microsoft" means the speaker owns 100 shares of Microsoft stock.

Market maker   A dealer who is regularly announcing its willingness to buy or sell a specified number of shares of a particular security at his or her stated bid or offer.

Market order   An order that is to be executed promptly at the best price currently available.

NASDAQ   National Association of Securities Dealers Automated Quotation system; the nationwide electronic quotation system for up-to-the-minute quotations on thousands of over-the-counter stocks.

New York Stock Exchange   Also called NYSE, or the "Big Board," it is the country's largest securities exchange, with over 2,000 issues listed. To have its securities listed on the NYSE, a company must meet certain minimum requirements.

Odd lot   An amount of stock less than the typical 100-share unit.

Offer   The price at which a person is ready to sell (sometimes called the **ask price**). The offer or ask price is opposed to the bid, the price at which one is ready to buy.

Order ticket   The form, required to be completed by a registered representative, that contains the customer's instructions to buy or sell plus the other qualifications imposed by the customer on the transaction.

Over-the-counter market (OTC)   The OTC market is a screen-based market operated throughout the United States. Dealers are linked via NASDAQ (or through pink sheets). Thousands of "unlisted" stocks and almost all bonds are traded OTC.

Primary market   The term used to describe the process by which new securities are issued and sold by the company, as opposed to the trading of already issued securities.

Program trading The simultaneous execution of transactions involving large baskets of stock, index options, and index futures. Most commonly used to take advantage of price discrepancies that develop among these instruments.

Quotation Also called a quote, it includes a bid to buy and an offer to sell a security in a given market at a given time.

Regular-way settlement Industry term for the normally accepted settlement date for secondary market transactions. The generally accepted regular-way settlement for securities traded in the United States is the third business day after the trade date. There are two main exceptions: open-closing transactions in listed options, and round-lot transactions in government and money market securities, settle the next business day.

Seat A figure of speech for a membership on an exchange. Price and admission requirements vary from exchange to exchange.

Secondary market Term used to describe the trading of securities among investors following their initial issuance and sale by the company in the primary market.

Settlement date The date on which funds are exchanged between banks or between the mutual fund and its broker after a trade.

Short Signifies an obligation to deliver a security at a future date. In a covered short, the person owns the security subject to the delivery obligation; in an uncovered or "naked" short, the person does not own the relevant security. "I am short 100 Microsoft" means the speaker owes 100 shares of Microsoft stock to someone else.

Specialist The member of a stock exchange who is responsible for maintaining a fair and orderly market for the particular stock(s) they have been allocated. Limit orders are left with the specialist, who maintains a book with these orders. Specialists both execute orders for other members and trade for their own account.

Specialist post Location on the floor of an exchange where specific securities are traded, and where, in most cases, the specialist is available to receive bids and offers or to give a quote for specific securities.

Spread The difference between the ask quote (offer to sell) and the bid quote (offer to buy) provided by a specialist, market maker, or dealer.

Stop loss order An order to sell if the price falls to a certain level—the **stop price**.

Street Popular term for Wall Street and the surrounding financial area. In recent years, the term has included all elements of the financial community, no matter where located. For example, "Here's the latest word from the Street."

Street name Popular term for a security registered in the name of a broker-dealer rather than in the name of the actual owner.

Volume The number of shares or bonds traded during a specific time. For example, the daily volume or weekly volume. Normally, volume figures are given for the principal marketplace for the security, although a wider base of measurement can be used.

6.1   U.S. Equity Markets Today*

Historical Development of the Current Equity Market Structure

The U.S. equity markets are larger, faster, and more complex than at any point in their history. This development reflects changes in the composition of market users (both customers and professional intermediaries) as well as in the structure of the markets themselves. The markets and users continue, however, to operate within the framework of a regulatory structure that was created 20 years ago under very different market conditions. Whether this structure still works is the primary focus of the Market 2000 Study.

The development of the current regulatory structure was triggered by the Commission's 1971 Institutional Investor Study.[1] In that study the Commission found that the securities markets had become increasingly active, complex, and susceptible to various practices that raised structural and efficiency questions. For example, by 1972, New York Stock Exchange (NYSE) volume had more than quadrupled over the past decade to the then dizzying figure of 16 million shares per day. The growing presence of institutional investors was reflected by the increase in block volume in NYSE stocks from 1% to 18.5% of trading during the same period. In the OTC market, the National Association of Securities Dealers (NASD) had modernized trading with the introduction of NASDAQ a year earlier. The markets were only a few years past the "paperwork crisis" during which a surge of volume nearly overloaded the securities processing capabilities of the major broker-dealers. Perhaps most importantly, institutional investors had developed arrangements and relationships with brokers on the regional exchanges and OTC market to avoid paying the NYSE's fixed commission schedule. These relationships raised the specter of a fragmented market structure in which multiple markets offering limited access traded the same securities without publicly disseminating quote and trade information.

In response to these developments, in 1972 the Commission issued its Statement on the Future Structure of the Securities Markets (Future Structure Statement).[2] The Commission concluded that trading should be concentrated in a central market system where competing market makers would generate the best prices, comprehensive disclosure would show where and how to obtain best execution for orders, all qualified broker-dealers would have access, and professionals acting as agents would put their customers' interests before their own.[3]

Three years later Congress adopted the Securities Acts Amendments of 1975 (1975 Amendments)[4] to enact the goals of the Future Structure Statement and to preserve and strengthen the U.S. securities markets. With these Amendments Congress directed the Commission, with due regard for the public interest, the protection of investors, and the

---

*From *Market 2000: An Examination of Current Equity Market Developments*, Division of Market Regulation, United States Securities and Exchange Commission, January 1994, pp. 4–12.

maintenance of fair and orderly markets, to facilitate the establishment of the national market system (NMS) for securities.[5] The Commission would not dictate the design of the NMS; that would be left to competition. Instead, the Commission would work with the markets to achieve the NMS goals.

The phrase "national market system" is not defined in Section 11A of the Securities Exchange Act of 1934 (Exchange Act) because Congress believed that it was essential to provide the Commission with "maximum flexibility in working out specific details" of the system.[6] Nevertheless, Congress established goals for the NMS. Section 11A states that new data processing and communications techniques create the opportunity for more efficient and effective market operations and that it is in the public interest and appropriate for the protection of investors and the maintenance of fair and orderly markets to ensure:

(i) economically efficient execution of securities transactions;
(ii) fair competition among brokers and dealers, among exchange markets, and between exchange markets and markets other than exchange markets;
(iii) the availability to brokers, dealers, and investors of information with respect to quotations for and transactions in securities;
(iv) the practicability of brokers executing investors' orders in the best market; and
(v) an opportunity, consistent with the provisions of clauses (i) and (iv), for investors' orders to be executed without the participation of a dealer.[7]

The efforts of the Commission and the markets to facilitate the establishment of the NMS led to significant improvements in market operations. For example, the Commission abolished fixed commission rates, and the markets established a consolidated quotation system, consolidated transaction tape, and the Intermarket Trading System (ITS) to link markets for listed securities. Investors benefited directly from these efforts: trading costs were reduced, particularly as fixed commission rates were eliminated, and increased market transparency enabled investors to monitor the quality of trade executions. In addition, investors benefited as higher levels of transparency and lower costs contributed to greater liquidity.

The U.S. equity markets have changed dramatically, however, since the adoption of the 1975 Amendments. The changes include growth in trading volume, advances in trading technology, the increasing prominence of institutional investors, the introduction of derivative products, and the globalization of securities markets (among other changes). These changes have resulted in an increasing array of markets, dealers, and products to trade securities. Many of these alternatives operate outside the exchanges and NASDAQ. Some industry participants are concerned that the splintering of trading among various markets and dealers has fragmented the equity markets and frustrated the achievement of the NMS. In addition, various market participants have complained that the regulatory structure has not kept pace with market developments. As a result, many believe that issues such as payment for order flow, proprietary trading systems, the growth of third market trading, and changes in NASDAQ warrant an evaluation of the viability of the NMS as envisioned by Congress in 1975.

An analysis of these and related issues, however, first requires an understanding of the current state of the equity markets. The various markets and their users are described next.

Developments in the Users of the Markets

The predominant trend during the past 20 years has been the growth in number, size, and diversity of equity market users. This trend is best illustrated by changes in the investor base. Individual investors continue to be active and are increasing in number. From 1975 to 1990, the number of shareholder accounts increased from 25 million to 51 million. Although individual investor participation in the markets is still widespread, instead of directly purchasing stocks, retail investors often participate indirectly through an institution, such as a mutual fund, public pension plan, private pension plan, or insurance company.

Institutions representing millions of individual investors now own over $2.9 trillion of U.S. equities. The "institutionalization" of the market has accelerated since the 1970s, although it may now be leveling off.[8] In 1975, institutions owned 43% of the shares of U.S. equities; by 1992, they owned slightly under 50% [see table 6.1.1 on page 278 for updated figures through 1996—ed. note].

The growth of mutual funds illustrates the widespread extent of indirect participation by individual investors.[9] Between 1975 and 1992, mutual funds' share of U.S. equities more than doubled. During roughly the same period, the number of equity funds grew from 276 to 1,232; the number of accounts in equity funds tripled from 8.9 million to 26 million; and the dollar value of assets in equity funds soared from $34 billion to $585 billion. In addition, hedge fund activity increased substantially.

Pension plans, too, have grown. From 1975 to 1992, the amount of U.S. equities held by private and public pension plans grew from $132 billion to $1.3 trillion. The equity holdings of one of the largest public pension plans are almost equal to the combined equity holdings of all the public pension plans in 1975.[10] The growth of pension plans has been accompanied by a marked rise in equity assets committed to passive management. From 1975 to the beginning of 1992, the amount of passively managed U.S. equity assets grew from under $2 billion to $231 billion.[11] During this period the percentage of total assets indexed by the top 200 pension plans increased from 2.5% to 14.4%.[12]

As the size and activity of institutional customers grew, so did market intermediaries. Equity trading by the larger broker-dealers has increased significantly over the past 20 years. In 1975, the amount of revenues that broker-dealers derived from trading amounted to $1.3 billion. By 1992, this amount had grown to $22.5 billion.[13] Aided by telecommunications and computer technology and the growth of institutional assets, the equity trading desks of large broker-dealers are now influential forces in the equity markets. They have facilitated the growth in global trading. Together with the pension funds, they also have sparked the growth in stock index derivatives.

Another trend over the past 20 years has been the change in the handling of individual investor accounts. Technology has enabled broker-dealers and the markets to automate the handling and processing of customers' orders. Automation of the order entry, routing, execution, and reporting functions allows broker-dealers and the markets to handle an exponentially greater volume of order flow than existed 20 years ago.[14] For example, a customer's order to buy 100 shares of a stock at the market price in 1975 could have taken up to an hour to travel from the branch office to the firm's trading desk, to the firm's broker on the floor of the exchange, to the specialist post, and back through the firm to the customer. Today the entire process—from the entry of the order to notification of the execution—can take less than a minute and is often completed while the customer is still on the telephone.

Whether handled by a discount or a full-service broker, a customer's retail order rarely receives personalized handling. Instead, the order usually is routed to a specific market or market maker through a predetermined routing algorithm employed by the broker-dealer. The customer's order is viewed by the broker-dealer as part of its overall order flow, which is packaged and distributed to specific locations.[15] Rather than determining for each individual order the best possible market or market maker, most retail firms automatically route their flow of small orders (i.e., orders under 3,000 shares) to a specified market or market maker. Apart from the particular stock and the type of order, a variety of other factors influence the routing decision for small orders. For example, broker-dealers may route orders to an affiliated specialist unit on a regional exchange or to their OTC market making desks for NASDAQ stocks. Some order flow is routed based on payment for order flow or reciprocal order flow arrangements. Other firms route orders only to the primary market. A few large broker-dealers internally cross their order flow, then route the resulting trades to a regional exchange. Regardless of their method of selecting a marketplace, retail firms believe that it is too expensive and inefficient to make individual order routing decisions.

Developments in the Equity Markets

The equity markets have changed in response to user's desires for better services, greater efficiency, and more competitive prices.[16] Users have pressed the organized markets and entrepreneurs operating independently of the markets to improve traditional trading services. The result has been a multitude of new services and products. Users are so different, however, that it is difficult for one particular market to accommodate them all. Consequently, the U.S. equity market has evolved into a multifaceted structure, with the primary markets—the NYSE, the American Stock Exchange (Amex), and NASDAQ—attempting to accommodate as many users as possible but losing some market share to competitors that provide a specialized service that the primary markets do not replicate (or do not replicate as competitively).

Trading in U.S. equities is discussed below.

Listed Stocks

There are approximately 2,900 stocks listed on exchanges in the United States [over 9,200 as of 1996—ed. note]. Companies on the NYSE account for 97% of the market value of listed companies; Amex companies account for 2%; and regional exchanges' companies account for under 1%. The NYSE and Amex provide an important price discovery function.[17] They also serve as the markets of last resort during times of market stress. In volatile market conditions, normal liquidity in the index derivative markets often diminishes, prompting market participants to channel their stock orders to the NYSE and Amex.[18]

The NYSE receives the majority of orders in NYSE-listed stocks. Although the NYSE market share in these stocks has declined over the past decade, the NYSE accounted for 70% of the total orders and over 79% of the volume in its stocks in the first six months of

1993. Block transactions, which often are negotiated off the floor of an exchange, account for half of NYSE volume and a third of Amex volume.

Orders for NYSE stocks also are executed in several other markets. For example, some blocks are sent to regional exchanges for execution, and blocks accounting for over two million shares a day are executed off the exchange after the close of regular trading hours. A portion of small orders for public customers is sent to the regional exchanges or third market dealers for execution. Together these two markets handle 29% of the total orders and 16% of the volume in NYSE stocks. Proprietary trading systems (PTSs) handle 1.4% of the volume in NYSE stocks, usually in the form of portfolio trades or block trades. Crossing of portfolio orders internally between accounts by large institutions or money managers can amount to a million shares on any given day. Ten million shares a day (3% of NYSE volume) are executed as program trades after the NYSE close, either on the NYSE's after-hours crossing session or through the foreign desks of U.S. broker-dealers. Other overseas trading by U.S. firms in NYSE stocks takes place primarily in London, either through the London Stock Exchange's Stock Exchange Automated Quotation (SEAQ) system and SEAQ International system markets (under one million shares per day), or through the U.S. firms' foreign desks (almost two million shares per day). [See table 6.1.2 on page 279 for 1996 data—ed. note.]

The five regional stock exchanges (the Boston, Chicago, Cincinnati, Pacific, and Philadelphia Stock Exchanges) compete for order flow with the NYSE and Amex. The overwhelming percentage of regional stock exchange business is in NYSE and Amex securities that the regional exchanges trade pursuant to grants of unlisted trading privileges (UTP) from the Commission.[19] The regional exchanges captured 20% of the orders in NYSE stocks and 16% of the orders in Amex stocks in the first six months of 1993. Most of this market share comes from small customer orders. During the 1970s and 1980s, the regional exchanges built automated systems that enabled member firms to route small public customer orders to the specialist posts at the regional exchanges. An order routed over these systems is exposed for a brief period to other markets; if no other market expresses an interest, the order is executed automatically at the ITS best bid or offer, regardless of the quote of the particular regional specialist. In recent years the regional exchanges have further solidified their share of the small order business by allowing their specialists to affiliate with firms with a broad retail customer base.

The regional exchanges also attract some block trades in listed stocks. A few regional specialists make markets in blocks, but most of the regional block trades are routed to regional exchanges to avoid the primary market's limit order book. Although the regional exchanges do not compete for order flow consistently on the basis of quotes, they have provided vigorous competition to the NYSE through lower transaction fees[20] and new services and products.[21]

Another competitor for trades in listed stocks is the so-called third market, which is OTC trading of exchange-listed securities. Third market transactions include, for example, executions of block trades off an exchange and transactions executed by third market makers who are not members of an exchange. The third market makers act much like NASDAQ market makers, seeking orders of a few thousand shares or fewer in the most active listed stocks from retail firms or discount brokers.[22] In 1989, the third market garnered 3.2% of reported NYSE share volume and 5.0% of reported trade volume. By 1993, third market volume had more than doubled to 7.4% of reported NYSE share volume and

9.3% of reported trade volume. A few third market makers have accounted for most of the increase in third market trading over the past several years.[23]

The competition for small order flow by regional exchanges and the third market reveals the value of these orders in today's markets. Small customer order flow is desirable to markets because the transaction volume (1) allows market makers to profit by capturing the bid-ask spread, (2) facilitates market making by specialists and dealers, and (3) provides revenue for the markets through consolidated tape fees. To draw small orders, the market centers offer brokers routing small retail orders a variety of inducements to ensure a constant stream of such orders. For example, the regional exchanges advertise their lower fees, speed of execution, and guarantee of primary market price protection. The regional exchanges also have facilitated the affiliation of regional specialists with large broker-dealers that have a retail customer order flow. Third market makers offer fast, inexpensive service and often provide cash rebates to firms with customer order flow. Similarly, the primary markets have promoted their ability to provide liquidity and to obtain executions between the spread. Recently, the NYSE began offering transaction fee credits.[24]

NASDAQ

The evolution in the markets for OTC stocks has been even more dramatic than in the exchange markets because of the growth of NASDAQ, an interdealer quotation system for the OTC market operated by the NASD, a national securities association registered under Section 15A of Exchange Act.[25] Since the beginning of its operation in 1971, NASDAQ has made tremendous strides in automating OTC market making and increasing the efficiency and transparency of the OTC market.

NASDAQ electronically links market makers around the country for over 4,000 issues.[26] In 1992, NASDAQ trading represented 42% of share volume and 29% of dollar volume of the U.S. equity markets. Its share volume makes NASDAQ the second-largest securities market in the world after the NYSE. Occasionally, NASDAQ's share volume exceeds that of the NYSE. In 1993, NASDAQ's dollar volume equaled 43% of the NYSE dollar volume.

It has been estimated that over 1,000 of the companies quoted on NASDAQ meet the financial listing standards for the NYSE; over 2,000 meet the equivalent Amex standards. These companies are aggressively recruited by the NYSE and Amex. Although most of the large capitalization companies are listed on the NYSE, a significant portion of the younger widely held companies remain on NASDAQ.[27] Over 52,000 market making positions are held by 472 active NASDAQ market makers. An average 11.5 market makers quote the typical NASDAQ security. For NASDAQ securities designated NMS (NASDAQ/NMS), this average increases to 12.3 market makers.

NASDAQ automates the display of dealer quotations. With the exception of its Small Order Execution System (SOES) and the SelectNet system, which allows market makers to use NASDAQ terminals to display and execute orders, executions for NASDAQ stocks still occur by telephone. PTSs, which offer automated executions and display of limit orders, have captured 13% of the volume (mostly institutional) in NASDAQ stocks.

As in the listed markets, the order flow of retail customers has become a valuable asset in the NASDAQ market. NASDAQ market makers offer a range of inducements, including cash rebates and automated services, to attract small-sized order flow. Most large broker-dealers execute as principal their customer orders in NASDAQ stocks in which they make a market.

Automated Trading Systems

Several types of automated trading systems offer institutions and broker-dealers the opportunity to trade off the exchanges and NASDAQ. The first are PTSs, which are screen-based trading systems used by institutions and broker-dealers. The sponsors of PTSs designed them to fulfill the needs of institutional investors not satisfied by traditional markets. Although use of these systems is growing, their market share is only 1.4% of NYSE share volume; they have, however, captured 13% of NASDAQ share volume. Almost all PTSs are regulated as broker-dealers.

A second type of automated trading systems is internal systems operated by large broker-dealers that cross their customers' orders and, in some cases, orders from other broker-dealers. The crossed orders for listed stocks are sent to an exchange for execution. Orders for NASDAQ stocks are submitted to the NASD for trade reporting.

Foreign Markets

Over the past 20 years it has become easier to trade securities around the world because of advances in telecommunications. The larger broker-dealers have established trading desks at the major securities markets around the world. As a result, hundreds of U.S. equities are traded on foreign stock exchanges, and the larger broker-dealers have the ability to route orders in U.S. equities around the world.

Available data indicate that trading of U.S. equities on foreign exchanges amounts to a few million shares a day. Otherwise, trading of U.S. equities abroad is not initiated in foreign markets but results from orders telephoned or faxed by U.S. broker-dealers to their foreign desks. These orders are typically for a large block in a single stock or a large basket of multiple stocks.[28] Based on available data, it appears that this "fax" trading currently amounts to approximately seven million shares per day in NYSE stocks.

Derivatives Markets

The derivatives markets, small in 1975, are now large markets that surpass the NYSE in terms of dollar trading volume. The equity derivatives market has evolved from a market primarily used for the hedging of market risks for institutional stock portfolios into a sizable market for trading by professional and institutional accounts.[29] It is well established that the stock, options, and futures markets are linked via market participants and the strategies they use.[30]

The Commission has examined the derivative markets in a variety of contexts and has made recommendations regarding the regulation of these markets.[31] The Commission continuously assesses the adequacy of regulation of derivative products. As a result of the separate attention that the derivatives markets receive from the Commission and other regulators, the Division has not specifically included derivative product regulation in the Market 2000 Study. Nevertheless, when examining the issues addressed in this Report, the Division was mindful of the growing importance of the derivatives markets and the fact that the stock index futures market now sometimes functions as a price discovery mechanism for the equity market.

Analysis of Equity Market Developments

The market for major U.S. equities has become somewhat dispersed among various competitors as users have sought alternatives to the NYSE, Amex, and NASDAQ when these markets would not or could not meet their needs. The resulting increase in market competition has created a veritable "menu" of systems in the equity markets.[32] This competition also has improved the efficiency and quality of the markets.

As the markets improved systems for trade routing, execution, reporting, and processing, the resulting efficiencies have translated into lower costs as commission rates have decreased and transaction fees have declined. New services have expanded the choices available to investors and professionals. Market participants no longer are limited to the primary markets but can select from numerous alternatives to satisfy their needs. To compete, the primary markets have improved their operations.

Technological innovations spurred by competition have contributed to increased market capacity. As a result, the substantial growth in trading volume can be handled efficiently. The equity markets are currently able to handle volume on a consistent basis that only several years ago could have strained the markets severely. Nonetheless, the market breaks of October 1987 and 1989 are a sobering reminder that volume can explode beyond predictable levels.

Market quality has improved substantially within the existing competitive environment. For instance, over the past several years, spreads for NYSE stocks have narrowed and depth has increased. This is true both for Standard & Poor's (S&P) 500 stocks and non-S&P 500 stocks. Although the percentage of volume and trades captured by the NYSE in stocks listed on that exchange has declined somewhat during the past eight years, the market quality of NYSE stocks has not been affected negatively. Similarly, the growth of NASDAQ has improved the liquidity and efficiency of the OTC market over the past 20 years.

Although alternative markets have provided a vigorous competitive challenge to the primary markets, the economic viability of the latter has not been jeopardized. The NYSE has announced record revenues for the first three quarters of 1993. The NASD also expects record revenues. This is due in part to record trading volume but also reflects the economic benefits that the NYSE and NASD receive from their primary market status. In 1992, the NYSE derived 40% of its revenues from listing fees, 13% from the distribution of market data to vendors, 11% from regulatory fees, and 16% from facilities fees, membership dues, and investments. Trading fees amounted to only 20% of the NYSE's revenues. Similarly, the NASD received 64% of its revenues from sources unrelated to trading volume. Although competition has reduced the NYSE's and NASD's respective market shares, it has not prevented them from operating successfully. Indeed, the NYSE's 70% share of orders and 79% share volume and NASDAQ's 90% market share of orders and 87% market share of volume would be envied in any other industry.

The competition for trading volume among markets has been beneficial to these equity markets; certain aspects of the markets, however, give rise to concerns. For instance, the profitability of retail orders that attracts such competition may stem in part from inefficiencies that keep spreads artificially wide and that prevent customers from receiving the best price for their orders. Similarly, the growing significance of NASDAQ raises questions as to whether a market designed for competing dealers in thinly traded OTC securities needs adjustments now that it includes widely held, actively traded securities. In addition, the growth in trading activity by institutional investors has made it more difficult for markets and regulators to balance the interests of retail, institutional, and professional participants. Finally, the ability of technology to blur the regulatory distinctions between exchanges, dealers, and brokers calls into question whether competition is being conducted on a level playing field. These problems are not yet serious, but they warrant resolution.

In summary, the Division believes that the U.S. equity markets are healthy and operating efficiently. The Division also believes that the alternative markets provide benefits that should be preserved. At the same time, regulatory attention is needed to address issues affecting market fairness and competitiveness.

Notes

1. SEC, *Institutional Investor Study Report*, H.R. Doc. No. 64, 92d Cong., 1st Sess. (1971) ("Institutional Investor Study").
2. SEC, Statement of the Securities and Exchange Commission on the Future Structure of the Securities Markets (Feb. 2, 1972), 37 FR 5286 (Feb. 4, 1972).
3. *Id.* at 5286.
4. Pub. L. No. 94-29, 89 Stat. 97 (1975).
5. 15 U.S.C. §78k-1(a)(1) (1988).
6. S. Rep. No. 75, 94th Cong., 1st Sess. 7 (1975) ("Senate Report").
7. 15 U.S.C. §78k-1(a)(1).
8. A recent survey indicates that the trend toward the institutionalization of the markets may have leveled off. See Leslie Scism, "Institutional Share of U.S. Equities Slips," *Wall. St. J.*, Dec. 8, 1993, at Sec. C, p.1, col. 4.
9. For a detailed discussion of the growth of mutual funds, see Division of Investment Management, SEC, *Protecting Investors: A Half Century of Investment Company Regulation* (1992).
10. The value of equities held by the state and local retirement funds in 1975 was $25.8 billion. See SEC, *42nd Annual Report* 188 (1976). In contrast, in 1992 the California Public Employees Retirement System had $22 billion invested in equities. See Letter from DeWitt F. Bowman, Chief Investment Officer, California Public Employees' Retirement System, to Jonathan G. Katz, Secretary, SEC (Oct. 15, 1992).
11. Compiled from various *Pensions & Investments Age* surveys.
12. Josef Lakonishok et al., "The Structure and Performance of the Money Management Industry," Brookings Papers: Microeconomics 373 (1992).
13. See SEC, *42nd Annual Report* (1976); SEC, *58th Annual Report* (1992).
14. Nevertheless, events such as the October 1987 market break test the limits of the markets' capacity to handle larger volume.
15. Of course, an investor's order that is large in size likely will receive individual handling by the broker-dealer. In addition, an investor has the option (rarely exercised in practice) of asking the broker-dealer to route an order to a specific market.
16. Study III contains a detailed description of the equity markets.
17. The NYSE, the Amex, and regional exchanges have automated many of their functions since 1975. As a result, they are able to handle exponentially greater volume than in prior years. At the point of order execution, however, the NYSE and the Amex largely remain an auction market with specialists handling the auction.
18. Division of Market Regulation, SEC, *Trading Analysis of October 13 and 16*, 1989, at 1 (1990) ("October 1989 Report").
19. The grant of UTP allows a market to trade a particular security, even though the issuer is not listed on that market. See Exchange Act Section 12(f), 15 U.S.C. §78l(f). An issuer does not pay listing fees to the exchange trading its securities via UTP.

20. As a result, the NYSE now offers transaction fee credits. Securities Exchange Act Release No. 31795 (Jan. 29, 1993), 58 FR 9244 (Feb. 19, 1993) (approving NYSE rule change that decreased transaction charges).

21. For example, the Pacific Stock Exchange operates an after-hours auction market until 4:50 P.M. (EST). Recently, the Chicago Stock Exchange began trading a basket of 20 stocks.

22. Under Rule 19c-1 of the Exchange Act, 17 C.F.R. §240.19c-1 (1993), the NYSE's off-board trading restrictions do not apply to orders handled by an exchange member as agent (other than agency crosses). This enables members to send such orders to third market makers who execute the orders as dealers.

23. Some third market firms handle institutional block trades.

24. See *supra* note 20. NYSE executives have indicated that new pricing policies for small trades since February have been successful in attracting volume. See "Big Board Market-Share Inched Higher in 1993," *Redemption Digest*, Dec. 29, 1993, at 1.

25. 15 U.D.C. §78oA.

26. See 1993 NASDAQ Fact Book & Company Directory. All the statistics cited for NASDAQ were obtained from this source.

27. As of November 11, 1993, 458 of the companies in the S&P 500 Index are NYSE companies, 37 are NASDAQ companies, and 5 are Amex companies.

28. Often the basket trade takes the form of an "exchange for physical" ("EFP"). An EFP involving stocks is the exchange of a long (short) futures position for an equivalent long (short) stock basket position. The EFP normally takes place after the NYSE close and is privately negotiated between the parties. See generally Division of Trading and Markets, Commodity Futures Trading Commission, *Report on Exchanges of Futures for Physical* (Oct. 1987).

29. Division of Market Regulation, SEC, *The October 1987 Market Break Report* xiv, 3–6 to 3–9 (1988) ("October 1987 Report").

30. See, e.g., *id.* at 3–4 to 3–9; "Report of the Presidential Task Force on Market Mechanisms," Fed. Sec. L. Rep. (CCH) No. 1267 (Jan. 12, 1988).

31. See, e.g., Securities Exchange Act Release No. 32256 (May 4, 1993), 58 FR 27486 (May 10, 1993) (Concept Release on derivative products); SEC, *Report on Intermarket Coordination Pursuant to the Market Reform Act of 1990* (May 1993, May 1992, May 1991); Division of Market Regulation, SEC, Trading Analysis of November 15, 1991 (Oct. 1992); SEC, Papers Relating to the Capital Adequacy of Securities Firms, Submitted to the Technical Comm. of IOSCO (July 16–17, 1991); October 1989 Report, *supra* note 22; October 1987 Report, *supra* note 33; Division of Market Regulation, SEC, *The Role of Index-Related Trading in the Market Decline on September 11 and 12, 1986* (1987); SEC, *Roundtable on Index Arbitrage* (1986); SEC, *Report of the Special Study of the Options Markets* (1978); SEC, *1988 Report to Congress on Actions by the Self-Regulatory Organizations Since the 1987 Market Break* (1988); "The Futures Trading Practices Act of 1991: Hearings on Title III of S.207 Before the Senate Comm. on Banking, Housing and Urban Affairs" (1991) (Testimony of Richard C. Breeden, Chairman, SEC); "Hearings on Intermarket Regulation Before the Senate Comm. on Banking, Housing and Urban Affairs" (1990) (Testimony of Richard C. Breeden, Chairman, SEC); "The Stock Market Reform Act of 1989: Hearings on H.R. 1609 Before the House Subcomm. on Telecommunications and Finance of the House Comm. on Energy and Commerce" (1989) (Testimony of Richard C. Breeden, Chairman, SEC); Richard C. Breeden, Address Before the International Swap Dealers Association Annual Meeting (Mar. 11, 1993); Mary L. Schapiro, The Growth of the Synthetic Derivative Market: Risks and Benefits, Address Before the National Options & Futures Society (Sept. 24, 1991).

32. Hans R. Stoll, *Debate over the Organization of the Stock Market: Competition or Fragmentation?* 2 (Financial Markets Research Center Policy Paper 92-01, 1992).

Appendix

Table 6.1.1
Holdings of U.S. equities outstanding (Market value in $ billions)

	Total	Households		Institutions	
		Value	% of total	Value	% of total
1965	735	616	83.8	119	16.2
1966	660	548	83.0	112	17.0
1967	835	682	81.7	153	18.3
1968	996	815	81.9	181	18.1
1969	850	587	69.1	263	30.9
1970	841	572	68.0	269	32.0
1971	988	651	65.9	337	34.1
1972	1,129	724	64.1	406	35.9
1973	887	536	60.4	351	39.6
1974	600	337	56.1	263	43.9
1975	800	454	56.7	347	43.3
1976	1,058	654	61.8	404	38.2
1977	942	556	59.0	386	41.0
1978	991	564	56.9	427	43.1
1979	1,175	690	58.7	485	41.3
1980	1,535	924	60.2	611	39.8
1981	1,423	830	58.3	593	41.7
1982	1,611	893	55.4	719	44.6
1983	1,920	1,015	52.9	905	47.1
1984	1,851	940	50.8	910	49.2
1985	2,360	1,155	48.9	1,205	51.1
1986	2,763	1,453	52.6	1,311	47.4
1987	2,779	1,418	51.0	1,361	49.0
1988	3,099	1,630	52.6	1,469	47.4
1989	3,810	1,929	50.6	1,881	49.4
1990	3,530	1,760	49.9	1,770	50.1
1991	4,864	2,653	54.5	2,211	45.5
1992	5,463	2,919	53.4	2,544	46.6
1993	6,278	3,285	52.3	2,993	47.7
1994	6,293	3,199	50.8	3,095	49.2
1995	8,345	4,286	51.4	4,060	48.6
1996	10,090	4,780	47.4	5,310	52.6

Note: Household sector includes nonprofit organizations.
Source: Federal Reserve Flow of Funds Accounts (revised)

Table 6.1.2
1996 market share data: NYSE stocks

	Avg. shares per day (millions)	Avg. shares per day (%)	Avg. transactions per day	Avg. transactions per day (%)
NYSE				
Regular hours	412.51	78.0%	296,064	73.1%
Crossing session 1	0.14	0.0%		
Crossing session 2	2.40	0.5%		
All regionals	44.38	8.4%	64,931	16.0%
BSE	5.76	1.1%	7,275	1.8%
CHX	15.37	2.9%	17,337	4.3%
PHLX	5.96	1.1%	8,084	2.0%
PSE	10.24	1.9%	18,964	4.7%
CSE	7.05	1.3%	13,271	3.3%
NASD	40.51	7.7%	43,417	10.7%
PTS				
Regular hours*	3.6	0.7%	543	0.1%
PTS after hours*	1.1	0.2%		
Overseas by NYSE firms				
Program trades	21.9	4.1%		
OTC (non-program)*	1.7	0.3%		
Foreign exchanges (non-program)*	0.7	0.1%		
Total	**528.94**	**100.0%**	**404,955**	**100%**

* As of 1993 (last available data)
Source: 1997 NYSE Factbook; SEC Market 2000 Report

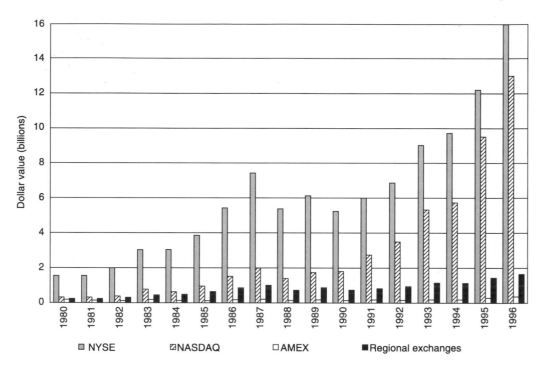

Figure 6.1.1 Average trading volume on U.S. stock markets 1980–1996

6.2   AOL Defection Illuminates Differences between NYSE and Nasdaq Markets*

Michael Brush

Since America Online Inc. (NASDAQ:AMER) announced last week that it is defecting from the Nasdaq stock market to the older, larger New York Stock Exchange, it has refused to explain its reasons for making the move. But given the recent round of Justice Department settlements regarding improper trading practices that have cast a shadow over Nasdaq, some may draw conclusions about why the company has pulled up stakes.

After all, what company would want to list on an exchange where market makers allegedly engage in anti-competitive practices like bullying clients or colluding to keep buy-sell spreads wide as a way to make more money?

Big-league corporations like Microsoft Corp. (NASDAQ:MSFT), Intel Corp. (NASDAQ:INTC), Apple Computer (NASDAQ:AAPL) and MCI Communications (NASDAQ:MCIC), that's who. If practices on the Nasdaq markets are so bad, why do so many huge corporations continue to list there when, according to tradition, they should have "graduated" to the NYSE years ago? And what are the pros and cons of each exchange, both for companies and investors?

To understand the answers to these questions, it is important to know some of the fundamental differences between the two markets.

The NYSE is known as an "auction market" because traders, acting as agents for investors, have the job of finding a buyer or seller to take the other side of each requested transaction. They earn their keep by charging investors a commission.

In the Nasdaq market, however, dealers buy shares directly from investors and then turn around and sell them at a markup. Known as the spread, that markup is their payment. Unlike the NYSE, Nasdaq assigns each stock about 10 or 15 dealers, known as "dealers in the box." They are obligated to make markets in the stock themselves, meaning they have to buy or sell a certain number of the shares at their quoted price, each time someone places an order.

So what do these differences mean for companies and investors? For investors, the two markets offer these advantages and disadvantages.

- **Regulation and information** The NYSE makes all companies report detailed financial information. "It has the greatest quality control of any exchange in the world," says a professor at a New York-based business school, who is conducting a study into market efficiency of the various exchanges and asked not to be identified.
- **Spread size** With a NYSE-listed stock you can typically turn around and sell it right away, if you wanted to, for just "one-eighth," or 12.5 cents, less than you bought it for. Nasdaq buy-sell spreads can be much higher, approaching 10% of the price of the stock, depending on the issue. That's important because it means your stock has to appreciate a lot more before you can sell it for a profit.

---

*From *Money Daily*, August 6, 1996. Reprinted with permission.

One way to save money when investing in a Nasdaq stock, even though this won't help reduce the spread, is to be sure to use the "dealer in the box," or appointed dealer for the stock. That way, you avoid the commission your broker will charge you for passing your trade on to that dealer, who you could contact on your own. Your broker is obligated to tell you who the assigned dealers are for each stock. On the other hand, if your broker works for a large firm, he or she may be better able than you to convince the dealer to offer a better price. Because dealers make more money when the spread is bigger, there is a built-in incentive to keep spreads wide, which is bad for investors.

- **Limit orders**   Because the NYSE has a centralized system for "limit orders"—or orders to buy or sell when a stock hits a certain price—they tend to get executed more efficiently. They're also more public: Limit orders placed for companies on the NYSE get posted openly for everyone to see, which adds depth to the market. In addition, once placed, they go into a queue and are executed according to the order in which they came in. In the Nasdaq, limit orders are handled individually by each dealer. Nasdaq is planning to correct this shortcoming soon by introducing Naqcess, its own version of NYSE's centralized limit order system.

For companies, the two exchanges offer the following pros and cons.

- **Hand holding**   Many firms like being on Nasdaq because of the stable of dealers committed to both making a market in their stock and researching their company. "By staying on Nasdaq, the companies know they will have five or ten people dedicated to maintaining liquidity and doing research," notes the business school professor. "They feel well-supported and that there is a deeper market for their stock. They think that if they were on the NYSE, Goldman Sachs, Morgan Stanley, and Merrill Lynch wouldn't be sitting there all day making a market in their shares."
- **Volatility**   Larger companies typically don't lose anything in terms of price volatility on Nasdaq because the market is considered efficient for stocks whose volume is over 50,000 a day, says the business professor. Below that, the spreads get bigger and each trade can move prices a lot more, bringing greater volatility. About 1,000 to 1,500 stocks out of the roughly 4,000 that trade on Nasdaq fit into this low-volume category.
- **Small stock advantages**   Still, Nasdaq's dealer market system is probably better for smaller stocks because dealers are obligated to keep a market in the stock. "For thinly traded stocks, the dealer market has the advantage of bringing dealer capital to the market to facilitate the trading process," says Robert Schwartz, New York University business professor and chairman of Nasdaq's economic advisory board.
- **Hard to say goodbye**   One of the drawbacks to listing on the NYSE is that once a company is there, it can be hard to get off the exchange because a minimum number of shareholders have to vote to delist.

6.3 Making the Best Use of Trading Alternatives*
Joshua D. Rose and David C. Cushing

The business of trading has always been considered more than an art, and it is rapidly becoming a science. This trend has been supported by the growth in quantitative strategies, the development of sophisticated and scientific trading techniques, and the increasingly technical and quantitative skill levels of investment professionals.

To trade effectively, traders must identify and evaluate their decision criteria. One crucial factor is understanding the sense of urgency. Traders must also understand the nature of the securities being traded: large-capitalization or small-capitalization; listed or OTC; and total trade size in issues, shares, and dollars. Each factor will have implications for deciding whether to trade patiently or quickly, as principal or agent, electronically or manually, and so forth. Throughout the trade, the current market conditions must be evaluated. In this presentation, we will discuss the alternatives available to traders and the keys to effective trading; we also will illustrate a typical trade, and take a look into the future.

Implementation Styles

Trades can be implemented in a variety of ways. The single-stock approach involves trading one stock at a time. A portfolio approach involves trading a large number of securities —say, 2,000 to 3,000—simultaneously as an indivisible unit. A hybrid approach is a combination of the two. From an evolutionary standpoint, traditional active management (stock picking) has lent itself to a single-stock implementation style. Over the years, however, the growth in passive and quantitative strategies has increased the prevalence of the portfolio approach.

The *single-stock approach* has the advantages of timely execution and a relatively high comfort level, because it has been done for a long time and people are familiar with it. Trading desks are generally staffed by investment professionals who know what they are doing, and they can spend time focusing on individual stocks and attempting to add value. This concentrated focus usually produces good results. The single-stock approach works well with relatively few orders. Some traders can manage 5 stocks in a day, and others can manage 50 stocks, but at some point, trying to trade too many individual orders produces diminishing returns. Because the single-stock approach is so labor intensive, it is inadequate for handling multiple orders.

The *portfolio approach* has the advantages of working well for multiple orders and allowing improved risk-management and hedging capabilities. In addition, the portfolio approach tends to reduce the overall costs of trading for portfolios that are potentially

---

Reprinted with permission from Execution Techniques, True Trading Costs, and the Microstructure of Markets. Copyright 1993, Association for Investment Management and Research, Charlottesville, VA. All rights reserved.

hedgeable. Disadvantages of the portfolio approach are that it does not necessarily work well for difficult trades and that it often requires substantial investment in technology. Not all trades are easy to implement. In trying to trade a large number of securities as a package, some individual issues are sure to have certain nuances or peculiarities about them of which the trader is not always aware. Over time, some of these peculiarities work for traders and some work against them. The portfolio approach requires, at a minimum, a personal computer and, at a maximum, a sizable trade-management system integrated with the portfolio-management system, the accounting system, and the back office.

Many traders and portfolio managers often combine the *single-stock and portfolio approaches*. Combining the two approaches often can yield the best results for institutions trying to minimize transaction costs.

How to trade is ultimately a function of a variety of factors. Maintaining flexibility and avoiding any overly structured approach may be necessary to get the job done most effectively. The trading process ultimately involves an ongoing, intelligent search for liquidity. This search involves a substantial, but important, investment in systems.

Trading Alternatives

Trades can be executed in a variety of ways. This section outlines the primary alternatives for trading using the single-stock and portfolio trading approaches.

Single-Stock Trading Alternatives

For the single-stock approach, the trading alternatives most frequently used are the institutional block market (upstairs market); the floors of major exchanges (specialists); the dealer market (which essentially entails trading with the broker-dealer firms as principals); crossing networks; and direct institution-to-institution trading.

- **Upstairs block market**   The upstairs block market entails lower transaction costs than some alternatives, because trades in the market often can be executed at or near the bid-offer spread. One disadvantage of the upstairs market is that it is inefficient for some transactions. It is generally more suitable for large-capitalization securities than for small-capitalization securities, for example. Finding the other side of a trade can be like trying to find the proverbial needle in a haystack. Another disadvantage is the exposure of the order to the marketplace, which often results in hidden market impact costs. The information content in the process of trying to match the other side of the trade can cause problems for some institutions.

- **Trading floors**   In the United States, the trading floors offer continuous, open-outcry markets and reasonable liquidity. A continuous market implies that liquidity is always available whenever the market is open. Proponents of call markets suggest, however, that one disadvantage of continuous markets is that order flow arrives at different points during the day. Thus, buyers and sellers may be like "two ships passing in the night." Order exposure can also be a problem, particularly for a large order. Trading against specialists is another disadvantage. Specialists may not have enough liquidity to help traders execute their trades. Thus, the liquidity of continuous markets may be more theoretical than real.

- **Dealer market** A single-stock trade in the dealer market is generally executed by a broker-dealer acting as principal. Advantages are immediacy and certainty of execution. An institution might ask for a bid or an offer on a certain stock, and the broker will buy or sell it at a certain price, but trying to find the other side of the trade in some of the agency capacities can be a time-consuming process. For traders with a sense of urgency, the dealer market can be a viable solution. One disadvantage of the dealer market is that it is typically high cost. Broker-dealers who act as principals are in business to make money trading, and the explicit and implicit costs—the commission cost plus the impact of the trade itself—are high. Another disadvantage is that the trader is (by definition) working against a broker-dealer.

- **Crossing networks** Crossing networks are used in only a small percentage of total trading volume, but this segment of the market is clearly growing. Some advantages of crossing networks include confidentiality, fair pricing, and low commission rates. Some networks execute trades at the midpoint of the bid-offer spread, and some at the last reported sale. The commission rates are generally lower than average institutional commission rates, which when combined with market impact savings allow for overall cost savings.

    One disadvantage of crossing networks is their lack of liquidity. Because these markets are still in their infancy, they offer less liquidity than other trading alternatives, and access can be difficult. Using crossing networks can also result in opportunity costs because the marketplace is bypassed during periods of activity in the securities being traded.

Portfolio Trading Alternatives

For portfolio-based approaches to trading, the alternatives include getting a guaranteed price (principal bid), using an agent or broker, and using a combined principal-and-agency approach.

- **Principal** Principal trades divide into two categories: cash only and derivatives related. Two forms of derivatives-related transactions are basis trades and exchange for physicals (EFPs). In a basis trade, a broker trades stock index futures in the broker's own account during the course of a day and then crosses the client's portfolio into the broker's account at the end of the day at a "basis," or spread, to the average futures price. The spread is based on fair value of the futures-cash basis. When the trade is complete, the client ends up with the desired cash portfolio, and the broker is left with the offsetting cash position hedged with futures. In an EFP transaction, the client starts off with futures and exchanges them with a broker for a "physical" or cash position. Alternatively, the client can start off with a cash position and exchange it for futures. Like basis trades, EFP transactions are priced relative to the fair value of the futures-cash spread. Unlike basis trades, EFPs must be posted on the relevant futures exchange, because a change of ownership of the futures is involved.

    These transactions are typically inexpensive, convenient, and relatively opaque to the marketplace. A limitation is that the basket being crossed or exchanged must track the index closely. Also, futures authorization is required for EFPs, which is not always easy to obtain.

    Another way to trade a list of stocks as principal is to get a straight guaranteed price from a broker. Typically, bids are solicited from several brokers in units of cents per share relative to a predefined benchmark. The most frequently used benchmark is closing price as of trade date. The client then selects the most attractive bid, and the portfolio is crossed from client to broker at the benchmark price net of the guarantee bid. Guaranteed bids have two major advantages: risk transfer from the client to the broker and convenience. Guaranteed bids, however, tend to end up being more costly than agency trading. Also, they possess potential for abuses such as front-running.

After a period of relative decline, principal bid activity made a resurgence in 1991. This resurgence has three explanations. One is increased concern about implementation shortfall, which makes investors want to complete their trades faster. Another is that liquidity in the marketplace as a whole recently has been on the decline. If liquidity is expensive or difficult to access, getting a principal bid for an entire list of stocks may end up being the easier and cheaper alternative. The third explanation is the proliferation of long/short, or market-neutral, strategies, because institutional restrictions on short selling make implementation as agent much riskier than for a straight long portfolio.

- **Broker**   Investors trade lists as agent because they believe that, in the long run, doing so is cheaper that other approaches. When list trading as agent, the money manager has two basic choices: "do it yourself" or hire a broker to manage the process. The main advantages of do-it-yourself trading are confidentiality and control. If a buy-side trader is working a large list of securities and does not want the market to know about it, do-it-yourself trading is probably the best choice. The disadvantages are that this method is labor intensive, is time-consuming, and requires investment in technology.

  An advantage of hiring a broker is the convenience of transferring the trade to someone who presumably has the expertise to handle such transactions. Compensation to the broker for providing this agency service can be structured in two basic ways: on a best-efforts basis, in which the commission rate is fixed, or on an incentive basis, whereby the better the broker does, the larger the commission paid, and vice versa. The main problem with incentive structures is the difficulty of defining an accurately calculated measure of trading skill. Thus, compensation may instead be based on the broker's ability to "game" the measure.

- **Combined principal and agency**   Of course, these approaches to list trading may be combined. Later on, we will provide an example in which breaking up a list and trading part as principal and part as agent might make sense.

Key to Effective Execution

The three keys to effective execution of a trade are liquidity, technology, and ideas. You seek liquidity and then apply technology and ideas.

Adequate liquidity is the controlling factor in effective execution. Some liquidity sources to consider in formulating trading strategy are exchange floors, crossing systems, block desks, and institutional order flow. To get liquidity, you must be willing and able to use whatever sources you can find.

Technology provides the support necessary for effective list trading. It is the key to trade-management capability, which means being able to account for trades and knowing where you stand; it provides the capability for useful real-time analytical and execution capabilities; it provides the conduit for transferring the trade data directly into the accounting system; finally, it allows traders to integrate all the various decision processes, which will reduce administrative delays and errors in trading.

Good execution depends on *good ideas*—a good trading strategy or game plan and good tactics. How do you time orders? What size trade do you send to the floor? What limit prices do you use? Ideas attempt to answer these types of questions. Because market timing is the factor with the largest effect on investment returns, ideas have the greatest potential for reducing costs. Of course, a large investment in time is required to design and test trading strategies that work, and that investment may exceed the perceived benefits.

Real-World Trading

The steps involved in executing a typical agency portfolio trade—pre-trade analysis, trade execution, and post-trade reporting—offer opportunities for cost savings.

Pre-trade Analysis

Effective trading requires comprehensive pre-trade analysis. The purposes of analysis are to control portfolio liquidity and to find a optimal split between the use of principals and agencies and between manual and electronic trading techniques.

Transaction costs savings can begin before a portfolio arrives on a trading desk by controlling portfolio liquidity. The approach is to use transaction-cost estimates as inputs to the portfolio-construction process. By incorporating this information, the portfolio manager can minimize the number of large, illiquid positions and make the portfolio more "digestible" by the market. Such improvements in liquidity, however, must be weighed against the likely increase in turnover resulting from liquidity-motivated purchases being sold in the next rebalancing.

After portfolio liquidity concerns have been addressed, the first trading-related step is to decide what portion, if any, of the list should be traded as principal and what part as agent. As mentioned previously, considerable savings can be achieved for some portfolios by intelligently combining principal and agency techniques. Ideally, traders would like to know which stocks are the most expensive to insure at the margin. These stocks would be the most logical candidates to be stripped out for agency trading, and the trader can then generate a reduced-cost principal bid for the balance. Table 6.3.1 illustrates the results of a marginal bid analysis for a $100 million mid-capitalization replicating portfolio. The cost of trading the entire list of 3,767,400 shares would be 14.23 cents share. By removing the 10 most expensive trades in the portfolio, the cost of guaranteeing the balance of 3,727,800 shares is estimated to drop to 13.80 cents a share. Thus, by removing approximately 40,000 shares, the overall commission amount decreases by about $18,000. The question then becomes: Is 45 cents a share ($18,000/40,000 shares) adequate compensation for taking on the risk of those 10 names? The answer to this question is frequently yes.

Another key decision to make before trading a list is: Which issues should be traded electronically and which should be traded manually? Table 6.3.2 shows a pre-trade analysis report that helps address this question. The orders are ranked by the expected difficulty of trading each stock. The expected difficulty, computed by Investment Technology Group, Inc. (ITG), is a weighted average of the trailing five-day average volume in the stock, the

Table 6.3.1
Combined principal-and-agency approach

Trade	Total shares	Initial bid	Removed shares	Cost of removed shares	New bid
A1	3,767,400	$0.1423	5,300	$1.2306	$0.1408
A2	3,762,100	0.1408	2,900	1.0381	0.1401
A3	3,759,200	0.1401	2,000	0.3710	0.1400
A4	3,757,200	0.1400	5,200	0.3636	0.1396
A5	3,752,000	0.1396	3,600	0.3349	0.1395
A6	3,748,400	0.1395	3,600	0.3326	0.1393
A7	3,744,800	0.1393	3,200	0.3088	0.1391
A8	3,741,600	0.1391	5,700	0.3059	0.1389
A9	3,735,900	0.1389	8,100	0.2963	0.1385
A10	3,727,800	0.1385	12,200	0.2867	0.1380

Source: Investment Technology Group, Inc.

bid-ask spread, and the absolute number of shares in the position. The difficulty measure is shown under the label "ITG comp." Factors and weights were selected empirically. The idea behind producing this ranking is to be able to draw a clean line through the list and say, "Most everything above that line should be traded manually, and most everything below it should be traded electronically." For example, we might not be comfortable trading 17,500 shares of International Multifoods electronically. A typical market in that stock has a depth of less than 1,000 shares, and the average daily volume is less than 10,000 shares. On the other hand, we might have no problem trading 9,300 shares of Exxon electronically.

Executing the Trade
After the key decisions are made in the pre-trade analysis, any remaining agency orders in the list are ready to be executed. At this stage, opportunities for saving money arise from managing information, crossing, and intelligent electronic trading.

• **Managing information** Effective management of information about the trading list and the progress of trades can reduce trading costs. Some important questions to track during the trading process are the following:

• What is the dollar balance of the trade? Have I bought more than I sold, or vice versa? Am I within the cash constraints of the portfolio?

• Am I out of risk balance? Are adverse sector bets developing in the list? Is the tracking error of the unexecuted portion of the list getting too high?

• What stocks are getting away? This question highlights a prime disadvantage of list trading. If you can get access to that information in real time and sort your lists to see which stocks are helping and which hurting the most, you can handle problems before they become disasters and take advantage of opportunities in stocks that are moving in your favor.

Table 6.3.2
Sample pre-trade analysis report

Company	Shares to be sold	Strike price 1	Latest close	× 5-day average volume	ITG comp
International Multifoods Corp.	17,500	27.0000	27.0000	2.04	5.41
American Business Products (Georgia)	7,800	26.5000	26.5000	2.18	2.37
St. Paul Companies, Inc.	24,500	74.6250	74.6250	0.83	1.08
Quantum Corp.	30,000	13.6250	13.6250	0.11	1.01
Sundstrand Corp.	24,500	33.5000	33.5000	0.16	0.83
American Building Maintenance (Indiana)	3,900	17.3750	17.3750	1.84	0.48
Unilever (Nevada)	20,300	111.0000	111.0000	0.29	0.47
RJR Nabisco Holdings Corp.	19,800	9.0000	9.0000	0.02	0.46
Merck & Co., Inc.	19,000	52.0000	52.0000	0.02	0.44
Grumman Corp.	17,900	20.8750	20.8750	0.49	0.42
Betz Labs, Inc.	5,300	53.2500	53.2500	0.07	0.40
Intel Corp.	10,700	58.5000	58.5000	0.01	0.36
Advanced Micro Devices, Inc.	7,600	9.1250	9.1250	0.03	0.26
McKesson Corp. (Delaware)	10,700	37.2500	37.2500	0.43	0.25
Quaker Oats Co.	10,600	60.2500	60.2500	0.09	0.25
Exxon Corp.	9,300	63.6250	63.6250	0.02	0.22
Gap, Inc. (Delaware)	7,900	31.8750	31.8750	0.01	0.18
Reebok International Ltd.	7,600	26.7500	26.7500	0.03	0.18
AAR Corp.	4,200	12.6250	12.6250	0.09	0.14
Data General Corp.	5,400	8.1250	8.1250	0.04	0.13
McDermott International, Inc.	5,000	21.2500	21.2500	0.05	0.12
Williams Companies, Inc.	4,700	33.1250	33.1250	0.04	0.11
Bear Stearns Companies, Inc.	3,435	16.1250	16.1250	0.02	0.08
Energen Corp.	2,300	17.6250	17.6250	0.46	0.08
V F Corp.	3,000	48.8750	48.8750	0.01	0.07
Enterra Corp. (Delaware)	1,400	18.0000	18.0000	0.10	0.06
Fingerhut Companies, Inc.	1,800	29.2500	29.2500	0.23	0.06
Federal Home Loan Mortgage	1,800	43.7500	43.7500	0.01	0.06
Parametric Technology Corp.	1,100	41.7500	41.7500	0.00	0.06
Schering Plough Corp.	2,300	62.2500	62.2500	0.01	0.05

Source: Investment Technology Group, Inc.

- Is arbitrage setting up? If you have a buy list on the floor at limit prices and it looks as if sell programs are about to set up, you may want to reduce or cancel your bids.
- How is the pace of trading? You may have explicit instructions from clients about how quickly to trade. More importantly, you may have input from clients about their estimates of the "half-life" of their alphas. Clients vary widely in their perceptions of how long the information behind their portfolio management will take to become impounded in stock prices. The pace of trading should reflect that perception. Post-trade analysis, which will be discussed later, can help identify whether a client's perception is accurate.
- What are my "leaves," or unexecuted share quantities? Even a small over- or under-execution can result in a trading loss that dwarfs any savings smart trading might bring.
- Is transient liquidity a factor? If I have 17,500 shares of International Multifoods to buy and an offering of 20,000 shares shows up, I want to know about it. I do not want to have somebody take that stock ahead of me and discover later I missed the boat. If I am alerted about this liquidity as soon as it becomes available, I have a much better chance of getting the first shot at it. Having that opportunity can help lower transaction costs.
- **Crossing** Another practice that can help reduce transaction costs is crossing. A simple quantitative example of the results of a cross involving slightly more than a million shares is as follows:

Shares	1,093,200
Principal amount	$34,830,294
Value of spread	$193,788
Spread saved	0.56 percent, or $0.18/share
Commission	$0.04/share
Net savings	$0.14/share

  When this savings of 14 cents a share is compared with the level of principal bids on comparable portfolios, transaction costs savings appear to be available through crossing.

  In our experience, crossing does not significantly change the risk or liquidity profile of a portfolio. A significant change could, of course, be considered evidence of a hidden cost of crossing, which would reduce the value of that 14-cent savings.

- **Electronic trading** Another way to lower transaction costs is to expand the use of computers in the trading process. One of the most important aspects of trading is being able to move orders quickly from one trading location to another—managing the logistics, getting the trades loaded into the trading system, getting them into crossing networks, getting them down to the floor, and changing limit prices to keep current with market conditions. Not only does electronic trading facilitate these tasks, it also allows efficient use of limit order models and implementation of "smart rules." Smart rules can help one stay pegged to the day's volume-weighted average price.

Post-trade Analysis

After a trade is completed, the paperwork begins. For settlement purposes, the client must receive a timely and accurate report about the execution. This report should detail the

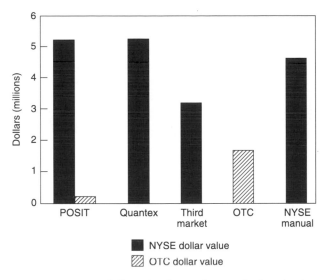

Figure 6.3.1 Portfolio value by trading method and primary exchange. Source: Investment Technology Group, Inc.

executed trades and include, at a minimum, name of the issue, buy or sell, shares, and average price.

Beyond the basic settlement report, a useful report to receive for the purpose of transaction cost control is a market impact analysis. This report should list for each issue the number of shares traded, the average price of the trade, and a benchmark price or prices. Typical benchmarks include the midpoint of the bid–offer spread as of the start of trading (as a proxy for impactless, immediate execution) and the previous night's close (for comparison with the cost of principal trading). Using two benchmarks, such as opening price on trade date and the intraday bid–offer midpoint, permits measurement of the opportunity cost or benefit of waiting to trade. The report should also show the net market impact for each issue in total dollars, cents per share, and percentage of volume.

Breaking executions down into analytically useful categories provides additional valuable information. A simple example is to look at buys and sells separately. Figure 6.3.1 shows an execution broken down by dollar amount executed in each market and trading method. Figure 6.3.2 shows the market impact produced by the use of each market and trading method. In this case, crossing resulted in 15 basis points of impact, the Quantex (an electronic execution system) impact was slightly more than 30 basis points, third-market block trading actually made a positive contribution to the bottom line, OTC trading had a small negative impact, and manual trading had a large negative impact. The client for whom this trade was executed typically crosses both in POSIT and in the third market as much as possible and so is apparently trading using the lowest cost execution vehicles for that investment style. If POSIT or third-market crossing showed up as a high-cost alternative, then this client should be advised to rethink how those vehicles are being used.

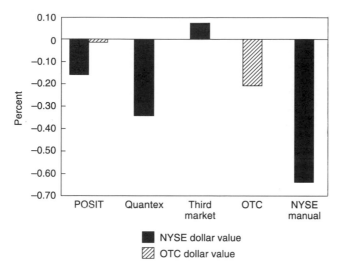

Figure 6.3.2 Market impact by trading method and primary exchange. Source: Investment Technology Group, Inc.

The Future

Looking to the future, we see the following:

- **Liquidity-driven trading**   This approach includes real-time optimization of trading lists based on available liquidity.
- **Factor-based trading**   In this type of trading, the underlying portfolio management style focuses more on factor exposure than an individual stock exposure, so liquidity is defined more in terms of the ability to obtain exposure to desired factors than it is to obtaining individual stocks.
- **Short-term trading models**   These models are short-term forecasts of individual stock alphas. This information can be included judgmentally in the trading process or as part of a more disciplined trading strategy to help improve the timing of trading decisions.
- **Machine-initiated trading**   A computer is programmed with criteria for making trading decisions and actually initiates trades. The primary application of this technique would be for small trades; the trader can then focus on the trades with larger potential for added value.
- **Systems integration**   This powerful trend is shaping the face of competition today. The systems being integrated in this case govern portfolio management, execution, and back-office functions. The strength of demand for system solutions is indicative of their potential to shift the responsibilities of traders away from paperwork and toward smart trading.

Conclusion

Many opportunities exist for saving costs in trading. The first is to trade in lists if possible. Many of the same benefits that accrue to investment portfolios (diversification and risk reduction) also accrue to portfolio trading. Be flexible about which avenues you use to trade. Do not overlook the ability of "singles and doubles," such as keeping a tight rein on dollar imbalances, to make a meaningful addition to cost savings; do not always go for the "home run" in cost savings. Keep abreast of new technologies, and use them to try to quantify expectations about trading costs and to measure results. Compare expectations of cost with what the trade actually costs. Do not underestimate the value of basic information management, such as keeping track of the stocks that are getting away, in reducing trading costs.

6.4   Big-Block Trading Pits Institutions, Dealers in a Fast, Tough Game*

Randall Smith

Welcome to the high-stakes game of block trading, a bruising, shadowy contest involving millions of shares of stock a day.

In one corner are institutional investors—pension funds, endowments, mutual funds, bank trust departments, insurance companies—and the money-management firms that handle some of these huge pools of capital. In the other are large securities dealers that in recent years have moved in to trade both with and against the institutions; some dealer firms themselves have amassed stakes of hundreds of millions of dollars. The two groups together have dramatically changed Wall Street.

Now, institutions and dealers account for an estimated 80% to 90% of all stock-exchange trading. As a result of their size and access to information, they have been able to seize the central role in the market and powerfully influence moment-to-moment stock prices. The individual investor, whose once-dominant position in the market has been steadily eroded over the years, has thus been put even further out in the cold. (see figure 6.4.1)

It is a fast-paced game. In a race for superior performance, institutions have stepped up their stock trading; the annual value of their trades comes to 61% of the value of their total holdings, up from just 23% in 1977.

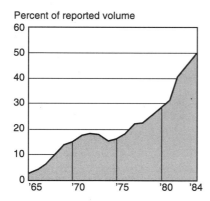

Figure 6.4.1   Block trading on the big board. Source: New York Stock Exchange

Much Criticism

This fast pace has been criticized because most institutions are supposed to be fiduciaries, managing the money of such diverse groups as factory workers, retirees, public employees, and wealthy individuals. Robert Monks, a former Labor Department pension watchdog, complains that institutions are running supposedly long-term investments "like a trading account." Some critics also believe that trading losses and transaction costs partly explain why so many money managers fall short of the market averages.

Usually, it is a businesslike game in which large trades are handled smoothly and straightforwardly. But it is also a game that is often played with sophisticated feints, bluffing, and misdirection.

By trading with institutions, dealers can earn hefty trading profits and commissions in the blink of an eyelash. However, they must also risk their own money by buying stocks from institutions for resale to other institutions or, occasionally, to the public. Such transactions often put dealers and institutions at odds; both try to disguise their activities and intentions so that they can make trades at favorable prices, while trying to find out what the other guy is up to.

Information about impending supply and demand is the coin of the realm. From the moment an institution indicates to a dealer that it wants to sell a stock until the moment the trade is completed, for example, that information can knock down the stock's price.

Stanley Shopkorn, the head of equities at Salomon Brothers Inc., says that in rare instances he charges an unusually high commission on a trade—and puts that commission into the sale price reported on the stock-market tape—so that the price will be higher. He says some stocks look more attractive to buyers if the last reported sale was an "uptick," an increase over the previous sale price.

"It's called tape dancing," Mr. Shopkorn says.

How It Works

According to Mr. Shopkorn, here is how it works: A seller wants to unload a big block of stock that last traded at $50.125. Salomon Brothers buys the stock and reports the trade at $50.25, up one-eighth from the last sale. But Salomon Brothers charges the seller a 25-cent commission instead of the normal rate of eight cents. After subtracting the 25-cent commission, the seller receives $50 a share.

Mr. Shopkorn says that if the seller paid the normal eight-cent commission, Salomon Brothers would bid only $50, down one-eighth instead of up one-eighth. The after-commission yield to the seller would be only $49.92 instead of $50. Moreover, a trade reported at an uptick price appears to have resulted from buyer interest rather than selling pressure.

"The uptick print will create a bigger rush" for the stock when Salomon Brothers puts it up for resale, Mr. Shopkorn says. "It's not to fool people. It's to create momentum on the tape." He adds: "The seller gets a better net price. The buyer gets the continued upward momentum in price movement. And the brokerage house, by effectively using the tape, earns a higher commission."

Although another trader says privately that he does the same thing, the practice is "clearly illegal under the general antifraud provision of the Securities Exchange Act of 1934," according to Michael Simon, assistant director of the market-regulation unit of the Securities and Exchange Commission.

"While nothing prevents institutions and brokers from negotiating specific commissions," Mr. Simon says, "the trade is incorrectly reported if the dealer charges a higher-than-normal commission merely to put an artificial price on the tape."

Mr. Shopkorn disagrees, contending that the practice is legal. "Regulatory standards require that transactions be within the current market range, and also that public orders on the books be satisfied. We meet those standards at all times," he adds.

Dealers have other tactics at their disposal. A few months ago, says Robert O'Hara, a trader at Goldman, Sachs & Co., the firm bought 65,000 shares of Teledyne at $260.50 from a big customer who had also asked several other dealers to bid competitively on the block. As soon as the $16.9 million trade crossed the tape with Goldman identified as the broker, Mr. O'Hara knew that other dealers would be watching to see whether Goldman had found a buyer of its own for the stock.

As it happened, Goldman didn't have a buyer. If that information had leaked out, it would have depressed the price of Teledyne, a volatile stock, and the value of Goldman's holding. Mr. O'Hara says he decided to sell the shares quietly on the New York Stock Exchange in small blocks of a few hundred shares each. And instead of using Goldman's own floor broker, he had the exchange specialist represent Goldman and sell the stock as if it were his own.

But some sellers aren't so lucky. Leaks about how much stock a big seller wants to unload occur "woefully too often" and pummel down prices, says James Mangan, Citicorp's head trader.

Although some practices may test the letter or spirit of stock-market rules, neither the Big Board nor the SEC discipline big dealers very often. Says Sheldon Richter, a Big Board surveillance manager: "These are all big boys, and they don't come crying."

Because market information is so sensitive, an institutional seller tends to call a dealer that can quickly buy an entire block. Usually the dealer must risk his own capital to buy all or part of it. The greater the dealer's buying power, the more calls it gets.

Two Kinds of Deals

A big dealer such as Salomon or Goldman Sachs will often buy an entire block at a price slightly lower than the last market sale and then try to find buyers among other institutions. A medium-sized dealer may agree to buy half a block for its own account and try to act as broker for the rest.

A typical transaction works like this: If the dealer buys half of 100,000 shares at $25 each, it pays $1,250,000 for the opportunity of making a commission of eight cents a share for both the purchase and sale sides of the entire trade, or $16,000. That is a 1.3% return in a matter of minutes. However, that return is wiped out if the stock goes down just three-eighths of a point before buyers are found. Or it doubles if the stock goes up three-eighths.

Dealers devote much time and money courting institutional traders and portfolio managers because most big trades are done by the first dealer the selling manager calls. If a manager calls several dealers to get the best bid on a sale, potential buyers may think that there are several sellers, and the price can drop.

It's no secret on Wall Street that dealers court institutional traders intensely, with expensive meals, limousines, sports and theater tickets, women, and cocaine. "These people are wined, dined, and bought," one Wall Street trader says.

Seeking Information

Dealers also try hard to ferret out institutional plans to buy and sell stock, not only in hopes of future commissions but for advance information on the prospective effect on supply and demand. If a dealer sees a big block of an airline stock traded, for example, he wants to know who bought and who sold.

Kenneth Garvey, the chief trader at Century Capital Associates, which manages about $1 billion of institutional money, says he once caught a dealer using a false identity phoning a Century clerk to find out whether Century was involved in a big trade.

Some shrewd traders try to outguess the market by watching the "elephants"—big institutions, with reputations for lacking trading skill, Mr. Garvey says.

Say an elephantine insurance company is known to own one million shares of a stock. If three 200,000-share blocks trade on successive days with that institution's favorite dealers, market watchers may conclude that the insurer is the seller and will continue the pattern by selling two more 200,000-share blocks soon. They also can think that then the price may rebound. Sometime before the last block is sold, a skillful trader might try to buy some of the shares, Mr. Garvey says.

Quick Changes in Plans

Frank Baxter, senior equity trader at J.P. Morgan & Co., says he can change his plans if the price of a stock that he is about to sell falls abruptly on anticipation of the sale. That may be true in some cases, but not all big institutions can change directions so adroitly if, for example, they decide to sell all their airline stocks.

To protect customers, dealers say they fire any employee who divulges what a client is doing. Jefferies & Co., a securities firm based in Los Angeles, is so security-conscious that it uses a three-digit code to conceal the identity of each customer.

Around the periphery of the dealer-institution arena hovers a hot-money group of traders known as hedge funds. They are private investment partnerships so named because they often hedge their bets by selling short—that is, selling borrowed stock in the hope of profiting by later buying back an equal number of replacement shares at a lower price. A hedge fund thus can short a stock with a bearish outlook or, if it expects a general market downturn, can sell short part of its portfolio. (Most institutions don't sell short as a matter of policy because it involves the risk of unlimited losses if the stock price rockets up.)

Hedge funds generate more commissions than many other customers because they do more trading. For example, one of the largest groups of hedge funds, run by Michael Steinhardt, has assets of about $400 million and generates more than $20 million annually in commissions, more than some institutions holding in excess of $10 billion in stocks. As a result, hedge funds are constantly getting calls from brokers asking whether they are interested in a particular trade.

But hedge funds want something in return. They "walk in every day with one purpose," says John A. Conlon Jr., the chief equity trader at E.F. Hutton & Co. They want to latch onto a trading opportunity, he says, "based on knowledge that should properly remain confidential—that is, the names and sizes of who's going to do what."

Hedge funds are masters of the cat-and-mouse game of extracting market information while obscuring their own intentions. And they use their commission money as bait. "You can get names," one hedge-fund operator says. If a securities-firm man resists, he adds, "you just tell him he can find another account to cover."

However, dealers themselves generally insist on being told the whole story about why a stock is being sold if they are going to buy some of it with their own capital. They also want to know exactly how many shares are being sold, so that they don't find out later that more shares are going to be offered soon thereafter and thus drive down the price. Clients that hide such information can get a reputation for "bagging the Street."

A Sharp Watch

Dealers try to keep close track of who bags them. Jacques Theriot of Smith Barney, Harris Upham & Co. says his firm generally tries to maintain a ratio of $6 in commissions for every $1 in trading losses generated by a specific customer. He says if the ratio drops to 3-to-1, someone from the firm may have a chat with the customer.

To find out whether they have been bagged on a particular trade, dealers say they occasionally depart from their rule that customer names are confidential. One may ask, "Was your seller on the last print a big Midwestern bank?" The other may reply, "It might have been." Or another might say, "I've bought his last 100,000 shares of Commodore five times."

Meanwhile, participants who were once at the center of all trading activity have been eclipsed. The upstairs dealers, with their bigger pools of capital, have taken much of the action from the specialists, who make markets in stocks at trading posts on the floor but don't have huge amounts of capital. Moreover, the upstairs trading rooms have become the real hotbeds of market intelligence. Michael Creem, a Big Board specialist, concedes, "The information has, in a way, moved off the floor."

Case Study: **Executing a Block Trade**

A fund trader has a fiduciary obligation to seek the best execution for fund orders. But best execution is a complex concept; it does not simply mean the lowest commission rate. A fund could pay a low commission while paying a higher purchase price for a stock and wind up worse off than an execution with a normal commission rate. Also, OTC trades are done "net" without any explicit commission.

Moreover, as mentioned in the introduction to this chapter, in selecting a securities broker, a fund trader is legally permitted to take into account the quantity and quality of research provided by different brokers to portfolio managers in the fund complex. In this regard, many fund complexes maintain a point system that rates the research of various Wall Street houses. Subject to the duty to seek best execution, fund traders will try to allocate fund orders to brokers who have provided the most useful research to the fund complex.

In a fund complex that is regularly trading, other factors may influence a fund trader's decisions. For example, a fund trader may be given buy orders in the same stock by several portfolio managers on the same day. The fund trader must find a way to allocate the purchases of this stock in a fair manner among the relevant funds. Alternatively, a fund trader may be asked to execute many orders from many funds over a short period. In such a situation, a fund trader needs to consider the relative time sensitivity of various trades.

This case study focuses on a fund trader who is trying to execute a block trade for a fund—a very large trade relative to the normal daily volume for that stock.

In-Class Team Discussion:

After reading and discussing the case study, your team should be prepared to answer the following questions:

1. Did Greg make a wise decision to go first to Kidder? Why? Were his reasons for going to Kidder short-term or long-term reasons?
2. In trying to sell Avantek alone, what were Greg's two main alternatives to the approach he took? What are the pros and cons of each alternative?
3. Why did Greg decide to include the Tandem buy in his proposal to Goldman Sachs? Was the Tandem buy more or less time sensitive than the Avantek sale?
4. Should Greg accept or reject Michael's offer? Should Greg make a counter-offer or go to a third dealer?
5. If Greg makes a counter-offer of selling Avantek at $24\frac{3}{8}$ and buying Tandem at $15\frac{1}{4}$, should Michael accept? Why or why not?
6. If Greg makes a counter-offer of selling Avantek at 24 and buying Tandem at $15\frac{1}{4}$, should Michael accept? Why or why not?

7. Is it reasonable for a mutual fund to incur higher transaction costs for larger trades? Aren't there economies of scale involved in executing a 180,000 share trade in Avantek versus an 8,000 or 100 share trade in Avantek?

8. How would the sale of Avantek be different if it were traded only on the New York Stock Exchange? Is the exchange or OTC market superior for executing block trades? From whose viewpoint?

6.5   At the T. Rowe Price Trading Desk*

Tuesday, August 21, 1984

It was 9:58 A.M. and the markets were about to open. Greg Donovan, one of two traders for the T. Rowe Price New Horizons Fund (and accounts holding similar securities) was going over the list of buys and sells that he was hoping to execute during the day. Greg thought the market would be up that day, especially after speculation on the part of the traders he had dealt with the previous day that several large institutions were in the process of increasing their equity positions. Greg saw his most difficult task being the sale of a large block of Avantek stock. Avantek, traded on the OTC, had been fluctuating around $25/share during the previous few weeks, after being as low as $18 in May. (Exhibit 1A.) The T. Rowe Price analyst covering the company thought that an earnings disappointment was imminent, and that news to that effect would cause the stock's price to plummet back into the teens. The analyst liked the stock on a long-term basis, however, and only wanted to trim down T. Rowe Price's current position of around 600,000 shares. Greg's instructions were to sell 183,000 shares at a price no lower than $23.

At 10:30 the Dow was up 7.50. Greg looked at the screen of his NASDAQ machine and saw that Kidder Peabody was the highest bidder for Avantek at $24\frac{5}{8}$. Several brokers were at $24\frac{1}{2}$ bid, with yet several others, including Goldman Sachs, at $24\frac{3}{8}$. (These bids were all for only 100 shares.) Goldman, knowing that T. Rowe Price had a large position in Avantek, had called earlier that morning to say that it was a buyer of the stock in sizeable quantities. Goldman was the largest and most preeminent OTC dealer, and would regularly offer to deal in large positions (50,000 shares or more) for its own account.

Greg decided to try Kidder first. Kidder, which had previously not committed much of its capital to the OTC market, had recently been moving towards becoming a more prominent player in this market. It had seemed to Greg that he might get a better execution from Kidder since a trade of this magnitude was the kind of trade on which they might even be willing to lose a little money in order to gain visibility. In addition, T. Rowe Price liked Kidder's research, and here was an opportunity to compensate them, in part, for that service.[1] Greg in any event often looked for opportunities to trade with brokers other than Goldman Sachs. This was because T. Rowe Price tended to get the best execution from Goldman, and so typically did a disproportionately large share of its trading through that firm; that is, out of proportion to the degree to which it availed itself of Goldman's research.

At 10:40 he somewhat nervously picked up the phone.

Greg (talking to Steve, a Kidder trader):   "Hi Steve, I see you're interested in some Avantek. How much do you want to buy?"

Steve: "Let me see. I'll call you right back."

Two minutes later.

Steve: "I can do 12,000 shares at [24]$\frac{5}{8}$."

Greg: "I am interested in a more medium sized quantity. Can you do better?"

Steve: "I don't really think so. But, let me look again. Don't do anything until I get back to you."

Ten minutes later.

Steve: "Look, the best I can do is 20,000 shares."

Greg: "That's not enough. It seems as if I am going to have to go elsewhere. Is that OK?"

Steve: (After a pause) "If I do more, say up to 35,000 shares, will you then deal?"

Greg: "No, that's still not enough. I'm just going to have to go elsewhere. OK?"

Steve: "I suppose you'll have to."

Greg was upset with himself. He had hoped to be able to do a large trade with Kidder. However, all Steve had done was to try to get him on the "hook," and he was not going to bite. The "hook" was a term traders used to describe a situation where if you did one trade with a dealer and had more of the same stock to trade, then by the implicit rules of the game you would be obligated to give that dealer a first right of refusal on what remained. This was because the dealer would typically have taken part of the other side of the trade on his or her own account, a position that would be endangered if you then went and off-loaded the rest of your position elsewhere. Greg was afraid that, if he did do an initial trade with Steve, the price of this lightly traded stock might fall by as much as one or even several dollars as Steve scurried around looking for more buyers knowing that he most likely had Greg on the hook for a lot more. Not all was lost at this point, however. By getting Steve to answer affirmatively when he had asked if he could go elsewhere, Greg had at least obtained an implicit commitment from Steve not to tell other traders of T. Rowe Price's intention to sell a large quantity of Avantek. At least, not immediately.

At this point Greg felt that his only option was to call Michael, a trader at Goldman Sachs. He wanted to move quickly and knew that Goldman would be willing to do the whole deal for its own account if necessary, as evidenced in particular by the early morning phone call. The trouble was that Greg now had to tell Michael that Steve already knew about the deal. Thus, since Goldman's position would now be riskier, Michael was unlikely to give him as good a price as he might have had Greg gone to him first.

Greg decided that perhaps the best way to approach Michael was to offer him a swap. For several weeks New Horizons had been adding to an already substantial long term position in Tandem (also traded OTC) and had done several of these trades through Michael. In fact, Goldman had mentioned that morning that they knew of a seller of Tandem. New Horizons and related accounts were interested in acquiring up to another 320,000 shares of this stock in the near term. It was up to Greg to choose how and when to acquire it. Greg's decision was to offer Michael both the Tandem purchase and the Avantek sale as a package deal.

At 11:25 he placed the call. At this point Kidder still showed up on the screen at $24\frac{5}{8}$ bid on Avantek, with Goldman at $24\frac{3}{8}$. During the course of the morning, small lots of Avantek stock had traded at levels as high as $24\frac{7}{8}$. (Exhibit 1C.) Tandem, being much more active, had traded in small lots in the range $15\frac{1}{4}$–$14\frac{7}{8}$, with a 10,000 share block having just traded at $14\frac{7}{8}$. (Exhibit 2C.) Currently, the lowest asking price for Tandem was $15\frac{1}{8}$ (Kidder, Salomon, Merrill), with Goldman asking $15\frac{3}{8}$. The Dow was up 11.81 for the day so far on volume of 40 million shares.

Greg: "I'd like to do a swap of 183,000 Avantek for 320,000 Tandem."

Michael: "Now those are the kinds of deals I just love! Is it a package deal? A one shot deal? What? I like one shot deals."

Greg: "One shot." Then, apologetically, "listen, I've already talked to Kidder but didn't give him any numbers. I did it because they're good on research. But, he only wanted to bid for medium size."

Michael: "I'll get back to you."

15 minutes later, Michael called back to say that the Tandem side of the deal was easy to do, but that the Avantek part was harder; no prices as yet. He called back once again at 12:22.

Michael: "I can do Avantek at $23\frac{1}{2}$ and Tandem at $15\frac{1}{4}$."

Background

T. Rowe Price Associates, Inc. was an independent investment counselling firm, founded in 1937 and located in Baltimore, Maryland. In 1984 the firm had $15.5 billion under management. This was divided about equally amongst fixed-income and equities, and also about equally amongst 12 mutual funds on one hand and separately managed accounts on the other, the latter consisting mostly of large corporate pension plan accounts.

The New Horizons Fund was founded in 1960 and, in 1984, was the largest and oldest emerging growth mutual fund in the U.S. The Fund's objectives were to invest in companies in the early stages of their corporate life cycle, and before they became widely recognized. On June 30, 1984, the Fund had $1.2 billion in assets, of which 88% was invested in the common stocks of 161 companies with five-year EPS growth rates estimated to be at least 25% per year. The remaining 12% was in short-term fixed-income securities.

The New Horizons Fund investment decisions were made by an investment advisory committee consisting of the president of the Fund, a trader (Greg), and five analysts who spent most of their time researching emerging growth companies. The analysts each managed a portion of the Fund corresponding to their areas of expertise, and could make individual stock selection decisions without prior committee approval. They were also responsible for coordinating and overseeing the trading in their stocks. The committee actively allocated the Fund's assets across these analysts, and based its decisions on their and the president's collective judgements. Generally it favored those sectors of the market with greater growth potential, better fundamentals and lower relative valuations.

T. Rowe Price employed six equity traders in all, including the head trader who had been with the firm for 25 years. Greg had the title of Vice President and had thus far spent 6 years at the firm, having previously had 10 years of trading experience elsewhere on the buy-side. In addition to serving on the investment advisory committee of the New Horizons Fund, he had some discretion to trade in stocks already owned by the Fund. For example, he could of his own accord increase an existing holding if there was a seller desperate enough to accept a very low price.

T. Rowe Price considered a college education to be a minimum qualification for a trading position, and would at times hire individuals with no previous trading experience. The salary and bonus levels for traders at T. Rowe Price were about in line with those of other large buy-side firms, where traders were typically paid somewhat less than their portfolio manager and analyst counterparts. However, remuneration was usually widely distributed within any one of these groups. Traders and analysts on the sell-side earned more on average than their buy-side counterparts, with a few earning relatively very high sums of money.

In 1983 the equity trading desk did about 23,000 trades, averaging $36,000 per trade, and totalling $8.1 billion. These trades were split 50-50 between purchases and sales. The market capitalizations of the companies traded averaged $5.5 billion. The New Horizons Fund accounted for 18% of this trading in companies whose market capitalizations averaged $750 million. (See exhibit 5.)

Recent Developments vis à vis Avantek and Tandem

T. Rowe Price's initial position in Avantek dated back to 1978 with the purchase of 320,000 shares at 1\frac{3}{4}$ (split adjusted) by the New Horizons Fund. The firm's position in this stock increased over the years, reaching 871,000 shares on March 31, 1984 (see exhibit 1D). The bulk of this increase occurred in portfolios other than New Horizons. Some selling and repurchasing took place during these years based on occasional near term fundamental concerns on the part of the Aerospace/Defense analyst covering the company.

In June 1984, this analyst travelled to California to meet with the managements of several New Horizons Fund holdings. Upon his return, he issued the following update on Avantek with the stock then trading at 23\frac{1}{8}$.

Volume at AVAK continues to increase in both military and commercial lines. The production problems on the high frequency amplifier lines appear to be resolved. AVAK shipped $3.0 million within the most recent month, up from recent periods under $2.0 million. A quarter-end push was clearly a factor, but I believe AVAK has made the strides it promised. Orders continue to flood in on the military side, although we should expect the rate to slow in coming quarters. On the commercial side, low noise amplifiers for the home satellite television (TVRO) market continue to sell in high volume. After holding up for a surprisingly long time, prices have finally collapsed, due in part to a flock of new entrants. AVAK is the low-cost producer and has steadily reduced costs on the TVRO line through engineering changes and limited automation. Operating margins, which exceeded 30% in 1983, should be no more than half that in 1984. TVRO should represent about 20% of sales this year. It is hard to tell where the TVRO market is going, but there is no reason to expect reduced pressure on prices. The potential for a serious problem exists with TVRO, and I will continue to monitor the situation closely.

On balance, I was very satisfied by my visit to AVAK. My calendar 1984 estimate of $0.89 is probably too low by a few cents. Sell-side estimates have come down to the $0.90–$0.95 level. With rising margins on the military side, AVAK should be able to deliver excellent earnings comparisons for the foreseeable future. I continue to be a buyer of AVAK below $18 and a seller at $24.

With the surge in the stock market in early August, Avantek rose above $24, and the New Horizons Fund and related accounts sold about 200,000 shares of Avantek between $24–$25 on August 2nd and August 3rd.[2] No further selling took place prior to August 21, 1984, when, based on further research by the analyst, a sale recommendation was written with the stock at 24\frac{5}{8}$. Excerpts are as follows:

The pricing on low noise amplifiers (LNA) for the home satellite television (TVRO) market continues to collapse. While this business represents only 22% of AVAK's revenues, it has had considerably higher margins than the company's other lines. I expect that the margin squeeze will cause third quarter EPS to fall below the $0.21 reported in the June quarter, which would be a major disappointment. I have revised my third quarter estimate downward to $0.18 from $0.23 (versus $0.11 a year ago). Although the TVRO problem may be a reflection of the seasonal summer slowdown, I see no way the company can make up the earnings in the fourth quarter. With the drop in my estimate for the year, and the possibility of a protracted profit squeeze in TVRO, AVAK's valuation goes from rich to ridiculous. I recommend immediate sale.

AVAK is a leading producer of microwave amplifiers, components, and telecommunications equipment. By product line, sales break out as follows: defense components—40%; telecommunications components and systems 24%; TVRO components—22%; and test equipment components—14%. Over the past year, AVAK's growth has come from defense components and TVRO. On the defense side, the company has been a major supplier of high frequency amplifiers to the electronic warfare systems contractors. The entire components industry was caught off guard by massive orders for high frequency amplifiers in 1982 and 1983. Everyone, AVAK included, had production problems, followed rapidly by earnings disappointments. AVAK bounced back most rapidly among all components suppliers. Part of this can be attributed to management, which turned around the high frequency product line. The second key factor, though, was diversification. AVAK's business was not dependent exclusively on the high frequency product line, and when profits were hurt, other lines took up the slack. The biggest boost came from TVRO, which uses a high quality amplifier to boost the satellite TV signal received in the owner's backyard.

The TVRO business came out of nowhere in 1982, and AVAK was perfectly positioned to address it. As the market grew, AVAK worked to become the low-cost producer, and now has about a 30% share, principally at the high end of the quality spectrum. New entrants have caused prices to collapse, but until this quarter, TVRO remained AVAK's most profitable business. The Japanese have just entered the market, having diverted unused direct broadcast satellite (DBS) capacity to TVRO. AVAK has a big head start, but I doubt that the seasonal upswing in September can overcome the margin pressures at work in the marketplace.

The problem here is that Wall Street has very high expectations for AVAK. Everyone is looking for a 50% EPS gain this year, followed by 35% or more next year. It is too early to tell what will happen in 1985, since military components margins could rise dramatically, but 1984 will not meet the consensus estimate of $0.90 without a miracle in TVRO. In any case, the good news is in the stock. This is a well-managed company with good products in good markets. It is my judgement that the stock price today is out of line with AVAK's prospects. I recommend sale, with an eye to repurchasing in the $18–19 range.

Regarding Tandem, the New Horizons Fund and related accounts began accumulating a position in the stock in late 1981 and early 1982, and reached a position of over a million shares at an average cost of approximately $22 per share by the end of 1982. Based on some short-term fundamental concerns, this position was reduced in the first quarter of 1983 by about 200,000 shares at an average sale price of $28–$29 per share. The analyst however remained intrigued in the longer term with Tandem's niche market position in fault-tolerant computers and continued to like Tandem's long-term growth prospects. The remaining position was held through the balance of 1983 and the stock performed quite well closing the year at \$35$\frac{1}{8}$. The company, however, experienced fundamental problems in the first half of 1984 relating to revenue shortfalls and the stock plummeted from \$35$\frac{1}{8}$ to a low of \$13 in August 1984. On August 1 the analyst issued the following comments on Tandem, with the stock at \$13$\frac{7}{8}$.

Tandem (TNDM) has once again disappointed with its latest quarterly EPS report and its stock has sharply retreated to mid-1980 price levels. I am concerned about TNDM's "anemic" revenue growth this year relative to my expectations of mid-1983 and now believe a 25% secular revenue growth forecast is much more reasonable than my prior 35% forecast. TNDM has been planning for 30%–35% revenue growth and operating profit margins have remained depressed as revenues have fallen short of budgeted amounts. I have reduced my FY1984 EPS estimate from \$1.01 to \$0.80 and my FY1985 estimate from \$1.60 to \$1.25. I have also reduced my secular growth rate assumption from 35% to 25%. In spite of the prevailing gloom about the company, I remain encouraged by TNDM's product capability, balance sheet strength, and much improved financial control. I believe TNDM will produce excellent investment returns from current levels over the next 12–24 months but would not expect TNDM to outperform other cyclically sensitive technology stocks near term. For those whose valuation instincts were better than mine over the past six months, my congratulations. At current price levels, however, I suggest another serious look, with the price being right but timing perhaps still premature.

New Horizons Fund and related accounts began adding to positions in Tandem in late July, accumulating another 600,000 shares prior to August 21, 1984.

Notes

1. Unlike trades on the NYSE and AMEX which were on a commission basis (10¢/share was typical for a large institution), OTC trades were done purely on a spread basis, i.e., the dealer found a buyer willing to pay an asking price and a seller willing to receive a bid price (hopefully lower than the asking price), and pocketed the difference.
2. Related accounts had sold approximately 70,000 shares between March 31 and July 31 for reasons unrelated to any research recommendations.

Exhibit 1A

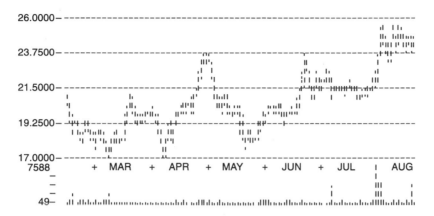

Avantek price and volume charts. February–August 1984. Note: Daily volume in hundreds of shares traded.

Exhibit 1B

Daily price ranges and volume for Avantek, July 26, 1984–August 20, 1984

Date	High	Low	Volume (100's shares)
July 26	$21\frac{5}{8}$	$21\frac{1}{4}$	125
27	$21\frac{3}{4}$	$21\frac{1}{4}$	439
30	$21\frac{5}{8}$	$21\frac{1}{2}$	668
31	$22\frac{3}{8}$	$21\frac{3}{0}$	1,053
Aug. 1	$22\frac{1}{2}$	$21\frac{3}{4}$	7,588
2	$23\frac{3}{8}$	$22\frac{1}{8}$	4,550
3	$25\frac{1}{4}$	$23\frac{3}{4}$	4,576
6	$25\frac{1}{2}$	$24\frac{1}{2}$	1,159
7	$24\frac{3}{4}$	$23\frac{7}{8}$	638
8	$24\frac{1}{2}$	$23\frac{1}{2}$	632
9	$24\frac{5}{8}$	$23\frac{1}{2}$	407
10	$25\frac{1}{2}$	$24\frac{3}{4}$	1,522
13	$24\frac{3}{4}$	24	555
14	$25\frac{1}{2}$	$24\frac{1}{2}$	1,003
15	$25\frac{1}{4}$	$24\frac{7}{8}$	410
16	$25\frac{1}{8}$	$24\frac{1}{8}$	587
17	$24\frac{3}{4}$	24	1,245
20	$24\frac{3}{4}$	$24\frac{1}{2}$	116

Exhibit 1C

Avantek trades on August 21, 1984 10:00 A.M.–12:20 P.M.

Time	Price	Shares (100's)
10.17	$24\frac{1}{2}$	5
10.53	$24\frac{1}{2}$	4
10.53	$24\frac{3}{4}$	10
11.03	$24\frac{7}{8}$	5
11.03	$24\frac{7}{8}$	45
11.33	$24\frac{5}{8}$	25
11.41	$24\frac{7}{8}$	1

Exhibit 1D

Institutional holdings in Avantek on 3/31/84** (Price = $19 7/8, 18.7 million shares outstanding)

	3-month chg in shares	Shares held	Value 000$
Aetna Life & Casualty Co	−61,500	255,000	5,069
Allstate Insurance Co	313,100	622,700	12,379
American Natl B&T/Chicag	1,400	25,700	511
Ameritrust Company	−10,900	0	0
Associated Banc-Corp	600	14,300	284
Bank of Boston Corp	31,405	263,655	5,241
Bank of California N A		43,000	855
Bank One of Dayton N.A.	−21,500	0	0
Campbell Advisors Inc	140,300	407,400	8,099
Campbell William G & Co.		43,400	863
Capital Research & Mgmt	233,000	233,000*	4,632
College Retire Equities	0	65,000	1,292
Comerica Inc		21,750	432
Dean Mitter Rey Intercap	35,600	125,600	2,497
Eaton & Howard Vance Snd	−2,184	26,033	518
Eberstadt Asset Mgmt Inc	121,800	371,500	7,385
Exxon Corporation	0	80,600	1,602
Fiduciary Tr Co/New York	−1,800	32,900	654
First Interstate Bancorp		20,420	406
First Manhattan Co	2,300	13,850	275
First Wisconsin Corp	0	26,500	527
Fleet National Bank	10,975	96,585	1,920
Franklin Resources Inc	0	12,000	239
G T Capital Management	11,200	117,000	2,326
Gardner & Preston Moss	−86,270	0	0
Hancock John Mutual Life	78,300	362,000	7,197
Harris Associates Inc	0	84,000	1,670
Harris Trust & Svgs Bank	−59,000	416,000	8,270
Hartford Stean Boiler	5,300	5,300*	105
Harvard College		4,000	80
Hongkong & Shanghai Bkg	−22,400	0	0
IDS Growth Fund Inc	0	500,000	9,940
IDS New Dimensions Fund	32,500	200,000	3,976
Investors Research Corp	175,000	175,000*	3,479
Jennison Assoc Capital	315,000	657,600	13,073
Kemper Finl Services	−181,900	94,300	1,875

Exhibit 1D (continued)

	3-month chg in shares	Shares held	Value 000$
Kidder Peabody & Co	3,700	27,700	551
Lincoln First Banks Inc		406,500	8,081
Merchants Natl Bk/Ced Rp	−900	25,000	497
Metropolitan Life Insur	0	9,500	189
Morgan Stanley Inc	124,344	460,844	9,162
National City Bk/Cleveld	0	11,000	219
Natl Westminster Bk Plc	0	31,000	616
Philadelphia Natl Bank		27,500	547
Price T Rowe Associate	38,735	871,410	17,324
Provident Life & Acc Ins	3,800	32,900	654
Reimer & Koger Assocs		51,900	1,032
Republicbank Corp	−96,100	15,785	314
Rice Hall James & Assoc	−15,500	0	0
Rothschild Asset Mgmt	−61,000	0	0
Russell Frank Co Inc	−31,300	0	0
Seligman J W & Company	−655,000	0	0
Shahmut Corporation		14,300	284
SIT Investment Assocs.		15,000	298
Smith Barney Inc		1,389	28
Sperry Capital Mgmt	10,000	110,000	2,187
State Street Resr & Mgmt	−89,100	204,900	4,073
Stein Roe & Farnham	−520	42,560	846
Torchmark Corporation	−60,000	0	0
Travelers Corp	0	55,000	1,093
USAA Investment Mgmt		25,000	497
United Missouri Bank/K C	0	56,000	1,113
United States Trust/N Y	2,000	13,800	274
United Virginia Bkshares	−92,800	102,450	2,037
University of Rochester	0	404,000	8,032
Welch & Forbes Inc	790	51,830	1,030
Wells Fargo Bank N.A.	−3,150	43,900	873
Wisconsin Investmt Board	0	60,000	1,193
59 Mgrs 45.9% Shs Out	138,325	5,857,261	170,715

Source: "The Spectrum 3," Computer Directions Advisors, Silver Springs, MD.
*New position.
**This was the most recently available data on 8/21/84.

Exhibit 2A

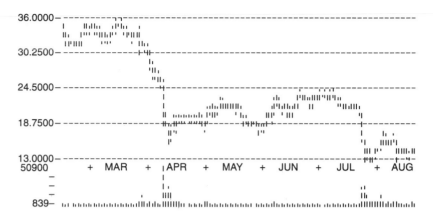

Tandem price and volume charts. February–August 1984. Note: Daily volume in hundreds of shares traded.

Exhibit 2B

Daily price and volume ranges for Tandem, July 26, 1984–August 20, 1984

Date	High	Low	Volume (100's shares)
July 26	$16\frac{7}{8}$	$13\frac{3}{8}$	26,807
27	$15\frac{3}{4}$	$14\frac{1}{4}$	14,909
30	$15\frac{3}{4}$	$13\frac{1}{4}$	7,759
31	$14\frac{1}{4}$	13	11,108
Aug. 1	$15\frac{1}{8}$	$14\frac{1}{4}$	11,240
2	$15\frac{5}{8}$	$15\frac{1}{8}$	9,057
3	$16\frac{3}{4}$	$15\frac{1}{4}$	134,43
6	18	16	7,646
7	$17\frac{1}{2}$	$16\frac{1}{8}$	4,615
8	$16\frac{3}{4}$	16	6,506
9	$16\frac{3}{4}$	16	4,849
10	$17\frac{5}{8}$	$16\frac{5}{8}$	10,791
13	17	$13\frac{1}{2}$	7,596
14	$15\frac{3}{8}$	$14\frac{1}{2}$	4,708
15	$15\frac{5}{8}$	$14\frac{1}{2}$	2,392
16	$15\frac{1}{2}$	15	5,806
17	$15\frac{3}{8}$	$14\frac{3}{8}$	4,084
20	$14\frac{7}{8}$	$13\frac{3}{4}$	3,209

Exhibit 2C

Tandem trades on August 21, 1984, 10:00 A.M. to 12:20 P.M.

Time	Price	Shares (100's)	Time	Price	Shares (100's)
10.00	15	25	10.36	15	5
10.01	$14\frac{7}{8}$	10	10.37	15	1
10.01	$14\frac{7}{8}$	5	10.41	15	4
10.03	$14\frac{7}{8}$	3	10.43	15	1
10.03	$14\frac{7}{8}$	5	10.43	15	3
10.03	$15\frac{1}{8}$	50	10.43	15	5
10.05	15	3	10.44	$15\frac{1}{8}$	10
10.05	$15\frac{1}{8}$	10	10.44	$15\frac{1}{8}$	10
10.06	$14\frac{3}{4}$	10	10.48	15	3
10.06	$15\frac{1}{8}$	5	10.49	15	25
10.06	$15\frac{1}{8}$	3	10.54	$14\frac{7}{8}$	1
10.06	$15\frac{1}{8}$	5	11.00	$14\frac{7}{8}$	32
10.07	15	1	11.01	15	2
10.07	$15\frac{1}{8}$	5	11.04	15	4
10.07	15	2	11.05	15	2
10.07	$15\frac{1}{8}$	13	11.09	15	1
10.07	15	10	11.09	15	3
10.08	$15\frac{1}{8}$	10	11.09	15	2
10.09	$15\frac{1}{8}$	10	11.18	15	5
10.11	$15\frac{1}{8}$	20	11.25	$14\frac{7}{8}$	100
10.11	$15\frac{1}{8}$	20	11.28	15	5
10.12	$15\frac{1}{8}$	9	11.30	15	5
10.14	$15\frac{1}{8}$	10	11.32	$14\frac{7}{8}$	270
10.20	$15\frac{1}{8}$	30	11.32	15	217
10.22	$15\frac{1}{8}$	100	11.32	15	5
10.22	$15\frac{1}{4}$	49	11.33	15	10
10.23	$15\frac{1}{8}$	25	11.36	15	1
10.25	$15\frac{1}{8}$	5	11.37	15	10
10.26	$15\frac{1}{4}$	3	11.42	15	10
10.26	$15\frac{1}{4}$	3	11.44	15	10
10.26	$15\frac{1}{8}$	10	11.44	$15\frac{1}{8}$	2
10.27	$15\frac{1}{8}$	5	11.48	15	1
10.27	$15\frac{1}{4}$	10	11.49	$15\frac{1}{8}$	10
10.31	$15\frac{1}{8}$	250	11.49	$15\frac{1}{8}$	20
10.32	$15\frac{1}{8}$	2	11.49	15	20
10.32	$15\frac{1}{8}$	18	11.49	$15\frac{1}{8}$	2
10.32	15	10	11.53	$15\frac{1}{8}$	2
10.21	15	10	11.54	$15\frac{1}{8}$	4
10.34	$15\frac{1}{8}$	3	12.15	$15\frac{1}{8}$	1
10.35	15	5			

Exhibit 2D

Institutional holdings in Tandem on 3/31/84**

	3-month chg in shares	Shares held	Value 000$
Aetna Life & Casualty Co	67,200	178,700	5,429
American Natl B&T/Chicag	85,900	138,300	4,202
American Security Bank	151,700	411,700	12,507
American Tel & Tel Index	39,600	39,600*	1,203
Ameritrust Company	−12,600	18,000	547
BEA Associates Inc		15,000	456
Bankamerica Corp	11,350	11,350*	345
Bank of Boston Corp	−2,200	176,020	5,347
Bank of California N A		61,900	1,881
Bank New England Corp	−3,000	11,256	342
Bank of New York	−22,550	28,035	852
Bankers Trust N Y Corp		401,350	12,193
Batterymarch Finl Mgmt	81,700	81,700*	2,482
Bernstein Sanford C & Co	1,587,815	1,587,815*	48,238
Boston Company Inc	0	10,810	328
Brokaw Capital Mgmt Co	−13,010	866,995	26,339
Capital Guardian Trust		75,100	2,282
Capital Holding Corp	−10,000	0	0
Capital Research & Mgmt	40,700	530,700	16,123
Centerre Bancorporation	100	78,000	2,370
Century Capital Assoc	−460,200	870,400	26,443
Chase Manhattan Corp	29,100	37,500	1,139
Cigna Corporation	−115,000	109,100	3,314
Citicorp	−60,572	571,070	17,349
College Retire Equities	60,000	170,000	5,165
Commerce Bankshares Inc	0	3,000	91
Criterion Group Inc	87,950	228,050	6,928
Crocker National Corp		170,400	5,177
Dauphin Deposit Bk & Tr	0	32,500	987
Dean Witter Rey Intercap	7,000	77,000	2,339
Donaldson Lufkin & Jen	−341,500	1,506,100	45,755
Duke Endowment	−9,900	17,100	519
Eaton & Howard Vance Snd	0	1,108	34
Eberstadt Asset Mgmt Inc	−100,000	425,000	12,911
Endowment Mgmt & Reserch	454,200	454,200*	13,799
Equitable Life Assur/Us	1,600	1,600*	49

Exhibit 2D (continued)

	3-month chg in shares	Shares held	Value 000$
Essex Investment Mgmt Co	−35,800	0	0
Exxon Corporation	22,100	22,100*	671
FMR Corp	−714,800	241,900	7,349
Fidelity Internatl Ltd	5,000	55,000	1,671
Financial Programs Inc		200,000	6,076
First Bank System Inc	−20,700	0	0
First City Bancorp/Texas	−12,200	0	0
First Interstate Bancorp		127,150	3,863
First Natl Bk/Palm Beach	−4,000	7,500	228
First Seneca Bank	−200	12,900	392
First Tennessee Natl Co	0	17,800	541
First Trust Co/St Paul	4,500	12,664	385
Frontier Capital Mgmt Co	−55,000	418,200	12,705
G T Capital Management	−6,600	240,900	7,319
Gardner & Preston Moss	10,128	10,128*	308
General Elec Invt Corp	−30,000	0	0
Geocapital Corporation	67,100	190,200	5,778
Hancock John Mutual Life	−1,100	204,900	6,225
Harris Trust & Svgs Bank	6,000	106,000	3,220
Hongkong & Shanghai Bkg	−3,550	89,075	2,706
IBM Retirement Plan	33,700	33,700*	1,024
IDS/American Express Inc	11,050	69,150	2,101
IDS Growth Fund Inc	0	880,000	26,734
Investors Research Corp	278,400	965,300	29,326
Investors Vari Paymnt Fd	−200,000	200,000	6,076
Irving Trust Company	−2,300	0	0
Jennison Assoc Capital	−256,600	3,788,670	115,100
Jundt/Capen Associates	48,600	82,500	2,506
Kemper Finl Services	375,000	1,272,800	38,668
Lehman Brothrs Kuhn Loeb	−210,000	0	0
Liberty Natl B&T/Okla Ct	0	10,000	304
Lincoln First Banks Inc		18,000	547
Lincoln Natl Corp	−122,925	31,200	948
Manufacturers Hanover Co	13,270	354,200	10,761
Manufacturers Natl Corp	100	35,400	1,075
Markston International	0	19,000	577
Mccohan Associates Inc		392,000	11,909
McRae Capital Mgmt	−17,100	0	0

Exhibit 2D (continued)

	3-month chg in shares	Shares held	Value 000$
Mellon National Corp		98,708	2,999
Merrill Lynch Asset Mgmt	66,300	134,300	4,080
Metropolitan Life Insur	1,500	1,500*	46
Morgan J P & Co Inc	26,000	127,000	3,858
Morgan Stanley Inc	−74,717	166,424	5,056
National City Bk/Cleveld	−6,000	52,000	1,580
National Life Insurance	−9,000	8,000	243
New York St Teachers Ret	0	118,000	3,585
Northern Trust Corp	4,800	29,250	889
Norwest Corporation	0	12,000	365
Oppenheimer Holdings Inc	−6,800	81,400	2,473
PNC Financial Corp	6,800	62,550	1,900
Pacific Mutual Life Ins	8,000	24,000	729
Potomac Asset Mgmt. Inc.	35,000	35,000*	1,063
Price T Rowe Associate	−428,900	863,245	26,225
Prudential Ins Co/Amer	113,000	113,000*	3,433
Prudential-Bache Secs.	22,272	22,272*	677
Rice Hall James & Assoc	−825	7,965	242
Rockefeller & Company	0	9,687	294
Rosenberg Capital Mgmt	−51,300	662,300	20,121
Rothschild Asset Mgmt	−28,400	154,600	4,697
Russell Frank Co Inc	−5,300	156,700	4,761
Safeco Corporation	−39,000	0	0
St Paul Companies Inc	−7,000	33,000	1,003
Scudder Stevens & Clark	−1,600	14,000	425
Sears Investment Mgmt	26,500	360,000	10,937
Seattle First Natl Bank	47,200	66,600	2,023
Shawmut Corporation		3,000	91
Siebel Capital Mgmt	140,000	176,300	5,356
Smith Barney Inc		95,755	2,909
Society Corporation	−150	8,450	257
Southtrust Bank/Alabama		35,000	1,063
State Street Boston Corp		42,500	1,291
State Univ Ret Sys/Ill		100,000	3,038
Stein Roe & Farnham	61,500	313,245	9,516
Toledo Trustcorp Inc		14,200	431
Trainer Wortham & Co	1,300	1,300*	39
Travelers Corp	35,000	93,400	2,837

Exhibit 2D (continued)

	3-month chg in shares	Shares held	Value 000$
United Missouri Bank/K C	0	678,000	20,598
United States Trust/N Y	−5,650	109,863	3,338
University of Texas Sys	2,500	20,000	608
Value Line Inc.	9,300	9,300*	283
Wachovia Corporation	−7,756	0	0
Wall Patterson Mcgrew	−30,250	0	0
Warburg Pincus Counsellr	0	20,000	608
Weingarten Mgmt Corp	40,000	40,000*	1,215
Weiss Peck & Greer		714,175	21,697
Wells Fargo Bank N.A.	118,405	214,705	6,523
111 Mgrs 65.3% Shs Out	826,205	25,607,490	777,955

Source: "The Spectrum 3," Computer Directions Advisors, Silver Springs, MD.
* New position.
** This was the most recently available data on 8/21/84.

Exhibit 3

Miscellaneous financial data on Avantek and Tandem (1983–84)

	Avantek	Tandem
P/E ratio	30	33
P/Book ratio	4.9	1.9
5-year EPS growth rate	27%	50%
Dividends	None	None
Revenues ($ mil)	119	464
L.T. debt/capitalization	2.3%	6.7%

Exhibit 4

The twenty-five largest holdings in the New Horizons Fund, June 30, 1984

Company	Initial purchase	Market value (000)	Percent of fund
Molex	1973	$ 24,663	2.1%
Home Depot	1983	24,087	2.0
Service Corporation International	1982	21,743	1.9
Liz Claiborne	1982	20,193	1.7
Analog Devices	1980	19,340	1.6
Toys "R" Us	1979	16,840	1.4
LIN Broadcasting	1981	16,147	1.4
Manor Care	1981	15,528	1.3
United Stationers	1982	14,368	1.2
Granger Associates	1983	13,887	1.2
Network Systems	1980	13,483	1.1
Kelly Services	1978	13,471	1.1
Intergraph	1981	12,932	1.1
Micom	1981	12,749	1.1
ACCO World	1983	12,445	1.1
Anixter Bros.	1983	12,371	1.1
Safety-Kleen	1983	12,218	1.0
Unitrode	1982	11,981	1.0
Viacom International	1979	11,446	1.0
Circuit City Stores	1983	11,415	1.0
Barry Wright	1982	11,267	1.0
Nordstrom	1978	10,971	0.9
Payless Cashways	1975	10,961	0.9
Esterline	1983	10,298	0.9
National Education	1982	10,265	0.9
Total		$365,069	31.0%

Exhibit 5

New Horizons Fund trading characteristics

	1983 First half	1983 Second half	1984 First half
Dollars traded ($ million)	806	652	411
Percent purchases	40%	50%	44%
Percent net trades[1]	54%	63%	67%
Total trades (thousand)	4	3	2
Avg. trade size ($ thousand)[2]			
Purchases	178	202	136
Sales	208	237	260
Avg. price volatility (%)[3]	35	35	35
Avg. share price ($)	28	25	18
Avg. company capitalization ($ billion)	0.9	0.6	0.4
Avg. comm.[4] (¢/shr)	8¢	9¢	7¢
Avg. comm.[4] (% principal)	0.29%	0.27%	0.35%
Avg. price impact of transactions[5] (% principal)			
Purchases: Commission trades	0.63%	−0.42%	−1.23%
net trades	−0.57%	0.28%	−0.30%
Sales: Commission trades	1.04%	−0.53%	0.24%
net trades	2.35%	1.38%	1.50%

1. Trades done on a spread rather than commission basis.
2. Average dollar value of a trade.
3. Annualized standard deviation of daily returns.
4. Commission purchase trades only.
5. Price impact as estimated by SEI Funds Evaluation, Inc. This is, roughly, the price at which the trade took place less the subsequent day's industry-adjusted closing price. For both purchases and sales, a positive number is a cost, and a negative number is a benefit. For net trades, these numbers are SEI's estimates of total transaction costs. Total costs for commission trades = price impact + commissions.

Exhibit 6

Performance record of the New Horizons Fund

Annualized compounded returns for periods ending 6/30/84	New Horizons	S&P 500
5 years	18.6%	14.0%
10	15.3	11.3
15	8.6	7.8
20	13.4	7.5
24	10.9	8.5

Figure 6.5.3 T. Price New Horizons Fund. P/E ratio of the fund's portfolio securities relative to the S&P "500" P/E ratio (10 months forward). This chart is intended to show the history of the average (unweighted) P/E ratio of the fund's portfolio companies compared with the P/E ratio of the S&P "500" index. Earnings per share are estimated by the fund's investment advisor from each quarter end.

III Marketing and Servicing of Fund Shareholders

7   Mutual Fund Marketing

Introduction

This is the first of three chapters addressing marketing to prospective shareholders and servicing existing shareholders. This first chapter covers marketing funds to prospective shareholders outside the retirement plan area. The second chapter discusses specific issues involving marketing to and servicing of retirement plan sponsors and/or participants. The final chapter will focus on servicing existing shareholders outside the retirement area.

There are three main distribution channels (plus the employer channel for retirement plans) through which investors purchase mutual funds: directly from a fund company; through an intermediary such as a broker-dealer or bank; and through a fund marketplace that offers funds from many complexes. These channels and the products offered through them have evolved as the needs of investors have changed. To understand the development and evolution of mutual fund marketing, it is useful to consider and apply five classic elements of the marketing mix: (1) Product, (2) Pricing, (3) Service, (4) Promotion, and (5) Distribution. Although these elements generally are integrated into a full marketing program, we will attempt to address each element briefly: the first three separately (service and pricing also are covered in more detail in subsequent chapters) and promotion/distribution together.

Product

The most popular mutual funds in the 1960s typically were diversified equity funds. These funds concentrated on groups of companies chosen by a given manager and were often defined by nothing more than that manager's investment philosophy. When the stock market sputtered in the late 1960s and early 1970s, investors began to pull their money out of equities and equity funds and put it into banks. At that time, banks were prohibited from paying more than a low interest rate (e.g., 4% or 5%) on deposits under $100,000. Mutual fund companies saw the opportunity to use pooled investment to purchase negotiable CDs above the $100,000 threshold and receive a higher rate of interest, which could then be passed on to fund shareholders. Fund companies introduced money market funds, which offered investors a low-risk instrument with high liquidity to compete against bank deposits, plus the ability to earn a return potentially greater than the interest rate available on bank deposits less than $100,000.

In the late 1970s, fund companies developed tax-free bond and money market funds that allowed investors to hold diversified pools of municipal debt and receive tax-exempt interest on the debt. Single-state tax-free funds allowed residents of a state to be exempted from both state and federal tax on the interest income distributed by such funds. National tax-free funds invest across states and allow shareholders to be exempted from federal income tax (and state income tax for bonds issued by entities of the shareholders' state of residence) on the interest distributed by such funds. These tax-free funds became especially popular with high net worth investors after the Tax Reform Act of 1986, which restricted or eliminated various tax shelters.

In the 1980s, as investor demand continued to grow, mutual fund complexes increased the variety of their products by introducing new types of funds to appeal to different types of investors. Complexes offered diversified domestic equity funds with different investment styles for investors with different risk tolerances—for example, growth and income funds for the more conservative investor and aggressive growth funds for the more adventuresome. As these investment-style funds gained in popularity, fund companies offered more focused funds to appeal to more specialized needs of investors. Investment managers introduced niche funds which allowed the investor to focus on a particular industry or market sector (e.g., a technology or a small-cap fund). Investment managers also introduced diversified international funds, which invested in established markets around the world. Today, niche international offerings are available—funds that invest in a particular country or region (e.g., a Latin America fund or a Germany fund).

Another product development, variable annuities, targeted insurance customers. While variable annuities have been around since the 1950s, only in the early 1980s did insurance companies look to mutual fund companies to provide investment options in variable annuity contracts—thereby creating a joint product for the fund and insurance industries. A variable annuity is a contract issued by an insurance company that allows a long-term investor to accumulate assets on a tax-deferred basis for long-term goals such as retirement. The annuity is considered "variable" because of the variable returns from the investment options available in the contract. Long-term investors can choose variable annuities that include specially designated investment options—such as mutual funds—from conservative money market portfolios to more aggressive bond and equity portfolios. In addition, the product provides some insurance protection for the sum of the contributions invested during the accumulation phase. Regardless of market fluctuations, the beneficiaries will typically receive at death at least the total contributions made to the variable annuity account.

Recently, asset allocation products have enjoyed increasing popularity. These products enable investors to buy one fund that invests across multiple asset classes—equities, bonds, and cash or money market instruments—rather than having to buy a fund from each asset class. At first, fund sponsors tended to offer a single asset allocation fund that invested in each asset class according to a strict or flexible asset allocation policy. Today, many complexes offer two or three funds with varied allocation across the asset classes in order to provide investors with different risk choices. For example, a conservative asset allocation fund may hold 30% equities, 40% bonds, and 30% cash, while a more aggressive such fund may hold 70% equities, 20% bonds, and 10% cash. A recent innovation, called a *lifestyle fund*, grows more conservative over time by reducing the fund's percentage in equities and increasing its bonds and cash as shareholders age.

With the proliferation in products as well as the increase in fund companies offering them, there are currently more mutual funds offered (over 6,000) than there are stocks listed on the New York Stock Exchange. Investors who used to hold one or two diversified funds can now purchase multiple mutual funds to build a diversified portfolio of funds—buying numerous niche funds while balancing various concerns and goals. One of the latest product developments, the *fund of funds*, extends this trend by having one "top" fund that invests solely in other funds, generally within the same complex. (The Investment Company Act of 1940 still severely restricts the ability of a fund complex to sponsor a fund that invests in other funds outside of a fund's own complex.)

2 Pricing

During the 1960s, when mutual funds were sold primarily by broker-dealers, the customer paid a high (e.g., $8\frac{1}{2}$%) sales charge or *load* to cover distribution costs. This was called a *front-end load* because it was subtracted at the time of the purchase of fund shares (i.e., on the "front-end"). During the 1970s, *no-load funds* became more popular as the stock market went into the doldrums. More fund sponsors began using a no-load structure initially to distribute money market funds and subsequently to entice investors back to stock funds. Without an up-front charge to cover distribution costs, a mutual fund sponsor may take years to recoup the advertising and promotion costs associated with attracting an investor to the fund.

In the early 1980s the SEC for the first time allowed funds to add a distribution charge, called a 12b-1 fee, to the annual fees charged to fund assets. This provided fund sponsors with a regular stream of revenue to cover the cost of advertising and promoting the fund to prospective shareholders. The increased asset base accumulated through efforts financed by 12b-1 fees may benefit fund shareholders by reducing fund expenses because they are spread over a larger asset base, and by providing more resources to support improved customer services. Furthermore, if 12b-1 plans are successful in attracting assets to a fund, positive cash flows may afford the portfolio manager greater ability to diversify investments and minimize the need to sell securities to meet redemptions. Arguments against 12b-1 fees include that existing shareholders are forced to cover the costs of bringing in new shareholders, and that over a period of years the present value of the total distribution charges in funds with high 12b-1 fees may exceed the level of the front-end loads. In addition, 12b-1 fees have been criticized when levied by large mature funds that are not aggressively promoting sales of fund shares.

As 12b-1 fees have proliferated, the total expense ratios of mutual funds have on average increased modestly, while front-end loads on average have declined from 8% to 4% or 5%. This increase occurred in part because 12b-1 fees are included in a fund's total expense ratio, but sales loads are not counted in a fund's expense ratio. In addition, some fund companies now charge sales loads and 12b-1 fees in various combinations. For example, a fund may charge a 4% front-end sales load together with an annual 12b-1 fee of 0.25% (25 basis points or 25 bp). Alternatively, a fund may charge a 75 bp annual 12b-1 fee together with a back-end load that is assessed when an investor leaves the fund or fund complex. Such back-end loads usually decline the longer an investor remains in a fund or fund complex (e.g., 5% after the first year, 4% after the second year, etc.).

The intermediary channel has used different combinations of loads and 12b-1 fees to create multiple pricing structures (called classes) for the same fund. The use of several classes for the same fund is designed to satisfy the needs of various groups of investors, while maintaining the economies associated with managing only one pool of securities. Class A shares generally carry a high front-end load and a relatively low (e.g., 25 bp) 12-1 fee. For investors who do not want to pay any up-front distribution charge, Class B shares of the same fund generally carry no front-end load but a relatively high 12b-1 fee (e.g., 75 bp) compared to Class A. To protect the annual revenue flow from the 12b-1 fees, Class B shares typically charge a back-end load that decreases the longer a shareholder stays in Class B. In addition, the same fund may have other classes—for example, an institutional Class I with no loads or 12b-1 fees for large institutional investors and fee-based financial planners.

Besides classes of shares, the fund industry has developed pricing innovations for both load and no-load funds. To encourage fund purchases, some load funds waive their front-end charges on any purchase made within a certain time period, while other funds waive loads for certain shareholders meeting specified criteria. For example, a fund may waive the load for all sales made to retirement plan participants and trust accounts. As long as segmenting a group of shareholders for the purpose of waiving a load is disclosed and is based on objective criteria, there is almost no limit to the categories of load waivers allowed. Most front-end load funds also offer load reductions for large purchases above certain dollar thresholds (called breakpoints). For instance, a 6% front-end load may be reduced to 4% for purchases above $300,000, to 2% for purchases above $600,000, and to 0% for purchases over $1 million. Moreover, complexes typically offer shareholders load credits if they exchange between two load funds in the complex. Thus, a shareholder would pay no sales charge to switch from a domestic growth fund with a 5% front-end load to an international bond fund with a 5% front-end load within the same complex.

No-load fund complexes have tried to attract investors by introducing funds with all-inclusive fees, often with guaranteed maximum fee levels. This pricing innovation is illustrated by the "Basic" funds of Dreyfus and the "Spartan" funds of Fidelity. For instance, Dreyfus might promise that the total expenses—advisory fee, transfer agency fee, and other fund expenses—of its Basic Money Market Fund will not exceed 40 bp per year. In addition, no-load funds have from time to time simply capped fees at a specified level to attract shareholders.

3   Service

For commodity products, differentiation is often based on service as well as on pricing. Some industry watchers feel that the proliferation of mutual funds has created a commodity-like atmosphere, and that this atmosphere will soon begin to drive down prices while leaving service as the differentiating factor. The industry continues to introduce new fund types and fund configurations, however, such as the asset allocation funds and fund of funds discussed above. Perhaps a fair conclusion is that certain types of mutual funds, such as money market funds and stock index funds, have become more like commodities with strong downward pressure on pricing and significant efforts toward service differentiation. (See chapter 9 for more detail on service.)

Broker-dealers were the initial service providers for investors and were responsible for educating the investor about the market while offering advice on the selection of mutual funds. Fund management companies provided broker-dealers with recordkeeping and other services through fund transfer agents. Once mutual fund sponsors began selling through direct marketing, they stressed convenience and access (as well as price) in an effort to compete with the personal "hand-holding" offered by broker-dealers. At the same time, direct marketers of money market funds focused on service differentiation relative to banks. Mutual fund sponsors introduced services to which bank customers were accustomed, such as checkwriting for money market funds. Toll-free 800 numbers were also largely employed by mutual fund sponsors, which lacked the network of branch offices offered by banks. In the process, the mutual fund industry helped to expand the bounds of customer servicing by offering 800 number assistance on a continuous basis—24 hours a day, 7 days a week. Customers could call at any time of night or day to speak to knowledgeable phone representatives about opening an account, purchasing or selling funds, or resolving problems.

Recent technological advances allow fund companies to route calls based on representative availability and provide representatives with access to extensive databases through workstations. Response times are quicker, representatives are better trained, and services provided have expanded. Many investors now use automated phone services to access account information, listen to market quotes, and place trades using push-button response systems. Voice-activated service is also becomings available, although currently on a limited scale. (See readings in chapter 12 on technology.)

While the majority of direct channel transactions are still effected via mail or phone, walk-in offices (called *investor centers*) and the Internet have provided additional points of contact. Direct marketers have opened a modest number of investor centers in key cities throughout the United States. These centers accept checks for fund purchases from those investors who feel more comfortable dealing in person than via mail or phone. These centers make available a broad array of disclosure documents and educational materials about the funds in the complex. They also provide the opportunity for customers to meet with a representative to discuss their asset allocation mix, tax objectives, or other personal issues.

Usage of the Internet by fund shareholders is increasing rapidly, as fund complexes improve their Web-based services and as investors become more comfortable with this medium. The Internet sites of fund sponsors provide a depth of information about individual funds (i.e., investment objective, historical performance, and manager's comments). Moreover, these sites often provide interactive services for the customer, such as a retirement "calculator" or an asset allocation tool. Currently, mutual fund sponsors are experimenting with ways to allow customers to effect fund transactions through the Internet. Such Web-based transactions will become more prevalent as fund sponsors resolve the information security challenges posed by Internet transactions. (See the class exercises in chapter 12.)

While direct marketers have established investor centers to provide a modicum of the personal service provided by broker-dealers, fund complexes sold primarily by broker-dealers have adopted some of the techniques of the direct marketers. Thus, Putnam has built a substantial telephone system to service the customers of its funds sold by broker-dealers. Similarly, Merrill Lynch has developed Internet tools to supplement its extensive network of retail offices selling mutual funds.

4 and 5   Promotion and Distribution

During the initial growth spurt in the sales of diversified mutual funds in the 1960s, sales were dominated by broker-dealers. This channel provided mutual fund sponsors with access to an established and accepted method of distribution with representatives who promoted the funds to both their existing and prospective clients. As mutual funds gained in popularity, new competitors entered the market. The intermediary channel expanded to include additional distributors such as investment advisers, banks, and insurance companies, each of which had an established customer base and their own methods of client contact and promotion.

During the 1970s money market funds were the catalyst for more investment management companies to exploit the direct distribution channel, selling funds through advertising and direct mail. Initially, promotional efforts focused on well-read investors—fund advertisements appeared in financial magazines and newspapers such as the *Wall Street Journal*. Today, direct marketers target investors from all professions and all walks of life through multiple sources, including television, print advertisement, and sponsorship of self-help seminars. Advertisements are designed to appeal to a broader audience—television ads run during prime-time television shows, print ads appear in local newspapers, and some mutual fund managers have become sponsors of sporting events.

During the late 1980s and 1990s, as the number of fund offerings grew tremendously, investors became increasingly interested in obtaining investment guidance and advice. Direct marketers responded by providing investors with more educational material, such as newsletters and asset allocation guides. (See exercise in chapter 2 for an example.) Broker-dealers responded by providing more personal advice and seminars as well as developing "wrap" accounts—initially for individual securities and subsequently for mutual funds. In a wrap account, the customer pays a yearly fee, ranging from 0.5% to 3.0% of assets under management, to a broker or other intermediary who allocates the customer's assets among appropriate individual securities and/or funds. That fee typically covers all transaction costs for purchasing or selling securities, but the fee is in addition to the normal expenses charged by any fund selected. Such wrap fee programs have become enormously popular among customers of broker-dealers, and low-cost versions of wrap programs have now been launched by direct marketers.

Independent of fund sponsors and large wirehouses, financial planners have proliferated to serve investors seeking financial advice. There are currently over 20,000 financial planners in the United States—from large, integrated firms to one-person shops. Some financial planners work only for a fee paid by the investor; others receive commissions and distribution fees from the sponsor of the products they sell. While a few financial planners deal almost exclusively with one fund complex, most prefer to select funds from many complexes.

For financial planners and investors generally, owning mutual funds from different complexes meant keeping track of multiple accounts and dealing with different service providers. It meant making multiple phone calls to rebalance portfolios, understanding various statement formats and aggregating tax reports from various sources. Therefore, financial planners and other investors wanted centralized access to all funds and periodic statements consolidating all their assets. These desires led to the development of the fourth distribution channel—the mutual fund marketplace, through which any customer may buy multiple funds from numerous fund families via a single brokerage account (the retirement channel, discussed in chapter 8, is considered the third distribution channel). The mutual fund marketplace concept was pioneered by Charles Schwab & Co., which caters heavily to financial planners. Fidelity Investments and Jack White & Co. have also developed extensive fund marketplaces, and other financial institutions are following suit.

Fund marketplaces provide benefits to fund sponsors as well as fund shareholders. These marketplaces offer sales opportunities for small money managers who may lack the resources needed to build a distribution network. For this opportunity, the small money manager typically pays to the operator of the fund network an annual fee of 25 bp to 35 bp (which may be paid by the small manager's fund in the form of a transfer agency charge and/or 12b-1 fee). The small money manager, however, generally does not know the name, address, or phone number of any fund customers obtained through the network. This information, and, more important, the customer relationship, is maintained by the operator of the fund network. From the perspective of the operator of a mutual fund marketplace, it provides a way to control a relationship with a customer who wants funds from other sponsors. The marketplace also provides a source of revenue to the marketplace operator, from fees paid by participating fund complexes or commissions charged to the customer. However, the advent of the fund marketplace has a significant disadvantage to the operator of the marketplace. Despite the breadth of their fund offerings, no complex is likely to capture all assets of its customers for its own funds.

The readings that follow cover the five classic elements described above and are designed to provide you with a more detailed look at mutual fund marketing (outside of the retirement plan market). Following the readings is a case study on the marketing choices confronting a bank seeking to sell mutual funds to its customer base. As explained in the readings, the bank sector of the mutual fund market is growing rapidly.

Questions

In reviewing the materials in this chapter, please keep in mind the following questions:

1. How important is the price of investment management services—the advisory fees—to most fund investors? Are advisory fees more or less important to shareholders of money market and bond funds as compared to shareholders of stock funds?
2. Would most investors prefer a high front-end load fund with no 12b-1 fee to a fund with a declining back-end load and a significant 12b-1 fee? Which pricing structure is better for which investors?
3. Should fund shareholders and sponsors focus on total returns or total returns after tax? What will be the effect on variable annuities of the new tax rate of 20% on long-term capital gains?
4. Are there too many types and classes of mutual funds? Why do sponsors keep launching new funds?
5. What are the differences among an asset allocation fund, a fund of funds, and a wrap program for mutual funds? What are the pros and cons of each from the customer's perspective?

6. Will the rise of fund marketplaces accelerate or decelerate the trend toward consolidation among fund sponsors? What are the pros and cons of fund networks from the viewpoint of the sponsor of a small fund?

7. What types of audiences are fund sponsors trying to reach? Will fund sponsors receive higher returns per dollar spent from advertisements in the *Wall Street Journal* than from commercials on television?

7.1   **Mutual Funds Are Sold Directly or by a Sales Force**
Frank A. Jones

A mutual fund is a pool of investors' dollars used to purchase a diversified portfolio of stocks and/or bonds under the supervision of professional managers....

There are some important decisions you need to make before you decide which types and sub-categories fit your needs.... But, assuming you have decided that you wish to buy three mutual funds—a growth fund, a growth and income fund and a short-term bond fund—what do you do now?

Where do you go to buy these funds? How do mutual funds market their products? It is time you take a look at a prospectus and performance records on different categories of funds and become familiar with the information available.

The Investment Company Institute is an association that represents about 3,500 mutual funds. The ICI divides mutual funds into two categories based on the fund's sales methods—funds sold direct and funds sold through sales persons.

- **Funds sold direct**   There are many mutual funds that offer their products direct to the investor by mail, telephone, or through their own offices. These funds are marketed by direct mail and through advertisements in newspapers and periodicals. Many of them can be bought through discount brokerage companies paying a small transaction fee or no fee. The advantage of using the discount brokerage company is the ease of buying and selling funds from different fund families without having to contact each one by mail. Direct-marketed funds are usually "no-load" funds. No-load funds pay no commissions to brokers when you buy or sell.

- **Funds sold through sales persons**   Many mutual funds are sold through extensive sales forces. The largest group of sales persons are stock brokers. Brokers have found that many customers, particularly smaller investors, are more comfortable with mutual funds than stocks and do not wish to make decisions on individual stocks. However, financial planners, life insurance agents, and bank personnel now offer mutual fund products to their clients.

No sales person will sell mutual funds without receiving a commission or some form of compensation. Usually the fund will impose a "front-end" sales load that can be as high as 8.5 percent, declining as the size of the purchase increases. A few funds now charge a "back-end" sales load of up to 5 percent, which often will decrease over five years if the investor does not sell the shares....

Direct marketers seem more successful in the aggressive growth funds and international funds. This may be that the more sophisticated and knowledgeable investors are comfortable with, and prefer, the flexibility of no-load funds.

If you believe you are widely educated and have the inclination to learn more about your investments in mutual funds, there are some decided advantages in purchasing no-load funds direct from the fund company. You will not pay any commission and the entire amount will go to work for you immediately.

If you decide to change to another fund because of poor performance, you can do so and will not incur any commission cost. If you have paid a commission, you will be less likely to switch.

The person who buys direct is more likely to be responsive to performance and not to be complacent about the investment. Monitoring your portfolio is necessary if you wish to optimize performance.

One of the best sources of information about mutual funds is the Morningstar organization in Chicago (800) 876-5005. They have publications that cover both direct-marketed funds as well as those sold by sales persons.

Morningstar is the recognized bible of the industry. It rates funds on a risk-reward performance basis comparing them to other similar funds.

Another less expensive publication is the no-load Fund Investor (914) 693-7420. This newsletter is published monthly showing performance of most of the no-load funds that can be purchased directly. They give phone numbers of the funds, usually 800 numbers, so that you can request a prospectus and performance report.

There are also investment advisers, registered with the Securities and Exchange Commission, who will help you establish a portfolio of funds to meet your financial objective using no-load funds. Generally such advisors charge a fee based on the assets under their management which will approximate 1 percent.

However, they also monitor the performance of funds in your portfolio regularly and, since they are using no-load funds, they will make changes when a fund is underperforming.

Many readers of this column may feel more comfortable using a stock broker or their banker to recommend a mutual fund. If you want the personal contact, are not concerned about paying a commission, plan to hold the fund for five or more years without concern about relative performance, then you should talk with a sales person who can give you the advice and help you need.

Is there any difference in the performance of no-load funds vs. load funds? There have been several studies comparing performance. I have never seen a study which can show, conclusively, that there is a difference.

The disadvantage with the load funds is the cost of changing if your broker recommends another fund. Performance of individual funds, even those with the same stated objectives, will vary greatly. Having the flexibility to switch to better performing funds at no cost is a decided advantage for no-load funds and for those investors who prefer to make their own decisions.

7.2   The Consumerization of the Mutual Fund Business*

Why do you choose one fund family over another? A solid performance record? A persuasive financial consultant? Product choice? Low annual fees? Does the image of a fund company projected in its print or television ad campaign impact your decision?

With more than 7,000 funds vying for your dollars, fund groups are spending more money than ever to promote brand awareness and distinguish themselves from the competition. In the first quarter of this year alone, the industry spent nearly $95 million on print and broadcast advertising. That's up 30% over the same period last year, according to Competitive Media Reporting, an advertisement-tracking firm. In 1996, fund families spent more than $264 million to burnish their image in the eyes of investors, up 43% over the previous year.

"There's been a gradual 'consumerization' of the investment business, where building a brand is no different than in any other market, such as detergents," says Bruce Brewington, equity analyst at Putnam, Lovell & Thornton, which follows publicly traded fund companies. "Why do people buy Tide over Surf or any of the other detergent products? I think the same thing is becoming more true in investment management."

From a fund family's perspective, the key is differentiation: distinguishing its funds and services from other families. But in the world of mutual funds, that's tough. A one-fund family like Kaufmann can tout performance ("#1 diversified fund since the market low of 1987"), but average returns in fund groups with dozens of funds tend to settle toward the mean. Fidelity could tout its extraordinarily diverse lineup of fund offerings, but, thanks to mergers, no longer can you count on the fingers of one hand the number of families with more than fifty funds.

Costs, too, tend to average out among families, and in a market that has soared nearly tenfold in the last decade and a half, few investors care that much about annual expense differences measured in hundredths of a percent per year.

Every fund group, ultimately, wants to preach confidence and trust. "I think what a fund family has to say," says Robert J. Powell, editor-in-chief of Boston-based *Mutual Fund Market News*, "is, 'I give better advice, more service, or I am more trustworthy. I put your interests ahead of our own much more than the other guy.' And that's really tough to do. But for the moment, that's the battleground."

We examined the strategies employed by the ten largest fund families, the most successful by the simple criterion that they have attracted the most assets. Their styles and strategies vary widely. But although there are differences, on the whole, their image-building and brand differentiation is soft and fuzzy.

---

*From *Mutual Funds*, August 1997, pp. 33–35. Reprinted through the courtesy of the editors of *Mutual Funds Magazine*, © 1998 The Institute for Econometric Research, 2200 SW 10th Street, Deerfield Beach; FL 33442. 1-800-442-9000.

Fidelity

The number-one firm with $500 billion of mutual fund assets, Fidelity is indisputedly the most widely recognized fund group and the one offering the most diverse lineup of funds, with more than 250 portfolios for investors to choose among.

Fidelity's logo—[a pyramid with a light shining from behind]—appears on its fund literature, as if to convey to investors that it can help them find direction. However, in recent years the fund group has shifted direction by demanding style consistency from portfolio managers, who previously had more leeway to swing for the fences. "Fidelity is in a very difficult position," says Powell. "It has to figure out a way to retain the tone and tenor of what made it so great, but not have that become the issue by which others sell against."

What made Fidelity great was its omnipresence (a fund for every need) and a history of excellent performance, achieved largely by the gun-slinging style of its star managers. But this backfired when some prominent managers made huge sector bets that proved disastrous (e.g., Fidelity Magellan manager Jeff Vinik's big bond and cash position in early 1996). Meanwhile, some say the competition has seized the opportunity to portray themselves favorably against the giant.

Vanguard

Vanguard gained the most market share in the past year, as investors hopped on the index-fund bandwagon. Some $8 billion flowed into Vanguard Index 500 in 1996 alone.

But index funds are no longer unique; lots of families offer them, even the pricey wirehouses. What's Vanguard got over everybody else? "Vanguard clearly is the low-cost provider," says Matt Beaudry, senior consultant at Financial Research Corp. "Its expense ratios traditionally have been the lowest in the industry. Plus, the firm offers excellent shareholder service."

"Its disadvantage at the moment is that it's not widely sold in the Schwab program, nor does it participate in any of the large broker-dealer outlets," observes Powell. Vanguard's penny-pinching expense ratios leave no room to pay the admission price to broker-sold programs.

Morgan Stanley Dean Witter

The investment community expects Dean Witter's recent merger with Morgan Stanley to catapult the firm from the shadows into the limelight. Last year, it was nagged by some of the financial press for compensating its sales force more for selling in-house products ahead of other funds. "It's hard to say to your customer, 'I put your interests ahead of the firm's,' when I get paid more to sell you a Dean Witter fund," observes one industry analyst.

The combined entity becomes the nation's largest securities firm, and a synergy had already begun to develop between the two firms prior to the official merger. "You might see the 'retailization' of some institutional products," Powell predicts.

American Funds Group

Managed by Los Angeles-based Capital Research & Management, American funds rarely advertise, yet three of its funds rank among the ten largest stock funds: Investment Company of America (third after Fidelity Magellan and Vanguard Index 500); Washington Mutual Investors (fourth place), and EuroPacific Growth (tenth). How do investors know about this group without splashy ads touting its performance record? Answer: A broad-based network of commission-based financial advisors.

All American funds are team-managed, with individual team members each charged with running a portion of a fund. Another distinguishing trademark of this group: It has bucked the trend toward multiple class shares, sticking to a classic front-end load structure. "If you're a typical investor and you trade in and out of funds every three years, certainly the shares would be costly for you," notes Powell. "But if you're a typical American fund shareholder, where you're staying in the fund ten or twelve-plus years, you have more than recouped the cost of that front-end load."

T. Rowe Price

At one time, each Price fund had its own animal mascot, but as the complex grew, it accumulated a zoo. From the menagerie, it culled its current symbol, the ram, connoting strength, and a single slogan, "Invest with confidence." The hoped-for image, says Alex Savich, manager of retail marketing at Price, is quality and consistent disciplined investment management that gives you high risk-adjusted returns. "Yes, performance is important, but make sure it's consistent and in line with the fund's objective, and that the performance has been achieved by not taking undue risks," he says.

"The company is one of the best service providers around," notes equity analyst Brewington. Much of its business revolves around 401(k) plans, and Price has responded to employer demands for information access, education, and service. "Investor education is very important, and T. Rowe stands out for providing the full range of services necessary to support a bundled defined contribution program," Brewington adds.

Putnam

A recent full-page ad placed by Putnam in a prominent financial publication appears to take dead aim at Fidelity. "Do you know what's in your mutual fund? A blue-chip growth fund could be buying IPOs. Or a stock fund could be heavily invested in Treasury bonds. At Putnam, when we create a fund and establish its investing 'style,' we take it seriously."

"Putnam is trying to portray itself as the prudent investors' fund firm," says Powell, "and it's doing that in part by saying, 'We don't have performance like Fidelity.'"

But Putnam spokesperson Janet Tosi says the disciplined investment theme has been in place for many years. "It has nothing to do with Fidelity," she says. "Everyone likes to interpret that, but we've been doing it longer than just the past year or two."

Putnam's modus operandi is sales via the broker channel, and its fees are among the steepest in the industry. Yet it was the number two market-share gainer over the past year, in part because of top performance records. Putnam New Opportunities, for example, is up 25% on an annualized basis over five years.

Franklin Templeton

Once upon a time, Franklin was known almost solely for its array of fixed-income funds. Then it married Templeton, and became a family of international acclaim. Last year, the entity bought Heine Securities, complete with star manager Michael Price of Mutual Series fame, and the lineup suddenly included blockbuster domestic equity funds. "Previously, Franklin was known for its income and tax-free investing," says Beaudry. "With the addition of Templeton and Michael Price, they're clearly a firm to watch for the future."

In print ads, Franklin's name is always accompanied by the visage of Benjamin Franklin. What's the point of this old-hat penny-wise message? "The biggest problem funds have is the ability to communicate trust," explains Powell. "I think there are probably few more trustworthy, well-respected images than that of Ben Franklin."

IDS American Express

Since its purchase of IDS in 1984, American Express has provided a full slate of financial services. Its salespeople consult with clients about insurance, estate planning, taxes, and, of course, investments. Last year, American Express Financial Advisors sold its one millionth financial plan. Its 8,400 planners select from among 350 load funds for their clients. "We don't have a cookie-cutter approach," says spokesperson Betsy Weinberger.

Amex recently signed golfer Tiger Woods to a $30-million contract to appear in its ads. The first spots will tout the company's financial services. "We expect Tiger Woods to reach a broad range of customers with a compelling message that supports our brand," Weinberger says.

So far, this firm has bucked the trend to provide clients access to no-load funds. Analysts say the firm should already be recognized for providing its "middle America" clientele with solid advice. The challenge is to move into the affluent market. The $30 million question: Can Tiger do that?

Merrill Lynch

Merrill Lynch, symbolized by the bull, takes pride in outperformance in bear markets. The marketing emphasis of its proprietary funds: Get rich slowly by investing in value-oriented funds.

In a bid to keep up fund sales, this wirehouse (as well as most other full-service brokerage houses) has recently implemented full-service financial planning, shifting the emphasis from commissions to a wrap-fee-based structure. Its widely admired sales force of 14,000 call themselves "financial consultants," and offer to help clients choose from among 4,000 funds in 81 families. "Merrill Lynch is the king of distribution," says Beaudry. Powell notes, "Its big disadvantage is that it's inhibited by its compensation structure."

Amvescap

AIM's February merger with Invesco has analysts speculating about what the future holds for the newly christened Amvescap PLC. Last year, sales were brisk for the advisor-and-broker-sold AIM family, known for its growth momentum investment style. The firm ranked among the top five market-share gainers in the past year, according to *Mutual Fund Market News*. No-load Invesco's strengths are in the international arena and 401(k) retirement plans.

"The new company can work in both sales channels, the traditional load and no-load, in addition to the defined contribution market and the international arena," says Brewington. "Right now, they're trying to establish and rebrand both Invesco and Aim funds. Aim has a very strong following. Invesco has strong brands overseas, so it's going to keep those brand names intact, and, in fact, increase advertising, marketing, and promotion to strengthen them."

7.3   Keys to Marketing Mutual Funds: Simplicity, Customer Service*
Peter Heap

Mutual funds should build up relationships with their shareholders—and make sure their customers never have to tell them the same thing twice, according to Don Peppers, president of consulting firm Marketing 1:1.

"Regular customers are those customers who value their relationship with you," he told the Investment Company Institute's general membership meeting here Wednesday.

"The more a customer buys from you, the more likely a customer will buy from you in the future."

But, he added, the relationship should include learning about a shareholder's individual characteristics—in other words, letting the customer teach the fund company.

Taking another tack, marketing strategies Jack Trout, president of Trout and Ries, asserted that mutual fund managers should keep their message simple, ideally using just one word.

For example, he said, BMW has built a campaign around the word "driving," while Domino's Pizza built a business on "home delivery."

Among fund companies, he said Franklin Resources' Templeton funds have "taken ownership" of worldwide investing.

"Keep it simple," Trout told the ICI session titled, "The New Marketing: Getting Customers ... and Keeping Them."

"The reason is, minds hate confusion," he said. "The best way to enter minds that hate complexity is to oversimplify your message."

As an example, he mentioned the rivalry between broker-sold mutual funds and no-load funds.

In customers' minds, the competition had come down to a "battle of oversimplified words, loads versus no-loads," Trout said.

But the word "load" is hard to defend, being "oppressive, burdensome," and smacking of justifying exorbitant fees, he added.

Trout recommended the well-tried tactic of escaping defeat by shifting the battlefield.

Load companies, he said, should exploit the difference between do-it-yourself investors and those who need advice, leaving the former to the no-load firms and aggressively pursuing the latter.

"Don't try to be everything to everybody," Trout cautioned.

The debate can then be recast in terms of "help versus no help," he said. And that view can in turn be converted into a marketing campaign with the slogan, "Broker-Sold Mutual Funds. They are Loaded with Help."

Once a firm has identified the single idea that will be its position, it must make sure it can back it with enough money to outgun the competition, make a long-term commitment,

---

and then configure its whole public image around that simple but powerful concept, Trout said.

For his part, Peppers said the means of selling products—including mutual funds—have changed from mass marketing to aggregate marketing.

Instead of trying to reach more and more people with the same product, the goal now is to improve the depth to which customers' needs are satisfied, he told the ICI conference.

Success, he added, is "measured not by how many customers you get, but by keeping the customers you have and growing them into bigger customers."

Computer technology makes this possible—although it is not essential, Peppers said. Firms can now keep databases of individuals' preferences and past transactions.

As an example, he mentioned a Chicago on-line grocery delivery service.

Although customers have to go through a long list at first, Peppers said the computer tracks what people buy, putting the most commonly purchased items at the top. Over time, shopping becomes much quicker—and the system can even remind customers when they may be running low on particular items.

Because the users have made an investment in teaching the service what groceries they buy, they are unlikely to switch to another company, even if it offers a lower price, Peppers said.

7.4   Boom Times with the Boomers
Michael J. McDermott

From now into the next century, one American will turn 50 years old every 8 seconds. That makes the country's 76 million baby boomers the mother lode of financial planning. Already sitting on a vast stockpile of resources, they are also in line for an extra windfall of some $1 trillion in inheritances over the next 10 years. At the same time, the continuing shift away from defined-benefit pension plans and toward defined-contribution vehicles such as 401(k) programs gives them direct control over a huge pool of retirement money. There's no doubt this is a group in serious need of financial guidance, but to whom will they turn to get it?

Clearly, direct marketers and other providers of financial services are just as aware as financial planners of the burgeoning market potential locked up in the baby boom, and they are mounting aggressive efforts to target it. Surprisingly, even the strongest proponents of self-directed investing acknowledge that the role of the professional financial planner is not likely to diminish. Indeed, the planner's importance may even grow considerably in this new environment. Planners themselves are positively bullish on the future, with many reporting record years recently and expecting more of the same to come.

"Most of the people I talk to say last year was their best year ever, and 1996 is even better," says Percy Bolton, a Los Angeles-based planner. "This is what I've been waiting 15 years for," adds James Bruyette, a certified financial planner and partner in Sullivan, Bruyette, Speros & Blayney in McLean, Va. "The demand we have been seeing is unprecedented. I think it's going to be great times ahead."

Even Sheldon Jacobs, publisher of *The No-Load Fund Investor* and a staunch proponent of self-directed investing, foresees no slackening in the demand for professional financial planning services. Although today's investors have access to a huge amount of information and new technology tools, their basic needs and concerns remain unchanged.

"Why should this generation split any differently than previous generations?" Jacobs asks. "Historically, the split has been about 60-40, with 60% wanting professional help and 40% preferring to go it alone. Unless I saw hard data contradicting that, I wouldn't expect it to change."

While many financial services firms are scampering to offer customers their own versions of financial planning, it is difficult and costly to duplicate the kind of customized, one-on-one service that a professional financial planner can provide, admits Steve Norwitz, spokesperson for T. Rowe Price Associates in Baltimore. "As an alternative, many of us are looking at ways to work with financial planners to the benefit of all involved," he says.

The largest generation of Americans in history is just now entering their prime saving years of 45 to 60. With homes purchased, children graduated from college and leaving the nest, and household income levels typically at their highest point, many boomers now can

From *Financial Planning*, October 1, 1996. Reprinted with permission.

start building substantial nest eggs. 'Flow of fund accounts' data from the Federal Reserve Bank peg the financial assets of households at $18 trillion in 1994, double the 1984 figure. Add in tangible assets such as real estate and the figure jumps to $29 trillion, with net worth representing $24 trillion.

Underlining the need for financial planning services is the disparity in household net worth data compiled by the Census Bureau. While the average net worth per household in 1994 was about $230,000, median net worth for all households was just under $38,000. For married-couple households, it was less than $62,000. The figures demonstrate that much of the net worth is concentrated among upper-income households, and Census Bureau data confirm that those households are found primarily among the older age groups. There is a veritable bonanza of wealth out there, and financial planners are in a terrific position to capitalize on it.

Brightening the outlook for planners is a variety of factors, including changing demographics, continued consolidation in the banking industry, the growing importance of small business to the economy and the emergence of self-directed pension funds as the retirement vehicle of choice.

"One of the most important demographic changes is the increasing wealth of women," Bolton notes, "They are used to cradle-to-grave relationships, and as they become more successful they are looking for the same kind of relationship with a planner."

Wooing female clients involves greater initial effort on the part of a planner because it is difficult to win their trust, Bolton warns. But once the relationship is established, women tend to follow the planner's advice and are less prone to second-guessing. "In our office, many of our female clients are professional women. They are used to making important business decisions and they are good delegators," he says. "Once they become comfortable with the relationship, they are more likely to refocus on whatever it is they do best and leave the money management to us."

Some observers point to the spread of technology, especially the Internet, as a potential threat to the financial planning industry—and not without some good reasons. Technology is making it easier and more convenient for individuals to manage their own investments, and convenience is one quality in strong demand among the baby boomers. At discount brokerage Charles Schwab & Co., for example, more than one-third of all transactions are already being completed by computer or telephone.

In one respect, that makes the female client potentially even more important to planners. Since surveys show that about 80% of regular Internet users are male, if this technology is going to have an impact on the financial planning business, that's the sector most likely to be affected. In fact, however, technology need not represent an impediment to business at all, Bolton argues. The spread of technology simply changes the nature of what planners do.

"In the '80s, it was all about product—mutual funds, money management, etc.," he says. "In the '90s, it's all about relationships—helping your clients understand risk, volatility, etc. All that requires intense handling. There are so many opportunities today to make deals, both good and bad, that you can't afford to make many mistakes. Your clients are being bombarded by people who want them to invest with them. Technology makes the money management part of our business easier. We have to focus more on managing the client."

That focus on relationships becomes an even more important competitive tool in light of the consolidation taking place in banking. As that industry becomes increasingly dominated by fewer, larger players, the kind of personalized service clients once came to expect from their local bankers is disappearing. Financial planners are uniquely positioned to step in and fill that void.

The growth of small business is driving demand for financial planning services on several fronts. It is creating new wealth, often for people with no real experience in managing it. It is spurring direct demand for services such as business plan preparation that financial planners can provide. And it is an important factor behind the increase in 401(k) and other self-directed retirement plans.

"There are so many 401(k) plans out there that are undeserved from a planning perspective right now that if I had the time I would start a business doing nothing but that," says Patrick O'Connor, a planner with Madison Financial Advisors in Stoughton, Wis.

A particularly ripe market is companies with 200 to 500 employees.

"A 401(k) company comes in, sells in idea and, after a meeting or two, gets everyone to switch over," says O'Connor. "Then no one knows what to do. There's no one there to service that need. The 401(k) company lays out the six investment options and gives a brief description of what they are, but it doesn't have the time or the financial incentive to provide the kind of in-depth help these people—many of whom are now first-time investors—really need. They whet people's appetite for this stuff, but then those people need help that just isn't available from the plan administrator."

Of course, there are many sources of outside help available to 401(k) investors, including bankers, insurance agents, and stockbrokers, O'Connor acknowledges. "But they all have a vested interested in a particular type of investment vehicle," he says. "The planner's advantage is that he represents an unbiased source of information and advice."

While it seems clear that the opportunities for professional financial planners are increasing rather than decreasing, it would be naive to ignore the fact that technology and the vast scope of information available to investors is making it easier for people who choose to do so to manage their own money. "I think that a higher percentage of investors in this country will be managing their own money in the future," says Bruyette. "However, the total number of investors is going to increase tremendously, and there will be a simultaneous increase in the number of people who are not able or willing to manage their money, especially as their assets increase in size. So demand for our services will continue to increase."

Jonathan Pond, a Watertown, Mass.-based planner with Financial Planning Information and the personal finance commentator on PBS's *The Nightly Business Report*, agrees with Bruyette's assessment. "Two developments that bode particularly well for planners are the aging of the baby boomers and the increasing size of the wealth they have accumulated. There is something about turning 50 that gets people thinking more seriously about these things, and that in turn gets them to seek out professional advice. As the amount of money they have saved increases and retirement age gets closer, they are more likely to turn to planners."

Many of these people also do some self-directed investing and utilize the planning services available through mutual fund companies, software, and brokerage houses, Pond allows. "The big thing the planner offers that none of these other sources can provide is an overview of all the client's investment," he says. "You really can't provide the caliber of advice an investor needs at this stage in life without a good grasp of the big picture."

Indeed, one reason why no-load mutual fund companies are opening financial planning divisions at a breakneck speed is that they are finding many baby boomer shareholders only feel comfortable making their own investments when the amount is relatively small. When they receive a six-figure inheritance or a large rollover that represents serious money, they are likely to seek professional advice.

Fear is definitely a factor in the planner's favor, Bruyette says, especially as nest eggs grow. "There is always that nagging fear, even among fairly sophisticated investors, that there is something out there they might have missed or some trap they might fall into," he says. "That drives a lot of people to the pros. Many people who are comfortable managing their assets when they total $100,000 become less comfortable when it gets up to half a million or a million dollars."

Diahann Lassus, a partner in Lassus, Wherley & Associates, a New Providence, N.J.-based CPA and family financial planning firm, also cites the fear factor as an important driver behind the growing demand for financial planning services. "We are seeing people who have done a good job on their own for the last 40 years now seeking advice because they are really scared. They don't want to make any mistakes now," she says. "With the speed of change today, the volatility of the markets and the number of investment choices they are facing, they want someone looking over their shoulder, even if it's just to say, yes, they're doing the right thing, or they need to make this minor adjustment."

While the high-net-worth and high-income ends of the market are both fairly well covered, Lassus sees strong opportunities in the middle-income sector. "These are the people who have the most difficulty getting cost-effective planning. To them, spending a couple of grand to have a plan done is a lot of money," she says.

One way planners can tap into that market is by leveraging off the services offered by direct marketers. "The automated plans provided by the fund companies can be a good starting point," says Lassus. "The key is for planners to provide real added value by delivering high-quality service in a cost-effective manner. The ones who do are the ones who will continue to grow in this business."

7.5   **Doing the Wholesaler Dodge***
Mark Henricks

Everybody wants a piece of Ray Johnson. The 21-year veteran with Prudential Securities in Scottsdale, Ariz., is besieged with calls, visits, and invitations from wholesalers of inside and outside mutual funds, managed money, annuities, and insurance products.

"I could have one every day if I wanted to," Johnson says of wholesaler meetings. In that, Johnson is no different from many brokers who face an ever-present flow of wholesalers through the office.

As a former mutual fund coordinator, Johnson is a little more expert than most at figuring out how to deal with these outside salespeople while minimizing interference. He's also perhaps better aware of how valuable a good wholesaler can be—if well-handled.

Look for the Edge

Johnson likes wholesalers who help him sell, prospect, and manage time. When he finds them, he works with them extensively. For example, Johnson points to a booklet from one wholesaler that describes, in detail, health and other issues that often arise as clients age.

"I've found that extremely effective for sending out to clients who raise the issue," says Johnson. "It allows me to add value."

To find wholesalers with value, Johnson goes to most officewide meetings wholesalers hold at his firm. From these, he tries to identify four or five with promise. He schedules meetings with the select few approximately quarterly in his office to see what they can help him with. But that's not all.

About every 18 months, Johnson visits the headquarters of his three most important wholesalers for a walk-through. "I find that extremely valuable because you're actually talking to the people managing the money," he says. "You can get a sense by talking to the secretaries, watching the way people work. It's extremely important."

The key to Johnson's in-depth work with wholesalers is knowing exactly what he wants, and limiting his selections to those who provide it. "If they don't add support, I don't need them."

Tap the Teachers

Dick Niebuhr, a branch manager with A.G. Edwards in Aberdeen, S.D., looks for wholesalers who can take him to school about funds, how to sell them and how to service clients.

"The wholesalers are the best teachers to have," explains Niebuhr. "They'll take the time to come out and work with you until you know the product inside and out."

Niebuhr points to several things he needs from wholesalers. A fund wholesaler can alert you to a large, long-term capital gain declaration planned for December, Niebuhr notes. "So we won't put people in those funds in the last quarter of the year."

Wholesalers also are sources of sales ideas that have worked for other brokers. One gem came from a wholesaler responding to a broker who asked what a particular fund was yielding that day. "He said, 'It's yielding X% for my clients who buy $100,000 or more.'" Pointing out in this manner that clients paid a lower commission on larger orders, producing a higher yield, increased sales of the product, says Niebuhr.

Equally important is assistance at unraveling back-office snags. Say a prospectus needs to be overnighted or a Social Security number changed. "They say it can't be done. You call the wholesaler, and it's done," Niebuhr says. "If you have problems with the back office, a good wholesaler will solve the problem almost immediately."

Niebuhr doesn't welcome all wholesalers or any wholesaler all the time. "Even with good ones, we limit their visits," he says. "There are probably four or five we see on a regular basis. By that, I mean twice a year. Outside of that, two or three times a year, we'll talk to a new wholesaler in a product line we do not know or are interested in. If we're interested, we'll see them again."

Data Mining

Stephen Edmondson of Prudential Securities in Indianapolis looks for hard, useful data from his wholesalers, and plays hard-to-get with those who don't provide it. "Some of the best ones I've seen provide lots of Ibbotson data," says the 11-year veteran. "Where they were very helpful was providing statistical information that I showed at seminars."

Edmondson doesn't mind having wholesalers present at his seminars, but draws the line at letting the wholesaler make the presentations. "People are there to see the financial adviser, not the wholesaler," he says. "It makes it too impersonal" to have an outsider speak.

Edmondson also looks for tips on consultative selling skills. "That's where the good wholesalers do the best job," he says, "helping financial advisers with that basic selling skill of collecting information first, and then fitting the wholesaler's product into a profile."

Not many wholesalers fit the bill, he says. "Based on my experience, only 10% of them are worth seeing," he says.

Personal Parameters

Glen Gatlin Jr. appreciates wholesalers who can help him understand fine points of funds. "When you're trying to differentiate one S&P 500 index fund from another, wholesalers can be important," notes the Dallas PaineWebber broker. "And I'll never get something in the mail that will have the impact of an individual wholesaler."

To control intrusions, Gatlin counts on screening by his office manager. Those who get through, call in the afternoon, not the morning. "In the morning, that guy's the last thing on your list," explains Gatlin. "To be honest, he's going to get one good ear."

Promising wholesalers are asked to set up an appointment for a meeting.

Gatlin limits the time they'll be able to talk to him. And he makes them stick to the time and the length.

"I tell the wholesalers very specifically that I'm glad to talk to them and I appreciate their time, but I need to know in advance and to schedule it," says Gatlin.

Expert Advice

As an expert on sales productivity and an 18-year veteran himself, Greg Voisen says to expect the same professional sales skills from a wholesaler that you expect from yourself.

Don't see those who drop by unannounced, suggests Voisen, president of Sales Solutions Systems, a Vista, Calif., sales training company, as well as North County Financial, a San Diego-area financial planning firm. Set up a time for a phone conference, preferably when the market's closed and you're not otherwise occupied. Early morning is a good time, Voisen says. Talk to them for a quarter of an hour, then ask them to follow up with a fax or mail.

"I haven't found a bunch of wholesalers doing that," notes Voisen. "They always want to call and get together for lunch, or come by in the morning for coffee and a bagel."

To get the biggest return, Voisen suggests attending conferences where many wholesalers are present. His broker/dealer, Union Pacific Securities, sponsors a four-day August meeting where reps can go for continuing education credits as well as to meet in breakout sessions with wholesalers.

Going to such a conference lets Voisen meet in person with a number of representatives in a single weekend. "It's a very effective, once-a-year use of your time," he says.

Just Skip It

Not everybody has wholesaler issues. "I don't deal with them much at all," says one Houston broker for Prudential Securities, explaining that nearly all his business is in individual stocks and bonds.

Other reps pass the buck. "I just let Merrill Lynch do all the due diligence for me," says one Louisiana Merrill broker who does a lot with the firm's Mutual Fund Advisor. "I focus more on the relationships."

The last word on dealing with wholesalers is that anything goes, as long it works for you. "You have to get your own individual style, and figure out how you want to work with people," says Johnson. "The key element is being able to get this information in a timely way that doesn't take away from your workday. Everybody wants a piece of you, but you have to control your own destiny."

7.6 To Sustain Fund Growth, Banks Stress Marketing*

Yvette D. Kantrow

Banks that manage mutual funds, realizing the days of easy growth are over, are looking to highly sophisticated marketing techniques to take them to the next level.

After seeing their advance into the fund business stall somewhat, banks got back on track in the 12-month period that ended June 30. Their fund assets swelled 27.7% to $434.1 billion, solidly in line with the 27.5% growth in the mutual fund industry at large.

The data, complied for *American Banker* by Lipper Analytical Services, Summit, N.J., showed that banks are slowly making strides in amassing equity assets—considered the cornerstone of a successful fund business. They also suggested that popular new offerings, such as asset-allocation funds, are helping banks attract more investors.

The findings come as larger banks are beginning to shed their status as newcomers in the mutual fund world. (See figure 7.6.1.)

Many banks that once relied on mergers and trust conversions to fuel their mutual fund asset growth have now racked up years of experience, giving them the skills and the credibility they need to doggedly compete for investors' assets. They are also adopting the marketing strategies that their more-established rivals have long employed.

"The larger bank holding companies advertise their mutual funds more now," said W. Christopher Maxwell, executive vice president and head of mutual funds for KeyCorp in Cleveland. "We have been much more effective in getting our message out within our own constituencies."

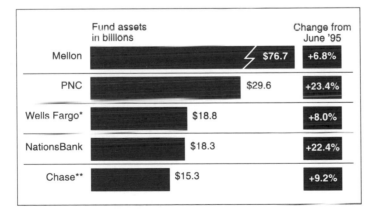

Figure 7.6.1 The upper echelon. Top banks in mutual fund management. *Reflects First Interstate Merger. **Reflects Chemical merger. Source: Lipper Analytical Services

---

*From *American Banker* 161, no. 153 (August 12, 1996). Reprinted with permission.

To be sure, the banking industry as a whole represents a shrinking sliver of the market for mutual funds. Banks' share of the $3.1 trillion fund universe slipped to 13.6% during the second quarter, down from 13.8% at the end of the first quarter, and from 15% in June 1995.

But the characteristics of the bank funds are starting to change—albeit slowly—to more closely resemble those offered by nonbank competitors. At the end of the second quarter, equity funds held 26.9% of bank fund assets, up from 23.2% one year ago. Shorter-term money market funds, meanwhile, held 56.3% of assets at June 30, down from 58% last year.

Bankers say that much of the increase in the coveted equity category comes from inflows, rather than performance gains. A number attribute the growth to the success of asset-allocation funds, which invest in a mix of stocks, bonds, and money market instruments that shift periodically as market conditions change.

At No. 17-ranked KeyCorp, for example, Mr. Maxwell said that assets in the bank's new KeyMap asset-allocation account doubled in the second quarter compared to the first.

"We introduced and promoted the product for the first time, but those levels of productivity are going to hold," Mr. Maxwell said. Equity funds represent approximately 31% of KeyCorp's $7.1 billion worth of proprietary fund assets.

R. Gregory Knopf, managing director of Unionbancal Corp.'s Stepstone Funds, tells a similar story. The San Francisco-based bank saw assets in its allocation account hit $36 million in the second quarter, up from $22 million at the end of March.

The bank has recently begun to market its asset-allocation account in conjunction with its Priority Banking Group, which serves the emerging affluent. A mailing by that unit offered free asset-allocation software to customers who came in to discuss the product with a broker.

Unionbancal, which at the end of the second quarter had $4.03 billion worth of proprietary fund assets, early next year plans to offer its funds through a toll-free telephone program dubbed "Funds Direct," Mr. Knopf added. Of course, banks are still somewhat reliant on mergers to help build fund assets. When Unionbancal merges the funds of Union Bank with Bank of California's early next year, assets in the fund complex will hit $4.5 billion, Mr. Knopf said.

And, a second wave of trust conversions now seems likely as President Clinton is poised to sign a tax-free common trust conversion measure into law.

But overall, bankers today are working to build assets through more active and sophisticated marketing plans. One of the industry's pioneers, Chase Manhattan Corp., plans to call more attention to the performance of some of the lesser-known equity funds in its Vista family this fall.

"We're going to do more in advertising to make people realize that Vista is a quality fund company," said Dave Klassen, vice president and equity portfolio manager for Vista Funds. "The thrust is to get people to know what we're doing."

7.7 Demystifying Variable Annuities*
Eric Uhlfelder

It walks like a mutual fund, talks like an insurance agent, and sheds taxes as a duck sheds water. What is it? One of the fastest-spreading products in the financial bazaar, the variable annuity. Snapped up by baby boomers seeking shelter from taxes, variable annuities have tapped into a mile-wide investment mainstream, growing from $23 billion in 1990 to $326 billion last year, according to Morningstar, the Chicago-based tracking service. But if you are thinking of joining the crowd, beware. Whether these annuities are for you depends heavily on three factors: your age, your tax bracket, and your tolerance for risk.

Annuities of the fixed sort, long a staple of insurance companies, ensure retirees a steady flow of money for an agreed term, often for life, and underlie the pension plans of many companies. But the payments, usually based on conservative investments, can fall behind inflation. So the industry came up with the variable annuity, which puts savings into mutual funds that can appreciate far more rapidly than can fixed-income investments. Long regarded as just another option for investors, the variable annuity has come into its own in the roaring nineties, propelled by the general popularity of mutual funds and the additional benefit of compounded tax-deferred returns.

That advantage stems from the right bestowed on insurance companies to reinvest income, interest, and capital gains free of taxes, in unlimited amounts. The investor's contribution, the principal, is taxed—that is, it is not tax-deductible, like an IRA—before it goes in; and accumulated interest, dividends, and capital appreciation are taxed when they are withdrawn, though often at the lower rate of post-retirement years. But in between, as long as the principal remains in the account, the money grows in a tax-sheltered mutual fund, faster than it would in a taxable account.

How much faster? That varies widely, as Richard B. Toolson, an associate professor of accounting at Washington State University, related recently in the *Journal of Taxation of Investments*. Seeking the break-even point, when returns from variable annuities and mutual funds are exactly equal, and after which variables are a better deal, Toolson compared examples under three scenarios: two tax brackets, 32% and 40%; different annual fees, ranging up to 1.50%; and yearly pretax returns of 6%, 8%, 10%, and 12%.

The result: As might be expected, the wealthier individuals in the 40% tax bracket benefited most, and did best of all by investing aggressively for a 12% return and watching costs. Under those optimum conditions, and with a readily available insurance fee of 0.75%, the break-even point was reached as early as five years, after which the variable annuities enjoyed a clear advantage, increasing every year. But for a more conservative investor in the same tax bracket, collecting an 8% return, that advantage came only after 10 years—and after 27 years for a cautious counterpart in a lower tax bracket who signed up for an annuity with fees of 1.25%.

---

*From *Individual Investor*, September 1997. Reprinted with permission.

The study illuminated a disturbing paradox. Conservative investors might be attracted to variable annuities for the main feature other tax shelters lack: death benefits, which guarantee at least the principal to the estate if the investor dies before age $59\frac{1}{2}$, and usually more thereafter. But if such investors then follow their nature and select havens for their money to grow in, they can lose out in the long run. Says James A. Shambo, former head of the personal financial planning division of the American Institute of Certified Public Accountants: "That's typical of what happens when the insurance industry comes up with a great idea. They intended something for specific people, but on the agent level, they sell it to everybody." Clearly, the onus is on the individual investor to choose wisely among the more than 100 insurance companies that offer access to 6,500 mutual funds (or sub-accounts, as they are called in the trade).

The Best Pool

The first comparison to make is costs. Insurance companies start with a yearly contract fee, usually no more than $50. But their big money comes from an annual insurance premium for providing the annuity and death benefits. That fee ranges from 0.15% of assets to 1.75%, and averages 1.27% for the majority of plans. Over time, the fees add up to serious money—and no one has yet discovered any correlation between costs and returns, surrender terms, or payout plans.

What's more, the fees are added to the expenses that the mutual funds already charge. The total should not exceed 2%, and it is worthwhile to look for funds that charge less. Nearly all of Vanguard's variable annuities cost investors less than 1% a year to hold, whereas the insurance premium alone of Fidelity Retirement Reserves is 1%,[1] and expenses are charged on top of that. The various layers of costs can easily amount to double the toll a mutual fund investor pays, sharply lengthening the time before an investor can reap any tangible benefit from the tax advantages.

The next decision is the selection of an insurance company that can deliver a wide array of mutual funds. That enables the customer to diversify among domestic, international, and specialty-sector funds managed by some of the most familiar names in the industry. An investor dissatisfied with the performance of one fund can shift money to another without incurring extra charges. As Jennifer Strickland, former editor of Morningstar's *Variable Annuity/Life Performance Report*, put it, "In mutual funds, you're trying to find the best fund; with variable annuities, you're trying to find the best pool of funds."

But before you dive into the pool, look twice. That a subaccount (a mutual fund run specifically for variable annuities) has a familiar name does not mean it is the same creature as the company's retail fund. For instance, Vanguard's Variable Annuity Plan Growth has a portfolio that is entirely different from Vanguard's U.S. Growth. Subaccounts with similar names can be run by different managers and be offered by different insurance companies, charge different fees and have different portfolios—and yield vastly varying results. So judge the subaccount on its own, looking for assets of at least $100 million and a track record of at least five years, with annualized returns for the latest five years in the top 20% of its peer group. Beating the average is a given requirement, and why anyone settles for less is a mystery of the human thought process. How has the fund done in the preceding two years? If it hasn't done exceptionally well during a time when the market has soared, then it might not be worthwhile.

Watch out for changes of portfolio managers. Fidelity's Equity Income annuity is the most popular subaccount in the industry: 29 insurance companies offer access to it, and its assets total more than $7 billion; that's huge by variable annuity standards. Its five-year annualized return of 16.70% is tops in its category. But last year, when the market returned 23%, Fidelity's Equity Income came up a disappointing 13.13%, following a turnover of managers.

Avoid tax-free investments such as municipal bonds (you receive lower returns and gain no advantage) and index funds. Because the gains from annuities are tax deferred, the tax benefits of low turnover typical of an index fund's passive management are lost. Ordinarily, such low turnover limits the taxpayer's capital gains. But in variable annuity accounts, high turnover, generation of income, and capital gains do not hurt the returns at all. In fact, according to Mark Mackey, president of the National Association for Variable Annuities, sharp subaccount managers can exploit those advantages by employing a high-turnover strategy to outperform a similar mutual fund portfolio. In 1995 Richard Hocy, who manages both the mutual fund and annuity versions of the Dreyfus Growth & Income fund, generated 25.03% for his mutual fund customers, and a spectacular 59.66% for his variable annuity investors.

Generally, growth-and-income and high-yield bond funds give the best long-term returns necessary to exploit the benefits of an annuity, according to data compiled by Morningstar. Growth-and-income subaccounts seem to offer the best of all worlds: substantial returns with low to moderate risk, achieved through investing in stocks with above-average yields and a decent shot at capital appreciation. As of January 1, the top five-year performer was Fidelity Retirement Reserves Equity Income, returning 16.80% annually.

Junk bonds ordinarily are risky, but subaccount managers have done well with them. Over the past five years, Fidelity Retirement Reserves High Income fund has been averaging 13.81%. But the truly remarkable statistic is that the worst junk bond five-year performer, Lincoln National American Legacy II High Yield Bond, produced respectable annualized gains of 9.55%.

Hard Questions

Putting your money in a variable annuity is the easy part. Getting it out is more complicated. Should you need it before age $59\frac{1}{2}$, you may well have to pay the IRS a 10% penalty, atop regular income tax, though that penalty is waived in extreme circumstances such as a medical emergency. Unless you have shopped carefully, you may also have to pay a hefty surrender charge to your insurance company. Generally, such charges should not exceed 7% or extend beyond seven years after each contribution. Death benefits also vary widely, from repaying just the principal if an investor dies before age $59\frac{1}{2}$ to guaranteed minimums that match the growing value of the portfolio at regular intervals. The amount paid for an annuity by no means ensures the level of payout and other benefits. . . .

[There are two ways to take money from an annuity contract. One is to make withdrawals. The other is to "annuitize" the contract, i.e., to have the insurance company make a series of periodic payments.

All withdrawals are fully taxable until all the investment earnings have been withdrawn. Further withdrawals are considered a return of principal and are not taxed. Taxable withdrawals are always taxed at the rates for ordinary income, even though the underlying mutual fund will usually have earned capital gains as well as dividend and interest income.

Taking all the money through withdrawals limits the life of the annuity, because federal tax law requires that all annuity contracts have a date on which all money remaining in the contract must be annuitized. Usually this date is set at age 85 or 90. If the contract is annuitized, generally a portion of each annuity payment is taxed as ordinary income, and the rest is a non-taxable return of principal.

For any contract that is annuitized, an annuity option must be elected. Many people who annuitize choose to receive annuity payments that are guaranteed to last either for their lifetime or for a specified period of years, whichever is longer. Others choose to receive annuity payments that last for a specified period of time, but do not continue beyond the end of the period even if the annuitant lives longer.

At death, not only is the remaining gain taxed as ordinary income on the deceased's final income tax return, but also the annuity's value is included in the deceased's estate, and the beneficiaries do not get a stepped up tax basis as they would if they inherited stocks from the deceased—ed. note]

Anyone looking ahead to such a situation might be better off choosing a short- to intermediate-term payment period, then creating a new, nonannuity portfolio. That way, with no insurance fees, the portfolio would be cheaper to run and would have distinct tax advantages. Where the tax-sheltered gains of an annuity are taxed as income at death, a new portfolio could be passed on to heirs tax free, since securities held directly by an investor can be bequeathed without income taxes and are valued at the market price at the time of death, not when they were purchased.

For investors seeking information on their own, Morningstar has teamed up with the Insurance News Network to create a Web site that tracks the variable annuity universe (www.insure.com). *The Wall Street Journal* publishes a thorough quarterly update and *Barron's* publishes data weekly. For the most complete data and analysis, Morningstar's *Variable Annuity/Life Performance Report* is available by monthly or quarterly subscription, as is its CD-ROM version, *Principia for Variable Annuity/Life*.

Judging by the explosive growth of variable annuities, it seems they are likely to continue to spread as baby boomers run out of other options for deferring their taxes. Even if Congress takes away some of the advantages of variable annuities by lowering the capital gains tax, or by raising the limits of 401(k) plans, which are a more flexible alternative, the time-tested variables will almost certainly continue to make waves in the investment mainstream.

Note

1.   Lowered to 0.8% (80 basis points) in 1997.

7.8 Buying Mutual Funds à la Carte: How Three Discount Brokers Are Slinging No-load Funds to the Masses*
Manuel Schiffres

The business of investing in no-load funds changed forever when, in 1992, Charles Schwab & Co. introduced the idea of buying any or all of them through one source, at no cost to the investor. Before then, if you wanted to own the funds of Scudder, Strong, and Janus, you had to deal separately with Scudder, Strong, and Janus, and then deal with a barrage of monthly statements. Or you could pay a transaction fee—a commission—to a discount broker such as Schwab to buy the shares for you from the no-load fund, in which case it was no longer a no-load fund.

Schwab's inspiration was to persuade fund companies to part with a portion of their management fees—at the outset, $2.50 per year for every $1,000 in assets invested. It seemed to be a good deal for everyone: Investors could shop for no-load funds in one place and combine many unrelated mutual funds in one account without being saddled with extra fees. For their part, fund companies would have more money to manage. And Schwab would collect a steady stream of fee income.

The big problem with the original Schwab program was its modest scope: It included just 86 funds from eight fund families. Since then, Schwab's OneSource program has mushroomed like the great bull market itself, to about 600 no-transaction-fee funds from more than 70 companies. Altogether, Schwab controls $65 billion in fund assets (not including the funds it sponsors), about half of which is in no-fee funds.

But Schwab isn't the only game in town anymore. Another dozen or so discounters have joined the no-transaction-fee bandwagon. Schwab's two most prominent rivals are Fidelity's discount brokerage unit and Jack White & Co. Fidelity recently offered 443 no-load funds without brokerage commissions from 48 companies (including 78 funds of its own). It controls $6.8 billion worth of non-Fidelity fund assets that were bought without brokerage fees. White, the quantity champ, recently offered 747 no-fee funds from 126 companies. White customers owned $3 billion worth of no-load funds for which they paid no brokerage fees.

The Big Choice

How do you choose from among the discounters? Assuming you're interested only in buying and selling funds, not in trading stocks or options, your first criterion should be the broker's lineup of no-transaction-fee funds. White clearly offers the most no-fee funds and is often the first to add new funds to its roster. Other firms are picky about the company they keep, but not White. Explains senior vice-president Peter Mangan: "Because past performance is no guarantee of future performance, we don't attempt to preselect funds. I can't think of a reason for not taking a fund."

But the number of no-transaction-fee funds offered may not be the decisive factor. Bear in mind that not every fund family is available on a no-transaction-fee basis at every discounter. Fidelity funds, for instance, may be bought without fees only through Fidelity Brokerage's FundsNetwork program. Oakmark, Scudder, and Twentieth Century funds are transaction-fee-free only through Schwab. White is the only firm of the Big Three to offer Lindner funds without fees.

For smaller investors, minimums—both to establish an account and to purchase funds—should be another consideration. Fidelity's basic brokerage account requires at least $5,000 in cash or securities, while the minimum to open an account at Schwab is $1,000 and at White, $500. Minimum initial investments per fund are $1,000 and up at Schwab and White, but are generally set at $2,500 at Fidelity. Minimums for subsequent investments drop as low as $250 at Fidelity and White and $500 at Schwab.

All three fund "supermarkets" allow you to invest additional amounts regularly in no-transaction-fee funds through bank drafts (the money automatically flows from your bank account to your brokerage account to purchase shares on a prearranged day of the month). Fidelity and Schwab require $100 or more per fund per transaction, and White requires $250 per fund.

Many prominent fund sponsors—Harbor, T. Rowe Price, and Vanguard, to name a few—don't participate in no-transaction-fee programs because they don't want to share their fees with the discounters (Fidelity and Schwab now command up to $3.50 annually for every $1,000 invested from the funds, while White charges $2.50 per $1,000.) Plus, as the president of Harbor, Ron Boller, puts it, "We don't like losing the connection to the customer." The funds don't know the names and addresses of the investors who buy their shares through these discounters.

Mark Whiston, the chief marketing officer at Janus, agrees that he would prefer to communicate directly with shareholders rather than have brokers do so. But Janus, he says, is pleased with the discount-brokerage channel, which supplied nearly $6 billion of its $32-billion mutual fund asset base.

Funds That Require Fees

If you don't want to limit yourself to no-fee funds, transaction charges become another consideration. Many no-load funds that are *not* available through a discounter's no-fee program can be bought for a small charge. This would include any T. Rowe Price or Vanguard fund. "It's a mistake to avoid such funds," says Eric Kobren, editor of *Funds Net Insight* newsletter (800-386-3763).

For now, Fidelity and White have the better deals on transaction fees. For all but the smallest purchases (these fees are also levied when you sell a fund), Fidelity charges $35. White charges the same amount on orders of $5,001 to $25,000 and $50 for anything above that. But Schwab charges 0.7% of principal on orders of up to $14,999. That's $70 on a $10,000 transaction. All three supermarkets offer discounts on trades made by personal computer or touch-tone phone. None permits automatic bank-draft purchases for transaction-fee funds. Besides, charging investors a fee for small regular contributions would make such plans unrealistic.

In addition to the basics influencing your decision, there are the frills. All three brokers let you buy funds on margin—that is, they allow you to borrow against your positions to leverage your investments. But only Fidelity (in the case of some of its Select sector funds) and White (in the case of certain transaction-fee funds) permit investors to sell funds short, a way of betting on falling prices.

When you're ready to sell fund shares, Schwab and White have a 3 P.M. (eastern time) deadline for receiving your order if you want that day's net asset value per share at 4 P.M. (a few funds have earlier or later cutoffs). Fidelity's cutoff for non-Fidelity funds is generally 30 minutes earlier. Schwab's restrictions on short-term trades are tougher than those of Fidelity or White.

For those who prefer to conduct business face to face, Schwab has 220 walk-in offices around the country, while Fidelity has 82. But White has just one office, at its San Diego headquarters. (For more details on differences among the discounters, see table 7.8.1.)

Table 7.8.1
What the Big Three are serving up

	Fidelity Brokerage	Charles Schwab	Jack White
No-transaction-fee funds	443	600	747
Fund families	48	70	126
Minimum to open account	$5,000**	$1,000	$500
Initial fund minimums	$2,500	$1,000 and up	$1,000 and up
Key fund families *unavailable* in no-transaction-fee programs*	Benham, Invesco, Lindner, Scudder, Twentieth Century	Fidelity, Lindner	Fidelity, Janus, Scudder, Twentieth Century
Transaction fees for funds not available on no-fee basis			
$2,500 transaction	$35	$39	$27
$10,000 transaction	$35	$70	$35
$50,000 transaction	$35	$175	$50
Short-term trade means shares held less than	six months	91 days	90 days
Policies on switching	After five short-term redemptions in a 12-month period, transaction fees apply for the rest of that period.	Transaction fee on short-term trades. Clients who make 15 short-term trades in a calendar year will pay transaction fees indefinitely.	Transaction fee on short-term trades. Clients who make 15 short-term trades in a calendar year will pay transaction fees on trades later that year.
Margin-loan rates			
$10,000	8.5%	8.5%	8.5%
$50,000	7.5%	7.5%	7.3%
Number of walk-in offices	82	220	1
800 number for information	544-9697	435-4000	323-3263

*Harbor, T. Rowe Price, USAA, and Vanguard are among no-load groups whose funds are not available on a no-transaction-fee basis at any of the discounters.
**for Plus account

A word about fees: There have been reports that the advent of fund supermarkets has been accompanied by rising costs. Neuberger & Berman, for instance, sells a class of funds through Fidelity's discount brokerage that has slightly higher expense ratios of 0.07 to 0.10 percentage point more per year than funds sold directly to investors or through Schwab. Schwab won't accept any sponsor into its OneSource program that wants to include a class of shares with a higher fee structure, says vice-president Matt Sadler. Nor, he adds, will it include any fund that is clearly passing on the costs of participating in OneSource to shareholders by raising its fees.

Whether fund fees overall have risen because of the supermarket phenomenon is subject to debate. But what's indisputable is that the discounters offer so much variety that constructing well-diversified portfolios under one account statement has never been easier.

Putting It Together

To illustrate that last point, we assembled sensible fund portfolios with the three biggest discount brokers. For the sake of variety, we used Schwab-sold funds for an aggressive portfolio, Fidelity for a less-ambitious stock plan and White for income-oriented funds. All of the funds we chose are run by experienced managers with superior long-term performance records.

Call the sponsor's phone numbers to get literature on the funds. Once you've set up your brokerage account, applications for the different funds aren't necessary.

Table 7.8.2

Schwab aggressive stock portfolio

	Allocation	800 number
Artisan International	20%	344-1770
Berger Small Company	20	333-1001
Montgomery Emerging Markets	10	572-3863
Selected American Shares	15	243-1575
Strong Growth	15	368-1030
Third Avenue Value	20	443-1021

Designed for risk-tolerant investors with long-term horizons, this portfolio divides domestic funds among rapidly growing small stocks (Berger Small Company); fast-growing bigger issues (Strong Growth); undervalued small companies, including troubled firms (Third Avenue Value); and cheap big stocks (Selected American). Artisan International is fairly new, but its manager, Mark Yockey, has been investing in foreign stocks since 1989. The Montgomery fund, which invests in companies in developing nations, such as Malaysia and Mexico, rounds out the portfolio. All of these funds require a minimum initial investment of $1,000, so you could replicate the portfolio with as little as $10,000.

Table 7.8.3
Fidelity lower risk stock portfolio

	Allocation	800 number
Baron Asset	20%	992-2766
Fidelity	20	544-8888
Janus	20	525-8983
Janus Overseas	20	525-8983
Royce Premier	20	221-4268

The U.S. funds in this group have shown themselves to be considerably less volatile than their counterparts in the aggressive portfolio. Baron Asset focuses on small growth companies, while Janus fund concentrates on larger ones. Janus' manager, Jim Craig, has shown a propensity to make adept shifts to cash before sharp market downturns. Fidelity fund's manager, Beth Terrana, is flexible in choosing between growth stocks and undervalued issues, but she seems to lean toward the bargains. Royce Premier invests in higher-quality, undervalued small stocks. Janus Overseas is relatively new, but its manager, Helen Young Hayes, has been on a roll with both Overseas and the more seasoned Janus Worldwide, which invests in both U.S. and foreign stocks. This portfolio, which contains no separate emerging-markets fund, requires $12,500 to replicate.

Table 7.8.4
Jack White income portfolio

	Allocation	800 number
Babson Value	10%	422-2766
Benham GNMA	10	345 2021
Cohen & Steers Realty	5	437-9912
Federated High Yield	10	341-7400
Fremont Bond	15	548-4539
Lindner Dividend	10	# #
Loomis Sayles Bond	15	633-3330
Strong Short-Term Bond	15	368-1030
Yacktman	10	525-8258

314-727-5305

The goal of this portfolio is to deliver a moderate amount of income along with some growth potential. It's about two-thirds invested in bond funds and the rest in lower-risk stock funds. The portfolio, which can be replicated with as little as $40,000, yields about 6%. The growth potential comes from the portfolio's stock funds: Babson Value, which as the name suggests, focuses on large, bargain-priced issues; Yacktman fund, which typically invests in steady growers at favorable values; Cohen & Steers Realty, which buys property-owning real estate investment trusts; and Lindner Dividend, an amalgam of undervalued stocks, convertible securities, and junk bonds.

The debt portion of the portfolio mixes different kinds of bonds, with varying maturities and quality levels. It includes a short-term bond fund, a high-yield (or junk) bond fund and a fund that invests in mortgage securities, whose principal is guaranteed by the Government National Mortgage Association. It also includes Loomis Sayles Bond, which owns medium-grade bonds and a smattering of junk bonds (including those issued in developing nations), and Fremont Bond, a high-quality, medium-maturity fund run by the well-regarded Pacific Investment Management Company.

Case Study: **Evaluating Strategies for Fund Distribution**

Banks have become a significant player in the mutual fund business—both as sellers of fund products and as creators of their own proprietary funds. In the 1980s, banks served primarily as selling agents for mutual funds advised by traditional investment management companies. Larger banks established broker-dealers to sell these funds in return for sales commissions and/or 12b-1 fees. Smaller banks sold these funds through the bank itself, which is permissible under federal banking and securities laws. By the 1990s, the larger banks began to create or expand their own line of mutual funds, which were sold through broker-dealer affiliates of the bank. For legal reasons, the underwriter of these funds was required to be an independent securities firm.

This case study is about a middle-size bank, which had recently established a relatively small line of its own proprietary funds. The bank also acted as selling agent for a range of third-party funds, advised by traditional fund management companies. The case study involves the efforts of a bank executive to think through what the bank's mutual fund strategy should be and how the bank should implement this strategy.

In-Class Discussion Questions

After reading the case study and discussing it with your team, please be prepared to answer the following questions:

1. What are the potential benefits to BayBank of entering the mutual fund business? Would entering this business pose a threat to BayBank's traditional banking business?
2. What comparative advantages would BayBank have over traditional fund companies, like Putnam or Fidelity, in growing a mutual fund business? What would be the barriers faced by any bank in successfully entering the mutual fund business?
3. Are there good reasons for BayBank to focus on growing its own full line of mutual funds? What would be the potential drawbacks of this strategy?
4. What would be the advantages of BayBank focusing exclusively on offering third-party funds? What would be the potential drawbacks of this strategy?
5. What are the alternative strategies (other than those mentioned in questions 3 and 4) that could be pursued by BayBank? Evaluate the pros and cons of each alternative.

7.9   BayFunds

In early June 1994, Judy Benson, Senior Vice President of BayBank's Investment Management Group (BBIM), was in the process of preparing the 1995–1997 strategic plan for the organization's line of mutual funds. Sixteen months earlier, BayBank had entered the mutual fund business successfully by launching BayFunds, a family of proprietary mutual funds. Now, Benson faced a new set of marketing issues in formulating a growth plan to develop the business further. Foremost among the questions that concerned her were: (i) how to extend the line of funds offered to meet changing economic conditions and (ii) what mix of proprietary and third party funds would be most effective in attracting and retaining customers. As she listened to the latest recording on the 1-800-BAY-FUND line, she was reminded of the many challenges involved in managing this complex business:

> Thank you for calling BayBank. You can call us 24 hours a day. Federal regulations require us to remind you that mutual funds, including BayFunds, are not FDIC-insured, are not deposits or obligations of, or endorsed or guaranteed by, BayBank, and may involve investment risk, including the possible loss of principal. Please select one of the following four choices at any time . . .

Company Background

BayBank, Inc., headquartered in Boston, Massachusetts, was New England's fourth-largest banking organization in 1993 with assets of more than $10 billion. Its predecessor, BayState Corporation, was organized in 1928 as a bank holding company. Through acquisition and branching, BayState emerged as one of the state's leading bank franchises in the mid-1970s, holding an 11% share of Massachusetts' deposits. BayState's decentralized organization was composed of a number of separate banks; each one had a distinctive character and operated within a unique marketplace. Under William M. Crozier, Jr., chairman and chief executive officer since 1974, BayState underwent significant change. Bank mergers, a consolidation of data processing and other major operations, and new unified advertising resulted in a substantial increase in the organization's operating efficiency. In 1976, BayState adopted the BayBank name, highlighting its recent transformation and newly-formed corporate identity.[1]

Crozier continued to build and strengthen BayBank's regional presence thereafter, using technology, for example, to advance the bank's retail distribution network. In the 1980s, BayBank launched one of the nation's most successful electronic banking programs that involved installing over a thousand automatic teller machines (ATMs) throughout the

---

region. The ubiquitous green and blue logo reinforced BayBank's commitment to banking with a widely-recognized symbol for convenient customer service.

In 1993, BayBank provided a full-range of commercial banking services to retail and corporate customers. The banks' extensive distribution system featured 201 full-service branches, a network of over 1,000 ATMs, and a 24-hour customer sales and service center (SCC) accessible by telephone. In 1993, BayBank's share of checking/NOW accounts in Eastern Massachusetts was 29%, almost three times that of the nearest competitor. Over 33% of the households in Massachusetts maintained at least one account with BayBank. Eighteen percent of households indicated in a recent survey that BayBank was their primary bank. Exhibit 1 provides a comparison of BayBank's customers with those of other Massachusetts banks. BayBank's retail bank penetration led all other banks in Massachusetts. Shawmut National Corporation and Fleet Financial ranked second behind BayBank, each with a 17% market share; Bank of Boston held a 13% market share. The latter three banks, however, were considered strong competitors of BayBank given their larger asset bases, broad distribution systems throughout the region, and substantial financial resources.

Over 750,000 Massachusetts households had a BayBank relationship. Core deposits included transaction accounts (demand, NOW, savings), money market deposit accounts (MMDAs), and certificates of deposit (CDs). BayBank's rate of total deposit balance growth had decreased since 1988, partially due to the New England recession that was characterized by high unemployment and falling interest rates. This environment led customers to seek higher-yielding alternatives to bank deposit accounts, such as mutual funds (see exhibit 2).

BayBank employed approximately 5,600 people (full-time equivalents) at year-end 1993. The organization's culture was one where setting goals and striving to meet them were highly valued and regularly practiced. BayBank's organizational structure consisted of three full-service commercial banks in Massachusetts and Connecticut and a number of subsidiaries that provided operational support. BayBank Investment Management, Inc. (BBIM) was incorporated and registered as an investment adviser with the Securities and Exchange Commission in the mid 1980s, but the predecessor division had been providing investment management advice to trust customers of the banking subsidiaries of BayBank for over 60 years. Currently, BBIM offered a range of investment products and services, to a diverse group of corporate, municipal, and personal trust customers. Although BBIM had achieved a favorable long-term performance record, BayBank's investment and trust business had not achieved as strong a position as its retail bank.

Mutual Fund Industry

A mutual fund was an investment vehicle that pooled money from many individuals and organizations and typically invested that money jointly in stocks, bonds, or money market securities. Each day, the fund calculated the market value of the stocks in its portfolio. That total, divided by the number of outstanding shares in the mutual fund, yielded the net asset value (NAV) per share, which measured how much each share of a mutual fund was worth. Mutual funds involved risk—their NAV could fluctuate daily as a result of market activity, portfolio trading, or changes in the interest rate or economic outlook.

Mutual fund managers decided when to buy, sell, and hold investments in the securities that comprised the funds. The limitations on the scope of a fund manager's decision-making authority varied and was governed by the investment guidelines for each mutual fund.

Mutual funds offered the individual investor several advantages over individual stock or bond market investments: professional fund management, minimized risk through diversification, liquidity, and fair pricing.[2] For such services, most mutual fund companies charged shareholders a management fee, typically 1% of assets under management, which depended on the types of assets in the fund. For example, the management fees for a money market mutual fund were substantially lower than for an international equity fund. Many funds also could charge annual "12b-1" fees, ranging from 0.05% to 0.75% of assets per year to cover marketing expenses and sales "loads," up to 8.5%, which were one-time fees measured as a percentage of the initial investment or of fund withdrawals, used to cover commissions to sales agents.[3] Mutual funds were also used by institutional investors (for example, in the investment of excess operating cash balances) and for defined contribution plans, such as the 401(k)s.

In 1993, there were about 4,500 mutual funds sold in the United States. The industry was highly concentrated with roughly 15 mutual fund complexes managing more than half of all mutual fund assets (see exhibit 3). Well-established families of funds with familiar brand names were Fidelity Investments, Putnam, Franklin/Templeton, Vanguard, T. Rowe Price, and Dreyfus. Fidelity alone managed more than $200 billion, while Vanguard was well-known as the low cost provider. These mutual fund companies were particularly strong in customer prospecting and many had established powerful reputations for successful funds management. Mutual fund complexes whose funds were sold directly (as opposed to the broker-dealer channel)—principally by print advertising and direct mail— had reached an effective saturation point in capturing additional market share and were looking for alternative distribution channels. Similarly, funds that relied on the broker-dealer network also were seeking to expand their distribution channels, since many investors were uncomfortable in receiving investment advice from a broker. In short, the advisory aspects of the distribution business—assessing customers' financial needs and risk tolerance, and then selecting, recommending, and reviewing investment choices—represented an area of opportunity which currently was not being fully exploited by the existing system.

Achieving economies of both scale and scope was critical for fund performance and growth. Large funds could realize scale economies by distributing the marketing, service, and operation expenses over an extensive asset base. The scope advantages of offering an extensive product line of funds were driven by consumer preferences for a variety of funds to satisfy individual investment diversification goals. Industry leaders were aggressively developing additional support services for their product families in an effort to attract new customers as well as to retain existing ones.[4]

Mutual funds could be classified into three broad categories: money market, bond/fixed-income funds, and equity funds. *Money market funds* included some of the most conservative noninsured investments, since any money market mutual fund had to adhere to maximum fund maturity and quality standards. *Income funds* typically sought current income, as opposed to total return, and were typically used by individuals to supplement other sources of income. *Equity funds*, on the other hand, sought long-term growth and were typically positioned to be used by individuals to meet long-term goals such as funding retirement or children's education. Within each of these three fund groups, there was several subcategories of fund types and each one had a specific investment objective. Well-established mutual fund companies offered extensive product lines that encompassed many of these sub-categories, including, for example, growth, asset allocation, and international coverage.

Demand for mutual funds increased dramatically during the 1980s. Assets grew at a rate of 17% compounded annually, as declining short-term interest rates motivated investors to move their financial resources out of bank deposits and into mutual funds, in search of higher yields.[5] By 1990, mutual funds had become the nation's third largest financial institution in terms of assets, trailing only commercial banks and life insurance companies. In 1993, total assets of mutual funds (including institutional assets) were roughly $2 trillion with 38% of assets in bond and income funds, 33% in equity funds, and 29% in money market funds. By 2000, the total mutual fund industry was projected to reach $3.6 trillion. Retirement plan assets were identified as one of the primary drivers of future industry growth. Mutual funds were expected to grow faster than the overall economy in the 1990s as a result of an anticipated increase in the savings rate and the entrance of the baby boomer generation into peak earning years.[6]

Bank Mutual Funds

Commercial banks entered the retail mutual fund market in earnest during the late 1980s. A fall-off in the growth rate of deposit balances and weak loan demand forced banks to seek alternative sources of income. Offering mutual funds enabled banks to retain customers who might otherwise depart in search of higher-yielding products. It also provided the banks with a new way to generate fee income through providing investment advice and selling funds.[7]

Initially, banks served only as a distribution channel for third-party funds. These funds were managed and marketed by mutual fund companies such as Fidelity or Putnam. Banks received a substantial part of the up-front sales load as compensation for selling the funds, as well as "trailer" income for retaining assets in the fund. In the early 1990s, banks began to take on the role of investment advisers for their own "proprietary" mutual funds. (An alternative strategy was to "private label" a fund. An outside fund company would manage and provide all support services, but a fund or class of an existing fund was created with a bank's own "brand name.") Thus, banks were offering both proprietary and third-party funds. Most banks started their own funds with converted trust assets. Proprietary bank funds were typically small and included only the three broad categories of funds—money market, bond, and equity portfolios. Most banks carried third-party funds because they enabled them to offer more "sophisticated" types of mutual funds to meet diverse customer needs, reinforced a bank's claim to objectivity in managing customers' investment goals, and enhanced profitability. Moreover, the brand names of third-party funds attracted bank customers who were seeking a convenient and simple way to invest in mutual funds while also satisfying their banking needs. Although third-party funds provided banks with a substantial source of fee income through sales loads, overall program profitability depended in part on whether the proprietary funds were sold on a load or no-load basis. Exhibit 4 provides an overview of several of Boston's bank fund families.

In 1993, one-third of *all* mutual funds were available through at least one channel within a bank, while banks accounted for 13% of all fund sales. Roughly 100 banks in the United States together sold over 1,000 proprietary funds. Bank of America managed the leading family of proprietary bank funds which consisted of 24 classes of funds and $10.4 billion in assets in 1993. Total bank-managed assets invested in mutual funds were $216 billion in 1993 (11% of the total mutual fund market), up 34% from the preceding year. Money market funds comprised the majority of these assets (67%) while equity funds held a minority share (13%). The skew toward money market funds was driven by the heavy institutional clientele base of most bank proprietary funds. Many individual customers also favored money market funds because, like CDs, these portfolios were relatively safe investments whose value tended to be stable. Total proprietary fund assets were expected to grow to $400 billion by 2000.

Banks moving into the mutual funds business naturally looked to their existing customer base as their principal source of prospects. However, the majority of bank depositors tended to be unsophisticated about making investments. Roughly 75% of bank depositors had never purchased an investment product. As a result, they were often attracted to conservative, low risk funds. Bank customers who had some investment experience represented a particularly attractive target opportunity. However, these investors also were less likely to move funds out of the hands of existing managers. A 1988 study by the Investment Company Institute (ICI) found that 80% of mutual fund buyers surveyed used only one distribution channel for three-fourths of their mutual fund purchases, suggesting that consumers had stable preferences for methods of investing in mutual funds.[8] A recent study conducted by Fidelity Investments found that 32% of investors who already owned funds were likely to buy funds from their own banks.[9]

Bank mutual funds could offer a number of potential advantages to consumers:

Consumer Preferences	*Bank Service*
One stop shopping	Bundled services
Simplified money management	Personal service
Face-to-face contact	Heritage as fiduciary, conservative
Reduced risk through diversification	Informed guidance
Simplified purchasing process	Ongoing client communications
Guidance after purchase	Local presence

Banks who sold their own line of mutual funds were often criticized for their seeming lack of investment knowledge and experience. How would banks respond to a major downturn in the stock market? Federal regulators were also concerned that selling uninsured products on the banking floor and/or under the aegis of a bank could be confusing to customers. Unlike traditional bank products, such as savings accounts and CDs, mutual funds were not covered by the Federal Deposit Insurance Corporation (FDIC). Furthermore, many banks used their own names or similar names to identify or brand their proprietary funds. This practice was one which those concerned about consumer protection believed might mislead customers and create an erroneous impression that their principal was protected by the FDIC or the bank.

The total mutual fund market in Massachusetts was strong among the state's households with an 11% penetration for money market mutual funds and 16% penetration for other mutual funds. This rate was greater than the national average, a reflection of the fact that Massachusetts had a higher than average percentage of its population earning more than $75,000 per year. The first mutual fund was started in Boston in 1929. Since then, the city had become a major center for mutual fund sales. Competition was fierce among Boston's leading fund companies: Fidelity Investments, Putnam, Eaton Vance, Colonial, Scudder, Pioneer, Keystone, and Mass Financial Services. By mid-1993, the four major banking organizations in New England had all introduced proprietary mutual funds. Fleet was the largest local competitor. Its Galaxy fund family, introduced in 1986, contained 15 funds and had over $3 billion in assets. Local banks considered their toughest competition to come from the Boston-based mutual fund companies, particularly when they were distributed as third-party funds along with a bank's own proprietary and private label funds.

Regulatory environment

As banks dramatically expanded their brokerage and investment advisory activities, they faced increasing regulatory scrutiny from both federal banking agencies and Congress. However, no branch of the Federal Government had yet obtained jurisdiction over bank sales of uninsured investments. Banks who offered mutual funds, unlike brokerage firms and investment advisory services, were not required to register with the Securities and Exchange Commission (SEC). Moreover, banks were not subject to either the registration and reporting requirements or the sales practice rules contained in the Federal securities laws.[10] Nonetheless, an investment adviser to a mutual fund (whether a bank, or a non-bank subsidiary such as BBIM) was subject to the SEC's governance. Accordingly, the SEC closely monitored banks' marketing of proprietary mutual funds and the National Association of Securities Dealers (NASD) had to approve certain types of advertising and sales literature for fund programs.

In early 1994, the federal regulatory agencies for banks and thrift institutions first issued joint guidelines on bank retail sales of mutual funds and other nondeposit investment products.[11] The guidelines outlined the steps banks should take in marketing their mutual fund products in order to minimize the potential for customer confusion over the risks they incurred when investing in these noninsured investment vehicles. Specifically, they contained explicit rules on the content, form, and timing of disclosures; advertising claims; the physical setting in which funds could be sold; and the qualifications, training, and compensation of personnel involved in making recommendations or referrals relative to the sale of mutual funds. The most stringent rules concerned the use of conspicuous verbal and written disclosures when selling, advertising, or otherwise marketing nondeposit investment products to retail customers.

Several Congressional representatives considered the banking agencies' guidelines to be insufficient, and, introduced bills to regulate bank sales of mutual funds and other nondeposit investment products. In October 1993, Henry Gonzales, Chairman of the House of Representatives' Banking Committee, proposed legislation (the "Depository Institution Retail Investment Sales and Disclosure Act") that would transform several of the agency guidelines into enforceable laws and at the same time, make others even more restrictive. For example, the Gonzales bill would prevent any bank from using its name or logo (or a "similar" one) for its mutual funds and prohibit nonlicensed bank employees from receiving any compensation for customer referrals. In November 1993, John Dingell, Chairman of the Senate Subcommittee on Oversight and Investigations, introduced the "Securities Regulatory Equality Act of 1993." That bill sought to require that banks engaged in securities activities register with the SEC as a broker-dealer and be subject to the securities laws and regulations like other participants in the securities business. If passed, the bill would, among other things, force banks to make all proprietary fund sales through licensed investment professionals.

Currently, branch sales staffs were allowed to sell mutual funds, although few did. Certain programs, like BayBank's, allowed nonlicensed bank personnel to make customers aware of the availability of mutual funds, to "make available" (rather than proactively sell) money market mutual funds and to refer them to the bank's licensed personnel. However, the bill, if passed, would restrict nonlicensed bank personnel to making only referrals. Although Congress was not expected to act on either of these bills in 1994, it was likely that, in the longer term, pressure for increased consumer protection would lead to some strengthening of current regulations.

Industry Marketing Research

In recent years, a number of studies had been undertaken to explore consumer decision-making with respect to investments. This research helped to expand industry understanding of the investment decision process. Earlier views were based primarily on standard economic models which emphasized a simple trade-off between risk and return. However, subsequent research indicated that these factors alone did not fully explain the variation in investment decisions observed.

A national consumer telephone survey conducted in 1992 examined attitudes toward the mutual fund investment decision, focusing on the selection criteria and information sources used by consumers in choosing among mutual funds.[12] As exhibit 5 indicates, the majority of investors surveyed rated published performance rankings as both the most important information source and the principal selection criterion used in allocating their investment dollars. Investors tended to view information about a fund's relative historical performance as a "proxy for anticipated future return."[13] Classifying investors on the basis of both the selection criteria and information sources used led to the segmentation scheme shown in exhibit 6.

However, evidence from a recent empirical study examining investment *behavior* suggests that consumer response to past performance is asymmetrical. The 20-year study of 690 equity mutual funds found that while exceptionally high performing funds attracted large inflows of new money, poorly performing funds did not suffer from a similar investment outflow. In short, there was a great deal of inertia in the movement of funds. That is, consumers appeared to be hesitant to reallocate their moneys, once the initial investment decision was made. In addition, the study found that demand for specific funds was sensitive to fee levels and, even more strongly, to the support services offered.[14]

BayFunds

In the early 1990s, under the leadership of William M. Crozier, Jr., Chairman of Bay-Bank, and Jack Arena, Vice Chairman of BayBank (who was responsible for the entire Investment Services Group at BayBank, including BBIM, mutual funds, trust, private banking, and Capital Markets), BayBank began investigating the possibility of entering the mutual funds market. Several factors influenced the bank's decision to move forward.

BayBank wanted to take advantage of the growing mutual fund market and the increasing recognition by customers that existing bank products alone would not allow them to build their savings sufficiently to satisfy long-term investment goals. Aware of the success other banks had experienced with mutual funds, BayBank believed that by also offering such funds, it could fill certain gaps in its overall product line and create cross-selling opportunities. Mutual funds could generate additional revenues from existing bank customers and aid in overall customer retention. They also offered long-term profit potential from earnings on fund sales and investment advisory services. The critical objectives for BayBank funds were:

1. **To leverage the BayBank franchise** The characteristics of BayBank's existing customer base closely resembled those of the typical mutual fund customer. Perceived as a stable institution with leading-edge service, BayBank believed it had the kind of trustworthy reputation customers valued most in a mutual fund provider.
2. **To increase fee income** Mature mutual funds had attractive gross contribution margins, ranging from 60% to 70%. They could also become a powerful vehicle for retaining customers who were eager to move their financial assets out of bank deposits.
3. **To provide an off balance sheet alternative for gathering the investment funds of retail customers** The mutual fund product line could allow BayBank to capture and retain the investment funds of retail customers who were becoming more sensitive about the interest rate environment and were seeking alternatives to traditional bank products.

In August 1991, BayBank introduced its first proprietary mutual fund, the BayFunds Money Market Portfolio, to its trust customers. Then, in February and March 1993, it rolled out BayFunds, a family of no-load funds, to the institutional and retail markets, respectively. The family included five proprietary funds and one private label fund, which covered the three broad categories of funds: three money market portfolios (one of which was a private label), two bond funds, and one equity portfolio. Also included in the new line of mutual fund products were 11 specialized third-party funds. The minimum investment required to open a BayFunds account was $2,500, although in order to invest through a BayBank IRA, only $500 was needed. Additional investments could be made in $100 increments.

The organization had invested in excess of five million dollars to develop and launch BayFunds. The startup costs included: systems development, training, marketing, advertising, legal expenses, and the building of a comprehensive compliance infrastructure. BayBank projected that its mutual fund business would break even on a cumulative basis by year three and be solidly in the black by year five.

The project represented a major effort within BayBank as it involved coordination among many different areas of the bank. Approximately 65 BayBank employees worked full-time on BayFunds, most of whom had been hired specifically to support the initiative, including a sales force, a compliance group, and administrative support personnel. Approximately 3,000 other BayBank employees were also involved in the program. The operation of BayFunds required a complex organization structure. Exhibit 7 presents the BayFunds' organizational chart. Two divisions of BayBank played key roles in BayFunds. BBIM served as the funds' investment adviser while BayBank Systems, Inc. (BBSI) functioned as their shareholder servicing agent.[15] In addition, Federated Management served as investment manager for the private label money market mutual fund.

Research on Demand for BayFunds

In the spring of 1992, BayBank commissioned a marketing research study to assess the demand for BayFunds. Telephone interviews with 700 BayBank retail CD and MMDA customers and 200 non-BayBank CD and MMDA customers were conducted in March and April 1992.[16] Data were collected on several issues, such as customers' attitudes toward BayFunds' service and delivery capabilities, third-party funds, and investment risk (see exhibit 8). The study confirmed that BayBank's customer base represented an excellent potential market for mutual funds. Results suggested that 5%–25% of BayBank's CD and MMDA customers would be interested in BayFunds. While 26% of those surveyed already owned at least one type of mutual fund, approximately 40% said they would be either "very likely" or "somewhat likely" to invest in a BayBank money market, bond, or stock mutual fund in the future. When asked the reasons for not investing in one of the three types of BayFunds, the most frequently cited reason was satisfaction with one's existing investment portfolio mix. In addition, the study, combined with previous marketing research, suggested a preliminary segmentation of the target market for BayFunds.

BayBank identified as its primary retail target market those BayBank customers with household incomes over $75,000 ("affluent customers"), with emphasis on those between ages 35 and 54. BayBank already had about 39% of this "affluent customer" segment in Massachusetts as customers—the highest market share of any commercial bank in Massachusetts. This segment of the *total* population accounted for 79% of all mutual fund assets nationally. Over 40% of these target customers surveyed planned to open a new mutual fund account or make an additional purchase within the next 12 months. These customers held an average of $130,000 in mutual fund assets which generated $750 in annual mutual fund revenue.

BayBank customers with incomes between $50,000 and $75,000 were classified as the secondary retail target market. In this second group, customers below age 40, the "emerging affluent," were identified as being an especially high potential sub-group, as they were expected to move into the primary target market as they grew older and became wealthier. Non-BayBank customers in these demographic groups and current BayBank small-business customers were also identified as important markets.

BayBank initially estimated the total retail market for BayFunds in Massachusetts to be roughly 150,000–220,000 BayBank customers and 450,000–600,000 non-BayBank customers. The former figures included 135,000 BayBank customers in the primary "affluent" target group (representing 18.1% of BayBank checking customers) and 71,000 in the secondary "emerging affluent" group (representing 9.5% of BayBank checking customers). The latter figures for non-BayBank customers were based on estimates of the potential penetration of the "affluent" and "emerging affluent" customers in Massachusetts who did not currently have BayBank relationships.

Product Line

BayBank offered its retail customers a product line that covered the three major categories of mutual funds: money market, bond/fixed-income, and equity. The BayFunds product line was designed to meet a variety of consumers' financial goals, including regular monthly income, retirement investment, tax-free investment, and long-term capital growth (see table A).

Table A
BayBank's proprietary funds

BayFunds	Fund type	Primary fund objective
Money Market Portfolio	Money market	Stability of principal
U.S. Treasury Money Market Portfolio	Money market	Stability of principal
Mass. Tax-exempt Money Market Portfolio[17]	Money market	Stability of principal
Short-Term Yield Portfolio	Bond	Current income consistent with preservation of capital
Bond Portfolio	Bond	Current income and capital appreciation
Equity Portfolio	Equity	Long-term capital appreciation

Exhibit 9 describes the investment objectives and anticipated customer profile for each of the six BayFunds. Combined, the six funds started with roughly $750 million in assets. Reaching a critical mass of $100 million per fund in invested capital soon after the launch, was essential to profitability. BayBank's existing Money Market Portfolio and the Massachusetts Tax-Exempt Money Market Portfolio exceeded the threshold level. Seed capital for the remaining four funds was drawn from several different existing pools of bank assets that were converted concurrent with the funds' launch.

"BayFunds" was selected as the name for BayBank's line of proprietary funds to foster an association between the bank and the funds and thereby leverage the positive image and reputation that BayBank had developed with respect to financial strength and convenience. BayBank took several steps to minimize the risk that the similarity of the bank and fund names might be a source of customer confusion over FDIC insurance of the funds:

- Customers were asked to sign an acknowledgment of understanding at account opening that BayFunds were not federally insured;
- All literature and advertising disclosed that BayFunds were not FDIC insured;[18] and
- Comprehensive training was given to both the branch staff and investment specialists.

The effectiveness of these programs was assessed in a 1994 study in which BayBank surveyed 358 of its BayFunds customers to establish whether they correctly understood the rules, regulations, and risks surrounding its proprietary fund family. The results indicated that BayFunds customers had a high level of understanding of the risks associated with mutual funds: 82% of respondents indicated that their BayFunds investment was not FDIC-insured while 72% of respondents reported that all mutual funds—regardless of who offered them—were not covered by the FDIC.

BayBank intended to employ the BayFunds name with all its proprietary funds. Research by ICI indicated that, overwhelmingly, new mutual fund customers stay with one family of funds, typically the one in which they initially invested. Although such umbrella branding was permitted under existing regulations, federal legislation which would prevent the use of either identical or similar names by banks for their mutual fund families was under consideration.

In addition to BayFunds, at inception BayBank also marketed 11 complimentary third-party funds, each with a distinct investment objective. As the mutual fund business had developed, BayBank had introduced 5 additional third-party funds to broaden its product line and meet the more specialized investment objectives of some of its target customers. Also, the third-party funds carried well-established names including: Putnam (10), Kemper Financial Services (4), and Eaton Vance (2). Descriptions for the 16 third-party funds BayBank offered are given in exhibit 10. Consumer research indicated that roughly 35%–50% of BayBank's customers (and 50%–60% of the bank's primary target customer group) would be interested in investing in third-party funds through BayBank.

BayBank offered several services to enhance the attractiveness of the BayFunds product line. First, BayFunds were available as companion products to various checking accounts. In order to facilitate the purchase and redemption of funds, customers could transfer money between the mutual funds and their deposit accounts. Relationship pricing was offered with one high-end checking account, BayPlus, which allowed customers to combine holdings in mutual funds and BayPlus accounts to satisfy minimum balances for all accounts. Second, depositors received a consolidated monthly statement summarizing BayBank checking and savings information along with BayFunds investment activity. BayFund shareholders also had access to 24-hour service, seven days a week, available through a toll-free number (1-800-BAY-FUND). By 1996, BayBank also contemplated using its ATM network to allow customers to perform certain BayFunds transactions.

Pricing

BayFunds' shareholders were charged an investment advisory fee to cover the management costs of the fund. Measured as a percentage of assets under management, this fee ranged from 0.20% and 0.70% based on the nature and complexity of each fund, with money market funds having the lowest fees. BayFunds retail customers were also charged a 0.25% shareholder servicing fee that covered all retail processing and statementing costs. Sales loads and 12b-1 fees were not levied by BayBank. While sales loads and 12b-1 fees were commonly charged by well-established non-bank fund providers—particularly those whose products where sold through the broker-dealer channels, BayBank believed that by not imposing such fees it would be able to compete effectively against its New England rivals and accelerate the penetration of its customer base. With the growth in third-party rating services, like Morningstar, Lipper, and *Consumer Reports*, consumers had become even more attuned to the impact of fees on returns and more skeptical of their influence on overall fund performance.

Sales and Distribution

Sales and service in the retail mutual fund business involved a number of processes that were typcially delivered by registered mutual fund representatives (in person or by telephone), or branch personnel ("making available"), and suported by direct mail, telemarketing, print advertising, and statement stuffers. BayBank's distribution strategy emphasized the use of personal selling in combination with a variety of other communication channels. Several research studies indicated that mutual fund customers were uncomfortable in dealing with financial matters and wanted help from a trusted expert to sort through investment alternatives and to determine how different products could assist them in meeting their financial goals.[19] In addition to personal contact and guidance in the purchasing of mutual funds, many customers also wanted the flexibility and convenience of alternative distribution channels—such as branch offices for opening mutual fund accounts and telephone and mail access for conducting routine transactions.

The BayFunds retail sales and distribution structure, outlined in exhibit 11, consisted principally of three components: investment specialists (ISs), BayBank's network of 200 branches, and the Customers Sales and Service Center (SSC). This distribution system was developed to meet the varying preferences of different target markets and to facilitate asset growth and business profitability. In 1992, BayBank began developing its new BayFunds salesforce and hired 32 registered ISs, professionals who had extensive experience in a variety of financial markets.[20] Twenty-nine of the ISs were assigned to a cluster of branches and were located off the banking floor at each of the branches. The other three ISs were assigned to the SSC. Five of the field ISs also served as team leaders, supervising the activities of a group of ISs. The team leaders reported directly to a sales manager. This type of sales force and the attendant sales management process was new to the BayBank organization.

ISs sold both proprietary and third-party mutual funds to BayBank's primary target market. The sales mix for a typical IS was 60% in BayFunds money market portfolios, 29% in fluctuating BayFunds portfolios, and 11% in third-party funds. ISs worked closely with the branch personnel who were their primary source of referrals. Roughly 60%–70% of their time was spent providing investment guidance to customers face-to-face. The remainder was spent serving as the primary resource for branch personnel. ISs averaged $50,000 in annual earnings, receiving almost 75% of their compensation as salary and about 25% as a bonus for selling mutual funds. This compensation arrangement, with such a large salary component, was not the norm for the industry. However, BayBank had decided that this compensation mix was the best way to ensure that the customer was receiving the most appropriate and objective investment advice. ISs were compensated slightly more for selling third-party funds because they involved a more complicated sales process and because of the higher cash flow to the broker-dealer. That is, the up-front payments to BayBank from the fund managers allowed BayBank to pay out larger commissions to its salesforce and, thereby, match its income and expenses at the time of sale.

Customer Service Managers (CSMs) and Sales and Service Associates (SSAs), located in the "platform" area of the branch, were only permitted to open money market mutual funds. They were not licensed to advise customers on any type of mutual fund, although they could refer customers interested in obtaining investment advice to the IS or to the center (SSC). CSMs and SSAs were encouraged to employ a "park and go" strategy, whereby they would open a money market account "at the door" and then refer the customer to the IS if he or she sought investment advice. Customer Service Representatives (CSRs), or tellers, could only make mutual fund referrals to the platform personnel; they were precluded by regulation from referring customers directly to the ISs. The branch sales staff was the critical link between customers and the ISs. The branch sales staff received one-time bonuses for opening accounts and for making referrals to ISs, a policy consistent with the compensation practice for traditional bank products. Although SSAs received substantial training, many were still uncomfortable dealing with funds. It was difficult for them to service customers interested in non-money market mutual funds while simultaneously adhering to the strict federal regulations that severely limited the amount and type of fund information they could provide to customers. SSAs were responsible for promoting many other BayBank products in addition to mutual funds. BayBank's product managers for credit cards and various deposit products, for example, aggressively competed for the branch staff's sales support.

The ISs and branches received extensive training prior to the BayFunds launch. The ISs, for example, were instructed in the mutual fund product line and in different selling techniques. Branch employees were trained to provide customers with information about mutual funds in general and specific BayFunds products so that they could increase the number of referrals made to ISs. BayBank believed that a strong on-going training program would ensure that its employees became increasingly confident in talking abut mutual funds. A secondary benefit of the training was in customer (and bank) protection—to ensure that the customer understood the risks associated with the product he or she was purchasing.

The SSC marketing efforts were targeted at BayBank's emerging affluent customer segment and non-BayBank customers. In addition to the three ISs, several service specialists were based at the SSC to serve those customers who preferred to conduct business over the toll-free BayFunds phone service. Advertisements and direct mail for BayFunds instructed customers interested in mutual fund sales or service to call the ISs at the dedicated toll-free number (1-800-BAY-FUND).

Marketing Communications

BayBank spent $2 million in mass media advertising and direct marketing to launch Bay-Funds. In the future, marketing communications for BayFunds were expected to amount to about one-half the prior budget, and might be allocated differently.

The introductory campaign was aimed at both BayBank and non-BayBank customers to create awareness of the bank's investment product offerings and capabilities, and specifically, to promote BayFunds (see exhibit 12). The ads sought to communicate that BayBank was a credible mutual fund provider. The media advertising budget for Bay-Funds in its first year, summarized in exhibit 13, emphasized local newspapers, magazines, and radio. The introductory campaign ran during March and April 1993 and was followed by a sustaining campaign for the remainder of the year. The newspaper and magazine ads described either the mutual fund product line or the role of the IS (see exhibits 14 and 15). The radio campaign focused on the availability and convenience of BayBank funds.

Direct marketing, consisting of detailed mutual fund information, was aimed at both the bank's primary and secondary retail audiences. BayBank sent out direct mailings coincident with the launch. These mailings were expected to produce a 2% response rate, generating 8,000 new accounts annually.

Marketing Challenges

By January 1994, total BayFunds assets had reached $1.2 billion (including both institutional and retail accounts), up 60% from the level at the launch date almost one year earlier. Retail asset balances grew from $18 million to $256 million over this same time period. BayFunds ranked 49th in size among the more than 100 bank proprietary fund groups and second in the region to Fleet's Galaxy fund family, which ranked 15th. Almost 14,000 retail BayFunds accounts had been opened since March 1993, of which 40% where money market fund accounts. The average account balances in each of the six portfolios remained fairly stable. The funds had been delivering returns fully competitive with their "peer" funds (see exhibit 16).[21]

Having successfully launched BayFunds, Benson now faced a new challenge in formulating the strategy for BayFunds future growth. She viewed this as a critical juncture in the life of BayBank's newest investment product. Benson had observed during the past year that proprietary funds did not completely satisfy the investment needs of bank customers. Most banks were attempting to expand their limited range of proprietary stock and bond funds in response to recent marketing research showing that many holders of money market funds were considering broadening their investment portfolios. Benson was not sure if she could match the relatively broader proprietary fund offerings of other local competitors without a heavy subsidy for new funds lacking sufficient seed capital. Most proprietary funds were dominated by money market offerings, which were less profitable than long-term bond and equity funds. Furthermore, the typical bank proprietary fund had an asset base smaller than the industry average, which also translated into lower profitability. Thus, both demand and cost considerations favored companies that offered a broad array of mutual funds. BayBank, however, was currently not well positioned with its BayFunds product line to meet these market challenges. While overall BayFunds sales had been strong during the first year, Benson believed, based on recent sales of new accounts, that the BayFunds group had not made sufficient progress towards establishing BayBank's proprietary equity and fixed-income funds.

Moreover, in addition to refining BayBank's mutual fund product line, Benson needed to reassess her market segmentation strategies to ensure a fit between BayBank's strengths and the target customers' varying needs. While short-term growth in assets was certainly a goal, Benson understood that the critical long-term challenge was to develop a stable and profitable customer base. Benson also recognized that she needed to address two related issues that had grown in importance since BayFunds' introduction. First, how could Bay-Funds be further integrated into the BayBank system? And how could she effectively grow the retail business while, at the same time, coping with the uncertain regulatory climate?

Re-Examining BayFunds Marketing Strategy

BayBank's strategy for launching BayFunds was based on the premise that it could successfully diversify by leveraging the bank's strong brand identity. By extending the BayBank brand to its new mutual fund product line, the organization believed it could enhance BayBank's core reputation, expand the customer franchise, and grow the overall business. Convenience and technological superiority were the core associations typically evoked by the BayBank name; they were the benefits BayBank regularly emphasized when marketing its existing products and services. Benson, however, wondered whether convenience and technology were the features that customers valued most when purchasing mutual funds, particularly since a substantial percentage of BayBank customers rarely visited a branch office where the majority of BayFunds sales were made.

Tracking studies of bank-managed mutual funds revealed that, unlike CDs, non-money market mutual funds tended to be held by customers for a considerable period of timc with remarkably stable average balances. In effect, most customers viewed mutual funds as long-term savings vehicles and, thus, in order to select an appropriate fund or combination of funds, they needed to do a careful assessment of their financial needs, resources, and risk tolerance. Consequently, Benson wondered if marketing for BayFunds shouldn't also emphasize this solution-driven sales approach. Historically, BayBank had concentrated on selling checking and savings account products and generating trans-actions; and, therefore, was not accustomed to this more relationship-oriented sales process. How else could the overall strategy be adjusted to reflect the characteristics of BayFunds which made it markedly different from those of traditional bank products?

Integrating BayFunds into the core BayBank franchise was, therefore, a challenging task for Benson that was critical to the success of the bank's mutual funds program. As Benson explained, "We need to establish mutual funds as another core BayBank product and facilitate the sales process so that it is treated as another bank product." In an effort to achieve this goal, Benson wanted to include mutual funds in several of BayBank's packaged product offerings, an effort which would necessitate closer interaction with other product management teams. She believed that additional packaging strategies would en-hance the worth of BayBank's existing product offerings and the positioning of BayBank as a full-service financial provider. BayFunds had been able to sell mutual funds to 10% of new BayPlus checking accounts. However, cross-selling with other BayBank products, such as payments and credit services, was less developed.

Managing in an Uncertain Regulatory Environment

During the first year of its operation, the BayFunds group spent 20% of its time addressing issues and requests emanating from regulatory bodies concerned with proprietary bank funds. New rules and standards were issued almost every month and they impacted almost every area of BayBank's mutual fund business. Examinations by the SEC and various banking agencies required substantial preparation, and could be scheduled with as little as one day's notice. As a result, Benson believed that the BayFunds team needed to be pro-active with respect to the mutual fund regulations and to anticipate potential regulatory and legislative action. Benson was in the process of recruiting someone who would assume responsibility for ensuring the bank's compliance with all of the regulations.

1994–1995 Strategic Marketing Plan

Against this background, Benson began the task of formulating a marketing program for 1995. Benson was particularly interested in pursuing a plan for the bank's mutual funds program that would facilitate BayFunds' becoming a core BayBank product, and achiev-ing business line profitability by leveraging BayBank's strengths. Profitability depended on both asset retention and growth, as well as the mutual fund product mix. It was well known that the best prospects for mutual fund sales were the bank's existing customer base. While about 21% of BayBank customers already owned some type of mutual funds, less than 2% invested in BayFunds, suggesting that the potential for growth was enormous. To date, the majority of sales had been in money market funds, rather than bond or equity funds. As exhibit 17 demonstrates, both the "source" (i.e., proprietary versus third party) and the type of mutual fund influenced product line profitability over time. At present, a significant portion of BayFunds' assets were vulnerable to factors such as market volatility, the high percentage of investment dollars in money market funds, and the runoff of existing 401(k) assets when employees terminated employment or retired. As a result, mutual fund product offerings, distribution channels, and compensation strategies had to be aligned with profitability objectives.

In developing the marketing plan, Benson identified several broad mutual fund initiatives she wished to pursue over the next 18 months (see exhibit 18). The most controversial prosposal advanced in the plan was expanding the bank's relationship with third-party vendors. To date, BayBank had offered third-party funds from Putnam, Kemper, and Eaton Vance with the objective of providing its customers with more extensive investment options. Significant opportunities existed, however, for BayBank to expand and leverage these existing relationships by either adding new third-party mutual funds or by entering into more exclusive partnerships.

For vendors, BayBank's extensive retail distribution network offered access to a large untapped customer market. Thus, several fund providers had expressed interest in becoming the bank's "preferred provider" which would allow them, among other things, to enhance the position of their funds by working closely with the bank's mutual funds salesforce. For BayBank, further development of its third-party relationships would result in several benefits. The organization could take advantage of vendors' expertise and resources in: training (for licensed and non-licensed personnel), regulatory compliance, strategic marketing, consumer education, and the development of customer-focused, solution-driven portfolios. Available at no out-of-pocket costs, these services could greatly reduce total marketing expenditures for mutual funds. All of the third-party vendors that BayBank considered as potential partners had strong, widely-recognized brand names.

At various times in early 1994, Fidelity, Putnam, Kemper, and Federated had each approached BayBank about entering into some form of a strategic relationship. Benson wondered about the possibility of co-branding between BayBank and a well-established vendor. While the opportunities for BayBank appeared to be numerous, Benson had some concerns about developing closer ties with third-party vendors. Once familiar with the bank and its customer base, could the vendor then take those customers away from BayBank? She also wondered about the impact these types of arrangements might have on the future growth of BayBank's proprietary funds.

In addition to pursuing third-party partnerships, Benson placed a high priority on expanding marketing and strengthening customer relationships. Whatever product line mix was chosen, the organization had to pay careful attention to its target segments. To encourage greater asset retention and more profitable asset growth, the organization needed to focus on developing long-term customer relationships. As a result, the mutual fund marketing group had to shift from a product-oriented to a process-oriented sales approach, whereby sales staffs and investment specialists together would encourage customers to consider their overall financial goals and the benefits of long-term investing. Benson planned to modify BayFunds advertising strategy by increasing direct marketing and revising its advertising message to be more solutions-focused. Exhibit 19 contains budgeted costs for a selection of the proposed marketing programs.

Benson was scheduled to present her proposed marketing plan for mutual funds to the senior executives of BayBank at a meeting to be held at the end of the month. In the course of working on her presentation, she came across the following press report:

Widely regarded as the premier retail bank in New England, [BayBank] is pulling every available lever: its 203 branches in Massachusetts and Connecticut, its 24-hour telephone sales and service center, private banking and community business development officers, and a newly-hired cadre of 'investment specialists' dedicated to mutual fund sales. (Jeffrey Marshall, "Hitting the Ground Running," *United States Banker*, 1992)

After reading the press clipping, she asked herself: Are we pulling all of the right levers at BayFunds?

Notes

1. See Christine Remey and Gregory Dees, "BayBank Boston," HBS Case No. 9-393-095.
2. Raymond Sczudlo, "Mutual Funds: Opportunities and Risks," *The Bankers Magazine*, March/April 1994, p. 26.
3. A 1993 regulation limited annual 12b-1 fees to 0.75% of assets under management with a per-account lifetime cap on these fees ranging from 6.25 to 7.25%, depending on other fees imposed. See Carole Gould, *The New York Times Guide to Mutual Funds* (New York: The New York Times Company, 1992), pp. 46–62.
4. J. William Bowen, "Strategies for Harnessing the Mutual Funds Boom," *The Bankers Magazine*, March/April 1994, pp. 21–23.
5. The six-month Treasury bill was 8.8% in 1989 and 3.2% in 1993.
6. Baby boomers represented the 78 million persons born in the United States between 1946 and 1964.
7. Sczudlo, *op. cit.*, p. 26.
8. "The Environment for the Investment Company Industry in the 1990s," Investment Company Institute, 1990.
9. Sczudlo, *op. cit.*, p. 26.
10. Attachment to the "Securities Regulatory Equality Act of 1993," prepared by John Dingell, November 4, 1993.
11. The four federal banking agencies—Board of Governors of the Federal Reserve System (Federal Reserve Board), the Federal Deposit Insurance corporation (FDIC), the Office of the Comptroller of Currency (OCC), and the Office of Thrift Supervision (OTS)—had in the past issued separate guidelines that addressed various aspects of the retail sale of bank-managed mutual funds.
12. N. Capon, G. J. Fitzsimons, and R. A. Prince, "An Individual Level Analysis of the Mutual Fund Investment Decision," Unpublished Working Paper, Columbia University, (1992): 1–8.
13. Ibid., p. 25.
14. E. Sirri and P. Tufano, "Buying and Selling Mutual Funds: Flows, Performance, Fees, and Services," HBS *Working Paper No. 93-017*, (1993): 3.
15. For regulatory reasons, BayBank Boston, N.A. serves as the investment adviser to one of the BayFunds portfolios.
16. The criteria for participation included having at least $7,500 in any one CD or at least $7,500 in an MMDA account.
17. Federated Investors, a mutual fund manager and an affiliate of the distributor of BayFunds, created a second class of its existing fund, Massachusetts Municipal Cash Trust, for use in the BayFunds program, for which Federated Management would serve as investment adviser. The Federated organization provides an array of services for BayFunds including administration, distribution, and portfolio record keeping.
18. In fact, all BayBank mutual fund customers were informed 17 times in the first year that their BayFunds shares were not FDIC-insured.
19. A study conducted in 1991 by the ICI revealed that only 28% of mutual fund investors were sufficiently comfortable with their own financial expertise to be willing to purchase mutual funds through direct marketing channels.

20. Anyone giving investment advice had to be registered with the NASD and be sponsored by a broker-dealer. At a minimum, all ISs had a Series 6 license which enabled them to advise on mutual funds and annuities only. Eventually, the ISs would all be Series 7 registered where they could advise on other investments besides mutual funds.
21. "Peer" funds are those designated by the investment community as closely comparable in investment objectives, management style, and risk profile for the purpose of fund comparisons.

Exhibit 1

1993 Demographic profiles of customers of various Massachusetts banks

	State of Massachusetts	BayBank	Bank of Boston	Shawmut	Fleet	Thrifts	Other commercial banks
Median age	39	35	41	41	39	40	42
Median income	$35,000	$41,000	$40,000	$33,000	$33,000	$33,000	$38,000
Percent with college education or greater	42%	64%	51%	39%	37%	35%	36%
Percent with professional/ managerial occupations	47%	60%	47%	42%	48%	43%	45%
Number in sample citing primary bank[a]	3,939[b]	699	205	266	306	1,285	330

Source: Company Records. U.S. Bureau of the Census, *Census of Population, General Population Characteristics, United States* (1990 CP-1-1), as reported in *Statistical Abstracts of the United States 1993*, Table 69.
a. 848 Households cited either no primary banking relationship or one of the following: other credit union, other finance company, other insurance company, mutual fund, out of state bank, or brokerage company.
b. There were approximately 2.3 million households in the state of Massachusetts in 1993—15% of which had annual household incomes of more than $75,000.

Exhibit 2

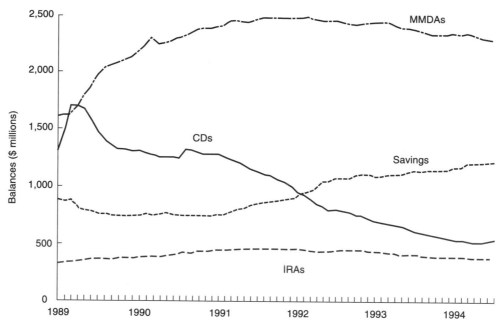

BayBank's deposit balance, 1989–1994 ($ billions)

Exhibit 3

Overview of leading mutual fund companies

Mutual fund management company	Parent company	1993 rank	1993 assets ($ billion)	1992 rank	1992 assets ($ billion)
Fidelity	FMR Corporation	1	237	1	164
Vanguard	Vanguard Group	2	130	3	93
Merrill Lynch	Merrill Lynch & Co., Inc.	3	117	2	108
Capital Research	Primerica	4	101	6	62
Franklin/Templeton[a]	Franklin/Templeton Group	5	92	5[a]	65
Dreyfus[b]	Dreyfus Corp.	6	74	4	76
Federated[c]	Federated Investors	7	68	9	45
Dean Witter InterCapital[d]	Dean Witter	8	59	7	53
Putnam	Marsh & McClennan Co., Inc.	9	59	11	41
Prudential	Prudential Insurance Co. of America	10	52	12	34

Source: Company records, *Hoover's Handbook of American Business 1994* (Austin, Texas: The Reference Press, 1993), "The Power of Mutual Funds," *Business Week,* January 18, 1993, p. 64; Timothy Middleton, "No Place Like Home," *Newsday*, March 14, 1994, p. 29.

a. 1992 ranking is for Franklin only, prior to late 1992 merger with Templeton.

b. Merged with Mellon Bank in 1993.

c. Sold by Aetna Life and Casualty in 1989 to management.

d. Spun off from Sears Roebuck, Inc., in 1993.

Exhibit 4

Proprietary fund families offered by Boston's leading banks, 1993

	BayBank, Inc.	Fleet Financial Group	Bank of Boston	Shawmut
BHC assets ($ billions)	$10.1	$47.9	$40.6	$27.2
Deposits ($ billions)	8.8	31.1	24.1	15.2
No. branches in Massachusetts	200	177	188	159
Total no. branches in New England (as of 12/93)	202	398	326	491
Proprietary fund family	BayFunds	Galaxy Funds	1784 Funds	Shawmut Funds
Date funds introduced	1991	1990	1993	1993
No. funds	6	17	8	9
Total fund assets ($ millions as of 3/31/94)	$1,240	$4,154	$844	$1,060
Investment advisory fees ($ millions 1993)	2.8	16.3	N/A	3.5
Loads	None	None	None	Front-end for equity funds
Initial investment	$2,500	$2,500	$2,500	$2,500
Product mix				
Bond	19%	54%	21%	22%
Stock	9%	22%	13%	25%
Money market	72%	21%	65%	53%
Blend	0%	3%	1%	0%
No. third-party funds	16	N/A	N/A	12

Source: Lipper Analytical Services, company records.

Exhibit 5

Importance of information sources and selection criteria in mutual fund investment descisions

Question: Please rate the importance of the following nine information sources when considering a mutual fund investment:

Information source	Mean rating[a]	Std. deviation
Published performance rankings	4.57	0.73
Advertising	3.13	1.21
Commission-based financial advisors	2.60	1.59
Seminars	1.89	1.34
Recommendations of friends/family	1.74	1.05
Recommendations of business associates	1.56	0.85
Fee-based financial advisors	1.34	0.91
Books	1.17	0.63
Direct mail	1.11	0.42

Question: Please rate the importance of the following nine selection criteria in selecting a mutual fund investment:

Selection criteria	Mean rating	Std. deviation
Investment performance track record	4.62	0.64
Fund manager reputation	4.00	0.77
Number of funds in family	3.95	1.06
Responsiveness to inquiries	2.30	1.08
Management fees	2.28	1.31
Investment management style	1.68	1.12
Additional services offered	1.38	0.92
Confidentiality	1.35	0.83
Community service record	1.09	0.48

Source: Adapted from Noel Capon, Gavan J. Fitzsimons, and Russ Alan Prince, *An Individual Level Analysis of the Mutual Fund Industry*, Unpublished Working Paper, Columbia University, (1992), Table 1. Statistics reported above are derived from a national sample of 3,386 households contacted via telephone in March 1991.

a. Rated on 5-point scale: 1 = not at all important; 5 = extremely important

Exhibit 6

Investor groupings based on information sources and selection criteria

| | Selection criteria groups | | | |
Information source groups	Price-insensitive performance	Service-substance	Price-sensitive performance	Totals
Commission-based advisees	32%[a]	1%	3%	37%
Advertising-driven investors	18%	0%	6%	24%
Knowledge-based investors	2%	4%	1%	8%
Ranking-only investors	17%	0%	14%	32%
Totals	70%	5%	25%	

a. Cell entries are the percentages of a national sample of 3,386 households classified into each of the subgroups indicated.

Groups	Criteria for assignment
Based on information source importance	
Commission-based advisees:	Ranked commission-based financial advisors as most important information source, on par with published performance. Advertising also ranked highly.
Advertising-driven investors:	Ranked advertising as high in importance as published rankings. Friends and family also very high.
Knowledge-based investors:	Ranked fee-based advisors as most important next to published rankings. Least reliant on advertising.
Ranking-only investors:	Published performance rankings are the most important source.
Based on selection criteria	
Price-insensitive performance:	Rankings close to sample mean, but less concern for management fees and responsiveness.
Service-substance:	Ranked responsiveness, management style, and confidentiality very high and track record lower than mean.
Price-sensitive performance:	Ranked track record, scope, management fees, and responsiveness very high.

Source: Adapted from Noel Capon, Gavan J. Fitzsimons, and Russ Alan Prince, *An Individual Level Analysis of the Mutual Fund Industry*, Unpublished Working Paper, Columbia University, (1992), Table 4.

Exhibit 7

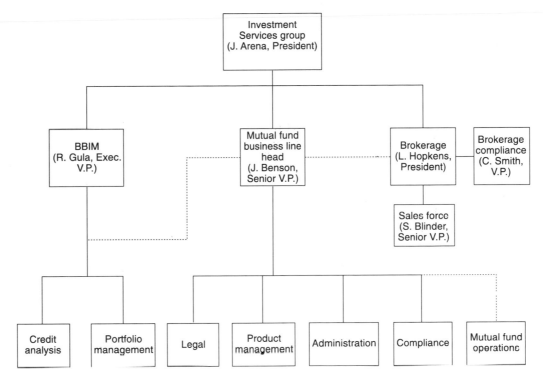

BayFunds organizational structure.

Exhibit 8

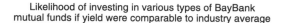

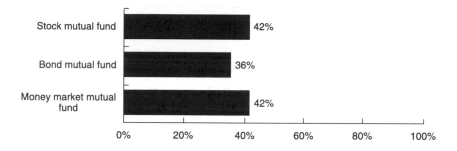

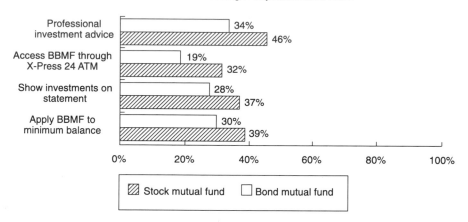

Likelihood of investing in different types of funds offered by BayBank. Note: Likelihood of investing includes those responding "somewhat likely" or "very likely" from a 1992 survey of BayBank and non-BayBank CD and MMDA customers. The base for the likelihood %'s with service enhancements is the number of respondents who already owned the particular type of mutual fund indicated. Source: Company records.

Exhibit 9

BayBank proprietary mutual fund portfolio

Type of fund					
Stable net asset value			Fluctuating net asset value		
Money Market Portfolio	BayFunds Shares—MA Municipal Cash Trust	U.S. Treasury Money Market Portfolio	Short Term Yield Portfolio	Bond Portfolio	Equity Portfolio
Fund objective Seeks high current yields by investing in a wide range of money market instruments, including commercial paper, bank CDs, obligations issued by the U.S. Government and its agencies, and repurchase agreements. Average maturity of the portfolio cannot exceed 90 days.[a]	Seeks a high level of income exempt from federal and Massachusetts taxes by investing in money market securities issued by the State of Massachusetts and its local governments. Average maturity of the portfolio cannot exceed 90 days.[a]	Seeks a high level of income by investing in U.S. Treasury and agency obligations, for which the repayment of principal and interest is guaranteed, as well as repurchase agreements backed by such obligations. Average maturity of the portfolio cannot exceed 90 days.[a]	Seeks a higher yield than a money market account while maintaining a relatively steady NAV. Invests in U.S. Treasury and federal agency obligations, high quality corporate debt obligations, bank CDs, commercial paper, and repurchase agreements. Average maturity of the portfolio is approximately one to two years but cannot exceed three years.	Seeks to provide current income and capital appreciation while applying conservative investment standards. Invests in U.S. Treasury, federal agency, investment grade corporate debt instruments, and repurchase agreements. Average maturity of the portfolio cannot exceed 12 years; but depending on market conditions, may have a much shorter maturity.	Seeks to provide long-term capital appreciation and to produce competitive performance rankings against a nationwide universe of equity portfolios. Invests in companies which display consistent and growing earnings, and are in solid financial condition.

Exhibit 9 (continued)

	Stable net asset value			Fluctuating net asset value		
Type of fund	Money Market Portfolio	BayFunds Shares—MA Municipal Cash Trust	U.S. Treasury Money Market Portfolio	Short Term Yield Portfolio	Bond Portfolio	Equity Portfolio
Customer appeal	Savings vehicle, liquidity for emergencies, expected expenses (i.e., tax payment, down-payment for auto, home), income, with no fluctuation in principal while earning a competitive yield.	Investors partly concerned with federal and Massachusetts taxes who are seeking a savings vehicle and liquidity with no fluctuation in principal.	Investors who are seeking safety associated with short-term U.S. Treasury securities, liquidity of a money market fund, and no fluctuation of principal.	Investors seeking higher yields than bank CDs and willing to accept modest fluctuations in NAV.	Investors seeking high current income to provide for current expenses. May also be appropriate as a conservative long-term savings vehicle. Investors must be willing to accept fluctuating NAV.	Investors seeking long-term total return for future needs (i.e., college savings, retirement, savings for a home, and long-term savings). May be appropriate for IRA or 401(k) plan customers.

Source: Company records
a. Subject to rule 2a-7 of the SEC.

Exhibit 10

B A Y B A N K
MUTUAL FUNDS AT A GLANCE

Investment Objective	Mutual Funds (Non-FDIC Insured)	Tolerance For Risk	Time Perspective
MONEY MARKET MUTUAL FUNDS Seek to preserve the value of your investment and to provide current income.	• BayFunds Money Market Portfolio • BayFunds U.S. Treasury Money Market Portfolio • Massachusetts Municipal Cash Trust – BayFunds Share	Low	Short-term (up to 3 years)
TAX-FREE INCOME FUNDS Seek to provide current income generally free from federal and Massachusetts income taxes consistent with safety of principal. Your return potential depends on the securities each fund holds and its average maturity.	• Eaton Vance Investment Trust – Massachusetts Limited Maturity Tax Free Fund • Eaton Vance Municipals Trust – Massachusetts Tax-Free Fund • Putnam Massachusetts Tax Exempt II	Low to Moderate	Short-term/ Intermediate-term (up to 5 years)
TAXABLE INCOME FUNDS Seek to provide current income consistent with safety of principal. Your return potential depends on the securities each fund holds and its average maturity.	• BayFunds Bond Portfolio • BayFunds Short Term Yield Portfolio • Kemper Investment Portfolios – Government Portfolio • Kemper Investment Portfolios – Short-Intermediate Government Portfolio • Putnam Adjustable Rate U.S. Government Fund • Putnam U.S. Government Income Trust	Low to Moderate	Short-term/ Intermediate-term (up to 5 years)
BALANCED FUNDS Seek income and long-term growth through a diversified mix of stocks and bonds.	• Eaton Vance Investors Fund • George Putnam Fund of Boston	Low to Moderate	Intermediate-term/ Long-term (3 years up to 10+ years)
GROWTH AND INCOME EQUITY Seek capital growth and current income through equity investments that typically pay above-average dividends.	• Eaton Vance Stock Fund • Putnam Fund for Growth and	Moderate	Intermediate-term/ Long-term (3 years up to 10+ years)
GROWTH EQUITY FUNDS Seek long-term capital growth; current income is secondary.	• BayFunds Equity Portfolio • Kemper Growth Portfolio • Putnam Voyager Fund	Moderate to High	Long-term (5 years up to 10+ years)
INTERNATIONAL AND GLOBAL FUNDS Seek long-term capital growth. Global Funds invest in domestic and foreign securities while International Funds are devoted exclusively to foreign securities.	• Kemper International Fund • Putnam Global Growth Fund	Moderate to High	Long-term (5 years up to 10+ years)

☎ CALL 1-800-BAY-FAST (1-800-229-3278) 24 HOURS

What Are Mutual Funds?

Mutual funds offer a convenient and timesaving way for individuals to invest, without undertaking the responsibility of personally selecting and following specific stocks and bonds. Mutual funds pool the money of many investors and pursue a variety of investment objectives.

Each fund's portfolio manager invests assets in a portfolio of different securities pursuing a specific investment objective.

Many kinds of mutual funds are available to meet your investment objectives. The funds that are right for you depend upon your financial goals, the time you have to achieve them, your tolerance for risk, and the return you're seeking.

Mutual funds carry varying degrees of safety or risk, depending on their objectives and investments. Unlike CDs or savings accounts, *mutual funds are not insured by the FDIC* and do not have a guaranteed rate of return. Additionally, the principal value of non-money market mutual funds is likely to fluctuate, so when fund shares are sold they may be worth more or less than the investor paid for them.

While no investment is 100% secure, mutual funds reduce the overall risk inherent in investing because the funds direct your money into many different securities. This means that your return is not tied to any single stock or bond.

For easy tracking of your fund's performance, daily market prices for shares of most mutual funds are listed in major newspapers.

*See the "Supplemental Information" section on the inside back cover of this Catalog for important mutual fund information.

Third-party funds available through BayBank. Note: In April 1994, BayBank added a 16th proprietary fund to its family—the Putnam Asset Allocation Fund, which offered investors a choice of one of three different asset mixes.

Exhibit 11

BayFunds sales and distribution strategy

	Distribution channels		
	Investment specialists	Branch	Sales and service center
Target segment	Affluent BayBank customers Household income $75K	All BayBank customers	Emerging affluent BayBank customers
Product	All BBMFs, third-party mutual funds Capital market and brokerage products	BBMFs—money market funds only	All BBMFs
Personnel	29 licensed ISs servicing branches	All SSAs and CSMs in branches	Sales center: • 3 investments specialists Service center • Investment service specialists
Role	Act as customers' "financial counselor," explain products, build trust, and help customers make decision Sell and open mutual funds	Answer questions, make BayFunds money market portfolios available Make referrals to IS for equity and bond portfolio sales Complete routine transactions (transfers, redemptions, purchases, etc.)	Sales center: • Generate awareness • Answer questions • Send out prospectuses and applications • Sell mutual funds • Follow up on leads • Open accounts (after customer receives prospectus) Service center: • Handle routine transactions (transfers, purchases, redemptions, information needs)
Relationship to other channels	Work with and train branch personnel to receive referrals	Make referrals to investment specialists	Receive referrals from branches and other groups in sales and service center

Source: Company records

Exhibit 12

Print ad for BayFunds launch, March 1993

Exhibit 13

1993 BayFunds advertising budget ($000)

	Budget
Print	
Spring	$862
Fall	170
Radio	140
Product of the month	60
Airport dioramas	35
Sales collateral	75
Direct mail & fulfillment	460
Applications	60
Brochures	180
Total budget	$2,042

Source: Company records

Exhibit 14

Mutual Funds Without The Mystique.

If you're interested in learning more about mutual funds and in making the investment decisions that are right for you, just speak to a BayBank Investment Specialist.

Every one of BayBank's licensed Investment Specialists has undergone very specialized training in mutual funds. That makes them highly skilled at answering your questions. Questions like these:

What are mutual funds? Mutual funds are a convenient and affordable way to participate in professionally managed and diversified portfolios. Mutual funds pool the money of many investors and pursue a variety of objectives. By investing in mutual funds, you gain the edge that only professional investment management provides.

How safe are mutual funds? Mutual funds carry varying degrees of safety or risk, depending on their objectives and investment practices. Unlike CDs or savings accounts, mutual funds are not insured by the FDIC and do not have a guaranteed rate of return. While no investment is 100% secure, mutual funds reduce the overall risk of investing because your funds are diversified across numerous stocks, bonds, or other securities and are managed by financial experts.

What types of mutual funds are available? Many types of mutual funds are available to meet your specific investment objectives. The funds that are right for you depend on your financial goals, the time you have to achieve them, and your tolerance for risk. Mutual funds can generally be classified into three categories:

MONEY MARKET: Money market funds are among the most conservative non-insured investments available. If you're looking for attractive current returns with minimal risk to principal, money market funds could be the right choice for you.

INCOME FUNDS: These funds seek high current income and capital appreciation. Income funds are designed for investors who can accept fluctuations in principal in return for potentially high current income and total return. You can choose from taxable and non taxable funds.

EQUITY FUNDS: These funds seek to achieve long-term capital appreciation with current income as a secondary objective. Equity funds may be the ideal choice for investors who can accept some fluctuations in share price in return for potential long term capital appreciation. Many people use equity funds to help meet long-term goals such as retirement or education.

How can BayBank help? With BayBank, it's as easy for you to buy and sell mutual funds as it is to do your everyday banking. We're just around the corner from where you live and work.

You can choose from a full selection of mutual funds available at BayBank, including BayFunds, a family of six no-load funds. Or choose from well-known mutual fund families such as Eaton Vance, Kemper Financial Services, and Putnam. One or more may be the right choice for reaching your investment objectives. A BayBank Investment Specialist will help you determine which funds meet your financial requirements.

For more answers to your questions about mutual funds, meet with a BayBank Investment Specialist at the nearest BayBank office. To speak to an Investment Specialist or to arrange for an appointment, simply call 1-800-BAY-FUND.

Call 1-800-BAY-FUND®

BayBank®
Day and night. Night and day.

BayFunds print ad

Exhibit 15

A Savings Alternative.

BAYFUNDS
SHORT TERM YIELD
PORTFOLIO

Mutual
Funds At
BayBank

BayFunds

The BayFunds Short Term Yield Portfolio can offer a potentially higher yield than savings accounts.

If you're concerned about current interest rates, consider the BayFunds® Short Term Yield Portfolio. This mutual fund seeks a higher level of income than savings accounts and CDs. Remember, however, that no mutual fund is FDIC insured; and the value of the shares you purchase may vary. But over the long run, the BayFunds Short Term Yield Portfolio may provide more price stability than investments in higher-yielding, longer-term bonds.

Investing in BayFunds is affordable too. There's no sales charge (or "load"), and all you need is $2,500 to open an account. Or only $500 with a BayBank IRA or when you have automatic transfers made from your checking or savings account.

With BayFunds, you'll enjoy the best in investing and banking convenience – including professional advice from BayBank Investment Specialists and 24-hour customer service. Plus, BayBank customers can get a consolidated statement that summarizes BayFunds activity with their checking and savings.

To invest in the BayFunds Short Term Yield Portfolio, call 1-800-BAY-FUND or stop by your nearest BayBank office. For more complete information about the fund, including charges and expenses, ask for a prospectus and read it carefully before you invest or send money.

1-800-BAY-FUND

BayFunds®

Mutual funds, unlike traditional bank products, are not federally insured and do not offer a fixed rate of return. In addition, they involve certain risks, including the possible loss of principal. A rise in interest rates can result in a decline in the value of your investment. BayFunds are not deposits or obligations of or guaranteed by BayBank, and are not federally insured or guaranteed. Federated Securities Corp., Distributor.

BayFunds print ad

Exhibit 16

BayFunds performance versus peers[a]

Total return—investment shares

Fund name	Quarter ending 6/29/93	Quarter ending 9/30/93	Quarter ending 12/31/93	Quarter ending 3/31/94	12 months ending 3/31/94
BayFunds U.S. Treasury Money Market Portfolio	0.64%	0.65%	0.65%	0.67%	2.64%
Peer group average[b]	0.63%	0.65%	0.65%	0.65%	2.61%
Number of funds in peer group	74	76	76	79	76
BayFunds Money Market Portfolio	0.60%	0.66%	0.66%	0.66%	2.70%
Peer group average[c]	0.71%	0.72%	0.73%	0.74%	2.94%
Number of funds in peer group	99	104	109	117	105
BayFunds Short Term Yield Portfolio	1.24%	1.68%	0.21%	0.11%	3.21%
Peer group average[d]	1.38%	1.61%	0.56%	(0.81%)	2.69%
Number of funds in peer group	95	90	100	106	86
BayFunds Bond Portfolio[e]	2.68%	3.45%	(0.77%)	(1.91%)	3.40%
Peer group average[e]	2.42%	2.70%	(0.12%)	(2.71%)	2.30%
Number of funds in peer group	81	88	99	117	90
BayFunds Equity Portfolio	1.22%	6.48%	(0.46%)	(4.68%)	2.27%
Peer group average[f]	0.72%	5.01%	2.26%	(3.44%)	3.79%
Number of funds in peer group	416	435	475	467	394
Ranking in peer group	181	143	407	330	225

Source: Lipper Analytical Services, company records.

a. Peer groups defined and measured by Lipper Analytical Services
b. U.S. Treasury Money Market Funds
c. Money Market Institutional Funds
d. Short Investment Grade Debt Funds
e. Intermediate Investment Grade Debt Funds
f. Lipper Growth Stock Funds

Exhibit 17

Projected fee income comparison by mutual fund type and source[a]

Proprietary funds with investment management fee[b]

| Year | Assets ($ millions) | | Product mix | | |
| | | | 90/10 | 70/30 | 50/50 |
	Year-end	New	Fee income ($)		
1	1,000	0	2,175,000	2,525,000	2,875,000
2	1,300	300	5,002,500	5,107,500	5,212,500
3	1,600	300	6,307,500	7,322,500	8,337,500
4	1,900	300	7,612,500	8,837,500	10,062,500
5	2,200	300	8,917,500	10,352,500	11,787,500

Third-party funds with loads[c]

| Year | Assets ($ millions) | | Product mix | | |
| | | | 90/10 | 70/30 | 50/50 |
	Year-end	New	Fee income ($)		
1	1,000		1,900,000	3,700,000	5,500,000
2	1,300	300	2,470,000	4,810,000	7,150,000
3	1,600	300	1,140,000	2,220,000	3,300,000
4	1,900	300	1,140,000	2,220,000	3,300,000
5	2,200	300	1,140,000	2,220,000	3,300,000

a. Product mix is ratio of money market funds to fluctuating NAV (equity and bond) funds.
b. Investment advisory fee of 40 basis points for money market funds, 75 basis points for fluctuating NAV funds. Calculations assume all new monies received at mid-year.
c. Front-end load of 20 basis points for money market funds, 200 basis points for fluctuating NAV funds. Loads applicable only to new monies to the funds. Calculations assume all new monies received at mid-year.

Exhibit 18

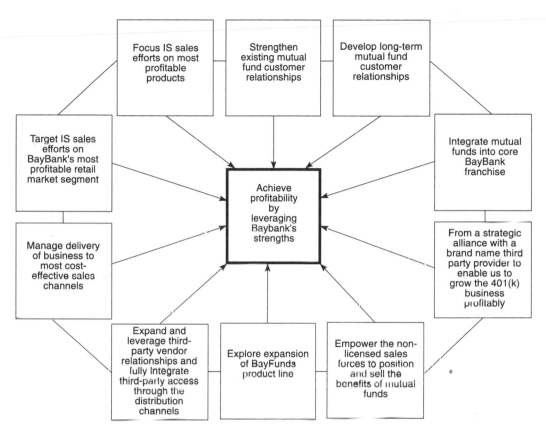

1994 1995 mutual fund initiatives

Exhibit 19

BayFunds marketing budget, 1994 and 1995 ($000)

	1994	1995
Advertising		
Print	$455	?
Direct mail	200	?
Product of the month	100	?
Seminars	100	?
New funds collateral	100	?
Sales support	75	?
Fulfillment	25	?
	$1,055	$750
Branch contests	$50	$80
Marketing research and systems consulting	$130	$155
Prospectuses and collateral materials[a]	$457	$515
Total budget	**$1,692**	**$1,500**

Source: Company records
a. Internal training is included in BayBank's corporate overhead budget, which amounted to $1,674,000.

8   Retirement Plans and the Fund Business

Introduction

This is the second chapter on mutual fund marketing. The first chapter discussed the traditional channel of broker-dealer distribution, the development of the direct marketing channel, and the recent creation of mutual fund marketplaces. The next chapter will address the servicing of non-retirement shareholders. This chapter will focus on distributing funds and servicing fund shareholders through retirement plans.

The retirement business can be seen as an additional channel to the three channels discussed in the previous chapter. The retirement channel is partially institutional and partially retail. This channel is institutional in that the initial sale is made to the employer, who determines which funds or fund complexes will be available to employees through the retirement plan. The retirement channel is retail in the sense that the actual sale of the funds is made to hundreds of thousands of plan participants, who must choose among mutual funds as well as other investment alternatives offered by the retirement plan.

For many years, the retirement market was dominated by insurance companies and banks as service providers. In more recent years, however, mutual fund companies have garnered an increasing share of the retirement market. As explained in the readings, the success of mutual fund companies has been linked to the rise of defined contribution (DC) plans and the leveling off of defined benefit (DB) plans. This shift from DB to DC plans is one of the most important trends in the U.S. financial markets and is starting to happen across the world. (See case study in chapter 13.) The growth of DC plans has spread equity ownership through mutual funds to millions of new investors who in the process have become interested more generally in mutual funds and the securities markets.

In DB plans, retirement benefits are typically set by a schedule based on the number of years worked by the participant and his or her average salary in the years immediately prior to retirement. To finance this benefit schedule, employers (and sometimes employees) make regular contributions to DB plans. Employers (or their investment managers) choose the investments for DB assets, and employees have no say in investing these assets. If the contributions to the DB plan and the investment performance of DB assets are together insufficient to meet the schedule of retirement benefits offered by a DB plan, the employer must make up the shortfall. If the employer sponsoring a DB plan goes bankrupt, participants in the employer's plan are guaranteed to receive only a low level of "basic benefits" from a federal insurance program administered by the Pension Benefit Guaranty Corporation (PBGC). If an employee terminates employment with the employer sponsoring a

DB plan, it is usually quite difficult for the employee to take with him or her any share of the plan's assets.

In DC plans, by contrast, participants typically decide how much to contribute to the plan; the employer usually (but not always) will contribute by matching some of the employee contributions. In DC plans, employers establish the array of investment alternatives available in the plan, but the participants choose the investments for their accounts. The retirement benefits of DC participants are determined by the amount of plan contributions and the performance of the investment alternatives chosen by the participants. In a DC plan, the employer is not obligated to provide any specific level of retirement benefits; the employer's obligation is limited to a selected level of contributions. If the retirement benefits of the employee are lower than desired because the plan investments selected by the employee did not perform well, the employee must make do with those benefits. If the employee leaves an employer sponsoring a DC plan, it is usually feasible for the employee to transfer all or most of his or her plan investment accounts to an individual retirement account (IRA) maintained by a financial institution.

The most popular type of DC plan is the 401(k) plan, named after a section of the Internal Revenue Code. The annual pretax deferral limit for participants in 401(k) plans will be $10,000 in 1998, which gradually rises in accordance with an inflation index. Additional contributions such as employer matches and employee after-tax contributions can bring the total contribution to the lower of $30,000 or 25% of the individual's compensation. This total limit may be reduced for highly paid executives, however, because of antidiscrimination rules—a complex set of rules designed to ensure participation by all levels of employees. The 401(k) plan is used by corporate employers, while other types of DC plans are available to municipal employers (457 plans), and to nonprofit institutions such as universities or hospitals (403(b) plans). Each of these other types of DC plan has somewhat different contribution and other requirements than a 401(k) plan.

In a 401(k) plan, an employer may choose to offer as few or as many investment alternatives as it pleases; however, an employer must offer at least three core investment alternatives in order to enjoy the benefit of a safe harbor established by the Department of Labor (DOL). The safe harbor protects employers from liability on the performance of the specific investments chosen by the employee as long as the employer provides a reasonable array of investment alternatives and sufficient information about such alternatives. The three investment alternatives required to meet the DOL safe harbor must be well diversified within their asset classes and have materially different risk/return characteristics. Three typical examples are: (1) a money market fund or other low-risk alternative such as a bank deposit or a fixed-rate contract offered by insurance companies; (2) an income alternative such as a government or corporate bond fund; and (3) a diversified stock fund.

Most 401(k) plans offer several stock and/or bond alternatives, a "safe" choice such as a money market fund or managed income portfolio, as well as employer stock. Mutual funds have become more attractive to plan sponsors than bank collective trust funds and insurance company commingled accounts for several reasons. First, these trust funds and insurance accounts are private investment vehicles often without daily valuations. By contrast, mutual funds provide daily purchases and redemptions based on prices published in the newspaper. Second, the large mutual fund complexes offer a broader array of equity and bond funds than most banks and insurance companies. Moreover, mutual fund managers have developed new products specially tailored to the needs of retirement plan participants—for example, the "lifestyle" funds that change their equity-bond mix as participants age. Third, fund sponsors have devoted considerable resources to improving participant communications and enhancing customer support. In particular, the direct marketers have transferred their technological and service experience from money market funds to the retirement area.

The strong trend is toward providing participants with more and more investment choices. Some large employers now offer 20 or 30 fund alternatives from the same complex. Other large employers have asked mutual fund sponsors to expand 401(k) plan offerings to include not only their own funds but also funds from other complexes—a development parallel to fund marketplaces. As investment choices have proliferated, 401(k) participants, like their retail counterparts, are increasingly seeking more guidance and advice about financial planning for retirement.

To encourage employee education about their investment alternatives, the DOL has issued an interpretive bulletin on educational materials. That bulletin allows mutual fund sponsors and other service providers to 401(k) plans to disseminate educational materials to plan participants without such dissemination constituting "investment advice." Under the Employee Retirement Security Act (ERISA), the key federal law regulating private pensions, a provider of "investment advice" becomes exposed to additional legal liabilities. In most 401(k) plans offering mutual funds, the employer asks the fund sponsor to provide plan participants with educational materials and recordkeeping services as well as an array of investment choices. More recently, employers have also asked mutual fund sponsors to supply administrative support for health and welfare plans and regular payroll, as well as for 401(k) plans.

There is tremendous downward pressure on fees in the 401(k) business as large employers have become increasingly demanding of service providers. Almost all mutual funds offered to 401(k) participants are no-load; even funds with loads typically waive them for retirement plans. Without sales loads, the principal revenue stream from retirement investors to the fund sponsor is the advisory fee and, to a lesser extent, the transfer agent fee. In addition, employers or plans often pay separate fees to mutual fund sponsors for providing recordkeeping and other administrative services. For example, some mutual fund sponsors have established trust companies to serve as trustees or custodians to 401(k) plans.

In contrast to large employers, a majority of small employers have historically not offered any type of retirement plan to their employees. While small employers were eligible for various types of regulatory relief in sponsoring retirement plans, they still complained about the cost and red tape involved in complying with government requirements for such plans. In 1996, Congress responded by creating the Savings Incentive Match Plan for Employees or SIMPLE—a streamlined type of DC plan for employers with 100 or fewer employees. Beginning January 1, 1997, eligible employers may elect to establish either a SIMPLE 401(k) or a SIMPLE IRA. Both are designed to have lower costs and less administration than traditional plans.

If an employer signs up for SIMPLE with a qualified financial institution, including a mutual fund sponsor, the employer has to transmit monthly payments to that institution only for employees who choose to participate. The employer must either make a limited matching contribution for participating employees, or make a minimum contribution for all employees. Employees participating in a SIMPLE plan may establish their own retirement accounts with the financial institution and choose among its investment alternatives. The employees deal directly with the institution, which provides almost all reports and services required for the SIMPLE plan. Certain fund sponsors have been quite successful in signing up small employers to participate in SIMPLE.

A few years ago, Congress passed incentives for plan participants who leave employment to "roll over" the assets in their DC plan accounts to an Individual Retirement Account (IRA), instead of withdrawing those assets for consumption. The law now requires a plan administrator to withhold 20% of plan withdrawals for departing employees, unless those withdrawals are transferred directly from the plan to a rollover account at a qualified financial institution. A qualifying rollover is not subject to income tax until the participant actually takes retirement distributions from the IRA. As a result of these tax incentives, plus changes in population demographics and early retirement practices, the rollover IRA market has exploded for mutual funds. At the end of 1996, rollover assets accounted for 38% of IRA assets held in mutual funds, which totaled $632 billion at that time.

More recently, Congress reinvigorated the IRA market for mutual funds by expanding the eligibility for up-front tax deductions to the traditional IRA and by creating a new type of IRA with a back-end tax benefit. In the early 1980s, when IRA tax deductions had been available to all Americans, fund sponsors had actively marketed IRAs to individual investors as a retail product. After 1986, when Congress had imposed strict income limitations on IRA tax deductions for taxpayers participating in an employer plan, IRA contributions had dropped sharply and fund sponsors had greatly reduced their advertising budgets for IRAs. In 1997, Congress enacted new rules under which (after a gradual phase-in over several years) a taxpayer with annual income of $50,000 or less ($80,000 or less for couples) may take a full tax deduction in the year of contribution of up to $2,000 to a traditional IRA even if the taxpayer participates in an employer plan. But the amount contributed and the earnings thereon will be taxed when distributed at retirement. Alternatively, a taxpayer with annual income of $95,000 or less ($150,000 or less for couples) is now fully eligible to contribute up to $2,000 a year to a back-end IRA. While taxpayers will receive no deduction in the year of contribution to back-end IRAs (Roth IRA), the earnings on assets in these IRAs are never taxed if they are held in the IRA for 5 years and distributed after age $59\frac{1}{2}$ or for another qualifying reason.

At approximately the same time, Congress almost doubled the size of the IRA market for nonworking spouses—a relatively affluent group of over 13 million taxpayers, many of whom already own mutual funds. Historically, a nonworking spouse and working spouse could together make annual IRA contributions of only $2,250. Moreover, the deductibility of that IRA contribution typically depended on whether the working spouse was an eligible participant in an employer-based retirement plan. In 1996, however, Congress enacted legislation allowing a nonworking spouse to make an annual IRA contribution of $2,000 in addition to the $2,000 IRA contribution of the working spouse. In 1997, Congress provided further that the nonworking spouse may receive a full tax deduction for an IRA contribution, regardless of the working spouse's pension participation, as long as the couple's total income does not exceed $150,000 per year.

The readings for this chapter describe in more detail the strong trend toward DC plans and the important role of mutual fund sponsors in that trend. The case study puts you in the position of a pension consultant advising different types of employers on the design of their 401(k) plans.

Questions

In reviewing the materials in this chapter, please keep in mind the following questions:

1. Why have employers wanted to shift from defined benefit to defined contribution plans? What is the difference in accounting treatment for the employer's future obligations under a DB plan versus a DC plan?
2. Why have employees accepted and often embraced the shift from DB to DC plans? What are the potential negative effects of this shift for employees?
3. Why is diversification so important for participants in DC plans? Is employer stock appropriate as one of several investment alternatives for DC plans?
4. If an employer demands that a fund sponsor provide funds from other families as well as its own family, how will the fund sponsor earn a reasonable profit from these other funds? How many funds are "too many" for a 401(k) plan?
5. Do you think that SIMPLE will lead most small employers to offer DC plans? What do you predict would be the objection of small employers to SIMPLE?
6. Would you be better off contributing $2,000 to a traditional front-end IRA than contributing $2,000 to your employer's 401(k) plan? Please state precisely the assumptions and/or conditions underlying your answer.
7. If you were age 30 and a nonworking spouse in a family with a total annual income of $100,000, should you contribute $2,000 to a traditional front-end IRA or to the new back-end IRA? Again, please state precisely the assumptions and/or conditions underlying your answer.
8. If you and your spouse earned $90,000 per year, should you each invest in a back-end IRA or in a variable annuity? Would your answer be different if you were going to choose a stock fund versus a bond fund?

8.1   401(k) Plans: How Plan Sponsors See the Marketplace*

Shift in Pension Coverage

Since the passage of the Employee Retirement Income Security Act (ERISA) in 1974, there has been a trend away from pension coverage under defined benefit plans (DB) and toward defined contribution plans (DC), particularly toward relatively new types of DC plans such as 401(k) and Employee Stock Ownership Plans (ESOPs). Defined benefit plans are designed to provide an employee with a specified benefit upon retirement. That benefit is specifically identified in the plan and typically constitutes a fixed percentage of the employee's salary, determined by the employee's age at retirement and his or her number of years of service with the employer. Because the employer is contractually bound to provide the defined benefit upon retirement, the employer bears all risk flowing from the investment performance of any investment vehicle used to fund the plan. To the extent that the plan's assets produce a positive investment return, the employer's exposure under the defined benefit plan is reduced. On the other hand, to the extent the plan's assets produce a poor investment return, the employer's exposure under the defined benefit plan increases.

Defined contribution plans, in contrast, do not promise employees a specified benefit upon retirement. Rather, under such plans, employers typically contribute a defined percentage of payroll (money-purchase plan) or a defined percentage of profit (profit-sharing plan) to a retirement account established for each employee. Since the employee's retirement benefit is the value of his or her account at retirement, the employee bears the entire risk of plan investment performance. Favorable investment performance will increase the benefit, while poor performance will reduce it.

The growth in DC plans relative to DB plans is evident when examining trends over the last few decades in number of plans and participants. Between 1975 and 1991, the number of active participants[1] in DB plans decreased slightly, from 27.2 million to 26.1 million, while the proportion of eligible employees that were active participants in these plans declined from 87 percent to 62 percent. The total number of private DB plans increased from 103,000 in 1975 to a peak of 175,000 in 1983, then dropped to 113,000 in 1990. Preliminary figures for 1991 indicate a further decline in the number of DB plans to 99,000. By way of contrast, the total number of DC plans (including those that are the primary benefit and those which are supplementary) increased almost three times between 1975 and 1991, from 208,000 to 609,000. Active participants in DC plans rose from 11.2 million to 36.3 million during the 1975 to 1991 period.[2]

The growth of defined contribution corporate retirement plans during the last decade has been dramatic. In 1983, DC plan assets accounted for 30.6 percent of total private

---

*Courtesy of Investment Company Institute, Research Department, Winter 1995, pp. 13–19, 89. Reprinted with permission.

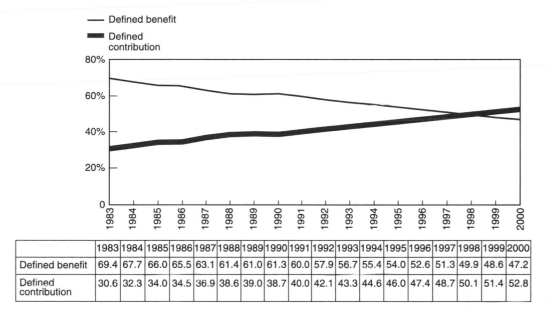

Figure 8.1.1 Distribution of private pension assets by type of plan, 1983 to 2000. Source: Employee Benefit Research Institute, 1983–1993; ICI projections, 1994–2000

pension assets. By 1993, they had grown to 43.3 percent of the total. By the year 2000, DC assets are projected to grow to 52.8 percent of private pension assets. (See figure 8.1.1.)

The disparity between the contributions to DB and DC plans is even more dramatic than that between the number of participants and the number of plans. DC plan contributions increased from $23.5 billion in 1980 to $82.1 billion in 1991, with $52.5 billion of the 1991 total accounted for by 401(k)-type plan contributions. The growth in contributions to DC plans is largely due to the growth of 401(k) plans. Without them, contributions to DC plans would have been only $29.6 billion in 1991.[3]

Among explanations for the growth in DC plans is the shift in employment from large unionized firms in manufacturing, which traditionally have provided DB plans, to smaller nonunion firms in the service sector, where DC plans are more common.[4] Another reason for the growth of DC plans relative to the growth of DB plans is that workers tend to change jobs more frequently than in the past, thus increasing the need for portable benefit plans. DC plans are deemed to be more portable than DB plans because DC plan participants are generally allowed to take distribution of benefits in one lump sum when they retire or terminate employment for other reasons.

In addition, tax laws and federal legislation, beginning with ERISA, have added to the cost and complexity of maintaining DB plans and decreased the benefit to employers. Prior to the enactment of ERISA, the employer's obligation to fund a retirement plan was largely a moral commitment rather than a legal requirement. Then ERISA imposed a mandatory funding requirement upon many types of plans, including defined benefit plans. As a result of this mandatory funding requirement, employers began to offer defined contribution plans which enabled them to satisfy their pension obligation simply by making a specified contribution on behalf of each employee. These DC plans also enabled employers to transfer to their employees the risk that the employer's contributions would not grow sufficiently to provide the employees with adequate retirement income.

In addition to the mandatory funding requirements imposed by ERISA in 1974, the growth of corporate DC retirement plans received further impetus from the tax law changes adopted in the Revenue Act of 1978. The Revenue Act of 1978 authorized employers to establish a new type of defined contribution profit-sharing plan commonly known as a 401(k) plan. This type of plan permits an employee to reduce his taxable income by electing each year to contribute a percentage of salary to the retirement plan. The contributions to the plan are not currently taxed as income of the employee, but are held in the employee's individual account until retirement, separation from service, or other specified events.

Because the contribution to 401(k) plans are wages deferred upon the employees' voluntary election, these plans also often offer employees the right to select the investment medium for their account from a range of choices. It is the individual employee, rather than the employer, who not only bears the risk of the investment performance of his or her account under a 401(k) plan, but in many cases who also selects the investment medium used to fund the account.

An additional advantage offered by 401(k) plans is they are more flexible than many other pension arrangements. Since each eligible employee can determine the amount of saving he or she does through the 401(k) plan, these plans are likely to be more attractive at firms with heterogeneous work forces. Finally, from the firm's perspective, 401(k) plans may cost less for a given level of employer contribution per participating employee than other DC plans. With other defined contribution plans, the employer must contribute on behalf of all eligible workers. Even though participation in 401(k) plans is high, not all eligible employees participate, thereby reducing the employer's overall contributions.[5]

Growth of 401(k) Plans

The growth of 401(k) plans has been phenomenal. Although there were no 401(k) plans in existence prior to 1978, by 1985 10.3 million participants had accumulated $105 billion. In the mid-1980s, 401(k) plans became increasingly popular and the trend away from DB plans toward DC plans accelerated. This shift can now be characterized as a shift from both defined benefit and non-401(k) defined contribution plans toward 401(k) plans. In 1983, only 3 percent of full-time workers received coverage under a 401(k) plan compared with 47 percent under other types of plans. By 1993, the coverage rate for full-time workers under 401(k) plans had increased to 27 percent, while coverage under other types of plans had fallen to 33 percent, with about 10 percent having coverage under both a 401(k) and another type of plan. The ratio of active 401(k) participants to DC plan participants increased from 16 percent in 1983 to one-third in 1986, and to close to 50 percent in 1993. (See figure 8.1.2.) Similarly, the ratio of 401(k) assets to DC plan assets almost tripled during the 10-year period, from 15 percent in 1983 to 44 percent in 1993.[6]

Among plans providing retirement benefits, 401(k) plans are a fairly recent innovation. The Revenue Act of 1978 added Section 401(k) to the IRS Code, effective for taxable years beginning after December 31, 1979, but this program was not widely used until the IRS

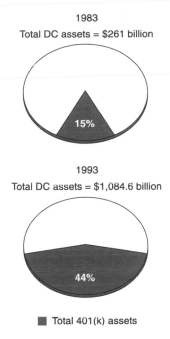

1983
Total DC assets = $261 billion

15%

1993
Total DC assets = $1,084.6 billion

44%

■ Total 401(k) assets

Figure 8.1.2   Ratio of 401(k) assets to defined contribution plan assets, 1983 and 1993

issued clarifying regulations in 1981. 401(k) plans are available only to employees of firms that offer such plans. Under this type of plan, participants can elect to defer part of their income on a pre-tax basis and have it held on their behalf in a trust until retirement. Taxes are also deferred until distribution. Because the saving is tax-favored, IRS rules restrict participant access to the funds. Elective deferrals may be withdrawn without penalty before age $59\frac{1}{2}$ only upon retirement, plan termination, separation from service, financial hardship, or disability. Otherwise, a 10 percent tax is imposed on lump-sum distributions paid to individuals before age $59\frac{1}{2}$ (in addition to income tax owed). The Tax Reform Act of 1986 (TRA-86) permits one-time election of five-year forward averaging for a lump-sum distribution received from a 401(k) plan after age $59\frac{1}{2}$.

Employers may contribute a matching percentage of employee contributions, make discretionary/profit-sharing contributions, or make no contributions at all. The TRA-86 set the employee deferral (or employee contribution) limit at $7,000 and indexed this limit for inflation in subsequent years. The contribution limit was $9,240 for the 1994 tax year. The TRA-86 also established new, tighter antidiscrimination requirements for 401(k) plans.

Much research has been done by Poterba, Venti, and Wise on the effect of 401(k) and IRA programs on household savings.[7] They concluded that contributions to both types of plans represent net additions to, and not substitutes for, other types of personal saving. This does not mean that IRAs and 401(k) plans are not used for personal saving, but they are generally used as vehicles for additional, targeted saving. In 1980, IRAs and 401(k)s accounted for less than 5 percent of targeted retirement saving, and employer-provided defined benefit pension plans accounted for 59 percent. By 1988, however, 401(k)s and IRAs accounted for 47 percent of retirement saving. Contributions to 401(k) plans eclipsed

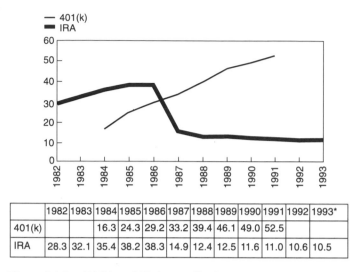

	1982	1983	1984	1985	1986	1987	1988	1989	1990	1991	1992	1993*
401(k)			16.3	24.3	29.2	33.2	39.4	46.1	49.0	52.5		
IRA	28.3	32.1	35.4	38.2	38.3	14.9	12.4	12.5	11.6	11.0	10.6	10.5

Figure 8.1.3 401(k) and IRA contributions, 1982 to 1993 (billions of dollars). Source: Department of Labor, IRS. 401(k) type plans (all plans with case or deferred arrangements which file the 5500 form). SEP contribution totals were included prior to 1987. *The IRA Reporter estimate.

contributions to IRAs as the leading form of tax-deferred individual retirement saving after the TRA-86 limited the tax benefits of IRAs for middle and high-income taxpayers. IRA contributions fell precipitously after 1986 and continued to decline through 1993, while contributions to 401(k) plans have continued their steady ascent reaching $52.5 billion in 1991. (See figure 8.1.3.) The research by Poterba, Venti, and Wise indicated 401(k) saving did not displace IRA saving, but IRA contributions were curtailed as a result of the 1986 tax reform. For many households, assets held through 401(k)s represent more than half of their financial wealth. The high participation rate for those eligible for 401(k)s, coupled with the tendency for most households to reach retirement age with few financial assets other than Social Security and employer-provided pension benefits, suggests that these accounts will play a very important part in the economic security of retirees in coming decades.

The rapid growth in defined contribution plans seems to have slowed recently, however, as the number of new DC plans increased by less than 2 percent between 1989 and 1991. While the number of 401(k) type plans continued to increase rapidly from 1989 to 1991, the rates of growth in 401(k) plan participants and assets were below the rates for all types of pension plans between 1990 and 1991. Much of the rapid growth in 401(k) plan participants and assets during the mid and late 1980s occurred among medium and large firms. During the 1990s, the expansion rate among the medium and large firms leveled off, indicating that a level of maturity, or potential for high growth, in the 401(k) market may have been reached for those segments.

In larger companies, 401(k) plans were often established by modifying an existing profit-sharing or thrift plan, presumably because 401(k)s provided more attractive opportunities for employees to defer taxable income. In most cases, these large companies offered a defined benefit plan as their primary retirement benefit, and the 401(k) was a supple-

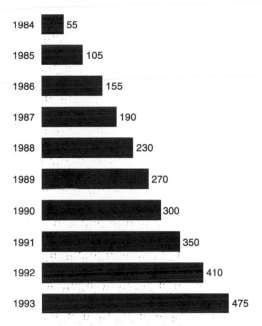

Figure 8.1.4 Total 401(k) plan assets, 1984 to 1993 (billions of dollars). Source: Access Research

mental plan.[8] Nearly two-thirds (64 percent) of plans with 1,000 or more participants are supplemental plans.

New 401(k) plan formation is still strong, although most activity is occurring among small companies. Almost half of the very small plans with fewer than 100 participants were installed since 1990. Smaller companies tend to use the 401(k) plan as the primary benefit for employees.

An estimated 210,000 corporations now sponsor 401(k) plans, with 18 million active participants out of 24 million eligible employees. The fact that these plans allow employees to defer income, to take advantage of employer-matching provisions where available, and to accumulate assets at the pre-tax rate of return are some of the factors that have made them the fastest-growing vehicle for retirement saving during the last decade. Assets have grown at a compound annual rate of 27 percent since 1984 to reach $475 billion in 1993 and are expected to grow by close to 15 percent per year to reach $1 trillion in 1999 (see figures 8.1.4 and 8.1.5). Growth in assets has slowed somewhat since 1990, not only because of a slowdown in investment returns but also because of high penetration among eligible employees, and the resulting slowdown in the growth of contributions among new participants. There is an overall participation rate of 75 percent, up from 62 percent in 1986. Participation is highly correlated with size in that it is lowest for very small plans (those with fewer than 100 participants) and highest among very large plans with 4,000 or more participants.

Adding to the prospect for further growth in 401(k) plans, as well as profit-sharing and other DC plans, are the new rules issued by the Department of Labor in October 1992. Under the ERISA Section 404(c), plan sponsors can achieve fiduciary relief, and therefore

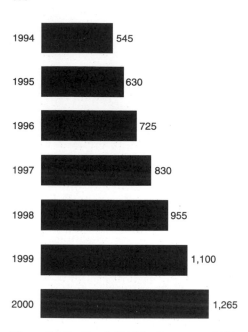

1994   545

1995   630

1996   725

1997   830

1998   955

1999   1,100

2000   1,265

Figure 8.1.5   Total 401(k) plan assets, 1994 to 2000 (billions of dollars). Source: Access Research

a measure of relief from liability in maintaining DC plans, by allowing participants to control the investment of assets in their 401(k) accounts. As long as the 404(c) regulations are satisfied, no fiduciary liability will arise for the plan sponsor by reason of the participants' investment decisions.[9]

Mutual Funds Become Active in 401(k) Market

The increasing use of 401(k) plans is shifting some of the burden of retirement planning from employer to worker. In this context, it's vital that workers contribute to their plans and thoughtfully select the investment choices for the money they set aside. Because employees take responsibility for investment decisions in many of these plans, it is important that they feel comfortable with their ability to access information about their investments. Participants want a full range of options under their individual account plans, the ability to transfer more frequently, and current and full information. Increasingly, plan sponsors have come to appreciate the advantages mutual funds can offer. They provide access to top professional portfolio managers, portfolio diversification, liquidity, portfolios managed according to a well-defined policy, well-documented track records, the diversified options necessary for compliance with ERISA Section 404(c), ease of administration, and the necessary recordkeeping and compliance-consulting services, and systems and procedures for communicating with, and educating, participants.

Mutual funds are particularly well-suited as investment vehicles for participant-directed defined contribution plans. For years mutual funds have been building a solid

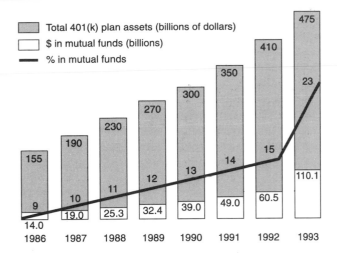

Figure 8.1.6   Trendline estimates of 401(k) plan assets invested in mutual funds

reputation and earning the trust of investors. They have developed the necessary technology (including 800 numbers) and shareholder communications to become very accessible to investors. Mutual fund complexes provide a range of investment alternatives and allow daily redemptions and purchases without restriction, often by telephone. In addition, fund companies have the refined marketing skills that are necessary for educating and communicating with participants.

As a result, demand by participants and plan sponsors for mutual fund options has increased substantially in the last several years. The amount of 401(k) assets invested in mutual funds and their share of the total market have grown steadily each year since 1986. In 1993, 401(k) assets invested in mutual funds jumped to over $110 billion, or 23 percent of the total 401(k) market. (See figure 8.1.6.)

This is an 80 percent increase over the $61 billion, and an 8 percentage point increase over the 15 percent of market share one year earlier. An investigation of major 401(k) market players revealed the steep increase in 401(k) assets invested in mutual funds in 1993 reflected not only greater marketing efforts by mutual fund companies, but also the conversion of some 401(k) separate accounts at insurance companies to institutional mutual funds, as well as some conversions of 401(k) commingled accounts at commercial banks to mutual funds.

The importance of the retirement market to the mutual fund industry is increasing and may even be the key to sustainable future growth in assets and earnings. As a result, the ownership structure of the industry and product demand have shifted a bit more toward retirement-oriented programs. Assets held in retail and institutional retirement accounts, of which 401(k) plans are a major segment, have grown to nearly one-third of total mutual fund assets. In 1993, 401(k) assets accounted for 5.3 percent of total mutual fund assets and 17.3 percent of all the retirement assets invested in mutual funds, up from 3.7 percent and 13.8 percent, respectively, the previous year. Cash flows[10] attributed to 401(k) plans also represented a substantial 15 percent of total industry cash flows in 1993. . . .

ERISA Section 404(c) Regulations

ERISA Section 404(c) provides that if participants exercise "control" over their plan assets, the plan sponsor will not be held liable for any losses incurred by the participant as a result of the participant's control of those assets. The Department of Labor in 1992 exercised its authority to issue regulations on the requirements plan sponsors must satisfy for participants to be deemed to have "control" over their plan assets. Compliance with the ERISA Section 404(c) regulations is optional, and failure to comply will not subject the plan sponsor to any adverse action by the Department of Labor or participants. However, fiduciaries of plans that do not comply will not be relieved from liability for the results of their participants' investment decisions. Section 404(c) regulation applies to virtually all participant-directed retirement plans established by employers for their employees, including 401(k) and profit-sharing plans. The regulations became effective for most plans beginning on January 1, 1994. State and local plans with grandfathered 401(k) plans are not subject to ERISA Title I and, hence, these regulations are not applicable to them.

To comply with the ERISA Section 404(c) regulations, plans must offer a diversity of investment vehicles and must permit changes in investments at least quarterly. At least three investment options with different risk/return characteristics must be offered by the plan. And, the retirement plan must offer diversification within and among such alternatives. Participants must also be given adequate information to make informed investment decisions. Even if plan sponsors comply with ERISA Section 404(c), they will continue to be responsible as ERISA fiduciaries for selecting and hereafter monitoring the investment vehicles that they offer to plan participants. And, of course, fiduciaries remain liable for losses that result from failure to carry out participants' investment instructions in a prudent manner.

Notes

1. Active participants of a pension plan are those who are currently contributing to the plan or have a positive balance in their account.
2. See U.S. Department of Labor, *Private Pension Plan Bulletin*, 1993 and 1994.
3. *Id.*
4. See Employee Benefit Research Institute, *Pensions in A Changing Economy* (1993).
5. See NBER, *Working Paper No. 4501*, L. Papke, M. Petersen, J. Poterba, *Do 401(k) Plans Replace Other Employer Provided Pensions?*, October 1993.
6. See U.S. Department of Labor, *Pension and Health Benefits of American Workers—New Findings*, from the April 1993 Current Population Survey, 1994.
7. See NBER, *Working Paper No. 4391*, J. Poterba, S. Venti, D. Wise, *Do 401(k) Contributions Crowd Out Other Personal Savings?*, June 1993.
8. Ibid., NBER *Working Paper No. 4501*, Papke, Petersen, Poterba.
9. An ERISA section 404(c) regulation was promulgated by the Department of Labor and became effective for most plans on January 1, 1994. The regulation's major provisions call for plan sponsors to offer employees at least three investments with wide-ranging risk and return characteristics, the opportunity to shift from one investment to another at least once every three months, and to give participants sufficient information to allow them to make informed investment decisions.
10. Cash flows or net flows = net sales plus net exchanges.

8.2   The State of the Defined Contribution—401(k) Market 1996*

Employees in all sectors of the U.S. work force share the need to establish nest eggs for retirement. However, the ability to offer innovative, cost-effective programs to augment existing defined benefit plans has been most pronounced in the corporate sector. Retirement options in the smaller public and the educational, or nonprofit markets are less advanced, but are quickly gaining ground. The demand-pull for name-brand mutual fund managers in the 403(b) and 457 markets and product features, sales, marketing, and service expectations usually associated with 401(k) plans are attracting new entrants.

Corporate Sector
Defined contribution plans most often associated with the corporate sector include profit-sharing plans, stock-bonus plans, money-purchase plans, and 401(k) plans. Established by the Employee Retirement Securities Act (ERISA) of 1974, a 401(k) plan is usually a profit sharing plan that includes a cash or deferred arrangement (CODA). Although synonymous with 401(k), the term CODA is rarely used anymore.

Strong indicators point to signs that the number of large 401(k) plans has matured and we anticipate that much of the growth in this marketplace will reside in the small- to mid-size plan segments. Figure 8.2.1 depicts 401(k) plan penetration by company size as of year-end 1995 and our projected estimates for the year 2000.

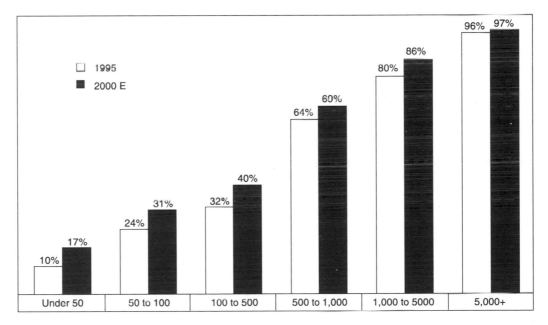

Figure 8.2.1   401(k) plan penetration by company size, 1995 and 2000 E. Source: Access Research, Cerulli Associates

---

* From *The Cerulli-Lipper Analytical Report*, pp. 17–19, 27–29, 111–118, 132–145.

While industry-wide demarcations vary, we define the small plan segment as plans having fewer than 200 lives (or $5 million in assets); the mid-size plan market as having between 200 and 1,000 lives (or $5 million to $25 million); the large plan market as having between 1,000 and 5,000 lives (or $25 million to $250 million); and the megaplan market as plans with over 5,000 lives (or more than $250 million).

Plan sponsors in virtually all market segments are becoming more sophisticated buyers, demanding higher quality, additional customization of services, and expanded investment offerings. This in turn requires an even greater investment in systems, technology, and human resources. Heavily entrenched full-service competitors like Fidelity Investments, The Vanguard Group, and State Street Bank & Trust (SSB&T) have exhibited a willingness to make such investments in order to protect established beachheads. These three firms manage approximately $246 billion or 31% of total 401(k) plan assets. We estimate that Fidelity currently commands roughly 15% of the 401(k) asset management market share, up from 10.5% in 1993. (See figure 8.2.2.) ...

Competition

Competition in the 401(k) market is intensifying. Within the context of a rapidly maturing marketplace, plans command more leverage than ever before. They are demanding higher quality, additional customized services, and expanded investment offerings. Providers who are unable to meet these requirements through additional investments in systems, technology, and human resources, are at a big competitive disadvantage.

The management of 401(k) plan assets is highly concentrated. The top 20 firms manage 77.2% of the 401(k) market's $800 billion in assets, while the top ten firms account for 55.8%. The top 20 firms are comprised of eleven investment companies (mutual fund companies, institutional money managers, and selected brokerage firms), six insurance companies, and three banks. (See table 8.2.1.)

Fidelity continues to be the dominant force in the 401(k) market managing roughly $120 billion as of year-end 1996. Total assets attributed to these plans were $106.6 billion at year-end 1995. The firm reportedly added more than 1,000 new plans in 1996, compared to approximately 900 new plans added in 1995. Roughly 100 of Fidelity's new plans in 1996 have assets exceeding $15 million. The remainder are smaller plans sold directly or through third-party intermediaries.

Fidelity's asset growth in 1996 reflects both new full-service business and fairly substantial alliance business, where the firm receives assets through formal arrangements with other full-service providers. Major new 401(k) clients include Shell Oil, United Technologies Corp., and Intel Corp. Shell Oil moved the administration, recordkeeping, trusteeship, and a significant proportion of its investment management for its $7 billion defined contribution plan to Fidelity as part of a total benefits administration outsourcing program.

Vanguard retains its position as the second-largest manager of 401(k) assets with approximately $68.3 billion, up from $53.3 billion in 1995. The firm plays up its reputation as a low-cost manager of mutual funds in the large plan marketplace and is generally perceived to be a higher-end service provider. While other major players in this segment of the market are developing institutionally-priced investment vehicles for more discerning plan

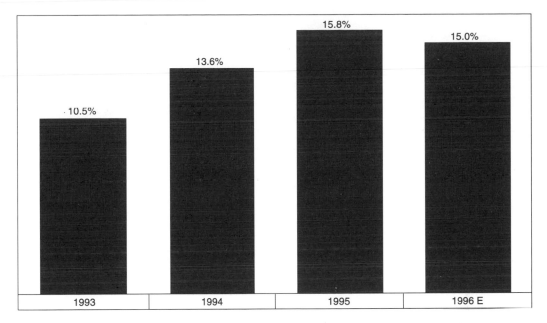

Figure 8.2.2 Fidelity's asset share of 401(k) market, 1993–1996 E. Source: *Pensions & Investments, CFO Magazine*, Cerulli Associates

sponsors, Vanguard has the luxury of supplying its widely popular (mostly indexed) mutual funds at little or no premium to separately managed accounts, commingled products, or institutional mutual funds. Unlike its two closest competitors (Fidelity and SSB&T), Vanguard has not made any moves into the area of Total Benefits Outsourcing.

SSB&T remains in third place with approximately $58.4 billion, an increase of $8.7 billion in 1996. Like Vanguard, SSB&T offers relatively low-cost investment management in the form of separate accounts, commingled trust products, and institutionally-priced mutual funds. The firm is successful in the megaplan market, playing off its master trust and custody relationships, and attractive indexed products managed by State Street Global Advisors. SSB&T is expanding its presence in the Total Benefits Outsourcing market through its joint venture relationship with Watson Wyatt Worldwide, now called Wellspring Resources.

One of the driving forces in the 401(k) market has been "branding" with the ultimate consumer—the plan participant. The old adage that a purchasing manager has never been fired for selecting IBM products is certainly relevant in the 401(k) market. Many plan sponsors gravitate to 401(k) offerings from companies like Fidelity, Vanguard, Merrill Lynch, and T. Rowe Price, because of the name recognition factor, which theoretically enhances employee participation.

Competition is forcing 401(k) providers to raise awareness at various levels of the sales process. While firms with significant retail recognition benefit from the inevitable spillover effect on corporate plan sponsors, investment consultants, and other intermediaries, all other credible players in the 401(k) market will need to dedicate substantial resources to branding initiatives. Industry trade publications such as *P&I*, *Institutional Investor*, and

Table 8.2.1

Top 20 leading 401(k) plan providers 1995 and 1996 ($ in millions)

Firm	Type of company	401(k) assets year-end 1995	401(k) assets year-end 1996
Fidelity Investments	Investment company	$106,600	$119,900
Vanguard Group	Investment company	$53,307	$68,300
State Street Global	Bank	$49,700	$58,400
Merrill Lynch	Investment company	$29,300*	$35,000*
Bankers Trust	Bank	$28,000	$33,000
Barclays Global Investors	Bank	$22,400	$32,800**
Prudential	Insurance company	$26,000	$27,000
UAM	Investment company	$14,000	$25,000
Principal Financial Group	Insurance company	$20,600	$24,500
T. Rowe Price	Investment company	$19,000	$22,500
CIGNA	Insurance company	$18,300	$22,000
Putnam Investments	Investment company	$12,000	$20,600
Aetna Retirement	Insurance company	$16,500	$20,000
MetLife	Insurance company	$18,200	$19,800
INVESCO	Investment company	$13,700	$18,000
American Century	Investment company	$11,900***	$16,300
Capital Research	Investment company	$11,000	$15,000
New York Life Insurance	Insurance company	$11,600	$13,500
American Express Institutional	Investment company	$10,500	$13,025
Dreyfus	Investment company	NA	$13,000
Top twenty total:		**$508,407**	**$617,625**
Other:		**$166,593**	**$182,375**
Total 401(k) assets:		**$675,000**	**$800,000**

* Includes outside funds
** Through November 1996
*** Includes assets of Twentieth Century Services and the Benham Group
Source: Cerulli Associates, *Pensions & Investments*

Plan Sponsor Magazine generally provide good access to corporate decision makers. However, this access is not cheap. Full page color advertisements in *P&I*, a biweekly publication, can cost as much as $15,000 per ad. . . .

Employee Education

Employee communications will come under extreme expense pressure as competition intensifies in the 401(k) market. Demands are being placed on vendors to deliver frequent, sophisticated employee communications as part of their standard programs—at no additional cost to either plan sponsor or participant. Companies looking to acquire additional

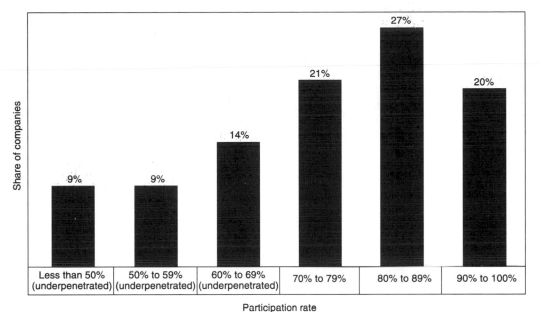

Figure 8.2.3 Employee participation rates in companies with 401(k) plans. Source: VIP Forum Research

market share must recognize the importance of the educational component in packages they design, particularly since it can serve to differentiate them from competing programs.

Nearly one-third of companies offering 401(k) plans have participation rates that are categorized as "under-penetrated," using a 70% rate as a benchmark measure. Approximately 20% of 401(k) plans have participation rates of 90% to 100%, while the greatest proportion of 401(k) plans have participation rates between 80% and 89%. (See figure 8.2.3.)

Improved educational initiatives should theoretically lead to greater participation rates and produce more profits for providers. A recent study by Buck Consultants reveals that employers who do not provide formal education programs for employees have an average participation rate of 77.5%, while those that do educate their employees have participation rates of 79.1%. (See figure 8.2.4.) While this minimal differential in participation rates is surprising, the profitability implications are compelling. A 401(k) provider who is able to increase participation rates by a relatively modest 1.6%, can expect to realize a 20-year net present value (NPV) advantage of $13,540 per participant. This equates to a $13.5 million 20-year NPV for a plan with 1,000 participants deferring 6% of salary on a consistent basis over time.

The trend towards more personalized, tailored communication materials has encouraged many plan sponsors and plan providers to use a wide variety of programs, including segmenting participants, mentoring, and unbundling provider services. Companies have enlisted the help of professional educators to improve the effectiveness of their communications.

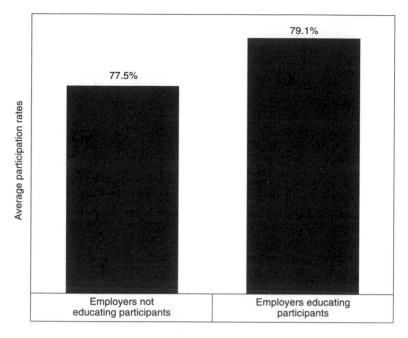

Figure 8.2.4   How employee education affects 401(k) participation 1995. Assumptions: 1,000 employees constant over time. Employees defer 6% of salary. Source: Buck Consultants, VIP Forum, Cerulli Associates

Segmenting participants is an important component of designing employee education. Increasingly, sponsors and plan providers use this technique to identify the specific educational needs of various groups of employees and address individual concerns. Plan sponsors typically target a variety of demographic data, such as age, earnings level, retirement goals, investment habits, and ethnicity. Segmentation is used to schedule enrollment meetings, participant focus groups, and to develop educational tools and other materials.

American Express takes segmentation to the extreme by classifying investors into 44 different demographic types from "East Coast" immigrants to "high-rise" renters. Although most participants fit into five or six categories, American Express claims its system allows it to identify each group's distinct behavioral characteristics. For example, "East Coast" immigrants respond best to video-based education because they are the second-highest renters of videos. American Express Institutional Services is also targeting the low savings rates of the Generation Xers through a pair of twenty-something cartoon characters reminiscent of "Beavis and Butthead" who discuss retirement investing. Putnam Investments targets younger participants by using sitcoms from the 60s and 70s to represent different stages of life. Plan sponsor Bell Communication Research's approach to segmenting investor behavior is to place greater emphasis on education for participants who are not investing properly. Bell seeks participants under 40 who are invested in cash, and those between 40 and 65 who have more than half of their plan assets in cash. Mellon's Dreyfus uses a consumer psychologist to gauge attitudes toward investing among participants in order to design its education strategy.

Scudder applies its segmentation approach to comprehensive 401(k) education through a program called Scudder University. Scudder's "curriculum" ranges from basic to advanced concepts and structures a series of ongoing workshops based on an evaluation of each company's specific educational needs. Some companies receive only a few days of programs each year, while others schedule classes for up to two weeks of training. In addition to standard "train-the-trainer" programs, Scudder's classes include "Pre-Retirement Workshop," "Introduction to International Investing," and "Leaving Your Job?"

Scudder separates employees into three categories: spenders, savers, and investors, and then targets each group using a number of interactive multimedia tools and workshops geared toward general plan awareness and the need to save for retirement. In the case of spenders, the multimedia tools and workshops focus on the need for long-term investing. Savers use Scudder's Retirement Plan Optimizer to help them learn to maximize their investment potential. Sophisticated investors can avail themselves of Retirement Blueprint, an interactive software package that allows participants to generate any conceivable "what if" scenario.

Scudder is also following another trend of staffing professional educators and human resource specialists. Six of Scudder's ten educational specialists have extensive training backgrounds in education and adult learning theory. Reliastar, the Minneapolis-based insurance, benefits, and investment services organization, took a similar tact by acquiring Successful Money Management Seminars (SMMS), which uses a professional training staff to provide retirement seminars for over 2,000 employers. Reliastar intends to leverage SMMS to help them deliver their services and provide more customized seminars for employers.

A growing number of plan sponsors and providers are developing plan mentors. This approach is based on the assumption that participants are intimidated by larger seminars and are more likely to respond to the experiences of their co-workers. Employees serving as mentors receive training in the fundamentals of retirement investing and are strategically placed within an organization to serve as resources throughout the workday.

Ingersoll-Rand Co., a New Jersey-based manufacturer, trained 120 employees, or nearly 1% of its 17,000 participants, to act as mentors to provide training seminars and educate their peers. Scudder University also incorporates a mentor program. Scudder selects employees, known as plan advocates, from various segments of a company based on their level of interest and ability to communicate. Scudder then trains them on the specific intricacies of their retirement plan.

Most large plan providers offer software packages to assist participants in determining their retirement needs. Fidelity Financial Planner (FFP) is an innovative comprehensive retirement and financial software package, that is developed jointly by Intuit Inc., the makers of Quicken, the leading financial planning software. In addition to the standard array of retirement planning and hypothetical tools, FFP encourages participants to import financial information from Quicken to create a personalized financial plan. FFP also provides employees with access to personal 401(k) information online and supports alternative planning for college or a second home. The software's cost to employees in $40. Although FFP is targeted to retail sales, sponsors can obtain volume discounts for employees.

Frank Russell offers its participants a low-tech, advice-oriented program. The paper-based LifePoints program provides participants with information on investing for retirement, helps them formulate a retirement plan, and guides them to a set of investments to match their needs. The program revolves around a fold-out "map" that participants use to pinpoint a stage in their life that involves retirement. The LifePoints program provides sponsors with customizable employee education kits, slide presentations for employee meetings, newsletters, and quarterly statement stuffers.

A number of providers now offer to unbundle their services by pricing employee education as a standalone service. CIGNA offers its 401(k) sponsors specialized financial education services from Price Waterhouse. A plan sponsor can use a program called Personal Financial Analysis which provides them with a more detailed view of a participant's financial situation. The information is gathered from a questionnaire and includes an individual's assets and liabilities, insurance needs, education-financing needs, and estate planning requirements. Customer service specialists are available at Price Waterhouse to answer participants' questions. The Savings Plan Report, offered in conjunction with CIGNA, as plan provider, and Price Waterhouse, analyzes 401(k) plan participants' savings rates and investment patterns and compares them to retirement income goals. It takes into account such non-401(k) income sources as social security and other retirement means. Analysis is based on data supplied by the individual's company and CIGNA. The cost to plan sponsors to use these programs is $10 to $250 per participant depending on the cost of the setup, number of participants, and degree of customization.

J.P. Morgan also provides an unbundled communication and education program to capitalize on its position as a top money manager. J.P. Morgan provides educational services to a select group of higher-end clients that consists of collateral materials and access to its investment communication desk which is staffed by trained personnel.

Advice and Guidance

Personal financial planning services in the 401(k) market appear under many guises. In the most common form, questionnaires qualify investors for specific asset-class allocations. After qualifying a participant based on risk and time horizon, a model portfolio of funds emerges. The plan participant does not relinquish discretionary control of the assets. Fees for these services are typically paid for by the plan participants, but plan sponsors pick up the tab in some cases.

FundQuest, a Boston-based retirement planning and asset allocation consulting firm, recently launched its employee education tool for 401(k) plan participants. The Personal Retirement Analysis (PRA) program is offered to participants through 401(k) plan providers as an independent service. The program uses software for asset allocation, savings projections, and retirement income gap analyses based on participants' specific goals and risk tolerance. Plan providers that adopt the PRA program pay FundQuest a fee for the service on a per-participant basis.

Detroit-based Pulte Home Corp., the nation's second-largest home builder, recently enlisted the services of Acumen Financial Inc. to provide each participant with a personal financial report. The report was customized using the employee's age, salary, current 401(k) contribution level, and investment strategy. The report determines what amount an employee needs to retire and identifies any shortfalls given the employee's current savings pattern. A survey of Pulte's plan participants found that 77% of respondents did not understand their retirement needs until the financial report qualified them. The reports are produced for a one-time setup fee of $10,000 and an additional $6 per report.

U.S. West Inc. offers its employees a similar service, analyzing employees' current retirement accounts through Bankers Trust. Bankers Trust has created a package that includes a wide variety of educational materials and three alternative portfolios based on three funds (conservative, aggressive, and moderate) offered by U.S. West. The sponsor avoided liability issues by not providing any recommendations on specific allocations.

One major mutual fund wrap program has worked its way into the qualified plan market. Smith Barney, again a trendsetter, was one of the first firms to actively promote personalized asset allocation services for its 401(k) participants, a segment of the qualified plan market for which stringent fiduciary liability issues such as ERISA apply. To receive approval from the Department of Labor, the firm had to commit to certain provisions, including a revised fee-structure that eliminated financial incentives for Smith Barney for recommending proprietary funds. An estimated 33% of Smith Barney's new assets in its consulting services division originated from non-IRA qualified plans.

Ayco Co., an Albany, NY-based financial advisor, offers a mix of employer and employee paid educational and financial planning services. Ayco's services vary by sponsor and combine telephone and focus group investment seminars. The program uses a participant questionnaire to generate recommendations for specific funds and allocations.

The Scarborough Group, Inc., a money manager in Annapolis, MD, has taken a more aggressive position by monitoring and making all discretionary allocation decisions for participants' retirement accounts. Scarborough requires all participants to sign disclaimers removing their employer from liability associated with poor performance. The annual program fee is $325, which is paid by the participant. Scarborough manages 401(k) assets for employees of companies such as General Motors, AT&T, Bell Atlantic, and U.S. West.

Financial advisors are responding to 401(k) participants' need for guidance by establishing networks of financial planners to offer advice. Many sponsors' use of financial advisors originates from personal financial relationships that have been established with top executives.

Boston-based Financial Answers Network (FAN) has assembled a network of certified financial planners (CFPs) and is marketing to defined contribution plan sponsors and providers. FAN works with sponsors to assist plan participants with their retirement contributions and asset allocation for one low cost. They offer unlimited financial guidance via telephone, newsletters, and reports through sponsors at an average annual cost of $5 per participant. Participants can meet with their CFP in person for an extra $25 per year.

FAN indemnifies sponsors and assumes liability for the investment advice offered by the CFPs in the network to address the DOL's guidelines prohibiting plan sponsors from providing investment advice. All financial advisors in the FAN network are registered investment advisors with a minimum of three years experience.

Data Translations, a Marlboro, MA-based plan sponsor allows employees to sign up for a three-month financial planning program with a CFP. The program consists of one face-to-face meeting and unlimited telephone conversations. Participants can choose from a list of several thousand CFPs. Data Translation's plan participants pay $18 a month for the service, but they are considering providing the service at no cost.

The 401(k) Forum provides specific asset allocation advice to plan participants through a customized Web page for each plan sponsor client, rather than face-to-face meetings. Participants who sign onto the Web page complete a risk-tolerance questionnaire that is then scored by a computer model, which recommends an optimum asset allocation. An education module is also available.

The 401(k) Forum is only offered through plan sponsors. The cost is between $9.99 and $19.99 per participant for unlimited online access, depending on the size of the plan and the number of participants. Two plan sponsors will beta test the new program by the end of Q2 1997. The Web page model does not currently offer participants online transaction capabilities allowing them to change either their portfolios or future contribution allocations. However, the two companies testing the system do offer employees a direct connection to the recordkeeping system where changes can be made via an internal computer network. Plans to help participants with advice on portfolio rebalancing are being considered for the future.

In December 1996, Mead Corporation announced that the 13,000 employees in its $400 million 401(k) plan will be given access to commission-based financial planners in late 1997. Although full details of the program are not yet available, Mead intends to use financial planners who agree to sell only 401(k)-related investments to employees who are participants in the 401(k) plan and who contribute an appropriate amount. The financial planning program will be implemented after Mead's total benefits administrator, Fidelity, develops an all-encompassing benefits statement for its employees.

Duke University contracted with Smith Barney in 1996 to make advice and guidance services available to its 403(b) plan participants. Duke has offered traditional investment education for years, but found that it was not enough. To set up the financial planning program, Smith Barney first evaluated all 200 funds offered by Duke and separated them into specific asset classes based on style analysis. After participants complete investor profile questionnaires, Smith Barney analyzes the results and makes specific recommendations. This service also includes ongoing telephone advice and monitoring, as well as an annual update to show employees how to rebalance their funds at year-end. . . .

Legal and Regulatory Update

Last year (1996) marked a relatively quiet year for generating pension legislation. Lack of national attention or urgency about retirement plan reform left both parties dealing with stalled initiatives that never made it out of their respective committees. Democrats were frustrated in their attempts to advance their "Families First" agenda which included measures to improve pension coverage, portability, and protection. Republicans were rebuffed in their attempt to repeal the 50% tax on corporate reversions for terminated defined benefit plans.

The two most prominent issues were discussions of social security reform and the need to provide pension relief to smaller companies, which culminated in the passage of the Small Business Job Protection Act of 1996. Additional perspective on these two significant events as well as some discussion on revenue-sharing practices relating to defined contribution plans follows.

Social Security Reform
In Washington, the retirement plan subject receiving the most attention is reform of the social security system. Once only whispered about by academics and economists, the

debate on social security reform was propelled into the national spotlight by unsubstantiated and often reckless discussions of the system's impending insolvency. These discussions, coupled with the government's inability to effectively communicate the issues to the general public have undermined the public's overall confidence in the system. In a recent study, The Employee Benefits Research Institute found that 79% of current workers lacked confidence in the ability of social security to maintain benefit levels comparable to those of today.

The need for a social security system overhaul to offset projected deficits is indisputable. The first baby boomers will reach retirement age in 2011. The social security trust now has assets in excess of $550 billion and that surplus is expected to grow to $2.8 trillion by the year 2018. At that point, however, the assets will shrink as the payouts to retirees begin to exceed payments into the system. Left unchecked, the trust fund will be depleted and revenues will cover only three-fourths of the cost of benefits.

Proposals to reform the system are as diverse and numerous. Some legislators claim that they could eliminate the projected deficit by simply adjusting the cost of living increase to current recipients. Others propose a far more aggressive approach, such as creating a 401(k)-type program to invest payroll contributions. One issue prevalent in most proposals is the need to invest at least a portion of the trust fund assets in the stock market. Currently, trust fund assets invest in long-term government securities and yield a real return of 2.3%. Proponents of the move to equity products contend that even if a small portion of the fund invests in stocks, which have historically yielded a rate of return of 7%, the deficit would easily be eliminated.

Arguably, the body of work with the most potential to influence policy is the Advisory Council on Social Security study of the system. The Council, convened by President Clinton, surprised many by unanimously recommending investing some social security taxes in stocks as a means to increase investment returns. The study maintains that private investment is crucial to the long-term solvency of the social security program as well as the national savings rate, and economic growth.

Recommendations most relevant to defined contribution plans are the proposals to create a self-directed account similar to the current 401(k) structure. In this proposal, individuals could direct a portion of their payroll tax into a personal savings account and invest the money in a vehicle of their choice. The purpose of the program is to address the potential demand by individuals for higher returns and greater control over their retirement savings.

The possibility of a social security asset inflow into the stock market is dramatic. Projected cash flows into the market vary from $1.2 trillion to $4.2 trillion by the year 2015. As expected, money managers, banks, and insurance companies are lobbying heavily for the move to equity products. Based on an average advisory fee of 0.50%, annual revenues to the investment management industry could range from $6 billion to $21 billion by the year 2015.

Specific company responses differ. American Express, American International Group, Alex Brown, and Quick & Reilly funded a study on social security privatization conducted by the Cato Group. SSB&T chairman Marshall Carter has written a book calling for wide-scale implementation of personal social security accounts among other reforms.

Impact of Savings Incentive Match Plan for Employees (SIMPLE) Legislation

Motivated by election-year politics and the desire to notch at least some retirement-based legislative progress, the president and Congress agreed on a bipartisan measure offering employers at small firms access to streamlined 401(k) plans. The program as structured is unlikely to contribute to greater penetration in the small plan segment. The Savings Incentive Match Plan for Employees or SIMPLE was signed into law in late August 1995 as part of the minimum wage bill. SIMPLE is designed to provide a low-cost, easy-to-administer retirement plan for any firm with 100 or fewer employees that does not have an existing tax-qualified pension plan. Eligible companies may elect either a SIMPLE IRA or SIMPLE 401(k). The new legislation took effect on January 1, 1997 and also applies to tax-exempt entities.

SIMPLE 401(k) offers distinct advantages over traditional 401(k) plans. It has few reporting requirements and offers greater flexibility than SARSEPs, but without the administrative burden of traditional 401(k) plans. A big draw for employers is the elimination of discrimination testing and top-heavy requirements that formerly limited contributions by highly compensated personnel.

The number of small businesses offering retirement plans is limited and industry excitement over the prospects of serving this untapped segment with low-cost 401(k)-type benefits is waning. Critics argue that SIMPLE's lower costs and greater flexibility are overshadowed by onerous employer contribution provisions. Firms must make mandatory employee contributions up to 3% as a trade-off for simplifying administration. Other differences reducing SIMPLE's appeal among small plan sponsors are 100% immediate vesting, a high 25% premature distribution penalty, a low participant deferral amount of $6,000 (compared to $9,500 for non-SIMPLE 401(k), SEPs, and SARSEPs), and mandatory conversion to a traditional 401(k) plan once a company grows beyond 100 employees.

The key to the SIMPLE plans' success and adoption will be whether organizations serving as trustees, such as mutual fund companies, banks, insurance companies, and brokerage firms are able to aggressively market them to small businesses. Initial response from the financial services industry appears to be tepid, especially for SIMPLE 401(k)s. The major mutual fund companies are much more excited about the prospects for simplified IRA plans, which benefit many companies with fewer than 50 employees who feel stuck in "retirement limbo."

The SIMPLE IRA plan lets small company employers establish Individual Retirement Accounts for each employee. The SIMPLE IRA provides all the benefits of a SIMPLE 401(k), but gives plan sponsors greater flexibility. Employers must match all participant contributions, but for rank-and-file employees this amount is likely to be less than the 3% mandatory minimum contribution that the SIMPLE 401(k) plan requires. Fidelity, T. Rowe Price, and MFS plan to introduce SIMPLE IRA plans. Advisors and pension consultants are leery of SIMPLE legislation and question the profitability of such plans, particularly SIMPLE 401(k) plans which require that an administrator or benefits consultant still has to review plan documents.

Fidelity recently launched a SIMPLE IRA featuring a variety of investment options (including a self-directed brokerage option for more sophisticated investors) and a dedicated customer service team for plan sponsors. The Fidelity SIMPLE IRA mutual fund package offers a select list of ten Fidelity no-load funds, including the recently introduced Fidelity Freedom Funds, which are funds-of-funds. Small business owners who choose the

Fidelity SIMPLE IRA brokerage option have access to Fidelity mutual funds as well as funds available through its FundsNetwork program. Additionally, participants can invest in individual stocks and bonds, CDs, and U.S. Treasuries.

Fidelity is also holding seminars to educate small business owners who are confused about retirement choices. The efforts are a response to a survey that revealed a low level of employer awareness regarding new SIMPLE legislation. The one hour seminars are held at Fidelity branch offices and led by retirement coordinators. The average attendance is 40 small business owners per seminar.

8.3   Emergence and Growth of Fund IRA Market [1980s Perspective]*

1   IRAs Helped the Fund Industry Growth in the 1980s

IRAs have broadened the market of funds and contributed to the growth the industry has experienced during the 1980s. Fund IRA assets have become a larger percentage of total fund assets for each year since 1982 when the retirement program was liberalized. Today [1987], fund IRA assets account for nine percent of total fund assets.

Substantial gains also occurred in the number of fund IRA accounts. At the end of 1981, for example, fund IRA accounts were slightly less than three percent of total fund accounts, whereas in April of 1987, they represented close to one-third of all accounts. IRA accounts grew at a faster rate than assets because shareholders are limited in the amount they may invest in their IRAs each year, but not in the number of accounts that they can own.

Like the fund industry in general, fund IRA assets and accounts have greatly benefited from the "bull" market of the 1980s. Historically high returns in both the stock and bond markets attracted investors who previously owned depository CDs, savings accounts, and MMDAs. Many of these investors are highly risk averse but because they know their IRAs will be invested for a longer period, they are more willing to tolerate short-term market fluctuations. Meanwhile, other, more experienced fund investors contributed to the industry's growth by opening additional accounts for their fund IRAs.

2   Funds Are Now a Major "Force" in the IRA Market

The success of mutual funds in attracting investors' IRAs is best seen in terms of market shares. In April of 1987, mutual fund IRAs accounted for $72.1 billion or 22.6 percent of all IRA assets. This represents more than a doubling of market share since the IRA program was liberalized in 1982.

The rise of mutual funds to the position of major "force" in the IRA arena brings with it certain market changes. Other financial institutions such as banks, thrifts, and insurance companies now recognize and directly compete against the fund industry. Part of the reason behind these institutions' new-found awareness of funds as competitors is the success of fund IRAs. This success has in part, been at the expense of depository and other competing institutions, and it has shown them that funds can adapt quickly to changing market conditions.

---

*From Investment Company Institute, "Mutual Fund Shareholders: Fund IRA Owners—A Market in Transition," Winter 1987–1988, pp. 4–12, 22. Reprinted with permission.

Gains in market share provide the industry with an opportunity to establish a base of "relationship customers," that is, shareholders who maintain more than one account. As shareholders who are relatively new to funds become more familiar with them through their IRA experiences, many may go on to purchase additional funds. Also, once a fund IRA is established, most investors will add money to it in subsequent years and many will hold onto their fund investment until retirement.

3 IRAs Introduce Many Investors to Mutual Funds

The growing popularity of IRAs has introduced many investors to mutual funds. One-half of all current fund IRA owners purchased their first fund since 1980, while only one-third of those shareholders who do not own fund IRAs purchased their first fund during the same period. An even larger difference exists for the first few years when the IRA program was liberalized—the 1980 to 1982 time period. For these years, the proportion of fund IRA owners who were first-time fund purchasers is almost twice the proportion of first-time fund purchasers who do not have fund IRAs. Many first-time fund purchasers during this period may have been attracted by high money market fund yields.

The IRA program has also helped to expand sales to investors who already owned funds or had owned them previously. The other half of the fund IRA population purchased their first fund sometime prior to 1980. These shareholders may have already owned a fund and bought another for their IRA, or they may have owned a fund previously and redeemed their shares, only to have recently purchased a fund IRA.

Shareholders who purchased their first fund prior to 1980 are more likely not to own fund IRAs. Sixty-two percent of this group of shareholders don't have a fund IRA. This is because many of these shareholders are older and retired, and no longer eligible for the IRA program.

4 Over One-Half of All Current Shareholders Own Fund IRAs

Mutual funds are a popular IRA vehicle for current fund shareholders. Fifty-four percent of all shareholders own fund IRAs. The remaining forty-five percent do not own a fund IRA. Those who do not may have an IRA in another type of financial product or they may not own any IRAs.

An earlier survey on IRA ownership conducted by the Institute in 1984 identified the main reasons why people generally do not own IRAs—whether they are fund IRAs or otherwise. Many of these reasons are applicable to fund shareholders. The two main reasons given in this earlier survey were: money to invest in an IRA was not available and savings could not be tied up until retirement.

Some of the less frequently given reasons for not owing IRAs included: other savings objectives, not eligible, and/or not interested. These responses, as well as those mentioned above, suggest that there may be certain demographic and life-cycle factors that affect a person's decision to own an IRA. Later sections of this report look specifically at the demographics of fund IRA owners in an effort to identify these factors.

5   Shareholders' Fund IRAs Are a Sizable Part of Their Total Fund Assets

Shareholders who own fund IRAs are off to a good start investing for their retirements. The survey found that these shareholders have over $12,000 in their fund IRAs as of the fall of 1986. This represents, in aggregate terms, almost one-third of these shareholders' household median fund assets and about eleven percent of their total financial assets.

Shareholders owning fund IRAs have a larger percentage of their total household financial assets invested in mutual funds—37.3 percent as compared to 32.7 percent—than do all fund shareholders. This is because they have more invested in fund IRAs and also have less household financial assets than the shareholder population in general. These trends are consistent with the demographic make-up of fund IRA owners. Specifically, fund IRA owners are in their capital formation years and many are still saving for retirement using their fund IRAs. . . .

6   Services Desired by Fund IRA Owners Reflect "Active" Investors

The services selected as important by fund IRA owners suggest that these shareholders are "active, hands-on" investors. The largest proportion of fund IRA owners identified telephone exchange privileges and the "family of funds" features as important when considering a mutual fund investment. These services along with fund IRA owners' next two most frequent choices—toll-free telephone service and mail exchange privileges—are mainly used by shareholders to reallocate fund assets and expedite transactions.

The notion that fund IRA owners are "active" investors who want investment flexibility is consistent with other survey data. Earlier findings showed that fund IRA owners more often purchase their funds without the assistance of salespersons. They do so primarily because they feel they are able to research and make their own investment decisions. Fund IRA owners are more likely to choose their own funds and also make their own redemption and exchange decisions.

Shareholders who do not own fund IRAs choose much different services as important. These shareholders-selected services that are more concerned with convenience when making fund purchases and redemptions, rather than those services designed for investment flexibility in different market climates. The market implications of these findings are important to consider. Fund IRA assets and accounts may not be entirely stable. Even though fund IRA dollars are long-term investments, shareholders may move their assets to other funds or even non-fund products in response to changing market cycles. It is clear, however, that many fund IRA owners would confine their moves—most likely for the sake of convenience—within a family of funds.

8.4 An Avalanche of New IRAs?*

Howard Gleckman with Jeffrey M. Laderman

For banks, mutual funds, and stockbrokers, 1998 promises to be the Year of the IRA. After spending a decade lobbying for a broad expansion of tax-advantaged individual retirement accounts, Wall Street now hopes to reap the benefits.

Some investment pros expect the tax law signed by President Clinton on Aug. 5 to boost annual IRA contributions fivefold to nearly $50 billion. Investment houses are about to inundate taxpayers with marketing designed to sing the praises of the new accounts. Merrill Lynch & Co. has already taken out big newspaper ads promoting the new bill. There's certainly a huge, untapped market out there: In 1985, before participation was curbed, 16 million taxpayers invested in the accounts. These days, barely 4 million do.

But the new law's complexity will make marketing tough. It expands existing accounts and creates two new ones, each with different tax advantages and eligibility rules. "We're challenged on how to cut through the clutter," says Douglas E. Harrison, T. Rowe Price Associates' marketing manager for individual retirement products.

The Roth IRA would let investors avoid taxes on earnings in the account but would not provide tax deductions for contributions that existing IRAs enjoy. That could be a more lucrative benefit for those patient enough to wait. Merrill Vice-Chairman John L. Steffens says marketing themes will center on: "Do you want a tax deduction now or an even bigger tax deduction in retirement, when you might need it most?"

While funds and discount brokers may have trouble communicating the complexity to their customers, full-service brokers see it as a marketing opportunity. Steffens calls IRAs "a terrific starter product" for attracting young investors.

Tax Windfall

Despite brokers' dreams, some experts think IRAs may have a surprisingly small payoff—for Wall Street and the economy. Skeptics warn that much of the money expected to pour into IRAs will merely be shifted from existing taxable accounts. There is some debate over the issue, but that helps explain what happened during 1982–86, when IRAs were quite popular, but the personal savings rate plummeted from 8% to 4%, where it has stayed.

If such shifting reoccurs, the result will be a tax windfall for savers but little new business for investment firms and a small boost in new savings available for investment.

How much new money will flow into IRAs is anyone's guess. But Wall Street—which lives by the axiom that investments are sold and not bought—is drooling at the opportunity to find out.

Class Exercise: **Designing an Investment Array and Communications Strategy**

As you now are aware, the employer-sponsor of a 401(k) plan has the legal obligation to design an appropriate array of investment choices for plan participants. If that array is properly designed and participants are provided with adequate information about the available choices, the employer-sponsor obtains the protection of a regulatory safe harbor from ERISA liability for the investment choices of plan participants.

In designing an appropriate array of investment alternatives for a 401(k) plan, the employer-sponsor should take into account the characteristics of its workforce. These include the age and sophistication of its employees as well as their attitudes toward investing: employees may be insecure, comfortable, or confident investors. In addition, to qualify for the protection of the regulatory safe harbor, an array must include a relatively "safe" choice such as a money market fund, a bank deposit, or a managed income portfolio.

The following reading provides strategies for successful participant investing, and the exercise puts you in the position of a consultant to four employers, each the sponsor of a 401(k) plan. Your job is to assess the investment alternatives offered by the plan and the actual choices made by plan participants, with a view to making recommendations for improvements. Each of the four companies has a different profile of employees.

In-Class Discussion Questions

After reviewing the following reading and the data provided for each company, you should be prepared to answer the following questions on each of the company plans:

1. How would you describe the participants in this company's plan in terms of their level of comfort with investment concepts and investment decision making?
2. Does the plan's current set of investment choices offer enough investment diversification to meet the needs of the plan participants? If so, why; if not, why not?
3. What changes, if any, would you recommend the company make in the menu of investment choices the plan offers to its participants?
4. What communication strategy would you recommend the company follow?

8.5 Keys to Employee Investing Success

Focusing on the Investor, Not the Investments

Every day defined contribution plan participants make investment decisions that will affect their income in retirement. Some make these decisions easily; others are less confident that they are making appropriate choices. By understanding that there are different types of investors with varying concerns, plan sponsors have an opportunity to provide employees with suitable investments—ones that improve the likelihood of being utilized effectively by participants.

This paper outlines strategies for successful participant investing, based on Benefits' many years of experience and research. It presents information about:

- how participants invest and the different types of investors (insecure, comfortable, confident);
- the importance of investment diversification and the difference it can make to the participant;
- the investment options that match investor levels of sophistication; and
- what plan sponsors need to consider in evaluating their plan's investment structure.

Our objective is to help plan sponsors simplify investment decision-making for employees by understanding how participants think, and by developing appropriate investment menus and well-thought-out communications programs.

Participants Matter Most

Defined contribution plans put the burden of making investment decisions entirely on the plan participants. But many participants have difficulty understanding investing. This may be because we often try to turn employees into *experts* who should be able to develop diversified portfolios, rather than *educating* them about investments that match their levels of comfort and understanding.

Benefits' customer service philosophy is based on the premise that "*participants matter most.*" This means that we work with plan sponsors to:

- understand how employees think about investing;
- evaluate the investment mix of their plans;
- evaluate their plans and decide if their investment options are simple and straightforward so that participants can understand them;
- develop communications programs that target different employee groups from the least confident investors to the most confident investors; and

- achieve desired participation levels, asset allocation and investment diversification results.

The cornerstone of these efforts should be an effective plan design that simplifies and demystifies investment decision-making for participants and effectively guides them to proper investment allocation and diversification.

The rest of this paper will address:

- how plan sponsors can determine the most optimal investment plan design;
- some sample investment structures; and
- how plan sponsors can achieve more of their objectives through a well designed, targeted communications campaign.

How Do Participants Invest?

In the early years of 401(k) plans, the emphasis was on participation—how to motivate the maximum number of employees to enroll. In recent years many plans have achieved high levels of participation and sponsors have turned their attention to ensuring their plans offer enough variety of investments and to helping participants achieve effective asset allocation and diversification. Over the long term, a properly allocated and diversified portfolio has tended to return more than one that is too heavily weighted in fixed-income securities, or company stock, with less risk to principal and inflation protection.

With the uncertain future of Social Security, defined contribution plans become a more significant portion of employees' nest eggs; plan sponsors recognize the need to help their participants make the most of their investment opportunities.

Benefits' research and experience with a diverse group of plan sponsors and participants have taught us:

- One can identify distinct groups of employees who think differently about investing and will respond to different investment messages.
- Well diversified investment options can be "packaged" and presented in a way designed to appeal to these distinct groups.
- Successful communications campaigns can be built around extensive investment menus. In several cases, investments were packaged, targeted to the needs of distinct groups, and accompanied by a communications campaign that delivered the right messages. The campaigns resulted in increased participation and improved asset allocation among participants.

The Importance of Diversification

Driven by a combination of management initiated effort to improve defined contribution plans and increasing employee bottom-up requests for a wider array and range of investment options, the average number of choices offered by Benefits, Inc. clients is now 9, compared to 3 or 4 five years ago. Indeed, many large companies offer 150 or more options. A big question, however, is whether these additional options are being used properly.

What is diversification, what is proper diversification, and why worry about it? Diversification in the investment context is the combination into a single portfolio of several types of investments with sufficiently different characteristics so that they normally behave differently in any particular investment environment. (They may also behave differently over time through varying environments.) The purpose of diversification is to reduce the risk inherent in any one type of investment or of multiple, but closely related investments. Risk in this context is the risk of a temporary decline of the investment's value or outright loss of value. More often than not, diversification is thought of in connection with protection against loss. But investment risk includes as well the loss of opportunity to offset the negative effects of inflation, as well as the opportunity for higher investment returns over time than many single types of investments can produce. Therefore, diversification can also be used to enhance opportunity for the future within acceptable bounds of risk of loss.

Table 8.5.1 illustrates the effect and potential benefits of asset class diversification over time. It shows the historical returns of a mix of stock and bond mutual funds as the percentage invested in growth mutual funds increases. Note that higher equity investment would have produced higher returns for all time periods shown, albeit with likely higher risk.

Many plan participants have long periods, say fifteen to twenty-five years, of employment still ahead. With an average current plan balance of $31,000, a return of 9.1% over 20 years, assuming no further contributions, amounts to $177,000, achieved through fixed-income funds with presumably low risk. On the other hand, a much more aggressive portfolio that is 75% in growth funds and only 25% in fixed-income returned 13.4% over the same period. Here the $31,000 grows to $383,000, an enormous difference. (Of course a portfolio that was 100% in growth funds would have resulted in an even greater amount of money.) The higher volatility of a 75/25 mix may be too great for many investors, but certainly not for all. Most participants should probably be somewhere in between.

Table 8.5.1
Longer time

	% Investment		Average annual percentage total return period ending 12/31/96*					
	Growth Funds avg.*	Fixed-income Funds avg.*	1 Year	5 Years	10 Years	15 Years	20 Years	25 Years
Higher equity investment/ higher risk	0	100	15.2	9.6	8.8	9.3	9.1	8.6
	25	75	19.1	11.2	9.9	10.2	10.2	9.5
	50	50	23.5	12.8	10.9	11.1	12.0	9.8
	75	25	27.7	14.4	12.0	11.7	13.4	10.9
↓	100	0	30.8	16.0	13.0	12.8	14.8	11.6

* Based on Lipper Analytical Services, Inc. Fixed-Income Funds and Growth Fund averages. Lipper is a nationally recognized mutual fund performance analysis firm. The Growth Funds average covers over 700 mutual funds with a growth objective. The Fixed-Income Funds average includes over 1500 funds. *Past performance is no guarantee of future results.* The table does not represent actual or future performance of any particular investment.

The difficulty, of course, is that there is no such thing as a one-size-fits-all diversification concept for defined contribution plan investors because every investor is uniquely different than every other investor. In the defined benefit retirement world, the employee does not play a role in investment decision making. He or she is only a potential beneficiary, not an investor, and all retirees can expect to receive a financial benefit based on a uniform formula that is the same for everyone. In the defined contribution world, however, without guarantees or formulas, the investor is everything and each individual's financial base in retirement is almost entirely dependent on the investment decisions and actions he or she made years earlier.

If some plan participants accumulate substantial assets, retiring comfortably due to good investment decisions, while others end their careers with little or nothing for opposite reasons, the company has no legal responsibility in either case. Having satisfied the responsibility to provide enough good quality investment tools so that virtually any employee can maximize opportunity with an appropriate level of downside risk, most plan sponsors believe the company also has a responsibility, to the greatest extent possible, to help employees understand how to use the available options. Given that all defined contribution plan options in a company are available to all employees, from the least to the most sophisticated, and the most to the least risk averse, plan sponsors have no easy task.

Numerous quantitative methodologies adopted from pension fund management practice are available and can be helpful. However, we believe such tools don't effectively work to help certain groups of participants select the particular investment options that are best for them from within the range of choices offered by the plan.

Participants Are Not All Alike

Recent client research by Benefits, Inc. shows that plan participants may be usefully grouped into three major segments based on their attitudes toward, and sophistication with, investment concepts. Plan sponsors should consider positioning options to relate to the needs of each segment.

Insecure Investors—40% of Participants

Insecure investors usually compose the largest single participant group. These individuals describe themselves as "beginner" investors. They express a lack of confidence and understanding in matters related to investing and doubt their ability to accumulate enough assets to retire. Their lack of confidence has pushed them into relatively "safe" investment choices such as money market, fixed-income, and managed income options. They tend to be the least well diversified. Some avoid participating in a 401(k) plan altogether because of their lack of confidence.

Options for Insecure Investors

Insecure investors need simple, easily understood choices that will not overwhelm them. The goal is to help them gain the potential benefits of a more balanced investment program.

The investment menu might include "ready-mix" options that provide appropriate asset allocation within a single fund. Several "ready-mix" options could be offered, each targeted to investors with a defined risk level and/or time horizon....

Comfortable Investors—28% of Participants

Almost three in ten respondents from the Benefits research say they are comfortable with their current investment/planning situation. These people make asset allocation decisions based on a sense of well-being about their financial security. They understand investing basics and the major types of investments. They believe they are saving enough money to retire and have not done a financial plan. However, many are risk averse and often not adequately diversified. This group often desires a limited selection of diversified individual fund choices and may be receptive to asset allocation offerings.

Options for Comfortable Investors
Investors in this group like to choose from an array of "mix-your-own" options. These are sometimes referred to as "core" options. Core options may include a broad spectrum of choice—from money market funds to aggressive equity funds. A "mix-your-own" or "core" menu might look as shown in figure 8.5.1.

Confident Investors—32% of Participants

One in three respondents provide a very confident investment self-profile. These people are willing to take risks when necessary. They are confident they know how to select investment options that meet their goals and consider themselves more investors than savers. Confident investors are not intimidated by a wide variety of investment choices, or even a self-directed brokerage option.

Options for Confident Investors
These investors may find the "ready-mix" or "core" options limiting. Core options may include a few broadly diversified funds that, together, constitute a broadly diversified portfolio—for example, fixed-income, growth and income, growth, and diversified international.

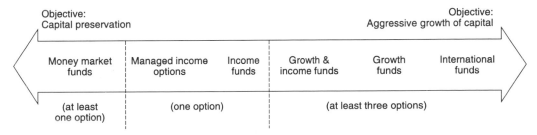

Figure 8.5.1 A "mix-your-own" or "core" menu investment objective spectrum

Table 8.5.2

Ready-mix options	Core options	Extended window options
Asset allocation Ready-mix funds	Money market fund Stable value option Bond fund Growth & income fund Growth fund Aggressive growth fund International fund	All or a subset of mutual funds All or a subset of FundsNet funds Brokeragelink

For their more sophisticated investors, plan sponsors should consider a third tier of expanded options. These are sometimes referred to as "window" or "extended" options, because they provide participants with a wide choice of investments beyond the core. Window options may include specialty funds that invest in certain market sectors, like small-cap companies, or in particular types of stocks like real estate or utilities. Funds could also include specialized international funds such as emerging markets, country, and region funds. . . .

Plan Investment Structure

The key to diversification and investment success is to be sure a portfolio consists of conservative, moderate, and aggressive investment options that are appropriate for each investor profile. A comprehensive plan, offering adequate opportunities for diversification for all participants could be structured as in table 8.5.2.

How Many Options?

Conventional wisdom suggests that plans offer a certain number of investments to participants. At Benefits, Inc., we prefer an alternative approach—one that focuses on the investors, not the investments. This means that:

- Employees define their investment style.
- Plan sponsors provide investments that can meet every employee's needs.
- A comprehensive communications program assists employees with their selection of suitable diversified investment options.

. . .

Conclusion

There are many different types of investors in defined contribution plans, with varying concerns and anxieties. If plan participants are going to be successful investors, they have to be confident in their investment decisions. To this end, we need to work with plan sponsors to provide a menu of options that meets every participant's investment need—

from the least sophisticated to the most sophisticated. In addition, we have to develop communications programs directed at various employee populations. With expanded investment options and targeted communications programs, we should be able to help investors make sound investment decisions which can help to give them the security they need for retirement.

8.6   Benefits Consulting to 401(k) Plans

The Situation

Benefits, Inc., is a global management consulting firm that is highly regarded for creativity and innovation in the areas of retirement plan design, benefits administration, and human resources. Benefits is known for its commitment to superior client service and has enjoyed tremendous growth over the last decade. In particular, Benefits has seen a huge rise in demand for consulting services related to corporate retirement plans.

In recent years, many U.S. companies have shifted from defined benefit retirement plans to defined contribution plans, which are increasingly in the form of 401(k) plans. From the employer's perspective, an important aspect of a 401(k) plan is the "safe harbor" provision in the Department of Labor's 404(c) Regulation, which limits the liability of plan sponsors offering an investment menu to participants in defined contribution plans. If the plan provides a "diversified array" of reputable investment alternatives and adequate information about investment choices, the plan sponsor will generally be protected from liability for specific investment alternatives chosen by plan participants.

Typically, plan participants allocated a disproportionate amount of their contributions to "safe" alternatives such as money market funds and managed income portfolios. Benefits, Inc., advises participants to invest the majority of their contributions in equity alternatives early in their working lives, and to shift away from equities as they approach retirement.

Set forth below is the "optimal" equity allocation (includes stock and balanced funds and company stock) recommended by Benefits, Inc.

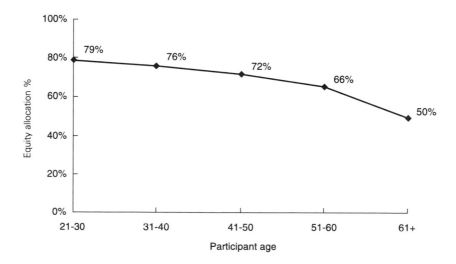

As part of their consulting services, Benefits often aids companies in establishing, administering, and educating employees about 401(k) plans. Currently, four plan sponsors have hired Benefits to evaluate and to make recommendations about improving their plans, with focus on investment alternatives and education campaigns.

Company no. 1:   Cosmetics, Etc.

Cosmetics, Etc., is a well-known fashion accessories manufacturer. Its employees are located mostly in five primary manufacturing sites in the south, with sales staff scattered across the United States. It has about 3,000 employees.

Cosmetics, Etc. senior managers' overall goal is to increase their plan's diversification, and they are considering several changes including plan design, fund options, and communications strategy.

The profile of Cosmetics, Etc.'s employees:

- 25% manufacturing, 30% sales/marketing, 45% administration
- Average age 40, sales and marketing employees are younger
- Heavy managed income/money market investment orientation
- Most in 2–3 funds, with very small nonmanaged income balances
- Some language issues among manufacturing staff
- Relatively low salaries

Cosmetics, Etc.'s current plan investment menu includes four options, and requires that the company match be automatically invested in the Managed Income Portfolio. This requirement has resulted in a plan where 64% of plan assets are in money market and managed income, with the remaining 36% split between the equity fund choices (see figure 8.6.1).

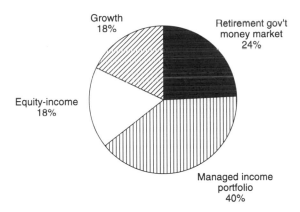

Figure 8.6.1   Plan investment options and percentage allocation

Company no. 2:   Financial Services, Inc.

Financial Services, Inc. is a financial services provider headquartered on the East Coast. It has five urban offices, with fifty small sites across the country. It has about 3,600 employees.

The plan sponsor's goal is to increase diversification, increase participation, and increase employee awareness and appreciation of the plan through better basic investment education. It particularly wants to target clerical workers, whom may be most in need of investment education.

The profile of Financial Services, Inc.'s employees:

• Majority of employees are clerical, with salary under $15,000, high school educated
• Small percent of highly compensated employees with salaries over $100,000 and post-graduate education
• Plan participation rate is 63%, with 67% of plan participants under the age of 40, 44% between ages 31 and 40
• 31% of participants have 1–2 funds, with no significant differences in investment choices by age
• Average assets per participant: $22,406

Financial Services, Inc. faces some unique challenges in its retirement savings plan. Its current plan investment menu includes eight options, but despite an attractive matching contribution (dollar for dollar up to 6% of salary), and a commitment from the company to promote the 401(k) plan, participation lags at about 63%. About 2/3 of its employees are under the age of 40, and these people are not significantly more aggressively invested than their older colleagues. Allocations for the various plan options are shown in figure 8.6.2.

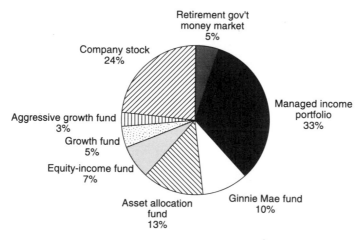

Figure 8.6.2

Company no. 3: Health Insurance, Inc.

Health Insurance, Inc. is a diversified Midwestern company that operates finance, insurance, and real estate businesses. The company has about 5,600 employees located throughout the midwestern states.

The plan sponsor's goal is to increase diversification of the plan assets. Its most important target is the female 30 to 40 year old clerical workers who make up a significant portion of the plan's participants. Health Insurance, Inc. feels that by reinforcing basic investment concepts to this core group the company can significantly improve its plan's asset allocation.

Health Insurance, Inc.'s employee profile:

*   Predominantly female, 30–40 years old
*   Clerical workers
*   Mostly high school educated, some college
*   75% participation rate

The current plan investment menu includes five options, with the allocation percentage shown in figure 8.6.3.

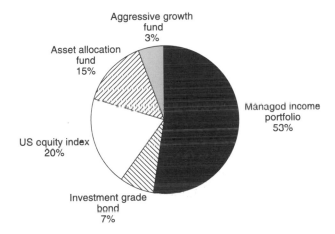

Figure 8.6.3

Company no. 4:   Smith & Jones

Smith & Jones is one of America's largest accounting firms, with 16,700 active participants in its plan. Smith & Jones is headquartered in the mid-Atlantic states and has multiple domestic and international offices.

The plan sponsor's goals are to increase employees' investment and retirement planning knowledge so that employees will be appropriately invested. The challenge is to reach the firm's well-educated employees, who are uninformed investors and who have little time available for investment education.

The profile of Smith & Jone's employees:

*   Generally well-educated population, but not investment sophisticated
*   15% administrative staff
*   Average age of employee: 33; 67% of employees between 21–40 years old

Their current plan investment menu includes nine options and has the percentage allocations shown in figure 8.6.4.

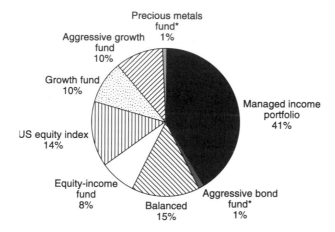

Figure 8.6.4   *Frozen to new contributions.

9   Servicing Fund Shareholders

Introduction

This is the third and final chapter on marketing mutual funds. We have already discussed selling mutual funds through broker-dealers, direct marketing, and fund marketplaces. We have also discussed marketing funds to participants in retirement plans and providing services to such participants. In this chapter, we will focus on providing services to fund shareholders outside of the retirement plan context.

Servicing of fund shareholders is a complex subject involving a number of definitional issues. First, servicing of shareholders is often intertwined with selling to fund shareholders. A customer who calls to check on his or her fund holdings may proceed to discuss buying another fund. Similarly, a broker-dealer may send material announcing a new fund in the same envelope as a customer's quarterly account statement. In this chapter, we will focus primarily on servicing customers after they have decided to buy fund shares; these servicing functions are primarily performed by the fund's transfer agent.

Second, servicing of fund shareholders is quite different in the broker-dealer context than in the direct marketing environment. In the broker-dealer context, the customer is connected to a named representative who is primarily responsible for providing services to the customer. By contrast, in the direct marketing context, the customer is serviced primarily by a relatively anonymous phalanx of telephone representatives and electronic systems. In this chapter, we will discuss the range of services offered by mutual fund complexes, including both broker-dealer and direct marketing organizations.

Third, servicing of fund shareholders is very different for retail investors as compared to institutional investors. While this introduction will focus primarily on retail investors, it is useful to outline the special servicing needs of institutional investors in mutual funds. Corporate treasurers, banks, and other institutions investing for their own account, or for fiduciary accounts, use specially designed money market funds for cash management. Such funds typically require a very high minimum account size (e.g., $100,000 or even $1,000,000) and charge relatively low expenses (e.g., 20 bp). For institutional shareholders in these funds, the critical servicing issue involves getting their monies invested and earning interest on the same day they are sent by wire to the fund's transfer agent. In addition, institutional shareholders of any type sometimes are investing in mutual funds on behalf of multiple beneficiaries, so these institutions want assistance from fund sponsors in maintaining sub-account records.

Having reviewed these definitional issues, we will look at servicing fund shareholders in chronological order, beginning immediately after a customer decides on a particular fund. The initial step is to fill out an application to become a fund shareholder. The fund's transfer agent or distributor provides the customer with the application in person, by mail, or via the Internet. When the fund's transfer agent receives the completed application, it establishes a computer file with the customer's name, address, phone number, and social security number as well as new shareholder account number. Now the customer is ready to purchase fund shares.

The transfer agent effects the purchase of fund shares by processing either the customer's payment for the shares (usually by check or wire) or an exchange between the customer's old fund and new fund choice. When a customer purchases a fund by check, the checks are typically sent for clearance to a collecting bank. The bank works closely with the fund's transfer agent, which computes how many shares are to be purchased from which fund. The challenge is to make sure that the fund actually has the cash available to invest promptly after the customer acquires the fund shares. When a customer effects a purchase by exchanging shares from an existing fund to a new one, the process is a little easier. The exchange typically is processed during an overnight cycle following the customer's call, and cash is transferred from one fund's account to the other's account early the next day.

The flip side of a fund purchase is a fund redemption. Most fund redemptions involve an exchange out of one fund into another—for example, from a stock fund into a money market fund against which checks may be written. A fund redemption may also involve a request for payment by check or wire, which is done by the transfer agency through a bank. The ability of a fund shareholder to redeem daily is one of the key distinguishing characteristics of a mutual fund from other financial products (e.g., bank CDs or insurance policies). Although a mutual fund may close to new purchases, it is required always to redeem shares at one daily price—usually as of 4 P.M. Eastern Time (ET). This requirement has profound implications for how mutual funds are run—a few of which are explored in the case study for this chapter. Because of this redemption requirement, mutual funds must invest most of their assets in liquid securities, which must be priced each day.

Another core servicing function is providing fund customers with information about their accounts and about their funds. When a customer purchases or redeems fund shares, the fund sponsor must send him or her a confirmation of that transaction. On a quarterly or monthly basis, each shareholder receives an account statement reflecting the status of his or her position in the fund. Most fund sponsors have made these account statements user friendly by consolidating all of the customer's positions in the fund complex. In January or February each year, the customer receives a summary of the prior year's transactions for tax purposes. This tax statement includes a breakdown of all fund distributions into taxable and tax-exempt income, and the various types of capital gain. In most of the large complexes, this tax statement also provides the average cost basis for fund shares redeemed during the prior year.

On a daily basis, mutual funds must compute their net asset values (NAVs) and disseminate them to fund shareholders. As a practical matter, this means pricing every fund in the complex at 4 P.M. ET prices in time to send these prices by 5:40 P.M. ET to the National Association of Securities Dealers (NASD) for its feeds to the newspapers. If a fund misses this deadline, it reports no NAV in the next day's newspaper (although it may generate a NAV in time for fund purchases and redemptions to be processed overnight during the nightly cycle). Every six months, each fund publishes: a report containing all its holdings, financial statements, and a performance report. These annual and semiannual reports also include a discussion of investment results, often in the form of an interview with the portfolio manager explaining why the fund has done well or poorly over the period. Approximately once a year, a fund shareholder receives an updated prospectus for any fund he or she holds. Every few years, a fund shareholder receives a proxy statement to vote on the election of fund directors or possibly a change in the fund's investment policies or fees.

Furthermore, most direct-marketed fund complexes send out periodic newsletters and magazines to their fund customers. These periodicals contain articles about subjects of interest such as changes in tax laws, new investment trends, and the introduction of new products or services. Similarly, fund sponsors selling through brokers and other financial intermediaries provide them with informational material (in addition to the annual and semiannual report as well as the updated prospectus) on the performance of the funds, trends in investing, and descriptions of new products or services. This material is passed along to fund shareholders by the broker or other financial intermediary.

Probably the most challenging servicing function is handling customer inquiries. These inquiries cover such a broad range of subjects—for example, estate taxes, address changes, and foreign stock prices—that it would be virtually impossible for any one representative to know enough. For this reason, fund complexes have established specialized service teams to deal with products requiring extra training, and have built computerized work stations so that representatives can call up answers to many questions. The most difficult inquiries involve customer complaints. The issues can range from errors on tax statements to misunderstandings about fund objectives to disputes about customer transactions. Most fund complexes have come to understand that efficient resolution of customer complaints is a key to customer satisfaction.

All these services are provided to fund shareholders by the fund's transfer agent, a company registered as such with the Securities and Exchange Commission (SEC). Many of the large fund managers have their own internal transfer agents in order to control as closely as possible the delivery and quality of shareholder services. Smaller and medium-size fund managers often hire third-party transfer agents (e.g., BFDS), because such managers cannot, or do not want to, make the large capital expenditures necessary to support shareholder servicing facilities. Such third-party vendors generally provide a standard menu of services less expensively than internal transfer agents, but the latter are more useful in making customer service a distinguishing competitive advantage. As explained in chapter 12, the fund industry has invested heavily in technology to handle the large volume of shareholder transactions, calls, and other services. These technologies include systems for call routing, workstations for telephone representatives, and Web sites for fund sponsors.

Transfer agents deliver services to fund shareholders pursuant to a contract negotiated with the fund's independent directors. They are involved because the cost of transfer agency services is a fund expense, part of the fund's total expense ratio, though usually much lower than the fund's advisory fees. There are many different pricing structures for transfer agency contracts: annual charges for each account, fees for each shareholder transaction, fees on asset size of account, and combinations of the above. Annual account charges are administratively simple, but do not reflect the volume of shareholder transactions. Although transaction fees reflect this volume, they are difficult to administer. Fees based on account size employ this measure as a proxy for service usage. Most servicing fees are charged to the fund and paid out of its assets as part of its expense ratio, although fees for special services (e.g., wire transfers or historical transcripts) may be charged directly to the shareholder making use of the service.

The fund's independent directors will also review the quality of services delivered by the transfer agent in connection with negotiating a service contract. While it is difficult to gauge accurately the quality of services delivered, it is possible to survey both objective and subjective measures of customer satisfaction. For example, fund complexes may compile statistics on the average number of seconds to answer a customer call or the accuracy of customer account statements. Independent firms may ask fund customers to rate specific components of service as well as overall satisfaction.

The readings for these chapters survey the types of pricing schedules and levels of fees employed by mutual funds. The readings also address a few of the quality issues regarding customer service in the fund industry. The case study involves "hot money," where a few shareholders create significant servicing costs and pricing issues for a fund investing primarily in Japanese stocks.

Questions

In reviewing the materials in this chapter, please keep in mind the following questions:

1. Why would a fund sponsor ever close a mutual fund? If a sponsor announces that a mutual fund is "closed," may existing shareholders still redeem their shares?
2. How can a fund sponsor value all of the fund's securities as of 4 P.M. ET in time to send in the fund's NAV by 5:40 P.M. ET? What happens if the fund's NAV in the newspaper is off by one penny per share?
3. What are the pros and cons of a transfer agent pricing structure based on the number of customer accounts? The number of shareholder transactions? The asset size of the account?
4. Should individual shareholders, rather than the fund, be charged for checkwriting, wire transfers, and exchanges? Should small accounts be charged higher transfer agent fees (in basis point terms) than large accounts?
5. What are the advantages and disadvantages of an internal versus external transfer agent? How should the fund's independent directors choose between the two?
6. How should the fund directors evaluate the quality of services provided by the transfer agent? Do you think customer satisfaction on a service survey would be influenced by fund performance?
7. When would you need the most staff for customer servicing (in terms of hours during the day and months during the year)? How would you address the potential customer service needs in anticipation of a sharp market correction (such as the market correction in October of 1987 or in October of 1997)?

9.1 Executive Summary from "The Service Quality Challenge: Understanding Shareholder Expectations"*

1. Overall, responding shareholders feel that mutual fund companies provide better service than other financial industries. Responding shareholders also think that fund companies are superior in providing high-quality investments. Banks are formidable competitors in many service areas, such as convenience and completing transactions in a timely manner. Table 9.1.1 shows that mutual fund companies are top-rated on a number of factors, including providing investments with high returns, innovative investments, and investments for retirement.

2. Although service quality is not key to attracting new customers to a fund company, it is a critical component of customer retention that has bottom-line implications. Figure 9.1.1 shows that individuals rating a fund company's customer service as either excellent or very good are more likely to increase their investments in that company than are customers rating service as either fair or poor. All other things being equal, mutual fund companies

Table 9.1.1

Type of company rated "best" on specific service and investment attributes**

Mutual fund companies	Banks	Brokerage firms
Understanding customer needs	Completing transactions accurately	Providing financial advice
Providing high returns on investments	Completing transactions in a timely manner	
Providing investments for retirement	Having courteous employees	
Providing innovative financial products and services	Providing convenient access to services	
Providing needed products and services	Providing safety and security for savings	
Helping customers with money management	Having the best reputation for service	
Providing the best investment value		

** Respondents' evaluations are based on their experience with, or perception of, each service provider and are not necessarily related to the purchase of mutual funds.

---

*From Investment Company Institute, "The Service Quality Challenge: Understanding Shareholder Expectations," Autumn 1994. Reprinted with permission.

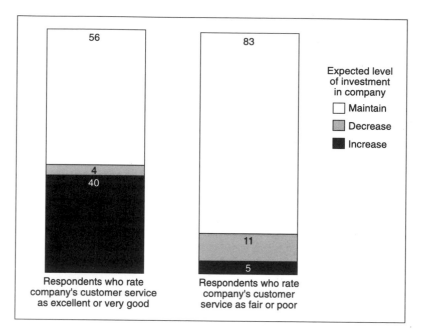

Figure 9.1.1 Relationship between respondents' assessment of customer satisfaction and their expected investment activity (percent of respondents). Note: For six months following survey

that invest in improving customer service should experience an increase in shareholder referrals and investments.

3. Of all fund-owning households contacted for this study, nearly half called or wrote to a mutual fund company for service in the 12 months preceding the survey. Respondents who contacted a company for service tend to be the types of shareholders that fund companies strive the hardest to retain. Table 9.1.2 shows that, when compared with all respondents, those who had a recent service contact own more funds and have greater assets invested in funds. Moreover, most respondents who had service contact typically own funds from several fund companies, making it easy for them to transfer their assets from one company to another. Hence, mutual fund companies should treat each shareholder service contact, whether by phone or by mail, as an opportunity to demonstrate superior customer service.

4. A relationship exists between shareholders' tenure with a fund company and their assessment of that company. Figure 9.1.2 shows that the longer respondents have owned funds with a company, the more favorable their evaluations of that company. By providing superior service during their contacts with shareholders, mutual fund companies can increase the likelihood that shareholders will continue to invest with them. One consequence of a highly tenured shareholder base should be improved company quality ratings.

5. It is important to shareholders that mutual fund companies handle their transactions and requests accurately, have knowledgeable employees, take responsibility for resolving problems, and make it easy to conduct transactions. Although fund companies are per-

Table 9.1.2
Respondents who had service contact compared with all respondents

	All respondents	Respondents who had service contact*
Median household financial assets**	$77,000	$105,000
Median assets invested in mutual funds	$25,000	$41,000
Average number of funds owned	3.5	6.1
Percent owning funds from more than one fund company	47%	72%

* In 12 months preceding survey.
** Excludes primary residence and assets in employer-sponsored pension plans.
Note: Respondent bases vary.

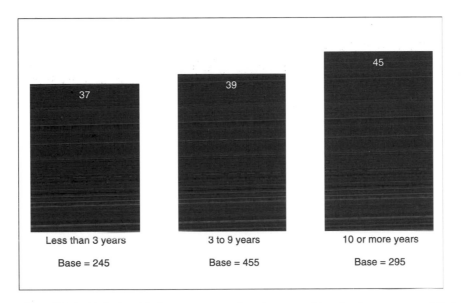

Figure 9.1.2 Relationship between respondents' tenure with a fund company and their evaluation of that company (percent of respondents rating fund company as an excellent one with which to do business)

forming well in these four areas, when measured against the ideal service relationship, both direct market and sales force companies do not meet respondents' expectations. Direct market and sales force fund companies do meet respondents' expectations in several other areas (see table 9.1.3).

6. Mutual fund companies' use of technology is well-ahead of respondents' preferences, indicating that investments in this area may be company-driven, not customer-driven. The most noticeable example where technology exceeds respondents' preferences is in fund companies' use of automated telephone systems. Very few respondents use automated systems to conduct transactions or to request information. Most prefer to conduct their

Table 9.1.3
Service areas meeting respondents' expectations

Direct market companies	Sales force companies
Handling transactions and requests in a timely manner	Making use of technology to facilitate access to services
Providing financial advice	Providing a variety of funds
Providing printed material and forms that are clear and easy to understand	

Note: Respondent bases vary.

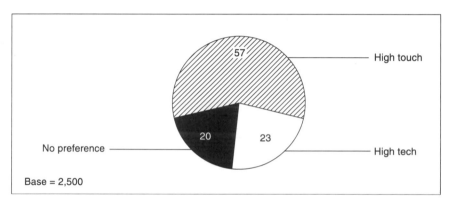

Figure 9.1.3 Classification of respondents according to their telephone service preferences (percent of respondents)

business with a telephone representative. Figure 9.1.3 shows that when respondents are classified according to their telephone preferences, most are "High Touch," not "High Tech." . . .

7. Mutual fund companies need to make shareholder communications, particularly prospectuses and annual reports, more "user friendly" for shareholders. Figure 9.1.4 shows that just over one quarter of respondents find prospectuses easy to understand, and only about two in five can easily understand annual reports. In contrast, two-thirds have no difficulty understanding account statements. The usefulness and format of prospectuses and annual reports are especially important to respondents, and both areas present fund companies with improvement opportunities.

8. Thirty percent of respondents contacted a telephone representative in the 12 months preceding the survey. When speaking with a telephone representative, respondents want to be treated as valued customers and have matters explained to them simply. Because telephone representatives already are doing an outstanding job on these and other aspects of personal telephone service, the opportunities to improve the quality of their service are relatively small. The two areas that offer the most room for improvement are completing shareholder requests during the initial phone call and eliminating the need to put shareholders on hold.

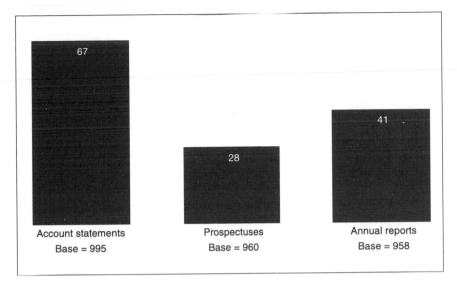

Figure 9.1.4 Respondents who strongly agree that account statements, prospectuses, and annual reports are easy to understand (percent of respondents)

9. In the 12 months preceding the survey, only 14 percent of respondents used an automated telephone system to conduct a transaction or to request information. For these respondents, ease of use and speed are the most important elements of an automated telephone system. While automated systems are meeting these needs, most respondents prefer to talk directly with a telephone representative. Hence, accommodating respondents' preferences by providing them with the option of a direct line to a representative may have a greater affect on fund companies' customer service quality ratings than marginal improvements to an automated system.

10. About three in ten respondents contacted a mutual fund company by mail in the 12 months preceding the survey. These respondents want their requests to be completed correctly the first time and want confirmation notices sent promptly. Mutual fund companies are meeting respondents' needs in these areas and should continue to focus on the accuracy and timeliness of handling service by mail. Respondents also would like fund companies to respond to their written requests by phone. For example, fund companies could respond by telephone to written letters of complaint. Because Securities and Exchange Commission (SEC) regulations require mutual fund companies to provide written confirmation of transactions, also calling to confirm transactions may not be cost effective.

11. Six percent of all respondents had a problem with a fund company in the 12 months preceding the survey. Although this is a small percentage, problem handling represents a critical component of service quality and is an area in which mutual fund companies could improve. Figure 9.1.5 shows that problem handling is the area where fewest respondents rate service quality as either excellent or very good. When problems occur, respondents feel that it is of primary importance that their mutual fund companies inform them of any delays in resolving problems. Respondents also want any correspondence relating to their

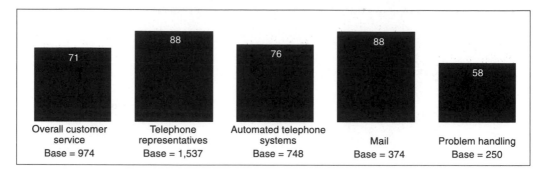

Figure 9.1.5 Quality ratings for key service areas (percent of respondents rating area as either excellent or very good)

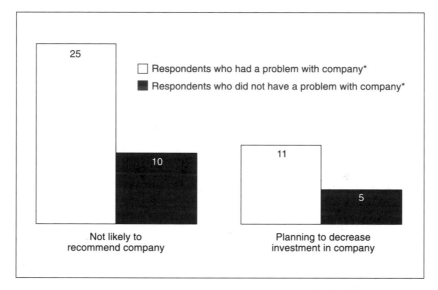

Figure 9.1.6 The impact of problems on a fund company's bottom line (percent of respondents). *In 12 months preceding survey. Note: Respondent bases vary

problems to be sent promptly, and, if at all possible, they want problems resolved immediately. To improve their problem handling, mutual fund companies should focus on resolving problems immediately and informing shareholders when that is not possible.

12.   Similar to customer service in general, shareholders with problems can have a significant effect on a fund company's bottom line. Figure 9.1.6 shows that, when compared with respondents who did not have a problem, those having a problem are much more likely to say they plan to decrease their investments in that company and are less likely to recommend that company to others.

13.   Problems are more likely to affect shareholders who are especially valuable to the mutual fund company—those who own multiple funds and who have significant mutual

Table 9.1.4

Respondents who had a problem with a fund company compared with all respondents*

	All respondents	Had problem with fund company
Median household financial assets**	$77,000	$143,000
Median assets invested in mutual funds	$25,000	$57,000
Average number of funds owned	3.5	8.5
Percent owning funds from more than one fund company	47%	81%

* In 12 months preceding survey.
** Excludes primary residence and assets in employer-sponsored pension plans.
Note: Respondent bases vary.

fund assets. Respondents with $250,000 or more invested in funds were three times more likely to have had a problem than were those who have less than $20,000 invested in funds. Similarly, respondents with more than ten funds were more likely to have experienced a problem than were customers who own less than ten funds. Table 9.1.4 compares the key characteristics of respondents who experienced a problem to all respondents.

9.2   Perceptions of Mutual Fund Company Service*

Respondents most frequently selected mutual fund companies as the best provider of service over banks, insurance companies, credit card companies, and brokerage companies. Nevertheless, banks are highly competitive, having been rated best on specific service dimensions, such as convenience and knowledgeable employees. Respondents describe their "ideal" mutual fund company as one that handles transactions and requests accurately. Although respondents rate direct market and sales force companies highly on this attribute, when measured against the ideal service relationship, fund company performance does not meet customer expectations.

A Comparison with Other Financial Services Providers

Respondents were asked to indicate which types of companies—mutual fund companies, banks, insurance companies, credit card companies, or brokerage companies—provide the best overall service. Figure 9.2.1 shows that the largest proportion of respondents, 40 percent, cite mutual fund companies as providing the best overall service. In contrast, only 27 percent mention banks and 21 percent mention brokerage companies. Only a few respondents point to credit card companies or insurance companies—7 percent and 6 percent, respectively.

In addition to selecting the type of financial services company that provides the best overall service, responding shareholders were asked to select one of the five company types

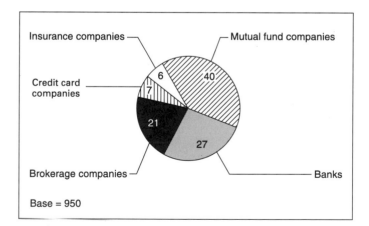

Figure 9.2.1   Best overall service provider (percent of respondents)

---

*Investment Company Institute, Chapter 1 of "The Service Quality Challenge: Understanding Shareholder Expectations." Reprinted with permission.

as the best at meeting 14 specific service and investment needs. With one exception, either banks or mutual fund companies are considered to be the best at meeting these 14 customer service and investment needs. For example, respondents rate mutual fund companies best at providing investments with high returns, investments for retirement, and the most investment value. Mutual fund companies are also considered best at providing innovative products and services and helping investors manage their money, although brokerages rate a close second on these two items.

Along with providing safety and security for savings, banks are rated best on factors that are more service-related than investment-related. For example, banks are rated best at providing convenient access to services, completing transactions in a timely manner, and having courteous employees. Banks and mutual fund companies are closely rated on their reputation for service and on completing transactions accurately.

Not unexpectedly, the largest proportion of respondents, 44 percent, rate brokerage firms as the best at providing financial advice. Mutual fund companies rank a close second —more than a third of respondents say that mutual fund companies are best at providing financial advice. Table 9.2.1 provides a comparison of the ratings of mutual fund companies, banks, brokerages, credit card companies, and insurance companies for all factors.

The Mutual Fund Company as a Company with Which to Do Business

Shareholders who participated in the study were asked to evaluate one mutual fund company with which they own funds on a variety of factors. For respondents owning funds from more than one fund company, the company was randomly selected. Respondents were classified as either evaluating a direct market or sales force company based on how they purchased shares of the company they evaluated. To provide individual company anonymity, the analysis only identifies the company as either a direct market or a sales force company.

One question asked the respondents to evaluate the fund complex as a company with which to do business. Given respondents' positive assessment of mutual fund companies in the cross-industry comparison, it is not surprising that respondents hold their individual mutual fund companies in high esteem. In assessing their particular mutual fund complex as a company with which to do business, 40 percent of respondents rate their company excellent and 39 percent rate it very good. Only 5 percent rate their company fair and just 1 percent rate it poor. Respondents who evaluated a direct market company more frequently rate the company highly than do respondents who evaluated a sales force company. Eighty-two percent of respondents evaluating a direct market company rate the company as either excellent or very good, compared with 76 percent of respondents evaluating a sales force company. Moreover, a higher proportion of those assessing a direct market company rate the company as excellent, while a higher proportion of those assessing a sales force company rate the company as very good.

The overall assessment of a mutual fund company varies across demographic groups. Older respondents evaluate their companies more favorably than do younger respondents. While 47 percent of those over 65 rate their particular mutual fund company as excellent, only 34 percent of those under 45 give the same rating. Respondents with less education

Table 9.2.1
Best at meeting specific service and investment needs* (percent of respondents rating provider as best)

Service needs	Mutual fund companies	Banks	Brokerage firms	Credit card companies	Insurance companies	Base =
Completing transactions accurately	37	**38**	20	4	2	838
Understanding customer needs	**34**	33	24	2	8	887
Completing transactions in a timely manner	28	**45**	21	4	2	916
Having courteous employees	27	**45**	20	2	6	841
Providing convenient access to services	23	**53**	17	6	2	967
Investment needs						
Providing high returns on investments	**62**	2	32	—	3	976
Providing investments for retirement	**62**	7	22	—	9	961
Providing innovative financial products and services	**40**	16	33	4	6	911
Providing needed products and services	**39**	33	22	3	2	947
Helping customers with money management	**39**	22	35	—	4	822
Providing financial advice	34	18	**44**	—	4	848
Providing security and safety for savings	29	**54**	11	—	6	959
Other						
Having the best reputation for service	34	**40**	18	2	6	916
Providing the best investment value	**58**	18	16	2	5	966

* Bold indicates institution with highest percentage ratings of "best."
Note: Respondents' evaluations are based on their experience with, or perception of, each service provider and are not necessarily related to the purchase of mutual funds.

are also more positive about their mutual fund company. Eighty-two percent of respondents without a college degree rate their particular company as excellent or very good, compared with 76 percent of those with at least some graduate school education. Additionally, respondents with lower incomes are more favorable toward the mutual fund company they assessed than are respondents with higher incomes. The longer respondents have owned funds with a company, the more favorable their assessment.

Respondents who had contact with their fund company in the 12 months preceding the survey, whether by mail or by phone, rate their particular company higher than do respondents who didn't have contact. Moreover, these higher ratings are consistent across all methods of contact.

The "Ideal" Mutual Fund Company

Respondents' assessment of the most important characteristics of a mutual fund company provides complexes with a sense of customer priorities. These priorities paint a picture of the "ideal" mutual fund company from the shareholder's perspective and indicate key areas to which companies could allocate resources. At the same time, they also point out areas to which mutual fund companies may be "over allocating" resources, and hence, may offer opportunities to reduce costs without significantly affecting customer satisfaction.

The importance ratings of the factors listed in table 9.2.2 shed some light on what responding shareholders value. The ratings of the 13 factors place them in three tiers. The first tier has only one factor—handling transactions and requests accurately. With a mean of 3.52, it is clearly the paramount issue for responding shareholders. This is true for respondents who evaluated a direct market company as well as those who evaluated a sales force company.

In the second and third tiers, both respondents evaluating a direct market company and those evaluating a sales force company rate the factors that make up an "ideal" mutual fund company about the same. The second and third tier factors are about the same in order of importance. The most significant difference between sales force and direct market company importance ratings is the emphasis placed on the role of employees. When compared with their direct market counterparts, respondents evaluating a sales force company rate the following as significantly more important: having knowledgeable employees, having employees that understand one's needs, and having employees who make shareholders feel like valued customers.

Evaluating Mutual Fund Company Performance on the Characteristics of the Ideal Company

Responding shareholders were asked to evaluate the mutual fund company they assessed on the same list of factors used to identify the important characteristics of the ideal mutual fund company. By comparing the performance scores of actual companies with the importance ratings of the ideal company, it is possible to determine where mutual fund companies are meeting respondents' expectations. Gaps where the differences between actual company performance scores and ideal company importance scores are positive indicate service areas where fund companies are exceeding respondents' expectations. The greater

Table 9.2.2

Importance ratings for the ideal mutual fund company (mean score*)

	All respondents	Respondents who evaluated a ...	
		Direct market company	Sales force company
Top tier factor			
Handles transactions and requests accurately	3.52	3.53	3.50
Second tier factors			
Has knowledgeable employees	3.32	3.24	3.39
Takes responsibility for resolving problems	3.28	3.30	3.29
Makes it easy to conduct a transaction	3.28	3.30	3.25
Handles transactions and requests in a timely manner	3.26	3.28	3.24
Provides printed materials and forms that are clear and easy to understand	3.17	3.13	3.19
Third tier factors			
Provides variety of funds	3.03	2.98	3.05
Has employees that understand your needs	3.01	2.91	3.07
Provides materials that help you make investment decisions	3.00	2.98	2.99
Has friendly and courteous employees	2.96	2.87	3.01
Makes use of technology to facilitate access to services	2.89	2.86	2.90
Makes you feel like a valued customer	2.85	2.74	2.92
Provides financial advice	2.79	2.60	2.96

*4 equals extremely important, 1 equals not at all important.
Note: Respondent bases vary.

the positive gap, the more fund companies are exceeding expectations on a particular service. Gaps where the differences between the performance scores and the importance scores are negative indicate areas where customer expectations are unmet. The greater the negative gap, the more fund companies are failing to meet customer expectations.

The following sections provide assessments of direct market and sales force companies' performance on the same factors used to describe the ideal fund company. In each section, the assessment of actual company performance is discussed first and is followed by an analysis of the positive and negative gaps between actual company performance and ideal company importance ratings.

Table 9.2.3

Comparison of direct market company with ideal fund company (mean scores for respondents who evaluated a direct market company)

	Actual company rating*	Ideal company rating**	Gap
Top tier factor			
Handles transactions and requests accurately	3.35	3.53	−0.18
Second tier factors			
Has knowledgeable employees	3.10	3.24	−0.14
Takes responsibility for resolving problems	3.02	3.30	−0.28
Makes it easy to conduct a transaction	3.23	3.30	−0.07
Handles transactions and requests in a timely manner	3.28	3.28	0.00
Provides printed materials and forms that are clear and easy to understand	3.11	3.13	−0.02
Third tier factors			
Provides variety of funds	3.16	2.98	0.18
Has employees that understand your needs	2.85	2.91	−0.06
Provides materials that help you to make investment decisions	2.99	2.98	0.01
Has friendly and courteous employees	3.13	2.87	0.26
Makes use of technology to facilitate access to services	3.07	2.86	0.21
Makes you feel like a valued customer	2.94	2.74	0.20
Provides financial advice	2.62	2.60	0.02

*4 equals excellent, 1 equals not good at all.
**4 equals extremely important, 1 equals not at all important.
Note: Respondent bases vary.

Direct Market Mutual Fund Company Performance

Table 9.2.3 shows that respondents who evaluated direct market companies rate them highest on transaction-related factors. Direct market companies received a mean score of 3.35 for handling transactions and requests accurately and a mean score of 3.28 for handling transactions in a timely manner. With mean scores of 3.23 and 3.16, respectively, making it easy to conduct a transaction and providing a variety of funds are two other factors on which direct market companies perform highly. At the other end of the spectrum, direct market companies received mean scores of 2.62 for providing financial advice and 2.85 for having employees that understand customer needs.

Comparing ideal company importance ratings with direct market company performance ratings indicates the service areas where direct market companies are meeting, exceeding, and failing to meet respondents' expectations. Among direct market companies, the largest negative gaps, indicating instances where customer expectations are unmet, include top and second tier factors such as taking responsibility for resolving problems, handling transactions accurately, and having knowledgeable employees. The largest positive gaps, indicating areas where direct market companies are exceeding their customers' expectations, are on third tier factors, such as having friendly and courteous employees, making use of technology to facilitate access to services, making a person feel like a valued customer, and providing a variety of funds from which to choose. As mentioned earlier, third tier factors are of less importance to respondents when describing their ideal mutual fund company. The positive gaps indicate that direct market mutual fund companies may have the opportunity to maintain, or perhaps even reduce, the resources allocated to product development and technology without negatively affecting their competitive position.

Instances where direct market company performance and ideal company importance ratings are similar indicate service areas to which direct market companies have devoted appropriate resources. For example, providing financial advice has a positive gap of only 0.02, which means that direct market shareholders are generally satisfied with the level of financial advice they receive from their fund companies. This is especially noteworthy because respondents who evaluated a direct market company give low performance ratings for this attribute, indicating that measuring performance alone does not provide the complete picture. Other factors on which direct market fund companies are allocating resources appropriately are handling transactions in a timely manner, providing printed materials that are easy to read, and providing materials that assist investment decisionmaking.

Sales Force Mutual Fund Company Performance
With a mean score of 3.17, sales force companies are rated highest on handling transactions and requests accurately. Other factors on which sales force companies are rated fairly highly include handling transactions in a timely manner and providing a variety of funds, both of which have a mean score of 3.08. Following closely, sales force companies received a mean score of 3.07 for making it easy to conduct a transaction. Factors with the lowest quality scores include providing financial advice at 2.78, having employees that understand customer needs at 2.84, and making shareholders feel like valued customers at 2.85.

Comparing ideal company importance ratings with sales force company performance ratings indicates the service areas where sales force companies are meeting, exceeding, and failing to meet respondents' expectations. Table 9.2.4 shows that several large negative gaps exist between sales force company performance and ideal company ratings, indicating some key areas where customer needs are currently unmet. Many of the negative gaps center around human resource-related factors. For example, having knowledgeable employees and taking responsibility for resolving problems have two of the largest negative gaps, −0.36 and −0.31, respectively. Handling transactions and requests accurately has a negative gap of −0.33. Two other factors with somewhat large negative gaps are providing printed materials that are easy to understand, which has a gap of −0.27, and having employees that understand your needs, which has a gap of −0.23.

Several areas exist where sales force fund companies are allocating appropriate resources. In these instances, sales force company performance and ideal company importance ratings are similar. For example, sales force companies have a positive gap of 0.03

Table 9.2.4

Comparison of sales force company with ideal fund company (mean scores for respondents who evaluated a sales force company)

	Actual company rating*	Ideal company rating**	Gap
Top tier factor			
Handles transactions and requests accurately	3.17	3.50	−0.33
Second tier factors			
Has knowledgeable employees	3.03	3.39	−0.36
Takes responsibility for resolving problems	2.98	2.29	−0.31
Makes it easy to conduct a transaction	3.07	3.25	−0.18
Handles transactions and requests in a timely manner	3.08	3.24	−0.16
Provides printed materials and forms that are clear and easy to understand	2.92	3.19	−0.27
Third tier factors			
Provides variety of funds	3.08	3.05	0.03
Has employees that understand your needs	2.84	3.07	−0.23
Provides materials that help you to make investment decisions	2.89	2.99	−0.10
Has friendly and courteous employees	3.05	3.01	0.04
Makes use of technology to facilitate access to services	2.90	2.90	0.00
Makes you feel like a valued customer	2.85	2.92	−0.07
Provides financial advice	2.78	2.96	−0.18

*4 equals excellent, 1 equals not good at all.
**4 equals extremely important, 1 equals not at all important.
Note: Respondent bases vary.

for providing a variety of funds, a negative gap of only −0.10 for providing materials to assist in investment decision-making, and no gap at all for making use of technology to facilitate access to services.

Opportunities for Improving Customer Perceptions

As mentioned previously, handling transactions and requests accurately is the most important factor to both direct market and sales force customers. Although direct market and sales force mutual fund companies receive their highest ratings on this factor, they are still not meeting customer expectations. This indicates that accuracy, and hence quality control, of all deliverables that shareholders receive from the mutual fund company, such as quarterly statements and confirmations, is of paramount importance. Based on these findings, all mutual fund companies should evaluate the need to tighten existing standards for accuracy so that customer expectations can be met. Additional resources needed to improve quality control could be reallocated from areas where shareholders rate performance higher than importance. Based on the survey results, two factors with "positive" performance gaps are offering a wide variety of funds and providing technology that facilitates access to services. Thus, mutual fund companies may be able to finance additional investments in quality control by maintaining, or perhaps even reducing, the emphasis placed on customer access-related technology and product development.

9.3   The Effect of Customer Service on Company Productivity*

Customer service can affect a fund company's bottom line. In fact, a strong relationship exists between excellence in a company's customer service and respondents' recent and expected investment activity in that company. Excellent customer service also increases the likelihood that shareholders will recommend the company to friends and relatives. (See figure 9.3.1.) To improve the quality of their customer service, direct market companies should concentrate on making it easier for shareholders to conduct a transaction, followed by improving their understanding of shareholder needs, and having knowledgeable employees. Sales force companies should focus on improving their understanding of shareholder needs, followed by completing transactions and requests accurately, and having friendly and courteous employees.

The Effect of Customer Service on the Decision to Invest

Those factors that contribute to a shareholder's decision to invest with a particular mutual fund company are of critical importance to that company. Previous ICI research has shown that investment performance is a very important factor. In this survey, service quality is found to be an important, but not a key, factor in attracting new customers.

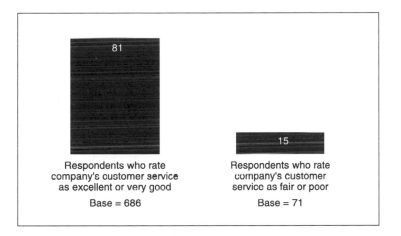

Figure 9.3.1   Relationship between quality of company's customer service and referrals (percent of respondents likely to recommend company to friends and relatives)

---

*Investment Company Institute, Chapter 2 of "The Service Quality Challenge: Understanding Shareholder Expectations." Reprinted with permission.

Table 9.3.1

Factors important in the decision to invest*

	All respondents	Respondents who evaluated a ...	
		Direct market company	Sales force company
First tier factor			
The investment performance of the family of funds	1.02	1.01	1.01
Second tier factor			
The reputation of the mutual fund company	0.55	0.46	0.62
Third tier factors			
Recommendations by someone you trust	0.28	0.14	0.35
The quality of customer service offered by the mutual fund company	0.23	0.14	0.30
The range of funds offered by the mutual fund company	0.14	0.08	0.16
The mutual fund company's sales charges and other fees	0.13	0.24	0.05
The range of services offered by the mutual fund company	0.00	0.00	0.00

*The score for each factor is based on a paired comparison.

An analysis of paired comparisons was used to identify which attribute is most important to shareholders when deciding whether to invest with a particular fund company: investment performance of funds, reputation, recommendations, quality of customer service, range of funds, sales charges and other fees, and range of services. These attributes were presented to respondents two at a time in various combinations. For each pair, respondents selected the attribute they considered to be the more important of the two. An average score was computed for each attribute based on respondents' answers. These scores identify how important each attribute is and by how much.

Table 9.3.1 shows that, with a score of 1.02, investment performance is by far the most important factor to both direct market and sales force company respondents when selecting a fund company. It is approximately twice as important as the next most important factor—reputation of the mutual fund company, which received a score of 0.55. While reputation is approximately half as important as investment performance, it is twice as important as any other factor, including the quality of customer service. As a result, company reputation can be considered a second tier factor, and one that offers some potential for attracting new customers. Customer service is clearly a third tier factor in the decision to invest. Overall, respondents rate it higher than several other third tier factors, including the range of funds offered, sales charges and fees, and range of services. With a score of 0.0, the range of services offered by a fund company is the least important attribute to respondents in the decision to invest with a particular company.

Table 9.3.2

Evaluation of company's customer service according to type of service contact* (percent of respondents)

	All respondents	Type of service contact with company			No service contact
		Phone only	Mail only	Phone and mail	
Excellent	32	43	24	42	23
Very good	39	37	45	40	40
Good	22	15	17	11	29
Fair	6	5	12	3	6
Poor	1	1	2	4	1
Base =	974	349	75	129	421

*For 12 months preceding survey.

Not surprisingly, respondents who evaluated a direct market company are concerned about sales charges and fees. This factor ranks third after performance and reputation for this respondent group. For those who evaluated a sales force company, recommendations and quality of service are less important than performance and reputation, but they are more important than sales charges and fees.

Evaluation of Customer Service

Thirty-two percent of respondents say that the customer service of the company they evaluated is excellent, 39 percent say it is very good, and 22 percent say it is good. Only 6 percent of shareholders rate the company's customer service as fair, and just one percent consider it poor. Respondent evaluations of direct market companies are higher than those of sales force companies. A total of 36 percent of respondents who evaluated a direct market company rate that company's customer service as excellent. This compares with 28 percent of those who evaluated a sales force company.

Table 9.3.2 shows that respondents' assessment of the company they evaluated varies depending on whether they had service contact with that company in the 12 months preceding the survey. Respondents who had no contact or only had contact by mail tended to give lower assessments than did respondents who had only phone contact or both phone and mail contact. For example, only 23 percent of respondents who had no service contact rated the company's customer service as excellent, compared with 42 percent of respondents who had both mail and phone contact with the company.

Several demographic patterns also emerged in respondents' assessment of the customer service of the company they evaluated. Older and less educated respondents rate customer service higher than do their younger and more educated counterparts. Predictably, loyal customers who have owned funds with the company they evaluated for ten or more years rate customer service higher than do customers who acquired funds more recently.

The Effect of Customer Service on a Company's Bottom Line

While the quality of customer service plays less of a role in the decision to invest in a mutual fund company than either fund performance or company reputation, it can affect shareholder behavior and, therefore, a fund company's profitability. For example, shareholders' customer service experiences can influence their decision to increase or decrease their investment with a particular fund company, as well as the likelihood of their recommending that company to their friends and relatives.

The survey examined the effect both of customer service on shareholders' recent investment decisions and on their future investment decisions.... The connection between excellence in service quality and increases in investment dollars is quite strong. Nearly four in ten respondents who rate their particular company's customer service either as excellent or very good say they increased their investment in that company in the six months preceding the survey. This compares with 22 percent of respondents who rate their particular company's customer service as either fair or poor. Respondents who give their particular company a fair or poor customer service evaluation are somewhat more likely to say they decreased their investment in that company when compared with respondents who give very good or excellent evaluations.

A similar pattern emerges for respondents' investment intentions. When asked about their purchase plans for the six months following the survey, more than four out of five respondents who rate their particular company's quality of customer service as either fair or poor say they expect to maintain their current level of investment in that company; only five percent expect to increase their level of investment. In contrast, 40 percent of respondents who rate the quality of service as either excellent or very good indicate that they plan to increase the level of their investment. Again, respondents giving lower quality evaluations are more likely to decrease their investments than are those rating the quality of service highly.

The quality of customer service also impacts customer referrals. Eighty-one percent of respondents who rate the customer service of the company they evaluated as either excellent or very good say they are likely to recommend that company to friends and relatives. In contrast, only 15 percent of respondents who rate the customer service of the company they evaluated as either fair or poor say they are likely to recommend that company to friends and relatives (see figure 9.3.1 at the beginning of this reading).

Opportunities for Improving Customer Service

It is important that mutual fund companies understand the primary factors that affect customer service for shareholders. These "key" drivers represent specific actions that mutual fund companies can take to increase their overall quality rating for customer service. Regression analysis was used to identify the key drivers.

Table 9.3.3 provides a list of key drivers of customer service for respondents who evaluated a direct market company. They are listed in order of importance, with the most important driver listed first. The ease with which a transaction or request can be completed is the most important driver of customer service for respondents who evaluated a direct

Table 9.3.3

Key drivers of customer service for respondents who evaluated a direct market company (in order of importance)

	Importance ranking*	Mean performance score**
Make it easy to conduct a transaction and request	1	3.23
Understand shareholder needs	2	2.85
Have knowledgeable employees	3	3.10
Have friendly and courteous employees	4	3.13
Use technology that facilitates access to services	5	3.07
Complete transactions and requests accurately	6	3.35
Provide information that aids investment decisionmaking	7	2.99

*As determined by least square regression analysis. The dependent variable is the evaluation of the quality of customer service. The independent variables are the performance ratings of the customer service attributes.

**4 equals excellent, 1 equals not good at all.

market company. This is followed by understanding shareholder needs, having knowledgeable employees, and having friendly and courteous employees.

Table 9.3.3 also shows the mean performance scores of direct market companies on the seven key drivers. Direct market companies are performing best on handling transactions and requests accurately and making it easy to conduct a transaction or a request for service, which are, respectively, the sixth and first most important key drivers of customer service. Direct market companies are not performing as well on understanding shareholder needs, the second most important key driver. Performance is also low for providing information that assists investment decisionmaking, which is the seventh most important key driver of customer service for respondents who evaluated a direct market company.

Using the importance and performance scores, it is possible to identify the opportunity available from each key driver to improve the overall customer service quality rating. Figure 9.3.2 shows the opportunity available to direct market companies for each key driver. As mentioned previously, 74 percent of respondents who evaluated a direct market company rate the customer service of direct market companies as either excellent or very good. The greatest opportunity for improving this rating is to make it as easy as possible for shareholders to conduct a transaction. If direct market shareholders are able to complete their transactions in the easiest way possible, the percent of respondents who rate direct market companies' customer service as either excellent or very good should increase 5.5 percentage points. In addition to making it easier to conduct a transaction, other key drivers that offer direct market companies considerable opportunity for improvement are increasing their understanding of shareholder needs and having knowledgeable employees. Complete improvement on all of the factors listed in figure 9.3.2 should improve the overall customer service rating so that all shareholders rate direct market companies' customer service as either excellent or very good.

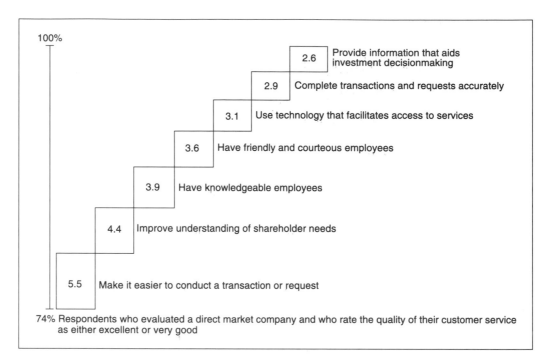

Figure 9.3.2   Opportunities for improving customer service for direct market companies (expected change in quality rating if each improvement is made)

For respondents who evaluated a sales force company, key customer service factors overlap substantially with the key factors of those who evaluated a direct market company, although their relative importance and performance ratings are different. The four key customer service factors that the two respondent groups have in common are: understanding shareholder needs, completing transactions accurately, having friendly and courteous employees, and providing information that assists investment decisionmaking.

Table 9.3.4 provides the seven key drivers for respondents who evaluated a sales force company. Understanding shareholder needs is the most important driver of customer service for these respondents, followed by accuracy in completing transactions, and having friendly and courteous employees.

Table 9.3.4 also shows sales force companies' performance ratings for each of the seven key drivers of customer service. Ratings are best on key drivers related to handling transactions and requests accurately and in a timely manner, which are, respectively, the second and seventh most important drivers of service quality. Sales force companies' performance is lowest on the most important driver of customer service—understanding shareholder needs.

Figure 9.3.3 quantifies the opportunities available from each of the seven key drivers of overall customer service quality. As mentioned previously, 68 percent of respondents who evaluated a sales force company rate the customer service provided by sales force companies as either excellent or very good. The greatest opportunity for sales force companies to increase this rating is to improve their understanding of shareholder needs. If

Table 9.3.4
Key drivers of customer service for respondents who evaluated a sales force company (in order of importance)

	Importance ranking*	Mean performance score**
Understand shareholder needs	1	2.84
Complete transactions and requests accurately	2	3.17
Have friendly and courteous employees	3	3.05
Provide printed materials and forms that are easy to understand	4	2.92
Take responsibility for resolving problems	5	2.98
Provide information that aids investment decisionmaking	6	2.89
Complete transactions and requests in a timely manner	7	3.08

*As determined by least square regression analysis. The dependent variable is the evaluation of the quality of customer service. The independent variables are the performance ratings of the customer service attributes. **4 equals excellent, 1 equals not good at all.

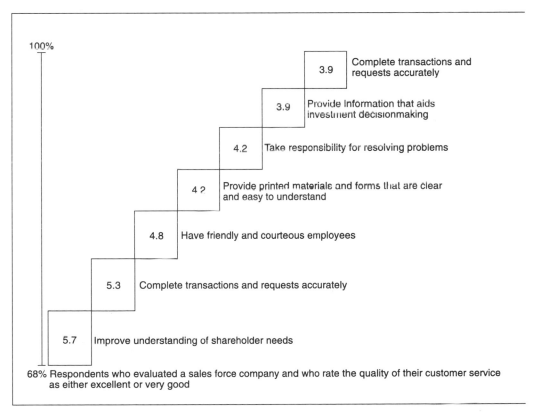

100%

3.9 — Complete transactions and requests accurately

3.9 — Provide Information that aids investment decisionmaking

4.2 — Take responsibility for resolving problems

4.2 — Provide printed materials and forms that are clear and easy to understand

4.8 — Have friendly and courteous employees

5.3 — Complete transactions and requests accurately

5.7 — Improve understanding of shareholder needs

68% Respondents who evaluated a sales force company and who rate the quality of their customer service as either excellent or very good

Figure 9.3.3 Opportunities for improving customer service for sales force companies (expected change in quality rating if each improvement is made)

sales force companies improve their understanding of shareholder needs, then the percent of shareholders rating customer service as either excellent or very good should increase 5.7 percentage points to 73.7 percent. In addition to better understanding shareholder needs, other key drivers that offer sales force companies considerable room for improvement are completing transactions and requests accurately, and having friendly and courteous employees. Complete improvement on all the factors listed in figure 9.3.3 should improve that overall customer service rating so that all shareholders rate sales force companies' customer service as either excellent or very good.

9.4　Rating the Fund Companies*
Nellie S. Huang

You're thinking about investing $5,000 in a mutual fund that a friend has enthusiastically recommended—the Dreyfus Disciplined Midcap Stock fund. So you pick up the phone and dial a toll-free number. Immediately, a customer-service rep named Ken answers the phone. You start hammering him with questions: Who's the fund manager? Has he run any other funds before? What are the fund's top 10 holdings? What's its track record over the last five years? Did the fund beat the Standard & Poor's 500-stock index last year? Question after question, the phone rep on the other end of the line has a ready answer. Too bad they were all for the wrong fund. We had called asking about the Disciplined Midcap fund. Ken, it seems, provided us with information about the Dreyfus Disciplined Stock fund. Big difference. Each fund has a different portfolio manager, different top 10 holdings, a different expense ratio. One fund invests in such blue-chip stocks as Coca-Cola, Philip Morris and General Electric. The other, the midcap fund, is heavily weighted in bank securities such as First Virginia, Barnett Banks, and City National.

"It is unfortunate and very rare that a Dreyfus representative would make a mistake like this," responds Patrice Kozlowski, a spokeswoman for the Dreyfus Corp. in New York. "The Disciplined Stock fund and the Disciplined Midcap fund are very similar-sounding funds. But we all make mistakes."

That's all fine and good, but when it comes to questions about investing your money, you don't want just answers—you want the right ones. Inaccurate information can mean the difference between a good financial decision and a bad one. Once you've opened up an account, of course, the need for those right answers and quick service grows exponentially—whether it's getting immediate access to your portfolio or help in deciphering an account statement.

Say, for instance, you want to roll over your IRA into another fund in the same family. Or you have a crucial, last-minute question about your short-term gains close to midnight on April 15. Will someone answer the phone that late? Perhaps you're closing on a house and you need money wired to you in two days without fail. Can your fund company deliver? Whether you have $500,000 or even just $500 parked with a fund company, the bottom line is you should expect great service.

True, most people *don't* use customer service as their top criterion in picking a mutual fund—the category runs a distant second, obviously, to the fund's money-making talent—but it's important nonetheless. After all, your money isn't the only thing you're worried about protecting—there's your time too. And of the 63 million mutual fund shareholders in the U.S., it's a fair bet that *not one* of them enjoys wasting three 10-minute phone calls to request a duplicate 1099-DIV form in order to file a tax return.

---

*From *SmartMoney*, September 1997 (with Brooke Deterline, Vera Gibbons, Eric R. Tinson, and Rob Turner) © 1997 by SmartMoney. A joint venture of the Hearst Corporation and Dow Jones & Company, Inc. All rights reserved.

For this reason we decided to investigate how well 15 major fund companies performed in the one category that has yet to be rated by Morningstar or Lipper: service. We started with the 11 largest fund companies, measured by net assets, and added to the mix four smaller companies that had at least one fund with more than $5 billion in assets. To be fair, we excluded brokerage firms and companies with exclusively broker-sold funds, such as Smith Barney, IDS, and Merrill Lynch, as their customer-service reps are less qualified to answer questions about accounts and specific mutual funds. (The brokers do it for them.) Also worth noting is that roughly half the fund companies in our survey—AIM Management Group, OppenheimerFunds, Franklin Templeton Group, Pimco Funds, Pioneer Mutual Funds, and Putnam Investments—are sold primarily through brokers, though investors can and do buy shares through the fund companies themselves.

Our next task was determining exactly what kinds of services investors need and most want from their fund company. We came up with five: accommodating and competent telephone-service representatives; a wide range of service offerings—e.g., the ability to check a fund's current net asset value (NAV) or get an update on the balance of your portfolio—from the fund's live customer service and 24-hour automated phone lines; clear and complete quarterly account statements; speedy delivery of prospectuses; and finally, a useful and easy-to-navigate Web site. Scoring in each of the five categories was from zero to 10, with 10 being the highest, although we also awarded fractional points to show the relative positions of funds in the rankings. (For example, a near-winner might receive a score of 9.9.) Finally, we added the scores for each company, giving equal weight to each category.

And the results? An authoritative win for Fidelity Investments. Out of a perfect score of 50, the Boston-based behemoth garnered a final score of 42.5, two points ahead of our second-place finisher, the Vanguard Group (another fund giant). (See table 9.4.1.) Although it isn't *that* surprising, perhaps, that Fidelity Investments was our survey winner—for many years, it's been a service leader in the mutual fund industry—it is truly remarkable that the company racked up perfect scores in three of our five ratings categories. In fact, if there's one word to describe the company's customer service across the board, it's "comprehensive." Everything you'd ever need as a shareholder—whether it's round-the-clock access to your fund accounts, a fact-filled account statement that explains, literally, *every* bit of data, or a Web site that lets you buy, sell, and exchange shares among accounts, Fidelity's automated service sets the bar.

"I'm sure we're unique," boasts Edward L. McCartney, president of Fidelity's retail investor services. "From our automated phone lines to the Web site, I can't identify and other company that offers the range of services we provide."

Nor could we. But that's not to say there isn't room for improvement. While the industry titan has plowed plenty of cash into its *mechanized* account management, it's customer-help line, well ... isn't quite as helpful. True, the firm has an army of some 900 agents to handle its shareholders' needs—more than any of its peers. But unfortunately, the ones we spoke to had trouble answering some very basic questions. For starters, no one could give us a load-adjusted return, year-to-date, for the company's flagship Magellan fund. Interested in a specific fund's top 10 holdings? Be advised, the ones the service rep gives you may well be two months old—or as one phone agent told us (with refreshing honesty, we might add): "They're current, but not real current."

Table 9.4.1
Service entrants: How fund companies stack up*

Rank	Fund family	Phone	Customer service reps	Range of services	Web site offerings	Account statements	Prospectus delivery	Total score
1	Fidelity Investments	800-544-8888	5.5	10.0	10.0	10.0	7.0	42.5
2	Vanguard Group	800-662-7447	10.0	3.5	9.3	10.0	7.5	40.3
3	Janus	800-525-8983	8.5	1.3	8.8	9.5	10.0	38.1
4	Scudder, Steven & Clark	800-225-2470	9.3	4.8	9.3	5.5	8.0	36.9
5	American Century Investments	800-345-2021	6.1	2.1	8.7	9.1	8.0	34.0
6	T. Rowe Price Investment Services	800-638-5660	6.6	3.4	9.6	7.3	7.0	33.9
7	Dreyfus Corp.	800-645-6561	5.6	7.4	6.2	4.6	10.0	33.8
8	Neuberger & Berman Management	800-877-9700	6.3	8.7	7.6	2.8	8.0	33.4
9	AIM Management Group	800-959-4246	9.9	1.8	6.7	5.9	9.0	33.3
10	OppenheimerFunds	800-525-7048	7.9	3.3	5.3	1.9	5.0	23.4
11	PBHG Funds	800-433-0051	4.6	0.5	6.7	1.9	8.0	21.7
12	Franklin Templeton Group	800-632-2301	5.2	1.3	8.0	0.0	5.0	19.5
13	Pioneer Mutual Funds	800-225-6292	6.6	3.0	6.4	2.8	0.0	18.8
14	Putnam Investments	800-225-1581	0.0	0.0	5.3	2.8	10.0	18.1
15	Pimco Funds	800-426-0107	1.5	0.7	0.0	2.8	6.0	11.0

*Fifteen leading mutual fund companies are ranked in five customer-service areas. Category scores are from zero (pathetic) to 10 (perfect).

The best answers we got from Fidelity reps were, surprisingly, about the company's own track record—particularly the Magellan fund's somewhat spotty recent history: When asked why the once-great Magellan fund had fallen on hard times, several reps were quick (and correct) to blame the fund's erstwhile heavy weighting in bonds during last year's market runup. Several, in fact, were just as candid about the former manager. (No, not Peter Lynch—Jeff Vinik, who left in June 1996 to start his own hedge fund.) Noted one rep: "Mr. Vinik had a lot of bonds in the fund, almost 10 percent. But we finally got rid of them."

While Vanguard's reps may have less gossip to work with—after all, a quarter of the firm's portfolios are straightforward index funds—they make up in data what they lack in "dish." The benchmark for the International Growth fund? They've got it. Capital gains distributions for the last three years straight? They'll rattle off the numbers.

We were equally impressed with the phone reps at tiny Neuberger & Berman Management. Though the company has just 20 funds and $19 billion under management, it outpaced not only its smaller fund rivals, like PBHG Funds, but stalwarts such as Franklin Templeton and Putnam—the fourth- and fifth-largest fund families, respectively, in the country.

Indeed, with a few remarkable exceptions, the biggest surprise of our survey was how *well* our group fared in service overall. Shockingly well, in fact. Only a few years ago, mutual fund companies thought of themselves as merely investment vehicles, plain and simple. Not as "service providers." Back then it was rare for a phone rep to know what a fund's top 10 holdings were—or even what sort of expenses were included in an expense ratio.

Take Vanguard, for example. Four years ago it took the company nearly two weeks to send out 5.4 million account-statement pages. Today it takes half that long to send out about twice as many.

Why the big improvement? Technology, for one thing: Many fund-company service agents now have access to scores of computer databases right at their desk. Very often, with the mere click of a button or two, your phone rep can pull up the most minute details on any fund—from the dividend history going back to 1970 to the fund's objective stated five different ways. A click of the mouse and he's got your account application or your last quarterly statement staring back at him from a 17-inch computer screen. Wait a few seconds more and he can provide you with an up-to-the-minute report on what the stock market's doing, or tell you what your average cost basis is or give you the latest 30-day yield of your government bond fund.

And that's just a start. At American Century Investments, you can ask a customer-service rep for the total return of the Ultra fund between arbitrary dates like June 2, 1994 and April 12, 1997—and get an answer in seconds. At Scudder, Stevens & Clark, the phone rep can fill you in on a fund manager's prior experience with other Scudder funds and then even break down what his performance was during those periods.

Even more impressive—and perhaps a tad scary—is that virtually all fund companies today use what is called "imaging" technology. Not only do they record each phone conversation between their customers and service reps, they can actually scan into their mainframe computers every bit of shareholder correspondence—even those that are scrawled by hand. The information is instantly organized per account so that when you call in to trace a redemption order, for instance, or to check up on an IRA rollover, any rep on the other end of the line can see exactly what you wrote or said in prior conversation.

But while fund companies have embraced such Big Brother technology with a near-religious conviction, it's up to the phone reps themselves, generally, to implement it. And glitches do happen all the time. Remember our Dreyfus phone rep, Ken? It was probably an errant click of his mouse that had him pulling up data on the Disciplined Stock fund instead of Disciplined Midcap.

9.5   Mutual Fund Transfer Agents: Trends and Billing Practices*

While investment performance remains the most significant distinguishing characteristic among fund complexes, the value of shareholder service continues to play an important role in solidifying shareholder loyalty. Ongoing pressure to achieve and maintain "best-in-class" service combined with technological advancements led to new rounds of capital and human resource investments by shareholder-servicing agents. Winning in today's ultra-competitive environment necessitates closer links between distribution channels and shareholder services to satisfy shareholder demands for access to more robust information from transfer agents, brokers, and retirement recordkeepers. The need for timely processing of shareholder transactions across these three generally distinct groups encouraged the development of "superstations," or front-end workstations, capable of directing all manner of shareholder transaction requests to the appropriate processing system.

Despite these growing pressures to provide expanded servicing capabilities, the results of the 1995 survey show a decrease of 8 percent in the average per-account charge, to $20.93 in 1995 from $22.77 in 1993. An analysis of open accounts only shows a smaller decrease of 3 percent, to $25.09 from $25.92. Some of the contributing factors to the decline in average per-account fees include the dramatic growth in lower-cost clearing-house accounts, such as: NSCC-Networked accounts; the decreasing costs of utilizing NSCC Networking; and increasing efforts by fund organizations to control fund expenses. Nonetheless, while per-account charges have decreased from 1993 levels, aggregate dollars spent by funds for transfer-agency services increased. Between 1993 and 1995, total dollar fees reported by funds in the survey increased by an average of 35 percent.

Discussions with transfer agent management indicate that the decline in per-account charges conflicts with the increased cost of servicing existing shareholders. Most executives believe this disparity reflects the time lag between negotiated transfer agent/shareholder service contracts and the investment in resources necessary to provide such services. This is a significant issue many organizations are currently addressing. In fact, six of the largest fund complexes recently established or are currently negotiating transfer agent fee increases. Finally, one of the effects of the broadening of distribution channels used by mutual fund organizations is the growth in sub-accounting arrangements. While some of these relationships may be in the form of sub-transfer agent arrangements, many are structured as service-agent arrangements whereby some of the services traditionally performed by the transfer agent are assumed by the service agent. The contractual arrangements for these services are varied. Fees traditionally charged by transfer agents are now being split among distribution fees, transfer agent or sub-transfer agent fees, and costs borne by the fund advisor. This reduces charges classified as transfer agent fees, and lowers the amounts reported by fund complexes in the survey.

Survey Results

The 1995 survey includes responses from 496 mutual funds representing 69 fund complexes....

Figure 9.5.1 illustrates the range of per-account charges for all funds included in the survey. While the range in which 80 percent of the funds are grouped remained relatively stable at $10–$38 in 1993 versus $10–$34 in 1995, the concentration of per-account charges in the $10–$22 per-account range became even greater.

Tables 9.5.1 to 9.5.8 present the per-account charges for all accounts and for open accounts only be transfer agent type, fund type, and distribution channel, respectively. These three factors have traditionally had the most significant impact on differentiating transfer agent fees.

Tables 9.5.5. and 9.5.6 present the average transfer agent per-account charges by fund type for the three survey periods. In general, per-account charges for all fund types have been moving closer together. Fixed-income fund per-account charges, calculated on an all-accounts basis, have for the first time surpassed money market per-account charges, possibly reflecting continued downward pressure on money market fund expenses as initially observed in the 1993 survey.

While continued emphasis on cost control is not limited to money market funds, its impact could be more significant for these funds given the relatively high transaction

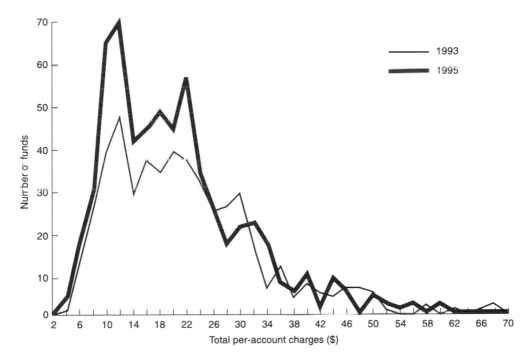

Figure 9.5.1   Concentration of per-account charges for all funds in the survey

Table 9.5.1
Average per-account charges (all accounts) by type of transfer agent

Type of transfer agent	1991	1993	1995
Internal	$22.34	$23.34	$21.39
External	$19.52	$21.18	$19.55
Combined average	$21.55	$22.77	$20.93

Table 9.5.2
Average per-account charges (open accounts) by type of transfer agent

Type of transfer agent	1991	1993	1995
Internal	$25.34	$26.39	$25.64
External	$23.08	$24.56	$23.42
Combined average	$24.76	$25.92	$25.09

Table 9.5.3
Average per-account charges (all accounts) by type of transfer agent

Type of transfer agent	Type of fund			1995 combined average
	Fixed- income	Equity	Money market	
Internal	$23.03	$19.54	$22.49	$21.39
External	$20.72	$17.86	$21.38	$19.55
Combined average	$22.51	$19.11	$22.18	$20.93

Table 9.5.4
Average per-account charges (open accounts) by type of transfer agent

Type of transfer agent	Type of fund			1995 combined average
	Fixed- income	Equity	Money market	
Internal	$27.58	$22.49	$29.30	$25.64
External	$25.23	$20.17	$27.66	$23.42
Combined average	$27.06	$21.89	$28.83	$25.09

Table 9.5.5
Average per-account charges (all accounts) by type of transfer agent

Fund type	1991	1993	1995	% change
Fixed-income	$22.34	$24.66	$22.51	−8.7%
Equity	$17.70	$19.57	$19.11	−2.4%
Money market	$27.14	$24.88	$22.18	−10.9%
All funds	$21.55	$22.77	$20.93	−8.1%

Table 9.5.6
Average per-account charges (open accounts) by type of transfer agent

Fund type	1991	1993	1995	% change
Fixed-income	$25.88	$27.15	$27.06	−0.3%
Equity	$20.31	$22.52	$21.89	−2.8%
Money market	$31.27	$30.28	$28.83	−4.8%
All funds	$24.76	$25.92	$25.09	−3.2%

Table 9.5.7
Average per-account charges (all accounts) by type of transfer agent

Distribution channel	1991	1993	1995
Broker (affiliate)	$11.11	$12.32	$14.55
Broker (independent)	$23.95	$24.81	$22.03
Retail	$24.36	$28.54	$26.77
Retail (captive)	$21.35	$22.41	$19.34

Table 9.5.8
Average per-account charges (open accounts) by type of transfer agent

Distribution channel	1991	1993	1995
Broker (affiliate)	$13.63	$15.07	$16.57
Broker (independent)	$26.94	$27.39	$27.05
Retail	$29.31	$34.01	$32.61
Retail (captive)	$22.64	$24.94	$22.21

volumes associated with money market shareholder accounts. In addition, transfer agents have steadily increased the use of fees charged directly to shareholders, such as low-balance accounts, account maintenance, and check-writing fees.

Out-of-pocket expenses are included in the calculation of total per-account charges. Out-of-pocket expenses declined 5 percent, from $4.48 to $4.25, continuing a trend observed in the 1993 survey when out-of-pocket expenses decreased 10 percent. There has been movement by some fund complexes to incorporate out-of-pocket expenses into basic fees. This trend bears watching in future surveys.

While both internal and external transfer agent per-account charges decreased by 8 percent, there was noticeable variance by fund types. Internally-serviced money market funds showed decreases of 14 percent, externally-serviced fixed-income funds decreased by 12 percent, and equity funds remained relatively flat. Cost pressures on yield-sensitive funds have continued during the past two years: internal transfer agents appear to be narrowing the spread between money market and fixed-income fund per-account charges. Continued growth in the number of fixed-income funds and intense competition between external transfer agents has likely led to greater fee sensitivity in this area. Consistent with prior surveys, internally-serviced funds report per-account charges that are 9 percent higher than comparable externally-serviced funds.

Historically, fund distribution channels have significantly affected transfer agent per-account charges. The decline in the average per-account charges for the retail, independent broker-dealer, and captive-sales-force distribution channels ranged from 6 percent to 14 percent. However, continuing a trend first observed in the 1993 survey, average per-account charges for affiliated broker-dealer-distributed funds increased. This distribution channel has historically had the lowest per-account charges, and, notwithstanding the 18 percent increase from $12.32 to $14.55, affiliated broker-dealer-distributed funds continue to report the lowest average per-account charges in the survey. During the past several years, these organizations have expanded traditional in-house fund and service offerings to become more competitive with "no-transaction-fee" or retail fund distribution channels. This has required additional investments in systems and other resources to coordinate and service outside fund offerings.

In the 1993 survey, recognition of the growing emphasis on multiple processing sites led to the creation of a "multi-region" transfer agent location category. In 1993, 17 percent of funds surveyed had multiple processing locations. This category increased to 24 percent in 1995, and may continue to grow in the foreseeable future. Multiple sites allow transfer agents the flexibility to shift workloads, provide expanded shareholder servicing hours without incurring significant overtime costs, and strengthen disaster recovery or business continuity plans.

Current Industry Perspectives

In addition to input received from survey participants, roundtable meetings were held in Boston and Denver with management personnel from 10 transfer agent organizations. These meetings reviewed preliminary data from the 1995 survey, and gathered management insights and perspectives on current issues and anticipated trends in the industry. The remainder of this summary discusses these observations within five broad categories:

technology, human resources, products and services, distribution channels, and fee structures.

Technology

During the past two years, transfer agents have continued to invest in technology and have realized significant operational and service-quality improvements. Despite the existence of proven automated work distribution (AWD) systems for several years, many complexes are just now implementing these systems. While AWD systems have proven to generate operating efficiencies, they require dedicated staffs to implement and significant investment in training and technology.

Beyond AWD system integration is the need to upgrade existing workstations to increase capacity and functionality. This is a significant cost, even when considered on a per-unit basis. Enhanced processing platforms have generally been developed in conjunction with expanded enterprise-wide computer system networks, commonly known as wide-area networks (WANs), which require significant costs to develop, implement, test, and secure. WANs have become even more critical as transfer agents expand operations to multiple sites.

Telephone systems continue to be upgraded, enabling more types of transactions to be processed by automated telephone systems. Furthermore, complexes are handling increased call volumes via automated voice response systems. As these systems become more robust, complexes continue to invest in upgrades to better distinguish services to existing and potential shareholders. Most complexes report an increased usage of these phone services by shareholders, and calls requiring shareholder representative assistance now tend to be more time consuming and complex.

The Internet has just begun to achieve market acceptance as an information gathering resource. While some complexes and service providers expect to launch limited transaction-processing capabilities on the Internet, the power of this tool has not been realized. Complexes are now investing in products and services that will fit this market segment as well as address concerns about confidentiality and security of transaction processing.

Complexes have also begun to address the Year 2000 problem, by reviewing their computer programs and developing an understanding of how their service agents are preparing for the turn-of-the-century transition. The solutions appear costly and may lead complexes to replace existing systems with newer client-server-based technology well ahead of the complex's previous plans.

Distribution Channels

During the past two years, virtually all fund complexes have placed increased emphasis on expanding distribution channels. As a result, the lines between traditional distribution channels have begun to intersect. Traditionally no-load complexes have established new load products or added low loads or 12b-1 plans to existing funds. Broker-dealer entities have begun to drop loads or participate in no-transaction-fee networks, providing greater product distribution but no sales commissions. The use of fund marketplaces is likely to expand during the coming years, and complexes will need to develop the means to distinguish their products and services from an increasingly broad array of funds available to their shareholders.

As the "fund-of-funds" concept continues to gain investor acceptance, the idea of managing a portfolio of funds has also grown more popular. This has been a positive factor in the growth of the role that financial intermediaries and advisors play in the distribution of fund products. Funds now view financial intermediaries and advisors as clients that must be supported by dedicated resources. Fund complexes will need to bring these networks of advisors and intermediaries into the automated, centralized facilities developed by the funds and brokerage industries in order to provide seamless service to fund shareholders.

The retirement marketplace has continued to expand for mutual funds, with no foreseeable roadblocks in the near future. Indeed, recently enacted federal legislation may make retirement plans more attractive to smaller businesses, perhaps increasing the use of mutual funds as retirement planning vehicles. The growing popularity of mutual funds in retirement plans has placed significant demands on complexes to develop participant services, or to form alliances with outside parties to provide such services. The systems and skills required to support plan participants differ from those needed to service retail shareholders, thus requiring additional investments in systems and resources that cannot leverage existing retail-oriented systems. As this market segment develops, perhaps the most important area of differentiation is service quality. Given that the investment options available to participants have expanded significantly, the future is likely to hold more competition for service providers, with participants demanding better services, greater plan flexibility, and reduced costs.

Products and Services

Complexes have focused on implementing many technological innovations over the past few years, including enhanced workstations, expanded voice-response phone systems, enterprise-wide networks, and automated work-routing systems. Progress has also been made through the development of sophisticated Internet homepages, more interactive processing, improved communication capabilities, and the creation of more complex products.

Up to this point, fund complexes have generally viewed Internet websites as marketing tools. They have, accordingly, developed tools and services which will distinguish their companies from competitors in the eyes of existing and potential shareholders. This has been evident in the use of software tools to assist shareholders in developing personal investment or savings plans in conjunction with the selection of appropriate funds to meet these highlighted needs. Some complexes have established open chat sessions with portfolio managers to encourage better communication of fund performance objectives or investment strategies. While these services allow the complex to build a closer relationship with individual shareholders, they also enable transfer agents to continue the trend of shifting transaction processing to outside parties, such as broker-dealers, third-party administrators, retirement plan sponsors and participants, and even shareholders. While these services are viewed in the marketplace as an additional benefit to shareholders, they may also help control transfer agent processing costs.

The ability to communicate with shareholders becomes more important as fund complexity increases. While sophisticated fund shareholders may already be familiar with sales charges, distribution fees, exchanges, wire redemptions, self-directed brokerage services, and other service options, many others are not. The proliferation of fund features requires fund complexes to better identify where and who owns their funds. Active shareholders will have a different service profile than shareholders investing solely through an employer-sponsored, defined-contribution retirement plan. In addition, as fund product design is refined to service different shareholder needs, through structural changes such as multiple classes or master/feeder organization, transfer agent systems will require modifications to properly record activity and provide data quickly for shareholder service needs. These initiatives, along with changing processing and servicing environments, will require some rethinking of traditional systems design as today's systems users comprise a broader range of internal and external parties.

Human Resources

For transfer agents, human resource issues have traditionally revolved around training and employee turnover. While still the case, the dynamics behind these issues have changed dramatically. As more routine clerical functions become automated, the complexity of tasks performed by shareholder service representatives has increased significantly. The growth in the number of funds, the diversity of fund offerings, the increased knowledge of shareholders, and an expanded array of shareholder services has necessitated more comprehensive training programs, more frequent product updates, and refresher courses. Consequently, more transfer agents require college graduates, possibly with prior work experience, for positions in customer service and transaction processing.

The fast pace at which increasingly complex processing systems have been introduced into transfer agent processing environments has necessitated the hiring of experienced technical personnel to maintain these systems. Successful implementation of new systems is dependent upon the quality of technical resources, as well as the availability of staff who possess requisite skills. This requires organizations to invest in and create stable work environments that minimize the impact of turnover and enable the organization to benefit from staff continuity on long-term projects.

Fee Structures

Fee structures have remained essentially unchanged from prior survey results, with the flat-fee billing structure remaining the predominant arrangement (comprising 56 percent of total responses). One reason for the continued predominance of the flat-fee billing structure may be the desire to simplify billing arrangements. Instances of complex billing arrangements necessitating substantial systems modifications to support the new structure, as well as increasing the risk of error, have been noted as reasons to maintain a flat per-account billing structure. In past years, other billing structures, such as flat-fee-plus-transaction charges or basis-point fees, seemed likely to increase in usage. However, funds' utilization of these structures has remained at levels observed in prior surveys.

Despite the desire to keep things simple, the growing complexity of distribution arrangements has necessitated a fairly diverse set of new billing relationships. Upon entering into a mutual fund marketplace, for instance, many fund complexes have negotiated a fee based on total or net assets in the program. Portions of these fees have, in some cases, been charged to the fund as transfer agent expenses and, in other instances, have been borne by the management company. Many complexes have not yet finalized these arrangements, nor have they completely decided how the arrangements will be reflected, if at all, as billings to the fund. The growth of financial intermediaries and retirement marketplaces has also led to the development of new billing arrangements for accounts created through these channels. Some complexes charge for services provided to these accounts at the intermediary or plan-sponsor level, while others charge on a per-account basis using a flat-fee or basis-point arrangement.

Case Study: **Controlling Hot Money**

A mutual fund may be thought of as a group of people who get together, pool their money, and hire someone to use the money for the purpose the group has agreed upon. Mutual fund shareholders agree to split the proceeds of their investment and also agree to split the costs of some basic services that they feel are important, such as customer phone service and fund annual reports. In a pooled investment, there are many different shareholders and many different relationships that must be considered—large investors, small investors, investors that are part of a retirement plan, etc. Each shareholder may have different servicing needs and preferences, but has agreed to pay for the average level of service required by the group.

The transfer agent of a fund incurs the ongoing costs of shareholder servicing such as transaction processing, updating account information, and mailing confirmation statements, which costs are charged directly to the fund. These ongoing servicing costs are spread on a pro-rata basis to all shareholders of the fund, regardless of an individual shareholder's contribution to the costs. Because fund shareholders would have great difficulty coordinating among themselves, they rely instead upon the fund's independent directors to protect shareholder interests and act as arbitrators when conflicts arise. Among other fiduciary tasks, the directors need to decide whether the services provided by the fund's transfer agent are worth the costs borne by all fund shareholders, or whether some of these costs should be borne by a particular set of shareholders.

The case study below presents one such dilemma for independent directors that involves conflicts between different groups of shareholders of the same fund. A Japan Fund has recently experienced high cash flow volatility, caused by short-term movement in and out of the fund by a small percentage of shareholders. The portfolio manager has been forced to spend more and more time managing this cash flow, and portfolio transactions have greatly increased as a result of the volatile cash flows. Also, increased shareholder activity has led to higher fund expenses for transfer agent services.

The situation facing the directors of the Japan Fund is further complicated by the significant time difference between the U.S. and Japanese stock markets. The fund focuses on Japanese securities, which are primarily traded on stock exchanges in Japan. These exchanges operate during Japanese business hours (rather than U.S. business hours) and close long before the U.S. business day begins—typically 2 A.M. Eastern Time (ET). Most U.S. mutual funds are priced daily at 4 P.M. ET to coordinate with the close of the New York Stock Exchange (NYSE). This leaves a 14-hour window between the last trade in a Japanese security and the valuation point of that security for the purposes of determining the net asset value of the fund.

At the next meeting of the fund's board of directors, you, as the chief financial officer for the investment adviser to the fund, are scheduled to make a presentation addressing these cash flow and pricing issues. The case study contains the material on both issues available to you. At your last staff meeting, you asked a select group of experienced employees to help you analyze the situation, evaluate alternatives, and develop recommendations to be presented to the board.

In-Class Discussion Questions

After a review of the materials provided, the group has determined that answers to the following questions are necessary:

1. What is the impact of the short-term trading on the Japan Fund during August of 1997? Please quantify, to the extent feasible, the various categories of costs imposed by short-term trading of the fund. Which fund shareholders bear these costs of short-term trading?

2. What are the disadvantages (opportunity costs and administrative costs) of controlling "hot money" in the Japan Fund? Who bears these costs?

3. Assuming that action is warranted, what strategy will you propose to the Japan Fund directors that is likely to reduce substantially the short-term purchases and redemptions (or their impact) by shareholders while minimizing the disadvantages identified above? (Please be specific and quantify your recommendation.) Alternatives may include:

   - Restricting the number of transactions per account
   - Restricting the manner in which redemption orders are taken
   - Adding a redemption fee to the fund
   - Adding a back-end load to the fund

4. What security prices are being used by the fund at 4 P.M. ET when net asset value is determined? What other prices could be used? What other valuation time could be used?

5. Review the SEC's forward pricing rule included in the case study (see exhibits 7 and 8). Is the fund's current pricing policy a violation of the literal words or underlying concerns of this rule? If not, is it possible for investors to "game" the fund's pricing policy? If so, how?

6. Look in the materials at the price movements in Nikkei futures traded in Chicago during U.S. business hours on 1/16/97 (exhibit 10). For that day, should you adjust the price of the Japan Fund or some or all of the securities it owns? Would you make a different valuation decision if the futures were up by the same amount or percent as they were down?

9.6 The Japan Fund

The Problem

Since the beginning of 1997, the U.S.-sold Japan Fund has experienced substantial cash inflows and outflows from investors, and portfolio manager David Smith has recently voiced his concern about the volatility. He also noted that extremely large shareholder orders seem to coincide more and more with news affecting Japan, and that cash flow management is taking up a large percentage of his time that might otherwise be spent selecting securities.

David thinks that perhaps some shareholders are trying to increase their profits by "timing" the market—quickly moving their money from one fund to another within the complex. Further, he speculates that these investors might be attempting to profit from the methodology used by the fund complex to compute the daily net asset value (NAV) of the fund by trading on stock price information that may become available between the time when the Japanese markets close and the time the fund values its holdings. David has requested that someone look into the shareholder trading activity and also analyze whether the pricing of the fund has encouraged or contributed to the cash flow volatility.

Background on the Japan Fund

Introduced on October 28, 1993, the Japan Fund is a nondiversified, SEC registered mutual fund sold with a 5% sales load and a 0.25% 12b-1 fee to U.S. investors. The fund's investment objective is to achieve long-term growth primarily through investment in securities of Japanese companies. The fund may hold any type of equity or debt securities, although it is expected that equity securities will normally account for the majority of the fund's investments. The Japan Fund may also invest in indexed and debt-like securities whose value depends on the price of foreign currencies, securities indices, other financial indicators, or underlying interests. As of August 31, 1997, the fund had assets of $125 million, and 12,500 shareholders with an average account size of $10,000. Currently, the average stock trade for the Japan Fund is 5,000 shares at $20 per share, and David Smith tends to hold no more than 3% of the fund's assets in cash, but occasionally may hold less for a day or two, depending on recent shareholder redemption activity.

The Japan Fund is managed by Global Management Company (Global), which also serves as manager of the following other mutual funds in the Global complex: Emerging Growth, Large-Cap Stock, Small-Cap Stock, S&P 500 Index, International, Emerging Markets, Europe, Latin America, and High Income Bond. Shareholders of any fund in the Global complex may sell their fund shares and buy shares of other Global funds, subject to any restrictions detailed in each prospectus. The shares exchanged will carry credit for any sales charge previously paid by the investor in connection with their purchase. Each fund reserves the right to terminate or modify the exchange privilege at any time in the future.

Regional international funds, which are relatively new offerings for Global, seem to have gained in popularity. Assets in the funds increased at a fairly steady pace the prior year, and the complex now has a few funds (listed above) that each focus on a non-U.S. region or country. Although these focused funds carry higher risk than diversified international funds, they have the potential for higher returns. Because they are more concentrated than diversified international funds, country funds may appeal to investors who want to take more personal control of their investments, potentially including more active traders. As a result, Global anticipated that the Japan Fund might experience higher shareholder volatility, but the recent wave of cash that has been moving in and out of the Japan Fund seems to be especially high.

Short-Term Trading

Global has found that short-term trading is somewhat more likely to occur in aggressive or volatile funds or funds that are concentrated in one type of investment. Investors that are looking to place a "bet" have more difficulty doing it in a diversified fund, where the manager has more discretion to move money among market sectors and possibly asset classes. Since most sector and country funds have relatively small shareholder bases, a small group of shareholders making short-term trades can cause significant cash flow volatility relative to the size of the fund.

Short-term trades affect various categories of fund expenses that are paid by all shareholders in the fund. The fund's expenses, as detailed in exhibits 1 and 2, include management fees, 12b-1 fees, transfer agent fees, and other expenses as well as brokerage commissions. Brokerage commissions are accounted for as an addition to the cost basis, or reduction in the proceeds from the sale, of the fund's portfolio securities and therefore reduce the gain (or increase the loss) realized by the fund.

Redemption Fees

Redemption fees are defined as fees paid to the fund (as opposed to loads, which are paid to the distributor). They may be imposed on all redemptions or on shares redeemed within a certain time period (e.g., 90 days), and are sometimes used to dissuade short-term trading and/or to compensate the remaining shareholders for the adverse effects of such trading. Redemption fees are typically charged on exchanges into other funds within the complex as well as full account liquidations (i.e., leaving the complex). Some funds are introduced with redemption fees initially, while others have redemption fees added only after experiencing heavy cash-flow volatility.

Global has previously determined the level of a redemption fee should be based on the trading costs associated with the type of portfolio, and has used estimates of turnover costs, including such factors as commissions, taxes, and bid/offer spreads. The company feels that redemption fees based on a holding period are clear-cut and precise, but such fees may affect people who sell after a short period even though they did not buy the fund as a short-term or market timing investment.

Back-end Loads

Back-end loads are a sales commission levied by some load funds when an investor sells mutual fund shares. These back-end loads are typically structured as a contingent deferred sales charge (CDSC), which often start at 5% or 6% of money withdrawn within a year of buying the fund and then decline by a percentage point or so each year until they disappear. Back-end loads are usually set to compensate the distributor for marketing and selling the fund, especially to protect anticipated annual flows of 12b-1 fees; however, back-end loads may also be used to dissuade short-term traders—funds may set a high back-end load for money withdrawn within a very short time-frame, and then revert to the more general schedule of yearly declining load amounts referenced above.

Like most other mutual fund complexes, Global grants investors the privilege to exchange in and out of funds within the complex, and also allows credit for any load paid when purchasing or redeeming one of the funds. For the purpose of calculating an applicable CDSC, most complexes also give credit to investors for the holding period of shares purchased in other funds of the same complex if those shares are exchanged into a fund with a CDSC.

General Mutual Fund Pricing

Most mutual funds sold in the United States are priced daily as of 4 P.M. ET to correspond to the closing of the NYSE, although the time of pricing is left to the board of directors of the fund. Since there is no secondary market in fund shares, a daily price means that investors can be assured of having their orders executed within 24 hours (during normal business days). While more frequent valuations are allowed, they may be prohibitively expensive for a fund manager, both from an administrative and operational perspective.

SEC rule 22c-1 (see exhibit 7) links the time of the NAV to shareholder trades by requiring that investor orders be executed at the next available share price after receipt of the order. For example, an investor that places an order at 11 A.M. to redeem 200 shares in the Japan Fund must be able to redeem those shares at the fund NAV calculated as of 4 P.M. ET that afternoon. However, an investor that places an order at 4:59 P.M. the same day to purchase $2,500 worth of shares in the Japan Fund will buy the shares at the NAV calculated as of 4 P.M. ET on the next day.

Pricing of the Japan Fund

The Japan Fund is open for business each day the New York Stock Exchange is open. The fund's NAV is normally calculated as of the close of business of the NYSE, normally 4 P.M. ET. The fund's NAV is the U.S. dollar value of a single share, and is computed by adding up the value of the fund's investments, cash, and other assets, subtracting its liabilities, and then dividing the results by the number of shares outstanding. Foreign securities are translated to U.S. dollar values using the applicable foreign exchange rate.

At 4 P.M. ET the last price offered for most securities held by the fund is 14 hours old, since the Japan exchanges close at 2 A.M. ET (earlier in the same day). Nevertheless, on most trading days, there is little change in Japanese stock market levels after Tokyo markets close at 2 P.M. ET and little activity in Japanese equity trading outside of Japan. As a result, there typically is little change in the yen-denominated prices of Japanese equities from the market's close in Japan to the market's close in the United States. To the extent that the fund owns Japanese securities that trade primarily in the U.S. markets (including American Depository Receipts for Japanese stocks, which are usually listed on the NYSE), they will be valued at their last trading price in the U.S. market at 4 P.M. ET.

Occasionally, however, significant events may occur after Japan's business day is over that can dramatically change Japanese equity values. When these unusual events occur, the Japan Fund may value its Japanese investments at a level reflecting their value at the U.S. market close—which may be more or less than their value at the end of Japanese trading hours. The ability to make this kind of adjustment is recognized in the prospectus for the Japan Fund, which states that the fund's Board of Trustees may use valuations other than closing local market quotations if prices have been materially affected by events occurring after the closing of a local market.

Summary

Portfolio manager David Smith has called to check on the status of his request, and the board of directors' meeting is coming up in a few weeks. Your staff members have gathered relevant statistics, documents, and articles (exhibits 3–13), and are busy conducting analyses of the topics to be discussed.

Exhibit 1

Global Japan Fund: expenses as of 6/30/97

Shareholder transaction expenses	
Maximum sales charge on purchases (as % of offering price)	5%
Maximum sales charge on reinvested distributions	None
Deferred sales charge on redemptions	None
Exchange fee	None
Annual fund operating expenses	
Management fee	0.80%
12b-1 fee	0.25%
Other expenses	0.52%
Total fund operating expenses	1.57%

Source: Global Japan Fund prospectus, June 30, 1997

Exhibit 2

Global Investment Company schedule for significant "other expenses" as of 6/30/97

Transfer agency (for shareholder transactions)	
Account fee	$10
Transaction fee	$12
Custodian (for Japan Fund transactions)	
Asset charge	2 bp
Transaction fee	$40
Pricing & bookkeeping	
Asset charge	5 bp
Transaction fee	None

Exhibit 3

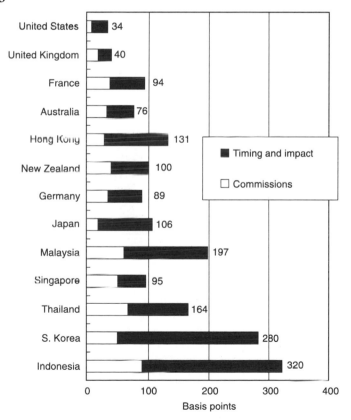

Listed equities: Total institutional transaction costs by country for one-way transactions. Source: Plexus Group

Exhibit 4

Global Japan Fund sales data ($)

Date	Gross sales	Gross redemptions	Net Sales
8/1/97	540,003	590,457	−50,454
8/4/97	698,457	1,589,497	−891,040
8/5/97	542,378	595,911	−53,533
8/6/97	480,573	1,441,264	−960,691
8/7/97	49,487	151,081	−101,594
8/8/97	957,845	3,985,150	−3,027,305
8/11/97	3,500,240	1,490,821	2,009,419
8/12/97	298,563	1,563,346	−1,264,783
8/13/97	249,448	1,511,611	−1,262,163
8/14/97	113,895	526,078	−412,183
8/15/97	113,799	1,010,743	−896,944
8/18/97	634,040	650,709	−16,669
8/19/97	16,023	569,273	−553,250
8/20/97	101,644	1,678,032	−1,576,388
8/21/97	3,422,587	469,827	2,952,760
8/22/97	99,348	4,100,354	−4,001,006
8/25/97	145,325	249,950	−104,625
8/26/97	140,652	914,240	−773,588
8/27/97	40,292	697,674	−657,382
8/28/97	12,345	380,198	−367,853
8/29/97	37,836	868,789	−830,953
Total	12,194,780	25,035,005	−12,840,225

Exhibit 5

Global Japan Fund: Redemption by holding period during the 46 months ended 8/31/97

Months following purchase	Percent of shareholders redeemed each month
1	10.0%
2	1.0%
3	1.0%
4	9.0%
5	9.0%
6–12	2.0%
13–46	0.5%

GLOBAL INVESTMENT COMPANY   *Retail Marketing*
Memorandum

TO: Chief Financial Officer

FROM: Heather Martin

DATE: September 10, 1997

RE: Japan Fund

Further to our discussion earlier today, I would like to strongly argue against the possible addition of fees or restrictions to the Japan Fund. In interacting directly with customers on a daily basis, I have the opportunity to observe first-hand their reactions to differing fees and restrictions on Global funds.

I find that additional fees on any fund are a deterrent to all existing and potential customers. To the average investor, a fee is a fee whether it is front- or back-end, targeted to short-term traders or not. As you know, the Japan Fund currently has a front-end load, and a redemption fee would, in my opinion, significantly reduce new monies coming into the fund and may spur redemptions from current shareholders. While most investors do correctly perceive a load as a sales charge (whether front- or back-end), they perceive a redemption fee as an additional fee charged by the management company (even though it is paid to the fund).

Imposing a limited transaction policy or making the redemption process more difficult would also put off potential shareholders and may frustrate current shareholders once they decide to redeem. One of the attractive features of the Global complex is that investors can place buy, sell or exchange orders for multiple funds with one phone call. Differentiating the Japan Fund by placing additional restrictions not found in other funds makes integrated servicing more difficult and more confusing to the customer. Anything that makes the redemption process for the Japan Fund more difficult than for other funds -- even if disclosed in the prospectus and verbally reiterated during phone orders -- has the potential to anger shareholders when they attempt to redeem and sour them on the entire Global complex.

Is short-term trading truly enough of a problem to warrant any of the actions mentioned above? In my opinion, the answer is clearly no.

Please feel free to contact me if you would like to discuss this further or have additional questions.

Exhibit 7

9.7   Pricing of Redeemable Securities for Distribution, Redemption, and Repurchase

SEC, Investment Company Act of 1940, Release no. IC-14244, File no. S7-39-84, 17CFR Part 270, November 21, 1984 (excerpt)

Rule 22c-1(b), as amended in 1979, requires investment companies issuing redeemable securities to compute the net asset value of shares (i) not less frequently than once daily on each day (other than days when no order to purchase or sell is received and no tender for redemption is made) in which there is a sufficient degree of trading in the investment company's portfolio securities that the current net asset value of the fund's redeemable securities might be materially affected by changes in the value of the portfolio securities, and (ii) at such specific time during the day as determined by a majority of the board of directors of the investment company no less frequently than annually.[1]

Rule 22c-1 was originally adopted in 1968 to require forward pricing of investment company redeemable securities.[2] The rule requires that an open-end investment company, for purposes of sales, redemptions, and repurchases of its redeemable securities, give investment orders the next computed prices of the net asset value after receipt of the order. Prior to adoption of rule 22c-1, investor orders to purchase and redeem could be executed at a price computed before receipt of the order, allowing investors to lock-in a low price in a rising market and a higher price in a falling market. The forward pricing provision of rule 22c-1 was designed to eliminate these trading practices and the dilution to fund shareholders which occurred as a result of backward pricing.

Notes

1.   17 CFR 270.22c-1(b).
2.   ICA release no. 5519 (October 16, 1968); 33 FR 16331 (November 7, 1986).

Exhibit 8

9.8 Putnam "No Action" Letter*

SEC-Reply-1: Securities and Exchange Commission
Washington, D.C. 20549
January 23, 1981

Response of the Office of Chief Counsel
Division of Investment Management

Our Ref. No. 80-327-CC
The Putnam Growth Fund
Putnam International Equities Fund, Inc.
File Nos. 811-781 and 811-1403

Based on the representations contained in your letter, we would not recommend any action to the Commission under section 22(d) of the Investment Company Act of 1940 (the "1940 Act") or rules 22e-1 and 2a-4 under the 1940 Act if The Putnam Growth Fund and Putnam International Equities Fund, Inc. ("the Funds") value their assets at 4:00 P.M. New York time and use as the values of their portfolio securities which are principally traded on foreign securities exchanges the next preceding closing values of such securities on their respective exchanges except when an event has occurred since the time a value was so established that is likely to have resulted in a change in such value, in which case the fair value of the securities as of 4:00 P.M. New York time will be determined by the consideration of other factors. In addition, based on the representations contained in your letter, we would not recommend any action under the aforementioned provisions if each of the Funds, a substantial majority of whose portfolio securities are not principally traded on Japanese exchanges, does not price its shares for sale or redemption as of those Saturdays that the Japanese exchanges are open for business.

Stanley B. Judd

Inquiry-1: Ropes & Gray
225 Franklin Street
Boston 02110

---

*Provided by the Securities and Exchange Commission.

Investment Company Act of 1940;
Section 22(d) and Rules 2a–4 and 22(c) (1)
October 22, 1980

Securities and Exchange Commission
Division of Investment Management
500 North Capitol Street
Washington, D.C. 20549

Attention: Joel H. Goldberg, Associate Director
Stanley B. Judd, Assistant Chief Counsel

Re: The Putnam Growth Fund
Putnam International Equities Fund, Inc.

Gentlemen:

The purpose of this letter is to request confirmation by the staff of the Securities and Exchange Commission that it will not recommend action by the Commission under Section 22(d) of the Investment Company Act of 1940 (the "1940 Act") and Rules 22(c) (1) and 2a–4 under the 1940 Act if The Putnam Growth Fund and Putnam International Equities Fund, Inc., value their assets invested in securities of companies principally traded in foreign companies in accordance with the procedure outlined below.

Facts:

The Putnam Growth Fund ("Putnam Growth") is a Massachusetts business trust which is registered under the 1940 Act as an open-end management company which had assets as of September 30, 1980, of approximately $690 million. The investment objective of Putnam Growth is to seek long-term growth of capital with current income as a secondary consideration. Under most conditions, common stocks have constituted a substantial majority of the Fund's investment. As of September 30, 1980, Putnam Growth had approximately $48 million, or 7%, invested in securities of issuers whose securities are primarily traded in foreign countries. As of that date, approximately 3% of the Fund's total assets were invested in securities of companies whose securities are principally traded on the Tokyo Stock Exchange. The Fund may invest up to 20% of its assets in securities of foreign issuers although to date the Fund has never invested in the aggregate more than 10% of its assets in such securities. Putnam Growth is owned by approximately 85,000 shareholders.

Putnam International Equities Fund, Inc. ("Putnam Equities") is a Massachusetts corporation which is registered under the Act as an open-end management company with assets as of September 30, 1980, of approximately $42 million. The investment objective of Putnam Equities is to seek capital appreciation by investing its assets primarily in common stocks. Up to 70% of Putnam Equities' assets may be invested from time to time in securities principally traded in foreign markets. As of September 30, 1980, investments of the Fund could be geographically divided as follows:

Australia	6.4%
England	2.4%
Germany	9.2%
Hong Kong	4.2%

Japan	26.4%
South Africa	6.9%
Switzerland	2.9%
Netherlands	4.6%
United States	37.0%

Putnam Equities is owned by approximately 13,000 shareholders.

Both Putnam Growth and Putnam Equities currently value their assets at 4:00 P.M. each day on which the New York Stock Exchange is open for trading. Securities which are principally traded in foreign countries are valued as of 4:00 P.M. New York time using as a basis for this valuation the next preceding closing values for such securities on the stock exchanges where such securities are principally traded. For many foreign securities there are American Depository Receipts ("ADRs") which reflect ownership in the underlying foreign security. Such ADRs are traded in the U.S. in the over-the-counter market and are valued daily as of approximately 4:00 P.M. New York time.* Where such ADRs exist and are actively traded, the Funds use such ADRs to value the underlying foreign security whether or not they in fact own the ADRs.

Both Putnam Growth and Putnam Equities are sold only in the United States. In the case of orders for purchases and sales through dealers, the applicable public offering price will be the net asset value determined as of the close of the New York Stock Exchange on the date the order was placed plus the applicable sales charge but only if the order is received by the dealer prior to the close of the Exchange and transmitted to the Funds' distributor prior to its close of business that date—normally 5:00 P.M. Boston time.

Both Putnam Growth and Putnam Equities are managed pursuant to contracts with The Putnam Management Company, Inc., which also acts as investment adviser to eleven other open-end and one closed-end investment companies. The pricing of the Funds' portfolios is done by Putnam Administrative Services Company, Inc., acting as agent for The Putnam Management Company, Inc.

The offices of Putnam Growth, Putnam Equities, The Putnam Management Company, Inc., and Putnam Administrative Services Company are not open for business on Saturday. No fund business is transacted on that day and there are no personnel regularly present to process orders to purchase shares or to determine prices of portfolio securities and make other calculations necessary to determine net asset value. To the extent necessary, investment matters on such days relating to foreign securities are generally followed by portfolio managers from their own homes. Mail addressed to the Funds or their shareholder servicing agent or principal underwriter at the street address is picked up Monday through Friday at a central post office in Boston and processed on those days. A clerical person picks up box mail each Saturday but the letters are not opened until Monday nor is there personnel present to open such mail on Saturday.

Discussion:

In response to comments of the Commission's staff in connection with certain registration statements of open-end investment companies which have recently or will soon become

---

*As of September 30, 1980, approximately one-third of Putnam Growth's foreign investments and one-quarter of Putnam Equities' foreign investments reflect ownership by the Funds of ADRs.

effective and in light of the response of the Commission's staff to the "no action letter" of Nomura Capital Fund of Japan and Nomura Index Fund of Japan of November 6, 1979 (the "Nomura Letter"), Putnam Growth and Putnam Equities have reviewed their pricing policies with respect to foreign securities. Such review has been made not only with respect to the practice of not pricing securities which are traded in the Japanese market on those Saturdays on which the Japanese Stock Exchange is open for trading but also generally with respect to the manner in which each Fund normally values its foreign securities on a regular business day. While each Fund believes that its procedures are appropriate and fair to all investors, we believe it is appropriate in light of the Nomura Letter to seek the views of the Commission's staff as to the current procedures followed by these two Fund.

Rule 22c–1(a) and (b) provides in part:

(a) No registered investment company issuing any redeemable security ... shall sell, redeem, or repurchase any such security except at a price based on the current net asset value of such security which is next computed after receipt of a tender of such security for redemption or of an order to purchase or sell such security; ...

(b) For the purposes of this rule, (1) the current net asset value of any such security shall be computed (i) no less frequently than once daily on each day (other than a day during which no such security was tendered for redemption and no order to purchase or sell such security was received by the investment company) in which there is a sufficient degree of trading in the investment company's portfolio securities that the current net asset value of the investment company's redeemable securities might be materially affected by changes in the value of the portfolio securities, and (ii) at such specific time during the day as determined by a majority of the board of directors of the investment company no less frequently than annually; ...

Rule 2a–4 under the Act provides in part:

(a) The current net asset value of any redeemable security issued by a registered investment company used in computing periodically the current price for the purpose of distribution, redemption, and repurchase means an amount which reflects calculations, whether or not recorded in the books of account, made substantially in accordance with the following, with estimates used where necessary or appropriate:

(1) Portfolio securities with respect to which market quotations are readily available shall be valued at current market value, and other securities and assets shall be valued at fair value as determined in good faith by the board of directors of the registered company....

As described above, Putnam Growth and Putnam Equities, at the time of their daily computation of net asset value at 4:00 P.M. New York time, utilize for purposes of determining the proper security value of portfolio investments traded principally in foreign countries the market values for such securities as of the close of trading on the principal exchanges where such securities are traded as of a time earlier in the day. For example, with respect to securities traded on the London Stock Exchange, trading has ceased as of 10:00 A.M. New York time and there are no current market quotations as of 4:00 P.M. New York time except those market quotations which are available from earlier in the day at the close of business of the London Stock Exchange. For this reason, Putnam Growth and Putnam Equities have used such earlier values for purposes of estimating the value of such securities as of 4:00 P.M. New York time.

We believe that the above procedure for valuing such foreign securities is consistent with the requirements of Rule 2a–4 (a) under the Act for either of two reasons. First, if one determines that portfolio securities traded in London and for which trading ceased approximately six hours earlier in the day are "portfolio securities with respect to which market quotations are readily available" then one is required to use "current market values" for such securities in computing current net asset value. Since no securities have generally traded in London since 10:00 A.M. New York time, the only current market values available for determining the value of such securities as of 4:00 P.M. New York time are the closing prices on the London Stock Exchange earlier in the day. Pursuant to the provisions of Rule 2a–4, Putnam Growth and Putnam Equities estimate the prices as of 4:00 P.M. New York time utilizing the earlier day London closing values as the basis for such estimates. Second, if one determines that as of 4:00 P.M. New York time the London securities are not "portfolio securities with respect to which market quotations are readily available" onc is then required to value such securities "at fair value as determined in good faith by the board of directors of the registered company." In this case, the Fund would in almost all instances use, for purposes of fair valuation, the closing prices of such London securities of approximately six hours earlier and estimate that as of 4:00 P.M. New York time such values reflect fair value of such securities as of that time. In either case, the valuation made at 4:00 P.M. New York time is being estimated based on market values which reflected closing values as of earlier in the day. Such method would clearly seem to be permissible under Rule 2a–4.

If, however, some extraordinary event were to occur after the close of business on the London Stock Exchange but prior to the close of business on the New York Stock Exchange on the same day and the Funds' officers, to whom authority for pricing the respective Funds has been delegated, determine that such closing prices are no longer a reasonable estimate of such securities values as of 4:00 P.M. New York time, then there would be made a fair value determination of the value of such securities as of 4:00 P.M. using other appropriate indicia of value or valuation of the Funds' overall portfolio would be suspended until early the next morning at which time current portfolio quotations for such London securities could be obtained with the previous U.S. closing prices used for U.S. securities.

The above valuation procedures of Putnam Growth and Putnam Equities avoid the abuses which forward pricing, as set forth in Rule 22c–1, was intended to limit. For example, an investor who enters an order to purchase shares of either Putnam Growth or Putnam Equities at 3:00 P.M. New York time will not be circumventing the requirement of Rule 22c–1 that such shares be purchased at a price which is next computed after the order is received. This is true even with respect to foreign securities, values for which will be established as of 4:00 P.M. New York time. This is not any less true because the Fund utilizes prices reflecting closing stock exchange values earlier in the day since the determination that such prices continue to be valid is made in fact after the order has been received. In those rare circumstances when the earlier London or other foreign markets' closing values are no longer deemed by the Funds to be accurate as of 4:00 P.M. New York time the Funds procedures for valuation as required by the Act would require that the Funds utilize fair value procedures for arriving at a 4:00 P.M. New York valuation and thus the valuation would continue to be made after the order has been received.

Further, the utilization of 4:00 P.M. New York time as the valuation time not only for Putnam Growth but also for Putnam Equities which may have a majority of its securities traded in countries outside of the United States is appropriate and consistent with the Act and the rules thereunder. As stated in Rule 22c–1, it is required that directors/trustees of each Fund determine the specific time during the day when a fund must value its assets. The utilization by Putnam Equities of 4:00 P.M. New York time is not only consistent with the provisions of Rule 2a-4 for the reasons stated above but also permits the Fund's shareholders to have a net asset value fixed at a time consistent with other mutual funds and which permits the maximum public distribution of such prices. To pick another time, for example 10:00 A.M. New York time (i.e., the close of business on the European markets) would mean that a shareholder who purchased his or her shares at 11:00 A.M. New York time would not be given a value for such purchase until 10:00 A.M. the next day and would not be able to read the price per share received in a newspaper until the following day or two full days after the order was entered. This approach would not seem to be beneficial for shareholders and would tend to underscore the reasonableness of the director's decision that a 4:00 P.M. New York time on the day the order to purchase or sell shares is received is the proper time for valuing Putnam Equities' securities. . . .

If you need any additional information in connection with the foregoing, please do not hesitate to contact the undersigned. Also, in the event that you have any difficulty taking the position requested in this letter, I would apreciate the opportunity to discuss this matter with you further at your convenience.

Sincerely yours,

Edward P. Lawrence

cc: Mr. Richard M. Cutler
Vice Chairman
The Putnam Funds

Exhibit 9

9.9 "Fair-Value" Pricing for Shares in Funds to Be Reviewed by SEC*
Charles Gasparino

The controversy surrounding "fair-value" pricing for mutual-fund shares has caught the eye of the fund industry's top cop.

The Securities and Exchange Commission, which regulates the $4.4 trillion mutual-fund business, plans to scrutinize the unusual pricing technique in the wake of last week's market turmoil and investor angst over the issue.

In fair-value pricing, fund companies largely disregard closing market prices of stocks and other securities to determine how much a mutual fund is worth. Instead, they rely on other bits of information, including the trading of futures tied to these securities, to determine stock prices and ultimately the price of mutual-fund portfolios.

At the moment, SEC rules allow fund companies to use this technique—instead of the more traditional approach of using closing share prices—to come up with a fund's net asset value, or NAV. However, following last week's upheaval in global markets, many investors are complaining that they bought or sold fund shares unaware that some fund companies, including giant Fidelity Investments, relied on the fair-value system. SEC officials now say they will reconsider the commission's policy.

"In light of the events of the last week," an SEC spokesman said in a statement, "the commission intends to review the operation of its rules of the pricing of fund shares in turbulent markets. We will be talking to the fund groups and may conduct examinations of the fund groups that use 'fair-market value' pricing methods. If it appears that the rules are not working in the best interest of fund shareholders, they will be revised."

In theory, SEC officials favor giving fund companies leeway in their pricing of fund shares. Gene Gohlke, an associate director with the SEC's Office of Compliance Inspections and Examinations, told a securities conference in New York Friday he believes fair-value pricing is a "reasonable approach," when market prices "might no longer be the best prices." The SEC, he said, had given its blessing to the practice in a "no-action" letter to Putnam Investments. Mr. Gohlke said Putnam wanted to be sure it wouldn't raise regulators' eyebrows if it considered post-closing events when pricing overseas stocks or bonds, or mutual funds with overseas holdings.

But in light of what happened last week, SEC officials said they are no longer sure that when put in practice, fair value works to the benefit of investors. "We will review how the policy worked, and if it didn't work—if it hurt investors instead of helping them—we may change it," the spokesman added.

Though fund companies have used fair-value pricing for several years, it became an issue last week when markets throughout the world gyrated for several days. As investors sought to profit from depressed prices in international markets by buying shares of over-seas funds, they discovered that some big fund companies weren't relying on the closing price of overseas markets. Instead, as the companies later explained, they were using a "fair-value" stock price to determine a fund's NAV, or price-per-share.

At the center of the storm was Boston-based Fidelity, the nation's largest fund com-pany. Fidelity normally uses closing market prices to determine the value of stocks in its mutual-fund portfolios and, ultimately, the portfolios themselves. But last Tuesday, Fidelity calculated a two-cent rise in the NAV of its Hong Kong & China fund, based on the futures market and other factors it believed had an effect on the value of the stocks in the portfolio. Earlier in the day, however, many investors, unaware of fair-value pricing, had purchased the fund based on the close of the Hong Kong market, which fell about 14% before the day's opening in New York.

"I lost $50,000 in profits," said David DeVault, a retired dentist from Houston, who was one of the angry investors tripped up by the pricing system. "They say they used fair-value pricing, but nobody knew about it."

Officials at Fidelity defended the move, saying the fair-value method helps protect long-term investors from market speculators who might buy the fund in an effort to capitalize on short-term market distortions. They said the company's disclosure documents clearly spell out that they may use fair-value in determining stock and fund prices.

As for the SEC scrutiny of the matter, "we welcome it," said Jerry Lieberman, Fidelity's senior vice president and chief financial officer. "What we're doing is the right thing."

That, he said, is because speculators can spot a profitable short-term investment because of time differences between overseas and U.S. markets. If, say, speculators believe that a rebounding U.S market will help support prices in Hong Kong later, they might purchase shares of Fidelity's Hong Kong fund—as many did last week—only to flip it the following day at a big profit when the Hong Kong markets recover.

That profit, Fidelity said, comes at the expense of long-term investors who don't gain as much from such short-term market movements. But Fidelity officials said that Tuesday evening, after U.S. markets rebounded, they managed to stymie "market timers" by devel-oping a fair-value price for the stocks in the Hong Kong fund that took into account futures trading foreshadowing a parallel recovery in Hong Kong. As a result, they said, the pricing was more accurate than the previous day's lower closing prices in Hong Kong.

Interestingly, Fidelity relies on fair-value pricing all of the time, one way or another, Mr. Lieberman said. Sometimes the fair value of a security is reflected in the close of the market; sometimes it reflects other factors such as futures trading or dealers' quotes.

To price bonds, many mutual funds actually rely on outside pricing services. These services use models that are programmed to add "variances" to prior-day prices, taking into account the difference in credit quality between the bond at issue and a Treasury security of similar maturity. In a pinch, when a bond is too hard to price that way, the model kicks it out; the pricing service has to turn to dealers instead.

Exhibit 10

Instances of 1997 intra-day Nikkei 225* futures price movements >150 points as of August 1997

Date	Chicago Nikkei futures open	Chicago Nikkei futures close	Previous Nikkei close	Next Nikkei open	Next Nikkei close
01/13/97	18,050	17,895	18,119	18,061	18,093
01/15/97	18,025	18,225	18,093	18,126	18,144
01/16/97	18,160	17,900	18,144	18,097	18,090
01/21/97	17,385	17,640	17,358	17,441	18,014
01/23/97	17,950	17,760	17,909	17,894	17,689
02/12/97	18,460	18,660	18,410	18,505	18,688
03/05/97	18,290	18,450	18,274	18,342	18,041
03/06/97	18,050	17,820	18,041	18,001	18,199
03/07/97	18,250	18,030	18,199	18,196	18,114
03/24/97	18,025	18,300	18,044	18,117	18,440
04/24/97	18,650	18,440	18,698	18,648	18,613
05/05/97	19,720	19,890	19,515	19,617	20,181
05/08/97	20,030	20,185	20,062	20,097	19,803
05/09/97	19,910	19,660	19,803	19,731	20,144
05/12/97	20,030	20,280	20,144	20,207	20,129
06/23/97	20,400	20,220	20,436	20,383	20,342
07/22/97	20,175	20,340	20,157	20,244	20,131
08/08/97	19,570	19,200	19,604	19,462	18,824
08/15/97	19,430	19,050	19,326	19,213	19,041
08/20/97	19,195	19,375	19,252	19,320	19,157
08/21/97	19,150	18,900	19,157	19,074	18,650

*The Nikkei 225 stock average is a price-weighted benchmark that tracks the continuous price-only performance of 225 actively traded companies listed on the Tokyo Stock Exchange's first section.

Exhibit 11

Asia equity market trading hours: Eastern Time (May through September) vs. local time

Country	Eastern time	Local Time
New Zealand (+16)	5:30 PM–11:30 PM	9:30 AM–3:30 PM
Australia (+14)	8:00 PM–2:00 AM	10:00 AM–4:00 PM
Japan (+13)	8:00 PM–10:00 PM// 11:30 PM–2:00 AM	9:00 AM–11:10 PM// 12:30 PM–3:00 PM
Singapore (+12)	9:00 PM–12:30 AM// 2:00 AM–5:00 AM	9:00 AM–12:30 PM// 2:00 PM–5:00 PM
Taiwan (+12)	9:00 PM–12:00 AM (M–F)// 9:00 PM–11:00AM (S)	9:00 AM–12 Noon// 9:00 AM–11:00 AM
Philippines (+12)	9:30 PM–12:10 AM	9:30 AM–12:10 PM
Hong Kong (+12)	10:00 PM–12:30 AM// 2:30 AM–3:55 AM	10:00 AM–12:30 PM// 2:30 PM–3:55 PM
Thailand (+11)	11:00 PM–1:30 AM// 3:30 AM–5:30 AM	10:00 AM–12:30 PM// 2:30 PM–4:30 PM

Exhibit 12

9.10   Fund Companies Look for Ways to Discourage Market Timers*
David Weidner

Some mutual fund companies are working harder to keep fast-moving, fickle investors out of their funds.

The companies are targeting "market timers," those investors who pour large amounts of "hot money" into a fund but can pull it out just as quickly, depending on market conditions.

Funds are cracking down on market timers as the popularity of fund supermarkets has allowed inexpensive or no-fee trades that are harder to track. Supermarkets put more funds at risk to the perils off momentum traders.

"There are fewer and fewer places market timers can go," said Patrick J. Carolan, senior account manager for GT Global, Inc. in San Francisco. "Companies are being a lot more careful."

Small fund companies view market timers as an industry scourge. While new investments help build assets, market-timer redemptions can quickly gobble up a fund's cash reserves, playing havoc with investment strategies. Funds with less than $100 million in assets are particularly at risk.

Market timers don't affect bigger funds of $1 billion or more as much because such investments are only a small percentage of such a large fund.

To slow the pace of market timers, some companies have instituted delays, periods ranging between 90 days and one year, where investors are kept from making trades. Other deterrents include watching trading activity, pre-investment screening, and redemption fees. In some cases, trades have been killed and investors banned from funds.

"The gist of these actions is to slow down the velocity of the trades," says Peter J. Moran, chief marketing officer at Turner Investment Partners, Inc. in Berwyn, Pa. "Market timers like mutual funds because there aren't many fees and it's convenient."

---

*Dow Jones News Service, June 27, 1997. © 1997, Dow Jones & Company, Inc.

Exhibit 13

9.11   Index Funds May Not Be So Easy to Exit*
Jeff Benjamin

Feeling a little skittish about the heady stock market? Queasy about Friday's 130-point decline in the Dow Jones Industrial Average? Thinking about moving a chunk of your money out of popular index mutual funds?

You may not be able to do it in a snap at some of the largest index-fund groups.

That's because many index funds have placed a number of annoying—though not insurmountable—obstacles in the way of nervous investors seeking quick redemptions.

Some impose redemption fees if shares have been held for a short time. Others, including Vanguard Group, don't allow investors to sell shares by telephone. Still others limit the number of times an investor can move in and out of a given fund.

Some other types of funds—volatile small-company and international funds as well as some big fund groups—also have restrictions on selling shares.

Fully Invested

But index funds tend to have more redemption limits, largely because of their particular structure: They basically mimic one or another stock-market index and thus are fully invested, keeping no cash around.

That means when investors redeem their shares, cash-poor index funds have to sell individual stocks and bonds, increasing operating expenses and potentially creating a capital-gains-tax obligation.

As index funds have attracted increasing amounts of money in recent weeks, thanks to the market's continuing surge, there's a growing concern in the mutual-fund industry that these same investors may be the first to flee if they become unnerved by a more volatile market.

Between April 2 and July 16, average weekly net flows of cash into index funds rose 77.4%, according to AMG Data Services, an Arcata, Calif., company that tracks fund cash flows. Index funds have 33.6% more total assets now compared with early April.

AMG Data President Robert Adler believes this is simply hot money chasing performance as opposed to more stable individual or institutional investors in it for the long haul.

"The asset base [of index funds] has grown so quickly," Mr. Adler says. "This isn't due to 401(k) money. This is due to momentum players."

If so, fickle investors had better watch out. Fund groups aren't going to make it easy for them to flee if the market crumbles.

"We do worry about mutual-fund investors pulling money out in the event of a correction," says Gus Sauter, who heads index-fund investing at Vanguard. "We think investors are expecting much higher returns than they'll ever receive. And we try to educate people that there will be pullbacks and they should see through the dip."

At Vanguard, which represents a full two-thirds of the assets of all index mutual funds, index-fund redemptions can't be made over the telephone. A Vanguard spokesman says this "is done for a market-timing reason," meaning the company isn't putting out the welcome mat for in-and-out investors.

Doubling of Assets

Vanguard has reason to worry about being flooded with short-term money: In the past year, for instance, assets in the showcase Vanguard Index Trust 500 Portfolio have doubled to $44 billion.

Newer index funds also have slapped restrictions on redemptions. Strong Funds in Milwaukee has a 0.5% redemption fee for shares held less than six months on its Strong Index 500 Fund, launched in May.

Tony D'Amato, director of retail marketing at Strong Funds, says the firm studied other fund groups' policies before it launched its own index fund and added the exit fee. There was concern that "some investors might choose to use an index type product as a timing vehicle," he says.

Redemption Fee

At T. Rowe Price Associates in Baltimore, the firm's stock-index fund was originally introduced to institutional investors in 1990. But in 1994, when the fund opened to individual investors, T. Rowe added a 0.5% redemption fee for shares held less than six months.

In addition, T. Rowe also has an "excessive trading" policy applied to all T. Rowe funds that discourages trading fund shares within a 120-day period.

Fidelity Investments in Boston likewise felt a need to tack on a 0.5% redemption fee for shares held less than 90 days when it introduced its Spartan Market Index Fund in 1990.

At Dreyfus Corp., the $1.2 billion Dreyfus S&P 500 Index Fund not only comes with a 1% redemption fee on shares held less than six months, but the fund also prohibits telephone exchanges.

Clearly fund groups are nervous. While they contend their investors take a long-term view, many fund groups nonetheless constantly monitor the investing habits of their shareholders through periodic client surveys.

Vanguard says it has studied its investor base to determine if its index fund might be attracting a disproportionate amount of short-term investors.

"We found that there really wasn't much difference between the newer investors and the existing shareholder base," the Vanguard spokesman says. "That's not to say they won't take their money out if there's an extended bear market. But many have taken the position that this is a long-term investment."

Not everyone is worried about jittery investors. Charles Schwab Corp. decided not to impose redemption fees when it launched the Schwab S&P 500 Investor Shares index fund in April 1996 (though three other Schwab index funds have such fees).

Bill Klipp, president and chief operating officer of Charles Schwab Investment Management, says a recent study of trading activity in S&P 500 Investor Shares produced a profile of investors who are in the market for the long haul.

"When you see a dip now, people want to put their money to work," he says. "Short-term dips now represent buying opportunities."

IV   Advanced Topics

10 Financial Dynamics of Mutual Funds

Introduction

While prior chapters have touched upon pricing, marketing, and servicing of mutual funds (see chapters 7, 8, and 9), this chapter will focus on the revenues and expenses of the mutual fund business. These will be analyzed from a variety of perspectives—the fund shareholders, the fund itself, the fund adviser, and the fund distributors.

As a prelude to this chapter, let us review the types of expenses for a fund and its shareholders, as well as the related revenue for the fund management company and its affiliates. It is useful to distinguish between expenses paid by shareholders as individual investors and expenses paid by the fund itself (which are borne by all fund shareholders). In general, fees related to distribution and redemption are paid by shareholders at the time of a specific event, while fees related to management and service are paid by the fund on an annual basis. But this general rule has a few exceptions—most important, 12b-1 fees, which are continuing distribution charges borne by funds as a percentage of their assets.

Sales loads are the most significant fees charged to shareholders individually. Sales loads are paid to the fund underwriters, usually affiliated with the fund management company, and mostly passed on to the broker who helped close the sale. The maximum sales load is $8\frac{1}{2}$%, though as a practical matter sales loads now average 4% or 5%. Historically, all sales loads were paid by shareholders when purchasing fund shares at the "front-end" of their investment—and therefore were called *front-end loads*. Most fund complexes give shareholders a credit for a front-end load paid to purchase shares of one fund if those shares are exchanged into another front-end load fund in the same complex. During the 1980s, fund complexes began to offer *back-end loads*, which the shareholder pays on redeeming fund shares. Most back-end loads decline the longer a shareholder stays in the fund. For instance, a shareholder might pay a 5% load after one year, a 4% load after two years, a 3% load after three years, a 2% load after four years, a 1% load after five years, and no load thereafter. Such declining back-end loads are called CDSCs, which stands for *contingent deferred sales charges*.

In addition, most funds waive loads for various categories of investors. For instance, most funds waive loads for purchases of fund shares by retirement plans and trust accounts. Furthermore, load funds usually reduce their sales charges for purchases above certain dollar limits (called *breakpoints*). For instance, a fund with a 4% load might reduce the load to 2% for purchases over $500,000 and to 0% for purchases over $1 million.

With the creation of no-load funds and rising shareholder concerns about loads of any type, the SEC in 1979–80 allowed the fund (rather than each shareholder) to pay annual distribution charges called 12b-1 fees to the fund underwriter. These 12b-1 fees are similar to periodic installment payments (accrued daily against fund assets), which can replace, in whole or in part, sales loads as a means of financing fund distribution. These 12b-1 fees usually range from 25 bp to 75 bp, plus an additional 25 bp "servicing" charge in some cases (25 bp or basis points = 0.25%). Thus, the maximum annual 12b-1 is actually 100 bp of fund assets. A 12b-1 plan (including service fees, if any) must be approved initially by fund shareholders and annually by the fund's independent directors; 12b-1 fees must appear in the fee table at the front of the fund's prospectus.

More recently, the fund industry has created funds with two or more classes of shares. While all classes share in the same investments and have the same portfolio manager, each class has its own distribution and service arrangements, resulting in different class expenses. In a typical situation, Class A of the fund would have a front-end sales load and a low 12b-1 fee. Class B would have no front-end load; instead it would have a combination of a high 12b-1 fee and a back-end load in the form of a CDSC. In the Class B situation, the fund sponsor typically advances a large commission to the broker-dealer selling the fund shares and then recoups that commission through the 12b-1 fees collected over several years. The CDSC is designed to protect that flow of 12b-1 fees to the fund sponsor in the case of a shareholder who leaves before paying sufficient 12b-1 fees to support the commission advance.

Beside Classes A and B, fund sponsors have developed classes with other pricing structures. Class C is sometimes described as a *level load* because it combines a high 12b-1 fee with a modest CDSC for one or two years. In Class C, there is typically no front-end load, though the fund sponsor usually advances a small commission to the broker-dealer. There could also be a Class I, called the *institutional class*, with neither loads nor 12b-1 fees. This class is designed for institutions with very large accounts and financial planners who are collecting a separate fee from their customers.

Although loads and 12b-1 fees are paid initially to the fund underwriter (usually an affiliate of the fund management company), the underwriter passes through (or "reallows") most of these loads and fees to the broker-dealers actually distributing the fund's shares. For example, if the shares of a fund advised by a Boston fund manager are distributed by a Wall Street wirehouse, the fund's underwriter owned by the Boston fund manager might reallow to the wirehouse 5% of the 6% load and 40 bp out of the 50 bp 12b-1 fee. The wire house, in turn, would pass on part of these fees to the individual representatives associated with each investor account.

The 12b-1 fee (but not the sales load) is one of several components of a fund's expenses, often expressed in basis points as the fund's total expense ratio (the ratio of the fund's total expenses to its assets on an annualized basis). The most important component is the management fee paid by the fund to its investment manager. As discussed in chapter 3, the management fee must be approved periodically by a majority of the fund's independent directors. Another fund expense is the transfer agent fee. As discussed in chapter 9, this fee may be paid to a transfer agent affiliated with the fund manager or to an external service provider. Other fund expenses include smaller amounts paid for fund audits, custody charges, director fees, registration fees, and sometimes proxy solicitations. By contrast, brokerage commissions are included as part of the capital costs of the fund's portfolio securities, rather than as part of the fund's total expense ratio.

Management fees, on average, are highest for stock funds and lowest for money market funds, with bond funds in the middle. In many fund complexes, management fees decline in terms of basis points as fund assets increase beyond a specified level (called *breakpoints*). For instance, an equity fund might have a management fee of 70 bp for the first $500 million of fund assets and then 65 bp for fund assets above that threshold. Such breakpoints may represent an agreement between the independent directors and the management company that there are potential economies of scale in managing a large fund as opposed to a small fund.

A relatively small number of mutual funds (principally stock funds) have management fees composed of a base rate plus or minus a performance fee. Under SEC rules, a performance fee for a mutual fund must be linked to an objective index. A performance fee also must be symmetrical—it must go down and up by the same formula relative to the index. For instance, a U.S. stock fund might have a base fee of 65 bp, with a performance fee of plus or minus up to 20 bp depending on the fund's performance relative to the performance of the S&P 500 index. By contrast, the typical management fee of "private" investment companies—usually called *hedge funds*—is 1% of assets plus a performance fee. Moreover, the performance fee is typically 20% of net realized gains, without any penalty for net realized losses.

Some mutual funds, primarily bond and money market funds, have *all-inclusive fees*. In this arrangement, the management company charges a single fee of a specified amount (e.g., 50 bp) and assumes responsibilities for all fund expenses including transfer agency and other annual expenses as well as management costs. Such all-inclusive fees effectively shift the risks and rewards of controlling the fund's total expenses from the shareholders to the fund management company. Alternatively, management companies may choose to "cap" or limit fund expenses to a specified rate, without necessarily including all services under a single all-inclusive management fee. This has much the same effect as an all-inclusive fee, but with the difference that an expense cap, unlike a management fee, can be changed without shareholder approval.

Fund sponsors impose other types of fees on shareholders, rather than on the fund, to modify their behavior or make them absorb certain fund expenses. Funds sometimes impose redemption fees on shareholders who leave the fund after a short period of time (e.g., 90 days or six months). (See the case study in chapter 9.) Such redemption fees go back to the fund to cover the transaction costs imposed on remaining shareholders by departing sellers. Similarly, some index funds impose fees on new purchasers to defray the fund's costs in acquiring more shares of companies in the index. In addition, some fund sponsors charge fees for specified types of transactions, such as wire redemptions or fund exchanges, or for specific types of accounts. Most fund sponsors charge shareholders a fee for serving as the custodian for an IRA or other retirement account, though such custodial fees may be waived for large accounts.

Small account fees are another charge that shareholders may incur as individual investors. These fees, designed to offset in part the relatively higher costs of servicing smaller accounts, are payable by shareholders to the transfer agent. For example, a transfer agent may deduct an annual maintenance fee of $12.00 from accounts with a value of less than $2,500 as of the last Friday in October. This fee is sometimes waived if the shareholder has aggregate assets in the complex above a certain amount (e.g., $50,000). To encourage shareholder maintenance of larger accounts, most funds have a minimum initial investment requirement (e.g., $2,500). Further, most funds reserve the right to close any account that falls below the minimum balance and send the proceeds back to the investor if he or she fails to re-establish the minimum balance within a specified time period, such as 30 days after notification.

There has been a heated debate on the question: Are mutual fund fees in the United States too high? The total expense ratios of mutual funds have on average risen over the last decade, despite the rapid growth in fund assets. To fund critics, this growth of assets should have resulted in lower expense ratios based on economies of scale. On the other hand, a significant component of the total expense ratio is now the 12b-1 fee, which is an alternative charge for distribution to sales loads. Sales loads have declined from a maximum of $8\frac{1}{2}\%$ to an average of 4% to 5%. Moreover, fund services to shareholders have greatly expanded over the last decade. The answer to this question depends heavily on the standard against which fund fees are judged. Fund total expense ratios in Canada, Europe, and the Far East are considerably higher than in the United States. But U.S. fund total expense ratios are higher than the fees charged by U.S. money managers to defined benefit pension plans. The profit margins of U.S. fund sponsors are higher than those in many industrial sectors, though roughly comparable to the profit margins in high technology and personal service companies.

The chapter begins with the fee table from the prospectus for a no-load fund and a load fund. The readings for this chapter describe in more detail the various types of expenses associated with funds, from the perspectives of both fund shareholders and fund sponsors. The case study focuses on mergers in the mutual fund industry, and asks you to recommend the management, servicing, and cost structure of the combined fund after a merger.

Questions

As you review the materials in this chapter, in addition to evaluating the debate on whether mutual fund fees are too high, please keep in mind the following questions:

1. Compare the fee tables for Putnam Voyager and Scudder Large Company Growth Fund in the readings. What is the distribution strategy, and how is it financed, for each fund?

2. In choosing among funds, should investors be more sensitive to the relative level of fees and expenses in stock funds versus bond or money market funds? What does your answer imply about a cost-control approach for fund sponsors?

3. Classes of shares allow the same fund to provide a variety of pricing and servicing arrangements. But how do we know whether investors and their brokers/financial planners understand the relative pros and cons of each class?

4. Sales loads are sometimes ignored in calculating fund performance, but 12b-1 fees are always included as a fund expense in performance calculations. Is this differential treatment justified?

5. Do you believe that mutual funds or fund complexes realize economies of scale at some asset level? If so, at what level? Will a mutual fund or a fund complex encounter diseconomies of scale if it becomes very large?

6. Should the SEC encourage or discourage performance fees for fund managers? What specific changes would you suggest with regard to the rules governing performance fees?

10.1   Scudder Large Company Growth Fund Prospectus: Expense Information*

How to compare a Scudder *pure no-load*™ fund

This information is designed to help you understand the various costs and expenses of investing in Scudder Large Company Growth Fund (the "Fund"). By reviewing this table and those in other mutual funds' prospectuses, you can compare the Fund's fees and expenses with those of other funds. With Scudder's *pure no-load*™ funds, you pay no commissions to purchase or redeem shares, or to exchange from one fund to another. As a result, all of your investment goes to work for you.

1) **Shareholder transaction expenses:** Expenses charged directly to your individual account in the Fund for various transactions.

Sales commissions to purchase shares (sales load)	NONE
Commissions to reinvest dividends	NONE
Redemption fees	NONE*
Fees to exchange shares	NONE

2) **Annual Fund operating expenses:** Expenses paid by the Fund before it distributes its net investment income, expressed as a percentage of the Fund's average daily net assets for the fiscal year ended October 31, 1996.

Investment management fee	0.70%
12b-1 fees	NONE
Other expenses	0.37%
Total Fund operating expenses	1.07%

Example

Based on the level of total Fund operating expenses listed above, the total expenses relating to a $1,000 investment, assuming a 5% annual return and redemption at the end of each period, are listed below. Investors do not pay these expenses directly; they are paid by the Fund before it distributes its net investment income to shareholders. (As noted above, the Fund has no redemption fees of any kind.)

1 Year	3 Years	5 Years	10 Years
$11	$34	$59	$131

See "Fund organization—Investment adviser" for further information about the investment management fee. This example assumes reinvestment of all dividends and distributions and that the percentage amounts listed under "Annual Fund operating expenses" remain the same each year. **This example should not be considered a representation of past or future expenses or return. Actual Fund expenses and return vary from year to year and may be higher or lower than those shown.**

*   You may redeem by writing or calling the Fund. If you wish to receive redemption proceeds via wire, there is a $5 wire service fee. For additional information, please refer to "Transaction information—Redeeming shares."

Figure 10.1.1

---

*From the Scudder Large Company Growth Fund Prospectus, October 31, 1996.

10.2   Putnam Voyager Fund Prospectus: Expenses Summary*

About the fund

EXPENSES SUMMARY

Expenses are one of several factors to consider when investing. The following table summarizes your maximum transaction costs from investing in the fund and expenses based on the most recent fiscal year. The examples show the cumulative expenses attributable to a hypothetical $1,000 investment over specified periods.

	Class A shares	Class B shares	Class M shares
Shareholder transaction expenses			
Maximum sales charge imposed on purchases (as a percentage of offering price)	5.75%	NONE*	3.50%*
Deferred sales charge (as a percentage of the lower of original purchase price or redemption proceeds)	NONE**	5.0% in the first year, declining to 1.0% in the sixth year, and eliminated thereafter	NONE

Annual fund operating expenses

(as a percentage of average net assets)

	Management fees	12b-1 fees	Other expenses	Total fund operating expenses
Class A	0.49%	0.25%	0.28%	1.02%
Class B	0.49%	1.00%	0.28%	1.77%
Class M	0.49%	0.75%	0.28%	1.52%

The table is provided to help you understand the expenses of investing and your share of fund operating expenses. The expenses shown in the table do not reflect the application of credits that reduce fund expenses.

Figure 10.2.1

---

*From the Putnam Voyager Fund Prospectus. November 30, 1996.

Examples

Your investment of $1,000 would incur the following expenses, assuming 5% annual return and, except as indicated, redemption at the end of each period:

	1 year	3 years	5 years	10 years
Class A	$67	$88	$110	$175
Class B	$68	$86	$116	$188***
Class B (no redemption)	$18	$56	$96	$188***
Class M	$50	$81	$115	$209

The examples do not represent past or future expense levels. Actual expenses may be greater or less than those shown. Federal regulations require the examples to assume a 5% annual return, but actual annual return varies.

*   The higher 12b-1 fees borne by class B and class M shares may cause long-term shareholders to pay more than the economic equivalent of the maximum permitted front-end sales charge on class A shares.

**   A deferred sales charge of up to 1.00% is assessed on certain redemptions of class A shares that were purchased without an initial sales charge. See "How to buy shares — Class A shares."

***Reflects conversion of class B shares to class A shares (which pay lower ongoing expenses) approximately eight years after purchase. See "Alternative sales arrangements."

Figure 10.2.1 (continued)

10.3   Sorting Out Costs*

The most important consideration in selecting a fund is its potential to perform well. If your manager has a superior knack for picking stocks, you will make money. Even so, you need to keep an eye on sales charges and expenses, which can seriously erode your returns, especially if the manager isn't faring well. A fund with higher costs than its peers is like a sailboat held back by excess weight.

Common sense tells us that lower expenses translate into a higher bottom line—in this case larger net returns for the shareholder. Higher costs will exert an even bigger drag when compounded over many years. A slight difference in the compounding rate (or the sum being compounded) can make a big difference in the amount accumulated over a long period. Lower-cost funds put more money to work for the investor. That's why it's important to study expenses carefully and to try to find the most efficient portfolios around, all else being equal.

Kinds of Costs

Four basic types of fees or expenses are generally associated with funds. They are:

1. Sales charges, which include front-end loads, back-end loads (the so-called "contingent deferred sales charges") and ongoing "asset-based sales charges," popularly known as 12b-1 fees.
2. Ongoing service fees that are paid by a fund company to brokers and other salespersons for personal assistance to clients, which consists mainly of investment advice. The service fee may be considered as an additional 12b-1 component.
3. Ongoing management and administrative costs. This category includes the manager's take as well as the various costs of running the fund, such as custodian and transfer-agent fees.
4. Costs associated with trading the securities in the portfolio. More frequent trading results in higher transaction expenses.

Portfolios with no charges in categories 1 and 2 above are known as "pure" no-load funds.

How Funds Are Distributed

To understand the purpose and impact of commissions, you need to know how funds are sold. Basically, there are two marketing avenues: through a sales force and directly by the fund complex.

---

*From Albert Fredman and Russ Wiles, *How Mutual Funds Work.* © 1993 Prentice Hall. Reprinted with permission of Prentice Hall.

The most common method of selling funds is through a sales force, in which case the fund's underwriter acts as a wholesaler or distributor to broker-dealers. These companies, in turn, sell shares to the public through their branch offices. A number of brokerages also offer their own private-label funds, including Dean Witter, Merrill Lynch, PaineWebber, Prudential Securities, and Smith Barney Shearson. These same firms also sell independent load funds, from companies such as American Funds, Colonial, Franklin, MFS, Pioneer, and Putnam. Independent funds are not directly affiliated with a particular brokerage firm or with other financial services organizations. Insurance agents, financial planners, and bank representatives also market these products.

Almost anytime you buy through a sales force, you pay a commission, most of which compensates the salesperson and that individual's firm for guiding you through the fund-selection process.

Direct-marketed funds sell shares to investors without any middleman. They deal with prospective and existing shareholders through the mail, by phone, bank wire, or (in a few cases) at one of their local offices. These funds attract investors primarily through advertising and direct mail, as well as by word of mouth and favorable publicity. Buyers of no-load portfolios do their own research and make selections without the assistance of a salesperson.

Scudder, Stevens & Clark introduced the first no-load fund in 1928. Load portfolios dominated the industry until the 1970s, however, when a major movement toward lower costs was started to stimulate investor interest in a lackluster market environment.

In earlier decades a clear distinction existed between load and no load funds. The former frequently charged an 8.5 percent up-front commission on both initial and subsequent purchases. The latter charged nothing. But the introduction of 12b-1 fees by the Securities and Exchange Commission in 1980 changed things. The two types of products started to blur. Whereas you used to have just two flavors, chocolate and vanilla, you now find a rather confusing assortment of different flavors, or pricing structures, to choose from.

The main thing to remember about fees is that you don't get something for nothing. If you need help from a broker or other salesperson in selecting funds and managing your portfolio, you're going to have to pay for it—in one form or another. The prospectus discloses the details of the fund's pricing up-front, and should be studied carefully. Today there are more inclusive caps or limits on what funds can charge, which have been imposed by the SEC and the National Association of Securities Dealers (NASD).

Front-End Loads

As the name implies, the front-end load is applied up-front. The average front-end sales charge ranges from 4 percent to 5 percent. Suppose you invest $10,000 in a fund with a 5 percent up-front charge. The load would be $500, or 5.26 percent of the $9,500 actually invested.

You can easily spot funds with front-end loads in the daily newspaper listings. The offer price, also known as the "asked" price, would be greater than the fund's NAV, sometimes called the "bid." The former represents the NAV plus the applicable up-front sales charge.

Taking the offer price and NAV from the newspaper table, you can calculate the maximum front-end load. First, subtract the NAV from the offer price, then divide the

Table 10.3.1
Commission schedule for ABC Load Fund

Purchase amount	Sales commission as a percentage of:	
	Public offering price	Net amount invested
Less than $50,000	5.00%	5.26%
$50,000 but less than $100,000	4.00	4.17
$100,000 but less than $250,000	3.00	3.09
$250,000 but less than $500,000	2.00	2.04
$500,000 but less than $1,000,000	1.00	1.01
$1,000,000 or more	0.00	0.00

difference by the offer price. A fund with an offer price of $20 and an NAV of $18.80, has a front-end load of 6 percent: ($20.00–$18.80)/$20.00. Incidentally, once each week *The Wall Street Journal* provides the maximum initial charge for front-end load portfolios in its listings.

With larger purchases, this sales charge generally declines as specified quantity discounts or "breakpoints" are reached. Typically, you would pay a full load on investments up to some minimum threshold, which could range anywhere from $10,000 to $100,000. The breakpoints are listed in the fund's prospectus. Table 10.3.1 illustrates a commission schedule for a fund with a maximum 5 percent load. With some products, the charge disappears completely on very large purchases, usually $1 million or more.

The commission table will also specify the dealer's cut as a percentage of the public offering price. Usually, the broker and his or her firm collect most, if not all, of the load. For example, the dealer commission on our hypothetical fund in table 10.3.1 might be 4 percent for purchases of less than $50,000. So, if an individual makes a $10,000 investment, he or she would pay a $500 commission, $400 of which would go to the broker and his or her firm.

If a fund has no other sales charges, it could still have an 8.5 percent front-end load, but virtually none do. Some or all of the charge has been shifted from an up-front payment to an ongoing, annual 12b-1 fee, with a back-end load attached.

Ongoing Sales and Service Charges
SEC Rule 12b-1 allows funds to charge an annual levy for distribution costs, including advertising. The logic is that portfolios with the resources to promote themselves more actively will be able to attract more assets and thereby benefit more fully from economies of scale. A 12b-1 fee may also be charged for ongoing personal investor services rendered by a salesperson.

Some funds that formerly imposed 8.5 percent front-end loads reduced or eliminated those charges when they began to use the 12b-1 plan. The maximum permissible 12b-1 charge had been 1.25 percent annually up to mid-1993 but since then has dropped to 0.75 percent for the distribution component (technically, the "asset-based sales charge"). In addition, there can be an ongoing "service" fee of up to 0.25 percent annually to compensate the registered representative or other salesperson for investment advice. For all practical purposes, lumping the 0.75 percent maximum sales charge and the 0.25 percent maximum service fee results in an annual limit of 1.0 percent that can be charged against assets for sales and service.

Incidentally, a fund with no front-end and deferred loads cannot be represented by a salesperson as "no-load" unless its combined asset-based and service fees do not exceed 0.25 percent of net asserts yearly.

Well over half of all mutual funds today have the 12b-1 feature in one form or another. Sharp criticism has been voiced against 12b-1 plans. As one fund manager put it, the biggest negative is that the costs of gathering new money come out of the pockets of existing shareholders. Why should these investors be required to help pay for advertising? After all, it is management that really benefits most directly from new money, in the form of greater total fees. As a rule, you should avoid all funds with 12b-1 charges above 0.50 percent for sales and service combined; the longer you remain in a fund the more burdensome high 12b-1 fees become. You can be sure that most institutional investors won't have anything to do with funds that impose 12b-1 fees.

Contingent Deferred Sales Charges

The back-end load or contingent deferred sales charge (CDSC) is often used along with a 12b-1 plan for funds sold by middlemen. The idea here is to effectively guarantee some form of commission for the broker. If the investor remains in the fund for many years, the salesperson would be compensated through the ongoing service fee referred to above. But if the customer sells shortly after purchase, the broker gets paid through the CDSC.

The CDSC applies only if shares are redeemed during the first several years after purchase. If you hold the fund long term this exit fee—which decreases periodically in steps—usually disappears. For example, the CDSC might be 5 percent if shares are redeemed within the first year, 4 percent in year two, and so on until it phases out entirely after the fifth year. The CDSC is commonly levied against the value of the original investment. It may, however, apply to the redemption proceeds if the price of the shares has declined.

By looking carefully at individual fund listings in the newspaper, you can identify those with contingent deferred sales charges as well as 12b-1 fees. Watch for the following letters placed after the portfolio's name: **r** denotes a CDSC or a redemption fee may apply; **p** denotes a 12b-1 fee; and **t** indicates a redemption charge may apply and a 12b-1 fee exists. In other words, both the **r** and **p** footnotes apply. [Ref. figure 1.2.4 on page 19.]

Other Fees

You'll occasionally encounter funds with other charges. Here are three.

Redemption Fees   Unlike the CDSC, this is usually a relatively small percentage, such as 1 percent of the amount sold, and it typically remains at a fixed level. Sometimes the purpose is to discourage investors from selling soon after they buy. This charge is relatively uncommon. A handful of otherwise no-load portfolios impose a small redemption fee.

Fees on Reinvested Dividends   Most funds allow shareholders to reinvest both dividends and capital gains distributions into additional shares at NAV without paying any commissions. A few portfolios, however, do charge a fee on reinvested dividends.

Exchange Fees   There is usually no fee for moving your money between portfolios within a given fund family, although some companies charge $5 and a few $10 per telephone exchange.

Flexible Pricing

The flexible pricing structure available today with an increasing number of broker-marketed funds gives investors a choice of how they can pay their sales charges. The earliest form of flexible pricing, called dual pricing, was introduced in 1988 by Merrill Lynch. You can choose between two different fee structures with Class A and B shares.

In general, the Class A shares charge a front-end load ranging from, say, 4 percent to 6 percent, while the Class B shares have no front-end commission but do impose a contingent deferred sales charge or redemption fee. Typically, a 12b-1 fee would also apply to the Class B shares. It may apply to the A shares as well. But if the A shares do carry one, it would be lower than on the B shares.

In most cases, funds structure their A and B shares so that it's not so easy to determine the best option. This requires a careful cost analysis. You would need to consider such factors as the size of your investment and how long you intend to keep your money in the portfolio. For example, a large investor may get a quantity discount on the A shares of a particular fund, but not on the B. In any event, avoid funds with high 12b-1 fees if you expect to stay in for some time.

Going beyond A and B shares, it's becoming more common to see other pricing options, like "level loads." In fact, you can find A, B, C, and D shares, all based on the same portfolio. At present there are no industry standard definitions for the C and D shares. Giving buyers different options make it easier for a company to sell its funds. Critics have called the proliferation of confusing choices "fee madness."[1] The bottom line is that you don't get something for nothing. Read the prospectus carefully. And if your salesperson can't answer your questions satisfactorily, it may be best to look for one who is more knowledgeable.

Operating Costs

Ongoing management and administrative costs appear as a part of the expense ratio. The management company subtracts these operating costs bit by bit rather than in one lump sum. They stay in force for as long as you own a fund.

Management Fees
Management fees, common to virtually all portfolios, are charged by the advisory firm for the security analysis and portfolio management functions it performs. These fees generally range from 0.4 percent to 1 percent annually. At 1 percent, the expense would amount to $10 million each year on a $1 billion portfolio. A fund collecting relatively large management charges would make a statement such as the following in its prospectus: "Such fee is higher than that charged by most other investment management companies." Is the extra expense worth it? That depends on the size of the fee and the company's track record.

A detailed discussion of management expenses can be found in the fund's prospectus. In many cases, the adviser might state that it plans to reduce the fee percentage as the asset base swells. For example, the ABC Growth Fund may have a management fee of 0.7 percent for the first $100 million of assets, 0.6 percent for the next $400 million, and 0.5 percent for amounts above $500 million. Watch out for companies that do not reduce their management charge as the portfolio grows. Make sure the fund is passing along to shareholders the economies of scale that it realizes.

Other Recurring Expenses

Mutual funds tack on several other ongoing expense items in addition to the management fees and any sales or service fees. Most apply to all funds. They include:

- Shareholder servicing costs
- Custodian and transfer-agent fees
- Shareholder report costs
- Legal fees
- Auditing fees
- Interest expense
- Directors' fees

Expense items such as these are detailed in the fund's statement of operations, which is discussed later in this chapter.

When you add the 12b-1 charges, management fees, and other costs, you get the total operating expense. Divide this by the fund's assets (technically, average monthly net assets) and you would get the all-important expense ratio.

Some companies limit their expense ratio, often for competitive purposes. For example, the adviser might reimburse the fund to the extent necessary to maintain the number at a maximum 1 percent. This would be accomplished by waiving a portion of the advisory fee. Details would be reported in the prospectus and the annual and semiannual reports. Expense ratio limitations are more common among newer, smaller funds and may be temporary.

The Standard Fee Table

The SEC requires all fees charged by funds to be summarized in a prominently displayed table near the front of the prospectus. The fee table, which has been mandatory since 1988, is one of the most important parts of the prospectus and deserves careful consideration. It is divided into three sections:

1. A summary of shareholder transaction expenses.
2. A breakdown of the fund's operating expenses.
3. A standardized hypothetical example of the effect of fees over time.

The fee table for two hypothetical funds is illustrated in table 10.3.2 The funds are similar in all respects except that ABC features a 6 percent front-end load and no 12b-1 fee, whereas XYZ has no up-front charge but a 0.75 percent 12b-1 fee. The 12b-1 fee raises the annual expenses of XYZ.

Table 10.3.2
Sample prospectus fee table illustrations

Shareholder transaction expenses	ABC Fund	XYZ Fund
Max. sales load imposed on purchases (percent of offering price)	6.00%	0
Max. sales load on reinvested dividends	0	0
Contingent deferred sales charge	0	0
Redemption fee	0	0
Exchange fee	0	0

Annual operating costs (percent of average net assets)		
Investment advisory fees	0.70%	0.70%
12b-1 fees	0	0.75
Other expenses	0.50	0.50
Total operating expenses	1.30%	1.95%

Hypothetical example

You would pay the following expenses on a $1,000 investment in each fund assuming (1) a 5% annual return and (2) redemption at the end of each period:

	Year 1	Year 3	Year 5	Year 10
ABC Fund	$72	$99	$127	$207
XYZ Fund	20	61	105	227

The 5 percent annual return and $1,000 investment used in the example are standardized numbers employed by all funds in their fee tables. This makes a meaningful comparison possible. Note that ABC has higher costs in the earlier years but lower later on. The 10-year expenses run $227 for XYZ versus $207 for ABC, proving that the 12b-1 charges can add up over the years. If you now assume XYZ is a pure no-load fund, without any 12b-1 fee, it would have a 1.2 percent expense ratio. Over 10 years, XYZ's total expenses would fall from $227 to $145.

Lower Costs Translate into Higher Returns

A less expensive fund will generate better results, other things being equal. Low fees are especially important to bond funds, since fixed-income investments normally don't produce the type of long-run performance available in the stock market. High sales commissions and management fees can turn an otherwise good bond portfolio into a laggard. In addition, there is more justification for paying a higher management fee to a talented stock picker with the ability to really add value. Bond fund managers enjoy less opportunity to move ahead of the pack, since bond results normally cluster within a narrower range. The annualized return on some funds may barely exceed the rate of inflation.

Statement of Operations

In addition to the fee table and expense ratio, you should examine a fund's statement of operations, which appears in its annual and semi-annual shareholder reports. It's wise to analyze this statement if the expense ratio appears excessive and you're not sure why. The statement of operations contains a detailed breakdown that allows you to see if the various expense items are in line with those of comparable funds. Also read all footnotes, as they give further information on items such as advisory fees and interest expense.

Beware of Layered Fees

Some funds invest in other funds, but they are not common, and their record has not been that great. In theory, at least, their overly diversified portfolios tend to produce mediocre results, and a double layer of fees puts a drag on performance. Exceptions exist, of course, including a few fund families that offer economical access to related portfolios, usually charging just one layer of fees. Vanguard Star, for example, has no management fee of its own. This balanced portfolio invests in seven other Vanguard funds: four equity, two fixed-income, and one money market, and only the management expenses of these portfolios apply—on a pro-rata, not a cumulative basis. Two other multifunds that impose just one layer of fees are T. Rowe Price Spectrum Income and Spectrum Growth. Each invests in up to seven other T. Rowe Price funds, offering a means of getting widespread diversification in a single purchase.

Why Do Individuals Purchase Commission-Laden Funds?

It might seem odd that some people would willingly pay a sales charge, even though competitive no-load products are available. After all, it's apparent that the load hurts performance since it reduces the net amount of money invested. What you pay in commissions is gone. It cannot work for you. Yet roughly half of all fund purchases are made through a sales force. How can this be?

In truth investors buy commission funds for any of several reasons, some of which make a lot of sense and some of which don't:

- Many people learn about particular investment products through a knowledgeable salesperson. A casual investor might not understand the diversification merits of, say, an international stock fund, or may not be aware of low-risk CD substitutes, such as a short-term bond portfolio. It might require a broker, selling load products, to bring these investments to the person's attention.
- Some investors are gullible. They might fall for the old broker ruse that there's nothing free in life, so even no-loads have their hidden costs.
- Many individuals probably do not fully understand the impact of fees on performance. Instead, they think only about how much money they can make. Brokers often argue with some credibility that an up-front load won't make a big difference on a good-performing fund held many years.

- Many people simply do not have an interest in investments, so they need financial guidance. Perhaps they are too busy with their careers to educate themselves about financial matters.
- Some people just have a difficult time saying no to a charming salesperson with an exciting product.

We certainly won't go so far as to say, "Never invest in a load fund." In fact, purchasing a good one under the right circumstances can make a lot of sense. Some individuals definitely need the advice of a good broker or financial planner. Otherwise, they could be prone to making serious mistakes and losing lots of money. They might have trouble deciding not only what and when to buy, but when to sell.

Also, since load funds are actively marketed by a sales force, they sometimes attract more assets than equivalent no-load products, and may, therefore, have lower expense ratios.

And the load might not matter much to wealthier buyers, who can take advantage of quantity discounts. These discounts occur at specified breakpoints, as illustrated in table 10.3.1. Individuals investing $50,000, $100,000, $500,000, or $1 million would pay successively smaller sales charges. In many cases, the commission might be quite reasonable.

On this latter point, the fund may grant you a nice discount if you execute a "statement of intent." This lets you receive a lower commission, even if you don't invest everything at once. Typically, you have up to 13 months to invest enough cash to meet the breakpoint. This way, all purchases over that period would benefit from the lower rate. By spreading out your purchases over a number of months, you also benefit from dollar-cost averaging, which means you avoid the risk of making your entire investment at what could be the fund's high price for the year.

Affluent investors should seriously consider the best front-end load funds, along with the best no-loads. Also, individuals participating in thrift programs offered by their employers, including 401(k) and 403(b) plans, can buy load products at little or no commission because of the quantity discounts the employer can pass along to the workers.

Many well-established load funds have excellent long-term records. You can see the names of some of them on *Forbes* annual honor roll. On the other hand, there's no reason for anyone to consider high-cost funds with mediocre performance. The sad fact is there are far too many of them.

Expense Ratios Have Crept Upward

The mutual fund industry has grown astronomically in recent decades. Yet expense ratios over the same period have also risen, which suggest that investors aren't enjoying many economies of scale. The average expense ratio for equity funds has increased to about twice its level of the early 1950s.

Many funds have grown quite large, but their ratios haven't declined at all and sometimes have risen. This might seem illogical, since bigger portfolios should feature lower per-share fees due to economies of scale.

Several reasons explain why the trend of expense ratios has been upward in recent years:

- More funds have 12b-1 charges. In fact, none imposed these fees prior to 1980, when they were authorized by the Securities and Exchange Commission. Any 12b-1 fees, as noted earlier, are included in the expense ratio.
- Management fees have also been increasing. This advisory charge accounts for a large chunk of fund expenses.
- Funds are offering more shareholder service, which cost money. Families produce newsletters and other educational materials, maintain toll-free 800 numbers, and provide other benefits for a growing number of investors. Some families even operate walk-in investor centers in selected large cities.
- Perhaps most important, it can be complicated trying to analyze costs, as we've noted in this chapter. Thus, funds often can get away with increasing charges—or introducing new ones—because these changes may not be obvious to the average investor.

Note

1. Jason Zweig and Mary Beth Grover, "Fee Madness," *Forbes*, February 15, 1993, pp. 160–162 and 164.

10.4   Taking On New Loads*
Alan Lavine

Fund groups are radically changing their pricing strategies with the goal of increasing consumer business while at the same time attracting financial planners.

The Twentieth Century Group of Funds, traditionally a no-load fund group that charges a 1% management fee, for example, has added a new Adviser class of shares. It reduces the management fee to 75 basis points, but levies a 50 basis point "service plan" fee, which goes to the financial intermediary. These shares are designed for financial planners or small 401(k) plans that do business through discount brokerage firms' mutual fund supermarkets.

"We wanted to have a class of shares for the market that wants investment advice," says Brian Jeter, vice president of alternative distribution services at Twentieth Century. "We already have $6 billion in assets from firms we are reimbursing for services. More options in this marketplace will lead to more sales."

Sentinel Funds, with mutual fund assets of $2.2 billion and another $8.0 billion under management at various affiliates, sought to put some zip in its sales earlier this year with its new B shares. The basic B share structure has no front-end load, a 1% level load and a contingent deferred sales charge, or CDSC, in the early years.

But Sentinel Funds has added a new type of trailing commission and lowered break points. Beginning in the 13th month after the initial investment, registered reps with $100,000 to $200,000 of B share assets under management receive a 10 basis point trail. With assets of $200,000 to $1 million, the rep earns 25 basis points and over $1 million, the trail becomes 50 basis points. Meanwhile, shareholders get reduced CDSCs at break points of $250,000 and $500,000—down from an original $1 million threshold.

Give Them Perks

Shareholders can also combine assets in Sentinel funds to reach those break points. The CDSC is waived if money is moved from stock or bond funds into the Treasury money fund as well as for distributions, redemptions due to death, mandatory retirement, and 403(b) loan withdrawals and redemptions to 10%.

"We want to pay people more who do business with us," says Jeffrey Lauterbach, senior vice president with Sentinel Management Co. in Wilmington, Del. "About a third of our projected sales of $250 million will come from B shares this year."

A number of insurance agents and financial planners want the ability to put the Sentinel Common Stock Fund, a traditionally low-risk growth and income fund, into a fee-based management account. Lauterbach says that becomes advantageous with B shares,

---

*From *Financial Planning Magazine*, November 1996. Reprinted with permission.

which over time can provide more than double the cumulative trail income than A shares. So financial planners can provide more services for the commissions received at a relatively reasonable cost.

"We made the A and B shares neutral after six years," Lauterbach says. "At conversion, when B shares become A shares, the accounts are virtually equal. That makes it an attractive investment for the long term."

Level-Load Sales Stay Level

Although Sentinel expects strong level-load sales industry wide, level-load share sales are paltry.

Front-end load funds still are the most popular, with net cash flows of $64 billion over the past 18 months, according to Financial Research Corp., a Chicago-based research company. Net cash flow into back-end load and level-load funds totaled $23 billion, with net cash flow into level-load funds alone reaching just $9 billion. The reason: Level loads are too expensive for long-term investors. They typically work best for holding periods under five years. Merrill Lynch & Co. is reportedly getting about 13% of its sales from its level-load C shares and expects that to rise to 20% over the next few years.

The Delaware Group of Funds, with assets of $11 billion, can attest to low sales of C shares. Late last year Delaware added 1% level-load C shares with an upfront 1% commission to the dealer and a 25 basis point trailing commission in the 13th month. But sales have been lackluster.

"Response to the C shares is a non-event," says William Hostler, senior vice president at Delaware. "But it's been popular with the younger reps who charge fees for assets under management. We added C shares to give reps greater choices."

Delaware, Hostler says, wanted brokers to have a wide range of pricing options. C shares were designed for clients who prefer to pay for all types of financial advice throughout the investment period.

Alphabet Soup

Fidelity Investments also made some drastic pricing changes after vociferous complaints from registered representatives about cutting its Fidelity Advisor Funds' front-end load to 3.5% from 4.5% in January.

The fund group recently overhauled its pricing set-up. They now have A, B, T, and, yes, I shares on their stable of seven equity funds and 10 fixed-income funds, with assets of $30 billion.

"We heard from a number of clients who prefer the increasing flexibility of selling a mid-load 12b-1 product," says Michael Kellogg, executive vice president of Fidelity Investments Institutional Services Co. "These changes accomplish that as they benefit shareholders with lower fees and expenses and maintain trail compensation levels for registered reps who provide service to their investors over the long term."

The Advisor Funds have a new class of A shares that carry a higher front-end sales charge and a lower 12b-1. The old class A shares are now T shares, which carry a lower front-end load and a higher 12b-1.

Reps who want high upfront commissions will select the A shares, which have a 5.25% maximum front-end sales charge and a 25 basis point 12b-1 fee. The dealer gets 4.60%; there's also a 25 basis point trailing commission.

The B shares carry a 25 basis point 12b-1 fee. B shares are sold with a contingent deferred sales charge of 4% in each of the first two years. It then declines to 3% in the third year, 2% in the fourth year, and 1% in the fifth year before automatically converting to A shares at the end of the fifth year. Three percent goes to the dealer, and there also is a 25 basis point trailing commission.

Those who want a moderately priced fund can choose T shares, which have a 3.5% front-end load and a 50 basis point 12b-1. The I shares, which have no load and no 12b-1, are designed for mutual wrap accounts. Three percent goes to the dealer and there is a 50 basis point trailing commission.

Which Loads Look Hot

It's too early to tell which class of shares will be the best sellers. But it appears as if Fidelity is covering all bases. The fund group recently introduced six new no-load Advisor sector funds for fee-based advisers. On the load side, Fidelity's Kellogg expects no one class of shares to dominate.

"A lot depends on the broker-dealer's preference for upfront income or higher trailing commissions," Kellogg says. "The higher trailing commissions are designed for registered reps who want to manage assets over the long term."

This month, the Franklin Templeton Group is expected to issue multiple class shares on the recently acquired Mutual Series funds, which has assets of $17 billion. The four Mutual Series funds include Mutual Beacon, Mutual Qualified, Mutual Discovery, and Mutual Shares, in addition to the Mutual European Fund, launched in July.

Existing shareholders in the Mutual Series funds, which are no-load and non-12b-1, will be offered a special class of shares, so they can continue to purchase shares no-load without the 12b-1 charge.

New shareholders, however, will have a choice of Class I or Class II shares. Class I shares are sold with a 4.5% front-end load and a 12b-1 fee of 35 basis points, with 25 basis points going to the dealer. The dealer commission is unchanged at 4%. Class II shares have a 1% front-end load, a 1% contingent-deferred sales charge for the first 18 months and a 12b-1 fee of 1%. The dealer will receive a 2% commission.

Although Mutual Shares' level-load shares pay higher compensation to the dealer, the fund group expects Class I shares to outsell Class II shares.

"It's better for long-term investors because it's less expensive," says Holly Gibson, a Franklin Templeton spokesperson. "Class II shares are designed for those who want to own their fund for five years or less. The Mutual Series funds are designed for long-term growth."

10.5 No Free Lunch: "Supermarket" Fees Lift Costs*
Ellen E. Schultz and Vanessa O'Connell

Many mutual-fund investors are unwittingly picking up the check for someone else's lunch.

Most investors are probably aware that the guy who vacuums down his food at the local Hogs "R" Us Buffet, so to speak, is being subsidized by the dieters. But what is increasingly clear is that similar cost-shifting is going on in the mutual-fund business.

It all starts with the vastly popular fund "supermarkets," such as those offered by Charles Schwab, Fidelity Investments, and Jack White. These fund smorgasbords allow investors to buy and sell mutual funds from dozens of companies without paying transaction fees.

Naturally there is a price tag for this all-you-can-eat deal. The mutual-fund companies must pay the supermarkets a distribution fee, typically 0.25% to 0.35% of the assets they bring in. And many fund companies are passing along the cost—to all of their shareholders, not just the supermarket shoppers.

"I'm actually subsidizing people going into the supermarkets," complains Scott Greenbaum, a financial adviser in Purchase, N.Y.

Why this happens: When a fund already exists, the fund companies can't just tag on an extra cost. That's because the supermarkets, to preserve their discount image, prohibit fund companies from distributing more-expensive versions (or "classes") of shares on their shelves. So instead, the fund companies may simply increase the annual expense ratio for the funds—even for investors who buy the fund outside the supermarkets.

The result is higher costs in some new funds. For example, Women's Equity Fund and Domini Social Equity Fund both added so-called 12b-1 distribution fees to their new funds to cover the eventual cost of paying Schwab and Fidelity.

"If we get into Fidelity's program, we'll have to pay 30 basis points," (or 0.30% of assets), says Linda Pei, president of Pro-Conscience Funds, San Francisco, the investment adviser that sponsors Women's Equity Mutual Fund. It's unusual for fund companies to openly discuss the fees they pay for supermarket distribution—let alone to admit that the supermarkets contribute to any increase in the funds' costs.

But that sensitivity may be changing. Jon Carlson, executive vice president of Yacktman Asset Management, and a director of the Yacktman Fund, says in an interview that the Yacktman Fund pays Schwab 0.30% a year to participate in its supermarket.

To help pay for this expense, the fund charges shareholders 0.15% a year (the amount is included in the annual expense ratio). Meanwhile, the other 0.15% is paid to Schwab by Yacktman Asset Management, the subsidiary that manages the money. (Some might argue that the shareholders ultimately pay the expense. That's because the fund pays Yacktman

---

Asset Management 0.64% of assets to manage the money; the subsidiary pays the Schwab costs from its fee).

Mr. Carlson is also refreshingly frank about another matter: how the costs of paying supermarket fees may increase the annual expenses on the fund. The Yacktman Fund raised its annual expense ratio this year to 0.94% from 0.90%. The reason: "Expense ratios are up because we're paying some of the Schwab expenses from the fund," he says.

The Yacktman Fund's recent fee increase "didn't please us," says a Schwab spokesman, who adds that Schwab is eager to preserve and promote its image as a low-cost fund distributor. Schwab goes as far as to pressure funds in its OneSource supermarket to keep fees steady, or lower them after joining the program, he says. Indeed, if funds fatten up with new assets when they join OneSource, the total expenses each shareholder pays may drift downward—but only if the fund fees are based on a sliding scale, with each new dollar charged at a slightly lower rate.

But there's little Schwab can do to keep fund groups from creating new funds with higher fees, or to prevent existing funds from boosting management fees now and again, especially if the funds don't admit they are raising expenses to pay Schwab and other supermarket operators. "Everyone deserves to get a dollar," the Schwab spokesman says.

10.6 Your Funds May Be Making You Rich ... But You're Also Getting Robbed*

Jason Zweig

Before you pat yourself on the back for all the money you've earned in mutual funds lately, you need to recognize that you're not the only one making out like a bandit. So are the fund companies that sold you your shares. Worse, many funds are collecting outlandish fees for mediocre investment performance.

The heart of the problem: As funds have grown bigger, they should have become more economical to own. And, in truth, many companies have passed along the savings to shareholders. Yet sadly, more than half of all stock and bond funds with 10-year records— 56% to be exact—have actually raised fees in that time. That's why I call today's rising expenses the Great Fund Stickup. What's more, you may not be a totally innocent victim. If you've been letting your focus on high returns distract you from deciding how much you should pay for performance—or even worse, if you've been voting yes when your fund company asks for a fee increase—then you're an accomplice in your own victimization.

How bad is this crime? If fund fees ought to be 20% lower—as I'm going to document —then you and your fellow fundholders are being overcharged by $5.3 billion a year. That's $14.6 million a day, a number so huge that it makes an old-time bank holdup look like a squabble over pocket change.

If those garish aggregates don't grab you, think of the Great Fund Stickup this way. The more a fund company charges you—even if it's just a tenth of a point here and another tenth there—the less you keep. That might not hurt so much when returns are squarely in double-digit territory, as they have been lately. But wait until the markets hit a rough patch; then those fees will either magnify your losses or take a proportionately bigger sliver of your smaller gains. Says Barry Barbash, chief fund regulator at the Securities and Exchange Commission: "I'd rather have investors think about expenses now than wait until their returns come down and they're unhappy with the result."

Believe me, it pays to scrutinize fund expenses as closely as you do total returns. Over the past decade, the 20% of U.S. diversified stock funds with the highest expenses charged an average of 1.85 percentage points more in annual fees than the cheapest 20%. But those priciest funds earned an annual average of 1.91 percentage points *less than* the cheapest group.

The moral: On average, the more you pay the less you get. (See figure 10.6.2.) Think of that the next time some hotshot fund manager tries to justify a price hike by citing his [or her] past investment results.

In a few minutes, I'll tell you how to defend yourself from the Great Fund Stickup. But first, some more facts:

---

*From *Money*, February 1997. Reprinted with permission.

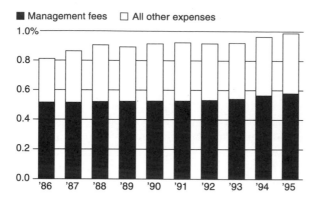

Figure 10.6.1   Fund fees keep rising ... Source: Lpper Analytical Services

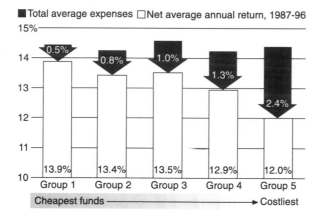

Figure 10.6.2   ... and the more you pay, the less you keep. Source: Morningstar

---

Funds Are Money Machines

You might still think it's quibbling to worry about 1% or 2% in annual fund fees. Far from it. This year shareholders like you will pay $26.7 billion in fees (on $3.2 trillion in assets) to cover all mutual funds' operating expenses. (Sales charges, or loads, are another thing altogether; we're not tackling them here.) Of that $26.7 billion, fees for investment management will hit $16 billion; another $10 billion or so will go for such expenses as accounting, legal, and marketing costs.

The bottom line? After you pay all these bills, the companies that run mutual funds post average net profit margins in the mid-20% range. That's more than triple the 7% net margin of the typical publicly traded U.S. company—and more than double what you can expect your funds themselves to earn over time. Want a comparison with names you know? Microsoft's 1996 net margin was 25.1%. Eat your heart out, Bill Gates. Fund giant Franklin Resources' 1996 net margin was 32.1%. "Managing money is the most profitable business in the United States," says Arthur Zeikel. He should know; he's president of Merrill Lynch Asset Management, the country's fourth largest fund sponsor.

These Money Machines Are Breaking a Basic Business Law

In most businesses, the more of a product you sell, the cheaper it becomes to produce and distribute. That's because the firm becomes more efficient as sales volume grows, reducing the cost per item. The more you pass on those reduced costs to your customers, the more competitive your product becomes.

But such economies of scale don't seem to hold for mutual funds. From 1986 through 1995 (the latest year with final data), total net assets of stock and bond funds rose nearly fivefold to $1.76 trillion. Did expenses drop? *Au contraire*. Stock and bond fund management fees (calculated as a percentage of assets under management) actually rose 11.8%, and overall expenses charged to shareholders have zoomed 22%.

The Fee Heist Isn't Limited to Newcomers Run by Struggling Fund Management Companies

Not at all. Some of the biggest funds run by some of the most muscular, widely known management outfits charge fees at least 75% higher than their category averages. Two extreme examples: $2.7 billion Alliance Growth B charges total annual expenses of 2.05% of assets (vs. 1.07% for the average growth fund), and $956 million John Hancock Special Equities B has total expenses of 2.20% (vs. 1.25% for the average small-company growth fund).

Have I got your attention? Now let's move on to the details of fund costs— and what you can do about them.

First off: What are "expenses" anyway? Again, we're not talking about sales commissions or "loads." Rather, the topic here is money that fund sponsors siphon out of your account to pay for day-to-day operations. Your fund has a board of directors, which hires an investment manager to run your money; a transfer agent to process the transactions; a custodian to hold the assets in safekeeping; accountants to check the books; and lawyers to keep everybody honest. The fund may also pay an annual fee to brokers and financial planners who help peddle its shares. By far the biggest of these charges is the management or advisory fee charged by the investment manager; it usually accounts for at least 60% of a fund's total expenses.

None of these people ever send you a bill. Instead, their fees are quietly, continuously subtracted from your assets. That's why you may never have noticed how much you're paying (or overpaying). You're not alone. According to a recent survey by the SEC and the Office of the Comptroller of the Currency, fully 81% of investors say they couldn't even hazard a guess about what their largest fundholding charges for expenses.

Quitely or not, these fees corrode your account. Let's say you invest $5,000 in N/I Growth, a stock fund that charges a reasonable 1% in total expenses. Now let's say the portfolio steadily rises in value by 10% over the next year. That should turn $5,000 into $5,500. But you will have only $5,445 to show for it. Why? Because N/I Growth's management company, Numeric Investors of Cambridge, Mass., deducts its fees, as all fund managers do, in daily nibbles over the course of each 12 months. That slows the growth rate of your investment by preventing all your money from working for you for the whole year; in this example, it reduces your 10% gross return to just 8.9% net. Even though you paid only slightly over $50 in fees, the cost ate up more than 11.7% of your $445 net return.

Now say you had bought PIMCo Advisors Target C, which charges a high 2% in annual expenses, and earned the same 10% gross return. Your net return would drop to just 7.8%—and your total expenses would devour an appalling 26.7% of your net return.

After a decade of 10% gross annual returns, an investor in N/I Growth would have turned his [or her] original $5,000 into $11,734. But an investor in the PIMCo fund, earning the same 10% before fees, would finish with only $10,616. This $1,118 gap, produced by the difference between the two funds' expenses, is a giant 22% of the $5,000 you started with. That's the black magic of decompounding, by which subtracting a small amount for fund expenses each year makes much of your future wealth vanish.

High expenses can also turn a stock fund into a bond fund. How so? If you're a stock investor paying 2% in fund fees plus another 1% to a financial adviser for monitoring your funds, your 3% annual costs are eating up the entire amount by which stock returns have exceeded bond returns in the long run. No wonder Morningstar president Don Phillips somberly told me, "I'm beginning to despair about the future of mutual funds as a low-cost option for investors."

Ralph Wanger, the co-manager of the outstanding Acorn Fund (total annual expenses: a very low 0.57%), agrees. "It's gotten to the point where the fund industry has a basic flaw in its design," he warns. "Unless fees come down, investors will get tired of being hosed, and they will find another way to invest."

Where did funds go wrong? In 1986, stock and bond funds had $383.9 billion in assets; by the end of 1995, they had $1.76 trillion—nearly quintupling in size. By all rights, that asset growth should have showered fund investors with economies of scale. It didn't. Back in 1986, the average stock and bond fund charged 0.515% in management fees and 0.810% in total expenses. By the end of 1995 (the latest available data), the average management fee had risen to 0.576%, while total expenses had bloated to 0.988%. (See figure 10.6.1.) Moreover, these numbers, from Lipper Analytical Services, are conservative because they are weighted by the size of the funds that make up the averages.

In short, far too many funds have been delivering *dis*economies of scale. Generally, running a fund becomes profitable for the manager once the portfolio hits $100 million or so in assets—so, beyond that point, there's room for fees to fall. Yet, according to Morningstar, 182 of the 2,555 stock or bond funds with $100 million or more charge at least 2% in annual expenses.

Ask the sponsors of funds like these why fees are high, and you'll get answers along these lines: Superstar portfolio managers can command several million dollars a year in pay; computers must be continually maintained and upgraded; every company in a portfolio must be researched (often by traveling to far-flung corners of the world); toll-free service lines must be staffed 24 hours a day. All of this costs tons of money.

Fair enough. But even so, investors in the United Kingdom could teach U.S. money managers a thing or two about pinching pennies. Foreign & Colonial Investment Trust, the world's oldest fund, began life in London in 1868, charging a maximum of 0.42% in annual expenses over its first five years. Today it charges just 0.47%—a 12% total increase in nearly 130 years. By contrast, as I've noted, the expenses at U.S. funds have increased nearly twice that much *in just 10 years.*

A little more history: Back in 1960, the managers of 73% of U.S. mutual funds paid for the funds' bookkeeping; 60% paid the funds' accounting fees; 11% paid for processing purchases and sales. Today most fund companies force their customers to pay those costs. But even after covering all those costs back then, fund managers still ran an average net profit margin of 18%. That's why I say that, given today's net margins in the 25% neighborhood, fund companies could easily cut their overall fees by at least 20%—$1 in $5— and still remain immensely profitable.

Just how lucrative is it to run a fund company? Well, even with his low management fees of 0.60% or so, Michael Price's investment firm, Heine Securities, earned $62.5 million in net income on its fee revenue of $95 million in the year ended last June. That's a net profit margin of 65.80%, or more than eight times higher than the average U.S. corporation's. That's one reason why Price was able to sell his firm, which was managing $17 billion, to Franklin Resources for as much as $800 million late last year—a rich price of more than 4% of total assets.

Another example: This year, Kaufmann Fund shareholders will pay their investment adviser, Edgemont Asset Management, at least $72 million in management fees. Assuming a net (pretax) margin of 50%—which, several sources tell me, may be conservative— Edgemont's two owners, Lawrence Auriana and Hans Utsch, will take home at least $18 million each in 1997.

To be fair, Kaufmann's total expenses have dropped from a steep 3.64% in 1991 (on $140 million in assets) to 2.17% in 1995 (on $3.2 billion) to 1.94% last year (on $5.34 billion at year-end). But the 1.50% management fee that Kaufmann shareholders pay to Edgemont is one of the highest in the business, and it has not fallen at all. "Someone has to have the highest fee," Auriana says, "and I guess we're the ones. Fortunately enough we've done pretty well for our shareholders." No argument there: Over the past five years, Kaufmann's 18.9% average annual return wallops its peers by 5.2 percentage points. Of course, the fund may not always perform so well in the future, but Auriana says firmly: "I see no reason to lower the [management] fee."

Yet plenty of managers have delivered above-average returns at below-average cost— and have cut those costs as their funds have grown. The American Funds' EuroPacific Growth, for instance, charged a total of 1.27% annually back in 1987 on $185 million in assets; by 1996, assets were up to $15.4 billion and expenses were down to just 0.95%. In 1987, on $1.1 billion in assets, Fidelity Growth & Income charged 1.09%; by last year, it had $23.7 billion in assets and expenses were down to only 0.75%. And T. Rowe Price Growth & Income charged 1.03% on $366 million in 1987; by 1996, its fees had fallen to just 0.83% on $2.5 billion.

Robert Marcin is co-manager of the MAS Value Fund (assets: $2.4 billion), which has beaten the S&P 500 by an annual average of 0.3 points over the past decade. His firm charges only 0.50% in management fees and 0.61% in total expenses. "A money manager can clearly run funds very profitably for 0.50% to 1% total," Marcin says. "Anyone who tells you otherwise is full of poop."

Marcin is right. Now here's what you should do.

Remember What You're Paying For

Over the long run, even the best managers—stars like Mario Gabelli, John Neff, and Michael Price—have a hard time beating the market average by more than one or two percentage points a year. A manager charging 2% in annual expenses has to outrun the market by more than two points just to stay even with the average. The higher the fees you pay, the worse are your odds of outperforming.

In the debate over whether the past returns of mutual funds can predict future returns, academics and fund analysts alike agree on only one thing: On average, funds that charge higher expenses will have lower returns. Since you can never be sure which funds will end up with the best future performance, but you *can* be certain which funds will have high expenses, you should avoid them.

Here are my rules of thumb on fund costs. First of all, if you want to work with a broker, don't begrudge [him or] her a fair sales commission, which tops out at about 5.75% on stock funds these days. Get it over with by paying up front, through the so-called Class A shares; if you choose another share class, the higher fees will eat away at your returns as long as you own the fund. Instead, zero in on the fund's annual expenses, which are disclosed in the beginning of the prospectus. (If you really can't abide the broker's sales load, then you should buy a no-load fund.)

For a bond fund, don't pay more than 0.75% in annual expenses; among the excellent high-grade choices in that price range are Harbor Bond, Benham GNMA Income, and Vanguard Total Bond Market. If junk or high-yield funds are your pleasure, pay up to 1% for good funds like Fidelity Capital & Income, Nicholas Income, and Vanguard High-Yield Corporate.

For a blue-chip U.S. stock fund, draw the line at 1% in annual expenses; Dodge & Cox Stock, Fidelity Fund, Janus Fund, and Vanguard Index 500 (or Vanguard Total Stock Market) all charge less than that.

For a small-cap fund, don't pay over 1.25% in expenses; good picks under that limit include Wanger's Acorn Fund, Babson Enterprise, and T. Rowe Price OTC.

For international stock funds, keep your costs below 1.5%; here you can choose from Scudder International, Vanguard International Growth, or Warburg Pincus International Equity.

All these funds have delivered solid returns without taking more than they should in expenses. Anytime you pay more than these guidelines, the odds are stacked against you.

Don't Let a Fund Manager Hold a Gun to Your Head

At the end of 1993, the American Heritage Fund had a phenomenal three-year annual average return of 48.9%. So when portfolio manager Heiko Thieme asked shareholders to approve a 67% increase in his management fee, they gave him the thumbs-up. Instead, they should have told Heiko to take a hike. In the three years since, the fund has lost an annual average of 24.3%. The lesson: Good returns can disappear in a flash, but expenses are forever. Don't buy the argument that hot results deserve to be rewarded with higher fees.

And that's why, when your fund company sends you a proxy statement, you must read it. You're being asked to vote on your future—and you can't take it lightly. My advice (and I'll admit it's uncompromising): If the proxy asks you to authorize an increase in the manager's investment advisory fee, you should *always* vote no. Then you should vote against the re-election of every single fund director on the ballot. These people have let you down by failing to make your fund more economical, and you should vote to fire them.

Only if you fight back like this will the fund industry begin to charge a fair price for its services. And if you don't, you'll have no one but yourself to blame.

Let me finish with this question: Would you let your accountant charge you 20% of your net income for filling out your tax return? Of course not. But, if stock returns revert to their long-term average of 10%, a fund company that charges 2% in annual expenses will be keeping at least 20% of your returns. Ask yourself: If I would never pay an accountant 20%, why on earth should I pay a fund manager than much?

It's not fair, and it makes no sense. Don't do it.

10.7   The Third White Paper: Are Mutual Fund Fees Reasonable?*

Outline of Analyses

Most sound analyses rely on using different bases to reach the same conclusions. However, in our world, the most powerful and insightful governor of the marketplace is competition. Thus, we first looked at external competitors to the mutual fund business both in and outside of the United States. Second, we looked at the competition within the mutual fund management companies for scarce resources, e.g., talent. Third, we looked at competition among funds.

Summary of Analyses

1. While expenses appear to be rising in aggregate, these apparently higher expenses are due to the large number of new high-expense funds, the inclusion of 12b-1 sales and service charges (often in place of front-end sales loads) and the shift in shareholder assets from money market funds to world equity and world debt funds. When properly adjusted, management fees are actually declining for older, more successful funds.
2. Based on pricing comparisons with alternative investment products, the cost of mutual fund service is less than that of mutual fund wrap accounts, individual securities wrap accounts, hedge funds, certificates of deposit, and funds registered outside of the U.S.
3. In general, fund management company profit margins are not rising despite asset growth. Margins are below their peak levels. The costs of competition for talent, as well as increased marketing and service expenses, are holding profitability down.
4. The profitability of mutual fund management companies is reasonable compared with other industries with high proprietary knowledge and service orientation.
5. While there has been tremendous asset growth in the fund industry, the average fund size has not grown significantly, certainly not enough to benefit from any economies of scale.
6. Older funds that have experienced significant growth in average fund size have passed along economies of scale through reduced expense ratios to their shareholders.

Alternative Investments

As investment analysts, we have great respect for markets' price-setting mechanisms. If buyers regard price as too high, then no transactions occur. Markets validate attractive

---

prices with increasing volume. The tremendous amount of assets that have flowed into open-end funds supports the idea that the market regards fund fees as reasonable. Mutual fund average monthly sales are now nearly twice as high as they were only four years ago. Are fund fees reasonable? Fund shareholders seem to be responding "Yes" with their money.

Mutual Fund Wrap Accounts

The recent increase in popularity of mutual fund wrap accounts, which add 1% to 3% in annual fees on top of fund fees, seems to contradict the idea that fund fees are too high. At the end of 1995, there was an estimated $19.3 billion in mutual fund wrap accounts, an increase of 60% from 1994. The marketplace would not support such a new product with its higher fees if the original product, individual funds, was viewed as overpriced.

Individual Securities Wrap Accounts

Individual security wrap accounts typically have annual fees between 1.5% and 3%. These fees are often more than twice as high as the median fee for non-money market open-end funds (1.2%).

Hedge Funds

Hedge funds generally charge 1%, plus up to 20% of gains. Operators of the hedge funds, on the basis of their higher fees, have the ability to hire good portfolio managers and analysts away from the mutual fund business. In order to be competitive many mutual fund organizations have had to raise their overall levels of compensation, particularly for well-known managers.

Certificates of Deposit

Bank certificates of deposit (CDs) are another alternative to mutual funds. The spread between the rate a CD investor receives and the rate at which a bank lends is in effect the "fee" an investor pays for the CD. For many banks, the long-term CD-to-Prime-rate spread is approximately 3%, again well over twice as high as fund fees. There are certainly very significant differences between bank CDs and managed accounts, including deposit insurance, banks' principal risk, and regulatory capital requirements. However, both funds and banks are active in a primary market (securities for the former and loans for the latter), and both deliver a return to their customers, after paying the cost of their operations. In a discussion about the reasonableness of fund fees, we believe it is valuable to look at the cost that customers bear in alternative vehicles for their money.

Funds Registered Outside of the U.S.

The Canadian fund average expense is 2.40%, compared with the U.S. median of 1.20%. Total expense ratios of European domiciled funds are more difficult to collect on a consistent basis, but we do have research on average equity fund management fees. Compared with equity funds of 21 European countries, the U.S. equity fund average management fee (0.75%) is lower than those in 19 countries.

Management Company Profit Margins; ROE Below Peak Levels

Advisor fees have been the subject of a number of law cases. In one of the two landmark Gartenberg cases the court suggested that the board had an obligation to determine that economies of scale were being shared with fund investors.

One way to discern whether advisors are benefiting from economies of scale is to analyze fund companies' profit margins. In a period of increasing volume, analysts usually expect to see profit margins expand. Given that expectation, we find it remarkable that seven out of eight of the publicly traded mutual fund management companies have pre-tax, after-marketing profit margins below their peaks. (See table 10.7.1.)

Upon closely examining profitability data for those advisors that report separate fund business financial data, one discovers that the average of each advisor's peak margin is well above the average of 1996 levels. (See figure 10.7.1.) Additionally, the five-year average return on equity (ROE) for public fund management companies tracked in Lipper Analytical's *Advisor Profitability Study* was 27.2%, again above the current 1996 level but still well below the peak. (See figure 10.7.1a.)

The ROE for the average mutual fund management company is in line with profitability measures for software manufacturers (28.6%) and pharmaceutical companies (33.3%). We believe that these two types of entrepreneurial businesses have some important similarities to the fund management business. These businesses are knowledge intensive, have low marginal cost of production, have high distribution costs, and have high continuing service responsibilities. We hasten to add that ROE analysis should be limited to public companies; private companies and partnerships may follow different practices, which would result in less meaningful ROE comparisons.

Management Company Purchases and Sales

All management companies have the option of growing their assets through starting new funds, growing old funds, or buying someone else's funds. If growing fund assets internally through new funds has become more expensive, then we would expect to see a rising demand, and rising valuation, for management company acquisitions.

We believe that, even for those management companies already in the fund business, new funds are expensive to start and grow. Therefore, we interpret the historically high valuations paid to acquire fund management companies by fund groups already in the business, e.g., Franklin's purchase price for Mutual Series of funds, as a confirmation that the knowledgeable buyer finds it more attractive to buy assets in existing funds than to launch new funds, even at record valuation levels for an inter-industry purchase.

Internal Competition

With low levels of barriers to entry, the fund business is highly competitive. Funds compete both in terms of performance and services provided. Both of these benefits are paid for by the shareholders. With the exception of front-end sales charges, fund expenses are deducted from net asset value before performance is measured. Fund expenses are required

Table 10.7.1
Profit margins and average return on equity: Public fund advisors

	Premarketing margin			After-marketing margin			Return on average stockholder equity		
	1995 %	Previous peak year	Peak year margin %	1996 %	Previous peak year	Peak year margin %	1996 %	Previous peak year	Peak year ROE %
Alliance Capital Mgt.	41.3	1995	40.9	27.3	1993	26.7	43.8	1991	48.0
Eaton Vance Corp.	30.6	1990	44.8	53.4	1987	59.8	18.5	1987	31.4
Franklin Resources Inc.	54.4	1987	70.8	46.6	1987	68.2	24.6	1986	85.4
John Nuveen Co.	46.3	1995	41.5	47.3	1991	47.6	24.4	1993	29.0
Pioneer Group Inc.	61.7	1987	77.8	5.6	1986	68.1	12.0	1987	32.0
T. Rowe Price Associates, Inc.	40.2	1995	38.9	30	1995	30.7	31.8	1986	43.9
Marsh McLennan Cos. (Putnam)	N/A	N/A	N/A	31.2	1988	35.0	25.9	1987	42.0
Phoenix Duff & Phelps Corp.	23.6	1994	34.8	19.5	1993	37.9	13.9	1993	*184.7
Averages	**42.6**		**49.9**	**32.6**		**46.8**	**24.4**		**44.5**

*Phoenix Securities Group and Duff & Phelps merged 11/95; peak year ROE is excluded from the average.

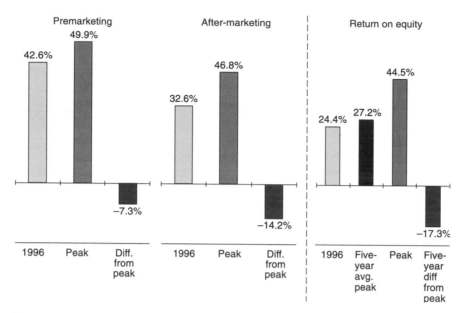

Figure 10.7.1 Average advisory margins, 1996 and peak year

Figure 10.7.1a Average ROE, 1996 and peak year

to be disclosed to investors and these expenses are quite visible in the front of the prospectus. Despite the intense competition of the fund marketplace and the high visibility of fund expenses, there exists considerable variation in individual mutual fund expenses, even within the same fund objective. For many investment objectives, the difference between funds in the highest quintile of expenses (top 20%) and the lowest quintile of fund expenses (bottom 20%) is approximately 100 basis points. In an intensely competitive marketplace with visible fees, any fund complex with higher prices must deliver superior perceived value or the fund complex will lose fund shareholders. We believe that competitive marketplace dynamics will continue to exert pressure on higher expense funds to deliver superior value (including returns and/or services) or risk falling into a consistent pattern of market share loss and redemptions.

Trends in Mutual Fund Expenses

There has been considerable discussion this year about the historical trend in fund expenses. Much of the discussion has centered around the observation that the asset-weighted expense ratio for all funds is higher than it was ten years ago. The conclusion reached by some commentators is that fund companies are being "greedy" by raising fees during a period of record inflow into funds. We believe that both the initial observation and the resulting conclusion are naive from a rigorous analytical standpoint.

The misguided conclusion results from a lack of understanding of two vital concepts: the dramatic changes in the fund universe over the past ten years and the nature of economies of scale in the fund business.

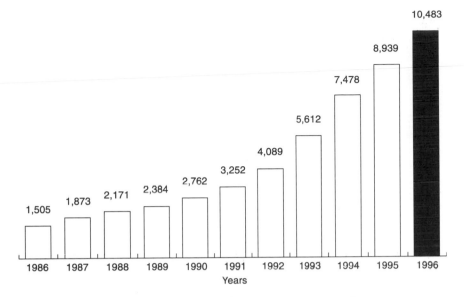

Figure 10.7.2   Total number of open-end mutual funds (year-end)

The universe of funds has changed significantly over the past ten years. Analysts must take into account these changes in order to comment thoughtfully on the trend in expenses. The four biggest changes in the fund universe from 1986 to 1996 have been:

1. A tremendous increase in the number of new funds. (See figure 10.7.2.)
2. World equity and world debt funds are more expensive to provide both management and custodian services than domestic funds. There has been a disproportionate increase in the number of new, high-expense world equity funds. (See figure 10.7.3.)
3. In the last ten years there has been a massive shift in the number of funds with front-end sales charges compared to ones with deferred sales charges (back-end loads). The fund investor pays for the intermediary advice through 12b-1 charges paid by the fund. (See figure 10.7.4.)
4. Ten years ago low-expense money market funds held almost half of the fund assets, with equity funds holding below a third. Today equity funds with their higher fees (more expensive managers and analysts) represent over half of all fund assets, and money market funds represent about a quarter of the total. (See figure 10.7.5.)

A Fresh Analytical Approach

Based on these major changes, we recommend that three analytical adjustments be made to the historical expense trend analysis. First, freeze the universe of funds in the study to those in existence for the whole observation period. Otherwise, any conclusion will be distorted by the growth of the newer, more expensive fund types, e.g., world equity funds.

Second, deduct the 12b-1 plan payments that have been added to many funds concurrent with a reduction of front-end sales charges. Otherwise, there will be an apparent

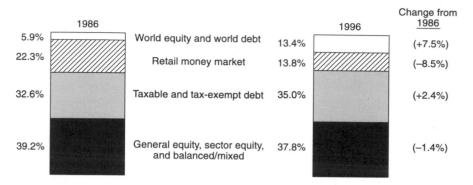

Figure 10.7.3 Proportion of all open-end funds in four major objective categories. ( ) denotes the absolute increase/decrease (+/−) since 1986

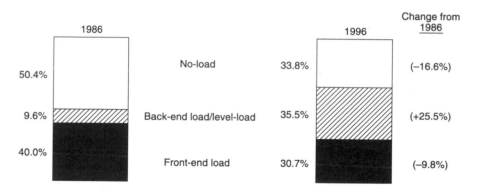

Figure 10.7.4 Proportion of all open-end funds with three major pricing structures. ( ) denotes the absolute increase/decrease (+/−) since 1986

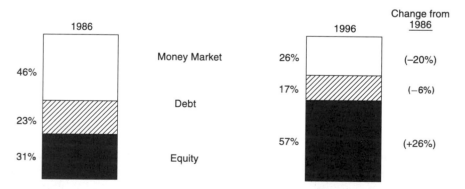

Figure 10.7.5 Proportion of all open-end funds with three major asset classes. ( ) denotes the absolute increase/decrease (+/−) since 1986. Note the substantial shift of assets into equity assets; both debt and money market assets decreased proportionally from 1986.

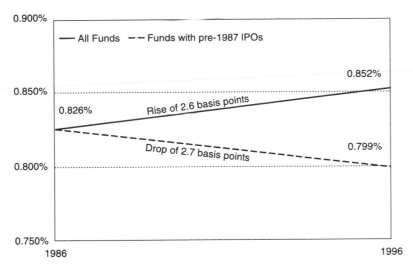

Figure 10.7.6 Average total expense ratios excluding 12b-1 plan payments from 1986 to 1996 for all open-end funds and all open-end funds in existence before 1987 (interim years between 1986 and 1996 were *not* plotted)

rise in fund expenses, when the actual effect to the investor of a 3% to 4% drop in the sales charge (from 8.5% to 4.5%–5.5%) is a lower total cost of ownership. The average front-end load fund, which has lowered its initial sales charge by 300 to 400 basis points, charges a 12b-1 plan payment of 31 basis points. Thus, an investor benefits from the combination of lower front-end sales charges and the initiation of 12b-1 plan payments for the first nine to 13 years. Since investors are holding their funds for a shorter period (6 to 8 years), they do realize a benefit.

Third, one should use median expense ratios, not total industry asset-weighted averages, when looking at all funds, or limit dollar-weighted averages to comparisons within investment objectives. Otherwise, investors' significant and voluntary shift from money market funds and other debt funds into stock funds will incorrectly portray an apparent rise in fund expenses.

New Funds Versus Old Funds

When these three analytical adjustments are made, the median expense ratio for funds that began in 1986 or before is *not* up, but down. Driving up median fund expenses are newer, higher-expense funds. In a nutshell, most older funds are not raising their expenses; in fact they are lowering them, and most newer funds have higher expenses. (See figure 10.7.6.)

We believe that behind higher expenses of newer funds are higher management fees. We studied 18 of the major investment objectives (all of the objectives with at least $25 billion in assets as of May 31, 1997). We compared the 1996 asset-weighted management fees for funds that were at least ten years old with "cohorts" based on their initial year of operation, including new share classes of only existing portfolios from subsequent two-year periods (1987–88, 1989–90, etc.). Out of 90 comparisons, the post-1986 cohorts had higher management fees than the old funds in 68 cases, or 76% of the observations.

Reasonable Expectations for Economies of Scale

The misunderstanding about the nature of economies of scale begins with the expectation that the tremendous growth in the asset size of the fund industry in aggregate should translate to a reduction in the average industry expense ratio. This expectation presumes an industry economy of scale, which does not exist. The fund industry does not have any economy of scale; individual funds do. One fund company's expenses do not go down (and may, in fact, go up) as a result of its competitors' assets going up.

We also do not believe that there is any economy of scale at the fund management company level. If a successful manager of state municipal funds raises assets in domestic equity funds, we would not expect to see any impact of those increased equity assets on the municipal funds' expense ratios.

The only economies of scale that we can see are at the individual fund level. We believe that these economies come from two sources: from a decrease in the level of some of the other operating costs (for example, custodian, directors, legal, registration) as a percent of fund assets and, to a more limited degree, from spreading the cost of investment management over more assets. However, we hasten to add that this second economy of scale is not linear. As the fund gets bigger, the fund company frequently will add more analysts and portfolio managers to manage the increased assets.

If we return to the expectation of a reduction in the average fund expense ratio as aggregate fund industry assets increase, this expectation would only be reasonable if the average fund size had increased significantly. However, there has not been such an increase. Over the past ten years, despite a near six-fold increase in total fund assets, the average fund portfolio size (for combined classes of shares) has only increased from $325.9 million to $488.3 million. If an individual fund increased its assets over ten years by this amount, one would expect to see little, if any, benefit from economies of scale leading to a lower expense ratio.

Older Funds Have Delivered Economies of Scale

If we examine the funds that began in 1986 or before we do see some examples of economies of scale. One reason for this may be that these older funds have grown significantly in size over the ten-year period. In 1986, these funds' average size was $325.9 million, and the average size grew to $1.188 billion in 1996. Thus, we do have evidence of some economies of scale passed through to fund shareholders as individual fund assets grew significantly.

Will Fund Shareholders Benefit Similarly with Newer Funds?

We see some reason to believe that some fund's total expenses will decline in the future.... Two trends are plainly obvious: on average, the newer funds are smaller, and on average, the newer funds have higher expenses. If the newer funds are successful in raising assets, then one could expect some future reduction in expense ratios similar to those of the older funds.

. . .

Case Study: **Balancing Interests in a Fund Merger**

Over the last few years, the merger activity in the mutual fund industry has been substantial and rising. In 1996, for example, there were 96 such acquisitions involving $530 billion in assets. These included 49 U.S. acquisitions, 17 U.S./cross-border acquisitions, and 30 foreign acquisitions. In 1997, there were 100 such acquisitions involving $740 billion in assets. These included 71 U.S. acquisitions, 12 U.S./cross-border acquisitions, and 17 foreign acquisitions. (Source: Investment Counseling, Inc., Seventh Annual Strategy Report.) Some of the mergers involved fund managers trying to fill out their line of products. An illustration is the acquisition of Templeton's management company, which has a strong reputation for international stock funds, by Franklin's management company with its heavy emphasis on bond funds. Other mergers involved institutionally oriented securities firms seeking more distribution to retail investors. An illustration is the acquisition of Dean Witter, a retail wirehouse, by Morgan Stanley with its institutional client base. Still others involve banks that want to gain a foothold in the mutual fund industry. An illustration is the acquisition of Dreyfus, an investment manager for a broad line of mutual funds, by Mellon National Bank. The article following the case study discusses several mergers in the mutual fund industry and the early results of the consolidations.

The acquisition of a fund management company raises difficult questions because, under the Investment Company Act of 1940, a change in control of an investment adviser to a mutual fund automatically terminates the advisory contract. Thus, the acquirer must obtain approval of a new or renewed advisory contract from the independent directors of the relevant funds as well as the shareholders of those funds. In reality, the acquirer is buying the assistance of the prior adviser in obtaining these director and shareholder approvals. In 1970, Congress enacted special rules for any acquisition of a mutual fund adviser, requiring that such an acquisition not impose "an unfair burden" on the mutual funds involved, and further that at least 75% of the directors of such funds be independent for at least three years after such acquisition.

After an investment manager for one set of mutual funds acquires an investment manager for another set of mutual funds and obtains the necessary director/shareholder approvals, the acquiring investment manager often re-examines the resulting product line. There may be overlap between mutual funds previously advised by the investment manager and mutual funds in the new complex. Alternatively, there may be small funds in the prior or new complex that have never been successful. Either case may lead to the possibility of fund mergers, which must be approved by the independent directors of both funds as well as the shareholders of the fund being merged out of existence.

The case study below presents this type of situation. American Guardian has recently acquired Best Management and now wants to consider merging two funds—one from American Guardian's prior complex and the other from the Best complex. At the year-end board meetings for both fund complexes, executives of Best American (the name of the combined management firm) must make recommendations on merging these two funds. Since fund mergers require director and shareholder votes, the rationale for the merger is extremely important. It must make sense for all major stakeholders—Best American, the independent directors and shareholders of both funds, as well as the brokers that sell them.

In-Class Discussion Questions

As a respected member of the CFO's staff, you have been requested to attend the pre-board meeting of Best American executives to map out a strategy. After reviewing the article and other materials provided, you should be prepared to answer the following questions:

1. a) What should be the advisory fee of the combined fund? Is a breakpoint a good idea?
    b) What would you recommend regarding the choice of portfolio manager?
2. a) What should be the proposal for distribution fees—sales loads and 12b-1 fees—for the combined fund?
    b) What changes, if any, should be made to the brokers' compensation structure?
3. a) How much asset growth is needed to pay for the sales force expansion?
    b) What level of fund sales would you project for next year?
4. a) What service fees should be proposed for the combined fund?
    b) Should the fund use an external or internal transfer agent?
    c) How much investment in service development seems reasonable over the next few years?
5. In light of the answers to the above questions, what does the combined P&L look like (see schedule B in the case study materials)?
6. Should Best American offer a Class B pricing structure—declining back-end load with 12b-1 fee—for the combined fund?
    a) What factors should management consider in this decision?
    b) How would you price the Class B share so that it would be comparable to Class A? (Schedule C provides a comparison of Class A and Class B pricing for a competitor which has both classes of funds, but which has a different pricing structure than either American Guardian or Best Management.)

Note: You should frame your answers in the context of each major stakeholder for these important decisions. You should state why the proposed merger and resulting business decisions make sense for:

- The independent directors of both funds,
- The shareholders of both funds,
- The brokerage firms that sell both funds, and
- Best American

10.8   Best American Management

Earlier this year, two mutual fund management companies, American Guardian, Inc., and Best Management, Inc., entered into an agreement under which American Guardian would purchase all of the issued and outstanding stock of Best Management and merge Best Management into American Guardian. Although the companies are now combined, there are still two separate boards of directors for the funds. Each fund complex retained the same independent board members previously elected by the shareholders, but company-appointed directors were re-evaluated and will be consistent for both boards. The combined entity, Best American Management, is now in the process of reviewing existing products and services and looking for opportunities to leverage its increased size.

American Guardian was a 30-year old Boston-based mutual fund complex. This fairly staid, conservative company was well-known but had not been particularly innovative in fund distribution or shareholder servicing. It had historically chosen to distribute mainly through broker/dealers, and outsourced its transfer agent process. The relatively new CEO of American Guardian firmly believed that in today's highly competitive environment, mutual fund complexes must "grow or die." He saw an acquisition as a necessary step to ensure that his firm's products and services would be attractive to investors and their advisors in the future.

Best Management was a fast-growing Boston-based mutual fund complex. The 15-year old company was recognized as a leader in the use of technology, having invested millions in upgrading its internal transfer agent/shareholder servicing affiliate. Rapid growth had begun to strain the firm's capabilities, however, and further investment in shareholder servicing was needed for coming years.

Both complexes had several funds, and a review of Best American Management's newly combined product line reveals that a few of the funds have very similar investment objectives and holdings. In particular, there are now two domestic equity growth funds, sold through the intermediary channel. (See schedule A.) The possibility of merging these two funds, American Patriot Growth and Best Western Growth, is currently under discussion by Best American Management.

American Patriot Growth; Class A (front-end load), has $3 billion in assets and has outperformed 45% of its peers over the past 3 years. The fee structure consists of a 58 basis point (bp) advisory fee, a 25 bp 12b-1 fee (all of which is paid out to the selling broker-dealer) and a 15 bp transfer agent fee. Total fees are slightly above the industry median for this type of fund (see schedule A). In addition, the fund carries a 5% load, 4.5% of which is retained by the broker that sold the fund. Gross sales for the most recent 12 months are negligible. Fund profitability for American Patriot Growth is forecast to be positive for the year (see schedule B).

Best Western Growth; Class A (front-end load), has above average performance, and has received favorable press coverage recently. The fund has $2.5 billion in assets and has beaten 72% of its competitors in the prior three years. Best's fee structure for domestic equities consists of a 44 basis point (bp) advisory fee, 35 bp 12b-1 fee (30 of which is paid out to the selling broker-dealer), and a 19 bp transfer agent fee. Total fees for the fund are above the industry median (see schedule A). Best Western Growth also carries the same load structure that American Patriot Growth does. Currently, gross sales are running at 10% of assets, and Best Western Growth is forecasted to produce a marginal profit for the year (see schedule B).

As there has been increased attention on fees throughout the industry, both broker-sold funds have come under some adverse scrutiny of late for their total expense ratios of nearly 1% (100 bp). Management of the new firm has been considering introducing a "breakpoint" pricing structure to the advisory fee of a potentially combined fund to help address this issue. For example, one idea being considered (after establishing a base advisory fee) is a reduction of 1 bp of advisory fee once combined assets reach $6 billion, and an additional 1 bp for every $3 billion increase in assets thereafter.

Since both funds are distributed through the intermediary channel, any merged fund would also be sold through the existing network of broker-dealers. American Guardian's funds were primarily sold through Merrill Lynch and Dean Witter. Although Best Management also had a good relationship with Merrill Lynch, the majority of sales were made through Salomon Smith Barney. In general, brokers receive at least a 25 bp 12b-1 fee on Class A securities from most fund companies, in addition to the front-end load of 4.5%. Any attempt to reduce these fees would likely be met with resistance, and might hinder the brokers' willingness to promote the fund(s).

As summarized in schedule B, both funds currently incur 25 bp of investment management expense, which includes portfolio management, research, trading, and investment support. The portfolio manager of American Patriot Growth has been with the fund for many years. He has indicated a willingness to shift into a different role with the combined firm, should management so desire. The impact of his total compensation and related expenses on the fund management expense is approximately 2 bp. The portfolio manager of Best Western Growth is viewed as a rising star within the industry. She is very popular with the brokerage firms, and has a good performance record for the short term and longer term. The impact of her total compensation and related expenses on the fund management expense is approximately 1.5 bp.

American Patriot Growth most recently spent 10 bp on sales support, while Best Western Growth spent approximately 15 bp. These expenses consist of a wholesaling sales force and other support for the brokers who sell the fund. American Patriot Growth has 3 wholesalers and Best Western Growth has 5. The senior sales executive for the combined firm believes that all of them will stay on, and hopes to be able to add 2 more wholesalers to gather additional assets, while eliminating redundancies and inefficiencies in the combined sales area. On average, fund sponsors must spend $200,000 to $250,000 per year to pay and support a wholesaler.

Best Western Growth spends considerably more than American Patriot Growth on servicing (25 bp vs. 17 bp) because they have chosen an "internal" transfer agent strategy, while American Patriot Growth uses an "external" third-party servicing agent. American Patriot Growth's service quality is considered to be adequate, while Best Western Growth's is above average. The head of operations, who was with Best Management, has estimated that he could service American Patriot Growth with an incremental spending level of half that incurred by Patriot Growth in the last year; however, the expected cost to continue growing and enhancing its internal servicing capability is substantial. After combining these servicing resources, he estimates that operations expense will grow in line with the expected growth in assets for the next 3 to 5 years.

At the December board meetings, company executives must present their recommendations for changes to these funds. This week's Funds' Operations meeting will focus on merging the two similar domestic equity funds. Since fund mergers require director and shareholder votes, the rationale for the merger is extremely important. It must make sense for all major stakeholders—Best American, the shareholders of both funds, and the brokers that sell them.

Schedule A

	Am. Guardian (Patriot Growth)	Best Mgmt (Western Growth)	Industry median
Distribution channel:	Intermediary	Intermediary	
Type of funds sold:	Domestic equity growth/cap. app. Class A	Domestic equity growth/cap. app. Class A	
Transfer agent:	Outsourced	Internal	
Size of fund:	$3B	$2.5B	
Current Fees (%):			
Advisory fees	58 bp	44 bp	52 bp
12b-1 fees	25 bp (25bp to B/D)	35 bp (30bp to B/D)	25 bp (25bp to B/D)
Service fees	15 bp	19 bp	17 bp
Total expense ratio	98 bp	98 bp	94 bp
Load structure			
Front-end	5% (4.5% to B/D)	5% (4.5% to B/D)	5% (4.5% to B/D)

Schedule B
1996 Pro-forma P&L

	American Patriot Growth		Best Western Growth		Newly merged fund (1-year forward)	
	$000	bp	$000	bp	$000	bp
Annualized average assets	3,000,000		2,500,000			
Projected gross sales	0		250,000			
Revenue:						
Sales loads, net (50 bp on sales)	0	0	1,250	5		
Management fees	17,400	58	11,000	44		
Subtotal net advisory fees	17,400	58	12,250	49		
12b-1 fees, net	0	0	1,250	5		
Fund accounting/Transfer agent fees	4,500	15	4,750	19		
Subtotal service fees	4,500	15	4,750	19		
Total revenue	21,900	73	18,250	73		
Expense:						
Fund management	7,500	25	6,250	25		
Sales support	3,000	10	3,750	15		
Fund accounting/Transfer agent	4,500	15	6,250	25		
Subtotal operations expense						
Total expense	15,000	50	16,250	65		
Pretax income	6,900	23	2,000	8		
After tax income (40% tax rate)	4,140	14	1,200	5		
After tax margin	18.9%		6.6%			

Schedule C Comparison of share class pricing for competitor X

A Share	Initial investment		$10,000	Sales charge		4.00%	12b-1 fees		0.40%
	Growth rate		8%	Commission		3.75%	Broker re-allowance		0.20%
	NPV discount rate		10%				Advisory fee + other exp.		0.70%
	Year 1	Year 2	Year 3	Year 4	Year 5	Year 6	Year 7	Year 8	Year 9	Year 10
Beginning investment	$9,600	$10,262	$10,971	$11,727	$12,537	$13,402	$14,326	$15,315	$16,372	$17,501
Net appreciation	$662	$708	$757	$809	$865	$925	$989	$1,057	$1,130	$1,208
Shareholder ending value	$10,262	$10,971	$11,727	$12,537	$13,402	$14,326	$15,315	$16,372	$17,501	$18,709
Sales charge	$400	$0	$0	$0	$0	$0	$0	$0	$0	$0
12b-1 fees	$40	$42	$45	$49	$52	$55	$59	$63	$68	$72
NPV of distribution-related expenses	$436	$471	$505	$538	$571	$602	$632	$662	$691	$719
NPV of distribution-related expenses retained	$43	$61	$78	$94	$110	$126	$141	$156	$170	$184
Sales charge commissions	$375	$0	$0	$0	$0	$0	$0	$0	$0	$0
12b-1 trailer	$20	$21	$23	$24	$26	$28	$30	$32	$34	$36
NPV broker compensation	$393	$411	$428	$444	$460	$476	$491	$506	$520	$534

Schedule C (continued)

B Share

Initial investment	$10,000	CDSC 4, 3.5, 3, 2.5, 2, 1, 0%	12b-1 fees*	1.00%
Growth rate	8%	Commission 3.75%	Broker re-allowance	0.20%
NPV discount rate	10%		Advisory fee + other exp.	0.70%

	Year 1	Year 2	Year 3	Year 4	Year 5	Year 6	Year 7	Year 8	Year 9	Year 10
Beginning investment	$10,000	$10,630	$11,300	$12,012	$12,768	$13,573	$14,428	$15,337	$16,395	$17,526
Net appreciation	$630	$670	$712	$757	$804	$855	$909	$1,058	$1,131	$1,209
Shareholder ending value	$10,630	$11,300	$12,012	$12,768	$13,573	$14,428	$15,337	$16,395	$17,526	$18,736
CDSC on redemption	$400	$350	$300	$250	$200	$100	$0	$0	$0	$0
Ending value w/redemption	$10,230	$10,950	$11,712	$12,518	$13,373	$14,328	$15,337	$16,395	$17,526	$18,736
12b-1 Fees	$103	$110	$117	$124	$132	$140	$149	$63	$68	$73
NPV of distr-related exp.	$94	$184	$272	$357	$438	$517	$594	$623	$652	$680
w/redemption	$457	$474	$497	$527	$563	$574	$594	$623	$652	$680
NPV of distr-related exp. retained	($300)	($227)	($157)	($90)	($24)	$39	$100	$115	$129	$143
w/redemption	$64	$62	$68	$81	$100	$95	$100	$115	$129	$143
Sales charge commissions	$375	$0	$0	$0	$0	$0	$0	$0	$0	$0
12b-1 trailer	$21	$22	$23	$25	$26	$28	$30	$32	$34	$36
NPV broker compensation	$394	$412	$429	$446	$463	$478	$494	$509	$523	$537

* converts to the A share 12b-1 schedule at the beginning of year 8

10.9   **When Your Manager Sells Out, Should You?***
James M. Clash

A wave of consolidation is washing over the mutual fund business. So far this year funds totaling more than $125 billion in assets have changed hands. To hear the consolidators tell it, mergers are good because they bring fund investors economies of scale and breadth of choice within a fund family. Will these promises be fulfilled? It is instructive to consider some of the bigger recent mergers. The results are not encouraging.

Take the Dreyfus funds, purchased in December 1993 by Pittsburgh's Mellon Bank. In the three years before the merger, the 12 domestic stock funds at Dreyfus performed, on average, on a par with the S&P 500 index. In the three years since, these funds, on average, have underperformed the index by a stunning seven percentage points a year.

Then there's the American Capital/Van Kampen merger in August 1994. In the 26 months prior to the marriage, the 11 stock funds here outperformed the S&P 500 index by an average of two points annually. In the 26 months since the merger, the funds have underperformed, by two points annually. (See table 10.8.1.)

Do fund shareholders at least benefit from economies of scale? Not really. Average expenses at both the Dreyfus and American Capital families are just about where they were before they changed hands, notwithstanding that assets are up.

Even the Templeton family seems to be suffering from postmerger letdown. These mostly international funds, founded by the revered investor John Templeton, are still market beaters, but they have seen a sharp falloff in how much they beat their benchmarks.

Table 10.9.1
Dreyfus and Amcap

Fund family	Average return		Average expenses (per $100)		Average assets ($mil)	
	before	after	before	after	before	after
Mellon/Dreyfus	−0.1	−7.2	$1.11	$1.14	$481	$535
American Capital/Van Kamper	1.8	−1.7	1.30	1.35	477	648

Mellon/Dreyfus: Premerger Dec. 31, 1990, to Nov. 30, 1993. Postmerger Nov. 30, 1993, to Oct. 31, 1996.
American Capital/Van Kampen: Premerger June 30, 1992, to Aug. 31, 1994. Postmerger Aug. 31, 1994, to Oct. 31, 1996.
All numbers are annual averages. Returns are domestic equity, against the S&P 500 index, in percentage points.
Note: These two families, consisting mainly of U.S. stock funds, petered out after recent mergers.
Source: Morningstar, Inc.

---

*Reprinted by permission of *Forbes Magazine*. © Forbes Inc., 1996.

San Mateo, Calif.-based Franklin Resources bought control of the Templeton family for $786 million on Oct. 30, 1992. The move gave Franklin, then primarily a bond fund firm, an instant international equity presence—and reputation—that helped market the combined firm's assets.

Templeton's two star managers, Mark Mobius and Mark Holowesko, signed what were essentially four-year employment contracts and were given fat cash bonuses and salary increases. Sir John Templeton, already cutting back from daily operations, bowed out almost entirely when the acquisition was finalized.

Not long after the merger, trouble began. Templeton's managers were not happy with the new bonus structure; suddenly their bonuses weren't linked just to their equity performance but to Franklin bond managers' performances, too. Templeton Chief Executive Thomas Hansberger quit in 1993 to found a rival institutional firm, Hansberger Global Investors, and took a bunch of Templeton staffers with him. Recently there has been further attrition as employment contracts begin to expire.

What has all this meant to Templeton's shareholders? All four of Templeton's big open-end international equity funds with at least four years on each side of the merger (a combined $27 billion in assets) show postmerger return declines against their respective benchmarks. (See table 10.8.2.) The average drop in relative annual performance: a stunning six percentage points.

What about the hoped-for economies of scale? They didn't happen. While average assets in these four Templeton funds have more than doubled, expenses have not gone down. They have increased by a third, from an average of $0.84 per $100 of assets annually to an average of $1.12.

This is not to say that the Templeton funds are a disaster for investors. Even with the relative petering out of their returns, the four still beat their Morgan Stanley benchmarks for international investing. Expenses, although higher, are still below the average for international funds. But the simple fact is that they are not the winners they once were.

Table 10.9.2
Templeton

Fund	Average return		Average expenses (per $100)		Average assets ($mil)	
	before	after	before	after	before	after
Templeton Global Small Cos I	5.8	0.4	$1.05	$1.29	$858	$1,326
Templeton Growth I	7.7	1.9	0.74	1.03	2,581	5,815
Templeton World I	4.6	2.9	0.74	1.02	4,187	5,334
Templeton Foreign I	13.8	1.1	0.83	1.12	937	5,391

Premerger Oct. 31, 1988 to Oct. 31, 1992. Postmerger October 31, 1992 to Oct. 31, 1996.
All numbers are annual averages. Returns are in percentage points versus Morgan Stanley World Index, *except Templeton Foreign (versus Morgan Stanley EAFE)*.
Note: These Templeton international stock funds, representing $27 billion in combines assets, have cooled significantly versus their comparison indexes since Franklin bought Templeton in 1992. But they've all managed to beat their benchmarks.
Source: Morningstar, Inc.

Mark Holowesko, president of the global equity group at Templeton, explains the postmerger weakening of performance as a consequence of too small a dose of Japanese stocks. He says expenses are up because the funds are invested in more countries, some of them—like Russia and Poland—very expensive to research. Holowesko says he plans to stay. Templeton's departure was not as traumatic as it may have seemed; the founder had already ceded most stock picking decisions in the late 1980s.

There has always been a question about whether fund buyouts are good for shareholders of the acquired firms. But this year, with a record half-dozen big fund acquisitions announced—including $50 billion-plus American Capital/Van Kampen by Morgan Stanley, and $57 billion AIM Management Group by Invesco—the stakes have risen.

Arguments for consolidation are simple. First, lower expenses should be realized through economies of scale from combining back-office operations. Second, increased purchasing clout with a larger asset pool should result in better access to Wall Street research. Finally, if the fund family being acquired is small, consolidation can free money managers from diversions like marketing so they can spend more time picking stocks.

Arguments against consolidation are less tangible. James Margard, chief equity strategist at $3 billion Rainier Investment Management, a pension fund manager in Seattle, maintains that stock pickers are much sharper when they're independent. "They get complacent once they cash out and buy the big sailboat," says Margard, 44, who has been approached by several firms interested in gobbling up his 15-year-old company, which also runs the excellent mutual fund Rainier Core Equity Portfolio. So far, he has resisted. "My investors are better off when I'm hungry," he says.

There's also the potential for disharmony when two corporations merge, and it can affect the performance of money managers, even causing some to quit. When Merrill Lynch bought $9 billion Hotchkis & Wiley this year, most of the bond department left.

What should you do if your fund company sells out? If the portfolio manager of a fund you are in stays put, it probably makes sense to give the new owners a chance. But keep a close eye on the situation. Franklin just paid some $610 million for Heine Securities, operator of the excellent Mutual Series funds run by Michael Price. Supposedly Price's attention has been secured by a five-year contract and up to $193 million in performance incentives. But Price can go part-time after just one year, so his heart may not be in the job after that.

The other thing to watch for is the cost of ownership. If expenses climb, consider departing. The hitherto no-load Mutual Series funds have often been on the *Forbes* Best Buy list for U.S. equity funds. They will have a hard time staying there: Effective Nov. 1, Franklin began charging a sales commission of up to 4.5%.

11 Mutual Funds as Institutional Investors

Introduction

In this chapter, we will look at the governance implications of substantial fund investments in publicly traded companies. We will focus on the role of mutual funds as shareholders in these companies, rather than on customers as shareholders in mutual funds. To minimize confusion, we will refer to shareholders of a fund as *customers* and reserve the word *stockholders* for the role of funds relative to publicly traded companies. In addition, we will see that mutual funds as stockholders face similar issues to pension funds, bank trust departments, and other institutional investors in relation to corporate America.

For most of the twentieth century, the stockholders of publicly traded companies were relatively passive. Although they technically owned the company, the stockholders (other than a few insiders) were so atomized and diffuse that they generally had great difficulty in changing or influencing the decisions of company executives. If stockholders disagreed with the policies pursued by a publicly traded company, they simply sold the stock—what is known as the *Wall Street Rule*.

Within the last two decades, however, institutional investors such as mutual funds have come to own a majority of the common stock of most publicly traded American companies. Table 11.0.1 details the growth of institutional holdings in the largest 1,000 U.S. corporations by market capitalization over the last decade. Table 11.0.2 quantifies the percentage of equity in these largest 1,000 U.S. corporations owned by institutional investors.

Equity mutual funds, in particular, have become larger stockholders of publicly traded companies, especially during the last few years. This trend over the last decade is quantified in table 11.0.3. As of 1996, the equities owned by U.S. mutual funds exceeded 14% of all publicly held corporate equity in the United States.

Despite the enormous equity holdings of institutional investors, they still follow the Wall Street rule in most situations when they are dissatisfied with the performance of a publicly traded company. Institutional investors are geared to portfolio investing in a diversified group of stocks; they do not have the time, expertise, or inclination to become involved in the operational management of many companies. Yet, as the equity holdings of institutional investors have increased, they have become unwilling to remain as passive shareholders in all situations. Moreover, institutions pursuing strategies of investing in accordance with an index may not be in a position simply to sell the stock if they are dissatisfied with management policies. The result is the phenomenon of institutional activism toward publicly traded companies. This phenomenon has been most regularly and dramatically represented through the activities of a relatively small group of public pension

Table 11.0.1
Institutional investor concentration of ownership in the largest 1,000 U.S. corporations by bracket: 1987–1996

U.S. corporations by market capitalizations	Average institutional holdings (percent)						
	1987	1990	1992	1993	1994	1995	1996
Top 1–50	48.7	50.1	52.1	47.2	62.7	52.9	56.3
Top 51–100	58.6	59.2	58.8	63.9	64.3	61.8	69.8
Top 101–250	52.3	54.7	55.8	58.9	60.1	58.4	62.4
Top 251–500	50.7	51.1	55.0	57.6	58.2	59.0	62.3
Top 501–750	45.2	47.5	50.0	55.7	58.6	59.4	59.8
Top 751–1000	37.7	44.6	49.7	52.4	52.4	52.5	52.5

Source: *The Brancato Report*. Calculated from the *Business Week* Top 1000 data base

Table 11.0.2
Institutional investor concentration of ownership in the largest 1,000 U.S. corporations by percentage of holdings: 1987–1996

Percentage of equity held by institutional investors	U.S. companies (percent)						
	1987	1990	1992	1993	1994	1995	1996
Over 90%	0.4	0.3	0.9	3.5	3.7	4.2	5.5
Over 80%	2.3	3.0	7.3	13.4	14.1	15.8	17.2
Over 70%	10.7	15.9	22.7	31.8	30.5	31.0	35.5
Over 60%	22.7	33.4	40.2	48.5	48.7	50.1	62.9
Over 50%	44.9	50.4	58.8	63.0	63.5	65.0	67.5
Over 40%	64.2	65.4	72.1	75.4	75.5	75.7	79.5
Over 30%	76.9	78.9	84.3	86.0	85.8	86.5	87.5
Over 20%	88.5	88.5	92.2	92.4	91.7	92.9	92.1

Source: *The Brancato Report*. Calculated from the *Business Week* Top 1000 data base

plans, such as the California Public Employees' Retirement System (CalPERS), the Florida State Board of Administration, the Wisconsin Investment Board, and the New York State Common Retirement Fund. From time to time, however, investment advisers to large mutual funds have become quietly involved in an effort to persuade corporate executives to change their policies.

It is important to distinguish such institutional activism from fiduciary diligence. It is generally accepted as a fiduciary obligation of investment managers diligently to review proxy statements, vote on issues in accordance with their clients' interests, and report back to the appropriate authority (e.g., trustees or board of directors). The Department of Labor has expressly elaborated this duty in letters and releases addressed to pension fiduciaries under the Employee Retirement Income Security Act (ERISA). By contrast, the SEC—the primary regulator of mutual funds—has not published a rule or release on

Table 11.0.3

Mutual funds' holdings of U.S. publicly held equities outstanding 1987–1996

Year	Holdings (billions of dollars)	Share of total (in percent)
1987	182	6.5
1988	188	6.1
1989	251	6.6
1990	233	6.6
1991	309	6.3
1992	401	7.4
1993	607	9.7
1994	710	11.3
1995	1,025	12.2
1996	1,460	14.5

Source: SIA, *Securities Industry Fact Book* (1997)

proxy voting by fund managers. Nevertheless, most advisers to large mutual funds follow written proxy voting guidelines, which have been set or approved by the independent directors of the funds. The fund adviser typically processes and votes all proxies for shares held by the funds, and submits annual or semiannual reports on its proxy voting record to the independent directors. Some boards have a special committee of independent directors on proxy voting issues; other boards review these issues through the full board.

Proxy voting guidelines are designed to cover issues arising in connection with non-routine items proposed by company management or put forward through stockholder resolutions. One important set of subjects involves takeovers and takeover defenses. These include votes on super-majority vote requirements for mergers, the staggering of elections for board seats, and the adoption of *poison pill plans*. When someone acquires more than a specified percentage (e.g., 15% or 20%) of a company's voting shares without director approval, a poison pill plan grants all other stockholders the right to purchase more company shares at a huge discount (e.g., one cent per share), making the company "hard to swallow." Another important category of nonroutine votes involves basic stockholder rights. These include the right to call a special meeting of stockholders and the authorization of new shares for the company to issue. Still another category of significant proxy issues involves those aspects of executive compensation that are put to a stockholder vote. These include the adoption of plans for awarding stock options and restricted shares as well as the approval of performance criteria for a company to receive a tax deduction for an executive's compensation of over $1 million in any one year.

In most cases, the advisers to mutual funds vote to support the recommendations of company management. They rarely vote against management nominees for directors, and they generally support management's position regarding company proposals or stockholder resolutions on other subjects. However, investment advisers must vote fund shares in what they believe is the best interests of their fund customers. Thus, investment advisers to funds may from time to time disagree with management when there is a takeover bid or a proxy fight between an outside organization and company management. If a stockholder resolution is properly worded and raises a significant corporate issue, investment advisers also must diligently consider whether to support the stockholder or management on such a resolution.

Investment advisers to mutual funds rarely initiate proxy fights or propose alternative slates of directors, and they almost never actively plan a takeover attempt. As explained by the readings, investment advisers face significant legal and operational constraints on engaging in such control-oriented tactics. For example, if certain directors of publicly traded companies represented mutual funds, the funds would be severely constrained in trading the company's securities by insider trading laws. From time to time, however, investment advisers to mutual funds do more than vote on issues put forward by others. If an investment adviser to a mutual fund decides to pressure a company on an important stockholder issue, the adviser would most likely meet with company management to discuss the issue. In addition, under the SEC's current rules, an investment adviser to a mutual fund is permitted to discuss that issue with other institutional investors as long as they do not agree to act in concert and no one solicits a proxy from another.

Some commentators have urged mutual funds and other institutional investors to become shareholder activists on social issues such as smoking or clean air. But mutual fund managers have stayed focused on financial aspects of corporate performance (including financial implications of social issues). The main exception is the small group of "ethical" or "green" funds designed to avoid "socially objectionable" stocks. Other commentators have suggested that institutional investors should bring about fundamental changes in the American system of corporate governance. But, again, mutual fund managers have been more interested in obtaining good financial returns than in pursuing political or ideological reforms.

SEC chairman Arthur Levitt has provided some guidance on institutional activism to mutual fund advisers and directors. Set forth below is an excerpt from his speech "Mutual Fund Directors: On the Front Line for Investors" (March 21, 1994):

Mutual fund management must decide how active it should be and under what circumstances. I recognize that funds that invest in a large number of companies cannot possibly take an active role in every matter submitted to shareholders. The costs would far exceed the benefits. But when a shareholder vote raises issues that are tied directly to a stock's price, the case for involvement is obvious.

Directors should look carefully at whether it is in investors' interest that a fund exercise its franchise in matters as critical as anti-takeover measures, proxy fights for control of a portfolio company, and elections. Funds also may find it advisable to consider executive compensation proposals, when those proposals are submitted to shareholders for approval.

Fund directors should ask the adviser about its policies for participating in the governance process. What kind of system does the adviser have for identifying issues that might require shareholder activism? How does the adviser reach its decision on how to cast its ballot?

I am not suggesting that directors generally should be involved in determining how a fund votes its shares in a particular matter. Rather, as in other areas, directors should ask the hard questions about overall policies and their implementation.

The materials in this chapter will explore both the types of objectives associated with institutional activism and the range of strategies available to implement those objectives. The case study involves a set of proxy fights between an insurgent group and company management in which institutional investors played the decisive role.

Questions

In reviewing the materials for this chapter, please keep in mind the following three hypothetical questions:

Hypothetical no. 1   In the Exxon proxy statement is a stockholder proposal recommending that "Exxon's directors adopt a no oil spill policy to the maximum extent feasible." How should you vote as the manager of the Value Mutual Fund, which owns 3% of Exxon's outstanding common stock? Why?

Hypothetical no. 2   A new independent director, a distinguished business school professor, suggests that the policies of all equity funds in the complex be revised (after approval by the funds' customers if required). At present, the fundamental policy limits each such equity fund to acquiring less than 5% of the outstanding common stock of any publicly traded company, and the complex's internal management policies limit all equity funds in the complex together to acquiring less than 15% of the outstanding common stock of any publicly traded company. The new director suggests that these percentages be changed to 10% and 35% respectively. What are the arguments for and against these suggestions?

Hypothetical no. 3   Suppose a software company is sued for allegedly failing to disclose promptly that its new Internet browser had significant bugs. The suit is brought by a plaintiff's law firm on behalf of a class consisting of all buyers of that company's stock during the month of April, just before the company disclosed the bugs. A growth fund bought 2% of the software company's common stock on April 1 at $100 per share. The stock dropped immediately to $80 per share after the company disclosed the bugs and stayed at $80 per share. At the time of the acquisition, the stock of the software company constituted $\frac{1}{2}$% of the growth fund's total assets of $1 billion. Should you as the investment manager of the growth fund take over control of the class action? Note: Congress recently passed a statute allowing the largest shareholder of a company to be a "presumptive plaintiff" in a class action against the company. The presumptive plaintiff may choose to control the class action, including hiring counsel, approving briefs, and negotiating settlements.

11.1   Pension Funds Flex Shareholder Muscle*
Ed McCarthy

Pension fund shareholder activism forces some companies into value-added reform, but some believe involvement in corporate governance issues has negligible value.

The era of the passive pension fund manager is over. In today's climate of institutional shareholder activism, it's not enough to earn solid returns on your portfolios. You also have to address corporate governance and performance issues—or you might be accused of neglecting your fiduciary duties.

It has been hard to ignore the increasing level of institutional investor activism during the past few years. Several large pension funds, including the California Public Employees' Retirement System (CalPERS) and other public employee funds, have voiced dissatisfaction repeatedly with the Archer-Daniels-Midland Co.'s board. The *Wall Street Journal* gave front page coverage to the poor but impressively durable performance of Champion International Corp.'s chairman and the efforts of pension fund shareholders to get him thrown off the board. William Patterson, corporate affairs director for the International Brotherhood of Teamsters, reports that his group will publish a list of America's worst-performing corporate board members. It is not just U.S. companies that are receiving attention, either: CalPERS has announced plans to expand its activism in Britain, France, Germany, and Japan in 1996.

There is no denying the new wave of pension fund shareholder activism. Advocates justify the movement by claiming that it produces rewards far in excess of its costs. Critics contend that activism is a waste of pension fund resources. Which view is right, and what are the implications for fund managers?

Background

In the January 1995 Council of Institutional Investors' (CII) newsletter, Sarah A. B. Teslik, the Council's executive director, looked back 10 years to the organization's founding. She notes that 1985 was a hostile climate for discussing shareholders' rights:

- "CEOs said publicly and proudly that the only right shareholders had with respect to their stock was the right to sell."
- "Words like proxy and directors hadn't entered the governance dictionary."
- "No public or union pension fund ever had filed a shareholder proposal."

The situation was about to change, though. The emergence of hostile takeovers and the resulting poison pills and greenmail payments spurred institutional shareholders to action. CalPERS launched its first initiatives, targeted at poison pills, in late 1987. For the

---

*From *Pension Management*, January 1, 1996. Reprinted with permission, Intertec Publishing Corp. ©
1996.

rest of the '80s and early '90s, public funds continued to be the most active group. In recent years, Taft-Hartley funds have increased their activities and corporations are showing more interest. CII's membership roster reflects these trends, growing from 20 members in 1985 to over 100 members today, including more than 20 corporate funds.

The shift into indexing gave impetus to the activism movement. If a fund's equity portfolio is locked into an index like the S&P 500, the fund has limited options for increasing its return above the index's results. One method is to improve the performance of the stocks in the index. That has led activists recently to focus much of their attention on those firms whose long-term results have lagged behind the S&P or some other industry benchmark. Their logic is straightforward: If we improve the laggards' performance, we improve the index's performance and our indexed fund will benefit. Stephen Nesbitt, a senior vice president with Wilshire Associates, has researched this change in focus in his study of CalPERS' activities. Mr. Nesbitt notes that before 1990, CalPERS focused largely on poison pill and confidential voting issues. In 1991 and 1992, performance-related issues dominated CalPERS' agenda.

A third factor moving funds towards activism was the 1994 release of the Department of Labor's (DOL) Interpretive Bulletin 94-2 (IB 94-2). This bulletin stresses "that the voting of proxies is a fiduciary act of plan asset management." IB 94-2 also discusses shareholder activism:

The Department believes that, where proxy voting decisions may have an effect on the economic value of the plan's underlying investment, plan fiduciaries should make proxy voting decisions with a view to enhancing the value of the shares of stock, taking into account the period over which the plan expects to hold such shares.

... the Department believes that active monitoring and communication with corporate management is consistent with a fiduciary's obligations under ERISA where the responsible fiduciary concludes that there is a reasonable chance that such activities by the plan alone, or together with other shareholders, are likely to enhance the value of the plan's involvement, after taking into account the costs involved.

Given the convergence of market trends and the DOL's bulletin, it is not surprising that pension fund activism is increasing. The key question remains: Does activism benefit the pension fund? Are we making money yet?

Critics of activism argue that if a company is producing a good return for its shareholders, why worry about issues like the firm's governance structure? Proponents counter that a firm that consistently overlooks its shareholders will not produce acceptable returns for very long. "There are some reasonable, common sense measures that protect shareholders," according to Linda Priscilla, international representative with the Laborers International Union of North America. "These include board independence. If the board is not independent, problems will develop. Another issue is directors' compensation, which should be in the form of stock."

Nancy Mayer, general treasurer of the State of Rhode Island and chair of the State Investment Commission, agrees some situations require intervention. "We should be active if we see a company that isn't doing well financially but whose officers and directors are doing very well. As shareholders we shouldn't sit back and watch a CEO run a company into the ground."

Mr. Nesbitt of Wilshire Associates believes that activism can benefit pension funds. He examined the performance of 42 firms that CalPERS targeted from 1987 to 1994. The results were striking. He found that the targeted companies had underperformed the S&P 500 by an average cumulative 66% for the five years before CalPERS took action. That works out to a 7.9% annual total return shortfall for the stocks in the study. After CalPERS initiated its actions, the returns went in the other direction, showing an average cumulative 41.3% excess return (7.1% annual) over the S&P 500 for the subsequent five-year period (see "CalPERS' corporate governance activities"). Mr. Nesbitt's conclusion: Even after adjusting for risk and industry factors, the CalPERS-targeted firms significantly outperformed the market, on average.

Mr. Nesbitt updated his original research in 1995 and found the results favored the "CalPERS Effect" even more than his 1994 study indicated. He attributes the findings to several causes. "Why do these stocks outperform the market after CalPERS targets them? I think there are a couple of reasons," he says. "One is that, in some cases, CalPERS and other institutional investors are catalysts for change, which may result in better operating performance at the company. Many cases have to do with breaking up the company, getting rid of a poorly performing division, and paying out cash flow.

"Second, I think the market perceives an outside investor like CalPERS as being a legitimate catalyst," adds Mr. Nesbitt. "Even though no real change happens immediately, just having a large institutional investor publicly voice concern about the company's performance may help bid up the price of the stock in the expectation that something real will happen."

The Lens investment fund points to its own record as further proof that activism can produce measurable returns for investors. Nell Minow, a principal with the firm, describes its investment approach as a variation on traditional value investing themes. "We see what we do as a traditional value approach with one important difference," Ms. Minow says. "The difference is that a value investor will pick a company based on the idea that someday something will happen and those values will be realized. We invest along the same basic value criteria, but then we will take steps to make sure the value gets realized sooner rather than later. Rather than invest in a stock and hope it goes up, we spur management and the board to do a better job. We have invested in seven companies in our history. All had major restructurings, all but one replaced the CEO, one company replaced the CEO twice, and all of them responded to our requests that they do better."

The firm uses a variety of methods to encourage change in its portfolio companies. These methods include publicity campaigns, coordination with other institutional investors, proxy contests, and shareholder litigation. The Lens fund approach seems to be working so far. Its annualized return over the fund's first three-year period ending July 31, 1995 was 23.4% versus the S&P 500's 13.1%. The principals currently have $15 million of their own funds under management, but they have commitments for another $75 million from outside investors.

Not Convinced

Not everyone is convinced that pension fund activism pays. Professor Wayne Marr of Social Science Electronic Publishing edits the *Journal of Applied Corporate Finance*.

Mr. Marr is skeptical about the long-term impact of institutional activism. "I've co-authored papers that look at governance issues, and it appears that institutional shareholder activism has very little influence, if any," Mr. Marr reports. "The result that we find to be most striking and significant is not unexpected. In our research, we've looked at a whole host of accounting measures and among all of them, the only thing that seems to have a long-term effect is poison pills. Staggered boards, eliminating greenmail, etc., don't seem to make a difference over the long run. We think a lot of that has to do with the fact that no one has found an effective way to get around the poison pill. So now you are seeing corporate governance activists taking a leading role in this area."

Mr. Marr sees a role for activism, but he does not believe it is appropriate for pension funds. "We're not saying poison pills are bad in every situation. The problem is trying to identify those situations where a poison pill is good and doesn't interfere in the long-run operations of the company. That's where activism can play a part," he says. "If a firm like the Lens fund can go in and identify the companies that truly are not in need of takeover protection, it's possible they can raise the value of those firms by being active. If they pick the wrong firm, there is very little value to be gained, because you are not trying to put the company in play as was common in the 1980s.

"It's a question of identifying those firms that are not in need of takeover protection, where you can go in and change the firm's governance profile," he adds. "That's the crux of it, and that's tough to do, especially if you are running a fund and monitoring 1,500 companies. Clearly, if you are going to go in and change the profile of a well-run firm, the value to be gained is probably zero or negative."

11.2   Management Focus: Not Awakening the Dead*

Pension funds and other institutional investors have become a powerful force in corporate America. Institutions now control more than half the shares in big American companies, up from just 16% in 1965, and they increasingly use their muscle to tell companies what to do.

Thus institutions routinely put pressure on companies to curb "excessive" salaries for executives, to make boards more independent, or even to sack poorly performing managers. The California Public Employees' Retirement System (CalPERS), an Dollars 80 billion pension fund that sets the pace among activists, complies an annual list of "crummy companies," judged by their stock performance and management style, and sends its people in to grill their bosses and directors. A study in 1995 by Korn/Ferry International found that 21% of the directors surveyed (and 32% of those at companies worth Dollars 5 billion or more) had been formally contacted by institutional investors; many more had been contacted informally.

Fans of shareholder activism argue that it is a crucial mechanism for making companies more accountable. In the past, shareholders were too diffuse and disorganised to have much impact; today, institutions have both the time and the resources to bring greedy or incompetent bosses to book. No wonder America's Labour Department is keen to foster shareholder activism.

But have institutional investors really changed the way companies are run? And have they improved companies' performance? Activists' fans point to 1992–93, when institutions claimed the scalps of the bosses of six American giants, including General Motors, American Express, and IBM. They have also forced large pay cuts on the bosses of ITT, General Dynamics, and USAir. More recently, activists have begun to try to engineer more wide-ranging corporate reforms. In March 1995 the College Retirement Equities Fund bullied W.R. Grace into cutting the size of its board, from 22 to 12, and imposing a mandatory retirement age of 70, as well as getting rid of its chairman and replacing half the directors.

More evidence for the impact of activism comes from Spencer Stuart's annual Board Index, which tracks the composition of the boards of 100 leading companies. It shows that the past five years have seen a net loss of 91 insiders and a gain of two outsiders. Two professors at Columbia Business School, Gerald Davis and Gregory Robbins, find that today's outside directors are much more likely to lose their jobs if their firms perform badly than were their predecessors in the 1980s. The proliferation of "directors' schools" at American universities also suggests that companies are demanding more of their directors.

But whether all this activity has actually helped to improve firms' performance is less clear. Research on the subject has been sparse, and two of the most widely quoted studies

---

*From *Economist*, August 10, 1996. Copyright © 1996 The Economist Newspaper Group, Inc. Reprinted with permission. Further reproduction prohibited.

point to opposite conclusions. A 1992 study by Wilshire Associates, a pension consulting firm, found that shares in companies targeted by CalPERS had substantially outperformed the Standard and Poor's [S&P] 500 index. A policy that had cost the pension fund around Dollars 500,000 had resulted in profits of Dollars 137m above the S&P's average.

But the following year a study of 1,000 leading companies in 1988–92 by Covenant Investment Management, a firm that gives advice to private investors, cast doubt on a central tenet of the shareholder movement by finding that firms with fewer outside directors did better than those with more. Now a new study, as yet unpublished, to be presented at the annual meeting of America's Academy of Management on August 12th, tilts the balance of evidence still further towards scepticism.

Catherine Daily, a professor of management at Purdue University, and three other management professors, studied the performance of a random sample of 200 Fortune-500 companies in 1990–93, a period when institutional activism was at its height. They gauged a company's performance in terms of return on equity, return on investment, and a measure that compared its performance with that of other firms exposed to similar risks.

To test the links between institutional activism and the performance of firms, the authors:

- tried to determine whether performance was affected by the proportion of stock held by institutions, on the assumption that institutions are superior monitors of corporate performance;

- looked at the effect of ownership by public pension funds, since they include some of the most active shareholders;

- measured the effect of the most active institutions, such as CalPERS, the College Retirement Equities Fund, and the New York State Common Retirement Fund; and

- tested whether shareholder proposals meant to improve corporate governance actually lead to better performance.

The results of all these tests were negative. The authors conclude, flatly, that institutional activism "has no appreciable effect on firm performance. Even the most activist of institutions are unable to achieve performance gains in the aggregate." The authors suggest that a good deal of shareholder activism is little more than window-dressing: a public-relations ploy by institutions, rather than a genuine attempt to improve the performance of targeted firms.

These gloomy results are unlikely to put a stop to shareholder activism. Professor Daily concedes that institutional activists may at least do some good. Good corporate governance may not boost a firm's performance in normal circumstances, she argues; but it could increase a firm's chances of surviving a crisis.

Besides, institutional investors have little option. To do nothing would irritate their clients. They cannot easily adopt the traditional Wall Street practice of dumping under-performing shares. They often hold so many shares that selling would depress the market. They may have inside knowledge that circumscribes their ability to trade. And many now adopt an "indexing" strategy—passively holding the shares in a market index rather than incurring the costs of frequent trading.

It may therefore be too soon for shareholder activists to stop prodding. But they should perhaps be a bit more humble about what their prods will achieve.

11.3   Fund Encourages "Good" Practices: CalPERS to List Top Corporate Citizens*

Vineeta Anand

The California Public Employees' Retirement System (CalPERS) is adding a new page to its corporate governance workbook by publicly praising top-performing companies that added the most jobs.

For years, the $100 billion fund has tried to shame poor-performing companies into doing better for their shareholders by naming them on its annual list of dogs. Now the fund hopes other companies will emulate those on its list of good corporate citizens.

The fund also intends to heap scorn on companies that use a "reverse Robin Hood" strategy of enriching top executives while shutting down operations and firing workers.

Apart from the two new initiatives in the upcoming annual meeting season, the fund will continue its efforts to develop baseline corporate governance standards and grade the nation's 300 largest companies against those.

What's more, the pension fund will, for a second consecutive year, train its sights for shareholder activism on 10 small poor-performing companies from the more than 1,500 companies in its investment portfolio. The fund will announce its hit list in January.

The agenda for the 1997 proxy season also includes an analysis of how directors contribute to companies' performance, a spokesman said.

Outside the United States, the fund will focus its corporate governance efforts on Japanese, British, German, and French companies in its portfolio.

The activist pension fund is using the carrot-and-stick approach for the first time to reward companies "that deserve praise for, over the long term, providing value to shareholders without sacrificing their work force," said Kayla Gillan, general counsel.

But Ms. Gillan underscored that companies can only land on the "good citizen" list if they first prove they are good investments for shareholders.

The fund's decision to praise companies that have added jobs while producing large returns for their shareholders comes at a time when many Americans are insecure about their jobs, and institutional investors have taken flak for goading companies to bump up their stock prices in the short term by laying off thousands of workers.

"One of the things we have been criticized for as institutional investors is that our corporate governance efforts are forcing companies to make quick fixes and force layoffs," said Brad Pacheco, a fund spokesman. "We are long-term investors and looking for something that rewards CEOs and employees and the shareholders," he said.

Labor Secretary Robert Reich was one of the first to point fingers at investors. "As corporations have focused more and more exclusively on increasing shareholders' immediate returns, the consequences have become obvious. The stock market has soared while pink slips have proliferated, health care and pensions have been cut, and the paychecks of most employees have gone nowhere," he said in a California speech.

The California pension fund began mulling its strategy in the spring, after AT&T Corp. announced plans to lay off thousands of workers as part of its restructuring, and some lawmakers suggested good corporate citizens be given preferential income tax treatment.

Richard H. Koppes, general counsel and deputy chief executive of the fund at the time, outlined the approach in a speech at the International Forum for Corporate Directors in San Diego earlier this year. Mr. Koppes blamed money managers, "the short-term investors of America," who react "swiftly and positively as layoffs are announced," for spurring companies to jettison their labor force. But corporations also must take their share of the blame, he said in the speech.

The fund plans to announce its list of good corporate citizens sometime next year, Ms. Gillan said.

Ms. Gillan said she was not ready to identify any stars that might be on the list. But the chances are good it will include Chrysler Corp., which has added more than 15,000 hourly workers in the last five years, as well as International Paper Co., Sara Lee Corp., Intel Corp., and Eastman Kodak Co., according to a source who did not wish to be identified.

And because of the giant California fund's influence as a trendsetter in corporate governance circles, it is a good bet that other activists might also consider adopting similar strategies.

Ms. Gillan said she had spoken to some members of the Council of Institutional Investors, the powerful Washington forum for shareholder activism, and the reaction had been "generally supportive."

Anne Hansen, deputy director at the council, said it is not inconceivable that the organization would prepare a similar list of good corporate citizens. "Our philosophy is on parallel tracks" with CalPERS, she said.

In fact, the theme of the council's conference next week is corporate responsibility, which the group defines as "a balance between the needs of the corporate community, shareholders, and employees."

"If you read between the lines, by doing such a conference, we would be underscoring our interest in supporting such an issue," Ms. Hansen said.

CalPERS' move in this direction is not surprising. Two years ago, the pension fund announced it would incorporate workplace issues into its corporate governance screening process for considering which companies to target at annual shareholder meetings.

"Both corporations and institutional investors have been taking a lot of heat for layoffs, and a counteroffensive is obvious at this time," said Patrick S. McGurn, director of corporate programs at Institutional Shareholder Services Inc., a Bethesda, Md., shareholder advisory firm.

At the same time, Ms. Gillan expressed concern that some companies "might have their priorities in the wrong place" by handing top executives "obscene amounts of pay" while firing workers and shutting down operations.

She cited The Warnaco Group, a New York-based apparel manufacturer as an example of the reverse Robin Hood strategy. Although the company announced plans to lay off workers and shut down some factories, Chief Executive Linda J. Wachner last year collected $16.6 million in pay, according to data from executive compensation expert Graef Crystal, cited in a Council of Institutional Investors' newsletter.

"That's the kind of situation we are going to be on the lookout for," Ms. Gillan said.

11.4   Institutional Investors: The Reluctant Activists*
Robert C. Pozen

In 1991, when the police unions were upset by the lyrics of a rap song by Ice-T, they lobbied institutional investors to vote against the directors of Time Warner Inc., the company that had released the song. Because institutional investors now own a majority of the voting stock of publicly traded companies in the United States, they have an influence on the way these companies are run. And given their influence, institutional investors are under increasing pressure to become activist shareholders on behalf of national competitiveness and various social causes.

At the same time, institutional investors have been criticized for intervening in the corporate governance process. As Charles Wohlstetter, former chairman and CEO of Contel, wrote about public pension plans in "The Fight for Good Governance" (HBR, January–February 1993), "In sum, we have a group of people with increasing control of the *Fortune* '500' who have no proven skills in management, no experience at selecting directors, no believable judgment in how much should be spent for research or marketing—in fact, no experience except that which they have accumulated controlling other people's money."

While Wohlstetter's claims are exaggerated, how *do* institutional investors act? What factors do they weigh when deciding to become activists? When should they vote with management, and when should they champion the cause of a competing interest? And—perhaps most important—what should corporate executives know about the way institutional investors make these decisions?

Most institutional investors do not set out to become activist shareholders, nor do they want to get involved with a company's operational issues. For most institutions, the approach to shareholder activism is straightforward: to decide whether and when to become active, an institutional investor compares the expected costs of a course of action with the expected benefits. The costs of activism depend primarily on the tools with which an institution exerts influence, from the high cost of waging a formal proxy fight to the low cost of holding informal discussions with management. The benefits depend partly on the probability of success and partly on the issue at hand, with more potential benefit from proposals directly affecting stock price and less from proposals for procedural reforms.

If corporate executives understood what motivates the decisionmaking of institutional investors, they would realize that institutions share their concerns about strategic positioning, succession planning, and long-term profitability. Corporate executives would also recognize institutions as their natural allies in responding to the legion of requests to pursue social or political agendas.

A Cost-Benefit Analysis of Shareholder Activism

Institutional investors have a fiduciary duty to try to achieve their client's objectives. Although these objectives vary, clients generally place their savings with institutional investors to earn higher returns than they could by investing on their own, to reduce risk by holding an interest in a large and varied pool of securities, and to maintain some degree of liquidity. Given their responsibility to clients, institutional investors must justify their activism in terms of achieving these objectives. That means becoming an active shareholder only if the expected benefits to clients—that is, increasing financial returns without taking large risks or unduly sacrificing liquidity—exceed the expected costs. While this approach sounds good in theory, in practice it is difficult to predict the results of institutional activism.

Measuring the Benefits of Activism

The best indicator of having achieved benefits for clients is an increase in a portfolio company's stock price. The next best indicator is an earnings increase, which is ultimately reflected in a higher stock price and/or higher dividend.

But the results of activism are not always so easy to interpret. Many forms of institutional activism involve trying to establish better procedures for corporate governance, such as a recent successful effort by the California Public Employees' Retirement System (CalPERS) to have the compensation committee of Advanced Micro Devices (AMD) be composed entirely of independent directors. While such procedural reforms are difficult to link directly to financial returns, they can be beneficial to an institution's clients if the new procedures lead to decisions that are more favorable to a company's shareholders. For example, with all independent directors, AMD's compensation committee is likely to align executive compensation more closely with shareholder returns through stock options or other devices.

If the price of a company's stock increases after an institutional investor's intervention, there is still the question of whether or not this intervention actually caused the price increase. Consider the case of Lens, Inc., a small activist-oriented institutional investment fund, and Robert Monks, its founder, who in late 1990 began pressuring Sears, Roebuck and Company to focus on its core business rather than attempt to combine a financial supermarket with a department store. After almost two years of pressure, Sears announced that it would concentrate on its retail business and sell Coldwell Banker, its real estate operations, as well as 20% of Dean Witter and Allstate, its principal financial holdings. Lens claimed that its efforts generated more than $1 billion in shareholder value because the price of Sears stock rose sharply over the two years. But the rise in the stock price generally followed the rise in the S&P 500 during the same period. Only two points are clear from Lens' efforts: the company's stock substantially lagged the S&P 500 before the campaign began, and the stock rose almost $4 on the day Sears announced it was selling its financial businesses. (See "Chronology of an Institutional Shareholder Campaign" at the end of this article.)

Measuring the Costs of Activism

The cost side of an institutional investor's cost-benefit analysis involves estimating the expenses of activism for these institutions and for their clients. These expenses are heavily influenced by the duties spelled out in the advisory contract between the money manager and the institution's board and by the more liberal requirements of the 1992 revisions to the SEC's proxy rules.

Most advisory contracts require money managers to perform normal proxy activity: reading proxy statements, making careful voting decisions, and sending reports to an oversight board. These contracts typically do not address the question of who pays for proxy activism undertaken by the institutional investor on behalf of its clients. In some cases, a money manager may justify imposing a charge on the clients' fund in addition to the advisory fee that clients pay to the money manager. For example, proxy activism may require hiring outside experts, such as appraisers, who will evaluate mineral rights held by a company proposing to go private. In other cases, such as travel expenses for meetings with company directors, the cost of activism is typically covered by the advisory fee.

Most such fees, however, are set on the assumption that institutional investors will usually function as passive money managers rather than as activists. The advisory fees of equity mutual funds average around 70 basis points (0.70%) per year, with a maximum performance fee of 10 to 20 basis points (0.10% to 0.20%). In other words, the fees do not cover heavy intervention on the part of the money manager. In contrast, advisory fees for a venture capital fund are typically composed of a 1% or 2% base fee plus 10% to 20% of all profits. This much higher fee is based on the assumption that venture fund managers will be actively involved with most of their portfolio companies.

An institutional investor can usually make a reasonable estimate of the out-of-pocket expenses associated with proxy activism. These include SEC filings of proxy solicitation materials; printing, mailing, and advertising these materials; professional fees for lawyers, proxy solicitors, and various consultants; and the extensive time and effort of the involved senior officials. The wild card is litigation. If a portfolio company sues one or more institutional investors for breach of a proxy rule or for acting in concert, the legal bills will be substantial regardless of the outcome. Litigation can also eat up lots of management time. The costs of litigation are hard to justify for institutional investors, since in most cases the benefits of activism are very difficult to predict.

By reducing the threat of litigation and the amount of necessary filings, the new SEC rules have significantly lowered the cost of proxy activism for institutional investors. According to these rules, an institutional investor, without any filings or mailings, can discuss voting issues with an unlimited number of other shareholders as long as the institutional investor does not solicit proxies from any of them. In late 1992, for example, the executive director of the Council of Institutional Investors called a number of council members to discuss the problems of Westinghouse's credit subsidiary, which had incurred large losses through aggressive lending. Representatives from several of these institutional investors then met with the management of Westinghouse to press for governance changes. The result of this very low-cost campaign: Westinghouse agreed to dismantle its poison pill, which would have deterred any large acquirer of Westinghouse stock by allowing all other shareholders to buy the company's stock very cheaply. Westinghouse also agreed to eliminate its staggered board, which would have prevented any potential insurgent from attaining control of a majority of the company's directors in one annual election.

The new SEC rules also allow an institutional investor to solicit proxies from a few large shareholders without mailing proxy statements to all shareholders. This focused approach was taken by Eagle Asset Management, a large holder of Centel and a virulent critic of its proposed merger with Sprint. Eagle mailed a 20-page booklet to Centel's 200 largest shareholders and lobbied them to vote against the merger. Eagle lost by less than 1% of the vote after spending only $250,000, much less than it would have spent on a series of mailings to all 5,000 Centel shareholders.

While the new SEC rules allow institutional investors to take on proxy issues without taking on tremendous expense, the rules do not solve the "free rider" problem. When an institutional investor spends substantial sums in pressuring a company to change its policies, the benefits of such activism are reaped by all stockholders, not just the clients of the active institution. While the value of Sears's shares as a whole may have risen by over $1 billion, how much of that gain was captured by Lens for its clients? And was that gain worth the expense of the battle?

As a practical matter, it is virtually impossible for the activist institutional investor to force all other benefiting shareholders to contribute to the effort. An activist institution can attempt to persuade a few large shareholders to share the costs of opposing a management initiative or of supporting a shareholder proposal. To take advantage of the new exemptions from proxy filings, however, an institutional investor cannot act in concert with other shareholders if together they hold more than 5% of a class of the portfolio company's voting stock. But the new SEC rules do not define "acting in concert," and the case law is very murky; no one really knows what this critical phrase means.

We do know that the new SEC rules have allowed more communication among institutional investors but have led to a more explicit rejection by them of group activity. If an institutional investor, for example, holds a large position in a company's stock and objects to a proposal on that company's ballot, the institution is likely to call other large holders to explain its objection. At the end of this conversation, however, both parties should state clearly that they will not be voting together or buying or selling securities together.

What's Worth Fighting For?

An institutional investor trying to decide whether or not to be an activist shareholder can use this cost-benefit approach to develop a ranking of voting issues and of the modes of proxy intervention. Voting issues can be ranked according to the potential benefits for institutional clients.

Stock Price

The highest potential benefits for clients come from voting issues in which stock price is directly at stake. Institutional activism that raises a company's stock price increases the financial returns for the institution's clients. In late 1987, for example, Hong Kong and Shanghai Bank, the majority shareholder of Marine Midland Bank, proposed to acquire the minority's shares in a cashout merger. Fidelity Investments thought the proposed price was too low, hired its own appraiser, and approached the special committee of independent directors of Marine Midland. As a result of this intervention, Hong Kong and Shanghai increased its offer by over $13 per share; this price increase directly delivered $12 million to the Fidelity funds as well as many millions of dollars to Marine Midland's other shareholders.

Antitakeover Measures

The adoption of most antitakeover measures tends to lower a company's stock price. To avoid these adverse price effects, the logic of cost-benefit analysis dictates that institutional investors should be prepared to devote some resources to opposing such measures. A possible exception is the poison pill, where companies may be able to demonstrate the need for a defensive position for a limited time. For example, as part of an informal settlement with institutional investors, Raytheon and Consolidated Freightways each announced that it would phase out its poison pill on a specified date within a few years and would not extend the poison pill or adopt a new one without the approval of a majority of shareholders.

Executive Compensation

Compensation packages heavily based on a company's financial performance usually correlate with positive returns for shareholders, although the adoption of a performance-based compensation package does not have the same immediate price effects as the adoption of an antitakeover measure. Institutional investors can vote directly on compensation issues only if a company is seeking approval of a stock option plan, a restricted stock plan, or a performance plan in order to deduct annual compensation of over $1 million under the 1993 tax act. Accordingly, it makes sense for institutions to vote for such a plan if properly designed and to lobby against non-performance-based plans. Last March, for example, the State of Wisconsin Pension Board urged the 160 largest shareholders of Paramount Communications to withhold their votes for members of Paramount's compensation committee because of the inverse relationship between executive pay and shareholder returns over the last five years. Although relatively few votes were withheld, the board reportedly believes that its campaign was an important factor in shaking things up at Paramount.

Governance Structures

It is difficult to prove the financial benefits of good governance structures such as the establishment of separate audit, compensation, and nominating committees composed entirely of independent directors, or shareholder rights to vote cumulatively or to call special shareholder meetings. If a company has a smart and strong CEO with appropriate compensation incentives, it may do well for years without these structures. But these structures are important safety valves when crises arise, when CEO succession is an issue, or when the business begins to go downhill. It is in the interest of institutional investors to make modest efforts toward promoting good governance structures as part of a long-term investment philosophy.

Procedural Frills

Some institutional investors have advocated procedural reforms that have not been shown to increase shareholder values or to play an important safety-valve function. One example is the shareholder advisory committee, which is either useless or will try to make decisions and thereby confuse the role of the board. Another example is the push for a chairman separate from the CEO: although this separation may be fruitful for a particular company, there is no evidence that as a general rule it benefits public companies.

Weighing the Modes of Institutional Activism

Using a cost-benefit analysis, institutional investors can also rank different types of proxy intervention, the tools of institutional activism.

Proxy Fights for Control

Proxy control fights, especially if they are successful, can have a positive effect on a company's share price. Yet institutional investors almost never initiate such fights because the costs are very high, and most institutional investors are legally prohibited from reaping the benefits of acquiring control of a company. Moreover, institutional investors have neither the staff nor the expertise to exercise operating control over even a handful of portfolio companies.

Proxy Campaigns Against Management Proposals

From time to time, institutional investors have been willing to incur the substantial costs of proxy campaigns against management proposals directly affecting share price, such as the opposition to the proposed merger of Centel and Sprint. But most of the opposition to antitakeover amendments has come from dissidents seeking to acquire control of the company. Without the potential benefits of acquiring control, institutional investors have generally been unwilling to launch proxy campaigns against antitakeover proposals. Institutions tend to be even more reluctant to expend large sums to defeat objectionable management proposals for compensation plans or governance procedures because, unlike issues that directly affect stock price, these have a weaker link to financial returns for institutional clients.

Shareholder Resolutions

Shareholders who follow the SEC's procedural requirements can place a proposal on a company's ballot. Sponsorship of a shareholder resolution is inexpensive because it is distributed at the company's expense as part of the proxy statement. As long as the resolution sponsor does not ask for proxy authorization, it may gather support orally without any SEC filings. As a result, shareholder resolutions have become a favorite mode of institutional intervention on a broad range of issues, including rescission of poison pills, performance measures for executive compensation, and expanded roles for independent directors. In 1987, the College Retirement Equities Fund (CREF) proposed a resolution calling for a shareholder vote at the next annual meeting to repeal poison pills at over a dozen companies. CREF's campaign reportedly involved total out-of-pocket expenses of less than $10,000 plus a modest amount of staff time and resources. At this price, a shareholder resolution could meet the cost-benefit test even if the benefits cannot be guaranteed.

Informal Jawboning

Even less expensive then a shareholder resolution is informal jawboning—direct discussions with management or public announcements by shareholders seeking improvements in a company's governance structure, changes in overall business strategy, or resolution of management succession issues. The costs of informal jawboning are limited to communications, travel expenses, and the time of the institution's representatives, but the benefits can be dramatic. For example, J.P. Morgan and Alliance met with the new CEO of

American Express to protest its retention of James Robinson as the company's chairman; a few days later, Robinson resigned. Portfolio managers at Wellington Management and Loomis, Sayles publicly expressed concern about the failure of the Chrysler board to name a successor to Lee Iacocca; in less than a week, the board named Robert Eaton the next CEO.

Explanatory Letters

The cheapest mode of institutional activism is voting "no" or withholding a vote and writing a letter explaining why to a company's CEO and/or directors. Companies are often willing to redesign their proposals in response to the reasonable concerns of a large shareholder. For example, Fidelity Investments usually votes against the adoption of stock option plans that give the company's directors total discretion on the pricing and timing of options issuance. After receiving letters from Fidelity explaining its position, many companies have been willing to incorporate pricing and timing criteria into their stock option plans.

Expansionists and Contractionists: Two Activist Philosophies

Many corporate executives are Contractionists. Like Charles Wohlstetter, they believe that institutional investors are intervening too frequently and too intensively in corporate decisionmaking and that institutional investors will ultimately try to micromanage their companies. Contractionists would be surprised to learn that their views are largely shared by institutional investors that take a cost-benefit approach to activism. Since these institutions are organized and paid as passive portfolio managers, they could not possibly become active in a large number of companies. In 1992, Fidelity Investments voted proxies for almost 3,000 companies but became actively involved in fewer than 12. Even CalPERS, the most outspoken of the public pension plans, becomes actively involved in fewer than 30 companies each year.

According to Contractionists, if institutional investors are dissatisfied with the decisions of company management, they should follow the Wall Street Rule of voting with their feet by selling that company's stock. In fact, most institutional investors dissatisfied with company management will sell the stock, because the expected benefits of activism do not warrant the expected costs. The Wall Street Rule is not viable, however, for those institutions employing a passive index strategy: approximately 10% of all institutional equity assets. Indexed investors, who in effect match their portfolios to market indicators, continued to be big holders of IBM, at one time a huge component of the S&P 500, even as the computer company turned in several years of dismal financial performance. By contrast, several nonindexed institutions bailed out of IBM when the company did not respond adequately to the trend away from mainframe computers.

Even most nonindexed institutions will become corporate activists only when company management proposes to take some action that portfolio managers view as depressing shareholder values over the long run. For example, institutional investors protested when Time, Inc., rejected a highly priced purchase offer from Paramount's Martin S. Davis and instead acquired Warner Communications, along with a very rich personal arrangement for Steven Ross, Warner's chairman.

Indexed investors will monitor the financial performance of their large holdings and will initiate discussions with management if that performance has been dismal over a period of three to five years. Since indexed investors cannot easily sell out, they will press these dismal performers on major structural issues rather than operational details. Such investors have successfully urged companies to refocus their core business strategies at Eastman Kodak, Sears, and U.S. Steel, and to replace their CEOs at General Motors, Goodyear, and IBM.

Corporate executive can avoid institutional activism by achieving good financial performance over the long term and explaining any short-term problems to their institutional shareholders. Although corporate executives complain that institutional investors do not understand the need for current expenditures to produce future benefits, institutions are actually big buyers of companies with large research budgets. But all research is not automatically good. If a company like Kodak spends millions on research that does not lead to enough successful products, institutional investors will lose faith in the research effort and company management.

Corporate executives should also be reluctant to make proposals to curtail the procedural rights of shareholders or to adopt antitakeover measures. Institutional investors strongly believe that the corporate governance process must serve as an effective means of holding management accountable. And although the takeover binges of the 1980s undoubtedly involved abuses of the governance process, the 1990s are a very different decade, without midnight raids and with much less junk bond financing. Moreover, the latest round of state antitakeover laws already provides corporate management with adequate protection against the abuses of the 1980s.

Most important, corporate executives should increase their efforts to talk directly with institutional investors about their shared goals. While many executives focus their communications efforts on Wall Street analysts, meeting periodically with their large institutional shareholders is equally critical. These meetings are often too important to be delegated to the investor relations office; they should include the CEO and the CFO. Ideally, these meetings should allow company officials to sound out new ideas and portfolio managers to articulate their perceptions of the company. As Lockheed treasurer Walter Skowronski reported last June about a series of such meetings, "Rational and commonsensical approaches by Lockheed met with rational and commonsensical responses from investors; the process was self-reinforcing over time."

At the opposite pole from the Contractionists are the Expansionists, who want institutional investors to play a larger role in corporate decision making. Most Expansionists are professors, public officials, or leaders of organized interest groups. Social Expansionists want institutional investors to push U.S. companies to follow social agendas; Block Expansionists want institutional investors to dominate U.S. companies along the Japanese-German model. Corporate executives should understand that, with a few exceptions, the proposals of neither the Social nor Block Expansionists pass the cost-benefit test for institutional investors.

Social Expansionists

Social Expansionists want U.S. corporations to take an active role in resolving a variety of social issues, such as protecting animal rights or cleaning up the environment. Given the nature of individual shareholding in most U.S. corporations, Social Expansionists turn to institutional investors as the only hope for pressuring corporations to get involved. However, the goals of Social Expansionists are fundamentally different from those of most institutional clients, who are generally seeking high financial returns. Therefore, executives can often gain support from institutional investors in opposing social issues unless these institutions are subject to contrary instructions from their clients or if pursuing these issues would create financial liabilities for the company.

Most clients of an institutional investor have not chosen it because of its societal views or expertise; they have chosen it because they believe it is likely to fulfill their financial goals. Accordingly, it would be an act of hubris for an institutional investor to vote its social preferences unless specifically directed to do so by its clients. For example, directions may come through a city ordinance prohibiting pension investments in South Africa, or through client selection of a "green" fund with limitations on investments stated in its prospectus.

Consider an institutional investor confronted with a request to vote against the incumbent directors of Time Warner because it released a song by Ice-T that seemed to condone attacks against the police. On the one hand, the police unions argued that this rap would encourage youths to beat up and shoot police officers. On the other hand, the civil libertarians defended Ice-T's First Amendment right to express his opinion of the police. Should an institutional investor resolve these complex issues in the context of a shareholder election of corporate directors, or should government officials resolve these issues in the context of a public forum?

An institutional investor may actively oppose the social actions of a U.S. company if they affect the financial performance of that company. An industrial company's practices of disposing of toxic wastes, for example, may be financially material if these practices create a large contingent liability. But an institutional investor will probably not support efforts by Social Expansionists to stop an industrial practice that is perfectly legal and poses no significant financial threat to the company. If Social Expansionists disagree with the current law on such an industrial practice, they should try to persuade the relevant agency or legislature to change the rules.

Block Expansionists

Block Expansionists have a different objective. They want institutional investors to acquire more than 25% of the voting shares of U.S. companies and become intensively involved with the management of these companies through board representation. In the view of the Block Expansionists, such intensive institutional involvement in U.S. companies would significantly enhance the economic competitiveness of U.S. industry. Block Expansionists explicitly or implicitly base their position on the success of the German and Japanese systems of corporate governance, in which very large shareholders keep close tabs on corporate managers.

Most executives would disagree with the Block Expansionist agenda, as would most institutional investors. If institutions acquired very large positions in a few U.S. companies, they would jeopardize the diversification objectives of their clients by dramatically increasing the risk of a large loss. This extra risk could be justified only if intensive institutional involvement with management decisions would likely cause these portfolio companies to achieve much higher financial returns. But most institutional investors have neither the expertise nor the resources to increase significantly the likelihood of achieving such extraordinary returns on a regular basis through intensive involvement with management decisions.

An expansive role for institutional investors is also inconsistent with the liquidity objectives of their clients. If institutions held more than 25% of a company's stock, they would have a very difficult time getting out of that stock. Furthermore, if an institutional investor had representatives on a company's board, securities law restrictions on insider trading and short-swing profits would severely impede the ability of that institution to sell that company's stock. While Block Expansionists may applaud locked-in stock positions as "patient capital," institutions want fairly liquid positions in order to meet redemption requests from clients or to reduce exposure to a particular industry.

To implement their ideas on a broad scale, Block Expansionists would have to persuade Congress to relax the current limits on institutional inventors substantially. Corporate executives would undoubtedly oppose such a relaxation as a threat to management control, and they would find allies in most institutional investors. Most institutions are not interested in regularly running the affairs of U.S. companies along the Japanese or German model. They are troubled by the specter of a few large banks or funds controlling the boards of the *Fortune* "500." Most institutions want to maintain the diversification and liquidity of a portfolio investor, as long as they can occasionally hold accountable the management of a poorly performing company.

Conclusions

As executives have watched institutional investors acquire an increasing percentage of their companies' shares, many have come to fear a slippery slope of institutional intervention—from questions about the wisdom of a merger one minute to advice about plant location or new product development the next. But institutional investors are not interested in day-to-day management of any portfolio company; they are reluctant activists. In a perfect world, institutions would never need to intervene in corporate governance because all their portfolio companies would be good performers. Even in this imperfect world, institutions overcome their built-in inertia only if the particular type of activism passes the cost-benefit test. Given the rigors of this test, activism turns out to be the best strategy in very few cases.

If corporate executives come to understand the modus operandi of institutional investors, these executives will realize that they do not need to worry about institutions taking control of U.S. corporations. In situations where company performance is down or a ballot proposal is controversial, executives should discuss these issues with their institutional shareholders as early as possible. In most other situations, executives can avoid institutional activism altogether by turning in good financial performance over the long term and designing proposals to enhance long-term shareholder values.

Chronology of an Institutional Shareholder Campaign

One of the best examples of the new brand of jawboning is Lens, Inc.'s efforts from 1990 to 1992 to pressure Sears, Roebuck and Company into changing its business mix and governance structure. Lens is a private company founded by Robert Monks, a wealthy investor who had previously headed the pension program at the U.S. Department of Labor.

Lens has attempted to raise capital from institutional investors to take large positions in public companies and improve their financial results through active intervention. But Lens' capital-raising efforts have so far been unsuccessful, and it has never owned more than $3 million in Sears stock.

Lens believed that because there was no synergy between Sears' retail and financial businesses, Sears should focus on one core business. Lens also believed that Sears' board, which was dominated by insiders, was not sufficiently accountable to shareholders. More-over, the trustees of the company's Employee Stock Ownership Plan (ESOP), which held 25% of the Sears voting stock, were the company's CEO and other Sears affiliates.

This situation met all of Lens' criteria for becoming an activist shareholder. The issues concerned the overall structure and direction of Sears; the obstacles to shareholder value could be addressed by shareholder activism; and the various institutions owning a majority of the company's stock provided Lens with potential allies. Moreover, there were five board seats open at the next election. Since Sears allowed its shareholders to concentrate their votes on one candidate, a practice known as cumulative voting, Lens could elect one director by winning the support of only 16% of Sears' shareholders.

Below is a chronology of Lens' jawboning campaign and the price of Sears stock on each date. (Also see figure 11.4.1.)

11/1/90 ($24.87): Lens writes to Sears to suggest that Lens founder Robert Monks be considered as a management nominee for the Sears board.

2/1/91 ($25.87): When Sears refuses to nominate Monks to the management slate, he is nominated by a shareholder associated with Monks. Sears reduces the size of its board, so that Monks needs the support of 24% of the company's shareholders to win a seat under cumulative voting.

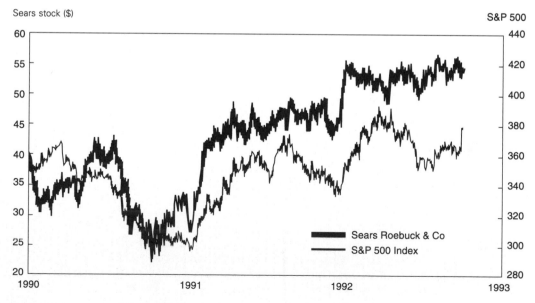

Figure 11.4.1 Sears rises during Lens' efforts: so does the S&P 500

5/9/91 ($39.50): Monks is not elected to the board, but he receives over 12% of the vote, primarily from institutional investors. Shortly after the election, the board decides to remove Sears' CEO from the board's nominating committee and to appoint independent trustees for the ESOP.

11/1/91 ($36.75): Individual and institutional shareholders sympathetic to Lens' critique of Sears propose five advisory resolutions to be voted on at the annual meeting scheduled for May 1992. Before that meeting, Lens solicits support for the resolutions by sending letters, making phone calls, and running a full-page advertisement in the *Wall Street Journal*.

5/14/92 ($43.25): At Sears' annual meeting, these five resolutions receive the following percentage of the votes cast:
Declassify the board: 41.2%
Establish confidential voting: 40.9%
Separate roles of CEO and chairman: 27.4%
Study divestiture: 23.7%
Institute a minimum level of stock ownership for directors: 19.3%

7/1/92 ($39.50): During the summer, Sears experiences various difficulties, including fraud charges at auto repair facilities and Hurricane Andrew losses at its Allstate unit. As part of a settlement of litigation brought by shareholders other than Lens, Sears appoints two new outside directors to its board, one the chairman of Philip Morris and the other the former CEO of Kellogg.

9/29/92 ($44.75): Sears announces that it will concentrate on its retail business, while selling all of Coldwell Banker as well as 20% of Dean Witter and Allstate. Sears stock rises $3\frac{7}{8}$.

Given its very small holding in Sears, Lens was not in a position to benefit from the stock price increase as much as institutions with larger stakes in the company. These other institutional investors were "free riders" on Lens' efforts to refocus Sears, through which Lens claims to have generated more than $1 billion in shareholder value for an expenditure of less than $500,000.

Others might debate that dramatic conclusion. While the price of Sears stock rose over the two years of Lens' jawboning efforts, so did the S&P 500. Lens' campaign clearly had some influence on the course of events at Sears during this period. It's impossible, however, to determine precisely how much of an effect Lens' activism had on Sears' decisionmaking or on the company's stock price. Perhaps Sears would ultimately have decided to focus on its retail business without the nomination of Monks or the divestiture resolution. In deciding to sell off its financial services businesses, perhaps the company was responding more to a general sense of shareholder dissatisfaction than to the specific votes on the advisory resolutions. Perhaps Sears actually moved more slowly than it would have in order to avoid the appearance of caving in to Lens' demands.

11.5   Agents Watching Agents: The Promise of Institutional Investor Voice*

Bernard S. Black

A   When Is Shareholder Voice Important?

Shareholder monitoring is one strand in a web of imperfect constraints on corporate managers. Other strands include the corporate control market, the product market, the capital market, the labor market for corporate managers, incentive compensation arrangements, creditor monitoring, the risk of bankruptcy if a company can't service its debt, fiduciary duties, and cultural norms of behavior.

There is an ongoing debate over the strength of these constraints on managerial discretion. Scholars who find little value in shareholder voting tend to see other constraints as strong. Others find much greater scope for managerial discretion. Brief discussion of the limits of other constraints is necessary, because the stronger the other constraints, the less room for shareholder monitoring to improve corporate performance.

Strong constraint proponents rely heavily on the market for corporate control. Hostile takeovers, though, are a clumsy way to discipline corporate managers. We incur the heavy costs of changing ownership, when all that was needed was new managers or closer oversight of the current managers. A company must be badly managed indeed to justify the typical 50% takeover premium. Moreover, some acquisitions reflect empire-building by the bidder's managers, rather than market discipline of poor target managers. And, hostile takeovers today face heavy legal obstacles, notably poison pills and strict antitakeover laws, that didn't exist a few years ago.

The other constrains can be powerful if a company or its management strays far off the profit maximizing path, but are often weak as long as a company functions reasonably well. Product market competition is strong in some industries, but weaker in others. Capital market constraints are weak for firms that can service their debt and rarely sell new equity. As for labor market constraints, most CEOs stay in their jobs until retirement. If a company is mismanaged, it doesn't help to know that the CEO may have trouble finding another job if the board won't fire him. Finally, if managers were tightly constrained, the systematic shortfalls in corporate governance discussed below wouldn't exist or would be much smaller.

These constraints complement but do not replace shareholder monitoring. The natural terrain for shareholder voice is where bankruptcy and capital market constraints are weak—for the not too badly run, fairly mature, public company that can service its debt and generate internally or borrow much of the cash it needs to fund new investments. Shareholder monitoring may prevent some companies from wandering too far off the profit path. It can be a quicker, lower-cost alternative to hostile takeovers or bankruptcy constraints.

---

*Originally published in 39 *UCLA L. Rev.* 811. © 1992, The Regents of the University of California. All rights reserved. [Footnotes deleted.]

If outside directors, in fact as well as in legal fiction, owe their primary loyalty to the shareholders, poorly performing CEOs may be replaced sooner. Fewer companies will flounder for years because their inbred managers can't adapt to new circumstances and won't look outside for help. We'll see fewer conglomerate mergers, which benefit empire-building managers but not diversified shareholders. Companies will return more of their surplus funds to shareholders for reinvestment elsewhere, instead of squandering them on perquisites or overexpansion.

Shareholder monitoring can affect the cost of capital. Better monitoring may reduce the risk, and hence the risk adjusted cost, of equity capital. Some scholars believe that Japanese and German firms have a cost-of-capital advantage for precisely this reason. If the same institutions provide both equity and debt capital, shareholder-debtholder conflicts will decrease, which may make lenders more willing to lend in times of crisis. Today American banks, unlike their foreign counterparts, almost never advance new funds to troubled borrowers.

Institutional voice can reduce both shareholder and manager myopia. If shareholders talk to managers, they may find that they share a common interest in long-term performance. Shareholders can be more patient if they know what managers are doing and know that they can do something if managers consistently fail to perform. Managers who talk to their large shareholders can worry less about shareholder impatience. And when managers talk long-term performance but don't deliver, managerial change will be more likely.

Shareholder monitoring can also strengthen other strands in the web. Shareholders can limit manager-sponsored antitakeover devices, thus preserving vitality in the corporate control market. If poor managers are more likely to be fired, the labor market for managers becomes a stronger constraint. Shareholders can develop better management compensation plans than managers currently choose for themselves. Legal constraints may become more important because institutions that own large stakes will be more willing to sue to preserve their voting power or to claim breach of fiduciary duty.

Changes such as these are, for me, the promise of institutional voice. The gains from oversight won't often be dramatic. They may occur indirectly, in ways that are hard to verify quantitatively. If we see, as we did in the 1980s, trends toward stronger boards of directors and less diversification, how much did institutional pressure contribute to these trends? But modest percentage gains can still be economically important because they will be spread over many companies.

Institutional voice requires institutions to hold larger percentage stakes and to be less diversified, but that is a minor cost. Today, many institutions take diversification to ridiculous lengths. Some own a thousand or more "names" when a hundred would elimate almost 99% of the firm-specific risk.

B What Institutional Shareholders Can Do

Institutional shareholders can't and shouldn't watch every step a manager takes. Only some issues warrant board attention. Even fewer warrant shareholder involvement. The shareholders can, though, structure manager incentives to be more congruent with shareholder incentives, discourage actions such as diversification that benefit managers but not shareholders, and step in when a CEO, having been given a fair opportunity to run the business, repeatedly falls on his or her face.

The institutions appear to understand that they can't micromanage individual companies. Moreover, their incentives discourage them from trying. Company-specific actions don't involve scale economies in monitoring. In contrast, shareholders have stronger incentives to take an active interest on issues for which scale economies will partly offset the incentives for passivity created by fractional ownership.

This section discusses ways that institutional shareholders can add value to the companies they own, *without* micromanaging. These include a variety of process and structure issues (subsection 1), mixed structural and company-specific issues (subsection 2), and targeting poor performers both to produce change at the targeted company and to send a warning to managers of other companies (subsection 3). Section C focuses on shareholder efforts to strengthen boards of directors, which is a central form of indirect monitoring. These actions all involve some scale economies.

In a number of areas, we have quantitative evidence of systematic shortfalls in corporate performance. Because these shortfalls are systemic, they are amenable to correction by diversified institutions. In a companion article, I review the empirical evidence on these shortfalls. Here, I draw on those results to discuss qualitatively how institutional shareholders can improve corporate performance.

I don't claim that institutions will be interested *only* in issues that involve economies of scale. Some company-specific issues will warrant attention on their own merits, especially for larger companies. Moreover, no hard-and-fast line divides company-specific issues from common issues. Instead, governance issues can be pictured as lying along a continuum from common to company-specific. A diversified institution can always classify more finely. It can vote, say, for poison pills at well-run companies and against pills at other companies, or oppose only pills with low percentage thresholds. Institutions presumably will subclassify companies as long as the gains from doing so outweigh the cost in reduced scale economies. In that calculus, the opportunity for deterrence, which preserves some scale economies for actions formally taken only at a few companies, may lead the institutions to target attention at poor performers.

1 Process and Structure Issues

Process and structure proposals currently on the shareholders' agenda include: issues related to board structure and composition (discussed in section C); confidential voting; asking managers to seek shareholder approval before taking various actions, such as selling a large block of stock, creating a leveraged ESOP, and adopting golden parachutes; rescinding or weakening poison pills; antitakeover amendments proposed by corporate managers; opting out of antitakeover statutes; and reincorporating in states with more desirable corporate law rules. Some of these issues involve direct monitoring. Others involve indirect monitoring through the board of directors or by strengthening other constraints on corporate managers.

The companion article collects quantitative evidence that a variety of antitakeover amendments and antitakeover laws have significant negative effects on stock prices. This suggests that these pro-incumbent rules decrease long-run company value. Institutional shareholders could defeat value-decreasing charter amendments—a process that is already underway. They could also try to roll back current entrenchment devices through bylaw changes, charter amendments, or reincorporation in a less pro-manager state. Weaker defenses may or may not mean more takeovers. But diversified shareholders will have a greater role in deciding which deals succeed and which fail. They ought, on average and over time, to make better decisions than target company managers.

Shareholders can also be more sensitive than managers to the effects of company actions on the political climate for business. For example, it may be sensible for any one oil company to risk an oil spill, but foolish for the industry as a whole, because the industry risks costly regulation. Diversified shareholders bear the costs of regulation for all portfolio companies. In contrast, most of these costs are an externality for any one company. Thus, there is some rough logic to investor concern about Exxon's environmental problems.

2 Mixed Issues

Many corporate governance issues involve both elements common to a number of companies, for which scale economies exist, and company-specific elements. One mixed issue is management compensation. A system where the average CEO's pay rises year after year, even if profits decline, can certainly stand some improvement. Large shareholders can keep CEO pay from exceeding the bounds of reason and decency. They can change the corrupt process of setting CEO pay, where the CEO hires a supposedly independent consultant to recommend a compensation plan to a compensation committee composed mostly of other CEOs. They can also promote pay structures that relate compensation to long-term performance.

Institutional investors can also be sensitive to the effects of executive pay levels on worker loyalty and public attitudes towards business. In contrast, each manager has an incentive to get the best deal he or she can. For some, such as Steve Ross of Time Warner, even public criticism may be a cost worth bearing in return for pay rich enough to warrant that attention.

A second mixed area is corporate diversification. Managers typically want their one-and-only company to grow. We have solid evidence, collected in the companion article, that corporate diversification is generally a bad idea, made worse by the common practice of overpaying for someone else's business. Few managers can manage several different businesses at the same time. Yet conglomerate acquisitions persist and many companies resist divesting noncore businesses. Diversified institutions are ideally situated to encourage greater corporate focus and resist diversification, especially for a company that is struggling in its own industry, or wants to enter a completely unrelated business.

Even beyond conglomerate acquisitions, many takeovers are misguided. Recent research sheds light on which factors predict that a takeover won't be value increasing. That lets the institutions assess the likely wisdom of a takeover bid, and follow up those judgments with pressure on the bidder to justify a suspect bid or abandon it. These judgments will be partly common, reflecting bid *type*, and partly company specific. Shareholders can also encourage directors to be more skeptical about a CEO's acquisition ideas. The many troubled takeovers highlight the potential for institutional oversight to serve as an alternative to takeovers. More voice may mean fewer deals.

Conversely, many value-increasing takeovers never happen because the target's managers want to remain independent. Here too, institutional pressure, based on a mix of judgments about bid type and assessments of particular transactions, could lead to greater target acceptance of value-increasing offers. Institutional oversight can also limit scorched earth defenses and thus reduce transaction and disruption costs.

An additional mixed area is corporate cash payout policies. Managers often like to hoard cash. Too often, they then spend it foolishly. Informed shareholders or directors can assess a company's capital needs and encourage payout of surplus funds, beyond a reasonable cushion for future adversity or opportunity. Shareholder oversight can also reduce the likelihood that managers will misspend the cash cushion they retain. Ongoing oversight may increase institutional willingness to provide capital in times of need, and thus reduce the cushion needed in ordinary times, with its inevitable temptations. Today, business groups oppose integration of the corporate and individual income tax because they fear shareholder pressure for cash payouts. Influential shareholders can put an end to such nonsense.

Conversely, some companies pay dividends they can't afford in an effort to fool investors about their profitability. Many utilities pay taxable dividends at the same time they're selling new shares. Dividend cuts also often lag far behind business reversals. Institutional oversight can make companies less likely to pay dividends they shouldn't.

3   Deterrence and Targeting of Poor Performers

A further way for institutions to pursue corporate governance issues is to target poor performers. One sees this pattern in, for example, CalPERS' vote against the ITT board to protest the rich pay of ITT chief executive Rand Araskog for a decade of mediocre performance, and in Robert Monks' 1991 campaign for election to the Sears Roebuck board.

On the surface, these actions seem company-specific. But on a closer look, they involve economies of scale. Deterrence goals can explain why diversified institutions care about the pay of a particular CEO or the makeup of a particular board of directors. By focusing on a few egregious cases, the institutions send a message to other managers to mend their ways, lest they too become a test case for institutional pressure. CalPERS' complaint about Araskog's pay mattered more for the message it sent to other companies and other directors, than for the few million dollars at stake at ITT. As Richard Koppes of CalPERS recently described his fund's strategy: "You focus on a few visible ones and make everyone else nervous."

C   Strengthening the Board of Directors

Much of the value of institutional voice is likely to come through improving boards of directors, many of which could surely stand improvement. The institutions have neither incentive nor ability to monitor many corporate actions directly. They can, however, hire directors to undertake company-specific monitoring for them. Directors can stop a misguided acquisition before it gets started; shareholders can only complain after the transaction is announced, when it may be too late. Directors can quietly remove a CEO; shareholders will find it harder to act quietly. If the current directors are part of a company's problem, institutional shareholders can prompt board turnover *before* a loan default or bankruptcy, much as they do today after a default.

Vigorous, independent directors won't cure all corporate ailments, but they should help at the margin. At a minimum, institutional voice might reduce the number of truly awful boards and compensation committees. The companion article collects evidence that even with today's imperfectly independent directors, boards with a majority of independent directors are more likely to fire an underperforming CEO, and less willing to endorse an overpriced takeover bid. Moreover, companies whose independent directors own little stock are more likely to become subject to a hostile takeover bid, suggesting breakdown in normal governance mechanisms. Thus, there is value in institutional efforts to ensure that more boards have a majority of independent directors, to insist that directors own a significant equity stake, and to strengthen boards in other ways.

1 Changes in Board Structure and Composition

The institutions are beginning to focus attention on boards of directors. Issues on the institutions' agenda include: should boards have a majority of independent directors; should companies have nominating and compensation committees composed entirely of independent directors; should shareholders be able to comment on management's nominees in the company proxy statement; should the positions of CEO and board chairman be separated; should a retired CEO stay on a company's board; should one limit how many boards one person sits on; should directors own a significant equity stake in the company they direct; and how should directors be compensated.

Many of these issues are controversial. Others, such as boards having a majority of independent directors, increasingly reflect the status quo. But the status quo can shift over time. Twenty years ago, many public company boards were controlled by insiders; today, almost all have a majority of *outside* directors, and many have a majority of *independent* directors (outside directors without close ties to the company). Most people think that's a change for the better. Institutional efforts are already affecting board structure. More companies are installing a majority of independent directors and an independent nominating committee, and the numerical dominance of outside directors is increasing. As a recent article put it, "it's muscle-flexing by large institutional investors that has helped shift the balance of power in corporate boardrooms toward independent directors."

Institutional pressure may also be moving boardroom culture toward greater willingness to challenge or replace a CEO or other corporate officers. Much of Myles Mace's classic and dismal depiction of what directors do and don't do still rings true, but not all. *Some* boards, perhaps most, function effectively. *Some* directors seem readier—though doubtless not ready enough—to fire the CEO if the need arises. It has become socially acceptable for directors to ask tough questions. Oversized boards are shrinking. News headlines such as "Taking Charge: Corporate Directors Start to Flex Their Muscle" or "More Chief Executives are Being Forced Out by Tougher Boards" attest to the change. Continued institutional pressure could presage further change.

2 Institutional Directors

In addition to general efforts to strengthen boards of directors, there are nascent efforts to place institutional representatives on boards of directors. I will call directors who are selected by a company's institutional shareholders, either formally or through informal agreement with the managers, *institutional directors*. Institutional directors are likely to owe more loyalty to the institutions which nominated them, and less to the current CEO. They may be quicker to react to declining performance, replace a weak CEO, oppose a costly acquisition, or question executive compensation.

Much of the value of institutional directors can be realized with minority representation. Often, it will be enough that the right questions are asked, even if the imperfectly independent directors who dominate most corporate boards control the answer. Reform can enable the institutions to more readily select a minority of directors. The existing legal impediments to exercising control will ensure that institutional voice won't often lead to majority board control.

Recently, there have been several tentative moves toward selection of institutional directors. In 1990, Lockheed and National Intergroup promised to add institutional representatives to their boards to gain support in proxy fights. Lockheed won its proxy fight and fulfilled its pledge. In 1991, Tiger Management ran a proxy fight and elected five directors to the board of Cleveland-Cliffs. The avowed goal was to install independent directors who would cast a critical eye on Cleveland-Cliffs' expansion plans. Robert Monks of Institutional Shareholder Partners sought election to the Sears board. He lost, but Sears promised to consult major shareholders in choosing new directors.

There have also been preliminary steps toward developing a registry of qualified directors, analogous to the British Institute for the Promotion of Non-Executive Directors (PRO NED). In 1990, CalPERS and Institutional Shareholder Services (ISS) began to develop a director database. Scott Paper and Armstrong World Industries have agreed, under institutional pressure, to help fund a clearinghouse for independent directors.

This is not a proposal for "public interest" directors or directors who represent non-shareholder constituencies. Most institutional directors probably will be cut from the same cloth as current directors. Business knowledge will be a prime qualification. The institutions could, however, elect some nontraditional directors. For example, they might push multinational companies to hire more foreign directors. Many institutional directors won't be employed by the institution that selects them. Insider trading liability and other legal risks make money managers reluctant to serve. Also, large institutions typically own stock in hundreds of companies. Their senior officers can serve on only a few boards.

It's too soon to say whether institutional directors will become common or how they will differ from current directors. The case for institutional voice, though, doesn't stand or fall on these details. Empowered institutions *could* elect institutional directors. They have incentives to do so if board functioning is improved thereby, and to choose good people for the job. The details should be left to them.

The value of institutional directors depends on how they interact with other directors. The value of minority directors has been long debated in the context of cumulative voting. Supporters argue that different points of view should be aired in the boardroom. Opponents contend that minority directors will be disruptive, ineffective, or both. There is reason to believe, though, that institutional directors will be a positive force. The institutions have no reason to create adversarial relations between institutional and noninstitutional directors. Most institutional directors are likely to be chosen informally, with institutions suggesting candidates to a company's nominating committee, or the committee choosing candidates from a central registry. And institutional directors haven't caused problems in other countries where they are common.

D   The Role of Blockholders and Trade Groups

Strengthening boards of directors is one form of indirect monitoring. Indirect monitoring can also involve encouraging or funding blockholders who will accept the legal risks involved in holding large percentage stakes, or financing trade groups. Such groups can facilitate informal coordination among the trade group members, and thus reduce the impact of legal barriers to joint action.

A number of "white squire" funds have sprung up in the last few years, funded largely by institutions, with the avowed goal of acquiring large equity stakes that will give them both the incentive and the ability to monitor company managers. They include Ken Miller's Lodestar Group, Harris Associates, Roy Disney's Trefoil Capital Investors, and Lazard Freres' Corporate Partners. Institutional Shareholder Partners and Batterymarch Financial Management are developing a fund that would seek governance changes in one or two companies at a time. And some leveraged buyout firms have taken minority stakes in some companies.

White squire funds and catalyst groups have promise but it's unclear whether they will succeed. Some may lack the staying power to engage in a multiyear battle with a resistant company—witness Harold Simmons' recent decision to bail out of Lockheed and Chartwell's sale of most of its Avon stake. And some efforts to form catalyst funds have failed for lack of money. Other shareholders will also worry that the catalyst will abuse control once it is obtained. In some proxy fights, institutions have split their votes, hoping that dissidents will obtain only minority representation on a company's board. Institutional reticence to cede control, however, reduces the returns from acting as a catalyst.

It's also possible for a single institution to hold a large stake in a single company. If the institution can be trusted not to abuse its power, other investors can rely on its monitoring efforts. Warren Buffett's Berkshire Hathaway is the prototype. Berkshire has bought large stakes in a number of companies, and Buffett took over as CEO of Salomon Brothers after a scandal forced the old CEO to resign. Other institutions are taking steps toward owning significant stakes in individual ventures. CalPERS, for example, recently paid $400 million for 20% of Catellus Corp., a commercial real estate developer, and invested $83 million in a joint venture with another developer to manage and develop industrial parks. This style of friendly investing isn't possible, though, when managers react to a large shareholder with instant hostility.

Corporate crossholdings could also let corporate managers watch each other. Double taxation of intercorporate capital gains hinders crossownership, but tax costs can be reduced by investing through the corporate pension plan. Labor Department and IRS clarification that cross-investments through pension plans can be prudent and won't be subject to unrelated business taxation might encourage such investments.

The need to aggregate power across institutions has led some institutions to rely on trade groups and independent advisers to coordinate governance initiatives. These organizations give voting advice, develop opinion papers on governance issues, sponsor research, and raise the salience of particular issues. Trade groups can also develop lists of director candidates and criteria for assessing director performance. The ISS director database is a step in that direction. This might seem innocuous, but the suspicion that the recent ISS-CalPERS director survey might be used to evaluate directors aroused strong business opposition. ISS is better positioned than many of its clients to withstand that reaction.

To be sure, trade groups can't do much without some direct institutional support. In Great Britain, for example, pension funds, mutual funds, insurers, and investment trusts each have their own trade group (e.g., the National Association of Pension Funds). The trade groups facilitate communication between shareholders and sometimes form committees to analyze particular troubled companies. These committees have successfully dealt with some specific situations, but at other times the trade groups have seemed to be paper tigers.

E Voting Versus Voice

Much of the value of institutional oversight will come through informal manager response to the wishes of large shareholders and through negotiated compromises. In many cases, compromise is essential. Electing institutional directors, for example, may require a few proxy contests. But if it routinely takes a full-scale contest, few institutional directors will be elected, and the directors who are elected will be less valuable.

There is reason to think that negotiated compromises will become common. Corporate and money managers often talk about the need for dialogue between shareholders and managers. The money managers, who are outside the walled citadel and want in, recognize the limited value of shooting arrows over the walls. The managers want the infidels to go away, but when pushed, often prefer compromise to a public fight. To date, many shareholder successes have come through negotiations with managers, in which the managers "voluntarily" adopt all or part of a shareholder proposal.

Informal shareholder pressure may already be having an effect beyond the limited number of explicit shareholder proposals. Boards of directors, though far from perfect, are more independent and vigilant today than in the past and more likely to question or fire an underperforming CEO. Shareholder pressure surely contributed to this shift. The massive negative publicity about CEO pay levels, fueled by institutional objections, is also having an effect. Compensation consultant Graef Crystal reports: "Outside directors . . . are confiding to friends that they have gotten the message [about CEO pay]."

Despite the importance of informal action, formal shareholder power is still essential. Compromises, after all, developed only after managers realized that they might lose if they pushed matters to a vote. Formal shareholder action at some companies also serves as a warning to other corporate managers whose companies haven't been targeted for shareholder action. It remains to be seen whether the new CalPERS approach of targeting companies for informal action *without* also submitting voting proposals will succeed as well as their prior strategy of combining informal action with a formal proposal.

. . .

Case Study: Fund Voting in a Proxy Fight

Institutional activism takes many forms, as we have seen. In most situations, mutual funds are drawn into the fray by the actions of others. Company management may put forward a proposal or initiate a structural change; or an opposition group may propose to buy the company or change the company's business strategy. The case study below presents such a situation where mutual funds and other institutional investors were drawn into a battle between an insurgent group and company management.

This case study involves two related initiatives by an insurgent group in relation to RJR Nabisco. RJR Nabisco is a conglomerate with both a tobacco business (RJR) and a food business (Nabisco). The tobacco business was subject to a broad range of legal suits along with other tobacco companies. The insurgent group, led by Bennett LeBow and Carl Icahn, owned slightly less than 5% of the voting stock of RJR Nabisco. The remainder of the stock was heavily concentrated in the hands of mutual funds and other institutional investors.

In the first initiative (First Act), the insurgent group put forth two shareholder proposals: (a) to spin off the Nabisco food business from the tobacco business, and (b) to restore the right of shareholders to call a special shareholders' meeting. Subsequently, in a second initiative (Second Act), the insurgent group proposed a slate of directors to replace the incumbent directors of RJR Nabisco.

In reviewing this case study and reading 11.7, assume that you are the manager of two mutual funds—Growth Fund and Environmental Growth Fund—each owning 1% of the outstanding common stock of RJR Nabisco, which is trading at $30 per share. The Growth Fund is a $10 billion fund and the Environmental Growth Fund is a $1 billion fund. The investment objective of the Growth Fund is to seek capital appreciation over the long term, and the investment objective of the Environmental Growth Fund is the same, while taking into account all aspects of environmental concerns.

In-Class Discussion Questions

You have been asked to vote shares of the two mutual funds on the above two shareholder resolutions and the election of directors. For each fund, please answer the following questions:

1. How will you vote? Will you vote the same for each fund?
2. What is the rationale for your vote? What is the difference between voting on shareholder resolutions and voting on director elections?
3. How would you evaluate the potential and probable benefits to your fund from engaging in shareholder activism on these votes? Please quantify your answer to the extent feasible.
4. What strategies or tactics would you utilize in support of your position? Would you talk to the insurgents, company management, and/or other institutional investors? Would you be prepared to solicit proxies or participate in any group actions?

11.6   RJR Nabisco Holdings Corp.*

First Act

Approval of the following shareholder resolutions submitted by Brooke Group, Ltd., a publicly traded company on the New York Stock Exchange, requires the written consent of a majority of RJR Nabisco Holdings Corp. common stock outstanding.

Brooke Group has initiated a consent solicitation through which shareholders are being asked to approve two proposals. The first item seeks adoption of a nonbinding resolution requesting that the board spin off the remaining 80.5 percent of Nabisco common stock immediately. The second resolution is a binding bylaw amendment proposal in which shareholders will vote on whether to restore the right to call a special meeting by written request of holders of 25 percent of the common stock outstanding. Brooke Group, which is controlled by Chairman and CEO Bennett LeBow, owns approximately 4.8 percent of RJR's outstanding common stock.

Item 1:   Approve Resolution to Spin Off Nabisco

This resolution is a nonbinding proposal through which shareholders would ask the board to spin off the remaining 80.5 percent share of Nabisco common stock in order to enhance the value of shareholders' investment by separating the company's food and tobacco businesses.

Table 11.6.1

Ownership information (February 6, 1996)

Beneficial ownership		Type of shares	Votes per share	Shares outstanding
Officers & directors	0.45%	Common stock	1.00	272,807,942
Institutions	64.33%	Series C conversion preferred stock	0.20	26,675,000
Wachovia Bank of North Carolina, N.A.	1.07%	ESOP convertible preferred stock	0.20	15,003,379

Source: Proxy Statement, CDA Investment Technologies

Note: The company has three types of voting stock. Each share of common stock entitles shareholders to one vote. Each share of Series C conversion preferred stock and ESOP convertible preferred stock entitles shareholders to one-fifth of a vote.

---

*Courtesy of RJR Nabisco Holdings Corp. © 1996 Institutional Shareholder Services.

RJR Management

RJR's board opposes the proposal, arguing that while it sees value in ultimately spinning off the remaining Nabisco stock to shareholders, it believes that the timing is wrong. RJR argues that a negative environment for litigation against tobacco companies could attract further litigation claiming that the spin-off is a fraudulent conveyance, meaning that the spin-off is intended to frustrate potential creditors rather than to effect a valid business strategy. Moreover, if the spin-off is viewed as not having a valid business purpose, it might not be tax-free to shareholders. The company also claimed that an injunction against the spin-off could block further dividend increases and stock buyback programs that could otherwise enhance shareholder value. Another reason for delaying a spin-off was RJR's perceived commitment to security holders that a spin-off would be delayed for a period of time in order to ensure the company's investment grade credit rating and overall financial integrity. RJR also questioned the integrity of the proponents, Mr. LeBow and Carl Icahn, who are well known for their involvement in financing corporate takeovers and their association with companies that have filed for bankruptcy protection.

Background

RJR implemented a partial spin-off of Nabisco in 1994 and used the proceeds to reduce the substantial debt burden that was its legacy from its debt-financed takeover by Kravis, Kohlberg and Roberts (KKR) in the mid-1980s. Following the partial spin-off, RJR retained an 80.5 percent stake in Nabisco. A shareholder proposal submitted at the 1995 annual meeting by a religious organization requested that the company engage in a full spin-off in order to achieve a full separation of the food and tobacco businesses. The board opposed the proposal as not being in the best interests of shareholders and because it would violate a board resolution in which it committed to not engaging in any distributions of stock of a subsidiary before December 31, 1996—and not before December 31, 1998, if such a distribution would cause the company's senior debt rating to be downgraded. The company also argued that it was taking other steps that would benefit shareholders, including a one-for-five reverse stock dividend intended to improve the market for RJR common stock, the introduction of a $0.375 quarterly dividend, and an exchange offer involving debt securities of RJR and Nabisco, Inc. The spin-off proposal was defeated and received little support from RJR shareholders.

Brooke Group approached RJR in May 1995 about a possible combination of its struggling Liggett tobacco business with RJR's tobacco operations in a merger that Brooke Group believed would permit RJR to spin off the remaining shares of Nabisco to RJR shareholders in a legally defensible transaction. Brooke Group reportedly asked for a 20 percent stake in the combined tobacco company and $350 million in preferred stock. RJR ultimately rejected the proposed transaction and may have also turned down a subsequent offer to buy Liggett from Brooke Group outright.

In August 1995, after talks broke down between Brooke Group and RJR, Brooke Group's wholly owned subsidiary, New Valley Corp., made a Hart-Scott-Rodino Act (H-S-R) filing to buy up to 15 percent of the company's outstanding common stock. Later that month, the board amended the company's bylaws to eliminate the right of shareholders to call a special meeting in response to a perceived threat of a takeover by LeBow and Icahn. On October 30, 1995, LeBow sent a letter to RJR announcing Brooke Group's intent to conduct a consent solicitation in which shareholders would be asked to vote in favor of a nonbinding resolution to spin off the remainder of Nabisco immediately. On November 20, 1995, Brooke Group made the necessary filings to preserve its right to run a slate of directors at the company's spring annual meeting.

RJR and Brooke Group Positions on a Spin-off

Brooke Group argues that the RJR board's fear of personal liability from litigation surrounding a potential spin-off is keeping Nabisco from being spun off and that the failure to carry out a separation of the food company is hurting the overall company's earnings and stock performance. Brooke notes that since RJR's initial public offering (February 1, 1991) through the date of the New Valley H-S-R filing, the company has had meager total returns of −0.5 percent, compared to 9.8 percent for the S&P Tobacco index and 9.8 percent for fellow food and tobacco products company Philip Morris. For the one-year period through the H-S-R filing RJR suffered a loss of 12 percent, while the S&P Tobacco index returned 28.6 percent and Philip Morris generated a 32.8 percent return for its shareholders. LeBow has stated that Brooke Group only wants to see RJR spin off Nabisco to increase his estimated $150 million investment in the company's stock and is not seeking to take control of RJR. Brooke Group cites recent studies and statistics demonstrating the apparent benefits of corporate spin-offs to shareholders. Brooke Group also expresses considerable doubt as to predictions of an improving litigation environment that will produce a more favorable time for a spin-off.

RJR does not refute Brooke Group's criticism of the company's past performance, but asserts that the litigation environment makes an immediate spin-off too risky. The company notes that the industry is currently faced with several lawsuits (*Castano, Engle*, and *Broin*) in which courts have upheld class certifications that could result in massive class action lawsuits against the industry, as well as a handful of state attorneys general cases in which states (including Florida, Mississippi, Minnesota, Maryland, and West Virginia) are seeking reimbursements for Medicaid expenses arising from alleged injuries and deaths due to smoking. The company believes that in the current environment, a spin-off would attract protracted litigation to prevent RJR from shielding Nabisco from a potential megaverdict arising from any of these cases. RJR CEO Steven Goldstone has publicly stated that he thinks that the company may make sufficient progress in these cases by mid-1998 that will make a spin-off less risky at that time.

RJR cautions shareholders not to throw their support behind Messrs. LeBow and Icahn given their reputation as corporate raiders and their involvement in certain companies which ended up in bankruptcy at some point, including SkyBox International Inc. (LeBow), MAI Systems Inc. (LeBow), and TWA (Icahn). RJR asserts that Brooke Group was forced by the company to disclose its attempts to work a deal to combine Liggett with RJR Tobacco and efforts by LeBow to form a consortium to take a controlling interest in RJR. . . .

Amendment of the Bylaw and RJR's Corporate Governance

RJR Management

Mr. Goldstone acknowledged that the elimination of shareholders' right to call a special meeting is an unpopular move with many of the company's institutional shareholders. However, he claims that most shareholders RJR has contacted do not intend to support the LeBow bylaw amendment, given the concerns expressed by the company that the dissidents' agenda is really to takeover RJR and not to improve the company's corporate governance. Goldstone said the board believed that this one potential defense against Mr. LeBow and Mr. Icahn is necessary given that relative to other S&P 500 companies, RJR has erected relatively few antitakeover defenses. He noted that the company does not maintain a poison pill, maintains cumulative voting in the election of directors, allows shareholders to act by written consent with a vote representing a majority of shares outstanding, and elects its board annually. RJR argues that the move to restrict the right to call a special meeting is aimed solely at the LeBow/Icahn solicitation and prevents the possibility of the dissidents calling a special meeting to vote on a takeover of RJR with support as low as 25.1 percent of shares outstanding. RJR also asserts that Brooke Group's corporate governance profile contains similar voting requirements to those adopted by RJR.

Brooke Group

Brooke Group complains that the bylaw amendment removing the right of shareholders, but not the board's right, to call special meetings was done in secrecy after Brooke Group met with RJR management and made known its intention to increase its stake in RJR. Brooke Group believes institutional shareholders will support its effort to restore their previous right to call a special meeting.

Second Act

Table 11.6.2
Ownership information (April 8, 1996)

Beneficial ownership		Type of shares	Votes per share	Shares outstanding
Officers & directors	0.46%	Common stock	1.00	272,982,782
Institutions	70.71%	Series C conversion preferred stock	0.20	26,675,000
Wachovia Bank of North Carolina, N.A.	1.07%	ESOP convertible preferred stock	0.20	15,003,379

Source: Proxy Statement, CDA Investment Technologies
Note: The company has three types of voting stock: common stock, Series C conversion preferred stock, and ESOP convertible preferred stock. Each share of common stock entitles its holder to one vote. Each share of Series C conversion preferred stock and ESOP convertible preferred stock entitles its holder to one-fifth of a vote. Wachovia Bank of North Carolina, N.A. beneficially owns 100 percent of the company's ESOP convertible preferred stock. Bennett LeBow and Carl Icahn together own approximately 6.6 percent of the outstanding common stock.

Item 1:   Elect Directors

Mr. LeBow's Brooke Group has nominated a ten-member slate to replace the current board of RJR. The LeBow slate has a three-prong platform:

- Effect an immediate spin-off of Nabisco.
- Increase the company's 1996 annual tobacco dividend from $1.50 to $2.00 per share and maintain a payout ratio of 60 percent of net cash flow.
- Revitalize the tobacco company under Ronald Fulford, former executive chairman of Imperial Tobacco, a subsidiary of Hanson PLC.

In addition, as a result of the terms of the recent Liggett Group Inc. tobacco litigation settlement of the Castano class action lawsuit and the settlement of a number of state attorneys' general suits against the industry to recover expenses of treating Medicaid patients, Mr. LeBow would offer RJR shareholders a first opportunity to consider a merger between Liggett and RJR that purportedly would extend the settlement to RJR and free the company from all current and future addiction-based liability claims.

The Brooke Group slate comprises ten nominees, five of whom (Bennett LeBow, Rouben Chakalian, Richard Lampen, Arnold Burns, and Barry Ridings) are employees or directors of Brooke Group or some affiliated organization. Mr. Chakalian has been president and CEO of Liggett since June 1994. Liggett is the manufacturer of *Chesterfields* and *Eve* cigarettes. Also providing the slate with tobacco industry experience is Peter Strauss, who was for three years (through December 1994) senior vice president, trade marketing (domestic) and international operations for the American Tobacco Co., which was merged into Brown & Williamson, a subsidiary of B.A.T. Industries, in 1994.

In addition to Mr. Strauss, the outside directors include shareholder advocate and former California Public Employees' Retirement System (CalPERS) CEO Dale Hanson, attorney Robert Frome, investment banker Barry Ridings, business professor William Starbuck, and Frederick Zuckerman, a former senior executive of IBM, RJR Nabisco, and Chrysler.

Cognizant that RJR and some shareholders are suspicious of Mr. LeBow's motives, Brooke Group's nominees have pledged that if they have not declared a spin-off of the remaining Nabisco shares held by the company within six months of their election, they will call a special meeting for the election of new directors. Brooke Group has also stated that it will not participate in the management of RJR Nabisco.

In addition, Brooke Group's slate has also pledged to adhere to a number of corporate governance policies, including the following:

- Any corporate transaction between RJR Tobacco and its subsidiaries and Brooke Group or its affiliates valued at more than $2 million (i.e., a Liggett/RJR merger) would require approval by a special committee of independent directors and RJR shareholders.
- No adoption of a staggered board or a poison pill.
- Adoption of confidential voting for future stockholder votes.

. . .

11.7   What Burns Holes in LeBow's Pockets?*

Jonathan R. Laing

The voice crackles with an excitement that's only accentuated by the scratchy connection from a car phone. "We've got a great message that institutional investors are really starting to turn on to," gushes Bennett S. LeBow, the one-time tanktown takeover artist who's now in the biggest battle of his life and clearly relishing it. "I'm an experienced fighter, and come April 17, I think a lot of people are going to get the surprise of their life."

That's the day, of course, he hopes to oust the board of giant RJR Nabisco Holdings at the company's annual meeting and install himself and his hand-picked slate of nine others as directors. LeBow is merely the latest barbarian at the gate of this once venerable tobacco and food concern. But his platform of breaking up the company to unlock value has seductive appeal to shareholders who've been saddled with years of disappointing earnings and slack stock performance following Kohlberg Kravis Roberts' $29 billion leveraged buyout of the firm in 1989.

LeBow's plan calls for RJR to immediately spin off to current shareholders the 81% stake it still holds in the Nabisco food operation. Then, LeBow figures, the food company's stock, freed of the immense litigation risks facing Reynolds and other tobacco companies, would bolt upward.

But it's difficult to imagine a more unlikely champion of shareholder value. Over the years, LeBow himself has proven a less-than-adept corporate manager. Two of his major corporate acquisitions of the mid-'Eighties, the computer concern MAI Systems and Western Union, ended up filing for Chapter 11 bankruptcy protection in 1993 while still under his tutelage. Heavy losses were inflicted on shareholders. LeBow denies any responsibility for this sad pass. He claims both MAI and Western Union were troubled, high-risk companies that he was, unfortunately, unable to save.

His current publicly-traded company, Brooke Group Ltd., is hardly in the pink of health. This despite the fact that Brooke's stock rocketed from $4 a share to $14 in a matter of weeks last fall after LeBow first announced his campaign to bust up RJR. The stock currently trades at around $9. Brooke's major operating unit, Liggett, is in free fall as a result of its shrinking share of the U.S. cigarette business. Liggett now holds about 2% of the market, and it is plagued by declining volume, poor distribution, a loss of pricing power for its important discount brands, and antiquated plant and equipment.

Meanwhile, the parent company Brooke is asphyxiating on some $400 million in consolidated debt that recently had to be restructured. As of last September 30 [1995], Brooke boasted a negative net worth of more than $325 million. And that number is likely to grow. In a notification of late filing last week, Brooke reported that it expects to post a net loss of $32 million for 1995. With performance like this, Brooke has another shot at being Fortune magazine's "Least Admired" company in the U.S., an accolade it last won in 1994.

---

*Reprinted by permission of *Barron's* © 1996 Dow Jones & Company, Inc. All rights reserved worldwide.

The deplorable operating results of LeBow-controlled companies never stopped him from enriching himself at the expense of fellow investors. Over the years he has feasted royally even as his companies hemorrhaged red ink. His combined annual compensation at Brooke and its various units exceeds $2 million. He also has never been averse to making sweetheart deals between his public companies and the private entities he controls. Brooke, for example, spent some $10 million in 1992 to buy LeBow's management company, which had been earning fancy fees for managing Brooke and its various subsidiaries. LeBow also benefited from having Brooke buy back shares from him in a deal that was not offered to other shareholders. In a sense, LeBow greenmailed his own company.

And, when it comes to maneuvering in bankruptcy court, few financiers shake and bake with the agility of LeBow. Though a minority shareholder of Western Union, or New Valley, as the company was renamed in 1991, LeBow wound up maintaining control of the company when it shocked the investment world by emerging from bankruptcy in 1995 with a cash kitty of $300 million after paying off all its creditors. An unexpected windfall from the sale of New Valley's funds-transfer business had made a minor bonanza out of what was expected to be a lugubrious court-ordered liquidation in which creditors and shareholders would be hosed.

Other equity holders cried foul and sued, charging that LeBow and Brooke had manipulated the bankruptcy process to their own benefit. But to no avail. Today, LeBow uses New Valley as his personal investment arm despite the fact that Brooke owns but 42% of the company's common.

Lavish Lifestyle

Lastly, LeBow has few qualms about using his debt-laden companies as personal banks for streams of loans to finance his lavish lifestyle of multiple homes and occasional hijinks. He outdid himself in 1989 when he chartered a plane to fly 150 friends to a $3 million party in London to christen his private yacht, which was modeled on one built for Queen Victoria. LeBow's guests reportedly were put up at Claridge's Hotel and were met at the harbor by a uniformed marching band.

At one point, LeBow's borrowing got so out of control that Brooke shareholders successfully sued to force LeBow to pay back some $16 million in outstanding loans, waive his right to $6.25 million in preferred dividends and limit increases on his annual salary for the next four years.

LeBow remains unrepentant. As he told *Barron's* last week, "The point to remember is that I would have paid every dime of the loans with contracted interest anyway. The lawsuit just accelerated the payback. Look, those were the swinging 'Eighties when everybody was living high. And by the way, you should know that RJR Chairman Mike Harper took some $40 million from the company last year, if you add up his salary, incentive compensation, bonuses, and other benefits. We'll fax you the numbers."

Of course, LeBow was stretching the truth a tad in his spirited rejoinder. The loans he was forced to repay all occurred in the Calvinist 'Nineties rather than the spendthrift 'Eighties. And the proffered fax on Harper's compensation got to the magic $40 million level only by lumping together two and a half years of Harper's salary, bonuses, option awards, insurance benefits, and perks. Clearly, all is fair in love and takeover battles.

LeBow's career of self-dealing has clearly paid off. His nearly 60% interest in Brooke alone has a current market value of more than $90 million.

Characteristically, he's mounting his epic proxy battle for control of multibillion-dollar RJR on the cheap. His partner in the effort, long-time raider Carl Icahn, put up some $350 million of the $500 million the pair used to accumulate its 18 million-share, or 6.6%, position in RJR's common. LeBow's contribution consists of $80 million supplied by New Valley—seemingly his sole remaining source of corporate liquidity—leveraged with some $70 million in margin debt. Both Icahn and LeBow are slightly underwater on their positions, based on RJR's recent trading level of around $31.

Yet the proxy fight being mounted by LeBow and Brooke can't be dismissed out of hand. Certainly RJR is taking the effort seriously, firing volley after volley of full-page ads in the *New York Times* and *The Wall Street Journal* trumpeting various claimed depredations of "LeBow—LeBogus" or "LeBow—LeBankrupt" and carpet-bombing its shareholders with all manner of anti-LeBow propaganda.

In February, the LeBow team shocked RJR by winning a consent solicitation of the company's shareholders in which more than half of RJR's outstanding shares voted in favor of a nonbinding resolution that the food unit should be immediately spun off. "It's the first time any *Fortune* 1000 company has ever lost such a solicitation," LeBow crowed to *Barron's*.

Perhaps even more worrisome from RJR's standpoint, Brooke also won a binding bylaw change that would allow any RJR shareholder to call a special shareholder meeting with the backing of just 25% of RJR's outstanding shares. This means that LeBow and Brooke can continue to push for changes in the composition of the RJR board and the like, even if they lose the proxy fight at the April 17 annual meeting. And they would no longer need a majority of the shares outstanding to pass new resolutions, as is needed in consent solicitations. Just a majority of the shares present and voting would suffice.

Moreover, last month LeBow thought he'd pulled off a considerable coup that would virtually insure a Brooke victory in the proxy battle. Breaking with previously sacrosanct tobacco-industry practice, LeBow's Liggett settled a clutch of major outstanding tobacco liability suits. The bucks involved were small, some 12% a year of Liggett's anemic pre-tax income, but the symbolism of the act was huge.

LeBow, of course, extracted a key concession from the plaintiffs' lawyers. They agreed that if LeBow were to win the proxy fight, they would allow the bust-up of RJR and the spin-off of the food unit to proceed without tying the deal up in court. Thus RJR could no longer claim that any spin-off would automatically trigger suits from plaintiffs' lawyers.

LeBow badly miscalculated, however. News of the Liggett settlement sent RJR and the other tobacco stocks careening lower. Industry giant Philip Morris slipped more than 10% in a matter of days, helping vaporize more than $10 billion in the tobacco industry's stock value. Investors panicked at the thought that Liggett's deal would, in the words of leading cigarette analyst Gary Black of Sanford Bernstein, "unleash a new flood of litigation." And who knew what damaging industry memos would surface now that Liggett was consorting with the enemy?

As a result, LeBow has likely cost Brooke victory in the proxy fight by alienating a number of large institutional shareholders in RJR who had backed Brooke's February consent solicitation. At least that's what Black and other analysts are hearing in their independent soundings of institutions. The doors at Fidelity and other major institutions are no longer open to LeBow, though he denies this is the case.

It's doubtful that LeBow would win the proxy fight anyway. For it's one thing to use LeBow to send a message to RJR management and quite another to actually hand over control of a major company to someone with as tainted a reputation as his. RJR's huge cash flow might prove too tempting.

RJR officials argue persuasively that LeBow has a hidden agenda in trying to take over RJR. They say his real intent is to unload the ailing Liggett on RJR at a fancy price.

There's plenty of evidence to back this contention. LeBow concedes that he began his saber-rattling at RJR only late last summer after the company spurned his proposal to merge Liggett into RJR's tobacco company for a price nearly four times what RJR considered Liggett's fair market value. So much for boosting RJR's shareholder value. Likewise, the briefing books that various Brooke nominees for RJR directorships received last December included financial tables assuming the two tobacco operations would be merged.

If Brooke fails in its effort to dump Liggett on RJR, which now seems likely, its business could continue to deteriorate and it, too, could someday join that long list of companies that LeBow has driven into bankruptcy court. That's what several sophisticated short-sellers are betting.

But any setback for LeBow would only be temporary, one suspects. For in bankruptcy court he would have his fellow Brooke investors and creditors just where he wants them.

12   The Role of Technology in Mutual Fund Complexes

Introduction

Technology has been one of the key drivers behind the growth of the mutual fund industry. Technology has enabled the industry to improve the quality of customer service, enhance information flows to portfolio managers, cope with exploding volumes of transactions, and introduce a broad array of new products. Moreover, technology has allowed the mutual fund industry to do all these things at a reasonable cost—after making substantial capital expenditures for the technology. This is largely because expensive labor-intensive functions have been replaced by automated systems that rely on ever-cheaper hardware and communications channels.

We will begin by looking at the effects of technology on the mutual fund industry from the 1960s to the 1990s, focusing on those changes that directly impacted customer services. Then we will review briefly those changes that had an impact on mutual fund portfolio managers and the investment process. Finally, we will look at some of the advanced technology that we can expect to see deployed over the next several years.

As discussed in earlier chapters, the mutual fund industry has grown and changed significantly over the last few decades. Technology has been one of the biggest enablers of this growth. In the 1960s and 1970s, advances in technology included the introduction of mainframe computers, on-line transaction processing, and telecommunications connectivity. Mainframes and on-line processing made it feasible for mutual fund sponsors to manage the records of their shareholders, and allowed these sponsors to move the transfer agency function in-house. Advances in telecommunications made it possible to establish 800 numbers and route incoming calls on a 24-hour basis to available customer service agents, who could provide information and handle investor orders over the phone.

The 1980s saw the improvement of voice response units, which, when linked to customer databases and trading systems via touchtone phones, began a trend toward customer self-service that continues today. Real-time data feeds, specifically geared to reflect transactions promptly, replaced "batch" services at the end of the day. Intraday fund pricing, in which a fund's net asset value is computed and published several times within the trading day, became a reality. The use of mainframe computers—whose demise had been regularly predicted throughout the decade—grew dramatically, driven by increased trading volumes and the growth of 401(k) systems that required the massive overnight number-crunching at which mainframes excel. At the same time, personal computers replaced "dumb" terminals on the desktops of company employees, and departmental "client-server" systems began to take on some traditional mainframe functions. Toward the end of the 1980s, these multiple layers of systems began to be interconnected by local area networks (LANs) and wide area nationwide networks. These networks allowed the integration of customer service functions, leading to automated workflow and problem tracking.

The proliferation of systems architectures that characterized the 1980s was a mixed blessing. As more services were offered to customers, it became increasingly difficult to present the appearance of a single unified entity. Customers expressed the need for integrated financial account statements, and for customer service representatives who could handle the full range of the company's offerings. At the same time, systems development was becoming more complex and expensive, as each system improvement required re-engineering of the complicated web of interconnections that had been created to maintain a "single face."

During the 1990s, the industry began to rationalize some of this technological hodge-podge. The departmental systems that were convenient but difficult to manage grew into *enterprise servers*—large computers based on the UNIX operating system, with the capacity and stability to become the next generation of mainframes. Mainframes themselves became cheaper and better oriented to their new role as the repositories of huge databases. On the desktop, graphical user interfaces (GUIs) brought a standardization and ease of use that allowed PCs to be provided to all employees with a minimum of training.

As hierarchical databases gave way to relational databases, they allowed applications to use data more flexibly. Single database management systems developed the capability to perform the very different jobs of high-volume transaction processing and data analysis across a wide variety of computer platforms. Data warehousing, in which a time-series of data "snapshots" provides an information base that supports analytical processing, began to be practical as the cost of computer disk storage declined.

As the cost of developing and maintaining systems became an increasing part of the overall cost of technology, interest grew in new technologies to support the development process. Ironically, the task of the programmer—the agent of automation—was itself a labor-intensive craft. New systems, called *fourth-generation languages* (4GLs), came into use.[1] These systems allowed programmers to use GUIs and tables of information to replace hand-coding of instructions. Until late in the decade, however, these 4GLs were not robust enough to work with high-volume core applications.

Home PCs proliferated, but did not become an important channel for the mutual fund industry until recently when the Internet exploded. In 1995, the Internet was a twenty-year-old technology, developed for the military and used primarily by the scientific and academic communities. But the broadening of the Internet's availability through the new World Wide Web changed everything. Since 1995, Web browsers installed on Internet-connected PCs have become the medium by which an increasing number of consumers obtain information and do business. These customers are currently held back by three factors: the availability of easy-to-use Web sites; the reliability and speed (i.e., bandwidth) of their connections to the Internet; and concerns about the security of their transactions.

New technological trends are rapidly eliminating these inhibiting factors. Mutual fund sponsors have established second-generation Web sites that provide better-organized information, more useful content, and simplified navigation. High-speed communications links—such as ISDN, cable-TV, and satellite links—are beginning to replace slower dial-up modem systems. Higher encryption standards for data transmission are making consumers feel more comfortable about entrusting their financial transactions to the Internet.

The World Wide Web presents an opportunity for new businesses, and a challenge to the dominant players of the securities industry. The battalions of customer representatives and the huge investment in capital equipment that now support large financial players present significant barriers to entry for newcomers. By contrast, a smaller fund sponsor can easily establish a presence on the Web with far less investment than was previously possible. The new technology is also driving down commissions and other fees, however, and the resulting lower margins may favor large suppliers who can use their size to achieve economies of scale. It remains to be seen whether the emergence of the Internet will tend to consolidate the positions of the current financial companies, or make way for a new generation of leaders.

Changes in technology have not only affected the services that mutual fund sponsors can provide their customers, but also have benefited investment professionals within the mutual fund industry. In the 1970s, newly available computing power allowed portfolio managers to use statistical packages and more current information to enhance investment decisions. In the 1980s, detailed financial information became available from multiple sources more frequently. Electronic spreadsheets and high-speed data feeds restructured the research process by providing new and more efficient techniques to analyze financial scenarios and models. In the 1990s, investment professionals within mutual fund advisers received a wealth of services to assist in managing money. Such services included market data and analytics packages (e.g., Bloomberg) as well as electronic company financial filings (e.g., 10K and 10Q) on CD-ROM and on-line via the SEC's Edgar system. The Internet created additional capabilities to support investment analysts, who gained electronic access to Wall Street research that was previously faxed or mailed to them. Traders in the 1990s began to view real-time video market reports (e.g., CNN) from their PCs, while simultaneously effecting trades across the globe from the same computer.

As these trends accelerate, technology will continue to be a major factor shaping the mutual fund industry. While no one can predict the future with absolute accuracy, some potential directions can be suggested:

- The maturation of voice recognition systems will bring new ease of use and capabilities to voice response unit (VRU) systems. Systems are already in place that permit customers to identify themselves by speaking a prearranged password into a phone, thus providing both memory-based and biometric security with greater convenience than today's PIN numbers. A customer can then proceed to ask basic questions about equities and mutual funds by speaking in a phone the names of these financial instruments. In the future, these systems will permit navigation by natural language recognition: Instead of "press one for this, press two for that," the customer simply will be able to say, "I want to buy Fund X" and the system will respond accordingly.

- The proliferation of incompatible systems will be eased by the emergence of platform-independent computer languages, such as the Java language, that will allow programs to execute anywhere, including on the desktop computer of a fund shareholder. The increased productivity of these new programming systems will power a new wave of automation that will further drive down costs for the mutual fund industry.

- The Internet will merge with other consumer media, so that it will become possible for a TV commercial featuring a mutual fund complex to end with an invitation to "click here" to open an account. Communications bandwidth will become so wide and cheap that customers will effectively be on-line all the time—thereby allowing information to be "pushed" to their computers without the need for any action on their part.

People will always be the most important part of the mutual fund industry, but in the future technology will change the nature of their work. Transaction processing, account queries, account setup, and asset allocation planning will increasingly be taken over by investors themselves, supported by the fund sponsor's representatives acting as advisers and guides to fund customers.

The readings in this chapter provide more background on the technological trends outlined above. First, a lengthy selection sets forth a framework for thinking about the role of technology in the mutual fund industry. The selection provides an approach to analyzing the relative importance of technology in different kinds of industries, as well as the positioning of firms within the maturity cycle of technology. Then, several shorter articles list the potential future technologies for the mutual fund industry, and discuss some of the issues involved in using these technologies. At the end of the chapter are two exercises, one that requires the use of a personal computer, and one that does not. The first explores Web sites of a few mutual fund complexes; the second involves the design of an on-line disclosure system.

Questions

In reviewing the materials in this chapter, please keep in mind the following questions:

1. What is the relative impact of information technology (IT) on industries such as defense, airlines, and banking? How would the mutual fund industry compare with these other industries in terms of IT?

2. How would a firm decide where to position itself within any industry in terms of strategic use of IT? Within the mutual fund industry, where do you think current players fall? Where might new entrants be positioned?

3. What are some of the concerns that must be addressed when setting up a Web site for a mutual fund sponsor? What is the main function of most current mutual fund sponsor sites? Do you anticipate that the current function will change; and if so, how?

4. How does the use of document imaging and representative workstations facilitate the delivery of products and services to fund shareholders? Will these two technological developments be rendered obsolete by the Internet?

5. What is the difference between a voice response unit and a voice recognition system? Would it be feasible for a voice recognition system to handle information requests, fund transactions, or problem resolution?

6. Do you think Microsoft will become an investment manager, securities broker, or transfer agent? What would be Microsoft's advantages in entering these fields, and what would be the significant barriers to its entry?

Note

1. Hardware codes were the first generation; symbolic assemblers the second; and English-like languages such as COBOL the third.

12.1 Manageable Trends*

Underlying Themes

This chapter discusses the nature and implications of ... six themes that reflect current insight into management practice and guidance for administrative action.

Because they represent what we believe to be the most useful ways to think about the forces driving how IT [information technology] is being used and managed within firms in the 1990s, these themes also provide the organizational basis for the chapters that follow. Our expectation is that additional experience and research with existing technologies and the emergence of new technologies will inevitably produce new—as yet unimagined—uses of IT in subsequent years.

Six manageable trends will be discussed in this chapter:

1. *IT influences different industries, and the firms within them, in different ways.* The type of impact strongly influences which IT management tools and approaches are appropriate for a firm.
2. *Telecommunications, computing, and software technologies are evolving rapidly and will continue to evolve.* This evolution will continue to destabilize the economic viability of existing IT-based systems and offer new types of IT application opportunities.
3. *The time required for successful organizational learning about IT limits the practical speed of change.* As the organization gains familiarity with a new technology, management's assimilation methods must change.
4. *External industry, internal organizational, and technological changes are pressuring firms to "buy" rather than "make" IT software and services.* This shift in the nature of the IT make-or-buy decision creates major IT management challenges.
5. *While all elements of the IT system life cycle remain, new technologies both enable and require dramatically different approaches to execution.* This significantly increases the complexity of the IT management challenge.
6. *Managing the long-term evolution of the partnership between general management, IT management, and user management is crucial for capturing the value of new IT-enabled business opportunities.*

Theme 1: Strategic Impact

It is increasingly clear that different industries are affected in fundamentally different ways by IT. In many industries, IT has enabled massive transformation of the strategy of the

---

*From Lynda M. Applegate, F. Warren MacFarlan, and James L. McKenney, *Corporate Information Systems Management*, 4th ed. (Irwin, 1996). Reprinted with permission of the McGraw-Hill Companies, Inc.

Box 12.1.1   Marketing (customer focus) question for managers

- Does the business require a large number of routine interactions each day with vendors for ordering or requesting information?
- Is product choice complex?
- Do customers need to compare competitors' product/service/price configurations simultaneously?
- Is a quick customer decision necessary?
- Is accurate, quick customer confirmation essential?
- Would an increase in multiple ordering or service sites provide value to the customer?
- Are consumer tastes potentially volatile?
- Do significant possibilities exist for product customization?
- Is pricing volatile (can/should salesperson set price at point of sale)?
- Is the business heavily regulated?
- Can the product be surrounded by value-added information to the customer?
- Is the real customer two or more levels removed from the manufacturer?

firm and the "value chain" of activities through which it is executed. Technology is now a core component of many of the products that we use every day. For example, today's car now includes over 50 IT components, and over 800 programmers at a major defense contractor are required to develop software for the control panels of airplanes and submarines; in addition, IT has revolutionized our notion of service. Supported by IT, retailers like L.L. Bean now distribute catalogs of their products—previously available only in standard paper format, now in interactive, multimedia CD-ROM and over the Internet—directly to customers who can order products by telephone (or the Internet) and pay for them using secure financial credit networks. Within the firm, computer-aided design and manufacturing (CAD/CAM); factory automation and control systems; and IT-enabled purchasing, distribution, sales, and marketing systems have enabled firms to simultaneously compete on quality, speed, and cost. The ability to create new IT-based products and services and to streamline, integrate, and time-synchronize internal operating and management processes is transforming industries and the firms within them. As industry leaders "raise the bar," many firms are finding that in the 1990s IT has become a strategic necessity.

Box 12.1.1 presents a series of questions for managers as they contemplate IT marketing (customer focus) opportunities. If the answer to most of the questions is no, IT probably would play a rather limited role in transforming marketing. Conversely, if the answer is yes, technology has played or will play major role. Box 12.1.2 provides a similar set of questions for managers contemplating IT opportunities in operations.

Figure 12.1.1 shows different approaches to the use of IT by industry leaders in different industries. In the airline industry, for example, the reservation system, heavily used by travel agencies, has given its leading developers, American Airlines and United Airlines, major marketing (customer focus) and operational advantages. It has also enabled better aircraft utilization, new services such as "frequent flyer" programs, and the development of joint incentive programs with hotels and car rental agencies. In addition, the ongoing

Box 12.1.2 Operations questions for managers

- Is there large geographic dispersion in sourcing?
- Is high technology embedded in the product?
- Does the product require a long, complex design process?
- Is the process of administering quality control standards complex?
- Is the design integration between customer and supplier across company boundaries complex?
- Are there large buffer inventories in the manufacturing process?
- Does the product require complex manufacturing schedule integration?
- Are time and cost savings possible?
- Is there potential for major inventory reductions?
- Are direct and indirect labor levels high?

operations of seat allocation, crew scheduling, maintenance, and so on, have been profoundly influenced by IT. When an IT system fails, airline operations suffer immediately. As figure 12.1.2 illustrates, some airlines invested less heavily in IT; some have paid a significant penalty in terms of their ability to differentiate their services in the eyes of the buying public and coordinate and cost-effectively deliver their services; in fact, failure to invest in IT has been cited as a leading cause for several airline failures.[1] Other airlines, such as Southwest, have pioneered radically different non-IT intensive ways of competing (frequent point-to-point flights, low labor costs, rock bottom prices, no food, no seat reservations, etc.).

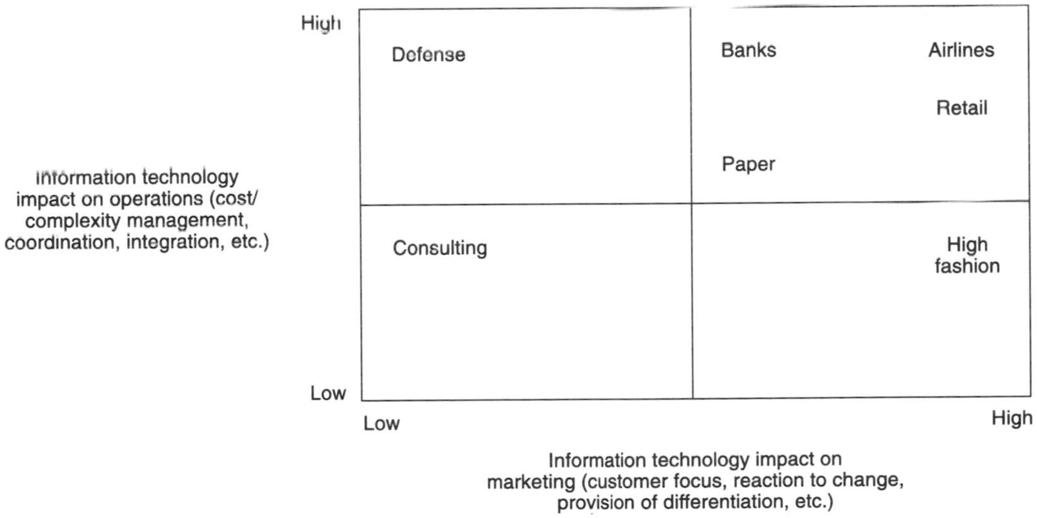

Figure 12.1.1 IT impact: Position of industry leaders

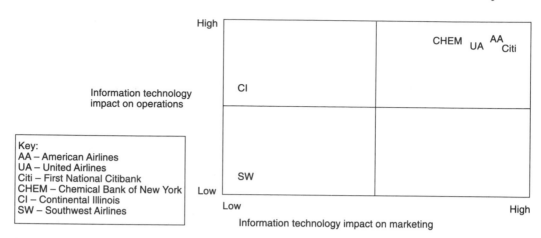

Figure 12.1.2   IT impact: Position of key players in airlines and banks

In the banking industry, several banks (e.g., Bank One, Citibank, and Chemical Bank) have moved aggressively to distinguish their products and services through effective use of information technology. Other banks, however, have used it primarily to transform the back office (e.g., check processing). The prime reason Tom Theobold, CEO of Continental Bank, gave for outsourcing the IT function in 1991 was that over the past 20 years, he had been unable to find a bank that had developed and maintained sustainable competitive advantage through use of IT.[2] The problem of defining the competitive potential of IT is further complicated by the fact that while some firms fail to reap competitive benefits from their IT investments, others dramatically change the basis of competition.

Figure 12.1.1 also shows the impact of IT on the leaders of several other industries. Defense, for example, with CAD/CAM, robotics, and embedded technology has been primarily affected on the operations side. The marketing impact on defense, however, has been considerably less significant, not only because of the much lower transaction rate, but also because the much higher transaction value introduces a different set of marketing forces that are less sensitive to technology's impact.

Conversely, retailing operations have been dramatically altered by bar coding and point-of-sale scanning technology that have enabled just-in-time ordering, massive cost-reduction programs, and major reductions in inventory levels. Quick response systems in retailing and efficient consumer response systems in grocery stores—which have been among the most exciting mid-1990s applications—have put great pressure on suppliers, distributors, and brokers to adapt their processes to survive. Similarly, display management, database marketing, and point-of-sale terminals that capture customer information at the time of a sale have made important marketing contributions. As mentioned earlier, the mid-1990s have seen the introduction of electronic-based catalogs through mediums such as CD-ROM and the Internet that have dramatically altered the concept of shopping. No longer must we go to a fixed location with fixed hours; today, shopping is done any time and any place....

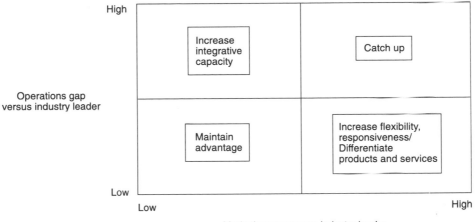

Figure 12.1.3

A Contingency Approach to IT Management

Figure 12.1.3 identifies the different competitive investment strategies facing industry players as they consider their relative position versus industry leaders and highlights the opportunities for using IT to transform marketing, operations, or both.

In summary, IT plays very different roles in different industry settings. (Figure 12.1.4 captures these differences.) Sometimes it has played a predominantly operational role, while at others its impact has been primarily on marketing. In many of these settings, industry leaders have been so aggressive that they have transformed the rules of competition, putting those who followed under great pressure. As the role of IT changes within the firm, leadership, organization design, and management processes also change.

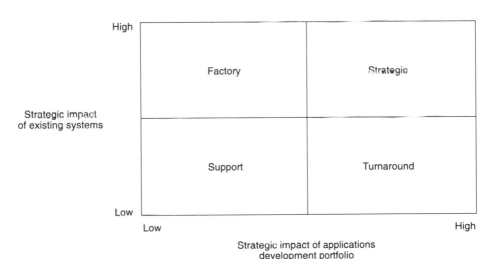

Figure 12.1.4

Two aspects embedded in the previous discussion have profound importance to the management of IT in an individual firm. The first is that for some firms, the second-by-second, utterly reliable zero-defect quality of its IT operations is crucial to the survival of the firm. Even small interruptions in service or disruptions in quality may have profound impact. In other firms, it would take significant disturbances in IT operations over an extended period to have a major impact on the firm's overall operations.

The second aspect, discussed earlier, is that whereas new IT development initiatives are of great strategic importance for some firms, for other firms, IT is useful but not strategic.[3] Understanding an organization's position on these two aspects is critical for developing an appropriate IT management strategy. Four categories of IT are identified.

Strategic

For a growing number of firms, IT is essential for executing current strategies and operations; in addition, the applications under development are crucial to future competitive success. It strategy, the backbone of such firms' competitive success, receives considerable attention. Banks, insurance companies, and major retail chains frequently fall into this category. Appropriately managed, these firms require considerably IT planning, and the organizational relationship between IT and senior management is very close; in fact, in some of these firms the head of the IT function, broadly defined, sits on the board of directors.

Turnaround

Some firms receive considerable IT support for operations, but are not absolutely dependent on the uninterrupted cost-effective functioning of IT to achieve operating objectives. The applications under development, however, are absolutely necessary to enable the firm to achieve its strategic objectives. A good example of this was a rapidly growing manufacturing firm. The IT used in its factories and accounting processes, though important, was not absolutely vital to its effectiveness. Nevertheless, the rapid growth in the number of products, number of sites, number of staff, and so forth, of the firm's domestic and international installations severely strained its operations, management control, and new product development processes. New IT applications were initiated to enable the company to define and implement new product initiatives, to streamline and integrate operations, and to restore management control. New IT leadership was sought and the position was redefined to encompass a more strategic role and to report to the CEO.

A second example of IT activity that can be classified as turnaround is found in a major pharmaceutical company. The firm recently implemented a major research computing center that provides sophisticated chemical modeling capabilities, which have facilitated several new major product discoveries, and it has streamlined the product-development process. But government regulations hamper the ability of the firm to take full advantage of the potential improvements in product-development cycle times; it still takes almost a decade from the time of invention to get a product to market; needless to say, a three-day interruption in IT service is unlikely to be disastrous.

Another firm entered the turnaround category by systematically under-investing in IT development over a period of years until its existing systems were dangerously obsolete; in fact, it was running on unique hardware platforms that its vendor was about to discontinue. Application development projects, initiated to rebuild the systems, were considered to be a matter of high corporate priority. Again, unevenness in system operations was irritating, but not life threatening.

Factory

Some firms are heavily dependent on cost-effective, totally reliable IT operational support to enable internal operations. System downtime causes major organizational disruption that can cause customer defections or significant loss of money. The CEO of an investment bank became fully aware of the operational dependence of his firm on IT when a flood above the data center brought all securities trading to a halt. Failure to ensure an off-site redundant data center crippled the bank's trading operations and caused massive financial losses. Needless to say, the CEO has a new appreciation for the importance of IT in running critical areas of business operations; a redundant data center was implemented shortly after the incident.

Firms in the factory quadrant of figure 12.1.4 are using IT, like the investment bank, to enable critical, time-dependent operations to function smoothly; but the IT applications under development, although profitable and important in their own right, are not fundamental to the firm's ability to compete. For the firms in this category, even a one-hour disruption in service has severe operational, competitive, and financial consequences. In the 1990s, mid-sized firms in this quadrant often turn to outsourcing to gain access to specialized expertise and costly security systems to help manage the risk.

Support

For certain firms some of which have very large IT budgets—the strategic impact of IT on operations and future strategy is low. For example, a large professional services firm spends nearly $30 million per year on IT activities that support more than 2000 employees; all agree that the firm could continue to operate, albeit unevenly, in the event of major IT operational failure. And the strategic impact of the IT applications under development, viewed realistically, is quite limited. Appropriately, IT has a significantly lower organizational position in this firm than in those in other arenas, and the commitment to linking IT to business planning activities, particularly at the senior-management level, is essentially non-existent. Until recently, although it keeps abreast of new technology, the firm, like its competitors, showed limited interest in the development and maintenance of a comprehensive IT strategy. Within the past two years, however, the firm spent a significant amount of money equipping 15,000 of its consulting professionals and field representatives with laptop computers, electronic mail, and a variety of specialized applications that allowed them to access and share information. Since the key to the firm's success lay in recruiting, developing, and retaining highly competent professionals with a broad range of skills and deep expertise within targeted areas, and in managing client relationships, this new IT initiative could shift the firm's focus toward the turnaround category. If successful, other firms within the industry may be forced to implement similar systems.

Surprisingly, we still find a large number of companies that senior management classifies as being in the support category. In spring 1995, 160 senior managers from firms located around the world were asked to classify their firms' approach to using IT—38 percent reported that their firm was positioned in the support quadrant; only 7 percent expected to be there five years in the future. (See table 12.1.1) . . .

Table 12.1.1
Senior manager perceptions of the role of IT within their firm (N = 160)

	1995	2000
Support	38%	7%
Factory	10	10
Turnaround	14	7
Strategic	38	76

Theme 2:   Integrating Changing Technology Platforms

At the heart of the IT challenge lies the dramatic, sustained, long-term evolution of IT cost/performance and the merging of a variety of technology platforms. IT applications that were nonexistent in 1989 were state-of-the-art by 1992 and by 1995 were routine; obsolescence is just a few years down the road.

The 1980s and 1990s saw the development of increasing communication and information storage capacities, which, in turn, supported an explosion of new types of software and IT applications. By the mid-1990s, many consider the useful life of a personal computer to be three years or less. The tremendous improvement in price/performance has enabled integration of video, voice, data, and graphics. This is radically changing the capabilities and potential uses of IT. For example, in 1995, full-motion digital video and voice annotations can be attached to documents, information reports, and spreadsheets.

But despite the integration in the classes of information, the separation of the management of computing, telecommunications, office automation, and broadcast technologies continues in many firms. The ability to capitalize on the real business opportunities afforded by the integration of these technologies can only come if we successfully merge the strategies, policies, and technology standards related to them. In this book, when we refer to IT departments, activities, or policies, we include all of these technologies. At present, many firms have begun the difficult process of coordinating these technologies; few have successfully integrated all of them.

There are three major reasons to manage these technologies—at least at a policy and standards level—as an integrated whole: (1) today's IT applications require an enormous number of physical interconnections among them (e.g., on-line information retrieval systems, electronic mail, and end-user programming require the physical integration of two or more of the technologies); (2) execution of IT application development projects utilizing technologies that are managed independently is exceedingly difficult;[4] and (3) efforts to identify potential business opportunities that take advantage of the emerging integration potential across these technologies are significantly hampered when the technology is managed separately.

The process of integrating technologies that were developed and managed separately is extremely complex. In many settings, integration will require a common operating and management process; some may choose to achieve integration at the senior management policy committee level, while requiring operating managers to work together as an interfunctional team. Failure to achieve management and operating integration can involve extraordinary expenses. This is especially true when integration involves PCs and local area networks (LANS). In fact, a recent study found that the cost of PC/LAN computing averaged $6,445 per user per year; this was 2.8 times higher than the $2,282 average cost per user per year of mainframe computing.[5] ...

Theme 3:   **Assimilating Emerging Technologies**

The task of implementing a portfolio of IT systems projects that are built around continually evolving technologies is an extraordinarily complex endeavor. Early involvement of end users whose daily activities will be influenced by the adoption of the technology has been shown to be a critical success factor. New IT innovations, however, are often complicated by the fact that user jobs may be eliminated by the new technologies that they are working so hard to help implement. Successful implementation of IT also often requires that users adopt new ways of performing intellectual tasks. To accomplish this, old procedures and attitudes must be abandoned, and new patterns must emerge and be accepted by individuals and work groups.

Since IT was first introduced in organizations, there has been an ongoing effort to understand the managerial issues associated with the evolution of IT and organization.... Successful implementation of a technology often requires that individuals learn radically new ways of performing intellectual tasks, causing changes in information flows as well as in individual roles. Frequently, this requires more extensive organizational changes involving structures, operating processes, management processes, human resource management systems, culture, and incentives. We describe the technology innovation and diffusion process within four phases.

Phase 1.   **Technology Identification and Investment**

The first phase involves identifying a technology of potential interest to the company and funding a pilot project. An alternative approach is to use the business-planning process to identify promising IT applications that require technology innovation and fund investigation of their potential as part of the budgeting process. The first approach involves a "grass roots" effort that can be used to define potential benefits and risks and system implementation difficulties early in the process and to garner support by demonstrating the potential payoff. The latter approach requires the commitment of senior management to serve as product champions for systems innovations early in the process. Because it is inappropriate to demand objective payoffs at the pilot project stage, top-level management commitment is often difficult to secure.

Phase 2.   **Technological Learning and Adaptation**

The objective during the second phase is to encourage user-oriented experimentation with the newly identified technology through a series of user-defined pilot projects. The primary purpose of the experimentation is to develop a broad base of user-oriented insights into how the new technology might be used to add value in the business and to make users aware of the existence of the technology. Frequently, the outcome of phase 2 provides a much different perspective on the technology than the one held by IT experts at the end of their phase 1 pilot.

The length of this phase varies with the type of technology, the characteristics of the users, the tasks for which the technology is used, and the organizational and environmental context.[6] For example, at one firm, a pilot project designed to test the use of handheld computers by the sales force was so successful that it progressed through phase 2 within several months and was fully deployed within 18 months. The technology, while new to the company, was not "new to the world"; the task that the technology would support was well defined, as was the influence of the technology on the task; careful attention was paid to involving and training both the users (and their bosses) from the start of the process, and incentives, compensation, and performance management systems were realigned to "fit" the new IT-enabled work process.

Phase 3.   Rationalization/Management Control

By the time a technology has reached phase 3, it is reasonably well understood by both IT personnel and key users. The basic challenge in this phase is to develop appropriate systems and controls to ensure that the technologies are utilized efficiently as they diffuse throughout the organization. In earlier phases, basic concerns revolve around stimulating awareness and experimentation; in this phase, they center on developing standards and controls to ensure that the applications are done economically and can be maintained over a long period of time. Formal standards for development and documentation, cost-benefit studies, and user charge-out mechanisms are all appropriate for technologies in this phase. Failure to develop and maintain these standards can be extraordinarily expensive.

Phase 4.   Maturity/Widespread Technology Transfer

By the time a technology enters the fourth phase, the required skills have been developed, users are aware of the benefits, and management controls are in place. A common pitfall in this phase is that enthusiasm for the technology dies while there is still opportunity to use it to add value. Lacking sufficient attention and resources, maintenance of existing applications may suffer and new value-creating uses may not be explored. Careful vigilance is also required in this phase to ensure that out-of-date technologies and applications are not extended beyond their useful life....

Theme 4:   Sourcing Policies for the IT Value Chain

A significant issue in repositioning IT over the past decade has been an acceleration of the pressures that are pushing firms toward greater reliance on external sources for software and computing support. Many call this outsourcing, but there is a wide variation in the definition of that word within the industry. Escalating costs of large-scale system development projects, limited staff, availability of industry-standard databases and networks, availability of software packages, and a dramatic increase in the number of potential applications have been some of the factors driving the trend to use outside sources—a trend that we believe will continue to accelerate throughout the 1990s. The realization that they do not develop their own word-processing or spreadsheet software leads managers to ask: "Do I need to develop my order-processing system? If I can specify the process, can I hire someone to write the code?" Facing significant pressure to focus on core competencies and the rapidly increasing complexity of technology management, many have expanded their thinking: "Do I really need to run my large computing centers and corporate networks? Can I safely delegate the operation of the infrastructure to enable me to focus my energy and resources on creating value-added IT applications?" Factors to consider as firms struggle with the answers to these questions are summarized in table 12.1.2.

The preference to buy rather than make has significantly influenced IT management practice as dissatisfaction with internally supplied services grows. The proliferation of end-user computing packages has resulted in the fact that in many firms in the mid-1990s less than 1 percent of all software has been developed by the IT group. The IT organization has increasingly turned into an in-house systems integration function, and new management processes are required. For example, internal management control systems must be checked to ensure that they do not motivate inappropriate "make" versus "buy" decisions. When software development is being outsourced, clear interorganizational project management systems and audit procedures must be in place to ensure that both parties are able to deliver on their commitments. Implementation risk on a fixed-price contract is strongly related to vendor viability. A "good" price is not good if the supplier goes under before completing the project. Provisions for "death" and "divorce" become critical in situations where a firm is outsourcing operational IT components (e.g., data centers, networks) since the normal length of these contracts is approximately 10 years.

Theme 5:   Applications Development Process

Traditionally, the activities necessary to produce and deliver information service have been characterized as a series of steps:[7]

1. Design—definition of the functions and relevant technologies
2. Construct—detailed design, programming and testing (or buy)
3. Implement—gain ownership by users, redesign processes, reorganize
4. Operate—execute processes, continuous training to exploit system
5. Maintain—upgrade technology, adapt system to changing requirements

... At one extreme are the traditional projects that were once the mainstay of the industry. These projects are noted for being large, requiring extensive development periods (often well in excess of 18 months) and significantly influencing the nature of work and organization across multiple areas of the business. These projects are inherently very complex. Often, the information required, how it will be processed, and the end results of the project are not clearly specified at the outset. In the 1990s, the traditional system life cycle continues to be appropriate for these projects, but the steps in the process are not performed in a highly structured and sequential fashion. There is a significant increase in the levels of interaction among a wide variety of IT and business professionals, each of whom brings different areas of expertise and management responsibilities; even vendors get in the act. This results in a much more interactive and iterative process; in addition, to manage complexity, these large projects are often subdivided into a number of smaller projects that may be managed in very different ways. For example, one team may use joint application development and rapid prototyping[8] to build the user interface for the system, while a second team conducts a pilot project of a portion of the system that will use a state-of-the-art technology that is new to the firm.

Table 12.1.2

IT sourcing: Pressures to "make/own" versus "buy"

Decision criteria	Pressure to "make/own"	Pressure to "buy"
Business strategy	IT application or infrastructure provides proprietary competitive advantage.	IT application or infrastructure supports strategy of operations, but is not considered strategic in its own right.
Core competencies	Business or IT knowledge/expertise required to develop or maintain an application is considered a core competency of the firm.	Business or IT knowledge/expertise required to build or maintain an IT application or infrastructure is not critical to the firm's success.
Information/process security and confidentiality	The information or processes contained within IT systems or data-bases are considered to be highly confidential.	Failure of routine security measures, while problematic, would not cause serious organizational dysfunction.
Availability of suitable partners	There are no reliable, competent, and/or motivated partners that could assume responsibility for the IT application or infrastructure. (Included are the financial viability of the partner, perceptions of quality of the partner's products and services, and perceptions of the ability to form a compatible working relationship over the life of the contract.)	Reliable, competent, and appropriately motivated vendors (or other partners) are available.
Availability of packaged software or solutions	The IT application or infrastructure required by the firm is unique.	Packaged software or solutions are available that would meet the majority of business requirements.
Cost/benefit analysis	The cost of purchasing the product or service and/or coordinating and controlling interorganizational relationships and operations is greater than the cost of performing the service in-house.	The cost of purchasing and managing the service is significantly less than the cost of performing the service in-house.
Time frame for implementation	There is sufficient time available to develop internal resources and skills to implement the IT application and/or to develop the IT infrastructure required by the firm.	The time required to develop internal resources and expertise and/or to implement the IT application or infrastructure project exceeds the organization's demand for the product or services.
Evolution and complexity of the technology	The firm is able to attract, retain, and develop the range of IT experts needed to implement IT applications and infrastructures at a reasonable cost.	The firm is unable to keep pace with the rapidly changing and increasingly complex technologies required by the firm.
Ease of implementation	Software development tools that provide rapid IT application development are available.	Tools to support rapid application development are not available or are viewed to be insufficient or ineffective.

At the other extreme are more focused projects that may involve the construction of a decision support system (DSS) for a group of end users. This type of project may use rapid prototyping and joint application development methods from the outset. Alternatively, a team may be working on the introduction and assimilation of a new technology using the phased approach to organization learning discussed earlier in this chapter. Finally, some projects may involve the use of computer-aided software engineering (CASE) tools.[9] The key to understanding the complexity of the applications development challenge in the 1990s is to appropriately select and implement a system development methodology based on the nature of the project and the experience and expertise of both business and IT professionals. In addition, it is critical to remember that all projects require careful management by both business and IT professionals throughout all phases of the project....

Theme 6: Partnership of Three Constituencies

Much of the complexity of IT management stems from managing the conflicting pressures of three different and vitally concerned constituencies: IT management, user management, and general management of the organization. The relationships between these groups vary over time as the organization's familiarity with different technologies evolves, as the strategic impact of IT shifts, and as the company's overall IT management skills grow.

IT Management

A number of forces have driven the creation of an IT department and ensured its continued existence. The IT department provides a pool of technical skills that can be developed and deployed to resolve complex problems facing the firm. An important part of its mission is to scan leading-edge technologies and to ensure that potential users are both aware of their existence and of how they could be used to solve business problems. Because many systems are designed to interconnect different parts of the business, IT professionals have become key integrators who can help identify areas of potential interconnection between the needs of different user groups and thus facilitate the development of integrated business solutions. From their earliest roots, IT has involved process analysis and redesign. As a result, in many firms, IT professionals are becoming the "business process reengineering" specialists—a role of increasing importance within firms in the 1990s. In a world of changing technologies and changing business opportunities, this unit is under continuous pressure to remain relevant. As end users become more involved in system development activities, a new relationship must be forged to ensure that the unique skills and expertise of both groups are utilized to their fullest to solve business problems.

User Management

Specialization of the IT function has taken place at a cost. System design, construction, operation, and maintenance tasks have become the responsibility of the IT department, yet the user continues to assume responsibility for the business activities that the systems support. This is an obvious point of friction. Additionally, in the past, the "mysterious" requirements of the technology alienated users from the system development and operations process, increasing the barriers to effective collaboration.

At times, vendors and consultants capitalize on this conflict by aggressively marketing their services directly to the users, who are then faced with the additional pressure of choosing among alternatives without fully understanding the criteria upon which to base their decision. Increasing user IT sophistication and experience, when coupled with the increasing availability of packaged, user-friendly software, has dramatically altered the conditions that initially led to IT specialization. In many firms, the boundaries are blurring as "hybrid" professionals with both business and technical expertise become more prevalent at both the user and IT specialist levels. But new state-of-the-art technologies continue to require specialized expertise. Appropriately, the relationship and apportionment of responsibilities between the IT specialist and user are being reappraised continuously. The management of these complex transitions is clearly general management's responsibility.

General Management

The broad task of general management is to ensure that appropriate structures, systems, and management processes are in place for ensuring that the overall needs of the organization are met. As IT assumes an increasingly visible role within an organization, executives' ability and interest in playing this role are a function of both their comfort with IT and their perception of its strategic importance to the firm as a whole. Since many have reached their positions with little exposure to IT issues or with exposure to radically different types of IT issues, they are often ill-equipped to assume this responsibility. It is important to note that much of this book is aimed at helping general managers assume a more active role in managing the information resource of the firm. As a new generation of managers with more experience and higher comfort levels with IT take on increasing responsibility, we expect more general managers will take a more active role.

In summary, as each group's perspective and attitudes evolve, some problems are solved while new ones arise. Managing the changing roles and relationships is one of the most complex issues facing all three groups as they attempt to harness the power of IT in the 1990s.

Notes

1. D. Copeland and J. McKenney, "Airline Reservations Systems: Lessons from History," *Management Information Systems Quarterly* 12, no. 2 (1988), p. 352.
2. R. Huber, "How Continental Bank Outsourced Its 'Crown Jewels,'" *Harvard Business Review*, January–February 1993, p. 121–29.
3. In the mid-1990s, few firms can be found for which IT is not strategic; however, the relative degree of strategic importance does continue to influence IT investment and management strategies.
4. Projects that involve integration across technology platforms are usually large, high-risk, and costly; in addition, success often depends on substantial organizational and work-related change.
5. International Technology Group, *Cost of Computing: Comparative Study of Mainframe and PC/LAN Installations* (Mountain View, CA, 1994).
6. L. Applegate, "Technology Support for Cooperative Work: A Framework for Introduction and Assimilation in Organizations," *Journal of Organizational Computing* 1, 1 (1991), pp. 11–39.
7. It is worth noting that this list of responsibilities remains with the firm irrespective of whether all or a portion of the system development process and IT operations/management is outsourced. The job of IT and business management is to ensure that those tasks are performed in the most effective and efficient manner, irrespective of where or by whom they are performed.
8. Joint application development is a system development methodology that involves both business users and IT professionals in all parts of the system design, development, and implementation process.

Rapid prototyping refers to the process of building a smaller version of the system that has limited functionality; this allows IT professionals and business users to better define requirements and test key areas of functionality prior to full-scale system development.

9. CASE tools are software programs that help system developers design and code business software. Some of the tools support designers in developing system specifications. Once those specifications are defined in the computer, the CASE tools automatically generate computer code—the instructions that tell a computer what to do—and then check the code for inconsistencies and redundancy. Others help developers, or even end users, design and implement information reporting or decision support systems. CASE tools often embody a specific approach to system development, which makes them more appropriate for some types of projects than for others.

12.2   Imaging Makes the Feeling Mutual*
Timothy Middleton

The elderly widow was extremely annoyed. Twice she had filled out an application to open an account with Twentieth Century Mutual Funds in Kansas City, and twice the account wasn't opened. In desperation she called the fund complex's toll-free customer service line. When she explained her problem to the phone representative, she was astonished to hear that the rep was looking at her two application forms, and that each was incomplete. The missing information was typed into the computer and the account was opened, instantly.

Actually, the telephone rep was looking not at the forms themselves, but at a high-resolution computerized image of them, complete with the envelopes they arrived in. The technology, called imaging, is new for the industry—and new technology is radically changing how responsive mutual fund companies can be when their customers call in.

"In pre-imaging days, it would have taken us time to pull the original documents and get them delivered," says Mary Smith, Twentieth Century's vice president for customer service. "This way we were able to look at it directly, on-line, and do follow-up immediately that otherwise would have taken much longer to do."

No-load mutual funds, which sell their shares directly to the public without sales charges, rely on the telephone to provide the kind of hand-holding that brokers provide in return for their commission. So while it's still possible to land in the voice-mail maze of automated systems—"If you want account balance information, press One"—the trend is toward direct contact with a real human being who is equipped to answer nearly any question you could ask.

"We feel our clients are always going to want the option of talking to a person," notes Bob DiStefano, vice president of information technology for Vanguard Group in Valley Forge, Pa. "And every one of our people has an intelligent workstation."

You can use the telephone to learn an awful lot about a mutual fund, whether you own it already or are just checking it out. With competition among funds at the boiling point, "you're in the driver's seat these days," says Don Phillips, publisher of the Morningstar Mutual Funds newsletter. Vanguard alone is spending upwards of $20 million to modernize the computer systems used by its telephone reps, so they'll have information at their fingertips.

What kind of information? You name it. Among the items available:

- Performance results—not for periods that make the fund look good, but for whatever you specify

- The bio of the fund manager, especially new ones

- Current yield, including the yield on equity funds

---

*From *Newsday* (Nassau and Suffolk Edition), January 9, 1994. © 1994 Timothy Middleton. Reprinted with permission.

- Detailed information on fund costs, including management fees

- The estimated amount of planned distributions

- Tax questions

- How to redeem shares

- Anything available in published form, like prospectuses and annual reports—and updated information on things like changes in major holdings

In fact, few mutual-fund investors take advantage of this abundant information. "Our typical call is for the account balance, or inquiring about a recent trade, or asking for the most recent price," says Ted Lowrie, senior vice president of Fidelity Retail Investor Services. Tax time—defined as now until April 15—is always a peak season.

Responding to customers' calls with useful information takes a prodigious amount of technology. Vanguard's reps have a monitor with a 21-inch, high-resolution screen. It is cabled to a workstation that makes a PC look like a video game, which in turn communicates with two interactive mainframes—one of them the biggest that IBM makes.

Fidelity has five telephone centers around the country. Together they receive 250,000 calls a day, and each of the more than 3,000 telephone reps has immediate access to a host of databases, some containing account information and others, records on the company's 170-plus funds.

With all this technology at their disposal, there's a lot that fund companies could tell you, but won't.

For example, has Jeff Vinik, manager of the Fidelity Magellan Fund, added to his big stake in Ford Motor, which he still owned on Oct. 31?

"We don't want customers calling in to ask what Jeff Vinik is buying today," says Lowrie. So, although Fidelity has the information, it is withheld from phone reps until it's stale. The same is true of some less-sensitive information, like portfolio turnover. "We wouldn't necessarily give that out," Lowrie says.

Twentieth Century is even more guarded. "We don't say when we're getting in and when we're getting out of anything," says Smith. "The only information that's available is the most recent annual or semi-annual report. It's a policy decision."

While you can expect to get answers to your questions 24 hours a day from a giant such as Fidelity or Vanguard or T. Rowe Price, smaller fund complexes, including Twentieth Century, staff the phones only during business hours. That's when all the complexes receive the bulk of their calls, anyway, they point out; before 4 P.M., trades can be executed at that day's closing price.

12.3   Why Invest on the Internet: An Introduction*
Peter G. Crane

A Brief History of Computers and Investing

Confusion in choosing where to invest is ubiquitous. As the amount of information and news affecting the investment world has grown, so has the need for sophisticated electronic tools to keep track of it all. Of course, since the dawn of investing, sophisticated market participants have used computing tools to gain an advantage over the competition. Today's worldwide financial system would be helpless without electronic assistants. But how did this relationship develop over the last 20 years?

Certainly, the large investment banks and trading houses, such as Goldman Sachs, Salomon Brothers, and Merrill Lynch, have had mainframe computers and state-of-the-art equipment tracking the markets for them for decades. The nature of finance—where split seconds and accurate data can mean millions—has kept it on the cutting edge of technology. But only since the dawn of the personal computer in the mid-1980s have the tools needed for extensive technical or fundamental research been available to smaller investors.

Beginning in 1985, discount brokers such as Charles Schwab and Quick & Reilly (who remain at the forefront of technology) began offering discounts for customers who used PCs to place orders. While these discounts also applied to their 800 number "tele-broker" services as well, they established a core user community that pushed for enhancements and the availability of more investment information. The PC, and then the spread of online services, fueled these trends.

Things have come a long way. Charles Schwab recently estimated that approximately 30 to 40 percent of investment trades will be transacted over the Internet within the next few years. At present, estimates of the total percentage of Schwab's trades placed via PCs range up to 25 percent. Commenting on why the companies themselves prefer the Internet over proprietary software, Schwab spokesperson Tom Taggart explains, "The Internet is a lot easier for companies to enhance and change."

In all, experts estimate that almost a million electronic brokerage accounts are now open, either directly through the Internet or via proprietary in-house software. This number will only grow in the coming months. Of the estimated total 60 million brokerage accounts and estimated 135 million mutual fund accounts open in the United States, up to half of these should be able to place transactions online by the end of 1997. And while mutual fund investors have traditionally lagged behind individual brokerage account customers (who trade individual stocks) in adapting to new technology, this is beginning to change.

The spread of mutual funds has coincided with the spread of PC use, so investors have come of age familiar with the benefits (and drawbacks) of electronic investing. Figure

---

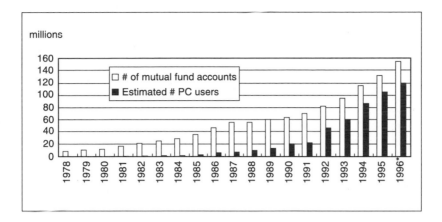

Figure 12.3.1 Mutual fund and PC use skyrocket. The exponential growth in fund PC use parallels fund use. *Author's estimate. Source: 1996 *Mutual Fund Fact Book*, Investment Company Institute, Washington, D.C.

12.3.1 shows the number of mutual fund shareholders plotted against the number of PC users over the last 20 years. As you can see, the growth in each group has been phenomenal over the past 10 years. At these rates of growth, almost every family in the United States will have at least one computer user and one mutual fund within two years (on average).

Using the PC for gathering information and tracking mutual fund investments is a natural fit. Even though volumes have been produced covering either computers or investing, there remains a void between the two subjects. The tremendous growth of the Internet's World Wide Web, in particular, has dramatically increased the availability of market information to the individual investor, while the equally impressive growth of assets invested in no-load mutual fund companies has provided a gigantic target audience. Thus, it is a fortuitous time to take advantage of today's technology.

Investing *with* computers is just now beginning to enter the mainstream, and yet the field has been ill explored. Many books and articles have focused on individual stocks and have missed the greater and safer opportunity in mutual funds.

Unfortunately, as the amount of information on investing has exploded, so has the potential for danger. Most of the investment recommendations in newspapers, magazines, and newsletters are written by self-interested parties. The writer often has investments in either the company or fund group, and the publisher often has advertising relationships with investment companies. Even though it is impossible to avoid all conflicts of investment advice, you should always be aware of the potential for self-interested commentary.

The Explosion of No-Load Funds on the Web

While mutual funds have seen incredible growth in the past 20 years, the biggest gains have come among the no-load funds—those that do not charge a sales commission. The spread of 401(k) plans also has been a major factor in this growth; employers have moved toward giving their workers more autonomy. In the interest of serving this market as well, we will concentrate on the biggest no-load fund groups—Fidelity Investments, The Vanguard Group, and Charles Schwab.

Although I do mention Web sites involving full-service brokerage firms and "load" funds, this group has a much lower profile due to the "do-it-yourself" nature of the Web. Though there are plenty of counterexamples, which we'll visit, you'll probably notice that most of the advertisements on the Web are from these no-load companies. The appealing demographic qualities of Webgoers are not lost on the no-load companies; they're self-starting, wealthier, and younger than the general populace.

The sheer number of mutual funds, however, has made it almost impossible to choose which ones are right for you. The last thing investors need is for the Web to give them even more choices. It doesn't have to be that confusing.

For the gigantic no-load mutual fund companies—Fidelity, Vanguard, and Schwab—the Web represents their dreams come true: no worries about mailing costs, an affluent, self-reliant clientele, and no toll-free phone bills the size of Rhode Island. The Web represents their ultimate sales tool. Thus it's no surprise that these companies are moving online *en masse*.

Conveniently enough, the only thing these financial powerhouses can't provide is specific investment advice and information, so the Web is a natural. The educational areas alone on the major no-load fund company sites have enough information to keep one reading for years. No single investment advisor or source can compete with the quality and comprehensiveness of these.

No-load mutual fund companies jumped onto the Web early, and they're there to stay. They've also moved forcefully onto the online services—America Online, CompuServe, and Prodigy. But the tremendous growth of the Web, in particular, has dramatically increased the availability of all types of market information to the individual investor.

What do computers and mutual funds have to do with each other, you ask? First of all, both have experienced tremendous growth over the past decade. Neither product existed at the turn of the century, and yet these two industries now affect practically everyone on the planet. More personal computers are being sold than television sets in America per year, while the average American household now owns shares in at least one mutual fund. However, both products remain mysterious to the average consumer.

The World Wide Web sites of fund groups—Fidelity, Vanguard, and Schwab, plus the upstart electronic deep-discount brokers—and of news providers and financial institutions are covered in depth. Mutual funds are a good choice because of their inherent advantages over all other investment types—their safety (through diversity), lower costs (through economies of scale), and ease of use.

No-load mutual fund families are the number one investment advice source on the Web. Though they are prohibited from giving specific investment advice, they provide plenty of helpful information. They make it easy for you to be your own investment advisor, attain better performance, and feel more comfortable about your financial situation.

Remember, the goal of this book is to give you the ability to harness the computer is order to simplify you finances, your investing, and your life. To help you avoid information overload, to avoid scam artists, and most of all to save time in entering the world of online investments, this book has been organized so that experienced investors and experienced Internet browsers both may move quickly past any introductory material.

12.4 Taking Mutual Funds Online*

Wesley R. Iversen

For the investment services industry, it's a happy coincidence that the phenomenal growth of the Internet has come during one of the strongest and most persistent bull markets in history. The confluence of trends has been a major factor in the rapid rise of Web-based stock trading, creating a fast-growing business for a widening cast of aggressive, on-line discount brokerage firms.

In step with the stock market's advance has come tremendous expansion in the U.S. mutual funds industry. Total mutual fund assets have more than tripled since 1990, rising to $3.7 trillion at the end of this year's first quarter, says the Investment Company Institute, a mutual funds industry trade group. The number of shareholder accounts, meanwhile, more than doubled between year end 1990 and year end 1996, rising to 151 million, the ICI says.

Unlike their brethren in the discount brokerage business, however, the mutual fund management companies have been slow to move transactions to the Web. Indeed, it was not a fund company, but rather Jack White & Co., a San Diego discount brokerage, that was the first to offer mutual fund sales on the Internet in March 1996. And by the time that Twentieth Century Funds (now American Century Investments) became the first funds management complex to roll out fund transactions on the Web last September, a number of other discount brokerages were already also hawking mutual funds on the Net. That group included San Francisco-based Charles Schwab & Co., the industry's largest discount brokerage, whose popular OneSource mutual fund supermarket has seen rapid growth lately in Web-based fund transactions.

Here They Come

Now, however, there are indications that the mutual fund industry may be ready to make a broad-based leap into Internet mutual fund transactions. Each of the top three no-load fund companies— Fidelity Investments, The Vanguard Group and T. Rowe Price—have recently rolled out Web-based account access and direct transaction capabilities for their retail shareholders and 401(k) plan participants. The technology allows shareholders the ability to buy, sell and exchange funds within a fund company on the Web. And where the big players go, the rest of the industry is sure to follow, industry sources say.

By various estimates, more than three quarters of all mutual fund management companies now have an Internet presence, although many are still using their Web sites primarily for posting sales and marketing information. In one recent survey of more than 100 fund companies by First Data Investment Services Group, a mutual funds transaction processing firm, 94% of fund company respondents had an Internet connection, 81% were using the Web to publish marketing material and 56% were using the Web for some kind of customer service, such as downloading prospectuses and electronic mail. Only 6% offered account access or on-line transactions to their retail customers.

But by 1998 at the latest, many believe that Internet account access and transactional capabilities will become a competitive requirement for fund companies. "I think most of the leaders will be there by the end of this year, and once that happens, then everybody else will have to have it," says Iang Jeon, vice president of electronic commerce at Boston-based Liberty Financial Companies Inc., whose Stein Roe & Farnham mutual fund operating company went transactional on the Web in late January.

Most agree that the Internet holds vast potential as a low-cost distribution channel for the mutual funds industry. The cost of delivering a fund prospectus electronically from a Web site amounts to less than a dollar, for example, compared to a cost of around $8 to process a telephone request and deliver a paper prospectus through the mail, points out Robert A. DiStefano, senior vice president, Information Technology Division, for Vanguard, based in Valley Forge, Pa. Similar savings will come in other phases of the customer service process, say industry sources.

But for some fund companies, the migration to cyberspace could also prove painful. If the fears of some industry officials pan out, one downside could be more volatility and higher costs for stock funds, caused by Web-empowered investors with a penchant for frequently trading in and out of funds.

Like It or Not

Whether the fund companies like it or not, some say, technology is on the way that will allow investors to execute direct electronic cross-fund exchanges on the Web-moving assets at the click of a mouse button straight from the coffers of one fund complex to those of another. On-line investors already have something close to that capability in the mutual fund supermarkets, though exchanges are limited to participating funds, and monies redeemed from one fund can typically not be reinvested into another fund until the next business day.

Indeed, most agree that as Internet fund trading moves toward the mainstream, it is certain to make mutual funds a more competitive arena. The Web puts a wealth of funds information at the fingertips of investors. And the powerful search-and-sort tools available at a growing number of funds-oriented Web sites will enable investors to more easily find funds that meet their exact investment criteria, sources note. It's a capability that some say will level the playing field, allowing small mutual funds with strong track records to compete more easily against funds from the better-known industry giants.

"It's going to put a lot of pressure on the performance of the bigger funds, because if somebody's able to search through thousands of funds, it's not necessarily the biggest funds that are going to come out on top when the search comes back," observes William L. Burnham, senior research analyst, electronic commerce, for Piper Jaffray Inc., a Minneapolis investment firm.

One early factor that slowed the fund industry's migration toward Web transactions was concern over security. But with advances in technology, and as consumers and fund companies alike gain more experience with the Net, the security issue is becoming less of a hurdle, sources say.

"Certainly, security was the number-one issue that we had with launching our service. But we went through an extensive amount of testing and a lot of back-end work, and we certainly wouldn't launch anything that we didn't feel was secure for our shareholders," says Charlene S. Vedros, marketing manager, electronic commerce, at American Century, Kansas City, Mo.

But even when fund company management is comfortable with Web transaction security, some consumers still need to be convinced. Mark J. Mitchell, marketing manager for interactive services at Baltimore-based T. Rowe Price, notes that before his company launched Web transactional service in April, "we were getting tons of e-mail from people demanding and asking for Internet access to their accounts." More than 65% of T. Rowe Price shareholders own PCs. But Mitchell says the company has learned through focus groups that while e-mail traffic may reflect the views of its more computer-savvy consumers, it is not necessarily representative of all of T. Rowe Price's computer-enabled shareholders.

"What we're hearing is that lots of people are comfortable getting basic fund and pricing information, but they're not as comfortable with conducting transactions," Mitchell says. "So I think that one of our challenges is to help people increase their comfort level in accessing and using these systems."

Third-Party Help

Security issues were a priority at First Data Investment Services Group when the processing company developed new Internet transaction technology for use by its 100-plus mutual fund company customers, says Robyn R. Thibodeau, director of electronic commerce for the Westboro, Mass., firm.

The First Data system, introduced in April, allows fund management companies to add shareholder account access and transaction capabilities to their Web sites. By clicking an icon on their fund company's home page, shareholders can be hyperlinked to First Data's server, which performs the requested transactions "The screens that we develop are customized for each management company. So from the shareholders' perspective, it's seamless. They don't even realize they've moved out of the management company site," Thibodeau explains.

Security features of the First Data system include proprietary encryption technology at both the application and network levels, as well as a requirement that shareholders' Web browser software be equipped with 128-bit encryption Secure Socket Layer technology, Thibodeau says. Customers gain account access by using a social security number/personal identification number routine. The system conforms to specifications developed by an ICI insurance underwriting committee covering mutual fund on-line transaction systems, Thibodeau adds. This means that fund companies using the First Data system will be able to obtain insurance through an ICI insurance subsidiary covering losses caused by certain types of on-line transaction fraud, she says.

As of mid-April, one fund management company—Wright Investor Services Fund, in Bridgeport, Conn.—had signed up to use the First Data Web transaction service.

Thibodeau expects that about 15 fund complexes will be running with the system by the end of the year....

For many smaller fund companies, the use of technology developed by a third-party vendor will likely be the most economical way to provide access and transactions on the Web. Winters declines to provide FAN pricing information. But Thibodeau says that up-front set-up and customization charges for the First Data technology will typically run from $2,000 to $5,000; operation costs will be on a per-transaction basis, priced at less than 50 cents each for both inquiries and financial transactions; an annual maintenance fee will run from $20,000 to $50,000, depending on options.

Spending Millions

With infrastructure costs that can run into the millions of dollars for an extensive Web site with transactional capabilities, only the large fund companies can afford to develop their own. Both Fidelity and Vanguard are going that route. "We see this as an important service to our clients going forward that we know is going to be around for a long time," says Vanguard's DiStefano. "We wanted to control the quality and the security of that service, so we chose to build it ourselves," he explains.

Vanguard entered the on-line world with a site on AOL in January 1995 and followed with a Web site on the Internet in December that year. From the beginning, Vanguard has emphasized investor education at its on-line venues. "We opened the Web site on day one with about 1,200 pages of content and it has grown to about 9,000 pages now," DiStefano says. The company launched account access for shareholders on AOL in May 1996 and at its Web site in January this year; Vanguard planned to launch transactional capability on its Web site for both its retail and 401(k) institutional customers in May.

On-line shareholder response has been strong, says DiStefano. "We're seeing a rapid acceptance by people who want to register for access, and it's happening still both on AOL and on the Web." On-line contacts now account for more than 15% of total client contacts received by Vanguard, he adds. That compares to 52% made through automated voice response systems, and 33% through contacts with human Vanguard associates.

Like others, DiStefano sees great long-term potential in the Net as a low-cost service and distribution channel. "Vanguard, and the direct marketers in general, are centralized service organizations with an international client base and a really complicated message. When you add to that Vanguard's interest in low cost, you really couldn't invent a better service and education medium than the Internet," DiStefano observes.

Despite its positive impacts, however, on-line technology does not get top grades all around at Vanguard. John C. Bogle, Vanguard chairman and founder, has recently criticized some aspects of the technology.

In a widely publicized speech in April, Bogle said that there is no evidence that the vast amount of information on the Web has helped investors do a better job of picking funds. And he decried a trend, attributed in part to the rise of on-line transaction technology, by which investors are abandoning their once-held view of mutual funds as long-term investments, but instead now think of funds more like stocks to be traded in and out of more frequently.

Bogle was particularly critical of mutual fund supermarkets, which he referred to as "the great fund casino—the no transaction-fee mutual fund marketplace in which funds can buy a computer billboard and permit shareholders to turn their shares over rapidly and without apparent commissions." Though the supermarkets may charge no transaction fee to shareholders for trading, the "hidden" cost is the annual fee of 25 to 35 basis points paid by the fund companies to the supermarket on the assets of funds held there—a cost that is ultimately borne by all of the funds' shareholders, Bogle said.

Supermarket Mania

For consumers, a mutual fund supermarket provides the convenience of one-stop shopping, offering an array of mutual funds from multiple management companies along with consolidated record keeping and statements. And while the supermarkets have been around for a number of years, some see the rise of the Internet adding fuel to the already successful concept. The supermarkets "have been gaining tremendous momentum as a product, and moving that onto the Internet just makes it all the easier for customers to select among different mutual funds and to rank and rate them," says Piper Jaffray's Burnham.

A number of on-line brokerage operations, including Fidelity and Jack White, have set up fund supermarkets. But Charles Schwab's OneSource is by far the largest and most visible of the group. Started in 1992, OneSource fund assets have more than tripled since year end 1994, rising from $12.5 billion to $41 billion at the end of this year's first quarter. The $15 billion that flowed into OneSource during 1996 was more than triple the amount of funds in all the other supermarkets combined, points out James Marks, vice president, equity research, for Credit Suisse First Boston Corp., in New York.

Through OneSource, Schwab currently offers no-transaction-fee trading in more than 720 no load funds from 87 fund families, including its own Schwab-managed funds. The discount brokerage also offers fee-based trades on an additional 700 funds that are not part of the OneSource program.

Schwab makes funds available through various channels, including its 243 branches, its touch-tone telephone and direct connect PC trading systems and—since last July, on the Schwab Web site. OneSource fund trading lately has been picking up rapidly on the Web, says Jeffrey M. Lyons, Schwab senior vice president, mutual fund marketing. By mid-April, more than 5% of OneSource transactions were executed on the Web, up from around 1% last November, Lyons says.

The OneSource site provides one-stop shopping for consumers, including information and tools to rank and evaluate funds, which can then be purchased, redeemed or exchanged on the site. But Lyons says he doesn't believe the supermarket concept encourages frequent in-and-out trading of funds. "We certainly haven't seen that kind of behavior exhibited with our investors," he says. In fact, OneSource rules discourage frequent trading by imposing transaction fees on funds held for less than 90 days, Lyons notes.

"The Internet is obviously going to make things easier for investors, but I think by empowering investors, there are going to be more upsides than downsides," Lyons concludes.

Credit Suisse's Marks notes that the success of OneSource has put many fund companies in a difficult position. Even though funds stand to pick up additional assets through their participation in the program, they do so at the expense of losing hard-won brand equity to OneSource. "After all, it is OneSource that brought the fund to the consumer's attention, and it is OneSource that the consumer will return to with more funds to invest or to move existing funds," Marks says in a recent research report on Schwab.

While perceptive fund sponsors realize the risk, the success of the OneSource program leaves them with little choice but to participate; the alternative is to risk losing market share to competitors who do participate in the program, Mark says. "It's dancing with the devil. But you've got to dance," Marks observes. "There's no other place to go."

Salvation

Despite the fears by some that OneSource could get between the fund management companies and their customers, Schwab's Lyons says that participation in OneSource and other supermarkets has been a salvation for some small fund companies. By providing better visibility and distribution, among other things, the supermarkets have allowed the smaller companies to remain viable against their larger competitors, Lyons says.

In agreement is Cebra Graves, editor of the Morningstar.net Web site operated by Morningstar Inc., the Chicago mutual funds research company. In the early 1990s, mutual fund industry experts were predicting an era of consolidation, says Graves. Conventional wisdom at the time was that the large fund companies would swallow the smaller ones in a struggle for survival, and that the boutique fund companies would disappear entirely, Graves says. "But the Internet and the fund supermarkets have changed that completely, where now, even the smallest fund companies—if they can put together a winning record—are going to get plenty of assets in the door," Graves observes.

While Schwab today has grabbed a healthy lead as a one-stop shopping spot for mutual funds on the Web, Graves expects to see others making a run for the business. "Schwab right now has the upper hand. But they're going to be facing a lot of competition five years from now from some big players like Intuit and Microsoft," Graves predicts....

Consumer Power

In the end, the migration of mutual fund companies to the Internet may mean that individual investors will have a greater role in determining the fund industry's direction—as well as the winners and losers. In recent years, some power has already flowed from the fund management companies as a group to the distribution companies such as Schwab and others that cater to investors' desire for convenience and choice, as well as low cost. And some believe that the move into cyberspace will only accelerate the trend.

One case in point could involve the issue of cross-fund exchanges between different fund management companies. At DST Systems, Winters says that his company currently has no plans to add the capability to its FAN system for the Internet, in part because mutual fund complexes aren't asking for it. "I don't think we have a lot of fund groups that would be real interested in offering the ability to their shareholders to redeem out of their fund family and go to another fund family," he notes.

But at First Data Investment Services Group, Thibodeau says that her company plans to build a cross-fund exchange capability into its Internet transaction product. The reason: First Data research shows that consumers will demand the capability.

Jeffrey A. Viezel, for one, is a believer. As director of electronic distribution for New York fund management company The Dreyfus Corp., Viezel says his company is "actively working" on an Internet mutual funds trading capability. And when the service is launched, the ability to transfer funds from a Dreyfus fund to another company's funds will definitely be among the transactions offered, Viezel says.

"We're going to provide it because it will be easier for our clients to keep their assets under Dreyfus." The capability will be offered under The Lion Account, a new Dreyfus all-in-one investment account with services including check writing, electronic bill payment, access to financial planning advice and stock trading, as well as to mutual fund investing.

"If clients want to keep their money in The Lion Account but switch it from a Dreyfus to a non-Dreyfus fund, I want to make it easy for them to do that," Viezel says, noting that the alternative is far less palatable. "If you don't give them that ability," he figures, "they're going to wind up taking all their money out and moving it to another company that will."

12.5   Ex-Novell CIO Leads Franklin*
Robert Sales

With another merger in the works, Franklin Resources' CIO Gordon Jones is sizing up technology for the mutual fund giant.

Back in the old days, when financial institutions used to value stocks and shares by hand, Gordon Jones was there, toiling away as a trust administrator at Lloyds Bank in London. Now, as chief information officer of mutual fund giant Franklin Resources Inc., Jones has worldwide responsibility for all of his firm's voice, video and data communications. "We've got a global [communications] network that spans from Moscow to South Africa to Taiwan.... So I do appreciate computers these days," quips Jones, a 49-year-old husband and father of two.

On top of his CIO title, Jones is also vice president of information services and technology at Franklin Resources—the holding company that oversees Franklin Templeton Investor Services, among other firms. What's more, Jones, who holds an MBA in management studies from England's Buckingham College of Higher Education, may soon have his technology oversight significantly broadened.

At press time, Franklin—which merged its Franklin Funds unit with Templeton in 1992—was on the verge of acquiring Heine Securities, an aggressive manager of mutual funds based in Short Hills, N.J. Jones, who says the deal is expected to be completed "any day now," describes Heine as a domestic equities specialist. "We've been very strong on the international [equities] scene with Templeton and very strong in fixed income securities with Franklin. So this [acquisition] complements [our] portfolio admirably," says Jones.

When the deal for Heine is finalized, it will provide yet another obstacle for Jones to hurdle in his quest to deploy a "seamless" technology environment. "The challenge these days is to provide connectivity behind the workstation, irrespective of where the particular information is—[such as] what box its on," he says.

While transparent access to information is a goal, Jones' says Franklin takes a cautious approach towards implementing emerging technologies—only doing so when it can improve service levels and/or reduce costs for its business units. "I think that we cannot be cavalier in technology, using unproven software," says Jones, a resident of Danvile, Calif., who enjoys playing soccer in his spare time. "But ... we've got to really evaluate all areas of the business that can benefit from technology ... [because] IT is becoming an enabler of making businesses more effective."

With 27 years of experience in the computer industry, Jones knows a little something about what makes businesses tick. In fact, in 1992—during his five-year stint as CIO and vice president of IS at networking vendor Novell Inc.—he was ranked as one of the top 100 CIOs by CIO Magazine.

---

*From *Wall Street & Technology*, December 1996. Reprinted with permission.

Jones worked at Novell until February 1995, when he took over as CIO of Franklin. Prior to joining Novell, Jones spent 14 years as a vice president at Lex Service Group, a multi-national electronics and automobile distributor.

According to Jones, those lengthy apprenticeships helped him develop a high technology I.Q. and an international business presence—attributes which he utilizes while making everyday decisions in his current post. "In the last 14 years, I've either reported to presidents of companies or CFOs. So I'm always looking at IT investments and what they can do for the business."

Strategic Building

One of the IT issues Jones constantly ponders is whether to build Franklin's applications internally or buy them from third-party vendors. "We do very rigorous make versus buy decisions," says Jones. "We want to focus our internal development on the features that provide [us with] a strategic edge." Among the applications that Franklin develops internally are research and trading systems.

On the other hand, Franklin relies on off-the-shelf systems to support its general ledger and portfolio accounting and management system needs. Currently, the firm makes use of systems supplied by a pair of portfolio accounting vendors: MaxData Corp. and Colonial. However, Jones says that Franklin is evaluating a variety of systems to standardize on one portfolio accounting platform in the not-too-distant future. "We have an initiative under way to move to a single portfolio accounting system ... and we're looking at different vendors at the moment," he says.

Franklin is still in the process of defining its "unique" portfolio accounting requirements, says Jones, and expects to make its selection within the next six months. Jones, who says Franklin has narrowed the vendor field down to "a short list," declines to specify which vendors are in the running.

But whoever snatches up the Franklin portfolio accounting contract will score a huge victory. The contract would call for the winning vendor to support a minimum of 500 users, with room for growth. Franklin currently has in the neighborhood of $125 billion in assets under management, but Jones says that figure will rise to roughly $160 billion when the firm finalizes its purchase of Heine Securities. Meanwhile, other vendors who figure prominently in Franklin's future technology plans include the tandem of AT&T/Lucent Technologies. "Since I've been on board, we've invested over $6 million in AT&T/Lucent [telephone] switches and voice mail," says Jones, a member of AT&T/Lucent's customer advisory board.

Besides making use of AT&T/Lucent's PBXs and voice mail systems, Franklin also plans to roll out the vendors so-called telephony server application programming interface. This system, which connects PBXs to servers, will allow users to "point and click" with a mouse on their computer screens and have any call routed to their phone sets "within one second," according to Jones.

In addition to purchasing a variety of third-party applications, Franklin also outsources a handful of its technology functions. Jones says that since he came on board, Franklin has outsourced its cabling, hardware desktop support and some of its software desktop support. Jones says he prefers to think of outsourcing as a "partneringtype" relationship in which a firm is leveraging its "core, fundamental" technology support with a vendor's experties. "I hate the word outsourcing, because it sort of implies that people are going to lose their jobs," he says.

A Mixed Environment

... Unlike some of his CIO contemporaries, Jones sees a future for mainframes at his firm. The fact that mainframes provide "more horsepower and higher bandwidth," Jones says, is one of the primary reasons Franklin has not migrated to a fully client/server architecture.

"We do still use mainframes because of the sheer volume of shareholder accounts. We've got over 4 million accounts in our mainframe," says Jones.

While mainframes support Franklin's shareholder accounting systems, other areas—such as sales automation and reporting—are supported by a client/server architecture. And Jones says that Franklin's mainframe and client/server systems work "in concert" with each other.

During his typical 65-hour plus work week, Jones—who says he tries to "free up Saturdays" for his family—also must figure out a way to recruit and retain talented technology staff, all within the parameters of a limited budget.

Franklin's annual technology budget, Jones says, is roughly $80 million—considerably less than budgets of certain rivals, such as Fidelity Investments. "But I've always found throughout my career that it's not how much you spend, but how wisely you spend on technology," say Jones.

Class Exercises: **Using the Internet to Benefit Shareholders**

Although changes in technology affect all areas of mutual fund complexes—from accounting to investment research and trading to shareholder communication—the most visible change to fund shareholders in recent years is probably the establishment of Web sites and use of the Internet.

While it is easy to establish a Web site, creating a successful one requires careful thinking about format and content. A visually appealing site that lacks information is practically useless; a site filled with information that is extremely difficult to navigate is unappealing. In the last few years, mutual fund sponsors have progressed from merely establishing a presence on the Internet to creating dynamic, informative sites that seek to attract and retain investors through investment tools and delivery of services.

This chapter contains two class exercises that focus on the mutual fund industry's use of the Internet. The first requires the use of a computer to evaluate Web sites of fund complexes. The second, which does not require a computer, involves the design of an Internet-based system for dissemination of fund information. Both exercises should help you better understand how mutual fund sponsors utilize technology—in particular the Internet—to better serve shareholders. The exercises should also help you understand how advances in technology present new opportunities (and sometimes challenges) for the mutual fund industry.

12.6   Exercise 1: Finding Fund Information through a Web Site

This exercise encourages you to examine how a mutual fund sponsor uses an established site on the World Wide Web to communicate information about the marketplace as well as its products and services to its existing and potential customers. In particular, you will explore the Web pages maintained by several mutual fund sponsors to determine how a diversified mutual fund complex attempts to use the Web as an effective mechanism to service its retail and institutional customers in a manner that both reduces customer servicing costs and serves as a useful marketing tool.

To visit a Web site, you will need Internet access capability from your personal computer with a modem, either through an on-line service (such as America Online or The Microsoft Network) or a direct Internet Service Provider. Currently (1997), if you plan to view personal account information or trade stocks or mutual funds, you will require an Internet browser that supports at least 40-bit (but preferably 128-bit) encryption. The current versions of the most popular browsers that you might purchase from a retail outlet in the United States, or receive from your Internet access provider, usually support such encryption levels. Once you have gained Internet access, most fund sponsor addresses (or *URLs*) are in the following format: www.sponsorname.com

---

In-Class Discussion Questions for Class Exercise 1

You are in the position of an individual seeking information about several competing funds and fund complexes. After browsing through Web sites of several mutual fund sponsors, you should be prepared to answer the following:

1. *Fund comparisons*   From information available through the fund advisers' Web sites, please answer questions about the following funds: Putnam Fund for Growth and Income, Fidelity Growth and Income, and Vanguard Windsor:
   a) How can each of these funds be purchased? Do they have sales loads or 12b-1 fees?
   b) Which fund has the lowest annual fees? Which fund has the highest? What are the main differences?
   c) Which fund has the highest total return for 1 year? 5 years? 10 years? Would you reach a different conclusion if loads were taken into account?
2. *Web site comparison*   Based on what you find while navigating through several fund sponsors' Web sites (assigned or chosen at your discretion), discuss the following:
   a) Were there any navigational features—e.g., hyperlinks or icons allowing easy movement from screen to screen—that made one site stand out from the others? Were any sites particularly difficult to obtain information from, and if so, why?
   b) Based on information available on the sites you visited, is the quality of information provided high enough to enable you to make a fund purchase decision? If not, what else is needed?

    c) What tools are made available through the Web sites to help you establish a general savings plan? Are there specific tools available for college planning? For retirement? For other needs?

3. *Electronic commerce*   Fund sponsors originally established Web sites for electronic delivery of educational information. With this in mind, please answer the following questions:

    a) What is the primary function(s) of mutual fund Web sites today?

    b) What are the transaction capabilities of these sites? What are the security issues that mutual fund sponsors or investors face in transacting over the Web?

    c) What types of informational or transactional capabilities are *not* available today through a mutual fund Web site? What on-line capabilities should be available for mutual fund investors in the future?

12.7   Exercise 2: Delivery of Disclosure Documents On-line

Federal securities laws require that mutual fund shareholders receive annual prospectus revisions as well as annual and semiannual reports. In addition, federal securities laws require that shareholders receive notification of material amendments to prospectuses.

SEC Releases in October 1995 and May 1996 set forth guidance on how a mutual fund may satisfy its delivery requirements electronically. The releases contain examples that illustrate and provide guidance on how to deliver disclosure documents on-line.

In this exercise, you are an employee in the electronic marketing department at a large mutual fund sponsor, Company ABC, that sells funds directly to investors and has a site on the Internet containing mutual fund advertising as well as servicing and educational information. The head of electronic marketing realizes that significant cost savings can be realized if Company ABC is able to deliver disclosure documents to shareholders over the Internet instead of mailing the documents to shareholders. Your boss asked you to lead a project to design a system so that Company ABC can deliver mutual fund disclosure documents to shareholders over its Web site.

You should keep in mind that in order to comply with the delivery requirements, the releases state that the fund sponsor must provide (i) timely and adequate notice to shareholders that the disclosure documents are available; (ii) comparable access to the disclosure documents as provided in paper form (e.g., providing continuous accessibility or the opportunity for retention and making paper versions available); and (iii) evidence that the disclosure documents were actually delivered to the shareholder (e.g., obtaining the shareholder's informed consent either manually or electronically).

In-Class Discussion Questions for Exercise 2

After reviewing the attached excerpts and examples from the October 1995 and May 1996 SEC Releases, you should be prepared to explain how you would set up a program to deliver the following documents to shareholders on your Web site:

1. Annual fund prospectus revisions;
2. Annual and semiannual fund reports; and
3. An unscheduled material change to the fund prospectus resulting from the addition of an annual account fee or a redemption fee.

12.8   Examples from Release no. IC-21399 (October 1995)

(43)   Example: A fund places its prospectus on its Internet Web site and revises the electronic version whenever the prospectus is modified. The fund materially amends the prospectus and decides to send a postcard or e-mail to persons to whom the prospectus has been delivered through electronic means or who have consented to electronic delivery notifying them of the availability of the amended prospectus.

Response: This procedure provides for delivery of the prospectus to those who have consented and to those to whom the prospectus has been previously delivered (if the fund expects those persons to be able to receive the amended prospectus). Alternatively, the fund could choose to satisfy its prospectus delivery requirements by sending a paper copy of the amended prospectus to investors in the fund, including investors who consented to receive documents electronically.

(46)   Example: A fund transmits annual and semi-annual reports over an electronic bulletin board system. The fund makes the current versions of these materials available and informs investors who have consented to electronic delivery of this fact. The fund provides separate notification each time a shareholder report is posted by including the notification in the preceding quarterly account statement or shareholder newsletter. The notice informs investors of a date by which the report will be available.

Response: Notification to shareholders in a statement or newsletter delivered within the preceding quarter would be considered sufficient notice under Section 30(d) of the Investment Company Act[1] and the rules thereunder to constitute delivery.

(50)   Example: A fund provides its prospectus, annual and semi-annual reports through an Internet Web site. After one year, the fund decides to terminate the Web site.

Response: The fund may cease making its prospectus available through the Web site as soon as the fund no longer plans to rely on electronic delivery for satisfying its prospectus delivery requirements[2] Generally, an annual or semi-annual report should be available until superseded by a later report. The fund in this example could terminate the posting of the most recent report when it is superseded by a new one, or earlier if it provides a replacement paper copy to shareholders who received the report electronically.

Notes

1.   15 U.S.C. 80a-29(d).
2.   Continued sales of fund shares or delivery of sales literature or application forms to investors who had received the prospectus electronically would require delivery of paper prospectus to those investors. Funds should consider whether paper prospectuses should also be sent to other investors (e.g., recent purchasers).

12.9   Examples and Excerpt from Release no. IC-21945 (May 1996)

IV   Additional Securities Act, Exchange Act, and Investment Company Act Examples

The October Interpretive Release included a series of examples illustrating the general concepts set forth earlier in that release in order to provide guidance in applying those concepts to specific facts and circumstances. The Commission is publishing here the following, additional examples to provide further guidance and illustration. These examples are based on questions that have been raised with the staff by industry representatives since the publication of the October Interpretive Release. Any party (whether or not a registered investment company) may look to these examples for guidance....

(5)   Example: A fund places its prospectus on its site on the World Wide Web or some other electronic system. Shareholders provide a written, revocable consent to receive prospectuses electronically through the system. The consent informs shareholders that the current version of each prospectus will be available continuously on the system and that the fund will use the quarterly account statement or quarterly newsletter as the means of notification of prospectus amendments. It also states that another means of notification may be used, but only after shareholders have been notified of the change by the then current means of notification.[1] The fund replaces its prospectus with an annual amendment updating the fund's financial information and making other changes.[2] The fund has provided notification that the prospectus will be updated by including notification in the preceding account statement or shareholder newsletter; the notification provides the approximate date on which the amendment will be available. A subsequent amendment to the fund's prospectus reflects the addition of a redemption fee. Notification of the prospectus amendment has been included in the preceding statement or newsletter.[3]

Response: Just as the use of a newsletter or statement in example 46 in the October Interpretive Release constituted sufficient notice for effective delivery of the semi-annual reports required under the Investment Company Act of 1940, the use of a newsletter or statement here would constitute sufficient notice for effective delivery with respect to the scheduled prospectus update....

A.   General

This discussion is intended to complement the discussion in the October Interpretive Release and to provide general guidance concerning issues under the Exchange and Advisers Acts. The Commission believes that broker-dealers, transfer agents, and investment advisers should be able to satisfy their obligations under the federal securities laws to deliver information required under the Covered Delivery Requirements by electronic distribution. The framework set forth in the October Interpretive Release is applicable to such electronic distribution.

In the October Interpretive Release, the Commission stated that it would view information distributed through electronic means as satisfying the delivery or transmission requirements of the federal securities laws if such distribution results in the delivery to the intended recipients of substantially equivalent information as such recipients would have if the required information were delivered to them in paper form.[4] The Commission is not specifying the electronic medium or source that broker-dealers, transfer agents, and investment advisers may use.

Like paper documents, electronically delivered documents must be prepared and delivered in a manner consistent with the federal securities laws. Regardless of whether information is delivered in paper form or by electronic means, it should convey all material and required information. If a paper document is required to present information in a certain order, for instance, then the information delivered electronically should be in substantially the same order.[5]

Moreover, regardless of whether information is delivered in paper or electronic form, broker-dealers and investment advisers must reasonably supervise firm personnel with a view to preventing violations.[6] Thus, broker-dealers and investment advisers should consider the need for systems and procedures to deter or detect misconduct by firm personnel in connection with the delivery of information, whether by electronic or paper means.[7]

The Commission believes that, as a matter of policy, a person who has a right to receive a document under the federal securities laws and chooses to receive it electronically, should be provided with the information in paper form whenever specifically requesting paper.[8]

In the October Interpretive Release, the Commission discussed issues of notice and access that should be considered in determining whether the legal requirements pertaining to delivery or transmission of documents have been satisfied,[9] and stated that persons using electronic delivery of information should have reason to believe that any electronic means so selected will result in the satisfaction of the delivery requirements.[10] The Commission believes that broker-dealers, transfer agents, and investment advisers should apply the same considerations in using electronic media to satisfy their delivery obligations under the Covered Delivery Requirements.

1 Notice

Broker-dealers, transfer agents, and investment advisers providing information electronically should consider the extent to which electronic communication provides timely and adequate notice that such information is available electronically.[11] When information is delivered on paper through the postal mail, recipients most likely will be made aware that they have received information that they may wish to review and, therefore, separate notice is not necessary. Information transmitted through electronic media, however, may not always provide a similar likelihood of notice that information has been sent that the recipient may wish to review.[12] Broker-dealers, transfer agents, and investment advisers, therefore, should consider whether it is necessary to supplement the electronic communication with another communication that would provide notice similar to that provided by delivery in paper through the postal mail.

2 Access

The Commission believes that customers, securities holders, and clients who are provided information through electronic delivery from broker-dealers, transfer agents, and investment advisers should have access to that information comparable to that which would be provided if the information were delivered in paper form. Thus, the use of a particular medium should not be so burdensome that intended recipients cannot effectively access the information provided. Also, persons to whom information is sent electronically should have an opportunity to retain the information through the selected medium or have ongoing access equivalent to personal retention.[13]

3 Evidence to Show Delivery

Providing information through postal mail provides reasonable assurance that the delivery requirements of the federal securities laws have been satisfied. The Commission believes that broker-dealers, transfer agents, and investment advisers similarly should have reason to believe that electronically delivered information will result in the satisfaction of the delivery requirements under the federal securities laws. Thus, whether using paper or electronic media, broker-dealers, transfer agents, and investment advisers should consider the need to establish procedures to ensure that applicable delivery obligations are met.

Broker-dealers, transfer agents, and investment advisers may be able to evidence satisfaction of delivery obligations, for example, by: (1) obtaining the intended recipient's informed consent[14] to delivery through a specified electronic medium, and ensuring that the recipient has appropriate notice and access, as discussed above; (2) obtaining evidence that the intended recipient actually received the information, such as by an electronic mail return-receipt or by confirmation that the information was assessed, downloaded, or printed;[15] or (3) disseminating information through certain facsimile methods. In order to ensure that information is delivered as intended, broker-dealers, transfer agents, and investment advisers delivering information using either electronic or paper-media should take reasonable precautions to ensure the integrity and security of that information.[16]

Notes

1. A change in means of notification under such circumstances would also be effective in the case of notification of the availability of shareholder reports discussed in example 46 in the October Interpretive Release. October Interpretive Release, *supra* note 1.

2. Under section 10(a)(3) of the Securities Act, a fund that continuously offers its shares would have to amend its prospectus no less frequently than every 16 months in order to include updated financial statements.

3. With *unscheduled* material prospectus amendments for which such advance notice would not be feasible, the fund would need to use other forms of notification such as a postcard or e-mail message. See October Interpretive Release, *supra* note 1, example 43.

4. October Interpretive Release, *supra* note 1, at 53460. See also *supra* example 7.

5. For a discussion of how requirements to present information in a certain order may be applied to documents containing hyperlinks, see example 51 in the October Interpretive Release. *Id.* at 53466.

6. See Exchange Act § 15(b)(4)(E); Advisers Act § 203(e)(5). See also NASD Rules of Fair Practice § 27; NYSE Rule 342.

7. See, e.g., *In re: Bryant*, Securities Exchange Act Release No. 32357 (May 24, 1993), (Commission upheld a finding of the National Association of Securities Dealers, Inc. that, among other things, the failure to develop procedures to supervise a registered representative, who sent a false confirmation statement on behalf of the broker-dealer, and to enforce existing procedures constituted a failure to supervise on the part of the president of the firm).

8. For example if a person revokes consent to receiving information electronically, even following delivery of the information, a paper copy should be delivered upon request. Revocation, however, is not a prerequisite to requesting a paper copy. The Commission understands that it can be very costly

for broker-dealers to maintain records for long periods of time. This is particularly true with respect to information that is specific to a customer's account or to a transaction, such as the type of information defined below as Personal Financial Information. See *infra* section II.B. For this reason, the Commission has limited the time period that broker-dealers must preserve records required to be made under Exchange Act Rules 17a-3. 17 CFR 240.17a-3. Specifically, Exchange Act Rule 17a-4 requires broker-dealers to preserve records for a period of six years (3 years in the case of certain types of information), the first two years in an easily accessible place. 17 CFR 240.17a-4. For these same reasons, the Commission believes it is reasonable to expect that broker-dealers would provide customers with information in paper form upon request for a period of two years. Transfer agents and investment advisers are subject to similar recordkeeping requirements. 17 CFR 250.17Ad-6 and 240.17Ad-7; 17 CFR 275.204-2.

9. October Interpretive Release, *supra* note 1, at 53460-61.

10. *Id.* at 53461.

11. See *id.* 53460. See also *infra* section II.B.2. regarding additional requirements when broker-dealers, transfer agents, and investment advisers send certain types of information (defined as Personal Financial Information) to customers.

12. For example, if information is provided by physically delivered material (such as a computer diskette or CD-ROM) or by electronic mail, that communication itself generally should be sufficient notice. If information is made available electronically through a passive delivery system, such as an Internet Web Site, however, separate notice would be necessary to satisfy the delivery requirements unless the broker-dealer, transfer agent, or investment adviser can otherwise evidence that delivery to the customer or client has been satisfied.

13. For example, the intended recipient's ability to download or print information delivered electronically would enable a recipient to retain a permanent record. See October Interpretive Release, *supra* note 1, at 53460.

14. See *id.* at 53460. If a consent is used, the consent should be an informed consent. An informed consent should specify the electronic medium or source through which the information will be delivered and the period during which the consent will be effective, and should describe the information that will be delivered using such means. The broker-dealer, transfer agent, or investment adviser also should inform the customer that there may be potential costs associated with electronic delivery, such as on-line charges. Except where a manual signature is required under the penny stock rules, see *infra* note 50, broker-dealers may obtain consents either manually or electronically. In most cases in which a request for information is made through an electronic medium, consent to receive the requested information by means of electronic delivery may be presumed.

   In addition, if the broker-dealer, transfer agent, or investment adviser is relying on the consent to ensure effective delivery and the intended recipient revokes the consent, future documents should be delivered in paper.

15. For example, depending on the circumstances and the procedures used, customers' and clients' written consent or acknowledgement, as required under certain Exchange and Advisers Acts rules and discussed *infra* notes 28–29 and accompanying text, may serve as sufficient evidence to show delivery.

16. October Interpretive Release, *supra* note 1, at 53460, n.22.

13   Internationalization of Mutual Funds

Introduction

Internationalization is a trendy topic. Almost every week there is a conference about globalization of some aspect of the financial markets. Cross-border securities investments were actually modest until the early 1990s, however. As shown by figure 13.0.1, 1993 was the top year for net purchases of foreign securities by U.S. investors. Although U.S. investors sold down their foreign securities holdings during 1994 in light of the Mexican peso crisis, they have since then been building up these foreign positions. Meanwhile, foreign purchases of U.S. securities have continued to climb throughout the 1990s (as shown by figure 13.0.2).

When we think about internationalization of mutual funds, we must distinguish between U.S. mutual funds investing in foreign securities and U.S. companies selling fund shares to foreign investors. This chapter will address both. As explained below, investing abroad by the U.S. mutual funds has been progressing steadily, though there are special constraints that must be addressed. By contrast, selling fund shares overseas by U.S. companies is quite restricted; there really is no global market for mutual funds.

The Micropal tables in the readings provide statistics on the diversification potential of international investing. From a global viewpoint, it is naive to believe you are well diversified if you hold only an S&P index fund or a series of U.S. stock funds. The majority of the global market capitalization of publicly traded companies is still located outside of the United States, as shown by table 13.0.1. Although the capitalization of the Japanese stock markets dropped sharply as the Japanese "bubble" burst in the early 1990s, the market capitalization of many of the emerging markets (e.g., Latin America and Southeast Asia) have soared since 1989. Similarly, the United States accounts for less than half of the global market for publicly issued bonds, as shown by table 13.0.2. More fundamentally, a significant portion of the earnings of "U.S. companies" are actually from overseas. For instance, over 70% of the annual income of Coca-Cola is derived from foreign sources.

If American investors decide to put a substantial portion of their investable assets in foreign securities, they must decide whether to purchase individual foreign securities or mutual funds concentrating in foreign securities. Global funds may invest in U.S. as well as foreign securities, while international funds invest mainly in non-U.S. securities. (See table 13.0.3 on flows into U.S. global and international mutual funds.) Managers of diversified international stock funds frequently use as a benchmark the Morgan Stanley Capital International's EAFE (Europe, Australasia, Far East) index, which includes securities in over 20 developed countries. Managers of stock funds concentrating in developing countries

$ billions

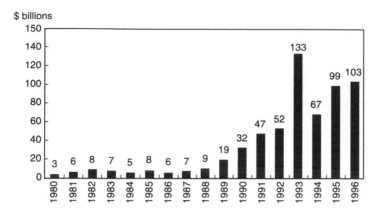

Figure 13.0.1 U.S. net purchases of foreign securities. Source: *SIA 1997 Securities Industry Fact Book*

$ billions

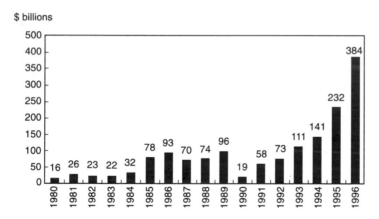

Figure 13.0.2 Foreign net purchases of U.S. securities. Source: *SIA 1997 Securities Industry Fact Book*

often use as a benchmark the Morgan Stanley Emerging Markets index. There are mutual funds investing in Latin America or other regions, or even in one foreign country such as India. In addition, many broadly diversified U.S. mutual funds hold significant positions in non-U.S. companies. For example, many health care funds have substantial holdings in European drug companies. In international and global funds, U.S. investors are taking currency risk. The performance of these funds is calculated in U.S. dollars and may be significantly influenced by changes in the value of the dollar relative to the value of other currencies. Although some international or global funds may partially hedge their currency positions, hedging is expensive and currency movements are notoriously difficult to predict.

When a U.S. mutual fund invests abroad, it confronts a host of special issues. To begin with, the research process is more difficult in most foreign countries than in the United States. The financial statements of many foreign issuers do not follow U.S. generally accepted accounting principles. While the company financial statements in certain large

Table 13.0.1
Global equity markets capitalization (market value in $ billions)

	Australia	Can.	France	Germany	Hong Kong	Italy	Japan	Neth.	Singapore	Switz.	U.K.	U.S.	Developed markets	Emerging markets	World
1980	60	118	55	72	39	25	380	29	24	38	205	1,448	2,552	186	2,738
1981	54	106	38	63	39	24	418	23	35	35	181	1,333	2,413	163	2,576
1982	42	104	28	69	19	20	417	26	31	37	196	1,520	2,579	149	2,728
1983	55	141	38	83	17	21	565	34	16	42	226	1,898	3,218	166	3,384
1984	49	135	41	78	24	26	667	31	12	39	243	1,863	3,296	146	3,442
1985	60	147	79	184	35	59	979	59	11	90	328	2,325	4,497	171	4,667
1986	95	166	150	258	54	140	1,842	84	17	132	440	2,637	6,276	238	6,513
1987	106	219	172	213	54	120	2,803	86	18	129	681	2,589	7,499	332	7,831
1988	138	242	245	252	74	135	3,907	114	24	141	771	2,794	9,240	489	9,728
1989	141	291	365	365	77	169	4,393	158	36	171	827	3,506	10,967	745	11,713
1990	108	242	314	355	83	149	2,918	120	34	160	849	3,059	8,785	615	9,399
1991	145	267	348	393	122	159	3,131	136	48	174	988	4,088	10,433	862	11,295
1992	135	243	351	348	172	129	2,399	135	49	195	927	4,485	9,922	913	10,835
1993	204	327	456	463	385	136	3,000	182	133	272	1,152	5,136	12,326	1,637	13,963
1994	219	315	451	471	270	180	3,720	283	135	284	1,210	5,067	13,209	1,915	15,124
1995	245	366	522	577	304	210	3,667	356	148	434	1,408	6,858	15,856	1,931	17,787
1996	312	486	591	671	449	258	3,089	379	150	402	1,740	8,484	17,933	2,226	20,159

Source: International Finance Corporation

Table 13.0.2

Global bond market capitalization (nominal value outstanding of publicly issued bonds, in U.S.$ billions or equivalent)

	U.S. dollar	Japanese yen	Deut-sche-mark	Italian lira	French franc	U.K. ster-ling	Cana-dian dollar	Others	All major markets
1985	3,119.0	1,082.9	427.2	276.4	174.4	210.8	131.0	511.5	5,933.2
1986	3,669.6	1,511.1	605.9	410.1	253.0	240.5	153.6	690.2	7,534.0
1987	4,165.7	2,120.6	811.5	540.1	336.8	332.7	192.9	902.3	9,402.6
1988	4,517.0	2,161.0	753.5	534.3	332.4	334.4	245.3	875.9	9,763.8
1989	4,949.6	1,980.8	847.5	606.1	455.5	302.7	282.5	943.5	10,368.2
1990	5,388.9	2,221.9	1,123.7	755.4	575.3	361.3	312.4	1,286.1	12,025.0
1991	6,238.1	2,502.5	1,257.0	867.5	653.5	375.8	360.6	1,773.2	14,028.2
1992	6,876.4	2,602.9	1,407.0	764.0	683.5	337.6	356.4	1,744.3	14,772.1
1993	7,547.2	3,044.0	1,590.8	780.7	748.6	436.6	393.0	1,765.6	16,306.5
1994	8,023.1	3,669.3	1,963.5	955.7	891.4	501.8	404.4	2,072.8	18,482.0
1995	8,837.3	3,807.4	2,282.9	1,084.4	1,024.0	540.9	424.1	2,482.0	20,483.0

Source: Salomon Brothers Inc

industrialized countries may be based on different but reasonable principles, the company financial statements in quite a few foreign countries provide less information on a less timely basis than in the United States. Moreover, the executives of most foreign companies are only gradually becoming comfortable with visits or phone calls from securities analysts.

If a portfolio manager of a U.S. mutual fund decides to buy foreign securities, the trading desk must then explore the various methods of purchasing such securities. The securities of some foreign companies are listed on U.S. stock exchanges through American Depositary Receipts (ADRs)—which represent interest in foreign securities actually held by a bank in a trust arrangement. But the best trading market for most foreign securities, even those with ADRs, is usually in their home country. The trading markets in most foreign countries are not as liquid or deep as the New York Stock Exchange, though the London and Tokyo markets are relatively efficient. In certain countries, such as Taiwan, foreign investors must obtain advance regulatory approval in order to buy shares of local companies, and may not hold more than a specified percentage of the outstanding shares of such companies. In addition, the restrictions against insider trading and securities manipulation are not as effective in many foreign markets as in the U.S. markets.

The shares of every U.S. mutual fund must be priced daily—for most funds, at 4 P.M. ET to coordinate with the close of the U.S. stock market. This requirement presents challenges to funds investing primarily in foreign markets that operate in different time zones. (See the case study in chapter 9.) A mutual fund must keep its portfolio sufficiently liquid in order to be prepared to meet potential redemption requests from fund shareholders. This requirement can pose problems in certain foreign countries where it is difficult to sell securities quickly. The independent directors of a mutual fund must generally approve the appointment of a bank as fund custodian as well as the terms of the custodial contract. It is

Table 13.0.3
Flows into U.S. mutual funds: International and global ($ millions)

	Net new sales net exch	Total net assets
International		
1990	5,034.0	14,323.5
1991	3,058.3	19,084.8
1992	5,115.4	22,916.5
1993	26,252.1	71,024.8
1994	27,186.0	101,744.6
1995	6,730.5	120.736.3
1996	29,780.2	177,414.4
Global equity		
1990	1,460.0	13,464.7
1991	120.4	17,285.7
1992	1,912.9	12,209.5
1993	12,224.9	43,269.7
1994	16,705.9	60,175.6
1995	4,962.2	76,001.6
1996	16,557.9	106,554.1
Global bond		
1990	5,638.1	12,411.3
1991	10,195.1	27,217.2
1992	−2,830.0	31,633.5
1993	4,520.1	38,235.2
1994	4,527.3	31,395.6
1995	−4,402.9	33,412.3
1996	−931.9	37,458.4

Source: Investment Company Institute

impractical, however, for the independent directors to develop sufficient expertise on the securities settlement procedures and the subcustodial arrangements of the fund's primary foreign custodian across the globe. As a result, the SEC has adopted special rules on the role of independent directors with regard to a fund's foreign custodial network.

Finally, the investment advisers to mutual funds investing in foreign securities must deal with the different political environment in many foreign countries. The political risks of international investing may include extreme price volatility because of a coup d'etat or a currency devaluation. From time to time, foreign markets have actually closed for extended time periods—in an infamous example, the Hong Kong market closed for four days during the 1987 market crash. On a less dramatic note, the concepts of shareholder rights and institutional activism are not accepted in many foreign countries. This is true in many emerging markets where the government maintains a controlling block in many publicly traded companies. It is also true in quite a few industrialized countries—for example, all

Table 13.0.4

International mutual fund survey, Quarter 4, 1996: Selected countries, Total net assets by type of fund (in millions)

Country	Equity U.S. dollars	Bond U.S. dollars	Money market U.S. dollars
Australia	9,843	1,260	7,633
Austria	2,279	28,434	—
Belgium	9,438	6,862	2,680
Canada	80,049	14,317	23,452
Denmark	4,361	4,654	
Finland			
France	58,427	157,224	242,185
Germany	36,759	75,675	20,033
Hong Kong	27,771	7,036	4,444
India			
Ireland			
Italy	21,687	51,049	47,286
Japan	100,383	187,048	122,740
Luxembourg			
New Zealand	1,278	2,032	422
Norway	4,781	1,667	3,006
South Africa	7,674	264	—
Spain	3,974	58,545	73,170
Sweden	26,097	4,999	—
Switzerland	29,894	18,273	—
United Kingdom	177,978	9,333	957

Source: Investment Company Institute

shareholder meetings in Japan are held on the same day to minimize the opportunities for shareholder dissent.

Whatever the challenges involved in foreign investing by U.S. mutual funds, they are modest compared to the constraints on mutual fund sales by U.S. companies to foreign investors. The fund industry in the United States is much larger than the fund industry in any other country, though mutual funds are becoming more popular throughout the world (see table 13.0.4). The financial sector of many industrialized countries has been dominated by universal banks, which have gradually become interested in mutual funds as sources of fee income. In many developing countries, the gradual emergence of a middle class with savings has spurred the growth of mutual funds or similar vehicles. The total or partial privatization of social security systems (e.g., in Chile and Australia) has also created a new customer base for mutual funds.

While most individual securities are traded around the world, there is no global market for the sales of mutual funds. It is virtually impossible to sell a U.S. mutual fund in most foreign countries because they impose incompatible tax, regulatory, and accounting requirements. For instance, Vanguard's Windsor Fund could not be publicly offered for sale in France or Japan; at best, it might be possible to make a limited number of private sales of Windsor Fund in those countries. Similarly, the SEC would not permit a French or Japanese mutual fund to be publicly offered to U.S. investors; those foreign funds could be sold only in a private offering to a limited number of sophisticated U.S. investors.

Instead of cross-border sales of existing mutual funds, investment advisers usually create "clones" of existing funds and customize them to foreign requirements. For instance, Dreyfus could create a British unit trust with similar investment parameters to its U.S. Government Fund and then sell that clone to British investors. In practice, however, there is no such thing as a perfect clone. Small differences in investment restrictions or pricing requirements can result in significant performance differences. Furthermore, the ordinary income and capital gains received by clone funds on their investments are taxed differently from country to country.

Regional movements toward harmonization for mutual funds have made some progress in the European Economic Community (EEC). Under the Directive on the Undertakings for Collective Investment in Transferable Securities (the UCITS Directive), any mutual fund registered in one EEC country (the country where the fund is situated) may be offered in another EEC country merely by filing a notice with the regulatory authorities of the latter country. It is up to the registering EEC country to assure that the fund complies with the minimum requirements set forth in the UCITS. But the EEC country where a fund is sold retains jurisdiction over advertising and in those areas "which do not fall within the field governed by this Directive." (See Article 44 of UCITs in the readings.)

In North America, clone funds are still the rule. A U.S. firm may establish a subsidiary in Canada and sell clone funds there. But a clone fund in Canada must be registered in every Canadian province where it is sold. Similarly, a Canadian firm may establish a U.S. subsidiary and sell clone funds here. But a clone fund must pay registration fees to all the relevant states as well as the SEC. Canadian trade negotiators argue that the United States is not providing "reciprocity" because Canadian banks (like U.S. banks) are prevented by the Glass-Steagall Act from underwriting mutual funds in the United States. By contrast, U.S. banks (like Canadian banks) are allowed to underwrite mutual funds in Canada. The U.S. trade negotiators argue that Canadian and U.S. banks are receiving "national treatment" in both countries with respect to mutual fund underwriting.

For many years, Mexico prohibited U.S. firms from selling even clone funds in Mexico. As discussed in the materials, however, the North American Free Trade Agreement (NAFTA) now requires Mexico to treat U.S. financial firms in a similar fashion to Mexican financial firms (after a transitional period). The problem is that Mexican mutual funds, run by Mexican or U.S. firms, are permitted to purchase only Mexican securities. By contrast, wealthy Mexicans typically maintain a brokerage account in a U.S. firm to purchase and sell individual U.S. securities.

The Far East remains the region with the most restrictions on the sale of clone funds by U.S. firms. From 1960 to 1990, the Japanese government limited mutual fund managers to fifteen Japanese firms. Most of those firms were affiliated with Japanese brokers, which were the only distributors of mutual funds. While Japanese brokers have provided intense personal advice and service to their customers, they have been notorious for switching shareholders out of funds after approximately one year in order to earn another sales commission. In 1990, the Japanese government announced that it would allow foreign firms for the first time to manage yen-denominated mutual funds subject to many restrictions. These restrictions were so onerous that no U.S. firm registered a yen-denominated fund until 1995, when many of these restrictions were eliminated through a bilateral trade agreement between the United States and Japan. This trade agreement also permitted direct marketing of mutual funds, though the costs of mailers, phones, and newspaper advertisements are still two to three times higher in Japan than in the Unites States. Japan has recently indicated that it will allow banks to advise and market mutual funds to their customers.

Other Asian countries are more restrictive on foreign fund entry than Japan currently is, as explained in the readings. In some countries such as India and Thailand, a foreign firm needs a local joint venture partner in order to sell mutual funds to local investors. These joint ventures raise difficult problems of ultimate control, work allocation, and technological transfer. In other countries, foreign firms have only recently been allowed to enter the fund business and the terms of access are still quite burdensome. In Korea, for example, mutual fund shares may be sold only through branches of fund companies, rather than branches of the Korean broker-dealers that typically work with foreign fund firms. In addition, Korea imposes capital and personnel requirements on fund branches that would be very high for a start-up foreign venture. Many of these Asian countries defend these restrictions on the basis that, without them, foreign fund sponsors would allegedly drive their local counterparts out of business.

Such restrictions on foreign access to Asian markets constitute the prime subject of the multilateral negotiations on financial services. While these negotiations were expanded to cover services as well as products during the last round of negotiations (called the Uruguay Round), a country signing on to the General Agreement on Trade in Services (GATS) does not automatically promise to open its financial markets to foreigners. Rather, such a signatory country commits only to the market opening measures specified in the service schedules submitted by that country in the negotiation process. In 1995, when the Uruguay Round generally ended, the United States decided that the market-opening commitments of several Asian countries in their financial service schedules were inadequate. A few Asian countries even refused to commit not to roll back their existing modest measures to open their financial markets. As a result, the United States reserved the right to take an exemption from Most Favored Nation (MFN) treatment for countries signing the GATS. Under MFN, a GATS signatory would receive as full access to the U.S. financial markets as the foreign country with the best trading relationship with the United States—for example, Malaysia would have as good access to the U.S. financial markets as Great Britain does. By reserving the right to take an exemption from MFN on financial services, the United States indicated that it might not grant MFN treatment to signatory countries unless they made significant commitments to open their financial markets. In response, the GATS negotiations on financial services were extended through the end of 1997. Because the Asian and other countries are improving the commitments in their service schedules, it appears that the United States will now sign the GATS and generally grant the other signatories MFN treatment in financial services.

The readings outline some of the benefits and constraints on investing fund assets and selling mutual funds around the world. The case study for this chapter involves the export from the United States to Canada of a defined contribution business for mutual funds. It illustrates the challenges of exporting any mutual fund business, even between two contiguous countries where most people speak the same language.

Questions

In reviewing the materials in this chapter, please keep in mind the following questions:

1. If you think broadly about diversification, how much of your "capital" is located in the United States? Count not only your securities investments and pension holdings but also your real estate and insurance. Why worry about international diversification since the U.S. economy and stock market are so strong?

2. Going back to the discussion in chapter 1, what are the pros and cons of investing in mutual funds versus investing in individual securities? Which of the arguments are significantly different for investing in foreign versus U.S. securities?

3. Looking at the UCITS Directive, reproduced in the chapter readings: To what extent can a mutual fund situated (registered) in Luxembourg be sold under the same terms and conditions throughout the EEC? To what extent could Luxembourg apply stricter regulations to funds situated (registered) there than to funds situated (registered) in other EEC countries? Would Luxembourg have any incentive to impose such stricter regulations?

4. The EEC is gradually moving toward a common currency, though each EEC country will retain its own tax structure. Will a common currency lead to mutual funds offered throughout the EEC? Or does the EEC need a common tax regime to support pan-European mutual funds?

5. Is Mexico providing "reciprocity" or "national treatment" to U.S. mutual fund managers? Is it reasonable for U.S. trade negotiators to ask Mexico's regulators to allow all Mexican mutual funds, or some subset thereof, to purchase non-Mexican securities?

6. Should U.S. firms rely for fund sales on Japanese brokers, which continue to dominate fund distribution? Should they try to distribute funds through the extensive branch network of Japanese banks? Or should they build their own distribution networks (branches or direct) in Japan for their own funds?

7. Do you think U.S. fund sponsors would drive local sponsors out of the mutual fund business in Southeast Asia? What was the actual experience of foreign firms in Europe, Japan, and North America? How could the Asian concern about preserving local competitors be reconciled with the policies favoring free trade in financial services?

8. If the United States accepts MFN in financial services, would the SEC be permitted under the GATS to deny fund registrations to a foreign sponsor from a signatory country that prevented U.S. firms from selling funds in that country? If the United States opts out of MFN in financial services, how will British and German fund sponsors be assured of national treatment by the SEC?

13.1   Investing Abroad: Risks and Returns*
Ted Sickinger

Good Fundamentals

International investing is hardly new. But in the last 10 years international mutual funds have extended the concept's potential advantages to plebeian investors.

Today, with brokers jumping on the asset allocation bandwagon and diversifying their clients' portfolios among different asset classes, putting 10 percent to 25 percent of a client's assets in international investments is all the rage.

"It actually lowers your risk," said W. David Holthouse, a senior vice president and managed-account consultant at Everen in Kansas City. "A diversified portfolio means lower volatility overall."

It makes sense. Foreign economies do lag that of the United States. They often grow while the U.S. economy is stagnating, providing a potential buffer when U.S. markets are having a down year. Witness Japan's growth while the United States was in recession, or Japan's recent woes while the U.S. economy has been growing.

But the real motivation for investing abroad, Holthouse acknowledged, is the potential for higher returns. He's not looking for a bonanza, but with the strong run-up in U.S. stock prices over the last decade, he thinks some foreign markets look like bargains.

"There are parts of the world growing faster than the U.S.," he said. "I want to be part of that growth."

Few economists argue the assertion that foreign economies will outgrow ours for the foreseeable future. The World Bank projects that 70 percent of the growth in the world's real gross domestic product during the next 20 years will come from developing economies in Asia, Latin America, Eastern Europe and Africa.

It's not hard to see why.

There are more people abroad whose incomes are growing faster.

Education, literacy, health care and the percentage of skilled workers are increasing. Having acquired the basics of life, they now want the conveniences.

There is a vast need for infrastructure and technology investment in emerging economies.

Political liberalization is promoting privatization of industry, international trade and more open, market-based economies that permit foreign-equity investment.

Recognizing their cue at home, fund companies have been quick to offer up a raft of new fund offerings in the international arena.

Since 1992, the number of international funds — those invested almost exclusively in foreign securities — has grown fourfold, from 77 funds to 311, according to Lipper Analytical Services Inc., the New York-based mutual fund tracking service.

---

*From *The Kansas City Star*, March 31, 1996. Copyright 1996 The Kansas City Star Co. Reprinted with permission.

That's not counting global funds, which invest in U.S. as well as foreign securities. That adds about 150 more. And the total assets under management in the two categories has exploded.

But the distinction between funds doesn't stop at international and global. There are bond and equity funds, funds for different regions and countries, sector funds that invest in particular industries and permutations of all of them.

The most important distinction that investment professionals draw is between developed and emerging markets.

Emerging markets are generally less developed, less industrialized countries with less output of goods and serviced. Their capital markets are still in their infancy, and are consequently more volatile and riskier.

But they offer the promise of potentially greater rewards. For instance, between January 1987 and May 1993, Turkey's stock market rose 637 percent. Argentina's was up 1,374 percent. And Mexico's was up 960 percent, according to the Investor's Guide to Emerging Markets.

"Of course, these returns are calculated using the market indices and thus average all companies whether they rose or fell in price," said Mark Mobius, the book's author. "However, correct individual stock selections could have revealed even more spectacular results."

Hence the investment community's enthusiastic, if tempered, endorsement of emerging markets.

"We're currently suggesting that about 15 percent of your portfolio be in foreign stocks," Chalasani said.

Other firms such as Merrill Lynch suggest that an even higher percentage of foreign stocks—up to 30 percent—would be instrumental in decreasing the overall volatility of your portfolio.

"We also suggest that 60 percent of that 15 percent be in developed countries that you know well," added Chalasani. "Forty percent can be in developing countries.

"If you keep that 60–40 relationship, you're taking enough risk."

The Risks

Not all market watchers are enamored of the international landscape. Some say the average investor isn't equipped to analyze foreign investments and that fund companies are expanding their international and global offerings too fast to maintain asset and analytical quality.

"How many years' experience do most of these guys managing the international funds have?" asked John Kornitzer, president of Kornitzer Capital Management in Kansas City. "They decide, 'OK, you'll be the international manager,' and those guys haven't been around the world twice."

Kornitzer's point properly underscores the importance of carefully evaluating a fund's management team. But he has his own agenda: selling the Buffalo USA Global Fund, in which investors can secure some overseas exposure without ever leaving the dock.

Kornitzer's game plan is to invest in U.S. companies that generate more than 40 percent of their revenues or earnings abroad, companies such as Gillette, Coca-Cola, McDonald's, American International Group and Cummins Engine.

More often than not, he said, it is U.S. companies that benefit from the infrastructure building and growing consumer product demand overseas.

"This gives people a way to play the international market without subjecting them to currency and liquidity risks," Kornitzer said.

Currency and liquidity risk are just two of a long list of potential risks that are unique to investing overseas:

Currency risk   When you invest in foreign securities, you not only bet on the investment, but on currency fluctuations.

For instance, if you buy a Japanese stock that appreciates 10 percent but the yen depreciates against the dollar by 5 percent, your return is halved. The opposite also can occur.

Some countries, such as Hong Kong and Argentina, peg their currencies to the U.S. dollar, which mitigates currency risk if you are investing in a single country. Some funds hedge currency exposure with futures contracts. Avoid funds that use exotic securities known as derivatives.

Political risk   The political climate and government stability are still questionable in many emerging markets, such as China, Russia, Poland and Mexico. The result can be inadequate regulations, nationalization of assets, foreign exchange controls or other measures that make it difficult to repatriate principal, interest and dividends.

"Few of these people remember when countries such as Canada, Cuba, France and Venezuela nationalized their industry," Kornitzer said. "People forget the risks, but they're going to find out."

Inadequate accounting   Foreign companies are not subject to the same audit standards or reporting requirements that companies listed on U.S. exchanges must meet. Information can be insufficient or inaccurate. Changes in management, ownership or industry conditions can affect foreign operations.

Liquidity problems   The trading volume and market capitalization on most foreign markets are minuscule compared with U.S. markets. It can be difficult to find buyers for shares, or purchase prices can be unfair.

Higher costs   Most foreign markets are less efficient and have higher transaction costs than U.S. markets, where commissions are negotiable. Managing an international portfolio is also a costly proposition, as fund managers and analysts travel the world to investigate investments. Expenses come right off the top of the fund and can run as high as 3 percent, compared with about a 1 percent average for a domestic fund.

Despite the risks of investing abroad, investors such as Carl Mitchell are becoming a lot more comfortable with the concept. In fact, after seven years in emerging markets, Mitchell is thinking of increasing his international allocation to 25 percent from 15 percent of his portfolio.

"I don't think I'm an aggressive investor," he said. "It takes some discipline to ride out things like what happened in Mexico. But you have to buy into the concept that higher growth rates lead to higher returns in the long run."

13.2 Micropal's Perspective on the Prospects for the Global Fund Industry (excerpt)*

Christopher Poll

For all intents and purposes, the correlations among established markets (table 13.2.1) and developing Asian markets (table 13.2.2) are low.

Table 13.2.1[1]
Correlation of established markets 5 years to 30 June 1996 in U.S. dollars

	Cnda	Frn	Ger	HK	Jap	Sing	US	UK
Cnda	1.00							
Frn	0.30	1.00						
Ger	0.24	0.59	1.00					
HK	0.60	0.34	0.42	1.00				
Jap	0.27	0.33	0.17	−0.01	1.00			
Sing	0.41	0.35	0.45	0.62	0.25	1.00		
US	0.35	0.73	0.55	0.35	0.39	0.46	1.00	
UK	0.46	0.46	0.39	0.30	0.14	0.31	0.60	1.00

Table 13.2.2[1]
Correlation of developing Asian markets 5 years to 30 June 1996 in U.S. dollars

	Indo	Kra	Mly	Phil	Pak	Twn	Thi	Trk	India	SA
Indo	1.00									
Kra	0.07	1.00								
Mly	0.48	0.18	1.00							
Phil	0.62	−0.04	0.61	1.00						
Pak	0.13	−0.04	0.22	0.30	1.00					
Twn	0.31	0.23	0.39	0.47	0.02	1.00				
Thi	0.55	0.15	0.60	0.67	0.27	0.33	1.00			
Trk	0.33	0.05	0.20	0.22	0.09	0.19	0.20	1.00		
India	0.11	0.08	0.01	−0.03	0.04	0.01	0.16	0.06	1.00	
SA	0.22	0.04	0.31	0.44	0.22	0.30	0.28	0.05	−0.10	1.00

---

*Source: Standard & Poor's Micropal.

Emerging markets are often perceived as moving in harmony. This table (13.2.3) shows the divergence among Latin American stock markets. The reality is very different from the perception.

Table 13.2.3[1]
Correlation of main Latin American markets 5 years to 30 June 1996 in U.S. dollars

	Arg	Brz	Chl	Mex
Arg	1.00			
Brz	0.23	1.00		
Chl	0.27	0.16	1.00	
Mex	0.39	0.33	0.30	1.00

The pattern is evident across all markets throughout the world (see table 13.2.4). Investment ... is about the relationship of return to volatility. The developed and emerging markets not only have little correlation, but returns and volatility vary considerably.

Table 13.2.4
Return compared to risk over 3 and 5 years to 30 June 1996 in U.S. dollars

	Three years		Five years	
	Annual av. return %	Annual av. volatility	Annual av. return %	Annual av. volatility
USA	15	8	13	9
Japan	2	20	5	23
UK	10	13	8	15
France	10	15	11	15
Germany	16	14	10	14
MSCI World	14	10	13	10
Argentina*	18	35	31	57
Brazil*	27	41	31	52
Chile*	24	25	22	26
Mexico*	−4	41	5	36
Latin Am*	9	30	16	28
Turkey*	5	56	4	61
South Africa	9	18	7	18
Hong Kong	14	30	23	27
Singapore	11	17	13	16
India	15	29	12	37
Indonesia*	16	29	11	30
Korea*	4	23	4	27
Malaysia*	18	30	19	25

Table 13.2.4 (continued)

	Three years		Five years	
	Annual av. return %	Annual av. volatility	Annual av. return %	Annual av. volatility
Pakistan*	11	34	22	40
Philippines*	11	34	22	40
Taiwan*	22	40	5	39
Thailand*	16	34	19	31
Asia*	17	25	17	21

*Source: International Finance Corporation

Running these benchmarks through an optimiser produces the results in table 13.2.5. To be realistic, from a U.S. investor point of view, the portfolio was restricted to 50% in the S&P 500, 10% to other developed countries, and 5% to emerging markets.

Table 13.2.5
Optimal configurations for world equity markets with constraints,* 5 years to 30 June 1996

	Optimal world equity portfolio
Portfolio return	15.01
Portfolio risk (volatility)	8.51
Portfolio sharpe ratio	1.76
MS Belgium	5.00
MS Italy	1.37
MS Japan	0.07
MS Netherlands	5.00
MS New Zealand	2.37
MS Swiss	5.00
South African ISF	5.00
Indian Bombay SENatl Index	5.00
IFCI Brazil	1.85
IFCI Chile	5.00
IFCI Malaysia	5.00
IFCI Philippines	4.82
IFCI Turkey	0.57
IFCG Korea	3.95
S&P 500	50.00

*50% in S&P 500; max 10% in G7 countries; max 5% elsewhere

As shown by figure 13.2.1, the optimal portfolio over 5 years has a return of 15.01%, a volatility of 8.51, and a risk/return ratio of 1.76. This compares to a return of 14.39% from the S&P, a volatility of 9.51, and a risk/return ratio of 1.51.

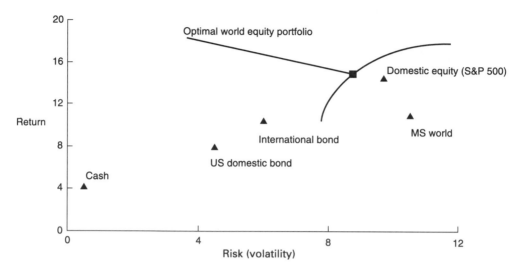

Figure 13.2.1 Asset allocation for world equity markets 5 years to 30 June 1996.

For the same return as the S&P, however, the volatility could have been reduced from 9.51 to 8.17—a 14% reduction—by investing 50% of the portfolio abroad. (These numbers are not great but remember that the United States has been on an unprecedented bull market run for the past five years, and 1994 was a particularly bad year for emerging markets.)

The three year returns to December 1995 illustrates better the benefits of non-U.S. investing from a U.S. investor's perspective, as shown in table 13.2.6. The figures over the past 3 years are even more marked in favor of non-U.S. diversification. The portfolio's annualized return is 18.23% with a volatility of 7.87 and a risk/return ratio of 2.31. The S&P over this 3-year period has an annualized return of 15.35%, volatility of 8.22, and risk/return of 1.87.

Table 13.2.6
Optimal configurations for world equity markets with constraints,* 3 years to 31 December 1995

Portfolio return	18.23
Portfolio risk (volatility)	7.87
Portfolio sharpe ratio	2.31
IFCI Brazil	5.00
IFCI Chile	2.45
IFCI Turkey	2.29
IFCG Korea	3.62
MSCI Belgium	5.00
MSCI Denmark	5.00
MSCI Finland	1.72
MSCI Germany	9.85
MSCI Italy	1.96
MSCI Netherlands	3.11
MSCI Swiss	5.00
South African JSE	5.00
S&P 500	50.00

* 50% in S&P 500: max 10% in G7 countries: max 5% elsewhere

Note

1. Correlation Coefficient: A measure (ranging in value from −1 to 1) of the association between a dependent variable and one or more independent variables. If one variable's values are higher than its average value when another variable's values are higher than its average value, their correlation is positive. By contrast, if one variable's values are lower than its average value when another variable's values are higher than its average value, their correlation is negative. A correlation coefficient is not necessarily a measure of causality, but it does indicate the strength of a relationship. A correlation coefficient of 1 implies that the variables move perfectly in lockstep; a correlation coefficient of −1 implies that the variables move inversely in lockstep; a correlation coefficient of 0 implies that the variable, as calibrated, are uncorrelated. (Source: Dictionary of Financial Risk Management, © 1996, Gary L. Gastineau.)

13.3 Council Directive of 20 December 1985 on the Coordination of Laws, Regulations and Administrative Provisions Relating to Undertakings for Collective Investment in Transferable Securities (UCITS)*

The Council of the European Communities,

Having regard to the Treaty establishing the European Economic Community and in particular Article 57 (2) thereof,

Having regard to the proposal from the Commission (¹).

Having regard to the opinion of the European Parliament (²),

Having regard to the opinion of the Economic and Social Committee (³).

Whereas the laws of the Member States relating to collective investment undertakings differ appreciably from one state to another, particularly as regards the obligations and controls which are imposed on those undertakings; whereas those differences distort the conditions of competition between those undertakings and do not ensure equivalent protection for unit-holders;

Whereas national laws governing collective investment undertakings should be coordinated with a view to approximating the conditions of competition between those undertakings at Community level, while at the same time ensuring more effective and more uniform protection for unit-holders; whereas such coordination will make it easier for a collective investment undertaking situated in one Member State to market its units in other Member States;

Whereas the attainment of these objectives will facilitate the removal of the restrictions on the free circulation of the units of collective investment undertakings in the Community, and such coordination will help to bring about a European capital market;

Whereas, having regard to these objectives, it is desirable that common basic rules be established for the authorization, supervision, structure and activities of collective investment undertakings situated in the Member States and the information they must publish;

Whereas the application of these common rules is a sufficient guarantee to permit collective investment undertakings situated in Member States, subject to the applicable provisions relating to capital movements, to market their units in other Member States without those Member States' being able to subject those undertakings or their units to any provision whatsoever other than provisions which, in those states, do not fall within the field covered by this Directive; whereas, nevertheless, if a collective investment undertaking situated in one Member State markets its units in a different Member State it must take all

---

*From *Official Journal of the European Communities*, no. L 375, December 12, 1985. Reprinted with permission.

necessary steps to ensure that unit-holders in that other Member State can exercise their financial rights there with ease and are provided with the necessary information.

Whereas the coordination of the laws of the Member States should be confined initially to collective investment undertakings other than of the closed-ended type which promote the sale of their units to the public in the Community and the sole object of which is investment in transferable securities (which are essentially transferable securities officially listed on stock exchanges or similar regulated markets); whereas regulation of the collective investment undertakings not covered by the Directive poses a variety of problems which must be dealt with by means of other provisions, and such undertakings will accordingly be the subject of coordination at a later stage; whereas pending such coordination any Member State may, *inter alia*, prescribe those categories of undertakings for collective investment in transferable securities (UCITS) excluded from this Directive's scope on account of their investment and borrowing policies and lay down those specific rules to which such UCITS are subject in carrying on their business within its territory;

Whereas the free marketing of the units issued by UCITS authorized to invest up to 100% of their assets in transferable securities issued by the same body (State, local authority, etc.) may not have the direct or indirect effect of disturbing the functioning of the capital market or the financing of the Member States or of creating economic situations similar to those which Article 68 (3) of the Treaty seeks to prevent;

Whereas account should be taken of the special situations of the Hellenic Republic's and Portuguese Republic's financial markets by allowing those countries and additional period in which to implement this Directive.

Has adopted this directive:

Section I   General provisions and scope

Article 1

1. The Member States shall apply this Directive to undertakings for collective investment in transferable securities (hereinafter referred to as UCITS) situated within their territories.
2. For the purposes of this Directive, and subject to Article 2, UCITS shall be undertakings:
   - the sole object of which is the collective investment in transferable securities of capital raised from the public and which operate on the principle of risk-spreading, and
   - the units of which are, at the request of holders, re-purchased or redeemed, directly or indirectly, out of those undertakings' assets. Action taken by a UCITS to ensure that the stock exchange value of its units does not significantly vary from their net asset value shall be regarded as equivalent to such re-purchase or redemption.
3. Such undertakings may be constituted according to law, either under the law of contract (as common funds managed by management companies) or trust law (as unit trusts) or under statute (as investment companies).
   For the purposes of this Directive 'common funds' shall also include unit trusts.

4. Investment companies the assets of which are invested through the intermediary of subsidiary companies mainly otherwise than in transferable securities shall not, however, be subject to this Directive.

5. The Member States shall prohibit UCITS which are subject to this Directive from transforming themselves into collective investment undertakings which are not covered by this Directive.

6. Subject to the provisions governing capital movements and to Articles 44, 45 and 52 (2) no Member State may apply any other provisions whatsoever in the field covered by this Directive to UCITS situated in another Member State or to the units issued by such UCITS, where they market their units within its territory.

7. Without prejudice to paragraph 6, a Member State may apply to UCITS situated within its territory requirements which are stricter than or additional to those laid down in Article 4 *et seq.* of this Directive, provided that they are of general application and do not conflict with the provisions of this Directive.

Article 2

1. The following shall not be UCITS subjects to this Directive:

- UCITS of the closed-ended type;
- UCITS which raise capital without promoting the sale of their units to the public within the Community or any part of it;
- UCITS the units of which, under the fund rules or the investment company's instruments of incorporation, may be sold only to the public in non-member countries;
- categories of UCITS prescribed by the regulations of the Member States in which such UCITS are situated, for which the rules laid down in Section V and Article 36 are inappropriate in view of their investment and borrowing policies.

2. Five years after the implementation of this Directive the Commission shall submit to the Council a report on the implementation of paragraph 1 and, in particular, of its fourth indent. If necessary, it shall propose suitable measures to extend the scope.

Article 3

For the purposes of this Directive, a UCITS shall be deemed to be situated in the Member State in which the investment company or the management company of the unit trust has its registered office; the Member States must require that the head office be situated in the same Member State as the registered office.

Section II   Authorization of UCITS

Article 4

1. No UCITS shall carry on activities as such unless it has been authorized by the competent authorities of the Member State in which it is situated, hereinafter referred to as 'the competent authorities'.

   Such authorization shall be valid for all Member States.

2. A unit trust shall be authorized only if the competent authorities have approved the management company, the fund rules and the choice of depositary. An investment

company shall be authorized only if the competent authorities have approved both its instruments of incorporation and the choice of depositary.

3. The competent authorities may not authorize a UCITS if the directors of the management company, of the investment company or of the depositary are not of sufficiently good repute or lack the experience required for the performance of their duties. To that end, the names of the directors of the management company, of the investment company and of the depositary and of every person succeeding them in office must be communicated forthwith to the competent authorities.

    'Directors' shall mean those persons who, under the law or the instruments of incorporation, represent the management company, the investment company or the depositary, or who effectively determine the policy of the management company, the investment company or the depositary.

4. Neither the management company not the depositary may be replaced, nor may the fund rules or the investment company's instruments of incorporation be amended, without the approval of the competent authorities.

Section III   Obligations regarding the structure of unit trusts

Article 5
A management company must have sufficient financial resources at its disposal to enable it to conduct its business effectively and meet its liabilities.

Article 6
No management company may engage in activities other than the management of unit trusts and of investment companies.

Article 7
1. A unit trust's assets must be entrusted to a depositary for safe-keeping.
2. A depositary's liability as referred to in Article 9 shall not be affected by the fact that it has entrusted to a third party all or some of the assets in its safe-keeping.
3. A depositary must, moreover:
(a) ensure that the sale, issue, re-purchase, redemption and cancellation of units effected on behalf of a unit trust or by a management company are carried out in accordance with the law and the fund rules;
(b) ensure that the value of units is calculated in accordance with the law and the fund rules;
(c) carry out the instructions of the management company, unless they conflict with the law or the fund rules;
(d) ensure that in transactions involving a unit trust's assets any consideration is remitted to it within the usual time limits;
(e) ensure that a unit trust's income is applied in accordance with the law and the fund rules.

Article 8
1. A depositary must either have its registered office in the same Member State as that of the management company or be established in that Member State if its registered office is in another Member State.

2. A depositary must be an institution which is subject to public control. It must also furnish sufficient financial and professional guarantees to be able effectively to pursue its business as depositary and meet the commitments inherent in that function.

3. The Member States shall determine which of the categories of institutions referred to in paragraph 2 shall be eligible to be depositaries.

Article 9

A depositary shall, in accordance with the national law of the State in which the management company's registered office is situated, be liable to the management company and the unit-holders for any loss suffered by them as a result of its unjustifiable failure to perform its obligations or its improper performance of them. Liability to unit-holders may be invoked either directly or indirectly through the management company, depending on the legal nature of the relationship between the depositary, the management company and the unit-holders.

Article 10

1. No single company shall act as both management company and depositary.

2. In the context of their respective roles the management company and the depositary must act independently and solely in the interest of the unit-holders.

Article 11

The law or the fund rules shall lay down the conditions for the replacement of the management company and the depositary and rules to ensure the protection of unit-holders in the event of such replacement.

Section IV   Obligations regarding the structure of investment companies and their depositaries

Article 12

The Member States shall determine the legal form which an investment company must take. It must have sufficient paid-up capital to enable it to conduct its business effectively and meet its liabilities.

Article 13

No investment company may engage in activities other than those referred to in Article 1 (2).

Article 14

1. An investment company's assets must be entrusted to a depositary for safe-keeping.

2. A depositary's liability as referred to in Article 16 shall not be affected by the fact that it has entrusted to a third party all or some of the assets in its safe-keeping.

3. A depositary must, moreover:

(a) ensure that the sale, issue, re-purchase, redemption and cancellation of units effected by or on behalf of a company are carried out in accordance with the law and with the company's instruments of incorporation;

(b) ensure that in transactions involving a company's assets any consideration is remitted to it within the usual time limits;

(c) ensure that a company's income is applied in accordance with the law and its instruments of incorporation.

4. A Member State may decide that investment companies situated within its territory which market their units exclusively through one or more stock exchanges on which their units are admitted to official listing shall not be required to have depositaries within the meaning of this Directive.

   Articles 34, 37 and 38 shall not apply to such companies. However, the rules for the valuation of such companies' assets must be stated in law or in their instruments of incorporation.

5. A Member State may decide that investment companies situated within its territory which market at least 80% of their-units through one or more stock exchanges designated in their instruments of incorporation shall not be required to have depositaries within the meaning of this Directive provided that their units are admitted to official listing on the stock exchanges of those Member States within the territories of which the units are marketed, and that any transactions which such a company may effect outwith stock exchanges are effected at stock exchange prices only. A company's instruments of incorporation must specify the stock exchange in the country of marketing the prices on which shall determine the prices at which that company will effect any transactions outwith stock exchanges in that country.

   A Member State shall avail itself of the option provided for in the preceding subparagraph only if it considers that unit-holders have protection equivalent to that of unit-holders in UCITS which have depositaries within the meaning of this Directive.

   In particular, such companies and the companies referred to in paragraph 4, must:

   (a) in the absence of provision in law, state in their instruments of incorporation the methods of calculation of the net asset values of their units,

   (b) intervene on the market to prevent the stock exchange values of their units from deviating by more than 5% from their net asset values;

   (c) establish the net asset values of their units, communicate them to the competent authorities at least twice a week and publish them twice a month.

   At least twice a month, an independent auditor must ensure that the calculation of the value of units is effected in accordance with the law and the company's instruments of incorporation. On such occasions, the auditor must make sure that the company's assets are invested in accordance with the rules laid down by law and the company's instruments of incorporation.

6. The Member States shall inform the Commission of the identities of the companies benefiting from the derogations provided for in paragraphs 4 and 5.

   The Commission shall report to the Contact Committee on the application of paragraphs 4 and 5 within five years of the implementation of this Directive. After obtaining the Contact Committee's opinion, the Commission shall, if need be, propose appropriate measures.

Article 15

1. A depositary must either have its registered office in the same Member State as that of the investment company or be established in that Member State if its registered office is in another Member State.

2. A depositary must be an institution which is subject to public control. It must also furnish sufficient financial and professional guarantees to be able effectively to pursue its business as depositary and meet the commitments inherent in that function.

3. The Member States shall determine which of the categories of institutions referred to in paragraph 2 shall be eligible to be depositaries.

Article 16

A depositary shall, in accordance with the national law of the State in which the investment company's registered office is situated, be liable to the investment company and the unit-holders for any loss suffered by them as a result of its unjustifiable failure to perform its obligations, or its improper performance of them.

Article 17

1. No single company shall act as both investment company and depositary.

2. In carrying out its role as depositary, the depositary must act solely in the interests of the unit-holders.

Article 18

The law or the investment company's instruments of incorporation shall lay down the conditions for the replacement of the depositary and rules to ensure the protection of unit-holders in the event of such replacement.

Section V   Obligations concerning the investment policies of UCITS

Article 19

1. The investments of a unit trust or of an investment company must consist solely of:
(a) transferable securities admitted to official listing on a stock exchange in a Member State and/or;
(b) transferable securities dealt in on another regulated market in a Member State which operates regularly and is recognized and open to the public and/or;
(c) transferable securities admitted to official listing on a stock exchange in a non-member State or dealt in on another regulated market in a non-member State which operates regularly and is recognized and open to the public provided that the choice of stock exchange or market has been approved by the competent authorities or is provided for in law or the fund rules or the investment company's instruments of incorporation and/or;
(d) recently issued transferable securities, provided that:
• the terms of issue include an undertaking that application will be made for admission to official listing on a stock exchange or to another regulated market which operates regularly and is recognized and open to the public, provided that the choice of stock exchange or market has been approved by the competent authorities or is provided for in law or the fund rules or the investment company's instruments of incorporation;
• such admission is secured within a year of issue.

2. However:
(a) a UCITS may invest no more than 10% of its assets in transferable securities other than those referred to in paragraph 1;

(b) a Member State may provide that a UCITS may invest no more than 10% of its assets in debt instruments which, for purposes of this Directive, shall be treated, because of their characteristics, as equivalent to transferable securities and which are, *inter alia*, transferable, liquid and have a value which can be accurately determined at any time or at least with the frequency stipulated in Article 34;

(c) an investment company may acquire movable and immovable property which is essential for the direct pursuit of its business;

(d) a UCITS may not acquire either precious metals or certificates representing them.

3. The total of the investments referred to in paragraph 2(a) and (b) may not under any circumstances amount to more than 10% of the assets of a UCITS.

4. Unit trusts and investment companies may hold ancillary liquid assets.

Article 20

1. The Member States shall send to the Commission:

(a) no later than date of implementation of this Directive, lists of the debt instruments which, in accordance with Article 19 (2) (b), they plan to treat as equivalent to transferable securities, stating the characteristics of those instruments and the reasons for so doing;

(b) details of any amendments which they contemplate making to the lists of instruments referred to in (a) or any further instruments which they contemplate treating as equivalent to transferable securities, together with their reasons for so doing.

2. The Commission shall immediately forward that information to the other Member States together with any comments which it considers appropriate. Such communications may be the subject of exchanges of views within the Contact Committee in accordance with the procedure laid down in Article 53 (4).

Article 21

1. The Member States may authorize UCITS to employ techniques and instruments relating to transferable securities under the conditions and within the limits which they lay down provided that such techniques and instruments are used for the purpose of efficient portfolio management.

2. The Member States may also authorize UCITS to employ techniques and instruments intended to provide protection against exchange risks in the context of the management of their assets and liabilities.

Article 22

1. A UCITS may invest no more than 5% of its assets in transferable securities issued by the same body.

2. The Member States may raise the limit laid down in paragraph 1 to a maximum of 10%. However, the total value of the transferable securities held by a UCITS in the issuing bodies in each of which it invests more than 5% of its assets must not then exceed 40% of the value of its assets.

3. The Member States may raise the limit laid down in paragraph 1 to a maximum of 35% if the transferable securities are issued or guaranteed by a Member State, by its local authorities, by a non-member State or by public international bodies of which one or more Member States are members.

Article 23

1. By way of derogation from Article 22 and without prejudice to Article 68 (3) of the Treaty, the Member States may authorize UCITS to invest in accordance with the principle of risk-spreading up to 100% of their assets in different transferable securities issued or guaranteed by any Member State, its local authorities, a non-member State or public international bodies of which one or more Member States are members.

    The competent authorities shall grant such a derogation only if they consider that unit-holders in the UCITS have protection equivalent to that of unit-holders in UCITS complying with the limits laid down in Article 22.

    Such a UCITS must hold securities from at least six different issues, but securities from any one issue may not account for more than 30% of its total assets.

2. The UCITS referred to in paragraph I must make express mention in the fund rules or in the investment company's instruments of incorporation of the States, local authorities or public international bodies issuing or guaranteeing securities in which they intend to invest more than 35% of their assets; such fund rules or instruments of incorporation must be approved by the competent authorities.

3. In addition each such UCITS referred to in paragraph 1 must include a prominent statement in its prospectus and any promotional literature drawing attention to such authorization and indicating the States, local authorities and/or public international bodies in the securities of which it intends to invest or has invested more than 35% of its assets.

Article 24

1. A UCITS may not acquire the units of other collective investment undertakings of the open-ended type unless they are collective investment undertakings within the meaning of the first and second indents of Article 1 (2).

2. A UCITS may invest no more than 5% of its assets in the units of such collective investment undertakings.

3. Investment in the units of a unit trust managed by the same management company or by any other company with which the management company is linked by common management or control, or by a substantial direct or indirect holding, shall be permitted only in the case of a trust which, in accordance with its rules, has specialized in investment in a specific geographical area or economic sector, and provided that such investment is authorized by the competent authorities. Authorization shall be granted only if the trust has announced its intention of making use of that option and that option has been expressly stated in its rules.

    A management company may not charge any fees or costs on account of transactions relating to a unit trust's units where some of a unit trust's assets are invested in the units of another unit trust managed by the same management company or by any other company with which the management company is linked by common management or control, or by a substantial direct or indirect holding.

4. Paragraph 3 shall also apply where an investment company acquires units in another investment company to which it is linked within the meaning of paragraph 3.

    Paragraph 3 shall also apply where an investment company acquires units of a unit trust to which it is linked, or where a unit trust acquires units of an investment company to which it is linked.

Article 25

1. An investment company or a management company acting in connection with all of the unit trusts which it manages and which fall within the scope of this Directive may not acquire any shares carrying voting rights which would enable it to exercise significant influence over the management of an issuing body.

   Pending further coordination, the Member States shall take account of existing rules defining the principle stated in the first subparagraph under other Member States' legislation.

2. Moreover, an investment company or unit trust may acquire no more than:
   - 10% of the non-voting shares of any single issuing body;
   - 10% of the debt securities of any single issuing body;
   - 10% of the units of any single collective investment undertaking within the meaning of the first and second indents of Article 1 (2).

   The limits laid down in the second and third indents may be disregarded at the time of acquisition if at that time the gross amount of the debt securities or the net amount of the securities in issue cannot be calculated.

3. A Member State may waive application of paragraphs 1 and 2 as regards:
   (a) transferable securities issued or guaranteed by a Member State or its local authorities;
   (b) transferable securities issued or guaranteed by a non-member State;
   (c) transferable securities issued by public international bodies of which one or more Member States are members;
   (d) shares held by a UCITS in the capital of a company incorporated in a non-member State investing its assets mainly in the securities of issuing bodies having their registered offices in that State, where under the legislation of that State such a holding represents the only way in which the UCITS can invest in the securities of issuing bodies of that State. This derogation, however, shall apply only if in its investment policy the company from the non-member State complies with the limits laid down in Articles 22, 24 and 25 (1) and (2). Where the limits set in Articles 22 and 24 are exceeded. Article 26 shall apply *mutatis mutandis*;
   (e) shares held by an investment company in the capital of subsidiary companies carrying on the business of management, advice or marketing exclusively on its behalf.

Article 26

1. UCITS need not comply with the limits laid down in this Section when exercising subscription rights attaching to transferable securities which form part of their assets.

   While ensuring observance of the principle of risk-spreading, the Member States may allow recently authorized UCITS to derogate from Articles 22 and 23 for six months following the date of their authorization.

2. If the limits referred to in paragraph 1 are exceeded for reasons beyond the control of a UCITS or as a result of the exercise of subscription rights, that UCITS must adopt as a priority objective for its sales transactions the remedying of that situation, taking due account of the interests of its unit-holders.

Section VI Obligations concerning information to be supplied to unit-holders

A. Publication of a prospectus and periodical reports

Article 27

1. An investment company and, for each of the trusts it manages, a management company must publish:
    *   a prospectus,
    *   an annual report for each financial year, and
    *   a half-yearly report covering the first six months of the financial year.
2. The annual and half-yearly reports must be published within the following time limits, with effect from the ends of the periods to which they relate:
    *   four months in the case of the annual report,
    *   two months in the case of the half-yearly report.

Article 28

1. A prospectus must include the information necessary for investors to be able to make an informed judgement of the investment proposed to them. It shall contain at least the information provided for in Schedule A annexed to this Directive, insofar as that information does not already appear in the documents annexed to the prospectus in accordance with Article 29 (1).
2. The annual report must include a balance-sheet or a statement of assets and liabilities, a detailed income and expenditure account for the financial year, a report on the activities of the financial year and the other information provided for in Schedule B annexed to this Directive, as well as any significant information which will enable investors to make an informed judgement on the development of the activities of the UCITS and its results.
3. The half-yearly report must include at least the information provided for in Chapters I to IV of Schedule B annexed to this Directive; where a UCITS has paid or proposes to pay an interim dividend, the figures must indicate the results after tax for the half-year concerned and the interim dividend paid or proposed.

Article 29

1. The fund rules or an investment company's instruments of incorporation shall form an integral part of the prospectus and must be annexed thereto.
2. The documents referred to in paragraph 1 need not, however, be annexed to the prospectus provided that the unit-holder is informed that on request he or she will be sent those documents or be apprised of the place where, in each Member State in which the units are placed on the market, he or she may consult them.

Article 30

The essential elements of the prospectus must be kept up to date.

Article 31

The accounting information given in the annual report must be audited by one or more persons empowered by law to audit accounts in accordance with Council Directive 84/253/

EEC of 10 April 1984 based on Article 54 (3) (g) of the EEC Treaty on the approval of persons responsible for carrying out the statutory audits of accounting documents (^{4}). The auditor's report, including any qualifications, shall be reproduced in full in the annual report.

Article 32
A UCITS must send its prospectus and any amendments thereto, as well as its annual and half-yearly reports, to the competent authorities.

Article 33
1. The prospectus, the latest annual report and any subsequent half-yearly report published must be offered to subscribers free of charge before the conclusion of a contract.
2. In addition, the annual and half-yearly reports must be available to the public at the places specified in the prospectus.
3. The annual and half-yearly reports shall be supplied to unit-holders free of charge on request.

B.   Publication of other information

Article 34
A UCITS must make public in an appropriate manner the issue, sale, re-purchase or redemption price of its units each time it issues, sells, re-purchases or redeems them, and at least twice a month. The competent authorities may, however, permit a UCITS to reduce the frequency to once a month on condition that such a derogation does not prejudice the interests of the unit-holders.

Article 35
All publicity comprising an invitation to purchase the units of a UCITS must indicate that a prospectus exists and the places where it may be obtained by the public.

Section VII   The general obligations of UCITS

Article 36
1. Neither:
   * an investment company, not
   * a management company or depositary acting on behalf of a unit trust,
     may borrow.
     However, a UCTIS may acquire foreign currency by means of a 'back-to-back' loan.
2. By way of derogation from paragraph 1, a Member State may authorize a UCITS to borrow:
   (a) up to 10%
   * of its assets, in the case of an investment company, or
   * of the value of the fund, in the case of a unit trust,
     provided that the borrowing is on a temporary basis;
   (b) up to 10% of its assets, in the case of an investment company, provided that the borrowing it to make possible the acquisition of immovable property essential for the

direct pursuit of its business; in this case the borrowing and that referred to in sub-paragraph (a) may not in any case in total exceed 15% of the borrower's assets.

Article 37

1. A UCITS must re-purchase or redeem its units at the request of any unit-holder.
2. By way of derogation from paragraph 1:
(a) a UCITS may, in the cases and according to the procedures provided for by law, the fund rules or the investment company's instruments of incorporation, temporarily suspend the re-purchase or redemption of its units. Suspension may be provided for only in exceptional cases where circumstances so require, and suspension is justified having regard to the interests of the unit-holders;
(b) the Member States may allow the competent authorities to require the suspension of the re-purchase or redemption of units in the interest of the unit-holders or of the public.
3. In the cases mentioned in paragraph 2 (a), a UCITS must without delay communicate its decision to the competent authorities and to the authorities of all Member States in which it markets its units.

Article 38

The rules for the valuation of assets and the rules for calculating the sale or issue price and the re-purchase or redemption price of the units of a UCITS must be laid down in the law, in the fund rules or in the investment company's instruments of incorporation.

Article 39

The distribution or reinvestment of the income of a unit trust or of an investment company shall be effected in accordance with the law and with the fund rules or the investment company's instruments of incorporation.

Article 40

A UCITS unit may not be issued unless the equivalent of the net issue price is paid into the assets of the UCITS within the usual time limits. This provision shall not preclude the distribution of bonus units.

Article 41

1. Without prejudice to the application of Articles 19 and 21, neither:
*   an investment company, nor
*   a management company or depositary acting on behalf of a unit trust
    may grant loans or act as a guarantor on behalf of third parties.
2. Paragraph 1 shall not prevent such undertakings from acquiring transferable securities which are not fully paid.

Article 42

Neither:

*   an investment company, nor
*   a management company or depository acting on behalf of a unit trust

may carry out uncovered sales of transferable securities.

Article 43

The law or the fund rules must prescribe the remuneration and the expenditure which a management company is empowered to charge to a unit trust and the method of calculation of such remuneration.

The law or an investment company's instruments of incorporation must prescribe the nature of the cost to be borne by the company.

Section VIII   Special provisions applicable to UCITS which market their units in Member States other than those in which they are situated

Article 44

1. A UCITS which markets its units in another Member State must comply with the laws, regulations and administrative provisions in force in that State which do not fall within the field governed by this Directive.
2. Any UCITS may advertise its units in the Member State in which they are marketed it must comply the provisions governing advertising in that State.
3. The provisions referred to in paragraphs 1 and 2 must be applied without discrimination.

Article 45

In the case referred to in Article 44, the UCITS must, *inter alia*, in accordance with the laws, regulations and administrative provisions in force in the Member State of marketing, take the measures necessary to ensure that facilities are available in that State for making payments to unit-holders, re-purchasing or redeeming units and making available the information which UCITS are obliged to provide.

Article 46

If a UCITS proposes to market its units in a Member State other than that in which it is situated, it must first inform the competent authorities and the authorities of that other Member State accordingly. It must simultaneously send the latter authorities:

- an attestation by the competent authorities to the effect that it fulfils the conditions imposed by this Directive,
- its fund rules or its instruments of incorporation,
- its prospectus,
- where appropriate, its latest annual report and any subsequent half-yearly report and
- details of the arrangements made for the marketing of its units in that other Member State.

A UCITS may begin to market its units in that other Member State two months after such communication unless the authorities of the Member State concerned establish, in a reasoned decision taken before the expiry of that period of two months, that the arrangements made for the marketing of units do not comply with the provisions referred to in Articles 44 (1) and 45.

Article 47

If a UCITS markets its units in a Member State other than that in which it is situated, it must distribute in that other Member State, in at least one of that other Member State's official languages, the documents and information which must be published in the Member State in which it is situated, in accordance with the same procedures as those provided for in the latter State.

Article 48

For the purpose of carrying on its activities, a UCITS may use the same generic name (such as investment company or unit trust) in the community as it uses in the Member State in which it is situated. In the event of any danger of confusion, the host Member State may, for the purpose of clarification, require that the name be accompanied by certain explanatory particulars.

Section IX   Provisions concerning the authorities responsible for authorization and supervision

Article 49

1. The Member States shall designate the authorities which are to carry out the duties provided for in this Directive. They shall inform the Commission thereof, indicating any division of duties.
2. The authorities referred to in paragraph 1 must be public authorities or bodies appointed by public authorities.
3. The authorities of the State in which a UCITS it situated shall be competent to supervise that UCITS. However, the authorities of the State in which 2 UCITS markets its units in accordance with Article 44 shall be competent to supervise compliance with Section VIII.
4. The authorities concerned must be granted all the powers necessary to carry out their task.

Article 50

1. The authorities of the Member States referred to in Article 49 shall collaborate closely in order to carry out their task and must for that purpose along communicate to each other all information required.
2. The Member States shall provide that all persons employed or formerly employed by the authorities referred to in Article 49 shall be bound by professional secrecy. This means that any confidential information received in the course of their duties may not be divulged to any person or authority except by virtue of provisions laid down by law.
3. Paragraph 2 shall not, however, preclude communications between the authorities of the various Member States referred to in Article 49, as provided for in this Directive. Information thus exchanged shall be covered by the obligation of professional secrecy on persons employed or formerly employed by the authorities receiving the information.
4. Without prejudice to cases covered by criminal law, an authority of the type referred to in Article 49 receiving such information may use it only for the performance of its duties or in the context of administrative appeals or legal proceedings relating to such performance.

Article 51

1. The authorities referred to in Article 49 must give reasons for any decision to refuse authorization, and any negative decision taken in implementation of the general measures adopted in application of this Directive, and communicate them to applicants.
2. The Member States shall provide that decisions taken in respect of a UCITS pursuant to laws, regulations and administrative provisions adopted in accordance with this Directive are subject to the right to apply to the courts; the same shall apply if no decision is taken within six months of its submission on an authorization application made by a UCITS which includes all the information required under the provisions in force.

Article 52

1. Only the authorities of the Member State in which a UCITS is situated shall have the power to take action against it if it infringes any law, regulation or administrative provision or any regulation laid down in the fund rules or in the investment company's instruments of incorporation.
2. Nevertheless, the authorities of the Member State in which the units of a UCITS are marketed may take action against it if it infringes the provisions referred to in Section VIII.
3. Any decision to withdraw authorization, or any other serious measure taken against a UCITS, or any suspension of re-purchase or redemption imposed upon it, must be communicated without delay by the authorities of the Member State in which the UCITS in question is situated to the authorities of the other Member States in which its units are marketed.

Section X   Contact Committee

Article 53

1. A Contact Committee, hereinafter referred to as 'the Committee', shall be set up alongside the Commission. Its function shall be:
   (a) to facilitate, without prejudice to Articles 169 and 170 of the Treaty, the harmonized implementation of this Directive through regular consultations on any practical problems arising from its application and on which exchanges of views are deemed useful;
   (b) to facilitate consultation between Member States either on more rigorous or additional requirements which they may adopt in accordance with Article 1 (7), or on the provisions which they may adopt in accordance with Articles 44 and 45;
   (c) to advise the Commission, if necessary, on additions or amendments to be made to this Directive.
2. It shall not be the function of the Committee to appraise the merits of decisions taken in individual cases by the authorities referred to in Article 49.
3. The Committee shall be composed of persons appointed by the Member States and of representatives of the Commission. The Chairman shall be a representative of the Commission. Secretarial services shall be provided by the Commission.
4. Meetings of the Committee shall be convened by its chairman, either on his own initiative or at the request of a Member State delegation. The Committee shall draw up its rules of procedure.

Section XI   Transitional provisions, derogations and final provisions

Article 54

Solely for the purpose of Danish UCITS, *pantebreve* issued in Denmark shall be treated as equivalent to the transferable securities referred to in Article 19 (1)(b).

Article 55

By way of derogation from Articles 7 (1) and 14 (1), the competent authorities may authorize those UCITS which, on the date of adoption of this Directive, had two or more depositaries in accordance with their national law to maintain that number of depositaries if those authorities have guarantees that the function to be performed under Articles 7 (3) and 14 (3) will be performed in practice.

Article 56

1. By way of derogation from Article 6, the Member States may authorize management companies to issue bearer certificates representing the registered securities of other companies.
2. The Member States may authorize those management companies which, on the date of adoption of this Directive, also carry on activities other than those provided for in Article 6 to continue those other activities for five years after that date.

Article 57

1. The Member States shall bring into force no later than 1 October 1989 the measures necessary for them to comply with this Directive. They shall forthwith inform the Commission thereof.
2. The Member States may grant UCITS existing on the date of implementation of this Directive a period of not more than 12 months from that date in order to comply with the new national legislation.
3. The Hellenic Republic and the Portuguese Republic shall be authorized to postpone the implementation of this Directive until 1 April 1992 at the latest.

    One year before that date the Commission shall report to the Council on progress in implementing the Directive and on any difficulties which the Hellenic Republic or the Portuguese Republic may encounter in implementing the Directive by the date referred to in the first subparagraph.

    The Commission shall, if necessary, propose that the Council extend the postponement by up to four years.

Article 58

The Member States shall ensure that the Commission is informed of the texts of the main laws, regulations and administrative provisions which they adopt in the field covered by this Directive.

Article 59

This Directive is addressed to the Member States.

Done at Brussels, 20 December 1985.

For the Council
The President
R. Krieps

Notes

1. OJ No C 171. 26. 7. 1976. p. 1.
2. OJ No C 57. 7. 3. 1977. p. 31.
3. OJ No C 75. 26. 3. 1977. p. 10.
4. OJ No L 126. 12. 5. 1984. p. 20.

13.4   NAFTA Opens Mexican Doors to U.S. Financial Services*
Robert C. Pozen

President Bush has signed the North American Free Trade Agreement (NAFTA), which now goes on the fast track for Congressional approval or rejection. While the legislators will surely engage in extensive debates on the environmental and labor implications of NAFTA, they should not overlook the significance of the treaty for U.S. financial services firms. NAFTA will open the door to Mexico for U.S. financial firms that have been virtually shut out of Mexico's rapidly growing financial market.

Under current Mexican laws, a U.S. firm may not directly or indirectly sell mutual funds to Mexican investors. A U.S. firm may not engage in cross-border sales by offering SEC registered funds on Mexican soil. Nor may a U.S. firm establish a Mexican subsidiary to sell customized Mexican funds—funds specially designed for Mexican investors and registered with the Mexican counterpart of the SEC.

U.S. brokers and U.S. banks are subject to similar restrictions under current Mexican laws on doing business in Mexico. With the exception of a few grandfathered firms, U.S. brokers and U.S. banks may not establish branches or subsidiaries to do business in Mexico. In 1990, U.S. firms were allowed to purchase a minority share of a Mexican broker or bank subject to stringent limits—each U.S. firm may hold no more than a 10 percent share and U.S. firms in the aggregate may hold no more than a 30 percent share.

By contrast, the U.S. financial markets are very open to Mexican firms interested in providing services to U.S. investors. Any Mexican firm may sponsor a customized U.S. fund for sale to U.S. investors simply by filing two registration statements with the SEC—one for the firm under the Investment Advisers Act and the second for the fund under the Investment Company Act. The SEC has no capital requirement for a foreign investment adviser and a capital requirement of only $100,000 for a U.S.-registered fund. The only constraint is that a Mexican registered fund may not be offered in cross-border sales to U.S. investors.

Similarly, a Mexican firm may establish a U.S. broker subsidiary by filing a registration statement under the Securities Exchange Act and supplying $25,000 in capital. And under the International Banking Act, a Mexican-owned firm may establish U.S. banking subsidiary subject to essentially the same requirements as U.S.-owned banks.

This gross disparity between America's wide open markets and Mexico's virtually closed markets would be largely remedied by NAFTA. It would allow immediately U.S. firms to establish wholly owned subsidiaries to sponsor and advise customized funds for Mexican investors subject to the same regulations as Mexican fund managers. These U.S. firms would be able themselves to distribute these customized funds or, alternatively, to rely on Mexican brokers to distribute these customized funds. Although U.S firms could

---

*From CDA/Weisenberger Mutual Funds Update, December 31, 1992.

not sell U.S. registered funds in Mexico, Mexican firms have never been allowed to make cross-border sales of Mexican registered funds to U.S. investors.

U.S. brokers and banks would also be allowed to establish wholly owned subsidiaries in Mexico, though they would be subject to market share limits until the year 2000. U.S. brokers in the aggregate would be limited initially to 10 percent of the Mexican securities market, which would rise to 20 percent by the year 2000. During this transition period, each individual U.S. broker would be limited to 4 percent of the Mexican securities market.

The market share limits on U.S. banks would be tighter because of Mexican concerns about potential U.S. dominance of the Mexican credit system. U.S. banks in the aggregate would be limited initially to 8 percent of the Mexican banking market, which would rise to 15 percent by the year 2,000. During this transition period, each individual U.S. bank would be limited to 1.5 percent of the Mexican banking market. After the transition period, U.S. bank acquisitions would remain subject to a 4 percent market share limit on the resulting institution.

The market share limits are one of the problems of NAFTA, in that they are unwise from a policy perspective and unworkable as a practical matter. How will the relevant Mexican market be defined, and who will enforce the allocation among competing U.S. firms? If appears that market share will be defined in terms of the capital of the Mexican subsidiaries or branches of a U.S. firm, or U.S. firms in the aggregate, relative to the total capital of Mexican brokers or banks as the case may be. It appears that these limits will be enforced by a Mexican government agency.

In this regard, it is important to recognize that the financial services provisions of NAFTA allows Mexican investors to purchase dollar-denominated financial instruments from U.S. offices of U.S. financial firms. Such cross-border transactions in financial services would not appear to be subject to the market share limits discussed above, which apply to the activities of the Mexican offices of U.S. financial firms. However, this point may be less significant than it seems, since the U.S. offices of U.S. financial firms may not solicit investors in Mexico. Moreover, under the financial services provisions of NAFTA, Mexican authorities have the right to define what constitutes solicitation with regard to Mexican investors.

In any event, while these market share limits are wrought with potential problems, they appear to be the price of U.S. admission to Mexico. Mexican officials are reportedly fearful that U.S. financial firms will overrun Mexico and put local firms out of business. Without these market share limits, Mexico apparently refuses to lift the current barriers to entry by U.S. financial firms.

Since NAFTA is being considered by Congress under fast track procedures, Congress may not pick and choose among treaty provisions. After the President submits the treaty to Congress, the President must wait 90 days to sign the treaty and then Congress has 90 session days to vote up or down on the legislation implementing NAFTA.

From the perspective of the financial services industries, Congress should approve NAFTA because, despite the market share limits on brokers and banks, it allows U.S. financial firms for the first time to have a reasonable opportunity to attract Mexican customers.

13.5   Go Forth and Multiply*

For all the glamour attached to being a fund manager, managing people's money is not that difficult. The hard part is persuading them to give it to you in the first place. A history of good investment performance helps, but on its own it is not nearly enough. In America, fund-management companies with successful track records are falling over one another in their efforts to market their products. But in most other places, that kind of wide-open competition has yet to take hold, for a number of reasons.

One is outright protectionism. In many emerging-market countries, fund-management companies are either forbidden to sell to locals, or forced to go through local inter-mediaries to do so. Even in countries with few explicit regulatory restrictions, however, a handful of powerful domestic intermediaries, combined with rigid financial markets, can make life difficult for foreigners.

Such barriers are all the more frustrating because it is almost embarrassingly easy to manufacture a good global mutual fund. All you have to do is set up a feeder fund in an accommodating offshore financial centre that will allow you to pass through the returns tax-free to your investors (who will, of course, dutifully report their gains to the local tax authority). Then you simply register versions of the fund everywhere, and you are ready to start selling.

In Europe, for example, most global fund houses have set up administrative centres in either Dublin or Luxembourg, which they use to process all of their funds sold throughout the region. The money, however, can be managed anywhere. If a fund house wants to see a global equity fund, for example, it might draw on a handful of its existing funds from different regions: say, a U.S. equity fund and a Latin America fund managed in New York; a Europe fund managed in London; and an Asia fund managed in Hong Kong. It then creates a new fund—call it the Global Equity Fund—which is registered in Luxembourg and combines shares in each of these other funds. Thanks to E.U. regulations, a fund registered in one member country can be sold in all the others, so the firm is now free to market its brand-new global fund throughout Europe.

Something for Nothing

The beauty of this arrangement is that it costs almost nothing to create the new mutual fund. The company is just selling extra shares in funds that are already being sold to other investors in other parts of the world. The only difference is that instead of selling the shares direct to European investors, it sells them to the composite fund in Luxembourg, giving the fund managers in each of the different regions a single new client, the Global Equity Fund.

Of course there will be costs associated with the new European fund—such as running the offshore administration centre, and marketing the fund to European investors. But if the company does a lot of business in Europe, and pushes a wide range of funds through that network, it can reap huge economies of scale. Moreover, by simply repackaging existing funds in different parts of the world, fund-management companies can begin to do something most other industries only dream about: sever the geographical link between "manufacturing" and distribution, without increasing costs or lowering quality. Ideally, a firm could simply manage each type of investment in those parts of the world that make the most sense for it, while still tapping a global market for their far-flung superstars.

Unfortunately, that ideal has not yet been attained. Outside Europe, the business of registering and distributing funds faces tight restrictions. Japan, for example, which accounts for roughly a third of the world's savings, allows only authorised securities firms to distribute investment trusts, the Japanese equivalent of mutual funds. Since 1990, foreign fund-management houses have at last been able to sell their funds to Japanese investors, but they must go through one of these intermediaries (four of which control most of the distribution). Financial deregulation may improve matters, but foreign fund managers face a long, tough climb.

Fortress Asia

It is the same story all over Asia. South Korea at last allowed foreign fund managers in earlier this year, after its admission to the OECD put pressure on the finance ministry to liberalise. Now, three foreign fund providers –Jardine Fleming, Merrill Lynch, and Fidelity—have been admitted, but only after signing exclusive deals with local securities firms through which they must distribute their products.

Two of Asia's biggest financial centres, Malaysia and Singapore, also restrict access to their markets in order to nurture their fledgling domestic fund-management companies. In Singapore, for example, a foreign fund cannot even register unless it is managed entirely in that market. This restriction defeats the entire purpose of global fund management, which is to provide investors in each country with an international selection of investment options, preferably drawing on managers in a number of different locations. Templeton, which runs a huge fund management operation from Singapore, had to clear several hurdles just to sell its global fund to Singaporean investors, even though the fund is a collection of smaller funds, many of which are managed in Singapore.

However, protectionist restrictions are not the only obstacle to the development of pan-Asian fund-management houses. Even when fund managers find ways round the regulatory barriers, they must then contend with the difficulties of distributing their products. The handful of fund houses with well-developed marketing skills—Jardine Fleming, Schroders, Fidelity, Templeton—are able to do a modest business selling funds direct to retail customers. But since mutual funds are still an unfamiliar product to many Asian investors, the main channel of distribution for them, and everyone else, is still the banks.

Consider HSBC, the world's biggest banking group and a colossus in the region. Its HongKong Bank unit has the capacity to distribute financial products throughout Asia, but mostly sells the products of the group's fund-management unit, HSBC Asset Management. After much negotiation and a few technical glitches, it has at last arranged to start selling the funds of a few other providers, possibly by the end of this year. Once again, however, it is only those fund managers with the most clout that have been able to gain access: Jardine Fleming, Fidelity and Bankers Trust, which does a thriving business in Australia.

Not surprisingly, there are hardly any retail fund-management companies with a pan-Asian pedigree. Jardine Fleming, a sister company of Britain's Robert Fleming, is the only firm which qualifies for that status. Fidelity seemed to be mounting a challenge, but its retail business has suffered of late.

Europe ought be much easier to crack, but turns out to be just as tough in its own way. EU rules on financial competition have largely eliminated the regulatory hurdles that make Asia such a nightmare (though fund managers grumble that too many still remain). Yet in most European countries distribution is sewn up by a handful of big intermediaries. For example, in France and the Netherlands, two of the bigger retail markets, 70–90% of mutual funds are sold through banks and life insurers. In Germany, the estimates range from 80% to 95%. (See figure 13.5.1.)

Most of these intermediaries have their own ambitions. The banks, for example, are anxious to offset their shrinking deposit base by turning mutual funds to their own advantage. Société Générale dominates distribution in France, along with Crédit Agricole;

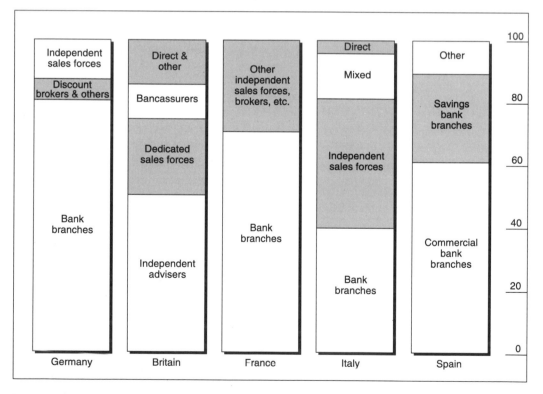

Figure 13.5.1 The devil you know: Sales channels for mutual funds. Source: Boston Consulting Service

but it also has a thriving fund-management operation of its own, which it is not about to undermine by hawking competitors' products. The same is true of ING, the Dutch bank-and-insurance group which in 1995 snapped up Barings, an investment bank with a big asset-management arm, after the British firm went bust.

German banks, too, have gone to great lengths to get into fund management. In 1995 Commerzbank purchased a British firm, Jupiter Tyndall; in the past few years Dresdner Bank has bought Kleinwort Benson in London and RCM in San Francisco; and it is almost a decade since Deutsche Bank acquired Britain's Morgan Grenfell. In Britain, Barclays Golobal Investors, part of the banking group, has become the world's fourth-biggest asset manager after acquiring Wells Nikko, an index-fund provider that was itself the product of a joint venture between an American and a Japanese firm. Since European banks tend to have sparse distribution networks outsider their home countries, none of these banks has been able to develop a pan-European presence in retail fund management. But they have been doing a great job keeping others off their home turf.

Insurance companies, too, have responded to the mutual-fund threat by developing their own retail funds, usually packaged in a life-insurance wrapper. These products require customers to forfeit some of the flexibility and liquidity of mutual funds, but they usually come with tax advantages attached. Like the banks, European insurers are short on cross-border distribution networks. Last year, for example, AXA, France's largest insurer, snapped up UAP, a French rival with a large presence in Germany. And Zurich Insurance, after acquiring America's Kemper in 1995, followed by Scudder, Stevens & Clark this year, has tried to portray itself as European asset manager, rather than an insurance outfit. It recently confirmed that it is in merger talks with BAT, a British tobacco and financial-services group.

Independent fund managers, or at least those that have not already sold out to the banks and insurers, have been hedging their bets. By signing deals with the banks, they have been able to reach the small cadre of customers dogged enough to pester their banks for third-party funds. And by combining their marketing prowess with direct-sales operations and independent financial advisers, they have tried to prise some customers away from the banks altogether.

Still, these efforts have as yet made only a dent in the European market. Fidelity, which has been managing Luxembourg-registered funds since 1990, is the only American mutual-fund firm in continental Europe's top 50; only a handful of British firms have made the list. As investor awareness grows, these efforts are likely to get a boost. Personal-finance magazines based on the American model, such as France's *Investir* and Germany's *Wertpapier*, are already providing the industry with a growing pool of informed and interested investors. The independents' prospects will stand or fall, however, with the way Europe's governments choose to reform their state pensions.

The Joys of Independence

If governments rely on employers to pick up the slack, and offer them a vehicle equivalent to America's 401(k) plans, then the independents will at last be able to give the banks and insurers a run for their money. They have the experience, the product variety, the information systems, the brand recognition and the service mentality that are required to operate these schemes. And although their rivals in the banking and insurance industries will try to milk their corporate contacts to win this business, the independent fund houses, especially the Americans, will be in the best position to offer the low-cost, trouble-free systems that employers cannot resist.

The independents won their first big battle in March, when France passed a law allowing workers (or their employers) to contribute up to 5% of their pay to a private pension plan. But the change of government in June put the law's status into doubt, and despite the compelling advantages of defined-contribution plans there is no guarantee that other European countries will continue down that route.

If they do not, the big independents will find life much more difficult. The worst result for them—as well as for individual investors—would be a shift towards traditional occupational schemes offered on a defined-benefit basis. At present, the market to manage these institutional funds tends to be dominated by domestic fund managers in each country. Since all that matters is the ability to manage money, rather than the administrative skills and service that go into defined-contribution schemes, domestic banks and insurers can take much better advantage of their client relationships.

Even in this event, however, not all independents would lose out. In the Netherlands, the only continental market with a large foreign presence, two big fund managers dominate the market: Wells Nikko and State Street. Both firms do a huge business managing passive funds, offering pension funds much lower costs than their active rivals at home or abroad.

Small independents would also benefit from a bigger institutional market, since distribution would become less of an issue. Many specialist fund managers, such as Global Asset Management, Guinness Flight, and John Govett, have competed successfully in Europe for contracts to manage specific portions of institutional customers' portfolios. The main losers from such a shift would be individual investors, who would miss out on the more direct involvement now enjoyed by their equivalents in America. Regardless of how employers handle their pension arrangements, the race for Europe's retail sector will be largely run between the banks and the independents. The banks will have convenience and distribution muscle on their side, but will have to work hard to emulate the independents' superior administration and service. In the end, their appalling lack of interest in serving customers may count against them.

Most independent fund houses, however, are convinced that they also have superior investment skills, which will help them win the day as Europe opens up.

13.6   Is America Being Shut Out Again?*

Robert C. Pozen

The world's trade negotiators, having reached a tentative agreement on agriculture, are pushing to conclude an agreement on other sectors by next month, when the Uruguay Round of the General Agreement on Tariffs and Trade is slated to be completed. For the American financial services sector, however, a quick completion of the Uruguay Round threatens to cast in concrete the current one-way street: American financial markets would remain open to all comers, while Asian markets would continue to restrict access.

Under the ground rules for service agreements, GATT does not grant foreigners the right to compete in domestic markets unless that right is included in a country's GATT service schedules. This creates a disadvantage for American and European financial institutions, whose markets are open to foreign banks and brokers that meet the regulatory standards of domestic institutions.

By contrast, Asian countries generally impose special restrictions on foreign access to their financial markets. For example, Korea has an outright prohibition on foreigners selling mutual funds to local investors, while Japan requires foreign fund companies to go through a multi-year application process without clear objective criteria for approval. Most Asian countries limit the number of foreign banks and/or the scope of their local activities, while many Asian countries have only recently begun to allow the entry of foreign securities dealers on any conditions.

Given these existing disparities, Americans and Europeans can improve their relative market access through the GATT negotiations only if the Asian make substantial commitments to open up their financial markets to foreigners. However, such commitments to date have been very thin.

For example, Korea has even refused to guarantee that it would maintain the limited market access it currently affords to foreign banks and securities firms. Other Asina countries with significant exports are trying to position themselves as third world economies in need of protection for local financial markets. Singapore and Thailand, despite having advanced financial centers, exclude virtually all of their domestic banking sectors and the dealer portions of their local securities markets.

If the Asian commitments on financial services do not substantially improve, the United States would be locking in current disparities by signing the Uruguay Round. It would be prohibited from using access to its financial markets as a basis for reciprocal negotiations wit Asian countries. Any special limits on Asian access to American financial markets would violate the most favored nation provision of GATT—a requirement to provide all signatories with the best market access afforded to any signatory. Thus, the most favored nation requirement would eliminate nearly all American leverage in bilateral negotiations with the Asians.

---

*From *The New York Times*, January 10, 1993. © The New York Times Co. Reprinted with permission.

What should be done? If the Asian countries do not make reasonable commitments to open their financial markets within the next month, the United States and Europe should claim a most favored nation exemption for financial services. At the same time, they should agree to maintain the current openness of their financial markets between themselves.

The United States would then be free to adopt a reciprocity statute like the Fair Trade in Financial Services Act, which last year passed the Senate but not the House. Under this Act, the Treasury would be required to evaluate whether American firms were being given fair access to Asian financial markets. If not, the United States could deny or condition licenses to Asian firms doing business in the American financial markets.

Although the United States negotiators are under intense international pressure to complete the Uruguay Round without taking major exceptions in any service sector, they should not allow Asia to become a "free rider" to the GATT agreement for financial services. By taking a most favored nation exemption for financial services, the United States would pave the way for tough bilateral negotiations based on trade reciprocity—the only viable method for getting equal access to Asian financial markets.

Case Study: **Transferring a Fund Business to a Foreign Country**

As discussed earlier in this chapter, U.S. firms may not sell U.S. registered mutual funds in most foreign countries. This is because each country tends to impose its own regulatory, accounting, and tax requirements on mutual funds sold there. As a result, U.S. firms must establish clone funds customized to meet the requirements of each country.

This case study examines what should be a relatively easy international transfer—the export of a defined contribution retirement system for mutual funds to Canada. After all, Canada is contiguous to the United States and most Canadians speak English. Canadian mutual funds operate in a similar fashion to broker-dealer sold funds in the United States, and Canadian defined contribution plans have features of both 401(k) and individual retirement account (IRA) plans in the United States. Furthermore, both Canada and the United States follow the Anglo-Saxon tradition of jurisprudence.

Nevertheless, as the case study demonstrates, even small differences in securities and pension laws between two countries can result in major challenges with respect to developing the computer systems needed to support defined contribution plans. For this reason, the questions for the case study are divided between regulatory and operational issues. In preparing for the case study, you may also wish to review chapter 8 on the retirement business in the United States and chapter 12 on technology in the fund industry.

In-Class Discussion Questions

After reviewing results of the studies that you commissioned in the case, you should be prepared to answer the following questions:

Regulatory Questions
1. What are the principal securities law differences in Canada that will affect the Canadian business and how will they affect:
   a) product offerings?
   b) employee communications?
   c) responsibilities of The Management Company (TMC) to educate or advise employees concerning their investments?
2. How does the "know your customer" requirement make the Canadian environment different from the U.S. environment?
3. Assuming that the Canadian retirement business will be based upon telephone service, how will you design a compliance system:
   a) what information do you need to know?
   b) how should it be collected?
   c) how will you update that information and keep track of each investor's personal circumstances?

d) what procedures will the phone representatives follow when a customer calls in a trade?

e) how will you design customer applications, confirmations, and statements to support the know your customer process?

Operational Questions

1. What are the important differences between CanHolder and Colossus? With respect to adaptability to the Canadian Know Your Customer requirements?

2. Which will be better suited for the Canadian environment? Which seems most likely to be ready six months from now?

3. What do you need to be able to deliver in six months? Assuming that you can persuade AmPride Canada to either a delay or to a phased launch, you will not need the entire system in place at one time.

a) What would you propose to do, delay and test the entire system or deliver the system on a just-in-time basis?

b) Would your answer vary if AmPride Canada's number one priority was to ensure a flawless roll out rather than to launch within 6 months?

13.7 The Management Company

Background

Your firm—The Management Company, or TMC—is a global mutual fund sponsor. It has established a mutual fund operation in Canada, selling Canadian mutual funds through Canadian dealers to their clients. TMC-Canada has met with significant success, establishing the TMC name and building an efficient transfer agency operation, among other things. TMC-Canada's operations currently revolve around a transfer agency system, called CanHolder. CanHolder is a computer system licensed from a Canadian firm, Canadian Data Services Corp. (CDS), that tracks investor account data, including purchases, withdrawals, exchanges, and dividends. Data are entered into CanHolder by telephone representatives taking instructions from full-service brokers (often called *dealers* in Canada) and by electronic feed from brokerage firms.

TMC-Canada's biggest sales season is the "registered retirement savings plan" (RRSP) season, starting on January 1 and ending 60 days later. Individual Canadians are allowed to invest up to $13,500 on a pretax basis in their RRSPs. Most Canadian investors take advantage of RRSPs, or a similar account. Many of them do so individually and through employer sponsored RRSPs. There are particularly popular, as the employer often makes matching or partial matching contributions. TMC-Canada has reported to management of TMC in the United States that the employer-sponsored RRSP marketplace offers significant opportunities for TMC-Canada.

Although Canada is TMC's first offshore defined contribution retirement business opportunity, TMC intends to establish defined contribution retirement businesses in England, Australia, Hong Kong, and over time Japan. TMC intends to offer customer service by telephone and mail, with investment vehicles in the form of mutual funds in each country. TMC assumes that the basic recordkeeping and reporting functions in each country will be similar. TMC's systems will have to accept employee and employer contributions, track share purchases, exchanges and withdrawals. Dividends paid by the underlying mutual funds must be posted and cost basis of each investment tracked over time. Each country will have local requirements that vary. They are as yet unknown, although work is now underway to determine local requirements in Canada.

TMC's U.S. retirement business has developed an enormous capacity for computing customer transactions—more than enough to handle the incremental transactions anticipated by a global retirement business, but the computer systems were necessarily programmed to satisfy the U.S. environment. Identifying the Canadian/U.S. differences will be an important part of your task. You have been asked to evaluate whether you should build separate systems for each of the four foreign countries, or if you should modify the U.S. system for each country. Your first assignment is Canada and you need a system that will be operational in six months.

TMC-Canada currently operates only CanHolder. CanHolder was designed to run on a small scale. It is currently running on a series of mini-computers and its "nightly run" is relatively slow. Even with recent enhancements—in the form of additional computing capacity—the nightly run for CanHolder still takes three hours. Yet local management will tell you that it is inexpensive to operate and to change. CanHolder will have to be changed because it was not designed as a retirement system. Enhancing CanHolder's functionality as a transfer agent system requires TMC-Canada to rely on CDS, the owner of the software, to deliver enhancements.

The U.S. retirement record keeping system is called "Colossus." Since it was designed in the United States, Colossus likewise does not have any Canadian-specific capability. Yet, Colossus is a proven workhorse. U.S. management has undying faith in the system. Colossus resides on mainframe computers and was designed to process enormous transaction volume. It can handle single U.S. retirement plans that have more employees in them than there are participants in the total Canadian defined contribution marketplace. Nothing can slow the system. It is as reliable as it is expensive to modify.

Your sales force reports back that they have just "signed their first client." It is a subsidiary of a U.S. multinational "AmPride Worldwide, Inc.," with facilities in each of your global target markets. (AmPride's slogan is "the American way all the way!") Your senior management reports that the Canadian account, "AmPride Canada" was won along with winning the U.S. account. Your firm won the $1 billion U.S. business because AmPride was "overwhelmed" by Colossus and since you were the only firm in the U.S. bidding process that was building a Canadian retirement company. At the final sales pitch, TMC's chairman personally guaranteed that the Canadian business would offer nothing less than "TMC Quality" to AmPride Canada. That seemed to clinch the deal. Press releases quickly followed.

AmPride understands that you will not be ready to take AmPride Canada's monthly payroll for six months. Employee statements will be prepared quarterly, and AmPride has accepted TMC's standard format. AmPride is considering limiting trades to four per year, and expects none during the first quarter. AmPride Canada's head of HR will be traveling for two weeks. She expects you to present your system to her on her return. AmPride's head of HR is reported by your senior management to be well aware that you are still in the design phase, and she is said to have only one priority—to launch within six months at all costs. You must decide whether to base your business on CanHolder or Colossus.

Knowing little about the Canadian defined contribution environment, you commission a series of studies: (1) an overview of the Canadian "DC" marketplace by Maple Leaf Consultants; (2) a memorandum from TMC's legal department on differences between Canada and the U.S. from a regulatory perspective; and (3) a study of the functionality needed for a DC computer system in Canada, including a "gap" analysis for each of CanHolder and Colossus.

Commissioned Study #1

A Maple Leaf Consulting Report to The Management Company:

The Canadian Defined Contribution Marketplace

I Industry Overview

A Mutual Fund Industry

Much has been written in recent years about the size and growth prospects of the Canadian mutual fund industry. As of year end 1996, the industry had approximately $235 billion in assets, compared to only $40 billion just six years ago, in 1990. Our forecasts call for industry assets to exceed $330 billion by the year 2000. Canada is a plainly a significant marketplace for mutual funds, although small in comparison to the $3 trillion U.S. fund marketplace.

Canada restricts public mutual fund offerings to funds whose prospectuses have been filed with the Canadian Securities Administrators. These funds must be Canadian, and must comply with provincial mutual funds regulations. Foreign funds, including U.S. mutual funds, may not be sold in Canada.

The Canadian mutual fund industry may be divided into three distribution channels. Banks account for the largest channel with a 46% market share. Dealers and financial planers hold an aggregate market share of 34%, and direct marketing firms hold only a 9% share.

The bulk of Canadian mutual fund investment takes place inside various types of retirement savings plans registered with Revenue Canada. This is probably the result of a number of factors, including the significance of tax deferral in a country with marginal tax rates of over 50%, the ease of mutual fund investing, and Canadian investors' increasing familiarity with mutual funds. Canadian mutual funds will continue to increase in popularity as an investment choice for both Canadian individual "registered retirement savings plans" (known as RRSPs) and employer sponsored group savings plans. RRSPs are the Canadian "equivalent" of an Individual Retirement Account (or IRA). Generally, there are both similarities between the Canadian and U.S. "equivalents," and very important differences, as will be explored further below.

There are a large number of Canadians who make use of vehicles other than individual RRSPs for a significant portion of their savings. Frequently, these people rely upon savings schemes provided by their employers. These savings schemes have traditionally been pension plans, either *defined benefit* (DB Plans) or *defined contribution* (DC Plans). More recently, there has been a sharp increase in the number of alternative employer sponsored savings schemes, such as *group retirement savings plans* (Group RRSPs), *deferred profit sharing plans* (DPSPs), *employee profit sharing plans* (EPSPs), *employer savings plans* (ESPs), and similar vehicles. As these DC Plans have became more prevalent, mutual fund companies are becoming more important participants in this segment of the market.

B How Big Is the Canadian DC Plan Market?

Canada is still early in the process of developing the DC Plan market place. At present, the main Canadian vehicle for employer sponsored savings are DB Plans, in which the employer makes all the contributions, makes the investment decisions, takes all the investment risk, and pays benefits to the employees on a predetermined formula, regardless of the actual returns in the pension plan. DB Plans account for the majority of employer sponsored savings plans, with more than $300 billion, or approximately 90% of the total amount invested in all employer sponsored savings plans. Their growth has, however, leveled off in recent years and most projections call for assets in DB Plans to hold steady at their current levels, with virtually no growth in the next decade. This stagnancy will, of course, result in a sharp decline in market share as employee savings continue to grow through other vehicles.

The diminishing popularity of DB Plans has been paralleled by the increasing prevalence of other types of retirement schemes, including most significantly DC Plans, Group RRSPs, and similar options. Currently, DC Plans and Group RRSPs are each estimated to have about $15 billion, or approximately 5% of the market. Growth projections are, however, very strong.

Growth of DC Plans and Group RRSPs will come from two sources: first, new plans that are established for employees with no current employer savings plan; and second, from the winding-up and conversion of existing DB Plans. Estimates show assets in DC Plans growing to approximately $75 billion (or almost 20% of the market) by 2000 and to close to $150 billion (25%) by 2006. Group RRSPs should enjoy almost as substantial a growth rate, doubling to $30 billion (7%) by 2000 and shooting up to close to $110 billion (or almost 20%) over the next 10 years to 2006. Clearly, there is a lot of money at stake, with even more to come.

Traditionally, the chief providers of DB Plans have been insurance companies, with a market share exceeding 60%. Their primary competitors have been trust companies, with a market share in the neighborhood of 25%. The remaining 15% of the market was taken up by mutual fund sponsors and investment dealers. This is, however, a very competitive business, with a large number of players (estimates typically suggest more than 50 participants in the Canadian market), few companies with a market share in excess of 5%, and none with greater than 10% market share.

With the shift from defined benefit to defined contribution schemes, which are frequently individual, self-directed vehicles, the competition for assets is likely to intensify further. Mutual fund sponsors and investment dealers, who have extensive experience catering to individual investors, are likely to vigorously challenge the traditional institutional providers, such as insurance and trust companies.

This shift represents an important new business opportunity for Canadian and foreign mutual fund firms, but it carries with it a variety of regulatory and practical challenges. In order to better understand these challenges, it is important to briefly survey the Canadian DP Plan environment.

II   Canadian Employer Sponsored Savings Plans

A   Shift to DC Plans

There are a wide variety of different workplace savings schemes in use in Canada. Traditionally, these schemes were primarily limited to DB Plans, but in recent years the growth has been in DC Plans (which are sometimes called *money purchase pension plans*). This shift in pension plans has been augmented by the increasing popularity of a variety of non-pension plans, such as Group RRSPs, DPSPs, EPSPs, and ESPs. Some of these are tax-sheltered plans registered with Revenue Canada (e.g., Group RRSPs) while others are simple, taxable savings plans (e.g., Employer Savings Plans). What all these plans have in common is that they are established and administered by the employer through the workplace. Generally, participation in the plans is dependent upon the employee meeting certain conditions, such as having attained a minimum length service and being in good standing. In a typical plan, employees may make contributions through regular payroll deductions and sometimes by lump sums as well. Often, part of all of the employee contribution may be matched by the employer, and in some cases the employer may make the entire amount of contributions on behalf of the employee, with no need for the employee to make any contribution.

B What Are They?

The types of employer sponsored savings scheme are limited only by the creativity of employers and, in the case of registered plans, the tolerance of Revenue Canada. Each plan must be examined carefully to ensure that is particular features are properly understood, because plans with similar names can have important differences.

Some of the more common types of employer sponsored savings plans are as follows:

Pension Plan (Defined Benefit) The DB Plan is the classic employer sponsored savings plan. Typically, the employer will determine all aspects of employee eligibility and entitlement, including the level of benefits. The employer will also take complete responsibility for making contributions to the plan and making all investment decisions for the pension plan assets. More importantly, the employer will assume all investment risk: If the plan earns less than what is required to provide the promised levels of payments to employees, then the employer will be liable for the shortfall; conversely, if the plan earns more than what is required to provide the promised levels of payments to employees, then the employer may (depending on the plan's particular provisions and subject to resolving legal issues about surplus entitlement) be able to enjoy the benefit of any excess gains.

Pension Plan (Defined Contribution) A defined contribution pension plan is very similar to a defined benefit pension plan, except for one fundamental difference: the employee assumes all investment risk. Employees are promised a certain level of contributions, rather than a specific level of final benefit. (Note that defined contribution *pension* plans ought to be distinguished from defined *contribution* plans, in general. The broader phrase, defined contribution plan, includes both pooled investment vehicles, such as defined contribution pension plans, as well as individual investment vehicles, such as Group RRSRs and similar plans.)

Group Retirement Savings Plan Group RRSPs are the major alternative to traditional pension schemes. A Group RRSP is, in fact, something of a misnomer, since *there is no true group plan.* In U.S. 401(k) plans, the employer-sponsored plan is a single separate trust for the benefit of all employees. The Canadian Group RRSP Plan consists of a series of individual RRSP trusts, one per employee; the employer provides a single prototype plan (registered with Revenue Canada) upon which all the individual RRSP trusts are modeled. From a legal perspective, the individual RRSP accounts are similar to self-directed RRSPs in a non-group context, except that each trust will have the same features and available investment options, since each trust in a Group RRSP is derived from the same template. This individual characterization is a fundamental difference from U.S. 401(k) plans and from DB Plans in both the U.S. and Canada: whereas 401(k) and DB Plans are collective investment vehicles, Group RRSPs are *individually administered trusts*. From a practical perspective, the benefits to an individual in utilizing an employer-sponsored group RRSP instead of an individual RRSP boils down to: employer contributions, automatic monthly payroll deductions, employer-sponsored educational materials, and a prescreened menu of investment alternatives that narrow the selection process.

Deferred Profit Sharing Plans   There are additional retirement plans in the Canadian marketplace, and employee participants in a Group RRSP may well also participate in one or more of these other plans. A popular adjunct to the RRSP is the Deferred Profit Sharing Plan (or DPSP). DPSPs are individual accounts, although they exist within a form of umbrella known as a *deferred profit sharing plan*. Like RRSPs, DPSPs are tax sheltered investment vehicles, but they are subject to different rules and restrictions. For instance, only employer contributions are permitted, that is, individual participants cannot contribute to their own DPSP accounts. DPSPs may, however, be similar to Group RRSPs in that the individual participants may be entitled to make their own investment selections, although it is common for a DPSP to require all investments to be allocated to the employer's stock or another limited alternative.

Employee Profit Sharing Plans   An EPSP is similar to a DPSP in that it is an individual account that exists within a form of umbrella known as an *employee profit sharing plan*. Like a DPSP, the ostensible purpose of an EPSP is to provide an incentive to employees by giving them some participation in their employer's profits. It is also similar to a DPSP in that investment choices may be very limited or may be entirely restricted, for example, only employer's stock. It differs from a DPSP, however, in that it is not tax-sheltered and employee contributions are permitted.

Share Purchase Plans   There are a variety of different plans through which employees may be able to acquire shares of their employer's stock, frequently on very favorable terms. The investment option in these plans is limited to employer issued securities and does not include pooled investment vehicles such as mutual funds; in this way, share purchase plans are fundamentally different from the other types of plans listed here.

Employer Savings Plans   This is a catch-all description for a variety of other employer sponsored savings schemes that do not fit into any of the above categories. ESPs are typically not tax-sheltered, but they are still administered by the employer and participation is limited to employees. Like Group RRSPs and DPSPs, individual participants are typically entitled to make their own investment choices, subject to any particular restrictions imposed by the plan.

For the purpose of analyzing the registration requirements arising under securities laws, the key difference between these various plans is whether they are truly pooled investment vehicles, such as pension plans, or are individual, self-directed accounts, such as Group RRSPs, DPSPs, EPSPs, and ESPs.

III   The Basic Business Requirements

A   What Type of Functionality Is Required?

The marketplace will demand that TMC-Canada offer all types of plans, whether Group RRSPs, DPSPs, EPSPs, and ESPs. Each employee's investments in each plan will need to be reported on a combined statement. The marketplace is increasingly driven by employers looking to outsource the employee benefit function. TMC has earned a reputation as a highly skilled outsource vendor in the U.S.. Maple Leaf believes that this is TMC's natural niche in Canada. A survey of human resources managers determined that the typical Canadian HR director is aware of the Colossus system. The typical HR director is looking to move to an outsource solution where a third party supplies telephone service on a continuous basis to employees, sends employee statements, performs tax reporting and shoulders all administrative and legal burdens. Most HR directors either want or are willing to offer mutual funds as the investment option for benefit plans. Nearly all are looking to offer DC Plans, or to add DC Plans to their existing DB Plan.

B   What Types of Products are Required?

Canada's late-blooming DC Plan marketplace is quickly learning by observing the state of the art in the United States. Accordingly, most HR directors expect that their DC Plan administrator will offer a wide array of funds, and will allow the employer to select funds from various sponsors.

IV   Conclusion

TMC-Canada is well positioned to launch a DC Plan administration business in Canada. To do so successfully and to capture market share it will need to offer more than the competition. It will need to offer a wide array of investment products as well as a high level of service.

Commissioned Study #2

The Management Company

Legal Department

To: Dudley Doright, TMC—General Counsel
From: John Dean, TMC—Associate Counsel
Date: June 30, 1997
Subject: TMC—Canada: Key U.S./Canadian Legal Differences

Question Presented: You have asked me to determine whether there are important differences between Canada and the United States applicable to a defined contribution retirement business. Specifically you have asked me to focus on whether Canadian law regulates DC Plans in a manner similar to the United States and if there are any new responsibilities that TMC will encounter in Canada.

I. The Canadian DC Plan Investment Process

A Relevant Regulations and Differences from U.S. Regulation

There are various bodies of applicable regulations in Canada, including securities regulations. This stands in contrast to the United States, which largely exempts U.S. 401(k) plans from securities laws on the theory that the supervisory function of the Department of Labor and the protections of ERISA provide a sufficient and unified regulatory environment. The Securities Act of 1933—which applies to U.S. public securities offerings—and the Investment Company Act of 1940—which governs U.S. mutual funds—do not apply to ERISA plans. This means that U.S. 401(k) plans are generally exempt from SEC oversight, although mutual funds offered through the plans are SEC regulated. As a practical matter, this means that participants in U.S. 401(k) plans are not required to receive prospectuses for U.S. mutual funds that are held in their plans. Prospectuses must be given by the mutual fund firm to the employer/plan sponsor acting as trustee of the plan. The U.S. theory is that the employer acts as a plan fiduciary and serves to protect employees.

Further, U.S. law limits the responsibility of the employer and the plan administrator for investment selection. So long as neither explicitly offer investment advice, the risk of investment decision making can be shifted to the employee. ERISA's section 404(c) provides a safe harbor for employers that offer a balanced range of mutual fund investment options to their employees. Having done that much, the employer has no duty to advise the employee on investment selection. The plan administrator, or another supplier, must be a registered broker dealer, but the broker dealer has no duty to advise either. The broker dealer's duty is to give suitable advice, if it chooses to make a recommendation. If the broker dealer acts as a "discount broker" and makes no recommendations, it need not get involved in the suitability of the employee's investment selections.

The theory behind the regulatory scheme in Canada is different. In Canada, there is no equivalent to ERISA, and in most defined contribution schemes there is no trustee acting for the employees. Each employee has his or her own RRSP or other DC Plan. Canada's securities laws are applied to protect these investors much the same as they would in any other mutual fund transaction.

Virtually all Canadian mutual fund transactions take place in one of two contexts: (i) the traditional individual, retail broker-client relationship; or (ii) a large-scale institutional environment. An example of the latter might be a DB Plan investing in a fund. Although various private placement exemptions from securities laws may apply to large-scale institutional trades, retail trades are the subject of Canadian securities regulation.

The individual retail relationship typically involves a personal one-on-one relationship with a broker; to place a trade, the individual calls his or her registered broker, who then places the order for the individual's account.

The problem with Group RRSPs (and similar vehicles) is that they don't fit well into either of these traditional relationships. They are neither as individual and personal as the traditional retail broker-client scheme nor are they as impersonal and sophisticated as the traditional institutional scheme. An individual investing through his or her own account typically works within what has been described above as a "retail" relationship; this relationship places him or her squarely within the scope of the various provincial securities acts. The individual investing within a Group RRSP has a relationship that is clearly individual, as opposed to institutional, yet it is not as direct and personal as a classic retail relationship. This results in a degree of regulatory tension.

B Group RRSP Investing

Although participation in a Group RRSP is unlike being a member of a DB Plan, it is also unlike traditional individual investing where someone calls up a stock broker and buys a publicly traded security. This is the primary source of regulatory tension. Although the legal characterization of a Group RRSP participant is that of an individual investor, the reality is that the nature of the investor/registrant relationships and their working arrangements are unique.

The typical Group RRSP established with a mutual fund sponsor begins with negotiations between the employer company and the fund sponsor. The two parties agree to work together, determine what sorts of plans will be offered, design the particular features of the various plans, identify the investment options that will be made available to participants, and allocate the various administrative and operational responsibilities. In due course, introductory materials are prepared and distributed to employees to advise them of their new Group RRSP, its key features, and how they participate in it. The individual employees should then be required to open an account with the mutual fund sponsor. This is the stage at which, from a regulatory perspective, the process passes from the traditional world of institutional, employer-administered pension-like savings schemes into the realm of a more traditional individual securities trading relationship.

Once the account has been opened, the employee will generally conduct his or her transactions directly with the mutual fund sponsor, either by regular payroll deductions or through phone instructions to the fund sponsor. The vast majority of transactions are small purchases made by means of payroll deduction. The employer (or its agent) will process the regular payroll and make a record of the amount of the deduction made for each employee. This record, which is typically in the form of a tape or other computer file, is sent to the mutual fund sponsor, which processes the information and makes purchases for each individual's account in accordance with their previously provided instructions. In addition to these payroll deduction transactions, employees can also typically provide phone instructions to transfer amounts between funds, redeem a portion of their investment, or make a lump sum purchase.

C   The Key Differences in Administration

One of the most important differences between a U.S. 401(k) Plan and a Canadian Group RRSP scheme is that in a Group RRSP the employee must establish individual relationships with the dealers and other market participants. This is fundamental change. The significance of this change is that Canadian dealers have a duty to provide advice to their clients concerning the suitability of their transactions. This "suitability" duty requires the dealer to know his customer's individual circumstances and to evaluate each transaction in light of these circumstances. This is a very challenging responsibility to administer in the DC Plan administration environment.

In a DC Plan the bulk of transactions occur by way of payroll deductions. This is fundamentally different from the typical retail brokerage trade: the investor makes the purchase without ever speaking to a broker, and, in fact, interposing anybody between the creation of the payroll type and the purchase of the fund units is inconsistent with what both employers and employees expect and demand. Their desire is to have a process that is as automated as possible to maximize efficiency and minimize cost. Whereas the traditional retail broker-client relationship is quite personal and involves direct contract, the Group RRSP environment is more institutional. Technically, the relationship is an individual one, yet, as a practical matter, there is little need or desire for personal interaction.

II   Canadian Requirements

A   Basic Registration Principles

The basic regulatory scheme under Canadian securities law is well-established. Essentially, the rule is that one can only trade securities if registered to do so. This basic requirement is set out in section 25 of the *Securities Act* (Ontario) (the "Act) and comparable provisions in the legislation of other jurisdictions. The type of securities being traded determines the nature of the registration required.

In addition, each distribution of securities (which includes the issuance of new mutual fund units on a purchase) must be undertaken pursuant to a prospectus.

Since registration is necessary, a variety of obligations arise, including requirements to ensure suitability of investments for the client (the so-called "know your client" obligations). These know your client obligations are a fundamental part of the securities regulatory framework and are written in unequivocal terms. The registrant (e.g., the mutual fund provider) has a positive duty to ensure the suitability of investments made by its clients.

B   "Know Your Customer"—Canadian Rules

The law in Canada has not specifically addressed the DC Plan environment. Still, by statute the provinces have imposed an affirmative suitability regime. The Ontario Securities Act Regulation, for example, provides that each dealer "shall make such inquiries as ... are appropriate in view of the nature of the client's investment and the type of transaction being effected for its account, as to the general investment needs and objectives of each client and the suitability of a proposed purchase or sale for that client" (ON Reg. 1015: 114 [4] [b]).

Cases interpreting the Ontario regulation have found that the regulation creates a *limited but specific* statutory duty. That duty is discharged when the broker diligently makes a recommendation. Should the client then elect not to follow the recommendation, and if a loss is incurred; the broker will not be liable. See, *Srdarev v. McLeod Young Weir Ltd.* In *Srdarev*, the investor failed to recover losses because the facts demonstrated careful advice from his broker which the investor consciously ignored.

The most interesting Canadian case is *Varcoe v. Sterling*. Varcoe was a sophisticated investor who lost a small fortune trading futures in his own account that he managed himself. The Court found no advisory relationship between Varcoe and his dealer. The dealer never suggested that Varcoe trade futures in any way. Varcoe recovered his losses from the dealer nonetheless after demonstrating that the dealer failed to meet his duty to advise Varcoe of the unsuitable nature of Varcoe's trading. This failure to advise was demonstrated by the dealer's failure to warn Varcoe of his losses while they were arising through a so called "margin call." Varcoe traded futures and was obliged to maintain a deposit with his dealer equal to a percentage of his losses. As Varcoe's losses mounted, the dealer typically would have called Varcoe to ask for additional cash deposits. These "margin calls" would have had the effect of warning Varcoe of the magnitude of his losses. The Court found that since margin calls were customary and part of the dealer's procedures manual, failure to make margin calls was a breach of the dealer's duty. The Court stated, "If industry and the regulatory authorities permit member brokers to ignore or violate their own rules and blame losses on the cupidity of the customer, then it falls to the Court to provide a remedy."

The Court's remedy was to allow recovery for all losses over and above the client's trading limit, established at the time the account was opened, and to deny counterclaims for negative balances in the client's account.

The *Varcoe* case involved a Toronto Stock Exchange regulated broker that failed to follow its procedures or to make any effort at a suitability determination. The Court in *Varcoe* stated that the suitability role of a non-discretionary broker as fairly specific. The Court stated that, so long as a broker "applies the skill and knowledge relied upon and advises fully, honestly and in good faith, the broker . . . is not responsible if the transaction proves unfavorable." Moreover, if the client does not follow the advice or if the broker disagrees with the client's decision, the broker has no duty to refuse the order.

It is also noteworthy that the Investment Funds Institute Canada's own mutual fund dealer's course materials generally assume that mutual fund dealers have a suitability duty.

C "Know Your Customer"—U.S. Rules

In the United States TMC acts as a service provider to DC Plans that invest in mutual funds. TMC's role as broker is limited to acting as an order taker. The law in the United States is fairly clear. The NASD Rules of Fair Practice impose a suitability duty only when a broker makes recommendations. The NASD rule states that "[i]n recommending to a customer the purchase . . . of a security, a member shall have reasonable grounds for believing that the recommendation is suitable for such customer . . . ." U.S. Courts generally find no duty in the broker to determine suitability or to prevent unsuitable trading, so long as the broker does not have investment discretion or has not made a recommendation.

A second U.S. commodities case is worth noting, if only because it stands in contrast to the state of the law in Canada. In *Puckett v. Ruffenach, Bromagen & Hertz, Inc.* 1991 WL 191654 (Miss.), Mr. Puckett managed to lose $2 million trading futures. The Court noted that the futures commission merchant provided no advice, knew Puckett's trading was foolish and offered no warnings. The Court found no duty at common law to intervene in Puckett's debacle and no contractual responsibility, even assuming that is was customary for futures commission merchants to do so as an industry practice, and even assuming further that the futures commission merchant failed to follow internal procedures and ignored information about the clients' tolerance for losses on its account application. The Court stated "if society is to be free, it must demand of every person who, completely on his own, makes a mistake that he has no legal right to shift from his shoulders onto another's the suffering it causes."

III   Conclusion

TMC-Canada will need to design a "know-your-customer" compliance system for Canada. This will be new territory for TMC. I am sure none of our U.S. computer or phone systems are designed to track the sort of background information that will be needed. Ultimately the business unit will have to design a practical solution.

Commissioned Study #3

Project:	Global Pension Recordkeeping System-Canada
FSDM Module:	PPI
Deliverable:	Project Charter

Version: 2.0   Publication Date: 10/31/96
GPRs Doc ID:
CB010

Prepared by the GPRS Strategy Team

---

1 Introduction

1.1 Business Problem/Opportunity

As the pension plan industry expands world-wide, TMC has domestic and international companies that are positioned to take advantage of the growing market. As more pension plan business is managed by TMC, a cohesive technology strategy becomes an imminent requirement to support the rapidly growing business as well as accommodate a global retirement plan technology infrastructure. The effort to plan a global strategy and build a supporting system infrastructure has been named the Global Pension Recordkeeping Strategy/System (GPRS). On the other hand, GPRS is projected to be very costly. Therefore an alternative system solution has also been considered: enhancements to CanHolder.

Through the integrated efforts of TMC Systems, TMC-Canada and TMC, this project ultimately will deliver Canada-specific business functions supported by a core system as well as external sub-system interfaces.

Although the GPRS project eventually is intended for the end-to-end international solution, which includes other places such as the United Kingdom and Asia, the focus of this document will be on the Canada implementation, from a cost benefit perspective.

---

2 Objectives and Scope

2.1 Objectives

2.1.1 Business Objectives

- Provide TMC-Canada with an internal system that will ensure control over strategic business direction, product design, costs, services provided, and pricing.
- Proactively manage volume of new business and allow for system scaleability for increasing capacity.
- Ensure a higher level of quality service to pension plan providers and sponsors.

2.1.2 *Project Objectives*
*   Manage the increasing volume of pension plan business efficiently and cost effectively.
*   Provide a system infrastructure that is flexible enough to add recordkeeping processes and functions from other countries as TMC expands its business world-wide.
*   Implement the end-to-end Pension Recordkeeping System solution in Canada (and the UK and Asia in the future).

2.2 Scope
The full scope of the project is to provide system recommendations and solutions which allow TMC-Canada to implement all recordkeeping and administration functions associated with the delivery and servicing of retirement products.

---

3 Summary of Relative Advantages of CanHolder and Colossus

3.1 Narrative of the GPRS System Project
In April 1995 we began to examine whether the CanHolder transfer agency system (the home grown Canadian recordkeeping system) could be used by a single group plan in Canada and if so, whether it was adequate for future business growth in Canada. It is immediately apparent that CanHolder is not adequate as a global pension record keeping system, but it may be considered as a viable solution for Canada.

At the same time, we began to review Colossus. It is also apparent that Colossus has the potential to become the core for a global pension record keeping solution, supplying a range of functions for multiple countries, provided that country-specific applications were to be developed. Colossus would require country specific applications to be used in Canada. We also believe that the cost of a mainframe computer—projected to be in excess of $2.5 million—precludes using Colossus in a mainframe environment. Nor will a mainframe be needed. Two mini-computers, one for back-up, collectively cost $300,000 and have ample computing capacity. Accordingly, Colossus will have to be adapted to a PC/mini-computer environment.

3.2 Key Functionality Needs
We have identified two critical systems needs for the Canadian business: foreign content rebalancing and "know your customer" support functionality. We immediately compared the relative merits of both systems in respect of these criteria.

---

4 Foreign Content Rebalancing

4.1 Scope
In Canada, investment in foreign property, including mutual funds that hold foreign property, is restricted for registered plans such as RRSPs (including LIRAs and spousals), DPSPs, EPSPs, and MPPs. Foreign content must not exceed 20% of the assets in the registered plan, determined at the time of purchase on a cost basis. Foreign securities are foreign content for this purpose. Mutual funds that hold in excess of 20% foreign property are themselves considered foreign property when held by a registered plan.

If the foreign holdings in a registered plan are more than 20% of the plan's cost, then Revenue Canada will penalize the participant. If the participant holds funds over 20% foreign based in their registered plan, they will be fined monthly 1% of the value of the foreign content holdings in excess of the permitted 20%. The foreign content rules require compliance on the last day of each month, and violations during the month will not trigger the penalty. The formula used to calculate foreign content in a plan is the Adjusted Cost Base (ACB) which is: cost of (purchases–redemptions $+/-$ interfund transfer + income distributions).

4.2 Assumptions and Constraints

TMC-Canada has made a business decision to rebalance registered accounts to 20% foreign content holdings on a monthly basis to ensure that participants never exceed the 20% foreign content holdings and incur a tax penalty. This practice has been widely adopted by the competitors as well.

The following assumptions have been made:

- Month end is defined as the last business day of the month.
- System calendars must reflect Canadian holidays.
- Registered plans (RRSPs—including LIRA and Spousal DPSPs and DCPPs) are the only types of retirement plans that restrict investment in a foreign fund.
- At fund set-up, the retirement system (whether Colossus or CanHolder) will allow the funds to be designated as either Domestic or Foreign.
- At enrollment, participant accounts are set up for automatic rebalance to the domestic fund that has the highest market value for that month. However, participants may request that their foreign content excess be exchanged into a domestic fund other than the one with the highest market value. This would only involve a choice of at least one fund.
- The month end rebalancing program will not prevent participants from making exchanges into their foreign funds prior to month end or from making full or partial withdrawals that will alter the plan's content. However, when an exchange or with-drawal is initiated by telephone, there will be a warning on the workstation that the foreign content threshold may be exceeded and that this transaction will activate automatic month-end rebalancing. TMC-Canada will not allow participants to be out of balance by month end.
- The foreign content limit may be subject to change so there must be the flexibility to change the 20% to another amount.
- The TMC-Canada retirement system will calculate adjusted cost basis on a transaction by transaction basis and store the information.
- The percentage of foreign content in the plan will be displayed on the Workstation so the Employee Service Centre representatives can advise the participant. If the partici-pant requests the breakdown by fund, this will be available on the representatives' screens.

4.3 CanHolder and Foreign Content Rebalancing

4.3.1 CanHolder System Functionality

The current CanHolder system automatically rebalances participants accounts to 20% on a daily basis. This functionality was developed to support the TMC-Canada mutual fund business. TMC-Canada already offers an individual RRSP through brokers. These RRSPs are also subject to the foreign content requirement.

4.3.2   CanHolder System Description

The CanHolder system is currently rebalancing all registered plans on a daily basis if a transaction has occurred. The accounts are "rebalanced" by shifting assets from a fund that is foreign property to a fund that is not foreign property, meaning to a domestic fund that holds at least 80% Canadian securities. The CanHolder system transfers the excess foreign property amounts automatically to the TMC-Canada domestic fund option with the highest market value at the time. If, however,the participant specifies that they want their rebalanced amounts to be invested in a specifically designated domestic fund, then the CanHolder system will automatically rebalance excess foreign content amounts to the designated fund or to more than one fund. If the participant specifies, they have an option of having their foreign fund rebalanced to one domestic fund.

4.4   Colossus and Foreign Content Rebalancing

4.4.1   Colossus System Functionality

The Colossus system has no foreign content rebalancing capacity. Were Colossus to be selected a systems enhancement would be necessary and the solution functionality recommended would not be the same as that currently available on CanHolder.

4.4.2   Colossus Enhancements

The Colossus enhancements to accomplish foreign content rebalancing should be cost effective. Foreign content rebalancing necessarily involves rebalancing a portion of a registered plan. It is anticipated that initially plan balances will be small and the foreign content transactions will be even smaller. This implies a very large number of small transactions, which would be an inefficient and costly use of Colossus. Therefore, TMC-Canada has decided to rebalance on the Colossus system monthly thereby eliminating high transaction volumes involving small amounts of money.

During plan enrollment, participants are advised that TMC-Canada will automatically rebalance their accounts monthly to the domestic fund in their plan with the highest market value at the end of the month. Although this is the preferred procedure from an operational perspective, TMC-Canada must also provide the participant with the option to choose their domestic fund where excess foreign dollars will be transferred to. This feature will be too costly to automate and will require a manual process. Accordingly, this would only be done if there was a specific request and the participant would only be able to choose one domestic fund to rebalance to.

4.4.3   Proposed Solution

The following solution is possible within six months, the time frame specified by TMC in the AmPride negotiations.

Monthly, TMC-Canada will run a program to extract from all registered plans the Adjusted Cost Base (ACB) of every fund within each participant's plan. (The ACB calculation will be a Colossus function.) The program will also select a foreign fund indicator for each account. The program will sort the data by participant plan and calculate the percentage invested in Canadian funds vs. the percentage invested in foreign funds. When a participant's account is over 20% foreign content threshold, TMC-Canada will *manually* create the transactions to rebalance the account, that is, an exchange out of the foreign fund and an exchange into the Canadian fund with the highest market value (or chosen by participant) will be created. These transactions will be loaded into Colossus and the accounts will be rebalanced in that night's batch cycle.

4.4.4 Data and Additional Functionality Needed in Colossus Data needed:
- Daily calculation of ACB by participant by plan.
- Default for foreign rebalancing to go to the domestic fund with the highest market value.
- Workstation field for inputting a fund choice for rebalancing if the participant chooses one.
- The exchange screen will be modified to display into which fund the excess foreign content will spill for each participant.
- The withdrawal screen will be modified to display notice that the withdrawal may put the foreign fund content above the threshold.
- The user defined table will be updated to include the four-digit fund number of the Foreign content spill fund. However, screens will display a short name for the selected fund.
- Two new transaction codes—rebalance exchange in and rebalance exchange out. The new codes will distinguish these transactions from non-rebalancing exchanges.
- The foreign fund indicator must be stored on the fund file as a field.
- The account balance information screen may be changed so that the ACB for each plan can be displayed. These ACB figures should be displayed beside market value.
- On the workstation—need to see what percentage of their money is in foreign funds.

Additional functionality needed:

- Storage and calculation of Adjusted Cost Base(ACB) for every fund within a participant's plans.
- Default set up on Colossus, which tells TMC-Canada that each time a participant is over the 20% foreign content where the fund should be rebalanced to—based on the domestic fund at the end of the month with the highest market value.
- A field on Colossus for participants to choose where their foreign content will be rebalanced to if they insist on choosing. The choice would be for one domestic fund. This would be available on the workstation for the employee service center to input if the participant requests.
- When funds are set up on Colossus, an indicator must be available to distinguish between foreign or domestic.
- At month end, the local side would feed back to Colossus a transaction file for all interfund transfers which are a result of any plans being over 20% foreign content.

4.5 Conclusion
The CanHolder System can service the foreign content rebalancing requirements of TMC-Canada without enhancement. It will have a daily rebalancing capability and the ability to offer multiple investment options (i.e., spill funds) on an automated basis.

Colossus can be adapted to provide a partially automated foreign content solution within six months. The system will only operate monthly. This is adequate, but less sophisticated. It will also not allow accounts to maintain a constant foreign content exposure, as exposure will fluctuate during the month. The cost for the Colossus enhancements will be $75,000. Full automation will be achievable, after the six-month deadline for an additional $25,000.

5   Know Your Client and Risk Class for Funds

5.1   Scope

The Canadian Securities Administrators require that mutual fund companies track retirement plan member's investment profile. Thus TMC-Canada is required to inform a member if his or her choices of investments are "outside" his or her chosen risk level. Investment profile information is not carried on either CanHolder or Colossus today. Modifications will be required to carry and store investment risk information as well as other directives. This information, which will reside at the participant/plan level, must be stored and tracked for each member within each plan. A warning must be issued if the member is outside his or her chosen risk level.

5.2   Assumptions and Constraints

The TMC-Canada system will need to deliver the following functions:

- Store investor profile information for each member within each plan.
- Store risk class for each fund.
- View and maintain the investor profile information on the workstation.
- Track and monitor anything that may effect the member's portfolio.
- Warn a member if he/she is outside the chosen level of risk.
- Trigger a Risk Warning record for the "outside the member's chosen risk level" event.
- Create an Audit report (Investment Profile Audit Report) that contains all member's warned from the workstation and the reason for the warning.
- Create a Warning report for front-end investment mix changes that are determined to cause a member to be outside his/her chosen risk level.

5.3   CanHolder and KYC

CanHolder has no KYC functionality at present and will not offer an automated solution within the six-month time frame. Experience has shown that CanHolder's software owner, Canadian Data Services, is not able to timely enhance its systems to meet TMC's needs and time frames. CDS has estimated that a partially automated solution would be at least a seven-month project and that they would propose to allocate staff to the project in two months when other initiatives within CDS are expected to be completed. Full automation will take 24 months, since CDS already has other enhancements and releases scheduled. Accordingly, if CanHolder is TMC Canada's system, KYC will be manual, and after the fact.

TMC will be able to down-load transaction data and then compare it to asset allocations and customer profile rankings using largely manual processes and spread sheets.

Written warnings could then be mailed to customers recommending that they rebalance their portfolios to meet their risk profile. CanHolder will not allow real time KYC assessments at the time of the transaction.

5.4 Colossus and KYC

Colossus can be enhanced within the six-month timeframe to provide an automated and real time solution of KYC. Colossus can be modified using internal systems resources:

- To provide TMC-Canada with the ability to store member investment profile information for each member within each plan to which he or she belongs.
- To provide an automated process for tracking anything that might effect a member's portfolio. This automated process will determine if a member's current level of risk is within his/her chosen risk level. It will also trigger a Risk Warning record when an event out of a participant's risk level happens.
- To modify fund tables to include a fund risk indicator for each fund.
- To provide the capability of viewing and maintaining a member's Investor Profile, Investment Knowledge, and Net Worth information on the workstation at the participant level.
- To provide a "Pop Up" warning screen on the workstation. This would be used to notify a member that he/she is outside their chosen level of risk.
- To provide a front-end process that will detect investment mix changes that place a member outside of his/her chosen risk level. This event (out of participant's risk level) will trigger a Risk Warning record on the workstation.

5.5 Conclusion

Use of CanHolder will necessitate a manual process of monitoring KYC. This is a practicable and low cost approach, given the immediate needs of the TMC retirement business and the small number of accounts in the AmPride plans. This manual approach will not be capable of supporting large transaction volumes and will need to be replaced eventually. (We estimate that the manual system will be able to handle no more than ten employers and, depending on their number of employees, as few as five.) This manual process will be very labor intensive and will cost $100,000 per year to support on a fully loaded basis (assuming two full time employees.)

Automating CanHolder will take will in excess of six months. CDS will not take us on for two months, and the project will take an additional seven months. Their initial cost estimates for a customer software enhancement to fully support KYC is $150,000. It would be ready in two years.

Colossus offers the potential for an automated KYC system within the immediate 6 month time frame. Colossus will be capable of performing KYC on a real time basis and in large volumes. The enhancement will cost $100,000.

---

6 Modifying Colossus from a Mainframe to a Mini

Colossus was designed for and resides on a mainframe. The Canadian-specific enhancements to Colossus mandate working on the system off-line. In order not to interfere with the U.S. business, a copy of the Colossus source code will be made and modified off-line.

At the same time, the code will be rewritten in its entirety to suit a PC/mini environment. This project will require a significant programming resource. At the same time, the rewritten code will need to be tested in the new environment.

Our summary conclusion is that Colossus can be rewritten from Cobalt to Unix over a five-month period and that testing will take the balance of a month. Once accomplished, Colossus will be easily copied for use in other countries, and a key step in establishing a GPRS will have been accomplished. The cost of this process will be $250,000. It is reasonable to expect that the rewritten system will be unstable during its first three to six months, with brief systems interruptions arising from time to time until all weaknesses have been identified through use.

Index